ROTHMANS SNOOKER YEARBOOK 1988-89

ROTHMANS SNOOKER YEARBOOK 1988-89

Editor: Janice Hale

ROTHMANS

Queen Anne Press

A *Queen Anne Press* BOOK

© **Rothmans Publications Ltd 1988**

First published in Great Britain in 1988 by
Queen Anne Press, a division of
Macdonald & Co (Publishers) Ltd
3rd Floor
Greater London House
Hampstead Road
London NW1 7QX

A member of Maxwell Pergamon Publishing Corporation plc

Front cover photograph: Stephen Hendry (Eric Whitehead Picture Agency).

Back cover photograph: Stephen Hendry and Dennis Taylor at the Rothmans Grand Prix 1987 (Rothmans UK Ltd).

Black and white photographs: p. 102, p. 154: Colorsport; p. 309: Rothmans UK Ltd; all other photographs, Eric Whitehead.

British Library Cataloguing in Publication Data

Rothmans snooker yearbook. — 1988–89—
  1. Snooker — Serials
  794.7′35′05

  ISBN 0-356-15885-3

Typeset by SB Datagraphics, Colchester, Essex
(An Ician Communications Group company)

Printed and bound in Great Britain by Hazell, Watson & Viney Ltd,
Member of the BPCC Group, Aylesbury, Buckinghamshire

CONTENTS

ACKNOWLEDGEMENTS

The editor would like to thank the following for their assistance in compiling this book:
Clive Everton, editor of *Snooker Scene* magazine
Julie Kane, whose statistical research has been invaluable

FOREWORD
FROM ROTHMANS PUBLICATIONS LTD

Dennis Taylor, Steve Davis, Jimmy White and Stephen Hendry are names which are synonymous with quality. They also happen to be the four previous winners of the Rothmans Grand Prix snooker tournament, which takes place in Reading each year.

The link between Rothmans and quality is maintained in the publication of this, the fourth edition of the *Rothmans Snooker Yearbook*. It is *the* definitive reference work for the sport and already the first edition has become a collectors' item as snooker enthusiasts start to build an incomparable reference library.

Janice Hale continues her role as editor and this book reflects the hard work and enthusiasm which she puts into producing the facts and figures which we hope will give you many hours of enjoyment.

IN PRAISE OF SNOOKER

Eamon Dunphy

Sport has been my life. From play on Dublin's less salubrious streets as a kid, through a teenage apprenticeship with Man. United in the Law, Best and Charlton era, to a life as a journeyman pro with Millwall in the Second Division (and at various times York City, Charlton and Reading lower down), my life has been defined by sport, professional soccer in particular. Neither achieving nor aspiring to the French writer Albert Camus' eloquence with the pen, I can nevertheless subscribe to his declaration that 'almost everything I learned about life I learned playing football'.

Camus, a gifted amateur, played in goal for the Algerian University team. The lessons about life he was referring to have, I believe, to do with man's nature, his capacity to deal with success, failure, and all the shades of human existence in between. That truths are revealed through sport reflects on the world in which our sport is set. Much of man's activity outside the sports arena obscures – as it is designed to – the truth.

In business, politics, marriage, within family life, in the clothes we wear, the cars we drive and the neighbourhood we choose to live in (assuming we have a choice), we attempt to create an identity that is other than our own. All the pressures are to conform to some vague idea of what someone else has determined life to be. The net result is a lie to which we ourselves are often the most enthusiastic subscribers. In modern life this is accentuated by the public relations and advertising industries whose business is to persuade us that we are what we wear, eat, drink, drive and live in.

I love sport because it strips away worldly illusion and informs us about our true nature. Along with the Victorians I believe that sport is both character-forming and a revealer of truths about ourselves ... and others. What you drive won't help on a football pitch or around a snooker table. What church you worship at, where you went to school, the colour of your skin and the way you talk are all irrelevancies when the balls are set. Thus men and women learn about each other – and, more valuably, about themselves – through sport. Friendships are born, the cant and hypocrisy of the real world dissolve and racial, religious and cultural barriers are removed. Thus in a world where the shadows of greed, racial and religious bigotry and the terrorism that is bred by these things grows ever larger and darker, sport enobles and redeems the societies it serves.

No sport does this more compellingly than snooker. No sport is more revealing of those who play it because no other sport, golf perhaps excepted, makes such demands of mind and spirit, no sport tells so much truth. In team games you can hide, explain away your failures and inadequacies in terms of the shortcomings of those around you. Snooker, like golf, offers no such refuge.

My love affair with this beautiful sport has developed as my disenchantment with my first love, soccer, has deepened. British soccer is in terminal decline. The game that once enthralled the world is a casualty of the modern world with which, sadly, its rulers have failed to come to terms. Hooligans, on the terraces and in the boardrooms, have destroyed soccer. The great football cathedrals now resemble prison camps, with barbed wire, spiked railings and policemen everywhere, as the game is played out to a chorus of foul, abusive racial chants. The best players have left the English game to seek the fortunes abroad which maladministration prevents them earning at home.

Soccer, morally and aesthetically, is sick and decaying, to the point where many of the best British sportswriters – and many of its great players from the past – will have nothing to do with it. For men like Hugh McIllvanny, Ian Wooldridge, George Best, Danny Blanch-flower and John Giles, the love affair is over. For me too. Snooker has filled the void. For others, golf remains a solace for sporting love lost.

I discovered snooker on television. I saw a game that was Olympian in the demands it made of its best players. You had to be skillful, disciplined, able to concentrate and to play the shot of the moment, as well as plot ahead. As in all great sporting disciplines, snooker demanded nerve . . . the ability to do the business when failure to do it released the demons of self-doubt.

My greatest sporting moment of 1988 was seeing Sandy Lyle sink a ten-foot downhill putt to win the Augusta Masters. We need heroes, and Sandy's courage at this critical moment of his sporting life was inspiring. But there was something that mattered even more about his achievement; it was true in that it was gained without resort to artifice . . . no PR man could help, no advertising was required, no lie was present, no cheating necessary. Thus, too, Steve Davis's magnificent season in snooker, the arrival of Stephen Hendry, the rehabilitation of Terry Griffiths (in itself one of British sport's most warming stories of 1988).

Beyond mere sporting excellence, the snooker year provided something even more precious: the sight of sport played in the spirit God intended. Everything about this great game encourages man to be at his dignified, generous best. Both in bearing and manner the snooker player stands as the ultimate sporting personification of good manners.

Where else but the Crucible would a great sportsman do as Jimmy White did when he called a foul on himself in his magical match with Stephen Hendry? In golf, perhaps, but never in rugger or soccer, much less the Olympic Games, in preparation for which warehouses full of drugs are being consumed.

That the British Press has focused on drugs in snooker tells more about Fleet Street and its traditions than about the beautiful sport betrayed. Growing up, growing wiser, snooker has its problems. But they will pass. The game will endure, providing for new generations of kids (and older kids like me) the heroes we need in a world that hardly deserves them.

Eamon Dunphy, the former Millwall and Reading footballer, is the author of It's Only A Game *and writes a regular sports column for the* Irish Independent.

A YEAR IN SNOOKER POLITICS

Clive Everton, the Editor of *Snooker Scene*, gives his personal view of the events of the past season.

In a year in which snooker's backstage political manoeuvring all too frequently took precedence over on-table action, Barry Hearn was the chief catalyst of change, sometimes by design, sometimes through the chain effect of commercial initiative.

In the beginning, it was all very simple. The 38-year-old chartered accountant – with an appetite for action to match his zeal for profit – merely managed Steve Davis, but as his management stable grew to eight, so his sphere of influence expanded. In the absence of the WPBSA, or indeed another promoter opening up new frontiers for the game, or new sources of income to supplement the chief events on the British circuit, he opened them himself and thus became, as well as a manager, a promoter.

As a WPBSA board member he did his bit for the game at large, finding a sponsor, Goya, for its first ranking tournament of the 1985–86 season and through his own Matchroom company sponsoring the Welsh and Irish Championships in 1987. However, he never made any bones about being on the board primarily to represent the interests of his players – not quite the extraordinary position this might appear, since virtually every board member inescapably has a personal interest of one sort or another.

More significantly, it is how these vested interests are resolved which often determines whether that person can remain on the board. Hearn found an acceptable equilibrium for some time, but resigned when he came into direct commercial competition with the WPBSA.

The point of departure was, ironically, one of his few commercial failures – World Series – which was intended to be eight overseas tournaments linked by a points system. Embassy, the sponsors of the WPBSA's flagship event, the World Professional Championship, had an agreement that the WPBSA would not sanction the use of the word 'world' for any other snooker singles event. As a board member, Hearn was party to that agreement and thus felt bound to resign, not only because he himself was promoting a world event but because he would be in direct competition in terms of the sales of television packages overseas. As it turned out, there were very few of the latter and with only three of the eight events completed, World Series was called off.

An incidental casualty of this episode was Rex Williams, the WPBSA's apparently perennial chairman, who declined to resign after a 5-1 board room vote of no confidence had gone against him in September 1987. Dissatisfaction with his style of chairmanship was one reason for this; another was that he had been seen to ally himself too closely with Hearn, who was not only in commercial competition with the Association but whose activities might even threaten the WPBSA's function as a governing body. It had also been noted that Williams's own company, Rex Williams Leisure plc, had come under the effective control of Frank Warren, the boxing promoter, who had openly expressed a wish to move into snooker.

Williams resigned at the WPBSA's AGM in November and word soon started to filter out that a rival governing body was in the offing. Boxing has three world governing bodies, so it seemed quite on the cards that snooker could have two, but Ian Doyle, manager of Stephen Hendry and Mike Hallett, who emerged during the year as a rising political force within the game, declined to have anything to do with this.

Concurrently, Mark McCormack's International Management Group were attempting to establish a meaningful presence in the snooker business through Bill Sinrich, its head of European Development. IMG, through its television production and sales subsidiary, Trans World International, had worked with Hearn on a Straight Pool/Snooker/Nine Ball Triathlon in St Moritz, featuring Steve Davis and Steve Mizerak, which they sold to an impressive number of outlets, including Britain's Channel 4 and the American sports cable network, ESPN. They expected to be working with Hearn on World Series but Hearn, erroneously as it turned out, thought he could satisfactorily handle the television side of the operation himself.

The WPBSA was eager not to be seen to be lacking in terms of promoting snooker overseas, and announced two new world ranking tournaments for the 1988–89 season in Canada and Belgium and two more in South-east Asia and Australia for 1989–90. IMG offered the WPBSA £925,000 in prize money and back-up for these projects, but the WPBSA received this offer with unmistakable coolness. This effectively promoted a reconciliation between IMG and Hearn. Warren, whose plans to acquire a stable of players had not materialised, was nevertheless involved through Rex Williams being loosely linked both to himself and to Hearn and also because he could offer a large, prestigious venue, the as yet uncompleted London Arena in Docklands, in which he holds a substantial stake.

In February, Hearn, Warren and Sinrich announced two new promotions, a World Matchplay Championship in December 1988 and a Wimbledon-style World Open Championships for Summer/

Autumn 1989, featuring Men's and Women's Singles, Men's Doubles, Mixed Doubles and Junior competitions. Here was a direct challenge to the WPBSA's self-proclaimed, if hitherto generally accepted, status as professional snooker's world governing body. Hearn stated that the WPBSA was not a governing body but a limited company endeavouring to trade at a profit for a restricted number of players. Legally, he was right. Indeed, governing bodies in sport tend to hold their status more through the consent of the governed than through any legal muscle.

It was quickly clear, through perusal of its much discredited constitution, that the WPBSA could neither bring punitive action against Hearn or his players for playing in events of which it did not approve, or prevent them from playing in any WPBSA events for which they were suitably qualified.

When the new consortium announced its two new world events, the WPBSA fulminated in vain. They contemplated setting up a rival tournament and offering it to ITV for the slot previously occupied by the World Doubles Championship, which ITV no longer wanted. But without Hearn's players how attractive would it be? And even with its substantial assets, how many tournaments could the WPBSA fund or even part fund itself, particularly as outside funding was not materialising for its overseas ranking tournaments?

John Virgo, who had succeeded Williams as the WPBSA's chairman, took it upon himself personally to try to repair the rift between WPBSA and IMG. This in turn put IMG in the honest broker position between the WPBSA and Hearn/Warren. The outcome was the WPBSA's sanction, for a fee, of the World Matchplay and World Open, which would at least be some compensation for the shortfall from the WPBSA's ITV contract, which specified delivery not of three but four televisable events.

It became clear that the Hearn/Warren/IMG consortium would remain in place only for their two new world events. In March, Hearn had set up his own television production and distribution alliance, which again appeared to exclude TWI from much further business; Warren had not made any further independent move in the snooker market; and IMG, as had been their chief desire all along, were moving into a commercial relationship with the WPBSA.

The threat of a breakaway governing body had receded, not least because it was less difficult, with will and effort, to mould the WPBSA into shape than to start again from scratch. Hearn (and Warren) had effectively made the point that the governing body could not, through its wholly owned subsidiary, WPBSA Promotions Ltd, act in a commercially quasi-monopolistic fashion. The need had been acknowledged, on all sides, that the WPBSA must employ a properly qualified chief executive and move towards methods of conducting its day to day affairs which did not involve perpetual reference to a cumbrous board of players and their representatives, few of whom can contribute a desirable width of experience outside snooker.

The WPBSA, originally a player's trade union forced into becoming a governing body because there was no one, in the seventies, who could effectively perform this function, had not done at all badly in the first phase of development in the sport's new television age. But it had clearly emerged that this situation was inadequate for the game's growing organisational, political and commercial complexities. Some of snooker's detractors drew a simplistic connection between its organisational disarray and its imminent demise as a public entertainment, but grossly underestimated the game's greatest safeguard – its players and depth of grass roots support.

In terms of playing strength and public interest, snooker has never been in better shape; the problem is evolving methods of organisation which make best use of these prime natural resources, allowing commercial enterprise to flourish within the constraints of fair competition and fair play.

EDITOR'S REVIEW OF THE SEASON

Janice Hale

With an awesome authority, Steve Davis continued to dominate professional snooker. As a climax to his best among many excellent seasons he won the Embassy World Championship for the fifth time. He won three other ranking tournaments and headed both the ranking list and the money list.

Even before he had struck a ball in the World Championship, Davis was already assured of being world number one, so steadily and majestically had he accrued ranking points over the season and in 1986–87. He won the first ranking tournament of the season, the Fidelity International, an event enjoying its fourth sponsor in as many years; the third, the Tennents UK Open, for the sixth time, and retained the Mercantile Credit Classic, the fifth. For good measure he regained the Benson and Hedges Masters title, his second, whitewashing Mike Hallett 9-0 in the final at Wembley and for the fifth time took first prize in the Benson and Hedges Irish Masters. His prize money for the season was just £5,000 short of half a million pounds, a figure that would have been unimaginable ten years ago.

However, there were indicators of who may eventually take over the mantle of world number one. Stephen Hendry, still only 19, won the other two ranking events, the Rothmans Grand Prix and MIM Britannia British Open. In the former, he beat Davis 5-2 in the last 16. In the latter, Davis suffered an amazing 5-0 defeat at the hands of the veteran former world champion Ray Reardon. Hendry, who started the season ranked 23rd, ended it 4th, behind Davis, Jimmy White and Neal Foulds.

The immensely talented Hendry's confrontation with White in the second round of the Embassy World Championship provided the match of the championship. It went the full distance of 25 frames and produced 26 breaks over 40 with White taking the decider with a run of 86. White, though, failed to reach the final. He was beaten in the semifinals by Terry Griffiths, who thus reached the final for the first time since 1979, the year he won the title at his initial attempt.

In the space of three weeks early in the season, Dennis Taylor, the 1985 world champion, reached the final of the Rothmans Grand Prix – where he was beaten by Hendry – and won both the Canadian Masters and Barry Hearn's 'in-house' Matchroom tournament, a run of success which included two wins over Davis.

Away from the table and internal politics, drugs again were to the forefront when Cliff Thorburn failed a drugs test taken during the MIM Britannia British Open in Derby in February 1988. The WPBSA set the date for his disciplinary hearing just two days before the World Championship, only for the 40-year-old Canadian to appeal success-fully to the High Court for a postponement. He reached the semi-finals at Sheffield before Gavin Lightman QC, sitting for the third time as an independent one-man disciplinary tribunal, adjudged that he be fined £10,000, forfeit two ranking points and be barred from competing in the first two ranking events of the 1988–89 season. It was a penalty which many thought lenient especially in view of the WPBSA's published statement of what the penalties would be should a player be found to have been using a banned substance – in this case cocaine. Thorburn will however be free to play in the two new ranking tournaments which will be staged in Canada and Belgium in the 1988–89 season.

The ranking list will thus be based on performances in eight events for that season, with qualifying taking place for all eight on sixteen tables in Blackpool in June and September.

EDITOR'S NOTE

Because of the volume of statistics which modern snooker is constantly creating, the *Rothmans Snooker Yearbook* has had to limit to a certain extent which items are included under the various sections.

To qualify for inclusion in the 'Players' section, matches must have been played in a bona fide tournament with at least four competitors and be of the best of nine frames or more.

The 'Circuit' section is more comprehensive, and here we have tried to record at least the result of the final in events where either the number of frames was insufficient, or where the early rounds were played on a round robin basis.

RANKING LIST

As both the number of professionals and the number of tournaments have increased, the game's governing body, the World Professional Billiards and Snooker Association, have had to devise some form of ranking list, not only to quantify the standings of the players but also to enable them to seed tournaments.

The ranking list is drawn up at the end of each season and is based on performances over the past two seasons in events which are designated ranking tournaments.

To qualify for ranking status, a tournament must be open to all snooker professionals. For the 1987–88 season there were six ranking events: Fidelity International, Rothmans Grand Prix, Tennents UK Open, Mercantile Credit Classic, MIM Britannia British Open and Embassy World Championship. For the 1988–89 season two more events have been added, the Canadian Masters (expanded from an eight man invitation event) and the European Open.

When seedings are decided for each tournament, the defending titleholder is automatically seeded one with the world champion, if he is not the defending titleholder, two. The remaining seeds are then taken, in order, from the ranking list.

To separate players who tie on ranking points, merit points, 'A' points and 'frames won' in the first round have also been introduced to the system which also favours performances in the immediate preceding season.

Players seeded 1–16 are exempt until the last 32 of the World Championship but in the other five events, players seeded 1–32 are exempt only until the last 64.

The various points are awarded as follows. World Championship: winner – 10 ranking points; runner-up – 8 ranking points; losing semi-finalists – 6 ranking points; losing quarter-finalists – 4 ranking points; losers in last 16 – 2 ranking points; losers in last 32 – 1 ranking point (if qualifier), 2 merit points (if exempt); losers in last qualifying round – 2 merit points; losers in 2nd preliminary round – 1 merit point; losers in 3rd preliminary round – 1 'A' point; losers in 1st preliminary round; number of frames won. Other ranking events: winner – 6 ranking points; runner-up – 5 ranking points; losing semi-finalists – 4 ranking points; losing quarter-finalists – 3 ranking points; fifth round losers – 2 ranking points; fourth round losers – 1 ranking point; third round losers – 1 merit point; second round losers – 1 'A' point; first round losers: number of frames won.

WORLD RANKING LIST 1988

Figure in brackets denotes previous year's ranking

		1986–87				1987–88										
		Ranking Points	Merit Points	A Points	Frames	Fidelity	Rothmans	Tennents	Mercantile	MIM Britannia	World	Ranking Points	Merit Points	A Points	Frames
1(1)	Steve Davis	29	0	0	0	6R	2R	6R	6R	1M	10R	59	1	0	0
2(2)	Jimmy White	25	1	0	0	2R	1R	5R	2R	3R	6R	44	1	0	0
3(3)	Neil Foulds	26	1	0	0	1R	1M	1M	1R	2R	4R	34	3	0	0
4(23)	Stephen Hendry	12	1	1	0	4R	6R	1M	3R	6R	2R	33	2	1	0
5(6)	Terry Griffiths	15	0	0	0	1R	2R	3R	3R	1R	8R	33	0	0	0
6(4)	Cliff Thorburn	13	3	0	0	5R	1R	3R	1R	4R	6R	33	3	0	−2
7(13)	John Parrott	10	2	0	0	2R	4R	3R	5R	4R	2R	30	2	0	0
8(7)	Tony Knowles	12	3	0	0	2R	3R	2R	4R	1R	4R	28	3	0	0
9(16)	Mike Hallett	10	1	0	0	4R	1M	3R	1M	5R	2R	24	3	0	0
10(8)	Dennis Taylor	10	1	0	0	1R	5R	1R	3R	1R	2R	23	1	0	0
11(5)	Joe Johnson	13	1	0	0	1M	1R	4R	1R	2R	2R	23	2	0	0

12(10)	Silvino Francisco	14	0	0	0	2R	1R	2R	2R	1R	2M	22	2	0	0
13(11)	Willie Thorne	6	4	0	0	1R	3R	4R	1R	2R	2R	19	4	0	0
14(18)	Peter Francisco	9	2	0	0	1M	4R	1R	2R	1R	1R	18	3	0	0
15(19)	John Virgo	8	0	0	0	3R	1R	1R	1R	1R	1R	17	0	0	0
16(17)	Cliff Wilson	9	3	0	0	1R	2R	1R	1R	1R	1R	16	3	0	0
17(9)	Alex Higgins	10	1	0	0	—	—	2R	2R	1M	2M	14	4	0	0
18(12)	Rex Williams	10	3	0	0	1M	1M	1M	1M	3R	2M	13	9	0	0
19(26)	Eddie Charlton	5	3	0	0	3R	2R	1M	1M	1M	2R	12	6	0	0
20(32)	Tony Drago	5	1	2	0	1M	2R	1M	1R	1M	4R	12	4	2	0
21(24)	Eugene Hughes	8	2	0	0	3R	1M	1R	1M	1M	2M	12	7	0	0
22(15)	Dean Reynolds	11	1	0	0	1M	1M	1M	1R	1M	2M	12	7	0	0
23(35)	Dene O'Kane	6	0	3	0	1M	1A	2R	1A	3R	1A	11	1	6	0
24(14)	Doug Mountjoy	8	1	0	0	1M	1M	1M	1R	1M	2R	11	5	0	0
25(45)	Steve Newbury	2	4	2	0	1R	3R	1M	4R	1M	2M	10	8	2	0
26(29)	Barry West	5	2	0	0	1M	1M	1R	2R	1R	1R	10	4	0	0
27(28)	John Spencer	6	4	0	0	1R	1M	1M	1R	2R	2M	10	8	0	0
28(25)	David Taylor	7	2	0	0	1R	1M	1R	1R	1M	2M	10	6	0	0
29(41)	Robert Chaperon	3	4	0	0	1R	3R	1M	1M	1R	1R	9	6	0	0
30(31)	Steve Longworth	5	3	0	0	1R	1M	1R	1R	1M	1R	9	5	0	0
31(20)	Tony Meo	6	4	0	0	1R	1M	1R	1M	1M	2M	9	8	0	0
32(67)	Steve James	1	0	3	7	2R	1M	1A	1M	1R	4R	8	2	4	7
33(22)	John Campbell	4	3	0	0	1M	1M	2R	1R	1R	1R	8	6	0	0

	Player (prev. ranking)	1986–87				Fidelity	Rothmans	Tennents	Mercantile	MIM Britannia	World	1987–88			
	Figure in brackets denotes previous year's ranking	Ranking Points	Merit Points	A Points	Frames							Ranking Points	Merit Points	A Points	Frames
34(34)	Wayne Jones	6	2	1	0	1R	1M	1M	1A	1M	1R	8	5	2	0
35(56)	Joe O'Boye	1	5	0	0	3R	1A	1M	1M	3R	1A	7	7	2	0
36(27)	Dave Martin	4	3	0	0	1M	1M	1M	3R	1M	2M	7	9	0	0
37(21)	Kirk Stevens	4	4	0	0	1M	1R	1R	1M	—	1R	7	6	0	0
38(36)	Jim Wych	4	2	0	0	1R	1R	1R	1A	1M	1M	7	4	1	0
39(84)	David Roe	0	3	3	0	1R	1R	2R	1A	2R	1A	6	3	5	0
40(38)	Ray Reardon	5	2	0	0	1M	1M	1M	1M	1R	1A	6	6	1	0
41(—)	Martin Clark	—	—	—	—	2R	1R	8F	2R	1M	1M	5	2	0	8
42(44)	Tommy Murphy	2	5	1	0	1M	1A	1R	2R	1M	1M	5	8	2	0
43(40)	Danny Fowler	2	4	2	0	1M	1M	2R	1A	1M	1R	5	7	3	0
44(39)	Warren King	4	2	0	0	1M	1A	1M	1A	1A	1R	5	4	3	0
45(—)	Gary Wilkinson	—	—	—	—	1M	2R	1M	1A	2R	9F	4	2	1	9
46(48)	Graham Cripsey	1	5	1	0	1M	2R	1M	1M	1R	2M	4	10	1	0
47(33)	Bill Werbeniuk	1	6	0	0	1R	1R	1M	1M	1A	1R	4	8	1	0

ID	Name															
48(30)	Murdo Macleod	2	5	0	0	1M	1M	1M	1M	1M	2R	2M	4	11	0	0
49(46)	Tony Jones	2	4	1	0	1A	1M	1M	1M	2R	2R	1A	4	7	3	0
50(37)	Steve Duggan	4	2	1	0	1A	1A	1A	1A	1A	1A	2M	4	5	5	0
51(59)	Tony Chappel	0	6	1	0	1M	1R	1M	1M	1M	1M	2M	3	11	1	0
52(55)	Mark Bennett	2	2	0	12	1M	1M	1A	1R	1R	1A	2M	3	6	2	12
53(53)	Ken Owers	2	3	1	2	1M	1A	1A	1R	1R	1A	1M	3	5	4	2
54(43)	Paddy Browne	2	1	4	0	1A	1A	1A	1A	1A	1R	1M	3	2	8	0
55(60)	Ray Edmonds	0	4	3	0	1A	1R	1R	1R	1M	1A	1A	2	5	6	0
56(100)	Nigel Gilbert	0	1	4	1	2R	3F	1M	2F	1M	1A	1A	2	3	5	6
57(83)	Dave Gilbert	0	0	4	10	2R	1A	1A	1M	1M	1F	1A	2	2	7	10
58(93)	Mick Fisher	0	1	2	8	1A	2R	1A	1A	1A	1F	4F	2	1	5	13
59(65)	Pat Houlihan	1	0	0	16	1A	1R	1A	1A	1A	1A	1M	2	1	4	16
60(58)	Roger Bales	1	0	5	0	1A	1R	1A	1A	1A	1A	1A	2	0	10	0
61(54)	Jon Wright	2	2	1	2	1M	1M	1A	1M	1M	2M	2M	2	7	3	2
62(52)	Les Dodd	2	1	3	0	1A	1M	1M	1M	1M	1A	1M	2	5	5	0
63(42)	Marcel Gauvreau	2	3	2	0	1A	1M	1M	1A	1A	1A	1A	2	5	6	0
64(51)	Jack McLaughlin	2	3	1	0	1A	1M	1A	1M	1A	1A	1A	2	5	5	0
65(69)	Graham Miles	0	4	2	0	1A	1M	1A	1A	1A	1A	1M	1	7	4	0
66(80)	Robby Foldvari	0	2	4	0	1R	1M	1A	1A	1M	1M	2M	1	6	6	0
67(79)	Colin Roscoe	0	3	2	3	1M	1A	4F	4F	1M	1M	1A	1	5	4	7
68(68)	Paul Medati	0	5	2	0	1A	1A	1A	1A	1A	1R	1A	1	5	7	0
69(99)	Paul Gibson	0	1	4	6	1M	1R	1A	1A	1R	4F	1M	1	3	6	10

70(91) Brian Rowswell 1-3-7-1; 71(73) Vic Harris 1-3-5-10; 72(108) Martin Smith 1-2-3-22; 73(–) Jim Chambers 1-1-2-5; 74(88) Jim Donnelly 1-0-7-15; 75(57) Malcolm Bradley 1-7-5-0; 76(47) Mark Wildman 1-6-5-0; 77(49) Bob Harris 1-6-6-0; 78(63) Geoff Foulds 1-3-7-1; 79(64) Robby Grace 1-2-5-13; 80(66) Tony Kearney 1-1-8-10; 81(70) John Rea 0-9-2-5; 82(78) Mario Morra 0-7-3-10; 83(62) Fred Davis 0-6-7-0; 84(85) Bill Oliver 0-6-6-7; 85(77) Eddie Sinclair 0-6-4-11; 86(87) Jim Bear 0-5-4-2; 87(72) Jimmy Van Rensberg 0-5-6-0; 88(71) Matt Gibson 0-5-6-7; 89(81) Ian Williamson 0-4-6-4; 90(61) George Scott 0-4-8-0; 91(86) Gino Rigitano 0-3-6-11; 92(104) John Dunning 0-2-5-12; 93(–) Eric Lawlor 0-2-1-9; 94(92) Jim Meadowcroft 0-2-7-9; 95(97) Glen Wilkinson 0-2-5-10; 96(75) Ian Black 0-2-6-7; 97(74) Bernie Mikkelsen 0-2-5-0; 98(114) Paul Watchorn 0-1-6-14; 99(112) Jack Rea 0-1-5-16; 100(90) Mike Darrington 0-1-3-24; 101(116) Terry Whitthread 0-1-3-19; 102(–) Alain Robidoux 0-1-0-0; 103(76) Patsy Fagan 0-1-6-10; 104(94) Greg Jenkins 0-1-5-13; 105(98) Pascal Burke 0-1-4-16; 106(96) Frank Jonik 0-1-3-20; 107(101) Ian Anderson 0-1-3-4; 108(82) Mike Watterson 0-1-0-20; 109(102) Jim Rempe 0-1-0-4; 110(103) Billy Kelly 0-0-7-18; 111(106) Dennis Hughes 0-0-5-12; 112(111) Dave Chalmers 0-0-5-30; 113(118) Francois Ellis 0-0-4-19; 114(89) Jack Fitzmaurice 0-0-4-16; 115(95) Dessie Sheehan 0-0-4-35; 116(–) Anthony Harris 0-0-3-9; 117(–) Steve Meakin 0-0-3-9; 118(–) Jason Smith 0-0-2-17; 119(–) Robert Marshall 0-0-2-6; 120(113) Clive Everton 0-0-2-14; 121(115) Derek Mienie 0-0-2-19; 122(105) John Hargreaves 0-0-2-14; 123(–) Derek Heaton 0-0-1-13; 124(110) Paul Thornley 0-0-1-13; 125(117) David Greaves 0-0-1-28; 126(120) Mike Hines (NT) 0-0-1-6; 127(123) Maurice Parkin (NT) 0-0-0-21; 128(121) Bert Demarco (NT) 0-0-0-17; 129(124) Bernard Bennett (NT) 0-0-0-14; 130(119) Joe Caggianello 0-0-0-7; 131(107) Eddie McLaughlin 0-0-0-1; 132(–) Steve Mizerak 0-0-0-0; 133(109) Gerry Watson 0-0-0-0

For the 1987–88 season, Paddy Morgan, James Giannaros, Lou Condo, Mannie Francisco and Wayne Saunderson were non-tournament playing members of the WPBSA and did not compete on the circuit.

MONEY LIST 1987–88

The *'Ranking'* column takes into account the Fidelity International, Rothmans Grand Prix, Tennents UK Open, Mercantile Credit Classic and MIM Britannia British Open. *'Sanctioned'* consists of Carling Champions, Langs Scottish Masters, Canadian Masters, Hofmeister World Doubles, Benson and Hedges Masters, Benson and Hedges Irish Masters, Fersina World Cup and WPBSA-supported national professional championships. *'Others'* comprises events set up primarily or even exclusively for the members of particular management camps. They include Barry Hearn's Matchroom tournament, the Rothmans Matchroom League and the Tokyo and Hong Kong Masters and Howard Kruger's Kent Cup.

		World	Ranking	Sanctioned	Breaks	Total	Others
1	S. Davis	95,000	165,812	101,630	9,000	371,442	124,500
2	S. Hendry	7,125	141,031	52,116	8,916	209,189	50,500
3	J. White	28,500	60,656	51,257	7,250	147,664	44,500
4	T. Griffiths	57,000	27,343	53,745	4,040	142,128	44,500
5	C. Thorburn	28,500	57,828	55,520	250	142,098	17,000
6	Dennis Taylor	7,125	51,734	73,395	8,850	141,104	99,500
7	M. Hallett	7,125	60,906	64,375	3,125	132,406	135,531
8	J. Parrott	7,125	79,500	23,562	6,000	116,187	38,500
9	J. Johnson	7,125	31,703	63,145	–	101,973	8,750
10	N. Foulds	14,250	11,703	66,308	–	92,261	44,250
11	T. Knowles	14,250	35,156	24,270	–	73,676	12,500
12	W. Thorne	7,125	38,859	13,612	6,750	66,346	61,000
13	A. Higgins	4,007	10,312	31,307	–	45,627	8,750
14	P. Francisco	4,007	28,921	8,750	–	41,679	–
15	S. James	14,250	8,312	8,750	9,500	40,812	–
16	S. Francisco	4,007	17,812	18,916	–	40,736	–
17	D. Reynolds	4,007	7,453	25,375	–	36,835	13,250
18	S. Newbury	3,117	28,781	1,842	–	33,740	–
19	E. Charlton	7,125	14,437	11,853	–	33,416	–
20	T. Drago	14,250	10,640	5,383	1,500	31,774	10,250
21	R. Williams	4,007	13,812	13,395	–	31,215	–
22	D. Mountjoy	7,125	7,453	12,937	–	27,515	–
23	J. Campbell	4,007	11,437	11,409	–	26,854	–
24	J. Virgo	4,007	18,953	3,375	–	26,335	–
25	C. Wilson	4,007	15,159	6,937	–	26,104	–
26	E. Hughes	3,117	13,109	8,857	–	25,084	–
27	M. MacLeod	3,117	9,312	10,854	1,666	24,950	–
28	D. O'Kane	–	15,125	8,541	–	23,666	–
29	J. O'Boye	–	17,625	4,967	1,000	23,592	–
30	B. West	4,007	12,234	5,967	1,250	23,459	–
31	R. Chaperon	4,007	16,468	1,717	1,250	23,443	–
32	D. Roe	–	14,593	8,750	–	23,343	–
33	W. King	4,007	2,406	12,742	222	19,378	–
34	J. Wych	1,632	9,546	7,725	–	18,904	–
35	D. Martin	3,117	12,531	2,404	–	18,053	–
36	W.Jones	4,007	6,093	7,687	–	27,789	–
37	T. Meo	3,117	10,374	3,592	–	17,084	19,250
38	S. Longworth	4,007	10,374	2,404	–	16,787	–
39	J. Spencer	3,117	11,703	1,779	–	16,599	–
40	T. Chappel	3,117	11,437	1,842	–	16,396	–
41	David Taylor	3,117	10,374	2,750	–	16,242	–
42	K. Stevens	4,007	8,265	8,287	–	15,560	–
43	M. Clark	1,632	10,968	2,750	–	15,351	–
44	T. Murphy	1,632	9,328	4,342	–	15,302	–
45	G. Cripsey	3,117	10,906	1,217	–	15,240	–
46	B. Werbeniuk	4,007	7,468	3,717	–	15,193	–
47	D. Fowler	4,007	8,750	2,404	–	15,162	–
48	John Rea	–	4,812	6,566	1,666	13,045	–
49	Gary Wilkinson	–	11,406	562	–	11,968	–
50	G.Miles	1,632	6,015	2,187	–	9,835	–

		World	Ranking	Sanctioned	Breaks	Total	Others
51	R. Foldvari	3,117	4,562	2,106	–	9,785	–
52	T. Jones	–	8,437	1,217	–	9,654	–
53	R. Reardon	–	7,718	1,842	–	9,560	–
54	R. Edmonds	–	7,390	1,217	–	8,607	–
55	M. Bennett	3,117	4,609	775	–	8,501	–
56	P. Browne	2,906	1,632	3,900	–	8,439	–
57	M. Smith	1,632	4,484	1,779	–	7,896	–
58	J. Bear	1,632	4,156	1,900	–	7,689	–
59	M. Morra	1,632	3,281	1,250	1,500	7,664	–
60	F. Davies	3,117	3,937	562	–	7,617	–
61	J. McLaughlin	–	2,406	5,150	–	7,556	–
62	L. Dodd	1,632	3,937	1,779	–	7,349	–
63	K. Owers	1,632	3,296	2,404	–	7,334	–
64	D. Gilbert	–	5,406	1,779	–	7,185	–
65	J. Wright	3,117	3,281	712	–	7,110	–
66	J. Chambers	4,437	2,187	–	–	6,625	–
67	S. Duggan	3,117	1,531	1,779	–	6,427	–
68	B. Oliver	3,117	2,625	150	–	5,892	–
69	N. Gilbert	–	5,843	–	–	5,843	–
70	P. Gibson	1,632	3,781	150	–	5,564	–
71	M. Bradley	1,632	1,968	1,217	–	4,818	–
	M. Wildman	1,632	1,968	1,217	–	4,818	–
72	C. Roscoe	–	4,609	–	–	4,609	–
73	M. Gauvreau	–	2,843	1,717	–	4,560	–
74	P. Houlihan	1,632	2,906	–	–	4,542	–
75	M. Fisher	–	4,500	–	–	4,500	–
76	B. Harris	3,117	–	1,217	–	4,334	–
77	R. Bales	–	2,906	1,217	–	4,123	–
78	B. Rowswell	–	4,000	–	–	4,000	–
79	E. Sinclair	1,632	875	1,400	–	3,907	–
80	M. Gibson	–	1,312	2,400	–	3,712	–
81	J. Donnelly	–	2,421	1,250	–	3,671	–
82	E. Lawlor	–	2,843	712	–	3,556	–
83	V. Harris	–	3,390	150	–	3,540	–
84	I. Williamson	–	2,187	1,217	–	3,404	–
85	P. Medati	–	2,906	–	–	2,906	–
86	J. Dunning	–	2,843	–	–	2,843	–
87	B. Kelly	–	–	150	2,375	2,525	–
88	J. Van Rensburg	–	2,406	–	–	2,406	–
89	P. Watchorn	–	1,531	625	–	2,156	–
90	Glen Wilkinson	–	1,312	705	–	2,017	–
91	A. Kearney	–	1,312	625	–	1,937	–
92	G. Rigitano	–	1,093	650	–	1,743	–
93	M. Darrington	–	1,312	150	–	1,462	–
	J. Meadowcroft	–	1,312	150	–	1,462	–
94	I. Black	–	–	1,400	–	1,400	–
95	G.Scott	–	1,093	150	–	1,243	–
	T. Whitthread	–	1,093	150	–	1,243	–
96	R. Grace	–	875	150	–	1,025	–
	Jack Rea	–	875	150	–	1,025	–

The following players only won money in sanctioned events. Money total as follows: 97 J. Caggianello, F. Jonik, G. Watson £850; 98 E. McLaughlin £750; 99 D. Greaves, R. Marshall £712; 100 G. Jenkins £705; 101 D. Chalmers, D. Hughes, J. Smith £562; 102 I. Anderson £555; 103 B. Mikkelsen, P. Thornley £500; 104 P. Burke, P. Fagan, J. Fitzmaurice, G. Foulds, A. Harris, D. Heaton, D. Sheehan £150.

THE PLAYERS

(WS) = *World Series. Figure in brackets denotes previous season's ranking.*

IAN ANDERSON (Australia)

Born 2.4.46. **Turned professional** 1974. **World ranking** 107 (101).

1974	v Mans	1-8	1st round	World Championship
1975	v Condo	15-8	1st round	World Championship
	v Williams	4-15	2nd round	World Championship
1976	v Jack Rea	5-8	Qualifying	Embassy World Championship
1979	v S. Davis	1-9	Prelim	Embassy World Championship
1981	v Martin	3-9	Qualifying	Embassy World Championship
1982	v Houlihan	5-9	Qualifying	Embassy World Championship
	v Sinclair	2-5	Qualifying	Jameson International
	v David Taylor	1-5	1st round	Professional Players Tournament
1983	v King	6-10	Qualifying	Embassy World Championship
	v Oliver	9-1	Qualifying	Coral UK Championship
	v Dunning	2-9	Qualifying	Coral UK Championship
1984	v Watson	10-4	Qualifying	Embassy World Championship
	v Donnelly	6-10	Qualifying	Embassy World Championship
1985	v Kearney	10-8	Qualifying	Embassy World Championship
	v Browne	5-10	Qualifying	Embassy World Championship
	v King	2-8	Quarter-final	Australian Championship
1986	v Charlton	2-6	Quarter-final	Australian Championship
	v John Rea	1-5	2nd round	BCE International
	v Oliver	5-4	1st round	Rothmans Grand Prix
	v Murphy	5-4	2nd round	Rothmans Grand Prix
1987	v Charlton	2-6	Quarter-final	Australian Championship
	v Watterson	5-3	1st round	Fidelity International
	v Cripsey	4-5	2nd round	Fidelity International
	v Jenkins	5-2	1st round	Rothmans Grand Prix
	v Bales	1-5	2nd round	Rothmans Grand Prix
	v Donnelly	4-9	1st round	Tennents UK Open

ROGER BALES (England)

Born 15.8.48. **Turned professional** 1984. **World ranking** 60 (58). **Best professional performances** Last 32 1987 Rothmans Grand Prix, 1986 Dulux British Open, 1986 BCE International.

1984	v Sheehan	5-2	Qualifying	Jameson International
	v Murphy	5-4	Qualifying	Jameson International
	v Fisher	5-3	Qualifying	Jameson International
	v Reynolds	4-5	Qualifying	Jameson International
	v Higgins	1-5	1st round	Rothmans Grand Prix
	v Chalmers	9-2	Qualifying	Coral UK Open
	v E. McLaughlin	9-4	Qualifying	Coral UK Open
	v Gauvreau	8-9	Qualifying	Coral UK Open
1985	v Bennett	5-1	Qualifying	Mercantile Credit Classic
	v Kelly	5-3	Qualifying	Mercantile Credit Classic
	v Virgo	1-5	Qualifying	Mercantile Credit Classic
	v Dodd	3-9	Qualifying	Tolly Cobbold English Championship
	v Black	6-4	Qualifying	Dulux British Open
	v Higgins	3-6	1st round	Dulux British Open
	v Chaperon	7-10	Qualifying	Embassy World Championship

	v Drago	5-2	1st round	Goya Matchroom Trophy
	v Edmonds	5-0	2nd round	Goya Matchroom Trophy
	v S. Davis	2-5	3rd round	Goya Matchroom Trophy
	v Smith	5-1	1st round	Rothmans Grand Prix
	v Fisher	5-3	2nd round	Rothmans Grand Prix
	v Wilson	1-5	3rd round	Rothmans Grand Prix
	v Simngam	2-9	1st round	Coral UK Open
1986	v Parkin	5-0	1st round	Mercantile Credit Classic
	v Fowler	4-5	2nd round	Mercantile Credit Classic
	v V. Harris	9-7	2nd round	Tolly Cobbold English Championship
	v Knowles	4-9	3rd round	Tolly Cobbold English Championship
	v Parkin	5-1	1st round	Dulux British Open
	v Dunning	wo	2nd round	Dulux British Open
	v Dennis Taylor	5-4	3rd round	Dulux British Open
	v Williams	4-5	4th round	Dulux British Open
	v Gilbert	7-10	Qualifying	Embassy World Championship
	v F. Davis	5-4	2nd round	BCE International
	v Stevens	5-3	3rd round	BCE International
	v Wilson	1-5	4th round	BCE International
	v F. Davis	4-5	2nd round	Rothmans Grand Prix
	v Cripsey	6-9	2nd round	Tennents UK Open
1987	v Murphy	2-5	2nd round	Mercantile Credit Classic
	v Owers	5-6	2nd round	Tolly Ales English Championship
	v Gauvreau	0-5	2nd round	Dulux British Open
	v Spencer	3-10	Qualifying	Embassy World Championship
	v John Rea	2-5	2nd round	Fidelity International
	v Anderson	5-1	2nd round	Rothmans Grand Prix
	v Campbell	5-3	3rd round	Rothmans Grand Prix
	v Thorne	2-5	4th round	Rothmans Grand Prix
	v Dunning	8-9	2nd round	Tennents UK Open
1988	v John Rea	0-5	2nd round	Mercantile Credit Classic
	v D. Gilbert	2-6	2nd round	English Championship
	v Gary Wilkinson	1-5	2nd round	MIM Britannia British Open
	v Miles	7-10	Qualifying	Embassy World Championship

JIM BEAR (Canada)

Born 21.1.40. **Turned professional** 1983. **World ranking** 86 (87). **Amateur career** Runner-up 1982 World Amateur Championship.

1983	v Morra	9-8	2nd round	Canadian Championship
	v John Bear	9-5	Quarter-final	Canadian Championship
	v Stevens	8-9	Semi-final	Canadian Championship
1985	v Caggianello	4-5	1st round	Canadian Championship
	v Houlihan	5-2	1st round	Goya Matchroom Trophy
	v Donnelly	5-2	2nd round	Goya Matchroom Trophy
	v Johnson	1-5	3rd round	Goya Matchroom Trophy
	v Kearney	3-5	1st round	Rothmans Grand Prix
	v Demarco	9-1	1st round	Coral UK Open
	v Watterson	9-0	2nd round	Coral UK Open
1986	v Kearney	0-5	1st round	Mercantile Credit Classic
	v O'Boye	1-5	1st round	Dulux British Open
	v Burke	10-8	Qualifying	Embassy World Championship
	v Gauvreau	5-10	Qualifying	Embassy World Championship
	v Chaperon	3-6	1st round	Canadian Championship
	v Watchorn	5-1	1st round	BCE International
	v Duggan	4-5	2nd round	BCE International
	v B. Bennett	5-2	1st round	Rothmans Grand Prix
	v Fowler	5-2	2nd round	Rothmans Grand Prix
	v Williams	2-5	3rd round	Rothmans Grand Prix
	v Everton	9-1	1st round	Tennents UK Open
	v Edmonds	6-9	2nd round	Tennents UK Open

1987	v Jack Rea	10-5	Qualifying	Embassy World Championship
	v Gauvreau	5-10	Qualifying	Embassy World Championship
	v Mikkelsen	6-0	1st round	Canadian Championship
	v Wych	6-4	Quarter-final	Canadian Championship
	v Stevens	7-2	Semi-final	Canadian Championship
	v Thorburn	4-8	Final	Canadian Championship
	v Clark	2-5	1st round	Fidelity International
	v Greaves	5-0	1st round	Rothmans Grand Prix
	v B. Harris	5-3	2nd round	Rothmans Grand Prix
	v Thorne	1-5	3rd round	Rothmans Grand Prix
	v Chalmers	9-5	1st round	Tennents UK Open
	v B. Harris	9-4	2nd round	Tennents UK Open
	v Johnson	5-9	3rd round	Tennents UK Open
1988	v J. Smith	5-3	1st round	Mercantile Credit Classic
	v Scott	3-5	2nd round	Mercantile Credit Classic
	v A. Harris	5-2	1st round	MIM Britannia British Open
	v Houlihan	5-0	2nd round	MIM Britannia British Open
	v S. Francisco	0-5	3rd round	MIM Britannia British Open
	v Mienie	10-4	Qualifying	Embassy World Championship
	v G. Foulds	10-2	Qualifying	Embassy World Championship
	v F. Davis	4-10	Qualifying	Embassy World Championship

MARK BENNETT (Wales)

Born 23.9.63. **Turned professional** 1986. **World ranking** 52 (55). **Amateur career** 1985 Welsh champion. **Best professional performances** Last 32 1988 Mercantile Credit Classic, 1987 Embassy World Championship, 1986 Rothmans Grand Prix.

1986	v Smith	5-4	1st round	BCE International
	v Browne	5-1	2nd round	BCE International
	v Virgo	1-5	3rd round	BCE International
	v Watterson	5-1	1st round	Rothmans Grand Prix
	v O'Kane	5-2	2nd round	Rothmans Grand Prix
	v Macleod	5-1	3rd round	Rothmans Grand Prix
	v Browne	0-5	4th round	Rothmans Grand Prix
	v Sheehan	8-9	1st round	Tennents UK Open
1987	v Sheehan	5-3	1st round	Mercantile Credit Classic
	v Black	5-3	2nd round	Mercantile Credit Classic
	v Virgo	3-5	3rd round	Mercantile Credit Classic
	v W. Jones	3-6	1st round	Matchroom Welsh Championship
	v Morra	4-5	1st round	Dulux British Open
	v Hargreaves	10-6	Qualifying	Embassy World Championship
	v Mikkelsen	10-4	Qualifying	Embassy World Championship
	v W. Jones	10-3	Qualifying	Embassy World Championship
	v Werbeniuk	10-8	Qualifying	Embassy World Championship
	v Dennis Taylor	4-10	1st round	Embassy World Championship
	v Chalmers	5-0	2nd round	Fidelity International
	v White	3-5	3rd round	Fidelity International
	v Medati	5-4	2nd round	Rothmans Grand Prix
	v Hendry	1-5	3rd round	Rothmans Grand Prix
	v V. Harris	7-9	2nd round	Tennents UK Open
1988	v G. Miles	5-1	2nd round	Mercantile Credit Classic
	v Stevens	5-2	3rd round	Mercantile Credit Classic
	v Clark	2-5	4th round	Mercantile Credit Classic
	v Everton	6-0	1st round	Welsh Championship
	v Mountjoy	3-6	Quarter-final	Welsh Championship
	v Morra	2-5	2nd round	MIM Britannia British Open
	v Rigitano	10-4	Qualifying	Embassy World Championship
	v Wych	10-5	Qualifying	Embassy World Championship
	v Stevens	7-10	Qualifying	Embassy World Championship

IAN BLACK (Scotland)

Born 11.12.54. **Turned professional** 1981. **World ranking** 96 (75). **Best professional performance** 1981 Scottish champion.

1981	v Macleod	5-4	Quarter-final	Scottish Championship
	v E. McLaughlin	6-3	Semi-final	Scottish Championship
	v Gibson	**11-7**	**Final**	**Scottish Championship**
	v E. McLaughlin	5-3	Qualifying	Jameson International
	v Houlihan	4-9	Qualifying	Coral UK Championship
1982	v Parkin	9-6	Qualifying	Embassy World Championship
	v Williams	2-9	Qualifying	Embassy World Championship
	v Macleod	6-0	Quarter-final	Scottish Championship
	v Ross	6-4	Semi-final	Scottish Championship
	v Sinclair	7-11	Final	Scottish Championship
	v Fitzmaurice	3-5	Qualifying	Jameson International
	v Virgo	2-5	1st round	Professional Players Tournament
	v Fisher	3-9	Qualifying	Coral UK Championship
1983	v Morra	10-9	Qualifying	Embassy World Championship
	v Medati	10-4	Qualifying	Embassy World Championship
	v Mans	3-10	1st round	Embassy World Championship
	v E. McLaughlin	6-4	1st round	Scottish Championship
	v Macleod	2-6	Semi-final	Scottish Championship
	v King	3-5	Qualifying	Jameson International
	v Spencer	2-5	1st round	Professional Players Tournament
	v Williamson	9-6	Qualifying	Coral UK Championship
	v White	1-9	1st round	Coral UK Championship
1984	v Hines	5-10	Qualifying	Embassy World Championship
	v Browne	5-4	Qualifying	Jameson International
	v Watterson	5-3	Qualifying	Jameson International
	v Macleod	3-5	Qualifying	Jameson International
	v P. Francisco	4-5	Qualifying	Rothmans Grand Prix
	v Chappel	3-9	Qualifying	Coral UK Open
1985	v J. McLaughlin	0-5	Qualifying	Mercantile Credit Classic
	v M. Gibson	2-6	1st round	Scottish Championship
	v Bales	4-6	Qualifying	Dulux British Open
	v Chalmers	4-10	Qualifying	Embassy World Championship
	v Rigitano	5-4	2nd round	Goya Matchroom Trophy
	v Mans	5-4	3rd round	Goya Matchroom Trophy
	v Duggan	1-5	4th round	Goya Matchroom Trophy
	v G. Foulds	3-5	2nd round	Rothmans Grand Prix
	v V. Harris	3-9	2nd round	Coral UK Open
1986	v G. Foulds	2-5	2nd round	Mercantile Credit Classic
	v Gibson	5-0	2nd round	Dulux British Open
	v S. Davis	2-5	3rd round	Dulux British Open
	v E. McLaughlin	6-4	Quarter-final	Canada Dry Scottish Championship
	v Hendry	2-6	Semi-final	Canada Dry Scottish Championship
	v B. Harris	10-8	Qualifying	Embassy World Championship
	v Newbury	2-10	Qualifying	Embassy World Championship
	v Wright	5-1	2nd round	BCE International
	v Charlton	0-5	3rd round	BCE International
	v Morra	4-5	2nd round	Rothmans Grand Prix
	v Watterson	3-9	2nd round	Tennents UK Open
1987	v M. Bennett	3-5	2nd round	Mercantile Credit Classic
	v John Rea	1-6	1st round	Scottish Championship
	v Roe	0-5	2nd round	Dulux British Open
	v Williamson	10-8	Qualifying	Embassy World Championship
	v O'Kane	2-10	Qualifying	Embassy World Championship
	v N. Gilbert	3-5	1st round	Fidelity International
	v M. Smith	0-5	1st round	Rothmans Grand Prix
	v J. Smith	9-8	1st round	Tennents UK Open
	v Werbeniuk	5-9	2nd round	Tennents UK Open
1988	v P. Gibson	2-5	1st round	Mercantile Credit Classic

v M. Gibson	2-6	Quarter-final	Scottish Championship
v Gary Wilkinson	2-5	1st round	MIM Britannia British Open
v Fowler	1-10	Qualifying	Embassy World Championship

MALCOLM BRADLEY (England)

Born 8.7.48. **Turned professional** 1984. **World ranking** 75 (57). **Best professional performances** Last 32 1985 Goya Matchroom Trophy, 1987 Mercantile Credit Classic.

1984	v Darrington	5-3	Qualifying	Jameson International
	v Jack Rea	5-2	Qualifying	Jameson International
	v Morra	3-5	Qualifying	Jameson International
	v Jonik	5-1	Qualifying	Rothmans Grand Prix
	v Virgo	0-5	1st round	Rothmans Grand Prix
	v V. Harris	9-8	Qualifying	Coral UK Open
	v Kelly	9-6	Qualifying	Coral UK Open
	v Meadowcroft	9-7	Qualifying	Coral UK Open
	v Hallett	8-9	Qualifying	Coral UK Open
1985	v Browne	3-5	Qualifying	Mercantile Credit Classic
	v Williamson	9-8	Qualifying	Tolly Cobbold English Championship
	v Knowles	8-9	Qualifying	Tolly Cobbold English Championship
	v Morra	6-2	Qualifying	Dulux British Open
	v David Taylor	6-3	1st round	Dulux British Open
	v Fowler	5-4	2nd round	Dulux British Open
	v S. Davis	2-5	3rd round	Dulux British Open
	v Mienie	10-4	Qualifying	Embassy World Championship
	v Mikkelsen	10-9	Qualifying	Embassy World Championship
	v Wych	7-10	Qualifying	Embassy World Championship
	v John Rea	5-1	2nd round	Goya Matchroom Trophy
	v Hallett	5-4	3rd round	Goya Matchroom Trophy
	v Johnson	2-5	4th round	Goya Matchroom Trophy
	v Gibson	4-5	2nd round	Rothmans Grand Prix
	v Jenkins	9-3	2nd round	Coral UK Open
	v White	4-9	1st round	Coral UK Open
1986	v Oliver	5-3	2nd round	Mercantile Credit Classic
	v N. Foulds	3-5	3rd round	Mercantile Credit Classic
	v Gilbert	9-5	2nd round	Tolly Cobbold English Championship
	v S. Davis	3-9	3rd round	Tolly Cobbold English Championship
	v Jack Rea	5-1	2nd round	Dulux British Open
	v Higgins	3-5	3rd round	Dulux British Open
	v Gilbert	7-10	Qualifying	Embassy World Championship
	v Wilkinson	5-4	2nd round	BCE International
	v Wych	2-5	3rd round	BCE International
	v Wright	0-5	2nd round	Rothmans Grand Prix
	v Meadowcroft	9-2	2nd round	Tennents UK Open
	v Parrott	4-9	3rd round	Tennents UK Open
1987	v Rowswell	5-4	2nd round	Mercantile Credit Classic
	v David Taylor	5-1	3rd round	Mercantile Credit Classic
	v White	0-5	4th round	Mercantile Credit Classic
	v D. Gilbert	6-3	2nd round	Tolly Ales English Championship
	v Fowler	3-6	3rd round	Tolly Ales English Championship
	v O'Boye	1-5	2nd round	Dulux British Open
	v Rowswell	10-6	Qualifying	Embassy World Championship
	v O'Boye	10-7	Qualifying	Embassy World Championship
	v Wych	7-10	Qualifying	Embassy World Championship
	v J. Smith	5-1	2nd round	Fidelity International
	v Dennis Taylor	0-5	3rd round	Fidelity International
	v John Rea	1-5	2nd round	Rothmans Grand Prix
	v Watchorn	5-9	2nd round	Tennents UK Open
1988	v Everton	2-5	2nd round	Mercantile Credit Classic
	v Thorne	1-5	3rd round	Mercantile Credit Classic

v Lawlor	5-6	2nd round	English Championship
v Williamson	3-5	2nd round	MIM Britannia British Open
v Williamson	10-9	Qualifying	Embassy World Championship
v Werbeniuk	8-10	Qualifying	Embassy World Championship

PADDY BROWNE (Republic of Ireland)

Born 1.4.65. **Turned professional** 1983. **World ranking** 54 (43). **Amateur career** 1982 Republic of Ireland champion. **Best professional performance** Last 16 1986 Rothmans Grand Prix.

1983	v Murphy	2-5	Qualifying	Professional Players Tournament
1984	v Duggan	10-9	Qualifying	Embassy World Championship
	v Roscoe	10-4	Qualifying	Embassy World Championship
	v Sinclair	1-10	Qualifying	Embassy World Championship
	v John Rea	5-2	Qualifying	Jameson International
	v Black	4-5	Qualifying	Jameson International
	v Duggan	2-5	Qualifying	Rothmans Grand Prix
	v G. Foulds	9-5	Qualifying	Coral UK Open
	v King	5-9	Qualifying	Coral UK Open
1985	v Bradley	5-3	Qualifying	Mercantile Credit Classic
	v Everton	5-0	Qualifying	Mercantile Credit Classic
	v Miles	5-3	Qualifying	Mercantile Credit Classic
	v White	2-5	1st round	Mercantile Credit Classic
	v Newbury	0-6	Qualifying	Dulux British Open
	v Murphy	3-6	Qualifying	Irish Championship
	v Anderson	10-5	Qualifying	Embassy World Championship
	v Morra	6-10	Qualifying	Embassy World Championship
	v B. Harris	3-5	2nd round	Goya Matchroom Trophy
	v B. Harris	3-5	2nd round	Rothmans Grand Prix
	v Chalmers	9-4	2nd round	Coral UK Open
	v Thorne	6-9	3rd round	Coral UK Open
1986	v Everton	5-0	2nd round	Mercantile Credit Classic
	v Wilson	5-3	3rd round	Mercantile Credit Classic
	v Gauvreau	3-5	4th round	Mercantile Credit Classic
	v Hendry	5-0	2nd round	Dulux British Open
	v Spencer	5-0	3rd round	Dulux British Open
	v Charlton	1-5	4th round	Dulux British Open
	v Hendry	9-10	Qualifying	Embassy World Championship
	v Burke	4-5	1st round	Strongbow Irish Championship
	v M. Bennett	1-5	2nd round	BCE International
	v Sheehan	5-4	2nd round	Rothmans Grand Prix
	v Johnson	5-2	3rd round	Rothmans Grand Prix
	v M. Bennett	5-0	4th round	Rothmans Grand Prix
	v Hendry	3-5	5th round	Rothmans Grand Prix
	v Williamson	4-9	2nd round	Tennents UK Open
1987	v Dunning	5-1	2nd round	Mercantile Credit Classic
	v Campbell	2-5	3rd round	Mercantile Credit Classic
	v Rigitano	4-5	2nd round	Dulux British Open
	v Wright	6-10	Qualifying	Embassy World Championship
	v Jack Rea	5-3	1st round	Matchroom Irish Championship
	v Burke	6-2	Quarter-final	Matchroom Irish Championship
	v Dennis Taylor	1-6	Semi-final	Matchroom Irish Championship
	v Roscoe	2-5	2nd round	Fidelity International
	v Meadowcroft	3-5	2nd round	Rothmans Grand Prix
	v M. Smith	4-9	2nd round	Tennents UK Open
1988	v M. Smith	1-5	2nd round	Mercantile Credit Classic
	v Jack Rea	5-0	1st round	Irish Championship
	v Murphy	6-5	Quarter-final	Irish Championship
	v Dennis Taylor	5-6	Semi-final	Irish Championship
	v Chalmers	5-2	2nd round	MIM Britannia British Open
	v Martin	5-4	3rd round	MIM Britannia British Open

v O'Kane	2-5	4th round	MIM Britannia British Open
v Kelly	10-8	Qualifying	Embassy World Championship
v James	1-10	Qualifying	Embassy World Championship

PASCAL BURKE (Republic of Ireland)
Born 19.6.32. **Turned professional** 1982. **World ranking** 105 (98). **Amateur career** 1974 & 1976 Republic of Ireland champion.

1983	v E. Hughes	2-6	Quarter-final	Irish Championship
	v Meo	0-5	1st round	Benson & Hedges Irish Masters
	v Morgan	9-10	Qualifying	Embassy World Championship
	v G. Foulds	2-5	Qualifying	Jameson International
	v G. Foulds	5-4	Qualifying	Professional Players Tournament
	v Johnson	3-5	1st round	Professional Players Tournament
1984	v Kelly	10-7	Qualifying	Embassy World Championship
	v B. Harris	10-4	Qualifying	Embassy World Championship
	v Hallett	5-10	Qualifying	Embassy World Championship
	v Kearney	5-4	Qualifying	Jameson International
	v Newbury	0-5	Qualifying	Jameson International
	v Darrington	5-3	Qualifying	Rothmans Grand Prix
	v Meo	1-5	1st round	Rothmans Grand Prix
	v Longworth	4-9	Qualifying	Coral UK Open
1985	v Newbury	1-5	Qualifying	Mercantile Credit Classic
	v Chalmers	5-6	Qualifying	Dulux British Open
	v Kearney	6-4	Qualifying	Irish Championship
	v Higgins	0-6	Quarter-final	Irish Championship
	v Newbury	3-10	Qualifying	Embassy World Championship
	v Rempe	3-5	1st round	Goya Matchroom Trophy
	v Newbury	3-5	2nd round	Rothmans Grand Prix
	v Jenkins	5-9	1st round	Coral UK Open
1986	v D. Hughes	5-3	1st round	Mercantile Credit Classic
	v Chaperon	2-5	2nd round	Mercantile Credit Classic
	v Gilbert	1-5	1st round	Dulux British Open
	v Jim Bear	8-10	Qualifying	Embassy World Championship
	v Browne	5-4	1st round	Strongbow Irish Championship
	v E. Hughes	3-6	Quarter-final	Strongbow Irish Championship
	v Fitzmaurice	5-4	1st round	BCE International
	v T. Jones	5-4	2nd round	BCE International
	v Thorburn	0-5	3rd round	BCE International
	v Roscoe	5-3	1st round	Rothmans Grand Prix
	v Spencer	3-5	2nd round	Rothmans Grand Prix
	v Watterson	0-9	1st round	Tennents UK Open
1987	v King	0-5	2nd round	Mercantile Credit Classic
	v Scott	2-5	2nd round	Dulux British Open
	v Oliver	5-10	Qualifying	Embassy World Championship
	v Fagan	5-3	1st round	Matchroom Irish Championship
	v Browne	2-6	Quarter-final	Matchroom Irish Championship
	v Jack Rea	1-5	1st round	Fidelity International
	v Everton	5-1	1st round	Rothmans Grand Prix
	v Reardon	2-5	2nd round	Rothmans Grand Prix
	v Oliver	1-9	1st round	Tennents UK Open
1988	v Oliver	2-5	1st round	Mercantile Credit Classic
	v J. McLaughlin	3-5	1st round	Irish Championship
	v Darrington	4-5	1st round	MIM Britannia British Open
	v Sinclair	2-10	Qualifying	Embassy World Championship

JOE CAGGIANELLO (Canada)
Born 16.5.55. **Turned professional** 1983. **World ranking** 130 (119).

1983	v Sanderson	9-5	1st round	Canadian Championship
	v Thornley	9-7	2nd round	Canadian Championship
	v Stevens	0-9	Quarter-final	Canadian Championship

1984	v Darrington	10-7	Qualifying	Embassy World Championship
	v Oliver	7-10	Qualifying	Embassy World Championship
1985	v Jim Bear	5-4	1st round	Canadian Championship
	v Thorburn	2-6	Quarter-final	Canadian Championship
	v Hargreaves	5-2	1st round	Goya Matchroom Trophy
	v King	0-5	2nd round	Goya Matchroom Trophy
	v Watterson	1-5	2nd round	Rothmans Grand Prix
1986	v Watson	3-6	1st round	Canadian Championship
1987	v Dunning	7-10	Qualifying	Embassy World Championship
	v Gauvreau	6-3	1st round	Canadian Championship
	v Stevens	0-6	Quarter-final	Canadian Championship

JOHN CAMPBELL (Australia)

Born 10.4.53. **Turned professional** 1982. **World ranking** 33 (22). **Amateur career** 1979 Australian champion. **Best professional performances** Last 16 1986 Embassy World Championship, 1985 Rothmans Grand Prix, 1985 Goya Matchroom Trophy, 1986 Mercantile Credit Classic, 1986 Dulux British Open, 1987 Mercantile Credit Classic; 1987 Rothmans Grand Prix; 1985 Australian champion.

1983	v Watterson	10-6	Qualifying	Embassy World Championship
	v Donnelly	10-2	Qualifying	Embassy World Championship
	v Thorburn	5-10	1st round	Embassy World Championship
	v E. McLaughlin	2-5	Qualifying	Jameson International
	v Mountjoy	5-3	1st round	Professional Players Tournament
	v Miles	5-2	2nd round	Professional Players Tournament
	v Martin	5-0	3rd round	Professional Players Tournament
	v Knowles	3-5	Quarter-final	Professional Players Tournament
1984	v White	1-5	Qualifying	Lada Classic
	v Gauvreau	7-10	Qualifying	Embassy World Championship
	v G. Foulds	5-3	Qualifying	Jameson International
	v S. Davis	1-5	1st round	Jameson International
	v W. Jones	5-4	1st round	Rothmans Grand Prix
	v Thorburn	1-5	2nd round	Rothmans Grand Prix
	v Donnelly	9-6	Qualifying	Coral UK Open
	v White	7-9	1st round	Coral UK Open
1985	v Scott	4-5	Qualifying	Mercantile Credit Classic
	v O'Kane	4-6	1st round	Dulux British Open
	v Morra	10-9	Qualifying	Embassy World Championship
	v Charlton	3-10	1st round	Embassy World Championship
	v Charlton	5-4	Quarter-final	Winfield Australian Masters
	v Parrott	6-4	Semi-final	Winfield Australian Masters
	v Meo	2-7	Final	Winfield Australian Masters
	v Foldvari	8-5	Quarter-final	Australian Championship
	v King	9-6	Semi-final	Australian Championship
	v Charlton	**10-7**	**Final**	**Australian Championship**
	v Morra	5-2	3rd round	Goya Matchroom Trophy
	v Mountjoy	5-1	4th round	Goya Matchroom Trophy
	v Thorburn	0-5	5th round	Goya Matchroom Trophy
	v Van Rensberg	5-4	3rd round	Rothmans Grand Prix
	v Mountjoy	5-2	4th round	Rothmans Grand Prix
	v Knowles	2-5	5th round	Rothmans Grand Prix
	v Medati	9-7	3rd round	Coral UK Open
	v David Taylor	4-9	4th round	Coral UK Open
1986	v Donnelly	5-2	3rd round	Mercantile Credit Classic
	v Mikkelsen	5-2	4th round	Mercantile Credit Classic
	v N. Foulds	1-5	5th round	Mercantile Credit Classic
	v West	5-4	3rd round	Dulux British Open

v Medati	5-4	4th round	Dulux British Open
v S. Davis	0-5	5th round	Dulux British Open
v Van Rensberg	10-6	Qualifying	Embassy World Championship
v Reardon	10-8	1st round	Embassy World Championship
v Thorne	9-13	2nd round	Embassy World Championship
v Wilkinson	6-1	Quarter-final	Australian Championship
v Foldvari	8-3	Semi-final	Australian Championship
v King	3-10	Final	Australian Championship
v Duggan	3-5	3rd round	BCE International
v G. Foulds	5-0	3rd round	Rothmans Grand Prix
v Griffiths	1-5	4th round	Rothmans Grand Prix
v W. Jones	3-9	3rd round	Tennents UK Open
1987 v Browne	5-2	3rd round	Mercantile Credit Classic
v Spencer	5-3	4th round	Mercantile Credit Classic
v Griffiths	3-5	5th round	Mercantile Credit Classic
v James	1-5	3rd round	Dulux British Open
v Chappel	10-6	Qualifying	Embassy World Championship
v S. Francisco	3-10	1st round	Embassy World Championship
v Wilkinson	6-4	Quarter-final	Australian Championship
v Charlton	6-8	Semi-final	Australian Championship
v James	4-5	3rd round	Fidelity International
v Bales	3-5	3rd round	Rothmans Grand Prix
v Chambers	9-7	3rd round	Tennents UK Open
v M. Smith	9-8	4th round	Tennents UK Open
v Thorburn	4-9	5th round	Tennents UK Open
1988 v Murphy	3-5	3rd round	Mercantile Credit Classic
v W. Jones	5-3	3rd round	MIM Britannia British Open
v O'Boye	1-5	4th round	MIM Britannia British Open
v F. Davis	10-3	Qualifying	Embassy World Championship
v White	3-10	1st round	Embassy World Championship

DAVE CHALMERS (England)

Born 14.7.48. **Turned professional** 1984. **World ranking** 112 (111). **Amateur career** 1982 English champion.

1984 v Oliver	5-4	Qualifying	Jameson International
v Meadowcroft	1-5	Qualifying	Jameson International
v Andrewartha	5-2	Qualifying	Rothmans Grand Prix
v Williams	0-5	1st round	Rothmans Grand Prix
v Bales	2-9	Qualifying	Coral UK Open
1985 v Mikkelsen	1-5	Prelim	Mercantile Credit Classic
v Meadowcroft	9-3	Qualifying	Tolly Cobbold English Championship
v White	5-9	Qualifying	Tolly Cobbold English Championship
v Burke	6-5	Qualifying	Dulux British Open
v Griffiths	0-6	1st round	Dulux British Open
v Greaves	10-3	Qualifying	Embassy World Championship
v E. McLaughlin	10-9	Qualifying	Embassy World Championship
v Black	10-4	Qualifying	Embassy World Championship
v Hallett	1-10	Qualifying	Embassy World Championship
v Chaperon	2-5	2nd round	Goya Matchroom Trophy
v Scott	2-5	2nd round	Rothmans Grand Prix
v Browne	4-9	2nd round	Coral UK Open
1986 v Donnelly	0-5	2nd round	Mercantile Credit Classic
v Fisher	9-2	2nd round	Tolly Cobbold English Championship
v Hallett	1-9	3rd round	Tolly Cobbold English Championship
v Scott	1-5	2nd round	Dulux British Open
v F. Davis	6-10	Qualifying	Embassy World Championship
v Houlihan	1-5	1st round	BCE International
v Agrawal	5-1	1st round	Rothmans Grand Prix

	v Chaperon	2-5	2nd round	Rothmans Grand Prix
	v Oliver	6-9	1st round	Tennents UK Open
1987	v G. Foulds	4-5	1st round	Mercantile Credit Classic
	v Wright	5-6	1st round	Tolly Ales English Championship
	v Wildman	0-5	2nd round	Dulux British Open
	v T. Jones	1-10	Qualifying	Embassy World Championship
	v Fitzmaurice	5-4	1st round	Fidelity International
	v M. Bennett	0-5	2nd round	Fidelity International
	v Darrington	2-5	1st round	Rothmans Grand Prix
	v Bear	5-9	1st round	Tennents UK Open
1988	v Glen Wilkinson	3-5	1st round	Mercantile Credit Classic
	v Browne	2-5	2nd round	MIM Britannia British Open
	v Oliver	9-10	Qualifying	Embassy World Championship

JIM CHAMBERS (England)

Born 7.2.57. **Turned professional** 1987. **World ranking** 73. **Best professional performance** Last 32 1987 Rothmans Grand Prix.

1987	v Grace	4-5	2nd round	Fidelity International
	v Fitzmaurice	5-2	1st round	Rothmans Grand Prix
	v O'Boye	5-3	2nd round	Rothmans Grand Prix
	v Mountjoy	5-2	3rd round	Rothmans Grand Prix
	v Hendry	1-5	4th round	Rothmans Grand Prix
	v Roscoe	9-4	1st round	Tennents UK Open
	v Wildman	9-5	2nd round	Tennents UK Open
	v Campbell	7-9	3rd round	Tennents UK Open
1988	v Rowswell	2-5	1st round	Mercantile Credit Classic
	v P. Gibson	6-0	1st round	English Championship
	v Scott	6-2	2nd round	English Championship
	v Longworth	4-6	3rd round	English Championship
	v Roe	3-5	1st round	MIM Britannia British Open
	v Watterson	10-3	Qualifying	Embassy World Championship
	v Wright	2-10	Qualifying	Embassy World Championship

ROBERT CHAPERON (Canada)

Born 18.5.58. **Turned professional** 1983. **World ranking** 29 (41). **Amateur career** 1981 Canadian champion. **Best professional performance** Quarter-finals 1987 Rothmans Grand Prix.

1983	v Watson	9-5	1st round	Canadian Championship
	v Jonik	4-9	2nd round	Canadian Championship
1984	v Fowler	0-5	Qualifying	Jameson International
	v Kearney	5-1	Qualifying	Rothmans Grand Prix
	v Gibson	5-4	Qualifying	Rothmans Grand Prix
	v Martin	4-5	Qualifying	Rothmans Grand Prix
	v T. Jones	1-9	Qualifying	Coral UK Open
1985	v G. Foulds	3-5	Qualifying	Mercantile Credit Clasic
	v Fagan	6-5	Qualifying	Dulux British Open
	v Werbeniuk	6-1	1st round	Dulux British Open
	v W. Jones	5-2	2nd round	Dulux British Open
	v S. Francisco	2-5	3rd round	Dulux British Open
	v Bales	10-7	Qualifying	Embassy World Championship
	v Heywood	10-1	Qualifying	Embassy World Championship
	v Morgan	10-3	Qualifying	Embassy World Championship
	v F. Davis	9-10	Qualifying	Embassy World Championship
	v Thornley	5-1	1st round	Canadian Championship
	v Stevens	6-4	Quarter-final	Canadian Championship
	v Jonik	6-3	Semi-final	Canadian Championship
	v Thorburn	4-6	Final	Canadian Championship

	v Chalmers	5-2	2nd round	Goya Matchroom Trophy
	v S. Francisco	5-3	3rd round	Goya Matchroom Trophy
	v Macleod	4-5	4th round	Goya Matchroom Trophy
	v O'Boye	3-5	2nd round	Rothmans Grand Prix
	v J. McLaughlin	5-9	2nd round	Coral UK Open
1986	v Burke	5-2	2nd round	Mercantile Credit Classic
	S. Davis	1-5	3rd round	Mercantile Credit Classic
	v V. Harris	5-0	2nd round	Dulux British Open
	v Wilson	3-5	3rd round	Dulux British Open
	v Jonik	10-8	Qualifying	Embassy World Championship
	v Gauvreau	8-10	Qualifying	Embassy World Championship
	v Bear	6-3	1st round	Canadian Championship
	v Jonik	3-6	2nd round	Canadian Championship
	v N. Gilbert	5-3	2nd round	BCE International
	v Martin	5-4	3rd round	BCE International
	v Drago	5-1	4th round	BCE International
	v E. Hughes	0-5	5th round	BCE International
	v Chalmers	5-2	2nd round	Rothmans Grand Prix
	v Reardon	5-3	3rd round	Rothmans Grand Prix
	v Hendry	2-5	4th round	Rothmans Grand Prix
	v Dodd	9-4	2nd round	Tennents UK Open
	v David Taylor	8-9	3rd round	Tennents UK Open
1987	v Roe	5-4	2nd round	Mercantile Credit Classic
	v Stevens	3-5	3rd round	Mercantile Credit Classic
	v Fisher	5-2	2nd round	Dulux British Open
	v Stevens	4-5	3rd round	Dulux British Open
	v Fitzmaurice	10-2	Qualifying	Embassy World Championship
	v Spencer	4-10	Qualifying	Embassy World Championship
	v Morra	5-6	1st round	Canadian Championship
	v V. Harris	5-4	2nd round	Fidelity International
	v West	5-4	3rd round	Fidelity International
	v Parrott	1-5	4th round	Fidelity International
	v Rowswell	5-4	2nd round	Rothmans Grand Prix
	v Reynolds	5-4	3rd round	Rothmans Grand Prix
	v Houlihan	5-0	4th round	Rothmans Grand Prix
	v Fisher	5-2	5th round	Rothmans Grand Prix
	v Parrott	2-5	Quarter-final	Rothmans Grand Prix
	v Jack Rea	9-6	2nd round	Tennents UK Open
	v David Taylor	6-9	3rd round	Tennents UK Open
1988	v Medati	5-3	2nd round	Mercantile Credit Classic
	v N. Foulds	1-5	3rd round	Mercantile Credit Classic
	v Rigitano	5-2	2nd round	MIM Britannia British Open
	v Stevens	wo	3rd round	MIM Britannia British Open
	v T. Jones	4-5	4th round	MIM Britannia British Open
	v Marshall	10-3	Qualifying	Embassy World Championship
	v Murphy	10-5	Qualifying	Embassy World Championship
	v David Taylor	10-6	Qualifying	Embassy World Championship
	v Hallett	2-10	1st round	Embassy World Championship

TONY CHAPPEL (Wales)

Born 28.5.60. **Turned professional** 1984. **World ranking** 51 (59). **Best professional performance** Last 16 1987 Tennents UK Open.

1984	v Mikkelsen	4-5	Qualifying	Jameson International
	v Scott	5-1	Qualifying	Rothmans Grand Prix
	v Stevens	3-5	1st round	Rothmans Grand Prix
	v Houlihan	9-3	Qualifying	Coral UK Open
	v Black	9-3	Qualifying	Coral UK Open
	v Reynolds	9-6	Qualifying	Coral UK Open
	v Stevens	7-9	1st round	Coral UK Open
	v Giannaros	2-5	Qualifying	Mercantile Credit Classic

	v Williamson	6-5	Qualifying	Dulux British Open
	v S. Davis	5-6	1st round	Dulux British Open
	v Hines	8-10	Qualifying	Embassy World Championship
	v M. Owen	6-0	1st round	BCE Welsh Championship
	v Griffiths	0-6	Quarter-final	BCE Welsh Championship
1985	v Meadowcroft	5-2	2nd round	Goya Matchroom Trophy
	v Stevens	5-3	3rd round	Goya Matchroom Trophy
	v Wilson	0-5	4th round	Goya Matchroom Trophy
	v Dodd	5-2	2nd round	Rothmans Grand Prix
	v Mountjoy	1-5	3rd round	Rothmans Grand Prix
	v O'Kane	9-5	1st round	Coral UK Open
	v White	5-9	2nd round	Coral UK Open
1986	v Murphy	4-5	2nd round	Mercantile Credit Classic
	v Griffiths	4-6	Quarter-final	Zetters Welsh Championship
	v Fowler	4-5	2nd round	Dulux British Open
	v Wych	6-10	Qualifying	Embassy World Championship
	v Roscoe	5-3	2nd round	BCE International
	v E. Hughes	4-5	3rd round	BCE International
	v Kearney	5-1	2nd round	Rothmans Grand Prix
	v Meo	1-5	3rd round	Rothmans Grand Prix
	v Wilkinson	9-2	2nd round	Tennents UK Open
	v S. Davis	7-9	3rd round	Tennents UK Open
1987	v Wright	4-5	2nd round	Mercantile Credit Classic
	v Reardon	6-4	Quarter-final	Matchroom Welsh Championship
	v Mountjoy	2-9	Semi-final	Matchroom Welsh Championship
	v Kearney	5-3	2nd round	Dulux British Open
	v White	1-5	3rd round	Dulux British Open
	v Morra	10-8	Qualifying	Embassy World Championship
	v Duggan	10-3	Qualifying	Embassy World Championship
	v Campbell	6-10	Qualifying	Embassy World Championship
	v M. Gibson	5-2	2nd round	Fidelity International
	v Parrott	1-5	3rd round	Fidelity International
	v Jonik	5-4	2nd round	Rothmans Grand Prix
	v Spencer	5-1	3rd round	Rothmans Grand Prix
	v Griffiths	3-5	4th round	Rothmans Grand Prix
	v D. Gilbert	9-2	2nd round	Tennents UK Open
	v Reynolds	9-5	3rd round	Tennents UK Open
	v Longworth	9-6	4th round	Tennents UK Open
	v Johnson	4-9	5th round	Tennents UK Open
1988	v D. Hughes	5-3	2nd round	Mercantile Credit Classic
	v Johnson	2-5	3rd round	Mercantile Credit Classic
	v Roscoe	6-4	1st round	Welsh Championship
	v Griffiths	4-6	Quarter-final	Welsh Championship
	v Ellis	5-0	2nd round	MIM Britannia British Open
	v Hendry	1-5	3rd round	MIM Britannia British Open
	v N. Gilbert	10-8	Qualifying	Embassy World Championship
	v Miles	10-7	Qualifying	Embassy World Championship
	v Drago	7-10	Qualifying	Embassy World Championship

EDDIE CHARLTON A.M. (Australia)

Born 31.10.29. **Turned professional** 1960. **World ranking** 19 (26). **Best professional performances** Runner-up 1973 World Championship, 1975 World Championship; 1964–67, 1969–84 Australian champion.

1970	v Simpson	22-27	Semi-final	World Championship
1972	v David Taylor	31-25	Quarter-final	World Championship
	v Spencer	32-37	Semi-final	World Championship
1973	v Mans	16-8	2nd round	World Championship
	v Miles	16-6	Quarter-final	World Championship
	v Higgins	23-9	Semi-final	World Championship
	v Reardon	32-38	Final	World Championship

Eddie Charlton

1974	v Dunning	13-15	2nd round	World Championship
1975	v F. Davis	5-3	Quarter-final	Benson & Hedges Masters
	v Spencer	2-5	Semi-final	Benson & Hedges Masters
	v Werbeniuk	15-11	2nd round	World Championship
	v Thorburn	19-12	Quarter-final	World Championship
	v Dennis Taylor	19-12	Semi-final	World Championship
	v Reardon	30-31	Final	World Championship
1976	v Williams	4-1	2nd round	Benson & Hedges Masters
	v Reardon	4-5	Semi-final	Benson & Hedges Masters
	v Pulman	15-9	1st round	Embassy World Championship
	v F. Davis	15-13	Quarter-final	Embassy World Championship
	v Higgins	18-20	Semi-final	Embassy World Championship
1977	v David Taylor	13-5	1st round	Embassy World Championship
	v Thorburn	12-13	Quarter-final	Embassy World Championship
1978	v Thorne	13-12	1st round	Embassy World Championship
	v Thorburn	13-12	Quarter-final	Embassy World Championship
	v Reardon	14-18	Semi-final	Embassy World Championship
1979	v Higgins	2-5	Quarter-final	Benson & Hedges Masters
	v Mountjoy	13-6	1st round	Embassy World Championship
	v F. Davis	13-4	Quarter-final	Embassy World Championship
	v Griffiths	17-19	Semi-final	Embassy World Championship
1980	v Spencer	2-5	Quarter-final	Benson & Hedges Masters
	v Virgo	13-12	2nd round	Embassy World Championship
	v Stevens	7-13	Quarter-final	Embassy World Championship
1981	v Mountjoy	0-5	1st round	Benson & Hedges Masters
	v Mountjoy	7-13	2nd round	Embassy World Championship
	v Martin	2-5	3rd round	Jameson International
1982	v White	5-4	1st round	Benson & Hedges Masters
	v Higgins	1-5	Quarter-final	Benson & Hedges Masters
	v Wilson	10-5	1st round	Embassy World Championship
	v Werbeniuk	13-5	2nd round	Embassy World Championship
	v Knowles	13-11	Quarter-final	Embassy World Championship
	v Reardon	11-16	Semi-final	Embassy World Championship
	v Virgo	4-5	1st round	Jameson International
	v D. Hughes	5-2	1st round	Professional Players Tournament
	v Williams	5-2	2nd round	Professional Players Tournament
	v Meo	5-3	3rd round	Professional Players Tournament
	v Reynolds	5-2	Quarter-final	Professional Players Tournament
	v Reardon	7-10	Semi-final	Professional Players Tournament
1983	v Virgo	5-2	1st round	Lada Classic
	v S. Davis	4-5	Quarter-final	Lada Classic
	v Meo	5-3	1st round	Benson & Hedges Masters
	v Werbeniuk	5-3	Quarter-final	Benson & Hedges Masters
	v Thorburn	5-6	Semi-final	Benson & Hedges Masters
	v David Taylor	5-4	1st round	Benson & Hedges Irish Masters
	v S. Davis	1-5	Quarter-final	Benson & Hedges Irish Masters
	v Dodd	10-7	1st round	Embassy World Championship
	v Spencer	13-11	2nd round	Embassy World Championship
	v S. Davis	5-13	Quarter-final	Embassy World Championship
	v Johnson	5-2	1st round	Jameson International
	v Morra	5-3	2nd round	Jameson International
	v Thorne	5-0	Quarter-final	Jameson International
	v S. Davis	2-9	Semi-final	Jameson International
	v E. McLaughlin	5-0	1st round	Professional Players Tournament
	v Fisher	5-4	2nd round	Professional Players Tournament
	v Johnson	0-5	3rd round	Professional Players Tournament
1984	v Wilson	5-0	Qualifying	Lada Classic
	v White	5-3	1st round	Lada Classic
	v Wildman	4-5	Quarter-final	Lada Classic
	v White	2-5	1st round	Benson & Hedges Masters
	v Higgins	2-5	1st round	Benson & Hedges Irish Masters
	v Stevens	3-5	1st round	Tolly Cobbold Classic
	v Andrewartha	10-4	1st round	Embassy World Championship

v White	7-13	2nd round	Embassy World Championship
v David Taylor	5-4	Quarter-final	Winfield Australian Masters
v Knowles	0-6	Semi-final	Winfield Australian Masters
v Johnson	1-5	1st round	Jameson International
v Everton	5-1	1st round	Rothmans Grand Prix
v Parrott	5-1	2nd round	Rothmans Grand Prix
v Mountjoy	4-5	3rd round	Rothmans Grand Prix
v S. Francisco	9-4	1st round	Coral UK Open
v Thorne	7-9	2nd round	Coral UK Open
1985 v Macleod	1-5	1st round	Mercantile Credit Classic
v Spencer	3-5	1st round	Benson & Hedges Masters
v B. Harris	3-6	1st round	Dulux British Open
v Dennis Taylor	5-4	1st round	Benson & Hedges Irish Masters
v Knowles	3-5	Quarter-final	Benson & Hedges Irish Masters
v Campbell	10-3	1st round	Embassy World Championship
v Dennis Taylor	6-13	2nd round	Embassy World Championship
v Campbell	4-5	Quarter-final	Winfield Australian Masters
v Wilkinson	8-2	Quarter-final	Australian Championship
v Morgan	9-3	Semi-final	Australian Championship
v Campbell	7-10	Final	Australian Championship
v Gibson	4-5	3rd round	Goya Matchroom Trophy
v G. Foulds	5-1	3rd round	Rothmans Grand Prix
v Drago	3-5	4th round	Rothmans Grand Prix
v P. Francisco	5-9	3rd round	Coral UK Open
1986 v P. Francisco	1-5	3rd round	Mercantile Credit Classic
v Stevens	5-4	1st round	Benson & Hedges Masters
v Knowles	4-5	Quarter-final	Benson & Hedges Masters
v Gilbert	5-2	3rd round	Dulux British Open
v Browne	5-1	4th round	Dulux British Open
v Virgo	4-5	5th round	Dulux British Open
v Wilson	10-6	1st round	Embassy World Championship
v Stevens	12-13	2nd round	Embassy World Championship
v Anderson	6-2	Quarter-final	Australian Championship
v King	6-8	Semi-final	Australian Championship
v Black	5-0	3rd round	BCE International
v Knowles	1-5	4th round	BCE International
v Drago	4-5	3rd round	Rothmans Grand Prix
v V. Harris	9-2	3rd round	Tennents UK Open
v S. Davis	6-9	4th round	Tennents UK Open
1987 v Fisher	5-0	3rd round	Mercantile Credit Classic
v Williams	5-4	4th round	Mercantile Credit Classic
v Parrott	4-5	5th round	Mercantile Credit Classic
v Medati	5-4	3rd round	Dulux British Open
v Dennis Taylor	1-5	4th round	Dulux British Open
v King	4-10	Qualifying	Embassy World Championship
v Anderson	6-2	Quarter-final	Australian Championship
v Campbell	8-6	Semi-final	Australian Championship
v King	7-10	Final	Australian Championship
v Reardon	5-4	3rd round	Fidelity International
v Griffiths	5-2	4th round	Fidelity International
v N. Gilbert	5-0	5th round	Fidelity International
v Hallett	4-5	Quarter-final	Fidelity International
v Van Rensburg	5-3	3rd round	Rothmans Grand Prix
v Edmonds	5-3	4th round	Rothmans Grand Prix
v Knowles	0-5	5th round	Rothmans Grand Prix
v O'Kane	8-9	3rd round	Tennents UK Open
1988 v Roscoe	3-5	3rd round	Mercantile Credit Classic
v James	2-5	3rd round	MIM Britannia British Open
v B. Harris	10-4	Qualifying	Embassy World Championship
v S. Francisco	10-7	1st round	Embassy World Championship
v Knowles	7-13	2nd round	Embassy World Championship

MARTIN CLARK (England)

Born 27.10.68. **Turned professional** 1987. **World ranking** 41. **Best professional performances** Last 16 1987 Fidelity International, 1988 Mercantile Credit Classic.

1987	v Bear	5-2	1st round	Fidelity International
	v Duggan	5-2	2nd round	Fidelity International
	v Drago	5-2	3rd round	Fidelity International
	v Dennis Taylor	5-0	4th round	Fidelity International
	v O'Boye	2-5	5th round	Fidelity International
	v Williamson	5-1	1st round	Rothmans Grand Prix
	v Grace	5-1	2nd round	Rothmans Grand Prix
	v N. Foulds	5-4	3rd round	Rothmans Grand Prix
	v Fisher	4-5	4th round	Rothmans Grand Prix
	v Foldvari	8-9	1st round	Tennents UK Open
1988	v Wych	5-2	2nd round	Mercantile Credit Classic
	v Hallett	5-4	3rd round	Mercantile Credit Classic
	v Bennett	5-2	4th round	Mercantile Credit Classic
	v Newbury	2-5	5th round	Mercantile Credit Classic
	v G. Foulds	6-0	2nd round	English Championship
	v White	5-6	3rd round	English Championship
	v Fisher	5-1	1st round	MIM Britannia British Open
	v Grace	5-0	2nd round	MIM Britannia British Open
	v White	2-5	3rd round	MIM Britannia British Open
	v Parrott	1-5	Final	Kent Cup
	v Darrington	10-5	Qualifying	Embassy World Championship
	v Scott	10-4	Qualifying	Embassy World Championship
	v King	9-10	Qualifying	Embassy World Championship

GRAHAM CRIPSEY (England)

Born 8.12.54. **Turned professional** 1982. **World ranking** 46 (48). **Best professional performance** Last 16 1987 Rothmans Grand Prix.

1982	v French	1-5	Qualifying	Jameson International
	v B. Harris	6-9	Qualifying	Coral UK Championship
1983	v D. Hughes	10-2	Qualifying	Embassy World Championship
	v Meadowcroft	6-10	Qualifying	Embassy World Championship
	v Ganim	4-5	Qualifying	Professional Players Tournament
	v Darrington	3-9	Qualifying	Coral UK Championship
1984	v Parkin	10-4	Qualifying	Embassy World Championship
	v Gauvreau	1-10	Qualifying	Embassy World Championship
	v Thornley	5-3	Qualifying	Jameson Internaitonal
	v Dunning	3-5	Qualifying	Jameson International
	v Morra	3-5	Qualifying	Rothmans Grand Prix
	v Foldvari	9-7	Qualifying	Coral UK Open
	v Fitzmaurice	8-9	Qualifying	Coral UK Open
1985	v Medati	4-5	Qualifying	Mercantile Credit Classic
	v Bennett	9-0	Qualifying	Tolly Cobbold English Championship
	v David Taylor	5-9	1st round	Tolly Cobbold English Championship
	v O'Kane	4-6	Qualifying	Dulux British Open
	v Longworth	8-10	Qualifying	Embassy World Championship
	v Bennett	5-3	1st round	Goya Matchroom Trophy
	v Medati	5-2	2nd round	Goya Matchroom Trophy
	v Dennis Taylor	1-5	3rd round	Goya Matchroom Trophy
	v Hargreaves	1-5	1st round	Rothmans Grand Prix
	v Greaves	9-4	1st round	Coral UK Open
	v Dunning	wo	2nd round	Coral UK Open
	v Wilson	9-7	3rd round	Coral UK Open
	v Dennis Taylor	2-9	4th round	Coral UK Open
1986	v Drago	5-4	1st round	Mercantile Credit Classic
	v Newbury	5-4	2nd round	Mercantile Credit Classic

		Score	Round	Tournament
	v Spencer	5-1	3rd round	Mercantile Credit Classic
	v Higgins	2-5	4th round	Mercantile Credit Classic
	v Meadowcroft	9-1	2nd round	Tolly Cobbold English Championship
	v Wildman	5-9	3rd round	Tolly Cobbold English Championship
	v Darrington	5-4	1st round	Dulux British Open
	v Williamson	4-5	2nd round	Dulux British Open
	v Drago	4-10	Qualifying	Embassy World Championship
	v Houlihan	1-5	2nd round	BCE International
	v P. Gibson	5-3	2nd round	Rothmans Grand Prix
	v Parrott	4-5	3rd round	Rothmans Grand Prix
	v Bales	9-6	2nd round	Tennents UK Open
	v N. Foulds	7-9	3rd round	Tennents UK Open
1987	v Mienie	5-0	2nd round	Mercantile Credit Classic
	v Thorburn	0-5	3rd round	Mercantile Credit Classic
	v Dunning	6-1	2nd round	Tolly Ales English Championship
	v White	4-6	3rd round	Tolly Ales English Championship
	v Watchorn	5-4	2nd round	Dulux British Open
	v Werbeniuk	5-2	3rd round	Dulux British Open
	v Thorburn	2-5	4th round	Dulux British Open
	v Meadowcroft	10-9	Qualifying	Embassy World Championship
	v M. Gibson	10-4	Qualifying	Embassy World Championship
	v David Taylor	7-10	Qualifying	Embassy World Championship
	v Anderson	5-4	2nd round	Fidelity International
	v Werbeniuk	1-5	3rd round	Fidelity International
	v M. Gibson	5-2	2nd round	Rothmans Grand Prix
	v West	5-3	3rd round	Rothmans Grand Prix
	v P. Gibson	5-4	4th round	Rothmans Grand Prix
	v P. Francisco	1-5	5th round	Rothmans Grand Prix
	v P. Gibson	9-6	2nd round	Tennents UK Open
	v Thorburn	6-9	3rd round	Tennents UK Open
1988	v M. Gibson	5-4	2nd round	Mercantile Credit Classic
	v P. Francisco	2-5	3rd round	Mercantile Credit Classic
	v Greaves	4-6	2nd round	English Championship
	v Donnelly	5-4	2nd round	MIM Britannia British Open
	v E. Hughes	5-3	3rd round	MIM Britannia British Open
	v Hallett	2-5	4th round	MIM Britannia British Open
	v Meadowcroft	10-3	Qualifying	Embassy World Championship
	v Houlihan	10-4	Qualifying	Embassy World Championship
	v Longworth	2-10	Qualifying	Embassy World Championship

MIKE DARRINGTON (England)

Born 13.9.31. **Turned professional** 1982. **World ranking** 100 (90).

		Score	Round	Tournament
1983	v Williams	0-10	Qualifying	Embassy World Championship
	v Williamson	5-3	Qualifying	Jameson International
	v S. Francisco	2-5	Qualifying	Jameson International
	v Duggan	4-5	Qualifying	Professional Players Tournament
	v Cripsey	9-3	Qualifying	Coral UK Championship
	v Hallett	1-9	Qualifying	Coral UK Championship
1984	v Caggianello	7-10	Qualifying	Embassy World Championship
	v Bradley	3-5	Qualifying	Jameson International
	v Burke	3-5	Qualifying	Rothmans Grand Prix
	v Longworth	5-9	Qualifying	Coral UK Open
1985	v Hargreaves	2-5	Qualifying	Mercantile Credit Classic
	v Virgo	0-9	1st round	Tolly Cobbold English Championship
	v Scott	3-6	Qualifying	Dulux British Open
	v T. Jones	2-10	Qualifying	Embassy World Championship
	v Gilbert	5-2	1st round	Goya Matchroom Trophy
	v Sinclair	0-5	2nd round	Goya Matchroom Trophy
	v Greaves	5-2	1st round	Rothmans Grand Prix
	v Foldvari	5-3	2nd round	Rothmans Grand Prix
	v N. Foulds	0-5	3rd round	Rothmans Grand Prix

	v Foldvari	9-6	2nd round	Coral UK Open
	v Martin	3-9	3rd round	Coral UK Open
1986	v O'Boye	0-5	1st round	Mercantile Credit Classic
	v Fowler	3-9	2nd round	Tolly Cobbold English Championship
	v Cripsey	4-5	1st round	Dulux British Open
	v Meadowcroft	10-6	Qualifying	Embassy World Championship
	v Edmonds	5-10	Qualifying	Embassy World Championship
	v Jack Rea	4-5	1st round	BCE International
	v Watchorn	2-5	1st round	Rothmans Grand Prix
	v Whitthread	9-8	1st round	Tennents UK Open
	v Fowler	6-9	2nd round	Tennents UK Open
1987	v Roe	0-5	1st round	Mercantile Credit Classic
	v V. Harris	3-6	2nd round	Tolly Ales English Championship
	v James	3-5	1st round	Dulux British Open
	v Demarco	10-6	Qualifying	Embassy World Championship
	v Hendry	7-10	2nd round	Embassy World Championship
	v Kelly	4-5	1st round	Fidelity International
	v Chalmers	5-2	1st round	Rothmans Grand Prix
	v Kearney	0-5	2nd round	Rothmans Grand Prix
	v Watchorn	2-9	1st round	Tennents UK Open
1988	v Meakin	4-5	1st round	Mercantile Credit Classic
	v Meakin	3-6	1st round	English Championship
	v Burke	5-4	1st round	MIM Britannia British Open
	v Dodd	5-4	2nd round	MIM Britannia British Open
	v P. Francisco	1-5	3rd round	MIM Britannia British Open
	v Clark	5-10	Qualifying	Embassy World Championship

FRED DAVIS O.B.E. (England)

Born 14.8.13. **Turned professional** 1930. **World ranking** 83 (62). **Best professional performances** Winner World Championship 1948–49, 1951–56.

1969	v Reardon	25-24	Quarter-final	World Championship
	v G. Owen	28-45	Semi-final	World Championship
1970	v Reardon	26-31	Quarter-final	World Championship
1972	v Spencer	21-31	Quarter-final	World Championship
1973	v Greaves	16-1	2nd round	World Championship
	v Higgins	14-16	Quarter-final	World Championship
1974	v Werbeniuk	15-5	2nd round	World Championship
	v Higgins	15-14	Quarter-final	World Championship
	v Reardon	3-15	Semi-final	World Championship
1975	v Charlton	3-5	Quarter-final	Benson & Hedges Masters
	v Dennis Taylor	14-15	2nd round	World Championship
1976	v Thorburn	4-2	1st round	Benson & Hedges Masters
	v Spencer	0-4	2nd round	Benson & Hedges Masters
	v Werbeniuk	15-12	1st round	Embassy World Championship
	v Charlton	13-15	Quarter-final	Embassy World Championship
1977	v Mountjoy	2-4	Quarter-final	Benson & Hedges Masters
	v Pulman	12-13	1st round	Embassy World Championship
	v Fagan	0-5	2nd round	Super Crystalate UK Championship
1978	v Miles	3-4	1st round	Benson & Hedges Masters
	v Virgo	9-8	Qualifying	Embassy World Championship
	v Dennis Taylor	13-9	1st round	Embassy World Championship
	v Fagan	13-10	Quarter-final	Embassy World Championship
	v Mans	16-18	Semi-final	Embassy World Championship
	v Dunning	9-2	1st round	Coral UK Championship
	v Higgins	4-9	Quarter-final	Coral UK Championship
1979	v Mountjoy	2-5	1st round	Benson & Hedges Masters
	v Stevens	13-8	1st round	Embassy World Championship
	v Charlton	4-13	Quarter-final	Embassy World Championship
	v Edmonds	6-9	3rd round	Coral UK Championship
1980	v David Taylor	5-13	2nd round	Embassy World Championship

	v Wildman	9-6	2nd round	Coral UK Championship
	v Higgins	6-9	Quarter-final	Coral UK Championship
1981	v Stevens	5-4	1st round	Benson & Hedges Masters
	v Griffiths	2-5	Quarter-final	Benson & Hedges Masters
	v Edmonds	6-9	1st round	John Courage English
	v David Taylor	3-13	2nd round	Embassy World Championship
	v Williams	0-5	2nd round	Jameson International
	v Knowles	6-9	2nd round	Coral UK Championship
1982	v Reynolds	7-10	1st round	Embassy World Championship
	v Fisher	3-5	Qualifying	Jameson International
	v Sinclair	2-5	1st round	Professional Players Tournament
	v Hallett	7-9	1st round	Coral UK Open
1983	v Williams	1-10	Qualifying	Embassy World Championship
	v Kelly	5-1	Qualifying	Jameson International
	v Morgan	3-5	Qualifying	Jameson International
	v Fisher	4-5	1st round	Professional Players Tournament
	v Watterson	6-9	Qualifying	Coral UK Championship
	v Donnelly	10-5	Qualifying	Embassy World Championship
	v Werbeniuk	4-10	1st round	Embassy World Championship
1984	v Dunning	5-4	Qualifying	Jameson International
	v Virgo	3-5	Qualifying	Jameson International
	v V. Harris	1-5	Qualifying	Rothmans Grand Prix
	v Fowler	4-9	Qualifying	Coral UK Open
1985	v E. McLaughlin	1-5	Qualifying	Mercantile Credit Classic
	v G. Foulds	2-9	Qualifying	Tolly Cobbold English Championship
	v Longworth	1-6	Qualifying	Dulux British Open
	v Chaperon	10-9	Qualifying	Embassy World Championship
	v Williams	6-10	Qualifying	Embassy World Championship
	v Duggan	1-5	2nd round	Goya Matchroom Trophy
	v Simngam	2-5	2nd round	Rothmans Grand Prix
	v John Rea	9-8	2nd round	Coral UK Open
	v Werbeniuk	9-7	3rd round	Coral UK Open
	v Higgins	2-9	4th round	Coral UK Open
1986	v Kelly	5-3	2nd round	Mercantile Credit Classic
	v Stevens	5-2	3rd round	Mercantile Credit Classic
	v E. Hughes	3-5	4th round	Mercantile Credit Classic
	v D. Hughes	9-6	2nd round	Tolly Cobbold English Championship
	v Martin	8-9	3rd round	Tolly Cobbold English Championship
	v Kelly	5-4	2nd round	Dulux British Open
	v Macleod	4-5	3rd round	Dulux British Open
	v Chalmers	10-6	Qualifying	Embassy World Championship
	v P. Francisco	1-10	Qualifying	Embassy World Championship
	v Bales	4-5	2nd round	BCE International
	v Bales	5-4	2nd round	Rothmans Grand Prix
	v Higgins	0-5	3rd round	Rothmans Grand Prix
	v Rowswell	4-9	2nd round	Tennents UK Open
1987	v Fisher	2-5	2nd round	Mercantile Credit Classic
	v James	2-6	2nd round	Tolly Ales English Championship
	v Owers	3-5	2nd round	Dulux British Open
	v Owers	5-10	Qualifying	Embassy World Championship
	v Roe	3-5	2nd round	Fidelity International
	v Fisher	0-5	2nd round	Rothmans Grand Prix
	v Ellis	9-6	2nd round	Tennents UK Open
	v Virgo	4-9	3rd round	Tennents UK Open
1988	v Meakin	5-4	2nd round	Mercantile Credit Classic
	v Mountjoy	0-5	3rd round	Mercantile Credit Classic
	v N. Gilbert	6-5	2nd round	English Championship
	v Meo	3-6	3rd round	English Championship
	v D. Hughes	5-2	2nd round	MIM Britannia British Open
	v Spencer	0-5	3rd round	MIM Britannia British Open
	v Fitzmaurice	10-8	Qualifying	Embassy World Championship
	v Bear	10-4	Qualifying	Embassy World Championship
	v Campbell	3-10	Qualifying	Embassy World Championship

STEVE DAVIS M.B.E. (England)

Born 22.8.57. **Turned professional** 1978. **World ranking** 1 (1). **Best professional performances** Winner Embassy World Championship 1981, 1983, 1984, 1987, 1988, Coral UK Championship 1980, 1981, 1984, 1985, Tennents UK Open 1986, 1987; winner of 8 ranking tournaments, 17 non-ranking tournaments, 2 English Championships.

Year	Opponent	Score	Round	Tournament
1979	v Anderson	9-1	Prelim	Embassy World Championship
	v Fagan	9-2	Qualifying	Embassy World Championship
	v Dennis Taylor	11-13	1st round	Embassy World Championship
	v Dunning	9-3	2nd round	Coral UK Championship
	v Mountjoy	9-5	3rd round	Coral UK Championship
	v Virgo	7-9	Quarter-final	Coral UK Championship
1980	v Morgan	9-0	Qualifying	Embassy World Championship
	v Fagan	10-6	1st round	Embassy World Championship
	v Griffiths	13-10	2nd round	Embassy World Championship
	v Higgins	9-13	Quarter-final	Embassy World Championship
	v Hallett	9-1	1st round	Coral UK Championship
	v Werbeniuk	9-3	2nd round	Coral UK Championship
	v Meo	9-5	Quarter-final	Coral UK Championship
	v Griffiths	9-0	Semi-final	Coral UK Championship
	v Higgins	**16-6**	**Final**	**Coral UK Championship**
1981	v Mans	3-5	1st round	Benson & Hedges Masters
	v Dennis Taylor	5-2	Semi-final	Yamaha International Masters
	v David Taylor	**9-6**	**Final**	**Yamaha International Masters**
	v Meadowcroft	9-2	1st round	John Courage English
	v Spencer	9-7	2nd round	John Courage English
	v Edmonds	9-0	Semi-final	John Courage English
	v Meo	**9-3**	**Final**	**John Courage English**
	v White	10-8	1st round	Embassy World Championship
	v Higgins	13-8	2nd round	Embassy World Championship
	v Griffiths	13-9	Quarter-final	Embassy World Championship
	v Thorburn	16-10	Semi-final	Embassy World Championship
	v Mountjoy	**18-12**	**Final**	**Embassy World Championship**
	v Mountjoy	5-0	Quarter-final	Langs Scottish Masters
	v White	5-6	Semi-final	Langs Scottish Masters
	v Mans	5-3	3rd round	Jameson International
	v David Taylor	5-1	Quarter-final	Jameson International
	v Higgins	9-8	Semi-final	Jameson International
	v Dennis Taylor	**9-0**	**Final**	**Jameson International**
	v Higgins	5-2	1st round	Northern Ireland Classic
	v Griffiths	9-6	Semi-final	Northern Ireland Classic
	v White	9-11	Final	Northern Ireland Classic
	v Thorne	9-2	3rd round	Coral UK Championship
	v Werbeniuk	9-5	Quarter-final	Coral UK Championship
	v White	9-0	Semi-final	Coral UK Championship
	v Griffiths	**16-3**	**Final**	**Coral UK Championship**
1982	v Spencer	5-2	1st round	Lada Classic
	v Reardon	5-4	Semi-final	Lada Classic
	v Griffiths	8-9	Final	Lada Classic
	v Mountjoy	5-2	Quarter-final	Benson & Hedges Masters
	v Meo	6-4	Semi-final	Benson & Hedges Masters
	v Griffiths	**9-5**	**Final**	**Benson & Hedges Masters**
	v Griffiths	**9-7**	**Final**	**Yamaha International Masters**
	v Miles	5-2	Semi-final	Tolly Cobbold Classic
	v Dennis Taylor	**8-3**	**Final**	**Tolly Cobbold Classic**
	v Mountjoy	5-2	Quarter-final	Benson & Hedges Irish Masters
	v Higgins	6-2	Semi-final	Benson & Hedges Irish Masters
	v Griffiths	5-9	Final	Benson & Hedges Irish Masters
	v Knowles	1-10	1st round	Embassy World Championship
	v Knowles	5-4	1st round	Langs Scottish Masters

Steve Davis

v Dennis Taylor	6-1	Semi-final	Langs Scottish Masters
v Higgins	**9-4**	**Final**	**Langs Scottish Masters**
v Roscoe	5-0	1st round	Jameson International
v Reynolds	5-0	2nd round	Jameson International
v David Taylor	3-5	Quarter-final	Jameson International
v Williams	9-6	1st round	Coral UK Open
v Fagan	9-3	2nd round	Coral UK Open
v Griffiths	6-9	Quarter-final	Coral UK Open
1983 v Dennis Taylor	5-2	1st round	Lada Classic
v Charlton	5-4	Quarter-final	Lada Classic
v Spencer	5-4	Semi-final	Lada Classic
v Werbeniuk	**9-5**	**Final**	**Lada Classic**
v Wildman	5-2	1st round	Benson & Hedges Masters
v Mountjoy	4-5	Quarter-final	Benson & Hedges Masters
v Dennis Taylor	5-1	Semi-final	Tolly Cobbold Classic
v Griffiths	**7-5**	**Final**	**Tolly Cobbold Classic**
v Charlton	5-1	Quarter-final	Benson & Hedges Irish Masters
v Griffiths	6-2	Semi-final	Benson & Hedges Irish Masters
v Reardon	**9-2**	**Final**	**Benson & Hedges Irish Masters**
v Williams	10-4	1st round	Embassy World Championship
v Dennis Taylor	13-11	2nd round	Embassy World Championship
v Charlton	13-5	Quarter-final	Embassy World Championship
v Higgins	16-5	Semi-final	Embassy World Championship
v Thorburn	**18-6**	**Final**	**Embassy World Championship**
v Macleod	5-1	1st round	Langs Scottish Masters
v Higgins	6-2	Semi-final	Langs Scottish Masters
v Knowles	**9-6**	**Final**	**Langs Scottish Masters**
v E. Hughes	5-1	1st round	Jameson International
v Watterson	5-0	2nd round	Jameson International
v S. Francisco	5-1	Quarter-final	Jameson International
v Charlton	9-2	Semi-final	Jameson International
v Thorburn	**9-4**	**Final**	**Jameson International**
v Donnelly	5-1	1st round	Professional Players Tournament
v Hallett	2-5	2nd round	Professional Players Tournament
v G. Foulds	9-1	1st round	Coral UK Championship
v Thorne	9-3	2nd round	Coral UK Championship
v Meo	9-4	Quarter-final	Coral UK Championship
v White	9-4	Semi-final	Coral UK Championship
v Higgins	15-16	Final	Coral UK Championship
1984 v Spencer	5-2	1st round	Lada Classic
v Griffiths	5-4	Quarter-final	Lada Classic
v Parrott	5-4	Semi-final	Lada Classic
v Meo	**9-8**	**Final**	**Lada Classic**
v Meo	5-0	1st round	Benson & Hedges Masters
v Stevens	3-5	Quarter-final	Benson & Hedges Masters
v Meo	5-4	Quarter-final	Benson & Hedges Irish Masters
v Higgins	6-4	Semi-final	Benson & Hedges Irish Masters
v Griffiths	**9-1**	**Final**	**Benson & Hedges Irish Masters**
v Thorne	5-2	1st round	Tolly Cobbold Classic
v Stevens	5-4	Semi-final	Tolly Cobbold Classic
v Knowles	**8-2**	**Final**	**Tolly Cobbold Classic**
v King	10-3	1st round	Embassy World Championship
v Spencer	13-5	2nd round	Embassy World Championship
v Griffiths	13-10	Quarter-final	Embassy World Championship
v Dennis Taylor	16-9	Semi-final	Embassy World Championship
v White	**18-16**	**Final**	**Embassy World Championship**
v Thorburn	5-2	1st round	Langs Supreme Scottish Masters
v Higgins	6-4	Semi-final	Langs Supreme Scottish Masters
v White	**9-4**	**Final**	**Langs Supreme Scottish Masters**
v Campbell	5-1	1st round	Jameson International
v David Taylor	5-1	2nd round	Jameson International
v Higgins	5-1	Quarter-final	Jameson International
v E. Hughes	9-3	Semi-final	Jameson International

	v **Knowles**	**9-2**	**Final**	**Jameson International**
	v Morra	5-2	1st round	Rothmans Grand Prix
	v Miles	5-0	2nd round	Rothmans Grand Prix
	v David Taylor	5-1	3rd round	Rothmans Grand Prix
	v Reynolds	5-0	Quarter-final	Rothmans Grand Prix
	v Thorburn	7-9	Semi-final	Rothmans Grand Prix
	v Murphy	9-1	1st round	Coral UK Open
	v Meo	9-7	2nd round	Coral UK Open
	v White	9-4	Quarter-final	Coral UK Open
	v Stevens	9-2	Semi-final	Coral UK Open
	v **Higgins**	**16-8**	**Final**	**Coral UK Open**
1985	v S. Francisco	5-0	1st round	Mercantile Credit Classic
	v Higgins	5-2	2nd round	Mercantile Credit Classic
	v Reardon	5-1	Quarter-final	Mercantile Credit Classic
	v Thorne	8-9	Semi-final	Mercantile Credit Classic
	v Higgins	4-5	1st round	Benson & Hedges Masters
	v Fowler	9-3	1st round	Tolly Cobbold English Championship
	v Williams	9-2	2nd round	Tolly Cobbold English Championship
	v Virgo	9-2	Quarter-final	Tolly Cobbold English Championship
	v Meo	9-8	Semi-final	Tolly Cobbold English Championship
	v **Knowles**	**9-2**	**Final**	**Tolly Cobbold English Championship**
	v Chappel	6-5	1st round	Dulux British Open
	v Virgo	5-2	2nd round	Dulux British Open
	v Bradley	5-2	3rd round	Dulux British Open
	v O'Kane	5-1	Quarter-final	Dulux British Open
	v Stevens	7-9	Semi-final	Dulux British Open
	v E. Hughes	5-4	Quarter-final	Benson & Hedges Irish Masters
	v Higgins	2-6	Semi-final	Benson & Hedges Irish Masters
	v N. Foulds	10-8	1st round	Embassy World Championship
	v David Taylor	13-4	2nd round	Embassy World Championship
	v Griffiths	13-6	Quarter-final	Embassy World Championship
	v Reardon	16-5	Semi-final	Embassy World Championship
	v Dennis Taylor	17-18	Final	Embassy World Championship
	v Bales	5-2	3rd round	Goya Matchroom Trophy
	v Virgo	5-1	4th round	Goya Matchroom Trophy
	v Macleod	5-1	5th round	Goya Matchroom Trophy
	v White	3-5	Quarter-final	Goya Matchroom Trophy
	v Agrawal	5-0	3rd round	Rothmans Grand Prix
	v Fowler	5-1	4th round	Rothmans Grand Prix
	v Higgins	5-0	5th round	Rothmans Grand Prix
	v S. Francisco	5-2	Quarter-final	Rothmans Grand Prix
	v Thorburn	9-5	Semi-final	Rothmans Grand Prix
	v **Dennis Taylor**	**10-9**	**Final**	**Rothmans Grand Prix**
	v Griffiths	5-4	1st round	BCE Canadian Masters
	v Thorburn	8-1	Semi-final	BCE Canadian Masters
	v Dennis Taylor	5-9	Final	BCE Canadian Masters
	v Sheehan	9-1	3rd round	Coral UK Open
	v Drago	9-2	4th round	Coral UK Open
	v Meo	9-5	5th round	Coral UK Open
	v West	9-1	Quarter-final	Coral UK Open
	v White	9-5	Semi-final	Coral UK Open
	v **Thorne**	**16-14**	**Final**	**Coral UK Open**
	v Reardon	5-2	1st round	Kit Kat
	v Higgins	6-1	Semi-final	Kit Kat
	v Dennis Taylor	5-9	Final	Kit Kat
1986	v Chaperon	5-1	3rd round	Mercantile Credit Classic
	v Van Rensberg	5-1	4th round	Mercantile Credit Classic
	v P. Francisco	5-0	5th round	Mercantile Credit Classic
	v White	2-5	Quarter-final	Mercantile Credit Classic
	v Griffiths	2-5	1st round	BCE Belgian Classic
	v David Taylor	5-4	1st round	Benson & Hedges Masters
	v Thorne	5-4	Quarter-final	Benson & Hedges Masters
	v White	3-6	Semi-final	Benson & Hedges Masters

	v Bradley	9-3	3rd round	Tolly Cobbold English Championship
	v Martin	9-4	4th round	Tolly Cobbold English Championship
	v Virgo	9-2	Quarter-final	Tolly Cobbold English Championship
	v Meo	7-9	Semi-final	Tolly Cobbold English Championship
	v Black	5-2	3rd round	Dulux British Open
	v Martin	5-1	4th round	Dulux British Open
	v Campbell	5-0	5th round	Dulux British Open
	v Wych	5-2	Quarter-final	Dulux British Open
	v Higgins	9-3	Semi-final	Dulux British Open
	v Thorne	**12-7**	**Final**	**Dulux British Open**
	v Edmonds	10-4	1st round	Embassy World Championship
	v Mountjoy	13-5	2nd round	Embassy World Championship
	v White	13-5	Quarter-final	Embassy World Championship
	v Thorburn	16-12	Semi-final	Embassy World Championship
	v Johnson	12-18	Final	Embassy World Championship
	v Thorne	2-5	Semi-final	Camus Hong Kong Masters
	v Griffiths	6-2	Semi-final	Matchroom Trophy
	v Thorne	9-10	Final	Matchroom Trophy
	v John Rea	5-1	3rd round	BCE International
	v King	5-4	4th round	BCE International
	v Williams	5-4	5th round	BCE International
	v E. Hughes	4-5	Quarter-final	BCE International
	v M. Gibson	5-1	3rd round	Rothmans Grand Prix
	v Drago	5-1	4th round	Rothmans Grand Prix
	v Griffiths	5-2	5th round	Rothmans Grand Prix
	v Williams	1-5	Quarter-final	Rothmans Grand Prix
	v White	5-2	1st round	BCE Canadian Masters
	v Higgins	8-2	Semi-final	BCE Canadian Masters
	v Thorne	**9-3**	**Final**	**BCE Canadian Masters**
	v Chappel	9-7	3rd round	Tennents UK Open
	v Charlton	9-6	4th round	Tennents UK Open
	v Reynolds	9-5	5th round	Tennents UK Open
	v Drago	9-8	Quarter-final	Tennents UK Open
	v Higgins	9-3	Semi-final	Tennents UK Open
	v N. Foulds	**16-7**	**Final**	**Tennents UK Open**
1987	v Jenkins	5-0	3rd round	Mercantile Credit Classic
	v Virgo	5-2	4th round	Mercantile Credit Classic
	v Meo	5-2	5th round	Mercantile Credit Classic
	v Parrott	5-4	Quarter-final	Mercantile Credit Classic
	v Hendry	9-3	Semi-final	Mercantile Credit Classic
	v White	**13-12**	**Final**	**Mercantile Credit Classic**
	v Mountjoy	2-5	1st round	Benson & Hedges Masters
	v Gauvreau	5-0	3rd round	Dulux British Open
	v Virgo	4-5	4th round	Dulux British Open
	v Meo	5-2	Quarter-final	Benson & Hedges Irish Masters
	v Griffiths	6-2	Semi-final	Benson & Hedges Irish Masters
	v Thorne	**9-1**	**Final**	**Benson & Hedges Irish Masters**
	v King	10-7	1st round	Embassy World Championship
	v Reardon	13-4	2nd round	Embassy World Championship
	v Griffiths	13-5	Quarter-final	Embassy World Championship
	v White	16-11	Semi-final	Embassy World Championship
	v Johnson	**18-14**	**Final**	**Embassy World Championship**
	v Dennis Taylor	5-4	Semi-final	Riley Hong Kong Masters (WS)
	v Hendry	**9-3**	**Final**	**Riley Hong Kong Masters (WS)**
	v O'Kane	5-2	3rd round	Fidelity International
	v Meo	5-3	4th round	Fidelity International
	v Parrott	5-2	5th round	Fidelity International
	v Virgo	5-2	Quarter-final	Fidelity International
	v Hallett	9-3	Semi-final	Fidelity International
	v Thorburn	**12-5**	**Final**	**Fidelity International**
	v Miles	5-1	3rd round	Rothmans Grand Prix
	v Wych	5-1	4th round	Rothmans Grand Prix
	v Hendry	2-5	5th round	Rothmans Grand Prix

v Dennis Taylor	1-5	1st round	Labatts Canadian Masters (WS)
v Meo	6-5	1st round	Matchroom Trophy
v Dennis Taylor	3-6	Semi-final	Matchroom Trophy
v King	9-2	3rd round	Tennents UK Open
v P. Francisco	9-6	4th round	Tennents UK Open
v Higgins	9-2	5th round	Tennents UK Open
v Parrott	9-5	Quarter-final	Tennents UK Open
v Thorne	9-2	Semi-final	Tennents UK Open
v White	**16-14**	**Final**	**Tennents UK Open**
1988 v Dodd	5-0	3rd round	Mercantile Credit Classic
v Donnelly	5-0	4th round	Mercantile Credit Classic
v Higgins	5-0	5th round	Mercantile Credit Classic
v Hendry	5-3	Quarter-final	Mercantile Credit Classic
v Newbury	9-2	Semi-final	Mercantile Credit Classic
v Parrott	**13-11**	**Final**	**Mercantile Credit Classic**
v Reynolds	5-2	1st round	Benson and Hedges Masters
v Griffiths	5-0	Quarter-final	Benson and Hedges Masters
v Johnson	6-3	Semi-final	Benson and Hedges Masters
v Hallett	**9-0**	**Final**	**Benson and Hedges Masters**
v Reardon	0-5	3rd round	MIM Britannia British Open
v Johnson	5-0	Quarter-final	Benson and Hedges Irish Masters
v Higgins	6-2	Semi-final	Benson and Hedges Irish Masters
v N. Foulds	**9-4**	**Final**	**Benson and Hedges Irish Masters**
v Virgo	10-8	1st round	Embassy World Championship
v Hallett	13-1	2nd round	Embassy World Championship
v Drago	13-4	Quarter-final	Embassy World Championship
v Thorburn	16-8	Semi-final	Embassy World Championship
v Griffiths	**18-11**	**Final**	**Embassy World Championship**

LES DODD (England)

Born 11.2.54. **Turned professional** 1982. **World ranking** 62 (52). **Best professional performances** Last 32 1983 Embassy World Championship, 1986 Rothmans Grand Prix, 1987 Mercantile Credit Classic; runner-up 1987 Tolly Ales English Championship.

1982 v Macleod	5-1	Qualifying	Jameson International
v Fitzmaurice	5-3	Qualifying	Jameson International
v Mans	3-5	1st round	Jameson International
v Williamson	9-1	Qualifying	Coral UK Championship
v French	9-7	Qualifying	Coral UK Championship
v David Taylor	7-9	1st round	Coral UK Championship
1983 v Williamson	10-9	Qualifying	Embassy World Championship
v Charlton	7-10	1st round	Embassy World Championship
v Gibson	1-5	Qualifying	Jameson International
v Griffiths	3-5	1st round	Professional Players Tournament
v G. Foulds	7-9	Qualifying	Coral UK Championship
1984 v Giannaros	10-1	Qualifying	Embassy World Championship
v N. Foulds	4-10	Qualifying	Embassy World Championship
v Foldvari	5-3	Qualifying	Jameson International
v Wilson	5-1	Qualifying	Jameson International
v Reardon	4-5	1st round	Jameson International
v Medati	4-5	Qualifying	Rothmans Grand Prix
v Newbury	9-6	Qualifying	Coral UK Open
v Wilson	8-9	Qualifying	Coral UK Open
1985 v T. Jones	1-5	Qualifying	Mercantile Credit Classic
v Bales	9-5	Qualifying	Tolly Cobbold English Championship
v Thorne	1-9	1st round	Tolly Cobbold English Championship
v V. Harris	1-6	Qualifying	Dulux British Open
v O'Kane	7-10	Qualifying	Embassy World Championship
v Simngam	5-4	2nd round	Goya Matchroom Trophy
v N. Foulds	3-5	3rd round	Goya Matchroom Trophy

	v Chappel	2-5	2nd round	Rothmans Grand Prix
	v Thorburn	4-9	3rd round	Coral UK Open
1986	v Rigitano	3-5	2nd round	Mercantile Credit Classic
	v Oliver	5-9	2nd round	Tolly Cobbold English Championship
	v Jonik	5-4	2nd round	Dulux British Open
	v Thorne	2-5	3rd round	Dulux British Open
	v Fitzmaurice	10-6	Qualifying	Embassy World Championship
	v Watterson	10-1	Qualifying	Embassy World Championship
	v Mans	7-10	Qualifying	Embassy World Championship
	v Reynolds	2-5	3rd round	BCE International
	v Scott	5-2	2nd round	Rothmans Grand Prix
	v Stevens	5-4	3rd round	Rothmans Grand Prix
	v Hallett	2-5	4th round	Rothmans Grand Prix
	v Chaperon	4-9	2nd round	Tennents UK Open
1987	v Medati	5-4	2nd round	Mercantile Credit Classic
	v Mountjoy	5-4	3rd round	Mercantile Credit Classic
	v Wilson	4-5	4th round	Mercantile Credit Classic
	v Smith	6-3	2nd round	Tolly Ales English Championship
	v Knowles	6-2	3rd round	Tolly Ales English Championship
	v West	6-3	4th round	Tolly Ales English Championship
	v Hallett	6-5	Quarter-final	Tolly Ales English Championship
	v Johnson	9-5	Semi-final	Tolly Ales English Championship
	v Meo	5-9	Final	Tolly Ales English Championship
	v Fowler	1-5	2nd round	Dulux British Open
	v Newbury	7-10	Qualifying	Embassy World Championship
	v Morra	3-5	2nd round	Fidelity International
	v Kelly	5-2	2nd round	Rothmans Grand Prix
	v Parrott	1-5	3rd round	Rothmans Grand Prix
	v Medati	9-6	2nd round	Tennents UK Open
	v Dennis Taylor	8-9	3rd round	Tennents UK Open
1988	v Roe	2-5	2nd round	Mercantile Credit Classic
	v S. Davis	0-5	3rd round	Mercantile Credit Classic
	v Heaton	6-0	2nd round	English Championship
	v Virgo	3-6	3rd round	English Championship
	v Darrington	4-5	2nd round	MIM Britannia British Open
	v Medati	10-6	Qualifying	Embassy World Championship
	v Fowler	8-10	Qualifying	Embassy World Championship

JIM DONNELLY (Scotland)

Born 13.6.46. **Turned professional** 1981. **World ranking** 74 (88). **Amateur career**
1978 Scottish champion. **Best professional performances** Last 32 1988 Mercantile
Credit Classic, runner-up 1987 Scottish Championship.

1981	v Johnson	4-5	Qualifying	Jameson International
	v Sinclair	5-0	Quarter-final	Scottish Championship
	v Gibson	4-6	Semi-final	Scottish Championship
	v Medati	7-9	Qualifying	Coral UK Championship
1982	v Gibson	9-8	Qualifying	Embassy World Championship
	v Sinclair	9-8	Qualifying	Embassy World Championship
	v Reardon	5-10	1st round	Embassy World Championship
	v Macleod	5-6	1st round	Scottish Championship
	v Williamson	3-5	Qualifying	Jameson International
	v Watterson	4-5	1st round	Professional Players Tournament
	v Ross	9-5	Qualifying	Coral UK Championship
	v Knowles	6-9	1st round	Coral UK Championship
1983	v Sheehan	10-6	Qualifying	Embassy World Championship
	v Campbell	2-10	Qualifying	Embassy World Championship
	v Demarco	6-4	1st round	Scottish Championship
	v Sinclair	5-6	Semi-final	Scottish Championship
	v Bennett	5-1	Qualifying	Jameson International
	v Wilson	5-1	Qualifying	Jameson International

v David Taylor	5-3	1st round	Jameson International
v S. Francisco	1-5	2nd round	Jameson International
v S. Davis	1-5	1st round	Professional Players Tournament
v Murphy	4-9	Qualifying	Coral UK Championship
1984 v Watchorn	10-7	Qualifying	Embassy World Championship
v Anderson	10-6	Qualifying	Embassy World Championship
v F. Davis	5-10	Qualifying	Embassy World Championship
v G. Foulds	3-5	Qualifying	Jameson International
v Hargreaves	5-4	Qualifying	Rothmans Grand Prix
v Wilson	2-5	1st round	Rothmans Grand Prix
v Gibson	9-6	Qualifying	Coral UK Open
v Campbell	6-9	Qualifying	Coral UK Open
1985 v Watchorn	5-1	Qualifying	Mercantile Credit Classic
v Williams	3-5	Qualifying	Mercantile Credit Classic
v John Rea	2-6	1st round	Scottish Championship
v W. Jones	1-6	Qualifying	Dulux British Open
v Fowler	0-10	Qualifying	Embassy World Championship
v Jim Bear	2-5	2nd round	Goya Matchroom Trophy
v Kelly	4-5	2nd round	Rothmans Grand Prix
v Drago	8-9	1st round	Coral UK Open
1986 v Chalmers	5-0	2nd round	Mercantile Credit Classic
v Campbell	2-5	3rd round	Mercantile Credit Classic
v Wilkinson	5-4	2nd round	Dulux British Open
v Meo	3-5	3rd round	Dulux British Open
v John Rea	1-6	Quarter-final	Canada Dry Scottish Championship
v Smith	10-6	Qualifying	Embassy World Championship
v West	5-10	Qualifying	Embassy World Championship
v Murphy	2-5	2nd round	BCE International
v N. Gilbert	5-1	1st round	Rothmans Grand Prix
v King	2-5	2nd round	Rothmans Grand Prix
v N. Gilbert	8-9	1st round	Tennents UK Open
1987 v Watchorn	0-5	1st round	Mercantile Credit Classic
v Macleod	6-2	1st round	Scottish Championship
v Sinclair	6-4	Semi-final	Scottish Championship
v Hendry	7-10	Final	Scottish Championship
v T. Jones	2-5	2nd round	Dulux British Open
v W. Jones	3-10	Qualifying	Embassy World Championship
v M. Smith	3-5	1st round	Fidelity International
v D. Hughes	5-1	1st round	Rothmans Grand Prix
v W. Jones	3-5	2nd round	Rothmans Grand Prix
v Anderson	9-4	1st round	Tennents UK Open
v O'Boye	2-9	2nd round	Tennents UK Open
1988 v N. Gilbert	5-2	1st round	Mercantile Credit Classic
v Duggan	5-4	2nd round	Mercantile Credit Classic
v Macleod	5-4	3rd round	Mercantile Credit Classic
v S. Davis	0-5	4th round	Mercantile Credit Classic
v Macleod	5-6	Quarter-final	Scottish Championship
v Greaves	5-4	1st round	MIM Britannia British Open
v Cripsey	4-5	2nd round	MIM Britannia British Open
v J. Smith	4-10	Qualifying	Embassy World Championship

TONY DRAGO (Malta)

Born 22.9.65. **Turned professional** 1985. **World ranking** 20 (32). **Amateur career** 1984 Malta champion. **Best professional performances** Quarter-finals 1988 Embassy World Championship, 1986 Tennents UK Open.

1985 v Bales	2-5	1st round	Goya Matchroom Trophy
v Watchorn	5-2	1st round	Rothmans Grand Prix
v King	5-4	2nd round	Rothmans Grand Prix
v Macleod	5-3	3rd round	Rothmans Grand Prix
v Charlton	5-3	4th round	Rothmans Grand Prix

Tony Drago

	v Wilson	2-5	5th round	Rothmans Grand Prix
	v Gilbert	9-5	1st round	Coral UK Open
	v Donnelly	9-8	2nd round	Coral UK Open
	v Wildman	9-5	3rd round	Coral UK Open
	v S. Davis	2-9	4th round	Coral UK Open
1986	v Cripsey	4-5	1st round	Mercantile Credit Classic
	v Gauvreau	5-3	2nd round	Dulux British Open
	v Williams	1-5	3rd round	Dulux British Open
	v Cripsey	10-4	Qualifying	Embassy World Championship
	v P. Francisco	4-10	Qualifying	Embassy World Championship
	v Morra	5-3	2nd round	BCE International
	v Thorne	5-2	3rd round	BCE International
	v Chaperon	1-5	4th round	BCE International
	v Watchorn	5-3	2nd round	Rothmans Grand Prix
	v Charlton	5-4	3rd round	Rothmans Grand Prix
	v S. Davis	1-5	4th round	Rothmans Grand Prix
	v Morra	9-6	2nd round	Tennents UK Open
	v Williams	9-7	3rd round	Tennents UK Open
	v Virgo	9-6	4th round	Tennents UK Open
	v Thorne	9-5	5th round	Tennents UK Open
	v S. Davis	8-9	Quarter-final	Tennents UK Open
1987	v Jonik	2-5	2nd round	Mercantile Credit Classic
	v Oliver	5-1	2nd round	Dulux British Open
	v Johnson	0-5	3rd round	Dulux British Open
	v Sinclair	9-10	Qualifying	Embassy World Championship
	v Clark	2-5	3rd round	Fidelity International
	v Meadowcroft	5-1	3rd round	Rothmans Grand Prix
	v Thorne	2-5	4th round	Rothmans Grand Prix
	v Murphy	7-9	3rd round	Tennents UK Open
1988	v Scott	5-3	3rd round	Mercantile Credit Classic
	v Dennis Taylor	0-5	4th round	Mercantile Credit Classic
	v Roe	3-5	3rd round	MIM Britannia British Open
	v Chappel	10-7	Qualifying	Embassy World Championship
	v Higgins	10-2	1st round	Embassy World Championship
	v Dennis Taylor	13-5	2nd round	Embassy World Championship
	v Davis	4-13	Quarter-final	Embassy World Championship

STEVE DUGGAN (England)

Born 10.4.58. **Turned professional** 1983. **World ranking** 50 (37). **Best professional performance** Quarter-finals 1985 Goya Matchroom Trophy.

1983	v Darrington	5-4	Qualifying	Professional Players Tournament
	v Dunning	5-2	1st round	Professional Players Tournament
	v Reardon	2-5	2nd round	Professional Players Tournament
	v G. Foulds	8-9	Qualifying	Coral UK Championship
1984	v Browne	9-10	Qualifying	Embassy World Championship
	v T. Jones	5-2	Qualifying	Jameson International
	v Sinclair	0-5	Qualifying	Jameson International
	v Browne	5-2	Qualifying	Rothmans Grand Prix
	v S. Francisco	3-5	1st round	Rothmans Grand Prix
	v O'Kane	6-9	Qualifying	Coral UK Open
1985	v W. Jones	5-0	Qualifying	Mercantile Credit Classic
	v King	4-5	Qualifying	Mercantile Credit Classic
	v B. Harris	9-8	Qualifying	Tolly Cobbold English Championship
	v Hallett	4-9	1st round	Tolly Cobbold English Championship
	v Foldvari	4-6	Qualifying	Dulux British Open
	v T. Jones	8-10	Qualifying	Embassy World Championship
	v F. Davis	5-1	2nd round	Goya Matchroom Trophy
	v Reardon	5-3	3rd round	Goya Matchroom Trophy
	v Black	5-1	4th round	Goya Matchroom Trophy
	v Thorne	5-4	5th round	Goya Matchroom Trophy

	v Thorburn	2-5	Quarter-final	Goya Matchroom Trophy
	v Gauvreau	5-4	2nd round	Rothmans Grand Prix
	v Wildman	4-5	3rd round	Rothmans Grand Prix
	v Wych	5-9	2nd round	Coral UK Open
1986	v King	2-5	2nd round	Mercantile Credit Classic
	v Longworth	4-9	2nd round	Tolly Cobbold English Championship
	v Murphy	5-1	2nd round	Dulux British Open
	v Hallett	3-5	3rd round	Dulux British Open
	v Fisher	10-3	Qualifying	Embassy World Championship
	v Wych	5-10	Qualifying	Embassy World Championship
	v Bear	5-4	2nd round	BCE International
	v Campbell	5-3	3rd round	BCE International
	v Williams	4-5	4th round	BCE International
	v Whitthread	5-1	2nd round	Rothmans Grand Prix
	v Thorne	0-5	3rd round	Rothmans Grand Prix
	v O'Boye	4-9	2nd round	Tennents UK Open
1987	v Watchorn	5-1	2nd round	Mercantile Credit Classic
	v N. Foulds	5-3	3rd round	Mercantile Credit Classic
	v Werbeniuk	5-0	4th round	Mercantile Credit Classic
	v White	2-5	5th round	Mercantile Credit Classic
	v Fisher	6-0	2nd round	Tolly Ales English Championship
	v Meo	3-6	3rd round	Tolly Ales English Championship
	v P. Gibson	5-3	2nd round	Dulux British Open
	v Longworth	5-2	3rd round	Dulux British Open
	v Thorne	2-5	4th round	Dulux British Open
	v Roscoe	10-7	Qualifying	Embassy World Championship
	v Chappel	3-10	Qualifying	Embassy World Championship
	v Clark	2-5	2nd round	Fidelity International
	v P. Gibson	4-5	2nd round	Rothmans Grand Prix
	v Williamson	9-7	2nd round	Tennents UK Open
	v Higgins	4-9	3rd round	Tennents UK Open
1988	v Donnelly	4-5	2nd round	Mercantile Credit Classic
	v Williamson	6-2	2nd round	English Championship
	v Hallett	3-6	3rd round	English Championship
	v M. Gibson	2-5	2nd round	MIM Britannia British Open
	v A. Harris	10-4	Qualifying	Embassy World Championship
	v P. Gibson	10-9	Qualifying	Embassy World Championship
	v Virgo	5-10	Qualifying	Embassy World Championship

JOHN DUNNING (England)

Born 18.4.27. **Turned professional** 1970. **World ranking** 92 (104). **Best professional performances** Quarter-finals 1974 World Championship, reached final round robin group 1984 Yamaha International.

1972	v Houlihan	11-10	Qualifying	World Championship
	v Miles	11-5	Qualifying	World Championship
	v Pulman	7-19	1st round	World Championship
1973	v David Taylor	4-9	1st round	World Championship
1974	v David Taylor	8-6	1st round	World Championship
	v Charlton	15-13	2nd round	World Championship
	v Miles	13-15	Quarter-final	World Championship
1975	v G. Owen	8-15	2nd round	World Championship
1976	v Reardon	7-15	1st round	Embassy World Championship
1977	v Virgo	6-11	Qualifying	Embassy World Championship
	v Parkin	5-4	1st round	Super Crystalate UK Championship
	v Higgins	0-5	Quarter-final	Super Crystalate UK Championship
1978	v Fagan	5-9	Qualifying	Embassy World Championship
	v Greaves	9-3	Qualifying	Coral UK Championship
	v F. Davis	2-9	1st round	Coral UK Championship
1979	v Jack Rea	9-5	Prelim	Embassy World Championship
	v David Taylor	8-9	Qualifying	Embassy World Championship

		Score	Round	Tournament
	v Greaves	9-8	1st round	Coral UK Championship
	v S. Davis	3-9	2nd round	Coral UK Championship
1980	v Johnson	6-9	Qualifying	Coral UK Championship
1981	v Greaves	9-4	Qualifying	John Courage English
	v David Taylor	9-8	1st round	John Courage English
	v Thorne	0-9	2nd round	John Courage English
	v Bennett	9-6	Qualifying	Embassy World Championship
	v Fagan	9-7	Qualifying	Embassy World Championship
	v Stevens	4-10	1st round	Embassy World Championship
	v Gibson	5-3	Qualifying	Jameson International
	v Martin	2-5	1st round	Jameson International
1982	v Macleod	9-4	Qualifying	Embassy World Championship
	v Spencer	4-10	1st round	Embassy World Championship
	v Roscoe	2-5	Qualifying	Jameson International
	v Wildman	4-5	1st round	Professional Players Tournament
1983	v B. Harris	3-5	Qualifying	Jameson International
	v Duggan	2-5	1st round	Professional Players Tournament
	v Andrewartha	9-2	Qualifying	Coral UK Championship
	v Spencer	7-9	1st round	Coral UK Championship
1984	v Oliver	3-10	Qualifying	Embassy World Championship
	v Cripsey	5-3	Qualifying	Jameson International
	v F. Davis	4-5	Qualifying	Jameson International
	v D. Hughes	5-0	Qualifying	Rothmans Grand Prix
	v Mans	5-4	1st round	Rothmans Grand Prix
	v Knowles	1-5	2nd round	Rothmans Grand Prix
	v John Rea	3-9	Qualifying	Coral UK Open
1985	v W. Jones	6-10	Qualifying	Embassy World Championship
	v Everton	5-2	2nd round	Goya Matchroom Trophy
	v Meo	0-5	3rd round	Goya Matchroom Trophy
	v Agrawal	0-5	2nd round	Rothmans Grand Prix
1986	v West	3-10	Qualifying	Embassy World Championship
	v Demarco	5-4	1st round	BCE International
	v Newbury	4-5	2nd round	BCE International
	v P. Gibson	1-5	1st round	Rothmans Grand Prix
	v Kearney	9-6	1st round	Tennents UK Open
	v M. Gibson	2-9	2nd round	Tennents UK Open
1987	v B. Bennett	5-2	1st round	Mercantile Credit Classic
	v Browne	1-5	2nd round	Mercantile Credit Classic
	v Cripsey	1-6	2nd round	Tolly Ales English Championship
	v Watchorn	2-5	1st round	Dulux British Open
	v Caggianello	10-7	Qualifying	Embassy World Championship
	v Scott	7-10	Qualifying	Embassy World Championship
	v Sheehan	5-1	1st round	Fidelity International
	v W. Jones	1-5	2nd round	Fidelity International
	v Foldvari	0-5	1st round	Rothmans Grand Prix
	v Fagan	9-4	1st round	Tennents UK Open
	v Bales	9-8	2nd round	Tennents UK Open
	v White	0-9	3rd round	Tennents UK Open
1988	v Jonik	2-5	1st round	Mercantile Credit Classic
	v Williamson	5-6	1st round	English Championship
	v Jonik	5-3	1st round	MIM Britannia British Open
	v Scott	5-3	2nd round	MIM Britannia British Open
	v West	0-5	3rd round	MIM Britannia British Open
	v Rigitano	7-10	Qualifying	Embassy World Championship

RAY EDMONDS (England)

Born 28.5.36. **Turned professional** 1978. **World ranking** 55 (60). **Amateur career** World Champion 1972, 1974; English champion 1969, 1974. **Best professional performance** Quarter-finals 1979 Coral UK Championship.

1978	v Virgo	4-9	Qualifying	Coral UK Championship

Year	Opponent	Score	Round	Tournament
1979	v Meadowcroft	9-3	2nd round	Coral UK Championship
	v F. Davis	9-6	3rd round	Coral UK Championship
	v Werbeniuk	8-9	Quarter-final	Coral UK Championship
1980	v Hood	9-6	Qualifying	Embassy World Championship
	v David Taylor	3-10	1st round	Embassy World Championship
	v Hallett	8-9	Qualifying	Coral UK Championship
1981	v Hallett	9-3	Qualifying	John Courage English
	v F. Davis	9-6	1st round	John Courage English
	v Johnson	9-5	2nd round	John Courage English
	v S. Davis	0-9	Semi-final	John Courage English
	v Wildman	9-3	Qualifying	Embassy World Championship
	v Williams	9-7	Qualifying	Embassy World Championship
	v Spencer	9-10	1st round	Embassy World Championship
	v E. Hughes	5-4	1st round	Jameson International
	v Spencer	3-5	2nd round	Jameson International
	v Thorne	4-9	2nd round	Coral UK Championship
1982	v Reynolds	6-9	Qualifying	Embassy World Championship
	v D. Hughes	5-0	Qualifying	Jameson International
	v Miles	5-1	Qualifying	Jameson International
	v Spencer	2-5	1st round	Jameson International
	v Dennis Taylor	4-5	1st round	Professional Players Tournament
	v Fisher	8-9	Qualifying	Coral UK Championship
1983	v Jonik	10-4	Qualifying	Embassy World Championship
	v Reynolds	6-10	Qualifying	Embassy World Championship
	v Jack Rea	5-1	Qualifying	Jameson International
	v E. McLaughlin	5-1	Qualifying	Jameson International
	v Knowles	1-5	1st round	Jameson International
	v Stevens	1-5	1st round	Professional Players Tournament
	v Medati	7-9	Qualifying	Coral UK Championship
1984	v Greaves	10-0	Qualifying	Embassy World Championship
	v Van Rensberg	9-10	Qualifying	Embassy World Championship
	v Foldvari	1-5	Qualifying	Jameson International
	v Rigitano	3-5	Qualifying	Rothmans Grand Prix
	v John Rea	6-9	Qualifying	Coral UK Open
1985	v Hargreaves	5-2	Qualifying	Mercantile Credit Classic
	v Watterson	5-2	Qualifying	Mercantile Credit Classic
	v Johnson	4-5	Qualifying	Mercantile Credit Classic
	v Longworth	4-9	Qualifying	Tolly Cobbold English Championship
	v Mienie	6-1	Qualifying	Dulux British Open
	v Miles	1-6	1st round	Dulux British Open
	v Foldvari	10-3	Qualifying	Embassy World Championship
	v Wildman	10-7	Qualifying	Embassy World Championship
	v Stevens	8-10	1st round	Embassy World Championship
	v Bales	0-5	2nd round	Goya Matchroom Trophy
	v Kearney	5-2	2nd round	Rothmans Grand Prix
	v O'Kane	5-2	3rd round	Rothmans Grand Prix
	v Knowles	3-5	4th round	Rothmans Grand Prix
	v Van Rensberg	9-5	2nd round	Coral UK Open
	v Higgins	8-9	3rd round	Coral UK Open
1986	v Smith	2-5	2nd round	Mecantile Credit Classic
	v Smith	9-8	2nd round	Tolly Cobbold English Championship
	v David Taylor	9-6	3rd round	Tolly Cobbold English Championship
	v N. Foulds	4-9	4th round	Tolly Cobbold English Championship
	v Hargreaves	3-5	2nd round	Dulux British Open
	v Kelly	10-0	Qualifying	Embassy World Championship
	v Darrington	10-5	Qualifying	Embassy World Championship
	v Wildman	10-9	Qualifying	Embassy World Championship
	v S. Davis	4-10	1st round	Embassy World Championship
	v James	5-2	2nd round	BCE International
	v David Taylor	4-5	3rd round	BCE International
	v O'Boye	2-5	2nd round	Rothmans Grand Prix
	v Bear	9-6	2nd round	Tennents UK Open
	v White	4-9	3rd round	Tennents UK Open

1987	v Williamson	2-5	2nd round	Mercantile Credit Classic
	v Bennett	6-1	2nd round	Tolly Ales English Championship
	v Reynolds	3-6	3rd round	Tolly Ales English Championship
	v G. Foulds	3-5	2nd round	Dulux British Open
	v James	10-1	Qualifying	Embassy World Championship
	v Sinclair	10-6	Qualifying	Embassy World Championship
	v Macleod	7-10	Qualifying	Embassy World Championship
	v Sinclair	4-5	2nd round	Fidelity International
	v Sinclair	5-2	2nd round	Rothmans Grand Prix
	v Williams	5-3	3rd round	Rothmans Grand Prix
	v Charlton	3-5	4th round	Rothmans Grand Prix
	v D. Hughes	9-4	2nd round	Tennents UK Open
	v Macleod	9-4	3rd round	Tennents UK Open
	v Griffiths	5-9	4th round	Tennents UK Open
1988	v Foldvari	5-4	2nd round	Mercantile Credit Classic
	v Longworth	3-5	3rd round	Mercantile Credit Classic
	v Gary Wilkinson	3-6	2nd round	English Championship
	v Roe	1-5	2nd round	MIM Britannia British Open
	v Morra	8-10	Qualifying	Embassy World Championship

FRANÇOIS ELLIS (South Africa)

Born 11.9.59. **Turned professional** 1983. **World ranking** 113 (118). **Amateur career** South African champion 1979.

1986	v Mans	7-6	2nd round	South African Championship
	v Van Rensberg	8-2	Semi-final	South African Championship
	v S. Francisco	1-9	Final	South African Championship
	v Morra	3-5	1st round	BCE International
	v Wildman	1-5	2nd round	Rothmans Grand Prix
	v D. Hughes	6-9	1st round	Tennents UK Open
1987	v Morra	1-5	1st round	Mercantile Credit Classic
	v Smith	5-2	1st round	Dulux British Open
	v Medati	0-5	2nd round	Dulux British Open
	v Roe	4-5	1st round	Fidelity International
	v Sinclair	4-5	1st round	Rothmans Grand Prix
	v Sheehan	9-8	1st round	Tennents UK Open
	v F. Davis	6-9	2nd round	Tennents UK Open
1988	v V. Harris	1-5	1st round	Mercantile Credit Classic
	v Chappel	0-5	2nd round	MIM Britannia British Open

CLIVE EVERTON (Wales)

Born 7.9.37. **Turned professional** 1981. **World ranking** 120 (113).

1981	v Kennerley	5-4	Qualifying	Jameson International
	v Watterson	4-5	Qualifying	Jameson International
	v Gibson	9-7	Qualifying	Coral UK Championship
	v White	4-9	Qualifying	Coral UK Championship
1982	v Reardon	1-6	1st round	Woodpecker Welsh Championship
	v D. Hughes	4-9	Qualifying	Embassy World Championship
	v Watterson	1-5	Qualifying	Jameson International
	v Fagan	5-2	1st round	Professional Players Tournament
	v Thorburn	2-5	2nd round	Professional Players Tournament
	v Murphy	4-9	Qualifying	Coral UK Championship
1983	v Griffiths	1-6	Quarter-final	Woodpecker Welsh Championship
	v Wilson	1-10	Qualifying	Embassy World Championship
	v Andrewartha	1-5	Qualifying	Jameson International
	v Thorne	1-5	1st round	Professional Players Tournament
	v Watterson	6-9	Qualifying	Coral UK Championship

1984	v Mountjoy	1-6	1st round	Strongbow Welsh Championship
	v Parrott	2-10	Qualifying	Embassy World Championship
	v Mikkelsen	0-5	Qualifying	Jameson International
	v Houlihan	5-3	Qualifying	Rothmans Grand Prix
	v Charlton	1-5	1st round	Rothmans Grand Prix
	v Watchorn	6-9	Qualifying	Coral UK Open
1985	v Browne	0-5	Qualifying	Mercantile Credit Classic
	v Fowler	1-6	Qualifying	Dulux British Open
	v G. Foulds	2-10	Qualifying	Embassy World Championship
	v Reardon	2-6	Quarter-final	BCE Welsh Championship
	v Dunning	2-5	2nd round	Goya Matchroom Trophy
	v P. Francisco	0-5	2nd round	Rothmans Grand Prix
	v Murphy	4-9	2nd round	Coral UK Open
1986	v Browne	0-5	2nd round	Mercantile Credit Classic
	v W. Jones	2-6	1st round	Zetters Welsh Championship
	v Medati	1-5	2nd round	Dulux British Open
	v Miles	3-10	Qualifying	Embassy World Championship
	v Jenkins	3-5	1st round	BCE International
	v Rigitano	1-5	1st round	Rothmans Grand Prix
	v Bear	1-9	1st round	Tennents UK Open
1987	v W. Jones	0-5	2nd round	Mercantile Credit Classic
	v Roscoe	2-6	1st round	Matchroom Welsh Championship
	v Fitzmaurice	2-10	Qualifying	Embassy World Championship
	v Williamson	0-5	1st round	Fidelity International
	v Burke	1-5	1st round	Rothmans Grand Prix
	v Rowswell	4-9	1st round	Tennents UK Open
1988	v Meadowcroft	5-3	1st round	Mercantile Credit Classic
	v Bradley	2-5	2nd round	Mercantile Credit Classic
	v M. Bennett	0-6	1st round	Welsh Championship
	v Glen Wilkinson	2-10	Qualifying	Embassy World Championship

PATSY FAGAN (Republic of Ireland)

Born 15.1.51. **Turned professional** 1976. **World ranking** 102 (76). **Best professional performance** Winner 1977 Super Crystalate UK Championship.

1977	v Meadowcroft	11-9	Qualifying	Embassy World Championship
	v Reardon	7-13	1st round	Embassy World Championship
	v Jack Rea	5-1	1st round	Super Crystalate UK Championship
	v F. Davis	5-0	2nd round	Super Crystalate UK Championship
	v Meadowcroft	5-4	Quarter-final	Super Crystalate UK Championship
	v Virgo	9-8	Semi-final	Super Crystalate UK Championship
	v Mountjoy	**12-9**	**Final**	**Super Crystalate UK Championship**
1978	v Pulman	2-4	1st round	Benson & Hedges Masters
	v Dunning	9-5	Qualifying	Embassy World Championship
	v Higgins	13-12	1st round	Embassy World Championship
	v F. Davis	10-13	Quarter-final	Embassy World Championship
	v David Taylor	7-9	1st round	Coral UK Championship
1979	v S. Davis	2-9	Qualifying	Embassy World Championship
	v Hallett	9-4	2nd round	Coral UK Championship
	v Miles	9-5	3rd round	Coral UK Championship
	v Dennis Taylor	6-9	Quarter-final	Coral UK Championship
1980	v S. Davis	6-10	1st round	Embassy World Championship
	v Johnson	9-4	1st round	Coral UK Championship
	v Griffiths	8-9	2nd round	Coral UK Championship
1981	v Dunning	7-9	Qualifying	Embassy World Championship
	v Watterson	5-2	Qualifying	Jameson International
	v Higgins	3-5	2nd round	Jameson International
	v Hallett	5-9	Qualifying	Coral UK Championship
1982	v Murphy	2-6	Quarter-final	Irish Championship
	v French	9-6	Qualifying	Embassy World Championship

		Score	Round	Tournament
	v David Taylor	10-9	1st round	Embassy World Championship
	v Stevens	7-13	2nd round	Embassy World Championship
	v Watterson	1-5	Qualifying	Jameson International
	v Everton	2-5	1st round	Professional Players Tournament
	v B. Harris	9-6	1st round	Coral UK Championship
	v S. Davis	3-9	2nd round	Coral UK Championship
1983	v Murphy	6-4	Quarter-final	Irish Championship
	v Dennis Taylor	1-6	Semi-final	Irish Championship
	v Fisher	8-10	Qualifying	Embassy World Championship
	v Martin	0-5	Qualifying	Jameson International
	v Parrott	2-5	1st round	Professional Players Tournament
1984	v Higgins	3-5	Qualifying	Lada Classic
	v Wych	3-10	Qualifying	Embassy World Championship
	v Newbury	0-5	Qualifying	Jameson International
	v T. Jones	2-9	Qualifying	Coral UK Open
1985	v Williamson	5-1	Qualifying	Mercantile Credit Classic
	v Wildman	5-3	Qualifying	Mercantile Credit Classic
	v Griffiths	0-5	1st round	Mercantile Credit Classic
	v Murphy	6-2	Quarter-final	Irish Championship
	v Higgins	3-6	Semi-final	Irish Championship
	v Gibson	10-8	Qualifying	Embassy World Championship
	v Wilson	10-9	Qualifying	Embassy World Championship
	v Thorne	10-6	1st round	Embassy World Championship
	v Reardon	9-13	2nd round	Embassy World Championship
	v Mienie	5-4	2nd round	Goya Matchroom Trophy
	v White	2-5	3rd round	Goya Matchroom Trophy
	v Oliver	4-5	2nd round	Rothmans Grand Prix
	v B. Harris	9-2	2nd round	Coral UK Open
	v N. Foulds	5-9	3rd round	Coral UK Open
1986	v Fitzmaurice	3-5	2nd round	Mercantile Credit Classic
	v Fitzmaurice	5-4	2nd round	Dulux British Open
	v Mountjoy	5-1	3rd round	Dulux British Open
	v Parrott	0-5	4th round	Dulux British Open
	v Knowles	5-4	Quarter-final	Benson & Hedges Irish Masters
	v White	0-6	Semi-final	Benson & Hedges Irish Masters
	v Thornley	7-10	Qualifying	Embassy World Championship
	v Kearney	0-5	1st round	Strongbow Irish Championship
	v Sinclair	0-5	2nd round	BCE International
	v Grace	5-3	2nd round	Rothmans Grand Prix
	v Virgo	2-5	3rd round	Rothmans Grand Prix
	v Wright	0-9	2nd round	Tennents UK Open
1987	v Grace	3-5	2nd round	Dulux British Open
	v Oliver	2-10	Qualifying	Embassy World Championship
	v Burke	3-5	1st round	Matchroom Irish Championship
	v O'Boye	1-5	2nd round	Fidelity International
	v P. Gibson	0-5	1st round	Rothmans Grand Prix
	v Dunning	4-9	1st round	Tennents UK Open
1988	v Whitthread	2-5	1st round	Mercantile Credit Classic
	v Kearney	3-5	1st round	Irish Championship
	v D. Hughes	4-5	1st round	MIM Britannia British Open
	v Greaves	10-3	Qualifying	Embassy World Championship
	v B. Harris	1-10	Qualifying	Embassy World Championship

MICK FISHER (England)

Born 12.7.44. **Turned professional** 1982. **World ranking** 58 (93). **Best professional performance** Last 16 1987 Rothmans Grand Prix.

		Score	Round	Tournament
1982	v Murphy	5-1	Qualifying	Jameson International
	v F. Davis	5-3	Qualifying	Jameson International
	v David Taylor	1-5	1st round	Jameson International

	v Black	9-3	Qualifying	Coral UK Championship
	v Edmonds	9-8	Qualifying	Coral UK Championship
	v Reynolds	6-9	1st round	Coral UK Championship
1983	v Fagan	10-8	Qualifying	Embassy World Championship
	v E. McLaughlin	10-9	Qualifying	Embassy World Championship
	v Stevens	2-10	1st round	Embassy World Championship
	v E. Hughes	4-5	Qualifying	Jameson International
	v F. Davis	5-4	1st round	Professional Players Tournament
	v Charlton	4-5	2nd round	Professional Players Tournament
	v Parrott	0-9	Qualifying	Coral UK Championship
1984	v Thornley	10-8	Qualifying	Embassy World Championship
	v Gibson	7-10	Qualifying	Embassy World Championship
	v Bales	3-5	Qualifying	Jameson International
	v Newbury	0-5	Qualifying	Rothmans Grand Prix
	v Watchorn	9-5	Qualifying	Coral UK Open
	v Williams	8-9	Qualifying	Coral UK Open
1985	v Longworth	1-5	Qualifying	Mercantile Credit Classic
	v French	9-8	Qualifying	Tolly Cobbold English Championship
	v Meo	3-9	1st round	Tolly Cobbold English Championship
	v John Rea	0-6	Qualifying	Dulux British Open
	v Rigitano	2-10	Qualifying	Embassy World Championship
	v Mikkelsen	3-5	1st round	Goya Matchroom Trophy
	v Bales	3-5	2nd round	Rothmans Grand Prix
	v Simngam	4-9	2nd round	Coral UK Open
1986	v Jack Rea	5-3	2nd round	Mercantile Credit Classic
	v Higgins	0-5	3rd round	Mercantile Credit Classic
	v Chalmers	2-9	2nd round	Tolly Cobbold English Championship
	v J. McLaughlin	3-5	2nd round	Dulux British Open
	v Duggan	3-10	Qualifying	Embassy World Championship
	v Hines	2-5	1st round	BCE International
	v Wright	1-5	1st round	Rothmans Grand Prix
	v Greaves	9-4	1st round	Tennents UK Open
	v V. Harris	4-9	2nd round	Tennents UK Open
1987	v Demarco	5-0	1st round	Mercantile Credit Classic
	v F. Davis	5-2	2nd round	Mercantile Credit Classic
	v Charlton	0-5	3rd round	Mercantile Credit Classic
	v Whitthread	6-3	1st round	Tolly Ales English Championship
	v Duggan	0-6	2nd round	Tolly Ales English Championship
	v Chaperon	2-5	2nd round	Dulux British Open
	v Owers	5-10	Qualifying	Embassy World Championship
	v Newbury	0-5	2nd round	Fidelity International
	v Watchorn	5-4	1st round	Rothmans Grand Prix
	v F. Davis	5-0	2nd round	Rothmans Grand Prix
	v E. Hughes	5-4	3rd round	Rothmans Grand Prix
	v Clark	5-4	4th round	Rothmans Grand Prix
	v Chaperon	2-5	5th round	Rothmans Grand Prix
	v Wych	6-9	2nd round	Tennents UK Open
1988	v Owers	0-5	2nd round	Mercantile Credit Classic
	v Wright	2-6	2nd round	English Championship
	v Clark	1-5	1st round	MIM Britannia British Open
	v A. Harris	4-10	Qualifying	Embassy World Championship

JACK FITZMAURICE (England)

Born 25.4.28. **Turned professional** 1981. **World ranking** 114 (89). **Best professional performance** Last 32 1982 Embassy World Championship.

1981	v Bennett	5-1	Qualifying	Jameson International
	v E. Hughes	3-5	Qualifying	Jameson International
	v Gibson	6-9	Qualifying	Coral UK Championship
1982	v Morra	9-7	Qualifying	Embassy World Championship

		Score	Round	Tournament
	v Stevens	4-10	1st round	Embassy World Championship
	v Black	5-3	Qualifying	Jameson International
	v Dodd	3-5	Qualifying	Jameson International
	v Sheehan	5-1	1st round	Professional Players Tournament
	v Reynolds	0-5	2nd round	Professional Players Tournament
	v Kelly	0-8 retd	Qualifying	Coral UK Championship
1983	v E. Hughes	7-10	Qualifying	Embassy World Championship
	v Morgan	4-5	Qualifying	Jameson International
	v Martin	0-5	1st round	Professional Players Tournament
	v B. Harris	3-9	Qualifying	Coral UK Championship
1984	v Murphy	8-10	Qualifying	Embassy World Championship
	v O'Kane	4-5	Qualifying	Jameson International
	v John Rea	2-5	Qualifying	Rothmans Grand Prix
	v Cripsey	9-8	Qualifying	Coral UK Open
	v Parrott	6-9	Qualifying	Coral UK Open
1985	v G. Foulds	1-5	Qualifying	Mercantile Credit Classic
	v Greaves	9-3	Qualifying	Tolly Cobbold English Championship
	v Reynolds	2-9	1st round	Tolly Cobbold English Championship
	v Watterson	1-6	Qualifying	Dulux British Open
	v T. Jones	4-10	Qualifying	Embassy World Championship
	v Watterson	5-2	2nd round	Goya Matchroom Trophy
	v Macleod	1-5	3rd round	Goya Matchroom Trophy
	v Sinclair	5-3	2nd round	Rothmans Grand Prix
	v White	0-5	3rd round	Rothmans Grand Prix
	v W. Jones	3-9	2nd round	Coral UK Open
1986	v Fagan	5-3	2nd round	Mercantile Credit Classic
	v Dennis Taylor	1-5	3rd round	Mercantile Credit Classic
	v Miles	5-9	2nd round	Tolly Cobbold English Championship
	v Fagan	4-5	2nd round	Dulux British Open
	v Dodd	6-10	Qualifying	Embassy World Championship
	v Burke	4-5	1st round	BCE International
	v Mienie	2-5	1st round	Rothmans Grand Prix
	v Hines	9-4	1st round	Tennents UK Open
	v T. Jones	0-9	2nd round	Tennents UK Open
1987	v Wilkinson	2-5	1st round	Mercantile Credit Classic
	v Scott	6-2	2nd round	Tolly Ales English Championship
	v David Taylor	1-6	3rd round	Tolly Ales English Championship
	v Wilkinson	0-5	1st round	Dulux British Open
	v Everton	10-2	Qualifying	Embassy World Championship
	v Chaperon	2-10	Qualifying	Embassy World Championship
	v Chalmers	4-5	1st round	Fidelity International
	v Chambers	2-5	1st round	Rothmans Grand Prix
	v Lawlor	0-9	1st round	Tennents UK Open
1988	v M. Smith	2-5	1st round	Mercantile Credit Classic
	v Marshall	1-6	1st round	English Championship
	v T. Jones	3-5	2nd round	MIM Britannia British Open
	v Parkin	10-6	Qualifying	Embassy World Championship
	v F. Davis	8-10	Qualifying	Embassy World Championship

ROBBY FOLDVARI (Australia)

Born 2.6.60. **Turned professional** 1984. **World ranking** 66 (80). **Best professional performance** Last 32 1987 Rothmans Grand Prix.

		Score	Round	Tournament
1984	v Rigitano	5-2	Qualifying	Jameson International
	v Edmonds	5-1	Qualifying	Jameson International
	v Dodd	3-5	Qualifying	Jameson International
	v Gauvreau	2-5	Qualifying	Rothmans Grand Prix
	v Greaves	9-5	Qualifying	Coral UK Open
	v Cripsey	7-9	Qualifying	Coral UK Open

1985	v Houlihan	5-1	Qualifying	Mercantile Credit Classic
	v Jack Rea	5-4	Qualifying	Mercantile Credit Classic
	v Martin	5-2	Qualifying	Mercantile Credit Classic
	v Thorne	2-5	1st round	Mercantile Credit Classic
	v Duggan	6-4	Qualifying	Dulux British Open
	v Meo	0-6	1st round	Dulux British Open
	v Oliver	10-3	Qualifying	Embassy World Championship
	v Edmonds	3-10	Qualifying	Embassy World Championship
	v Robinson	7-2	2nd round	Australian Championship
	v Campbell	5-8	Quarter-final	Australian Championship
	v V. Harris	5-4	2nd round	Goya Matchroom Trophy
	v Spencer	4-5	3rd round	Goya Matchroom Trophy
	v Darrington	3-5	2nd round	Rothmans Grand Prix
	v Darrington	6-9	2nd round	Coral UK Open
1986	v Houlihan	4-5	2nd round	Mercantile Credit Classic
	v Kearney	5-2	2nd round	Dulux British Open
	v Werbeniuk	4-5	3rd round	Dulux British Open
	v Rigitano	10-6	Qualifying	Embassy World Championship
	v Miles	10-7	Qualifying	Embassy World Championship
	v Parrott	6-10	Qualifying	Embassy World Championship
	v Jenkins	6-3	2nd round	Australian Championship
	v Morgan	6-2	Quarter-final	Australian Championship
	v Campbell	3-8	Semi-final	Australian Championship
	v B. Harris	5-0	2nd round	BCE International
	v Dennis Taylor	1-5	3rd round	BCE International
	v W. Jones	3-5	2nd round	Rothmans Grand Prix
	v Spencer	6-9	2nd round	Tennents UK Open
1987	v Mikkelsen	1-5	2nd round	Mercantile Credit Classic
	v Mikkelsen	5-3	2nd round	Dulux British Open
	v Williams	4-5	3rd round	Dulux British Open
	v Wildman	5-10	Qualifying	Embassy World Championship
	v King	1-8	Semi-final	Australian Championship
	v Meakin	3-5	1st round	Fidelity International
	v Kearney	5-1	2nd round	Fidelity International
	v Williams	5-0	3rd round	Fidelity International
	v D. Gilbert	4-5	4th round	Fidelity International
	v Dunning	5-0	1st round	Rothmans Grand Prix
	v King	5-4	2nd round	Rothmans Grand Prix
	v Werbeniuk	1-5	3rd round	Rothmans Grand Prix
	v Clark	9-8	1st round	Tennents UK Open
	v Newbury	5-9	2nd round	Tennents UK Open
1988	v Greaves	5-3	1st round	Mercantile Credit Classic
	v Edmonds	4-5	2nd round	Mercantile Credit Classic
	v Heaton	5-1	1st round	MIM Britannia British Open
	v G. Foulds	5-3	2nd round	MIM Britannia British Open
	v Parrott	1-5	3rd round	MIM Britannia British Open
	v Rempe	10-4	Qualifying	Embassy World Championship
	v T. Jones	10-9	Qualifying	Embassy World Championship
	v Wildman	10-1	Qualifying	Embassy World Championship
	v P. Francisco	5-10	Qualifying	Embassy World Championship

GEOFF FOULDS (England)

Born 20.11.39. **Turned professional** 1981. **World ranking** 78 (63). **Best professional performance** Last 32 1986 BCE International.

1981	v French	2-5	Qualifying	Jameson International
	v Kelly	9-7	Qualifying	Coral UK Championship
	v Knowles	1-9	Qualifying	Coral UK Championship
1982	v Wildman	8-9	Qualifying	Embassy World Championship
	v Kelly	4-5	Qualifying	Jameson International

v Spencer	1-5	1st round	Professional Players Tournament
v Gibson	9-3	Qualifying	Coral UK Championship
v Williams	7-9	Qualifying	Coral UK Championship
1983 v Gibson	10-6	Qualifying	Embassy World Championship
v Meo	4-10	Qualifying	Embassy World Championship
v Burke	5-2	Qualifying	Jameson International
v E. Hughes	1-5	Qualifying	Jameson International
v Burke	4-5	Qualifying	Professional Players Tournament
v Duggan	9-8	Qualifying	Coral UK Championship
v Dodd	9-7	Qualifying	Coral UK Championship
v S. Davis	1-9	1st round	Coral UK Championship
1984 v Morra	2-10	Qualifying	Embassy World Championship
v P. Francisco	5-4	Qualifying	Jameson International
v Williamson	5-4	Qualifying	Jameson International
v Donnelly	5-3	Qualifying	Jameson International
v Campbell	3-5	Qualifying	Jameson International
v Murphy	1-5	Qualifying	Rothmans Grand Prix
v D. Hughes	9-7	Qualifying	Coral UK Open
v Browne	5-9	Qualifying	Coral UK Open
1985 v Chaperon	5-3	Qualifying	Mercantile Credit Classic
v Jonik	5-2	Qualifying	Mercantile Credit Classic
v Fitzmaurice	5-1	Qualifying	Mercantile Credit Classic
v Hallett	4-5	Qualifying	Mercantile Credit Classic
v F. Davis	9-2	Qualifying	Tolly Cobbold English Championship
v Parrott	4-9	1st round	Tolly Cobbold English Championship
v T. Jones	0-6	Qualifying	Dulux British Open
v Parkin	10-6	Qualifying	Embassy World Championship
v Everton	10-2	Qualifying	Embassy World Championship
v Roscoe	10-7	Qualifying	Embassy World Championship
v Johnson	6-10	Qualifying	Embassy World Championship
v Roscoe	3-5	2nd round	Goya Matchroom Trophy
v Black	5-3	2nd round	Rothmans Grand Prix
v Charlton	1-5	3rd round	Rothmans Grand Prix
v Sinclair	4-9	2nd round	Coral UK Open
1986 v Black	5-2	2nd round	Mercantile Credit Classic
v Werbeniuk	3-5	3rd round	Mercantile Credit Classic
v Watterson	9-1	2nd round	Tolly Cobbold English Championship
v N. Foulds	4-9	3rd round	Tolly Cobbold English Championship
v P. Francisco	2-5	2nd round	Dulux British Open
v Roscoe	3-10	Qualifying	Embassy World Championship
v V. Harris	5-4	2nd round	BCE International
v Werbeniuk	5-2	3rd round	BCE International
v N. Foulds	0-5	4th round	BCE International
v Wilkinson	5-3	1st round	Rothmans Grand Prix
v Mikkelsen	5-1	2nd round	Rothmans Grand Prix
v Campbell	0-5	3rd round	Rothmans Grand Prix
v Roe	1-7 *retd*	1st round	Tennents UK Open
1987 v Chalmers	5-4	1st round	Mercantile Credit Classic
v O'Kane	5-4	2nd round	Mercantile Credit Classic
v Martin	4-5	3rd round	Mercantile Credit Classic
v B. Harris	1-6	2nd round	Tolly Ales English Championship
v Edmonds	5-3	2nd round	Dulux British Open
v Wilson	3-5	3rd round	Dulux British Open
v Watchorn	10-6	Qualifying	Embassy World Championship
v Fowler	6-10	Qualifying	Embassy World Championship
v Jack Rea	1-5	2nd round	Fidelity International
v James	0-5	2nd round	Rothmans Grand Prix
v N. Gilbert	4-9	2nd round	Tennents UK Open
1988 v Whitthread	3-5	2nd round	Mercantile Credit Classic
v Clark	0-6	2nd round	English Championship
v Foldvari	3-5	2nd round	MIM Britannia British Open
v Bear	2-10	Qualifying	Embassy World Championship

NEAL FOULDS (England)

Born 13.7.63. **Turned professional** 1983. **World ranking** 3 (3). **Best professional performances** Winner 1986 BCE International; runner-up 1986 Tennents UK Open, 1987 Dulux British Open; semi-finals 1987 Embassy World Championship.

1983	v French	2-5	Qualifying	Professional Players Tournament
	v Roscoe	9-2	Qualifying	Coral UK Championship
	v Meadowcroft	9-2	Qualifying	Coral UK Championship
	v David Taylor	4-9	1st round	Coral UK Championship
1984	v French	10-5	Qualifying	Embassy World Championship
	v Dodd	10-4	Qualifying	Embassy World Championship
	v Meadowcroft	10-2	Qualifying	Embassy World Championship
	v Higgins	10-9	1st round	Embassy World Championship
	v Mountjoy	6-13	2nd round	Embassy World Championship
	v Bennett	5-0	Qualifying	Jameson International
	v Griffiths	3-5	1st round	Jameson International
	v Demarco	5-2	1st round	Rothmans Grand Prix
	v T. Jones	5-0	2nd round	Rothmans Grand Prix
	v Thorne	5-1	3rd round	Rothmans Grand Prix
	v Knowles	5-2	Quarter-final	Rothmans Grand Prix
	v Dennis Taylor	3-9	Semi-final	Rothmans Grand Prix
	v Fowler	6-9	Qualifying	Coral UK Open
1985	v Longworth	3-5	Qualifying	Mercantile Credit Classic
	v D. Hughes	9-3	1st round	Tolly Cobbold English Championship
	v White	7-9	2nd round	Tolly Cobbold English Championship
	v Hargreaves	6-1	1st round	Dulux British Open
	v Higgins	1-5	2nd round	Dulux British Open
	v Rigitano	10-8	Qualifying	Embassy World Championship
	v S. Davis	8-10	1st round	Embassy World Championship
	v Dodd	5-3	3rd round	Goya Matchroom Trophy
	v Knowles	5-3	4th round	Goya Matchroom Trophy
	v David Taylor	5-4	5th round	Goya Matchroom Trophy
	v Johnson	5-2	Quarter-final	Goya Matchroom Trophy
	v White	5-9	Semi-final	Goya Matchroom Trophy
	v Darrington	5-0	3rd round	Rothmans Grand Prix
	v Higgins	3-5	4th round	Rothmans Grand Prix
	v Fagan	9-5	3rd round	Coral UK Open
	v Johnson	9-8	4th round	Coral UK Open
	v Dennis Taylor	5-9	5th round	Coral UK Open
1986	v Bradley	5-3	3rd round	Mercantile Credit Classic
	v Hendry	5-4	4th round	Mercantile Credit Classic
	v Campbell	5-1	5th round	Mercantile Credit Classic
	v Mountjoy	3-5	Quarter-final	Mercantile Credit Classic
	v G. Foulds	9-4	3rd round	Tolly Cobbold English Championship
	v Edmonds	9-4	4th round	Tolly Cobbold English Championship
	v White	9-4	Quarter-final	Tolly Cobbold English Championship
	v Hallett	9-8	Semi-final	Tolly Cobbold English Championship
	v Meo	7-9	Final	Tolly Cobbold English Championship
	v Hargreaves	5-4	3rd round	Dulux British Open
	v Griffiths	3-5	4th round	Dulux British Open
	v P. Francisco	10-9	Qualifying	Embassy World Championship
	v Knowles	9-10	1st round	Embassy World Championship
	v Thorne	3-6	1st round	Matchroom Trophy
	v Miles	5-2	3rd round	BCE International
	v G. Foulds	5-0	4th round	BCE International
	v Owers	5-1	5th round	BCE International
	v Reynolds	5-2	Quarter-final	BCE International
	v E. Hughes	9-8	Semi-final	BCE International
	v Thorburn	**12-9**	**Final**	**BCE International**
	v Miles	5-1	3rd round	Rothmans Grand Prix
	v Wilson	5-0	4th round	Rothmans Grand Prix

Neal Foulds

	v Thorne	5-3	5th round	Rothmans Grand Prix
	v Meo	5-3	Quarter-final	Rothmans Grand Prix
	v Williams	8-9	Semi-final	Rothmans Grand Prix
	v Cripsey	9-7	3rd round	Tennents UK Open
	v Wych	9-3	4th round	Tennents UK Open
	v White	9-7	5th round	Tennents UK Open
	v Thorburn	9-2	Quarter-final	Tennents UK Open
	v Parrott	9-2	Semi-final	Tennents UK Open
	v S. Davis	7-16	Final	Tennents UK Open·
1987	v Duggan	3-5	3rd round	Mercantile Credit Classic
	v Dennis Taylor	2-5	1st round	Benson & Hedges Masters
	v Owers	3-6	3rd round	Tolly Ales English Championship
	v Roe	5-1	3rd round	Dulux British Open
	v King	5-4	4th round	Dulux British Open
	v Thorne	5-2	5th round	Dulux British Open
	v Virgo	5-3	Quarter-final	Dulux British Open
	v Knowles	9-2	Semi-final	Dulux British Open
	v White	9-13	Final	Dulux British Open
	v Virgo	10-4	1st round	Embassy World Championship
	v Dennis Taylor	13-10	2nd round	Embassy World Championship
	v Hallett	13-9	Quarter-final	Embassy World Championship
	v Johnson	9-16	Semi-final	Embassy World Championship
	v Johnson	4-5	1st round	Carling Champions
	v Griffiths	4-5	1st round	Langs Scottish Masters
	v P. Gibson	5-2	3rd round	Fidelity International
	v Hendry	2-5	4th round	Fidelity International
	v Clark	4-5	3rd round	Rothmans Grand Prix
	v Griffiths	5-4	1st round	Labatts Canadian Masters (WS)
	v White	7-8	Semi-final	Labatts Canadian Masters (WS)
	v Griffiths	6-2	1st round	Matchroom Trophy
	v Thorne	5-6	Semi-final	Matchroom Trophy
	v Fowler	5-9	3rd round	Tennents UK Open
1988	v Chaperon	5-1	3rd round	Mercantile Credit Classic
	v Virgo	3-5	4th round	Mercantile Credit Classic
	v Parrott	4-5	1st round	Benson & Hedges Masters
	v Gary Wilkinson	6-3	3rd round	English Championship
	v Fowler	6-1	4th round	English Championship
	v Thorne	6-2	Quarter-final	English Championship
	v West	9-6	Semi-final	English Championship
	v Reynolds	5-9	Final	English Championship
	v Fowler	5-3	3rd round	MIM Britannia British Open
	v P. Francisco	5-3	4th round	MIM Britannia British Open
	v Parrott	0-5	5th round	MIM Britannia British Open
	v Knowles	5-3	Quarter-final	Benson & Hedges Irish Masters
	v Griffiths	6-4	Semi-final	Benson & Hedges Irish Masters
	v S. Davis	4-9	Final	Benson & Hedges Irish Masters
	v W. Jones	10-7	1st round	Embassy World Championship
	v Mountjoy	13-1	2nd round	Embassy World Championship
	v Griffiths	9-13	Quarter-final	Embassy World Championship

DANNY FOWLER (England)

Born 30.7.56. **Turned professional** 1984. **World ranking** 43 (40). **Best professional performances** Last 16 1987 Tennents UK Open, Mercantile Credit Classic.

1984	v Chaperon	5-0	Qualifying	Jameson International
	v Andrewartha	5-0	Qualifying	Jameson International
	v Martin	5-0	Qualifying	Jameson International
	v Dennis Taylor	0-5	1st round	Jameson International
	v Reynolds	2-5	1st round	Rothmans Grand Prix
	v Demarco	9-3	Qualifying	Coral UK Open
	v Oliver	9-3	Qualifying	Coral UK Open

v F. Davis	9-4	Qualifying	Coral UK Open
v N. Foulds	9-6	Qualifying	Coral UK Open
v Reardon	2-9	1st round	Coral UK Open
1985 v Rigitano	5-0	Qualifying	Mercantile Credit Classic
v Murphy	5-0	Qualifying	Mercantile Credit Classic
v Meadowcroft	5-2	Qualifying	Mercantile Credit Classic
v Wilson	4-5	Qualifying	Mercantile Credit Classic
v Oliver	9-7	Qualifying	Tolly Cobbold English Championship
v S. Davis	3-9	1st round	Tolly Cobbold English Championship
v Everton	6-1	Qualifying	Dulux British Open
v Williams	6-4	1st round	Dulux British Open
v Bradley	4-5	2nd round	Dulux British Open
v Hargreaves	10-0	Qualifying	Embassy World Championship
v Donnelly	10-0	Qualifying	Embassy World Championship
v Parrott	2-10	Qualifying	Embassy World Championship
v Agrawal	5-2	2nd round	Goya Matchroom Trophy
v Thorne	1-5	3rd round	Goya Matchroom Trophy
v Jonik	5-4	2nd round	Rothmans Grand Prix
v Werbeniuk	5-1	3rd round	Rothmans Grand Prix
v S. Davis	1-5	4th round	Rothmans Grand Prix
v Wilkinson	9-6	2nd round	Coral UK Open
v Mans	9-2	3rd round	Coral UK Open
v Meo	2-9	4th round	Coral UK Open
1986 v Bales	5-4	2nd round	Mercantile Credit Classic
v White	1-5	3rd round	Mercantile Credit Classic
v Darrington	9-3	2nd round	Tolly Cobbold English Championship
v Johnson	7-9	3rd round	Tolly Cobbold English Championship
v Chappel	5-4	2nd round	Dulux British Open
v Virgo	1-5	3rd round	Dulux British Open
v Oliver	10-8	Qualifying	Embassy World Championship
v Scott	10-7	Qualifying	Embassy World Championship
v Macleod	10-6	Qualifying	Embassy World Championship
v Griffiths	2-10	1st round	Embassy World Championship
v J. McLaughlin	2-5	2nd round	BCE International
v Bear	2-5	2nd round	Rothmans Grand Prix
v Darrington	9-6	2nd round	Tennents UK Open
v Thorburn	7-9	3rd round	Tennents UK Open
1987 v Wilkinson	5-1	2nd round	Mercantile Credit Classic
v Knowles	5-4	3rd round	Mercantile Credit Classic
v Hallett	5-4	4th round	Mercantile Credit Classic
v Hendry	4-5	5th round	Mercantile Credit Classic
v Bradley	6-3	3rd round	Tolly Ales English Championship
v Meo	0-6	4th round	Tolly Ales English Championship
v Dodd	5-1	2nd round	Dulux British Open
v Knowles	4-5	3rd round	Dulux British Open
v G. Foulds	10-6	Qualifying	Embassy World Championship
v B. Harris	10-6	Qualifying	Embassy World Championship
v Parrott	3-10	Qualifying	Embassy World Championship
v Watchorn	5-1	2nd round	Fidelity International
v Knowles	4-5	3rd round	Fidelity International
v D. Gilbert	5-1	2nd round	Rothmans Grand Prix
v S. Francisco	1-5	3rd round	Rothmans Grand Prix
v Kearney	9-7	2nd round	Tennents UK Open
v N. Foulds	9-5	3rd round	Tennents UK Open
v Miles	9-4	4th round	Tennents UK Open
v Hallett	4-9	5th round	Tennents UK Open
1988 v Rigitano	2-5	2nd round	Mercantile Credit Classic
v Medati	6-1	2nd round	English Championship
v Spencer	6-3	3rd round	English Championship
v Foulds	1-6	4th round	English Championship
v Kearney	5-1	2nd round	MIM Britannia British Open
v N. Foulds	3-5	3rd round	MIM Britannia British Open
v Black	10-1	Qualifying	Embassy World Championship

v Dodd	10-8	Qualifying	Embassy World Championship
v Macleod	10-3	Qualifying	Embassy World Championship
v Knowles	8-10	1st round	Embassy World Championship

PETER FRANCISCO (South Africa)

Born 14.2.62. **Turned professional** 1984. **World ranking** 14 (18). **Amateur career** South African champion 1981–83. **Best professional performances** Semi-finals 1987 Rothmans Grand Prix, 1986 BCE International.

1984	v G. Foulds	4-5	Qualifying	Jameson International
	v Black	5-4	Qualifying	Rothmans Grand Prix
	v Spencer	5-2	1st round	Rothmans Grand Prix
	v Reynolds	4-5	2nd round	Rothmans Grand Prix
	v Sheehan	9-5	Qualifying	Coral UK Open
	v Williamson	9-2	Qualifying	Coral UK Open
	v Sinclair	8-9	Qualifying	Coral UK Open
1985	v Longworth	4-5	Qualifying	Mercantile Credit Classic
	v Kelly	6-3	Qualifying	Dulux British Open
	v Virgo	2-6	1st round	Dulux British Open
	v Demarco	10-4	Qualifying	Embassy World Championship
	v Murphy	10-4	Qualifying	Embassy World Championship
	v Meadowcroft	10-5	Qualifying	Embassy World Championship
	v Macleod	7-10	Qualifying	Embassy World Championship
	v Gibson	4-5	2nd round	Goya Matchroom Trophy
	v Everton	5-0	2nd round	Rothmans Grand Prix
	v Virgo	5-4	3rd round	Rothmans Grand Prix
	v W. Jones	5-3	4th round	Rothmans Grand Prix
	v Griffiths	2-5	5th round	Rothmans Grand Prix
	v Charlton	9-5	3rd round	Coral UK Open
	v Williams	7-9	4th round	Coral UK Open
1986	v Jonik	5-2	2nd round	Mercantile Credit Classic
	v Charlton	5-1	3rd round	Mercantile Credit Classic
	v Martin	5-2	4th round	Mercantile Credit Classic
	v S. Davis	0-5	5th round	Mercantile Credit Classic
	v G. Foulds	5-2	2nd round	Dulux British Open
	v White	5-4	3rd round	Dulux British Open
	v Longworth	5-2	4th round	Dulux British Open
	v Higgins	2-5	5th round	Dulux British Open
	v Drago	10-4	Qualifying	Embassy World Championship
	v F. Davis	10-1	Qualifying	Embassy World Championship
	v N. Foulds	9-10	Qualifying	Embassy World Championship
	v Grace	7-1	2nd round	South African Championship
	v S. Francisco	3-8	Semi-final	South African Championship
	v Wildman	5-2	3rd round	BCE International
	v Higgins	5-4	4th round	BCE International
	v Gauvreau	5-2	5th round	BCE International
	v S. Francisco	5-3	Quarter-final	BCE International
	v Thorburn	7-9	Semi-final	BCE International
	v Medati	5-1	3rd round	Rothmans Grand Prix
	v Knowles	3-5	4th round	Rothmans Grand Prix
	v Watterson	9-4	3rd round	Tennents UK Open
	v White	5-9	4th round	Tennents UK Open
1987	v Gauvreau	5-3	3rd round	Mercantile Credit Classic
	v Johnson	5-3	4th round	Mercantile Credit Classic
	v S. Francisco	1-5	5th round	Mercantile Credit Classic
	v Sinclair	5-3	3rd round	Dulux British Open
	v Mountjoy	3-5	4th round	Dulux British Open
	v O'Kane	5-10	Qualifying	Embassy World Championship
	v Newbury	2-5	3rd round	Fidelity International
	v John Rea	5-3	3rd round	Rothmans Grand Prix
	v Johnson	5-2	4th round	Rothmans Grand Prix

Peter Francisco

	v Cripsey	5-1	5th round	Rothmans Grand Prix
	v Thorne	5-3	Quarter-final	Rothmans Grand Prix
	v Dennis Taylor	4-9	Semi-final	Rothmans Grand Prix
	v Lawlor	9-4	3rd round	Tennents UK Open
	v S. Davis	6-9	4th round	Tennents UK Open
1988	v Cripsey	5-2	3rd round	Mercantile Credit Classic
	v Owers	5-0	4th round	Mercantile Credit Classic
	v Dennis Taylor	3-5	5th round	Mercantile Credit Classic
	v Darrington	5-1	3rd round	MIM Britannia British Open
	v N. Foulds	3-5	4th round	MIM Britannia British Open
	v Foldvari	10-5	Qualifying	Embassy World Championship
	v Thorne	6-10	1st round	Embassy World Championship

SILVINO FRANCISCO (South Africa)

Born 3.5.46. **Turned professional** 1978. **World ranking** 12 (10). **Amateur career** South African champion 1968, 1969, 1974, 1977. **Best professional performances** Winner 1985 Dulux British Open, 1986 South African Championship.

1982	v Ross	9-0	Qualifying	Embassy World Championship
	v Morgan	9-1	Qualifying	Embassy World Championship
	v Dennis Taylor	10-7	1st round	Embassy World Championship
	v Reynolds	13-8	2nd round	Embassy World Championship
	v Reardon	8-13	Quarter-final	Embassy World Championship
1983	v Kelly	10-5	Qualifying	Embassy World Championship
	v Dennis Taylor	9-10	1st round	Embassy World Championship
	v Darrington	5-2	Qualifying	Jameson International
	v Donnelly	5-1	2nd round	Jameson International
	v S. Davis	1-5	Quarter-final	Jameson International
	v Morra	5-3	1st round	Professional Players Tournament
	v Scott	5-1	2nd round	Professional Players Tournament
	v Knowles	0-5	3rd round	Professional Players Tournament
1984	v Thorburn	5-1	Qualifying	Lada Classic
	v Wildman	1-5	1st round	Lada Classic
	v Van Rensberg	10-3	Qualifying	Embassy World Championship
	v Meo	10-5	1st round	Embassy World Championship
	v Reardon	8-13	2nd round	Embassy World Championship
	v Kelly	5-3	Qualifying	Jameson International
	v Spencer	5-2	1st round	Jameson International
	v Virgo	5-2	2nd round	Jameson International
	v Knowles	6-9	Semi-final	Jameson International
	v Duggan	5-3	1st round	Rothmans Grand Prix
	v White	5-1	2nd round	Rothmans Grand Prix
	v Reynolds	1-5	3rd round	Rothmans Grand Prix
	v Sinclair	9-4	Qualifying	Coral UK Open
	v Charlton	4-9	1st round	Coral UK Open
1985	v T. Jones	5-1	Qualifying	Mercantile Credit Classic
	v S. Davis	0-5	1st round	Mercantile Credit Classic
	v Kearney	6-4	1st round	Dulux British Open
	v White	5-4	2nd round	Dulux British Open
	v Chaperon	5-2	3rd round	Dulux British Open
	v Meo	5-4	Quarter-final	Dulux British Open
	v Higgins	9-6	Semi-final	Dulux British Open
	v Stevens	**12-9**	**Final**	**Dulux British Open**
	v Medati	10-7	Qualifying	Embassy World Championship
	v Dennis Taylor	2-10	1st round	Embassy World Championship
	v Parrott	3-4	1st round	Winfield Australian Masters
	v Knowles	5-4	1st round	Langs Scottish Masters
	v Thorburn	0-6	Semi-final	Langs Scottish Masters
	v Chaperon	3-5	3rd round	Goya Matchroom Trophy
	v Kelly	5-2	3rd round	Rothmans Grand Prix
	v Martin	5-3	4th round	Rothmans Grand Prix

	v White	5-4	5th round	Rothmans Grand Prix
	v S. Davis	2-5	Quarter-final	Rothmans Grand Prix
	v Wych	9-8	3rd round	Coral UK Open
	v Martin	9-6	4th round	Coral UK Open
	v Griffiths	5-9	5th round	Coral UK Open
1986	v Hendry	4-5	3rd round	Mercantile Credit Classic
	v Knowles	1-5	1st round	Benson & Hedges Masters
	v T. Jones	5-2	3rd round	Dulux British Open
	v Macleod	1-5	4th round	Dulux British Open
	v Williams	10-4	1st round	Embassy World Championship
	v Knowles	10-13	2nd round	Embassy World Championship
	v P. Francisco	8-3	Semi-final	South African Championship
	v Ellis	**9-1**	**Final**	**South African Championship**
	v Newbury	5-4	3rd round	BCE International
	v Virgo	5-0	4th round	BCE International
	v Dennis Taylor	5-0	5th round	BCE International
	v P. Francisco	3-5	Quarter-final	BCE International
	v Spencer	5-4	3rd round	Rothmans Grand Prix
	v W. Jones	5-4	4th round	Rothmans Grand Prix
	v Newbury	5-2	5th round	Rothmans Grand Prix
	v Knowles	5-2	Quarter-final	Rothmans Grand Prix
	v White	6-9	Semi-final	Rothmans Grand Prix
	v Owers	9-3	3rd round	Tennents UK Open
	v Reynolds	8-9	4th round	Tennents UK Open
1987	v Van Rensberg	5-4	3rd round	Mercantile Credit Classic
	v B. Harris	5-3	4th round	Mercantile Credit Classic
	v P. Francisco	5-1	5th round	Mercantile Credit Classic
	v Hendry	0-5	Quarter-final	Mercantile Credit Classic
	v Knowles	5-2	1st round	Benson & Hedges Masters
	v Dennis Taylor	3-5	Quarter-final	Benson & Hedges Masters
	v Rowswell	5-0	3rd round	Dulux British Open
	v Wilson	4-5	4th round	Dulux British Open
	v Campbell	10-3	1st round	Embassy World Championship
	v Hallett	9-13	2nd round	Embassy World Championship
	v King	5-2	3rd round	Fidelity International
	v Werbeniuk	5-3	4th round	Fidelity International
	v E. Hughes	4-5	5th round	Fidelity International
	v Fowler	5-1	3rd round	Rothmans Grand Prix
	v Gary Wilkinson	3-5	4th round	Rothmans Grand Prix
	v Reardon	9-3	3rd round	Tennents UK Open
	v Wilson	9-1	4th round	Tennents UK Open
	v Griffiths	3-9	5th round	Tennents UK Open
1988	v Rowswell	5-3	3rd round	Mercantile Credit Classic
	v Longworth	5-2	4th round	Mercantile Credit Classic
	v Hendry	3-5	5th round	Mercantile Credit Classic
	v Griffiths	3-5	1st round	Benson & Hedges Masters
	v Bear	5-0	3rd round	MIM Britannia British Open
	v Gary Wilkinson	3-5	4th round	MIM Britannia British Open
	v Charlton	7-10	1st round	Embassy World Championship

MARCEL GAUVREAU (Canada)

Born 9.1.55. **Turned professional** 1983. **World ranking** 63 (42). **Best professional performances** Last 16 1986 Mercantile Credit Classic, 1986 BCE International.

1983	v Rigitano	6-9	1st round	Canadian Championship
	v Miles	3-5	1st round	Professional Players Tournament
1984	v Campbell	10-7	Qualifying	Embassy World Championship
	v Cripsey	10-1	Qualifying	Embassy World Championship
	v Macleod	10-6	Qualifying	Embassy World Championship
	v David Taylor	5-10	1st round	Embassy World Championship

	v Jonik	5-1	Qualifying	Jameson International
	v Parrott	5-4	Qualifying	Jameson International
	v Stevens	5-1	1st round	Jameson International
	v Thorne	3-5	2nd round	Jameson International
	v Foldvari	5-2	Qualifying	Rothmans Grand Prix
	v Parrott	3-5	1st round	Rothmans Grand Prix
	v Bales	9-8	Qualifying	Coral UK Open
	v Mans	9-6	Qualifying	Coral UK Open
	v Knowles	5-9	1st round	Coral UK Open
1985	v Giannaros	5-3	Qualifying	Mercantile Credit Classic
	v Sinclair	5-1	Qualifying	Mercantile Credit Classic
	v Higgins	3-5	1st round	Mercantile Credit Classic
	v Greaves	6-3	Qualifying	Dulux British Open
	v Stevens	3-6	1st round	Dulux British Open
	v Van Rensberg	10-9	Qualifying	Embassy World Championship
	v Reynolds	1-10	Qualifying	Embassy World Championship
	v D. Hughes	4-5	2nd round	Goya Matchroom Trophy
	v Duggan	4-5	2nd round	Rothmans Grand Prix
	v O'Boye	5-9	2nd round	Coral UK Open
1986	v Simngam	5-1	2nd round	Mercantile Credit Classic
	v David Taylor	5-3	3rd round	Mercantile Credit Classic
	v Browne	5-3	4th round	Mercantile Credit Classic
	v White	2-5	5th round	Mercantile Credit Classic
	v Drago	3-5	2nd round	Dulux British Open
	v Jim Bear	10-5	Qualifying	Embassy World Championship
	v Chaperon	10-8	Qualifying	Embassy World Championship
	v Williams	3-10	Qualifying	Embassy World Championship
	v Jenkins	5-1	2nd round	BCE International
	v Macleod	5-4	3rd round	BCE International
	v Reardon	5-2	4th round	BCE International
	v P. Francisco	2-5	5th round	BCE International
	v J. McLaughlin	3-5	2nd round	Rothmans Grand Prix
	v J. McLaughlin	8-9	2nd round	Tennents UK Open
1987	v Rigitano	5-0	2nd round	Mercantile Credit Classic
	v P. Francisco	3-5	3rd round	Mercantile Credit Classic
	v Bales	5-0	2nd round	Dulux British Open
	v S. Davis	0-5	3rd round	Dulux British Open
	v Bear	10-3	Qualifying	Embassy World Championship
	v Medati	3-10	Qualifying	Embassy World Championship
	v Caggianello	3-6	1st round	Canadian Championship
	v Williamson	1-5	2nd round	Fidelity International
	v M. Smith	5-3	2nd round	Rothmans Grand Prix
	v Virgo	1-5	3rd round	Rothmans Grand Prix
	v A. Harris	9-3	2nd round	Tennents UK Open
	v West	6-9	3rd round	Tennents UK Open
1988	v Morra	4-5	2nd round	Mercantile Credit Classic
	v Medati	1-5	2nd round	MIM Britannia British Open
	v P. Gibson	9-10	Qualifying	Embassy World Championship

MATT GIBSON (Scotland)

Born 7.5.53. **Turned professional** 1981. **World ranking** 88 (71). **Amateur career** 1980 Scottish champion. **Best professional performance** Last 32 1985 Goya Matchroom Trophy.

1981	v Hood	5-3	Qualifying	Jameson International
	v Parkin	5-3	Qualifying	Jameson International
	v Dunning	3-5	Qualifying	Jameson International
	v Demarco	5-3	Quarter-final	Scottish Championship
	v Donnelly	6-4	Semi-final	Scottish Championship
	v Black	7-11	Final	Scottish Championship

Silvino Francisco

	v Fitzmaurice	9-6	Qualifying	Coral UK Championship
	v Everton	7-9	Qualifying	Coral UK Championship
1982	v Donnelly	8-9	Qualifying	Embassy World Championship
	v E. McLaughlin	6-3	Quarter-final	Scottish Championship
	v Sinclair	2-6	Semi-final	Scottish Championship
	v Wildman	1-5	Qualifying	Jameson International
	v Martin	2-5	1st round	Professional Players Tournament
	v G. Foulds	3-9	Qualifying	Coral UK Championship
1983	v G. Foulds	6-10	Qualifying	Embassy World Championship
	v Macleod	5-6	1st round	Scottish Championship
	v Dodd	5-1	Qualifying	Jameson International
	v Scott	3-5	Qualifying	Jameson International
	v Morgan	4-5	Qualifying	Professional Players Tournament
	v Johnson	6-9	Qualifying	Coral UK Championship
1984	v Rigitano	10-7	Qualifying	Embassy World Championship
	v Fisher	10-7	Qualifying	Embassy World Championship
	v Johnson	3-10	Qualifying	Embassy World Championship
	v Medati	5-3	Qualifying	Jameson International
	v W. Jones	2-5	Qualifying	Jameson International
	v Chaperon	4-5	Qualifying	Rothmans Grand Prix
	v Hargreaves	9-8	Qualifying	Coral UK Open
	v Donnelly	6-9	Qualifying	Coral UK Open
1985	v T. Jones	0-5	Qualifying	Mercantile Credit Classic
	v Black	6-2	1st round	Scottish Championship
	v Macleod	4-6	Semi-final	Scottish Championship
	v Demarco	6-1	Qualifying	Dulux British Open
	v Wildman	1-6	1st round	Dulux British Open
	v Hines	10-7	Qualifying	Embassy World Championship
	v Fagan	8-10	Qualifying	Embassy World Championship
	v P. Francisco	5-4	2nd round	Goya Matchroom Trophy
	v Charlton	5-4	3rd round	Goya Matchroom Trophy
	v Reynolds	0-5	4th round	Goya Matchroom Trophy
	v Bradley	5-4	2nd round	Rothmans Grand Prix
	v Knowles	1-5	3rd round	Rothmans Grand Prix
	v Longworth	2-9	2nd round	Coral UK Open
1986	v Virgo	3-5	3rd round	Mercantile Credit Classic
	v Black	0-5	2nd round	Dulux British Open
	v Sinclair	6-4	Quarter-final	Canada Dry Scottish Championship
	v John Rea	6-0	Semi-final	Canada Dry Scottish Championship
	v Hendry	5-10	Final	Canada Dry Scottish Championship
	v Jenkins	10-4	Qualifying	Embassy World Championship
	v Morra	10-9	Qualifying	Embassy World Championship
	v Medati	6-10	Qualifying	Embassy World Championship
	v Hines	5-1	2nd round	BCE International
	v Mountjoy	3-5	3rd round	BCE International
	v Mienie	5-4	2nd round	Rothmans Grand Prix
	v S. Davis	1-5	3rd round	Rothmans Grand Prix
	v Dunning	9-2	2nd round	Tennents UK Open
	v Reardon	6-9	3rd round	Tennents UK Open
1987	v J. McLaughlin	3-5	2nd round	Mercantile Credit Classic
	v Sinclair	2-6	1st round	Scottish Championship
	v J. McLaughlin	1-5	2nd round	Dulux British Open
	v Kelly	10-9	Qualifying	Embassy World Championship
	v Cripsey	4-10	Qualifying	Embassy World Championship
	v Chappel	2-5	2nd round	Fidelity International
	v Cripsey	2-5	2nd round	Rothmans Grand Prix
	v Murphy	0-9	2nd round	Tennents UK Open
1988	v Cripsey	4-5	2nd round	Mercantile Credit Classic
	v Black	6-2	Quarter-final	Scottish Championship
	v Hendry	1-6	Semi-final	Scottish Championship
	v Duggan	5-2	2nd round	MIM Britannia British Open
	v Knowles	4-5	3rd round	MIM Britannia British Open
	v Watchorn	7-10	Qualifying	Embassy World Championship

PAUL GIBSON (England)

Born 9.6.63. **Turned professional** 1986. **World ranking** 69 (99). **Best professional performance** Last 32 1987 Rothmans Grand Prix.

1986	v Meadowcroft	5-2	1st round	BCE International
	v Hendry	2-5	2nd round	BCE International
	v Dunning	5-1	1st round	Rothmans Grand Prix
	v Cripsey	3-5	2nd round	Rothmans Grand Prix
	v Agrawal	9-6	1st round	Tennents UK Open
	v Mans	wo	2nd round	Tennents UK Open
	v Griffiths	3-9	3rd round	Tennents UK Open
1987	v B. Harris	3-5	2nd round	Mercantile Credit Classic
	v D. Hughes	6-3	1st round	Tolly Ales English Championship
	v Medati	2-6	2nd round	Tolly Ales English Championship
	v Agrawal	5-0	1st round	Dulux British Open
	v Duggan	3-5	2nd round	Dulux British Open
	v Morra	6-10	Qualifying	Embassy World Championship
	v Glen Wilkinson	5-3	1st round	Fidelity International
	v T. Jones	5-4	2nd round	Fidelity International
	v N. Foulds	2-5	3rd round	Fidelity International
	v Fagan	5-0	1st round	Rothmans Grand Prix
	v Duggan	5-4	2nd round	Rothmans Grand Prix
	v Hallett	5-4	3rd round	Rothmans Grand Prix
	v Cripsey	4-5	4th round	Rothmans Grand Prix
	v Rigitano	9-5	1st round	Tennents UK Open
	v Cripsey	6-9	2nd round	Tennents UK Open
1988	v Black	5-2	1st round	Mercantile Credit Classic
	v J. McLaughlin	4-5	2nd round	Mercantile Credit Classic
	v Chambers	0-6	1st round	English Championship
	v Roscoe	4-5	1st round	MIM Britannia British Open
	v Sheehan	10-9	Qualifying	Embassy World Championship
	v Gauvreau	10-9	Qualifying	Embassy World Championship
	v Duggan	9-10	Qualifying	Embassy World Championship

DAVE GILBERT (England)

Born 15.8.61. **Turned professional** 1985. **World ranking** 57 (83). **Best professional performance** Last 16 1987 Fidelity International.

1985	v Darrington	2-5	1st round	Goya Matchroom Trophy
	v Wilkinson	5-4	1st round	Rothmans Grand Prix
	v Williamson	5-4	2nd round	Rothmans Grand Prix
	v Johnson	2-5	3rd round	Rothmans Grand Prix
	v Drago	5-9	1st round	Coral UK Open
1986	v Watson	5-4	1st round	Mercantile Credit Classic
	v T. Jones	3-5	2nd round	Mercantile Credit Classic
	v West	9-8	1st round	Tolly Cobbold English Championship
	v Bradley	5-9	2nd round	Tolly Cobbold English Championship
	v Burke	5-1	1st round	Dulux British Open
	v Morra	5-4	2nd round	Dulux British Open
	v Charlton	2-5	3rd round	Dulux British Open
	v Bales	10-7	Qualifying	Embassy World Championship
	v Bradley	10-7	Qualifying	Embassy World Championship
	v T. Jones	10-7	Qualifying	Embassy World Championship
	v Martin	5-10	Qualifying	Embassy World Championship
	v James	2-5	1st round	BCE International
	v Rowswell	5-1	1st round	Rothmans Grand Prix
	v Newbury	1-5	2nd round	Rothmans Grand Prix
	v Owers	8-9	1st round	Tennents UK Open

1987	v Spencer	4-5	2nd round	Mercantile Credit Classic
	v Bradley	3-6	2nd round	Tolly Ales English Championship
	v Murphy	4-5	2nd round	Dulux British Open
	v O'Kane	2-10	Qualifying	Embassy World Championship
	v A. Harris	5-4	1st round	Fidelity International
	v Houlihan	5-3	2nd round	Fidelity International
	v Martin	5-2	3rd round	Fidelity International
	v Wilson	5-1	4th round	Fidelity International
	v Hendry	0-5	5th round	Fidelity International
	v Lawlor	5-2	1st round	Rothmans Grand Prix
	v Fowler	1-5	2nd round	Rothmans Grand Prix
	v Heaton	9-5	1st round	Tennents UK Open
	v Chappel	2-9	2nd round	Tennents UK Open
1988	v Jack Rea	5-2	1st round	Mercantile Credit Classic
	v B. Harris	5-4	2nd round	Mercantile Credit Classic
	v Wilson	3-5	3rd round	Mercantile Credit Classic
	v Whitthread	6-1	1st round	English Championship
	v Bales	6-2	2nd round	English Championship
	v Reynolds	3-6	3rd round	English Championship
	v Wright	5-2	2nd round	MIM Britannia British Open
	v Macleod	4-5	3rd round	MIM Britannia British Open
	v Heaton	10-2	Qualifying	Embassy World Championship (withdrew from 2nd round)

NIGEL GILBERT (England)

Born 20.3.59. **Turned professional** 1986. **World ranking** 56 (100). **Best professional performance** Last 16 1987 Fidelity International.

1986	v Agrawal	5-0	1st round	BCE International
	v Chaperon	3-5	2nd round	BCE International
	v Donnelly	1-5	1st round	Rothmans Grand Prix
	v Donnelly	8-9	1st round	Tennents UK Open
1987	v Smith	5-0	1st round	Mercantile Credit Classic
	v Van Rensberg	3-5	2nd round	Mercantile Credit Classic
	v B. Bennett	5-6	1st round	Tolly Ales English Championship
	v Houlihan	5-4	1st round	Dulux British Open
	v W. Jones	5-3	2nd round	Dulux British Open
	v Reynolds	2-5	3rd round	Dulux British Open
	v Sheehan	10-6	Qualifying	Embassy World Championship
	v O'Boye	5-10	Qualifying	Embassy World Championship
	v Black	5-3	1st round	Fidelity International
	v J. McLaughlin	5-4	2nd round	Fidelity International
	v Macleod	5-1	3rd round	Fidelity International
	v W. Jones	5-4	4th round	Fidelity International
	v Charlton	0-5	5th round	Fidelity International
	v Jonik	3-5	1st round	Rothmans Grand Prix
	v Sinclair	9-8	1st round	Tennents UK Open
	v G. Foulds	9-4	2nd round	Tennents UK Open
	v E. Hughes	7-9	3rd round	Tennents UK Open
1988	v Donnelly	2-5	1st round	Mercantile Credit Classic
	v A. Harris	6-3	1st round	English Championship
	v F. Davis	5-6	2nd round	English Championship
	v Sheehan	5-3	1st round	MIM Britannia British Open
	v Werbeniuk	5-1	2nd round	MIM Britannia British Open
	v Williams	2-5	3rd round	MIM Britannia British Open
	v John Rea	10-5	Qualifying	Embassy World Championship
	v Chappel	8-10	Qualifying	Embassy World Championship

ROBBIE GRACE (South Africa)

Born 14.6.54. **Turned professional** 1985. **World ranking** 79 (64). **Best professional performance** Last 32 1986 Tennents UK Open.

1986	v Parkin	10-8	Qualifying	Embassy World Championship
	v W. Jones	3-10	Qualifying	Embassy World Championship
	v P. Francisco	1-7	2nd round	South African Championship
	v Houlihan	5-1	1st round	Rothmans Grand Prix
	v Fagan	3-5	2nd round	Rothmans Grand Prix
	v Houlihan	9-6	1st round	Tennents UK Open
	v Medati	9-5	2nd round	Tennents UK Open
	v Macleod	9-6	3rd round	Tennents UK Open
	v Thorne	1-9	4th round	Tennents UK Open
1987	v Rigitano	4-5	1st round	Mercantile Credit Classic
	v Meadowcroft	5-4	1st round	Dulux British Open
	v Fagan	5-3	2nd round	Dulux British Open
	v West	2-5	3rd round	Dulux British Open
	v Jenkins	9-10	Qualifying	Embassy World Championship
	v Chambers	5-4	2nd round	Fidelity International
	v Thorburn	1-5	3rd round	Fidelity International
	v Clark	1-5	2nd round	Rothmans Grand Prix
	v Gary Wilkinson	5-9	2nd round	Tennents UK Open
1988	v Van Rensburg	3-5	2nd round	Mercantile Credit Classic
	v Clark	0-5	2nd round	MIM Britannia British Open

DAVID GREAVES (England)

Born 1.9.46. **Turned professional** 1973. **World ranking** 125 (117).

1973	v Bennett	9-8	1st round	World Championship
	v F. Davis	1-16	2nd round	World Championship
1975	v G. Owen	3-15	1st round	World Championship
1976	v Charlton	8-5	Qualifying	Embassy World Championship
	v David Taylor	1-8	Qualifying	Embassy World Championship
1977	v David Taylor	0-11	Qualifying	Embassy World Championship
	v David Taylor	4-5	1st round	Super Crystalate UK Championship
1978	v Barrie	3-9	Prelim	Embassy World Championship
	v Dunning	3-9	Qualifying	Coral UK Championship
1979	v Williams	2-9	Prelim	Embassy World Championship
	v Dunning	8-9	1st round	Coral UK Championship
1980	v Meadowcroft	1-9	Qualifying	Coral UK Championship
1981	v Dunning	4-9	Qualifying	John Courage English
	v Parkin	9-5	Qualifying	Embassy World Championship
	v Thorne	3-9	Qualifying	Embassy World Championship
	v E. McLaughlin	1-5	Qualifying	Jameson International
1982	v Morgan	2-9	Qualifying	Embassy World Championship
1983	v E. McLaughlin	7-10	Qualifying	Embassy World Championship
	v Martin	1-5	Qualifying	Jameson International
	v Andrewartha	5-2	Qualifying	Professional Players Tournament
	v Reynolds	1-5	1st round	Professional Players Tournament
	v Wildman	5-9	Qualifying	Coral UK Championship
1984	v Edmonds	0-10	Qualifying	Embassy World Championship
	v J. McLaughlin	3-5	Qualifying	Jameson International
	v King	0-5	Qualifying	Rothmans Grand Prix
	v Foldvari	5-9	Qualifying	Coral UK Open
1985	v T. Jones	2-5	Qualifying	Mercantile Credit Classic
	v Fitzmaurice	3-9	Qualifying	Tolly Cobbold English Championship
	v Gauvreau	3-6	Qualifying	Dulux British Open
	v Chalmers	3-10	Qualifying	Embassy World Championship
	v Simngam	2-5	1st round	Goya Matchroom Trophy

	v Darrington	2-5	1st round	Rothmans Grand Prix
	v Cripsey	4-9	1st round	Coral UK Open
1986	v Watchorn	5-4	1st round	Mercantile Credit Classic
	v Sinclair	1-5	2nd round	Mercantile Credit Classic
	v Medati	4-9	2nd round	Tolly Cobbold English Championship
	v Agrawal	3-5	1st round	Dulux British Open
	v Smith	4-10	Qualifying	Embassy World Championship
	v Rigitano	3-5	1st round	BCE International
	v Meadowcroft	2-5	1st round	Rothmans Grand Prix
	v Fisher	4-9	1st round	Tennents UK Open
1987	v Oliver	4-5	1st round	Mercantile Credit Classic
	v Roe	1-6	1st round	Tolly Ales English Championship
	v G. Foulds	3-5	1st round	Dulux British Open
	v Thornley	10-6	1st round	Embassy World Championship
	v Miles	7-10	2nd round	Embassy World Championship
	v Meadowcroft	1-5	1st round	Fidelity International
	v Bear	0-5	1st round	Rothmans Grand Prix
	v V. Harris	1-9	1st round	Tennents UK Open
1988	v Foldvari	3-5	1st round	Mercantile Credit Classic
	v James	6-5	1st round	English Championship
	v Cripsey	6-4	2nd round	English Championship
	v West	5-6	3rd round	English Championship
	v Donnelly	4-5	1st round	MIM Britannia British Open
	v Fagan	3-10	Qualifying	Embassy World Championship

TERRY GRIFFITHS (Wales)

Born 16.10.47. **Turned professional** 1978. **World ranking** 5 (6). **Amateur career** 1975 Welsh champion, 1977 & 1978 English champion. **Best professional performances** Winner 1979 Embassy World Championship, 1982 Coral UK Championship, 1985 & 1986 Welsh Championship, 1982 Lada Classic, 1980 Benson & Hedges Masters, 1980–82 Benson & Hedges Irish Masters, 1986 BCE Belgian Classic, runner-up 1988 Embassy World Championship.

1978	v Williams	8-9	Qualifying	Coral UK Championship
1979	v Bennett	9-2	Prelim	Embassy World Championship
	v Meadowcroft	9-6	Qualifying	Embassy World Championship
	v Mans	13-8	1st round	Embassy World Championship
	v Higgins	13-12	Quarter-final	Embassy World Championship
	v Charlton	19-17	Semi-final	Embassy World Championship
	v Dennis Taylor	**24-16**	**Final**	**Embassy World Championship**
	v Wilson	9-4	3rd round	Coral UK Championship
	v Higgins	9-7	Quarter-final	Coral UK Championship
	v Werbeniuk	9-3	Semi-final	Coral UK Championship
	v Virgo	13-14	Final	Coral UK Championship
1980	v Thorburn	5-3	Quarter-final	Benson & Hedges Masters
	v Spencer	5-0	Semi-final	Benson & Hedges Masters
	v Higgins	**9-5**	**Final**	**Benson & Hedges Masters**
	v Mountjoy	6-9	1st round	Woodpecker Welsh Championship
	v Mountjoy	**9-8**	**Final**	**Benson & Hedges Irish Masters**
	v S. Davis	10-13	2nd round	Embassy World Championship
	v Fagan	9-8	2nd round	Coral UK Championship
	v Dennis Taylor	9-7	Quarter-final	Coral UK Championship
	v S. Davis	0-9	Semi-final	Coral UK Championship
1981	v F. Davis	5-2	Quarter-final	Benson & Hedges Masters
	v Spencer	6-5	Semi-final	Benson & Hedges Masters
	v Higgins	6-9	Final	Benson & Hedges Masters
	v Reardon	6-9	Semi-final	Woodpecker Welsh Championship
	v Thorburn	6-5	Semi-final	Benson & Hedges Irish Masters
	v Reardon	**9-7**	**Final**	**Benson & Hedges Irish Masters**
	v Meo	13-6	2nd round	Embassy World Championship

Terry Griffiths

	v S. Davis	9-13	Quarter-final	Embassy World Championship
	v Spencer	5-2	3rd round	Jameson International
	v Higgins	2-5	Quarter-final	Jameson International
	v Stevens	5-0	1st round	Northern Ireland Classic
	v S. Davis	6-9	Semi-final	Northern Ireland Classic
	v Miles	9-4	3rd round	Coral UK Championship
	v Knowles	9-5	Quarter-final	Coral UK Championship
	v Meo	9-3	Semi-final	Coral UK Championship
	v S. Davis	3-16	Final	Coral UK Championship
1982	v Thorburn	5-1	1st round	Lada Classic
	v Higgins	5-1	Semi-final	Lada Classic
	v S. Davis	**9-8**	**Final**	**Lada Classic**
	v Reardon	5-3	Quarter-final	Benson & Hedges Masters
	v Higgins	6-4	Semi-final	Benson & Hedges Masters
	v S. Davis	5-9	Final	Benson & Hedges Masters
	v S. Davis	7-9	Final	Yamaha International Masters
	v Roscoe	6-2	1st round	Woodpecker Welsh Championship
	v Wilson	9-6	Semi-final	Woodpecker Welsh Championship
	v Mountjoy	8-9	Final	Woodpecker Welsh Championship
	v Meo	5-3	Quarter-final	Benson & Hedges Irish Masters
	v Reardon	6-3	Semi-final	Benson & Hedges Irish Masters
	v S. Davis	**9-5**	**Final**	**Benson & Hedges Irish Masters**
	v Thorne	6-10	1st round	Embassy World Championship
	v Reardon	5-3	1st round	Langs Scottish Masters
	v Higgins	5-6	Semi-final	Langs Scottish Masters
	v Williams	5-2	1st round	Jameson International
	v Higgins	5-2	2nd round	Jameson International
	v Stevens	3-5	Quarter-final	Jameson International
	v Roscoe	5-1	1st round	Professional Players Tournament
	v Watterson	5-2	2nd round	Professional Players Tournament
	v Sinclair	5-3	3rd round	Professional Players Tournament
	v White	2-5	Quarter-final	Professional Players Tournament
	v Johnson	9-1	1st round	Coral UK Championship
	v Dennis Taylor	9-7	2nd round	Coral UK Championship
	v S. Davis	9-6	Quarter-final	Coral UK Championship
	v Meo	9-7	Semi-final	Coral UK Championship
	v Higgins	**16-15**	**Final**	**Coral UK Championship**
1983	v Mountjoy	1-5	1st round	Lada Classic
	v Stevens	5-3	1st round	Benson & Hedges Masters
	v Thorburn	3-5	Quarter-final	Benson & Hedges Masters
	v Everton	6-1	Quarter-final	Woodpecker Welsh Championship
	v Reardon	4-9	Semi-final	Woodpecker Welsh Championship
	v Werbeniuk	5-3	Semi-final	Tolly Cobbold Classic
	v S. Davis	5-7	Final	Tolly Cobbold Classic
	v Mountjoy	5-4	Quarter-final	Benson & Hedges Irish Masters
	v S. Davis	2-6	Semi-final	Benson & Hedges Irish Masters
	v Wildman	10-8	1st round	Embassy World Championship
	v Thorburn	12-13	2nd round	Embassy World Championship
	v Thorburn	1-5	1st round	Langs Scottish Masters
	v Miles	5-2	1st round	Jameson International
	v Scott	5-0	2nd round	Jameson International
	v Spencer	5-4	Quarter-final	Jameson International
	v Thorburn	8-9	Semi-final	Jameson International
	v Dodd	5-3	1st round	Professional Players Tournament
	v Parrott	5-1	2nd round	Professional Players Tournament
	v E. Hughes	2-5	3rd round	Professional Players Tournament
	v Martin	9-4	1st round	Coral UK Championship
	v Hallett	9-5	2nd round	Coral UK Championship
	v Johnson	9-2	Quarter-final	Coral UK Championship
	v Higgins	4-9	Semi-final	Coral UK Championship
1984	v Reynolds	5-2	Qualifying	Lada Classic
	v Roscoe	5-2	1st round	Lada Classic
	v S. Davis	4-5	Quarter-final	Lada Classic

	v Werbeniuk	5-1	1st round	Benson & Hedges Masters
	v Spencer	5-4	Quarter-final	Benson & Hedges Masters
	v Knowles	6-4	Semi-final	Benson & Hedges Masters
	v White	5-9	Final	Benson & Hedges Masters
	v Andrewartha	6-1	1st round	Strongbow Welsh Championship
	v Mountjoy	5-9	Semi-final	Strongbow Welsh Championship
	v Werbeniuk	5-2	1st round	Benson & Hedges Irish Masters
	v Knowles	5-0	Quarter-final	Benson & Hedges Irish Masters
	v Dennis Taylor	5-4	Semi-final	Benson & Hedges Irish Masters
	v S. Davis	1-9	Final	Benson & Hedges Irish Masters
	v Mifsud	10-2	1st round	Embassy World Championship
	v Werbeniuk	10-5	2nd round	Embassy World Championship
	v S. Davis	10-13	Quarter-final	Embassy World Championship
	v Knowles	3-5	1st round	Langs Scottish Masters
	v N. Foulds	5-3	1st round	Jameson International
	v Higgins	4-5	2nd round	Jameson International
	v T. Jones	3-5	1st round	Rothmans Grand Prix
	v Wilson	6-9	1st round	Coral UK Open
1985	v Fagan	5-0	1st round	Mercantile Credit Classic
	v Williams	5-3	2nd round	Mercantile Credit Classic
	v Thorburn	4-5	Quarter-final	Mercantile Credit Classic
	v Werbeniuk	5-2	1st round	Benson & Hedges Masters
	v Higgins	5-1	Quarter-final	Benson & Hedges Masters
	v Mountjoy	2-6	Semi-final	Benson & Hedges Masters
	v Chalmers	6-0	1st round	Dulux British Open
	v Newbury	3-5	2nd round	Dulux British Open
	v Higgins	2-5	1st round	Benson & Hedges Irish Masters
	v Williams	10-3	1st round	Embassy World Championship
	v Higgins	13-7	2nd round	Embassy World Championship
	v S. Davis	6-13	Quarter-final	Embassy World Championship
	v Chappel	6-0	Quarter-final	BCE Welsh Championship
	v Reardon	9-3	Semi-final	BCE Welsh Championship
	v Mountjoy	**9-4**	**Final**	**BCE Welsh Championship**
	v Newbury	5-2	3rd round	Goya Matchroom Trophy
	v Spencer	5-1	4th round	Goya Matchroom Trophy
	v Parrott	1-5	5th round	Goya Matchroom Trophy
	v J. McLaughlin	5-4	3rd round	Rothmans Grand Prix
	v B. Harris	5-3	4th round	Rothmans Grand Prix
	v P. Francisco	5-2	5th round	Rothmans Grand Prix
	v Thorburn	1-5	Quarter-final	Rothmans Grand Prix
	v S. Davis	4-5	1st round	BCE Canadian Masters
	v T. Jones	9-5	3rd round	Coral UK Open
	v Reynolds	9-7	4th round	Coral UK Open
	v S. Francisco	9-5	5th round	Coral UK Open
	v Thorne	7-9	Quarter-final	Coral UK Open
	v Reardon	5-2	1st round	Kit Kat
	v Dennis Taylor	4-6	Semi-final	Kit Kat
1986	v V. Harris	3-5	3rd round	Mercantile Credit Classic
	v S. Davis	5-2	1st round	BCE Belgian Classic
	v Knowles	5-2	Semi-final	BCE Belgian Classic
	v Stevens	**9-7**	**Final**	**BCE Belgian Classic**
	v Higgins	5-4	1st round	Benson & Hedges Masters
	v Thorburn	2-5	Quarter-final	Benson & Hedges Masters
	v Chappel	6-4	Quarter-final	Zetters Welsh Championship
	v Wilson	9-1	Semi-final	Zetters Welsh Championship
	v Mountjoy	**9-3**	**Final**	**Zetters Welsh Championship**
	v Scott	5-3	3rd round	Dulux British Open
	v N. Foulds	5-3	4th round	Dulux British Open
	v Macleod	5-2	5th round	Dulux British Open
	v Thorne	4-5	Quarter-final	Dulux British Open
	v Thorne	2-5	1st round	Benson & Hedges Irish Masters
	v Fowler	10-2	1st round	Embassy World Championship
	v Higgins	13-12	2nd round	Embassy World Championship

	v Johnson	12-13	Quarter-final	Embassy World Championship
	v Dennis Taylor	4-5	Semi-final	Camus Hong Kong Masters
	v Meo	6-3	1st round	Matchroom Trophy
	v S. Davis	2-6	Semi-final	Matchroom Trophy
	v Medati	5-3	3rd round	BCE International
	v West	5-1	4th round	BCE International
	v Thorburn	4-5	5th round	BCE International
	v Morra	5-3	3rd round	Rothmans Grand Prix
	v Campbell	5-1	4th round	Rothmans Grand Prix
	v S. Davis	2-5	5th round	Rothmans Grand Prix
	v P. Gibson	9-3	3rd round	Tennents UK Open
	v O'Kane	9-0	4th round	Tennents UK Open
	v Knowles	6-9	5th round	Tennents UK Open
1987	v O'Boye	5-1	3rd round	Mercantile Credit Classic
	v Martin	5-4	4th round	Mercantile Credit Classic
	v Campbell	5-3	5th round	Mercantile Credit Classic
	v White	3-5	Quarter-final	Mercantile Credit Classic
	v Higgins	4-5	1st round	Benson & Hedges Masters
	v W. Jones	6-2	Quarter-final	Matchroom Welsh Championship
	v Newbury	6-9	Semi-final	Matchroom Welsh Championship
	v John Rea	5-2	3rd round	Dulux British Open
	v T. Jones	5-3	4th round	Dulux British Open
	v Dennis Taylor	4-5	5th round	Dulux British Open
	v Higgins	5-1	1st round	Benson & Hedges Irish Masters
	v Johnson	5-0	Quarter-final	Benson & Hedges Irish Masters
	v S. Davis	2-6	Semi-final	Benson & Hedges Irish Masters
	v Wych	10-4	1st round	Embassy World Championship
	v Higgins	13-10	2nd round	Embassy World Championship
	v S. Davis	5-13	Quarter-final	Embassy World Championship
	v Dennis Taylor	3-6	Final	British Caledonian Tokyo Masters (WS)
	v N. Foulds	5-4	1st round	Langs Scottish Masters
	v White	6-2	Semi-final	Langs Scottish Masters
	v Johnson	7-9	Final	Langs Scottish Masters
	v Wildman	5-1	3rd round	Fidelity International
	v Charlton	2-5	4th round	Fidelity International
	v Kearney	5-0	3rd round	Rothmans Grand Prix
	v Chappel	5-3	4th round	Rothmans Grand Prix
	v Parrott	4-5	5th round	Rothmans Grand Prix
	v N. Foulds	4-5	1st round	Labatts Canadian Masters (WS)
	v N. Foulds	2-6	1st round	Matchroom Trophy
	v Gary Wilkinson	9-5	3rd round	Tennents UK Open
	v Edmonds	9-5	4th round	Tennents UK Open
	v S. Francisco	9-3	5th round	Tennents UK Open
	v White	7-9	Quarter-final	Tennents UK Open
1988	v Van Rensburg	5-2	3rd round	Mercantile Credit Classic
	v Wilson	5-2	4th round	Mercantile Credit Classic
	v West	5-2	5th round	Mercantile Credit Classic
	v Newbury	4-5	Quarter-final	Mercantile Credit Classic
	v S. Francisco	5-3	1st round	Benson and Hedges Masters
	v S. Davis	0-5	Quarter-final	Benson and Hedges Masters
	v Chappel	6-4	Quarter-final	Welsh Championship
	v Wilson	9-7	Semi-final	Welsh Championship
	v W. Jones	**9-3**	**Final**	**Welsh Championship**
	v Morra	5-1	3rd round	MIM Britannia British Open
	v Hendry	1-5	4th round	MIM Britannia British Open
	v Williams	5-1	1st round	Benson & Hedges Irish Masters
	v White	5-2	Quarter-final	Benson & Hedges Irish Masters
	v N. Foulds	4-6	Semi-final	Benson & Hedges Irish Masters
	v Longworth	10-1	1st round	Embassy World Championship
	v Thorne	13-9	2nd round	Embassy World Championship
	v N. Foulds	13-9	Quarter-final	Embassy World Championship
	v White	16-11	Semi-final	Embassy World Championship
	v S. Davis	11-18	Final	Embassy World Championship

MIKE HALLETT (England)

Born 6.7.59. **Turned professional** 1979. **World ranking** 9 (16). **Best professional performances** Runner-up 1988 MIM Britannia British Open, 1988 Benson and Hedges Masters.

Year	Opponent	Score	Round	Tournament
1979	v Parkin	9-1	1st round	Coral UK Championship
	v Fagan	4-9	2nd round	Coral UK Championship
1980	v Stevens	3-9	Qualifying	Embassy World Championship
	v Bennett	9-4	Qualifying	Coral UK Championship
	v Edmonds	9-8	Qualifying	Coral UK Championship
	v S. Davis	1-9	1st round	Coral UK Championship
1981	v Edmonds	3-9	Qualifying	John Courage English
	v Jonik	9-1	Qualifying	Embassy World Championship
	v Meo	4-9	Qualifying	Embassy World Championship
	v Demarco	5-4	Qualifying	Jameson International
	v Knowles	2-5	1st round	Jameson International
	v V. Harris	9-4	Qualifying	Coral UK Championship
	v D. Hughes	9-6	Qualifying	Coral UK Championship
	v Fagan	9-5	Qualifying	Coral UK Championship
	v Stevens	4-9	2nd round	Coral UK Championship
1982	v Johnson	9-8	Qualifying	Embassy World Championship
	v Virgo	4-10	1st round	Embassy World Championship
	v Jonik	5-2	Qualifying	Jameson International
	v Wildman	2-5	Qualifying	Jameson International
	v V. Harris	5-3	1st round	Professional Players Tournament
	v Virgo	2-5	2nd round	Professional Players Tournament
	v Demarco	9-1	Qualifying	Coral UK Championship
	v F. Davis	9-7	1st round	Coral UK Championship
	v Reardon	8-9	2nd round	Coral UK Championship
1983	v Andrewartha	10-7	Qualifying	Embassy World Championship
	v King	10-6	Qualifying	Embassy World Championship
	v Spencer	7-10	1st round	Embassy World Championship
	v Roscoe	5-2	Qualifying	Jameson International
	v Morra	3-5	Qualifying	Jameson International
	v Kelly	5-0	1st round	Professional Players Tournament
	v S. Davis	5-2	2nd round	Professional Players Tournament
	v Meo	3-5	3rd round	Professional Players Tournament
	v Darrington	9-1	Qualifying	Coral UK Championship
	v Miles	9-4	1st round	Coral UK Championship
	v Griffiths	5-9	2nd round	Coral UK Championship
1984	v Dennis Taylor	5-4	Qualifying	Lada Classic
	v Knowles	3-5	1st round	Lada Classic
	v Burke	10-5	Qualifying	Embassy World Championship
	v Mountjoy	4-10	1st round	Embassy World Championship
	v O'Kane	4-5	Qualifying	Jameson International
	v Sheehan	5-1	1st round	Rothmans Grand Prix
	v Higgins	5-3	2nd round	Rothmans Grand Prix
	v Stevens	3-5	3rd round	Rothmans Grand Prix
	v Bradley	9-8	Qualifying	Coral UK Open
	v Mountjoy	2-9	1st round	Coral UK Open
1985	v G. Foulds	5-4	Qualifying	Mercantile Credit Classic
	v Reardon	3-5	1st round	Mercantile Credit Classic
	v Duggan	9-4	1st round	Tolly Cobbold English Championship
	v Meo	4-9	2nd round	Tolly Cobbold English Championship
	v Meo	4-5	2nd round	Dulux British Open
	v Chalmers	10-1	Qualifying	Embassy World Championship
	v Thorburn	8-10	1st round	Embassy World Championship
	v Bradley	4-5	3rd round	Goya Matchroom Trophy
	v Mikkelsen	5-3	3rd round	Rothmans Grand Prix
	v Johnson	4-5	4th round	Rothmans Grand Prix
	v Meadowcroft	9-1	3rd round	Coral UK Open

Mike Hallett

	v Stevens	5-9	4th round	Coral UK Open
1986	v John Rea	5-2	3rd round	Mercantile Credit Classic
	v Thorburn	3-5	4th round	Mercantile Credit Classic
	v Chalmers	9-1	3rd round	Tolly Cobbold English Championship
	v Knowles	9-5	4th round	Tolly Cobbold English Championship
	v Johnson	9-6	Quarter-final	Tolly Cobbold English Championship
	v N. Foulds	8-9	Semi-final	Tolly Cobbold English Championship
	v Duggan	5-3	3rd round	Dulux British Open
	v Higgins	1-5	4th round	Dulux British Open
	v Wych	10-7	Qualifying	Embassy World Championship
	v Dennis Taylor	10-6	1st round	Embassy World Championship
	v Johnson	6-13	2nd round	Embassy World Championship
	v O'Kane	1-5	3rd round	BCE International
	v V. Harris	5-2	3rd round	Rothmans Grand Prix
	v Dodd	5-2	4th round	Rothmans Grand Prix
	v White	3-5	5th round	Rothmans Grand Prix
	v King	9-5	3rd round	Tennents UK Open
	v Meo	9-4	4th round	Tennents UK Open
	v Higgins	7-9	5th round	Tennents UK Open
1987	v Mikkelsen	5-3	3rd round	Mercantile Credit Classic
	v Fowler	4-5	4th round	Mercantile Credit Classic
	v Williamson	2-6	3rd round	Tolly Ales English Championship
	v Owers	6-2	4th round	Tolly Ales English Championship
	v Dodd	5-6	Quarter-final	Tolly Ales English Championship
	v Rigitano	5-0	3rd round	Dulux British Open
	v White	2-5	4th round	Dulux British Open
	v Newbury	10-4	Qualifying	Embassy World Championship
	v Knowles	10-6	1st round	Embassy World Championship
	v S. Francisco	13-9	2nd round	Embassy World Championship
	v N. Foulds	9-13	Quarter-final	Embassy World Championship
	v Roscoe	5-3	3rd round	Fidelity International
	v Longworth	5-1	4th round	Fidelity International
	v White	5-4	5th round	Fidelity International
	v Charlton	5-4	Quarter-final	Fidelity International
	v S. Davis	3-9	Semi-final	Fidelity International
	v P. Gibson	4-5	3rd round	Rothmans Grand Prix
	v T. Jones	9-2	3rd round	Tennents UK Open
	v Meo	9-5	4th round	Tennents UK Open
	v Fowler	9-4	5th round	Tennents UK Open
	v Johnson	7-9	Quarter-final	Tennents UK Open
1988	v Clark	4-5	3rd round	Mercantile Credit Classic
	v Dennis Taylor	5-3	1st round	Benson & Hedges Masters
	v Higgins	5-2	Quarter-final	Benson & Hedges Masters
	v Parrott	6-5	Semi-final	Benson & Hedges Masters
	v S. Davis	0-9	Final	Benson & Hedges Masters
	v Duggan	6-3	3rd round	English Championship
	v Williams	6-3	4th round	English Championship
	v West	5-6	Quarter-final	English Championship
	v Williamson	5-0	3rd round	MIM Britannia British Open
	v Cripsey	5-2	4th round	MIM Britannia British Open
	v Macleod	5-2	5th round	MIM Britannia British Open
	v O'Boye	5-4	Quarter-final	MIM Britannia British Open
	v Parrott	9-8	Semi-final	MIM Britannia British Open
	v Hendry	2-13	Final	MIM Britannia British Open
	v Chaperon	10-2	1st round	Embassy World Championship
	v S. Davis	1-13	2nd round	Embassy World Championship

JOHN HARGREAVES (England)
Born 2.12.45. **Turned professional** 1983. **World ranking** 122 (105).

1983	v Morra	0-5	Qualifying	Professional Players Tournament
	v Williamson	4-9	Qualifying	Coral UK Championship

1984	v E. McLaughlin	5-10	Qualifying	Embassy World Championship
	v Houlihan	5-2	Qualifying	Jameson International
	v Kelly	2-5	Qualifying	Jameson International
	v Donnelly	4-5	Qualifying	Rothmans Grand Prix
	v Medati	9-6	Qualifying	Coral UK Open
	v Gibson	8-9	Qualifying	Coral UK Open
1985	v Darrington	5-2	Qualifying	Mercantile Credit Classic
	v Edmonds	2-5	Qualifying	Mercantile Credit Classic
	v Medati	8-9	Qualifying	Tolly Cobbold English Championship
	v N. Foulds	1-6	1st round	Dulux British Open
	v Fowler	0-10	Qualifying	Embassy World Championship
	v Caggianello	2-5	1st round	Goya Matchroom Trophy
	v Cripsey	5-1	1st round	Rothmans Grand Prix
	v Longworth	2-5	2nd round	Rothmans Grand Prix
	v Mienie	9-7	1st round	Coral UK Open
	v Meadowcroft	8-9	2nd round	Coral UK Open
1986	v Cripsey	5-1	1st round	Mercantile Credit Classic
	v Longworth	2-5	2nd round	Mercantile Credit Classic
	v Houlihan	5-9	1st round	Tolly Cobbold English Championship
	v Edmonds	5-3	2nd round	Dulux British Open
	v N. Foulds	4-5	3rd round	Dulux British Open
	v Mikkelsen	7-10	Qualifying	Embassy World Championship
	v Owers	3-5	1st round	BCE International
	v Roe	1-5	1st round	Rothmans Grand Prix
	v W. Jones	0-9	2nd round	Tennents UK Open
1987	v James	5-6	1st round	Tolly Ales English Championship
	v Parkin	5-4	1st round	Dulux British Open
	v John Rea	3-5	2nd round	Dulux British Open
	v M. Bennett	6-10	Qualifying	Embassy World Championship
	v Morra	4-5	1st round	Fidelity International

ANTHONY HARRIS (England)

Born 19.4.68. **Turned professional** 1987. **World ranking** 116. **Amateur career** 1986 English champion.

1987	v D. Gilbert	4-5	1st round	Fidelity International
	v Meadowcroft	3-5	1st round	Rothmans Grand Prix
	v Morra	9-8	1st round	Tennents UK Open
	v Gauvreau	3-9	2nd round	Tennents UK Open
1988	v Jenkins	5-4	1st round	Mercantile Credit Classic
	v T. Jones	2-5	2nd round	Mercantile Credit Classic
	v N. Gilbert	3-5	1st round	English Championship
	v Bear	2-5	1st round	MIM Britannia British Open
	v Mizerak	10-3	Preliminary	Embassy World Championship
	v Fisher	10-4	Qualifying	Embassy World Championship
	v Duggan	4-10	Qualifying	Embassy World Championship

BOB HARRIS (England)

Born 12.3.56. **Turned professional** 1982. **World ranking** 77 (49). **Best professional performances** Last 32 1985 Goya Matchroom Trophy, 1985 Rothmans Grand Prix, 1987 Mercantile Credit Classic.

1982	v Scott	4-5	Qualifying	Jameson International
	v Cripsey	9-6	Qualifying	Coral UK Championship
	v Watterson	9-3	Qualifying	Coral UK Championship
	v Fagan	6-9	1st round	Coral UK Championship
1983	v Wildman	7-10	Qualifying	Embassy World Championship
	v Dunning	5-3	Qualifying	Jameson International
	v Wildman	2-5	Qualifying	Jameson International

	v King	3-5	Qualifying	Professional Players Tournament
	v E. McLaughlin	9-8	Qualifying	Coral UK Championship
	v Fitzmaurice	9-3	Qualifying	Coral UK Championship
	v Reardon	7-9	1st round	Coral UK Championship
1984	v Sheehan	10-3	Qualifying	Embassy World Championship
	v Burke	4-10	Qualifying	Embassy World Championship
	v Watchorn	7-9	Qualifying	Coral UK Open
1985	v Duggan	8-9	Qualifying	Tolly Cobbold English Championship
	v Meadowcroft	6-1	Qualifying	Dulux British Open
	v Charlton	6-3	1st round	Dulux British Open
	v E. Hughes	4-5	2nd round	Dulux British Open
	v Rigitano	4-10	Qualifying	Embassy World Championship
	v Browne	5-3	2nd round	Goya Matchroom Trophy
	v O'Kane	5-3	3rd round	Goya Matchroom Trophy
	v Dennis Taylor	3-5	4th round	Goya Matchroom Trophy
	v Browne	5-3	2nd round	Rothmans Grand Prix
	v Spencer	5-2	3rd round	Rothmans Grand Prix
	v Griffiths	3-5	4th round	Rothmans Grand Prix
	v Fagan	2-9	2nd round	Coral UK Open
1986	v Morra	5-3	2nd round	Mercantile Credit Classic
	v Johnson	4-5	3rd round	Mercantile Credit Classic
	v T. Jones	5-9	2nd round	Tolly Cobbold English Championship
	v Sinclair	5-3	2nd round	Dulux British Open
	v Martin	1-5	3rd round	Dulux British Open
	v Black	8-10	Qualifying	Embassy World Championship
	v Foldvari	0-5	2nd round	BCE International
	v Jack Rea	5-0	2nd round	Rothmans Grand Prix
	v Mountjoy	2-5	3rd round	Rothmans Grand Prix
	v Jack Rea	9-5	2nd round	Tennents UK Open
	v Wych	6-9	3rd round	Tennents UK Open
1987	v P. Gibson	5-3	2nd round	Mercantile Credit Classic
	v Wych	5-3	3rd round	Mercantile Credit Classic
	v S. Francisco	3-5	4th round	Mercantile Credit Classic
	v G. Foulds	6-1	2nd round	Tolly Ales English Championship
	v Thorne	2-6	3rd round	Tolly Ales English Championship
	v Kelly	5-2	2nd round	Dulux British Open
	v Thorne	1-5	3rd round	Dulux British Open
	v D. Hughes	10-2	Qualifying	Embassy World Championship
	v Fowler	6-10	Qualifying	Embassy World Championship
	v James	0-5	2nd round	Fidelity International
	v Bear	3-5	2nd round	Rothmans Grand Prix
	v Bear	4-9	2nd round	Tennents UK Open
1988	v D. Gilbert	4-5	2nd round	Mercantile Credit Classic
	v M. Smith	4-6	2nd round	English Championship
	v Lawlor	2-5	2nd round	MIM Britannia British Open
	v Fagan	10-1	Qualifying	Embassy World Championship
	v Sinclair	10-0	Qualifying	Embassy World Championship
	v Charlton	4-10	Qualifying	Embassy World Championship

VIC HARRIS (England)

Born 16.8.45. **Turned professional** 1981. **World ranking** 71 (73). **Amateur career** 1981 English champion. **Best professional performances** Last 32 1987 Tennents UK Open, 1986 Mercantile Credit Classic.

1981	v Sheehan	1-5	Qualifying	Jameson International
	v Higgins	3-5	Quarter-final	Langs Scottish Masters
	v Hallett	4-9	Qualifying	Coral UK Championship
	v Johnson	4-9	Qualifying	Embassy World Championship
1982	v Hallett	3-5	1st round	Professional Players Tournament
	v M. Owen	9-4	Qualifying	Coral UK Championship
	v Johnson	8-9	Qualifying	Coral UK Championship

	v Sheehan	5-3	Qualifying	Jameson International
	v Virgo	2-5	Qualifying	Jameson International
1983	v Meo	0-10	Qualifying	Embassy World Championship
	v Medati	0-5	Qualifying	Jameson International
	v Thorburn	1-5	1st round	Professional Players Tournament
	v Houlihan	9-6	Qualifying	Coral UK Championship
	v Williams	6-9	Qualifying	Coral UK Championship
1984	v Van Rensberg	7-10	Qualifying	Embassy World Championship
	v Williamson	0-5	Qualifying	Jameson International
	v F. Davis	5-1	Qualifying	Rothmans Grand Prix
	v Knowles	1-5	1st round	Rothmans Grand Prix
	v Bradley	8-9	Qualifying	Coral UK Open
1985	v Newbury	3-5	Qualifying	Mercantile Credit Classic
	v Scott	7-9	Qualifying	Tolly Cobbold English Championship
	v Dodd	6-1	Qualifying	Dulux British Open
	v Mountjoy	6-5	1st round	Dulux British Open
	v O'Kane	3-5	2nd round	Dulux British Open
	v O'Kane	5-10	Qualifying	Embassy World Championship
	v Foldvari	4-5	2nd round	Goya Matchroom Trophy
	v Wych	5-3	2nd round	Rothmans Grand Prix
	v Higgins	1-5	3rd round	Rothmans Grand Prix
	v Black	9-3	2nd round	Coral UK Open
	v Spencer	5-9	3rd round	Coral UK Open
1986	v Roscoe	5-1	2nd round	Mercantile Credit Classic
	v Griffiths	5-3	3rd round	Mercantile Credit Classic
	v Williams	1-5	4th round	Mercantile Credit Classic
	v Bales	7-9	2nd round	Tolly Cobbold English Championship
	v Chaperon	0-5	2nd round	Dulux British Open
	v T. Jones	7-10	Qualifying	Embassy World Championship
	v G. Foulds	4-5	2nd round	BCE International
	v Kelly	5-3	2nd round	Rothmans Grand Prix
	v Hallett	2-5	3rd round	Rothmans Grand Prix
	v Fisher	9-4	2nd round	Tennents UK Open
	v Charlton	2-9	3rd round	Tennents UK Open
1987	v O'Boye	1-5	2nd round	Mercantile Credit Classic
	v Darrington	6-3	2nd round	Tolly Ales English Championship
	v West	3-6	3rd round	Tolly Ales English Championship
	v Sheehan	5-4	2nd round	Dulux British Open
	v E. Hughes	1-5	3rd round	Dulux British Open
	v Rigitano	6-10	Qualifying	Embassy World Championship
	v Marshall	5-1	1st round	Fidelity International
	v Chaperon	4-5	2nd round	Fidelity International
	v Gary Wilkinson	0-5	1st round	Rothmans Grand Prix
	v Greaves	9-1	1st round	Tennents UK Open
	v M. Bennett	9-7	2nd round	Tennents UK Open
	v Martin	9-7	3rd round	Tennents UK Open
	v Roe	5-9	4th round	Tennents UK Open
1988	v Ellis	5-1	1st round	Mercantile Credit Classic
	v Murphy	2-5	2nd round	Mercantile Credit Classic
	v J. Smith	3-6	1st round	English Championship
	v Thornley	4-5	1st round	MIM Britannia British Open
	v M. Smith	6-10	Qualifying	Embassy World Championship

DEREK HEATON (England)

Born 27.9.48. **Turned professional** 1987. **World ranking** 123.

	v Sinclair	3-5	1st round	Fidelity International
	v Houlihan	0-5	2nd round	Rothmans Grand Prix
	v D. Gilbert	5-9	1st round	Tennents UK Open
1988	v Sheehan	2-5	1st round	Mercantile Credit Classic
	v Meadowcroft	6-0	1st round	English Championship
	v Dodd	0-6	2nd round	English Championship

| v Foldvari | 1-5 | 1st round | MIM Britannia British Open |
| v D. Gilbert | 2-10 | Qualifying | Embassy World Championship |

STEPHEN HENDRY (Scotland)

Born 13.1.69. **Turned professional** 1985. **World ranking** 4 (23). **Amateur career** Scottish champion 1984, 1985. **Best professional performances** Winner 1987 Rothmans Grand Prix, 1988 MIM Britannia British Open.

1985	v West	5-4	1st round	Goya Matchroom Trophy
	v E. McLaughlin	3-5	2nd round	Goya Matchroom Trophy
	v O'Boye	4-5	1st round	Rothmans Grand Prix
	v Agrawal	2-9	Qualifying	Coral UK Open
1986	v Sheehan	5-2	1st round	Mercantile Credit Classic
	v Miles	5-1	2nd round	Mercantile Credit Classic
	v S. Francisco	5-4	3rd round	Mercantile Credit Classic
	v N. Foulds	4-5	4th round	Mercantile Credit Classic
	v D. Hughes	5-1	1st round	Dulux British Open
	v Browne	0-5	2nd round	Dulux British Open
	v Demarco	6-1	1st round	Canada Dry Scottish Championship
	v Macleod	6-5	Quarter-final	Canada Dry Scottish Championship
	v Black	6-2	Semi-final	Canada Dry Scottish Championship
	v Gibson	**10-5**	**Final**	**Canada Dry Scottish Championship**
	v Demarco	10-7	Qualifying	Embassy World Championship
	v Browne	10-9	Qualifying	Embassy World Championship
	v W. Jones	10-8	Qualifying	Embassy World Championship
	v O'Kane	10-9	Qualifying	Embassy World Championship
	v Thorne	8-10	1st round	Embassy World Championship
	v White	1-5	1st round	Langs Scottish Masters
	v P. Gibson	5-2	2nd round	BCE International
	v Parrott	5-3	3rd round	BCE International
	v Dennis Taylor	3-5	4th round	BCE International
	v Williamson	5-1	2nd round	Rothmans Grand Prix
	v E. Hughes	5-1	3rd round	Rothmans Grand Prix
	v Chaperon	5-2	4th round	Rothmans Grand Prix
	v M. Bennett	5-3	5th round	Rothmans Grand Prix
	v White	4-5	Quarter-final	Rothmans Grand Prix
	v Oliver	9-1	2nd round	Tennents UK Open
	v Higgins	8-9	3rd round	Tennents UK Open
1987	v Jack Rea	5-1	2nd round	Mercantile Credit Classic
	v Reardon	5-3	3rd round	Mercantile Credit Classic
	v Wright	5-1	4th round	Mercantile Credit Classic
	v Fowler	5-4	5th round	Mercantile Credit Classic
	v S. Francisco	5-0	Quarter-final	Mercantile Credit Classic
	v S. Davis	3-9	Semi-final	Mercantile Credit Classic
	v Demarco	6-2	1st round	Scottish Championship
	v John Rea	6-0	Semi-final	Scottish Championship
	v Donnelly	**10-7**	**Final**	**Scottish Championship**
	v Sinclair	2-5	2nd round	Dulux British Open
	v Darrington	10-7	Qualifying	Embassy World Championship
	v Rempe	10-4	Qualifying	Embassy World Championship
	v Martin	10-7	Qualifying	Embassy World Championship
	v Thorne	10-7	1st round	Embassy World Championship
	v Longworth	13-7	2nd round	Embassy World Championship
	v Johnson	12-13	Quarter-final	Embassy World Championship
	v White	5-2	Semi-final	Riley Hong Kong Masters (WS)
	v S. Davis	3-9	Final	Riley Hong Kong Masters (WS)
	v Dennis Taylor	3-5	1st round	Carling Champions
	v Johnson	2-5	1st round	Langs Scottish Masters
	v Gary Wilkinson	5-4	3rd round	Fidelity International
	v N. Foulds	5-2	4th round	Fidelity International
	v D. Gilbert	5-0	5th round	Fidelity International

v O'Boye	5-2	Quarter-final	Fidelity International
v Thorburn	1-9	Semi-final	Fidelity International
v M. Bennett	5-1	3rd round	Rothmans Grand Prix
v Chambers	5-1	4th round	Rothmans Grand Prix
v S. Davis	5-2	5th round	Rothmans Grand Prix
v Knowles	5-2	Quarter-final	Rothmans Grand Prix
v Parrott	9-7	Semi-final	Rothmans Grand Prix
v Dennis Taylor	**10-7**	**Final**	**Rothmans Grand Prix**
v Wych	7-9	3rd round	Tennents UK Open
1988 v Werbeniuk	5-2	3rd round	Mercantile Credit Classic
v Johnson	5-3	4th round	Mercantile Credit Classic
v S. Francisco	5-3	5th round	Mercantile Credit Classic
v S. Davis	3-5	Quarter-final	Mercantile Credit Classic
v Demarco	6-0	Quarter-final	Scottish Championship
v M. Gibson	6-1	Semi-final	Scottish Championship
v Macleod	**10-4**	**Final**	**Scottish Championship**
v Chappel	5-1	3rd round	MIM Britannia British Open
v Griffiths	5-1	4th round	MIM Britannia British Open
v T. Jones	5-3	5th round	MIM Britannia British Open
v White	5-4	Quarter-final	MIM Britannia British Open
v Thorburn	9-5	Semi-final	MIM Britannia British Open
v Hallett	**13-2**	**Final**	**MIM Britannia British Open**
v Wright	10-4	Qualifying	Embassy World Championship
v Reynolds	10-6	1st round	Embassy World Championship
v White	12-13	2nd round	Embassy World Championship

ALEX HIGGINS (Northern Ireland)

Born 18.3.49. **Turned professional** 1971. **World ranking** 17 (9). **Amateur career** 1968 Northern Ireland champion. **Best professional performances** Winner 1972 World Championship, 1982 Embassy World Championship, 1983 Coral UK Championship, 1978 & 1981 Benson & Hedges Masters, 1980 British Gold Cup; 1983 Irish champion.

1972 v Gross	15-6	Qualifying	World Championship
v Parkin	11-3	Qualifying	World Championship
v Jack Rea	19-11	1st round	World Championship
v Pulman	31-23	Quarter-final	World Championship
v Williams	31-30	Semi-final	World Championship
v Spencer	**37-32**	**Final**	**World Championship**
1973 v Houlihan	16-3	2nd round	World Championship
v Davis	16-14	Quarter-final	World Championship
v Charlton	9-23	Semi-final	World Championship
v Spencer	2-8	Semi-final	Norwich Union Open
1974 v Bennett	15-4	2nd round	World Championship
v F. Davis	14-15	Quarter-final	World Championship
v Dennis Taylor	5-1	1st round	Norwich Union Open
v Werbeniuk	5-4	Quarter-final	Norwich Union Open
v Reardon	8-9	Semi-final	Norwich Union Open
1975 v Werbeniuk	5-0	1st round	Benson & Hedges Masters
v Williams	3-5	Quarter-final	Benson & Hedges Masters
v David Taylor	15-2	2nd round	World Championship
v Williams	19-12	Quarter-final	World Championship
v Reardon	14-19	Semi-final	World Championship
1976 v Miles	1-4	2nd round	Benson & Hedges Masters
v Thorburn	15-14	1st round	Embassy World Championship
v Spencer	15-14	Quarter-final	Embassy World Championship
v Charlton	20-18	Semi-final	Embassy World Championship
v Reardon	16-27	Final	Embassy World Championship
1977 v Mans	4-2	Quarter-final	Benson & Hedges Masters
v Mountjoy	3-5	Semi-final	Benson & Hedges Masters
v Mountjoy	12-13	1st round	Embassy World Championship

Stephen Hendry

	v David Taylor	5-4	2nd round	Super Crystalate UK Championship
	v Dunning	5-0	Quarter-final	Super Crystalate UK Championship
	v Mountjoy	2-9	Semi-final	Super Crystalate UK Championship
1978	v Dennis Taylor	4-3	Quarter-final	Benson & Hedges Masters
	v Reardon	5-1	Semi-final	Benson & Hedges Masters
	v Thorburn	**7-5**	**Final**	**Benson & Hedges Masters**
	v Fagan	12-13	1st round	Embassy World Championship
	v Meadowcroft	9-6	1st round	Coral UK Championship
	v F. Davis	9-4	Quarter-final	Coral UK Championship
	v David Taylor	5-9	Semi-final	Coral UK Championship
1979	v Miles	3-6	Semi-final	Holsten Lager International
	v Charlton	5-2	Quarter-final	Benson & Hedges Masters
	v Mountjoy	5-1	Semi-final	Benson & Hedges Masters
	v Mans	4-8	Final	Benson & Hedges Masters
	v David Taylor	13-5	1st round	Embassy World Championship
	v Griffiths	12-13	Quarter-final	Embassy World Championship
	v Houlihan	9-3	3rd round	Coral UK Championship
	v Griffiths	7-9	Quarter-final	Coral UK Championship
1980	v F. Davis	5-1	1st round	Benson & Hedges Masters
	v Mans	5-1	Quarter-final	Benson & Hedges Masters
	v Reardon	5-2	Semi-final	Benson & Hedges Masters
	v Griffiths	5-9	Final	Benson & Hedges Masters
	v Reardon	**5-1**	**Final**	**British Gold Cup**
	v Meo	10-9	1st round	Embassy World Championship
	v Mans	13-6	2nd round	Embassy World Championship
	v S. Davis	13-9	Quarter-final	Embassy World Championship
	v Stevens	16-13	Semi-final	Embassy World Championship
	v Thorburn	16-18	Final	Embassy World Championship
	v Thorne	9-7	2nd round	Coral UK Championship
	v F. Davis	9-6	Quarter-final	Coral UK Championship
	v Reardon	9-7	Semi-final	Coral UK Championship
	v S. Davis	6-16	Final	Coral UK Championship
1981	v Mountjoy	5-1	Quarter-final	Benson & Hedges Masters
	v Thorburn	6-5	Semi-final	Benson & Hedges Masters
	v Griffiths	**9-6**	**Final**	**Benson & Hedges Masters**
	v Reardon	5-6	Semi-final	Benson & Hedges Irish Masters
	v S. Davis	8-13	2nd round	Embassy World Championship
	v V. Harris	5-3	Quarter-final	Langs Scottish Masters
	v Thorburn	2-6	Semi-final	Langs Scottish Masters
	v Fagan	5-3	2nd round	Jameson International
	v Mountjoy	5-1	3rd round	Jameson International
	v Griffiths	5-2	Quarter-final	Jameson International
	v S. Davis	8-9	Semi-final	Jameson International
	v S. Davis	2-5	1st round	Northern Ireland Classic
	v Martin	9-7	2nd round	Coral UK Championship
	v David Taylor	9-5	3rd round	Coral UK Championship
	v Meo	4-9	Quarter-final	Coral UK Championship
1982	v Dennis Taylor	5-1	1st round	Lada Classic
	v Griffiths	1-5	Semi-final	Lada Classic
	v Charlton	5-1	Quarter-final	Benson & Hedges Masters
	v Griffiths	4-6	Semi-final	Benson & Hedges Masters
	v D. Hughes	6-2	Semi-final	Irish Championship
	v Dennis Taylor	13-16	Final	Irish Championship
	v Wych	5-3	1st round	Benson & Hedges Irish Masters
	v Thorburn	5-4	Quarter-final	Benson & Hedges Irish Masters
	v S. Davis	2-6	Semi-final	Benson & Hedges Irish Masters
	v Meadowcroft	10-5	1st round	Embassy World Championship
	v Mountjoy	13-12	2nd round	Embassy World Championship
	v Thorne	13-10	Quarter-final	Embassy World Championship
	v White	16-15	Semi-final	Embassy World Championship
	v Reardon	**18-15**	**Final**	**Embassy World Championship**
	v Sinclair	5-1	1st round	Langs Scottish Masters
	v Griffiths	6-5	Semi-final	Langs Scottish Masters

v S. Davis	4-9	Final	Langs Scottish Masters
v Kelly	5-3	1st round	Jameson International
v Griffiths	2-5	2nd round	Jameson International
v French	5-3	1st round	Professional Players Tournament
v Reardon	2-5	2nd round	Professional Players Tournament
v Martin	9-7	1st round	Coral UK Championship
v Reynolds	9-8	2nd round	Coral UK Championship
v Spencer	9-5	Quarter-final	Coral UK Championship
v Reardon	9-6	Semi-final	Coral UK Championship
v Griffiths	15-16	Final	Coral UK Championship
1983 v Werbeniuk	4-5	1st round	Lada Classic
v Werbeniuk	4-5	1st round	Benson & Hedges Masters
v Jack Rea	6-3	Quarter-final	Irish Championship
v E. Hughes	6-2	Semi-final	Irish Championship
v Dennis Taylor	**16-11**	**Final**	**Irish Championship**
v White	5-2	Quarter-final	Benson & Hedges Irish Masters
v Reardon	3-6	Semi-final	Benson & Hedges Irish Masters
v Reynolds	10-4	1st round	Embassy World Championship
v Thorne	13-8	2nd round	Embassy World Championship
v Werbeniuk	13-11	Quarter-final	Embassy World Championship
v S. Davis	5-16	Semi-final	Embassy World Championship
v White	5-3	1st round	Langs Supreme Scottish Masters
v S. Davis	2-6	Semi-final	Langs Supreme Scottish Masters
v Martin	2-5	1st round	Jameson International
v Watterson	2-5	1st round	Professional Players Tournament
v Macleod	9-6	1st round	Coral UK Championship
v Medati	9-1	2nd round	Coral UK Championship
v Knowles	9-5	Quarter-final	Coral UK Championship
v Griffiths	9-4	Semi-final	Coral UK Championship
v S. Davis	**16-15**	**Final**	**Coral UK Championship**
1984 v Fagan	5-3	Qualifying	Lada Classic
v Parrott	2-5	1st round	Lada Classic
v Mountjoy	5-2	1st round	Benson & Hedges Masters
v Knowles	1-5	Quarter-final	Benson & Hedges Masters
v Charlton	5-2	1st round	Benson & Hedges Irish Masters
v Reardon	5-2	Quarter-final	Benson & Hedges Irish Masters
v S. Davis	4-6	Semi-final	Benson & Hedges Irish Masters
v N. Foulds	9-10	1st round	Embassy World Championship
v Stevens	5-2	1st round	Langs Supreme Scottish Masters
v S. Davis	4-6	Semi-final	Langs Supreme Scottish Masters
v Knowles	3-5	1st round	Carlsberg Challenge
v Sinclair	5-1	1st round	Jameson International
v Griffiths	5-4	2nd round	Jameson International
v S. Davis	1-5	Quarter-final	Jameson International
v Bales	5-1	1st round	Rothmans Grand Prix
v Hallett	3-5	2nd round	Rothmans Grand Prix
v T. Jones	9-7	1st round	Coral UK Open
v Williams	9-7	2nd round	Coral UK Open
v Thorne	9-5	Quarter-final	Coral UK Open
v Thorburn	9-7	Semi-final	Coral UK Open
v S. Davis	8-16	Final	Coral UK Open
1985 v Gauvreau	5-3	1st round	Mercantile Credit Classic
v S. Davis	2-5	2nd round	Mercantile Credit Classic
v S. Davis	5-4	1st round	Benson & Hedges Masters
v Griffiths	1-5	Quarter-final	Benson & Hedges Masters
v Bales	6-3	1st round	Dulux British Open
v N. Foulds	5-1	2nd round	Dulux British Open
v Thorburn	5-2	3rd round	Dulux British Open
v E. Hughes	5-2	Quarter-final	Dulux British Open
v S. Francisco	6-9	Semi-final	Dulux British Open
v Griffiths	5-2	1st round	Benson & Hedges Irish Masters
v Stevens	5-3	Quarter-final	Benson & Hedges Irish Masters
v S. Davis	6-2	Semi-final	Benson & Hedges Irish Masters

v White	5-9	Final	Benson & Hedges Irish Masters
v Burke	6-0	Quarter-final	Irish Championship
v Fagan	6-3	Semi-final	Irish Championship
v Dennis Taylor	5-10	Final	Irish Championship
v Reynolds	10-4	1st round	Embassy World Championship
v Griffiths	7-13	2nd round	Embassy World Championship
v Thorburn	5-4	Semi-final	Carlsberg Challenge
v White	3-8	Final	Carlsberg Challenge
v White	0-5	1st round	Langs Scottish Masters
v D. Hughes	5-1	3rd round	Goya Matchroom Trophy
v Murphy	5-2	4th round	Goya Matchroom Trophy
v Dennis Taylor	1-5	5th round	Goya Matchroom Trophy
v V. Harris	5-1	3rd round	Rothmans Grand Prix
v N. Foulds	5-3	4th round	Rothmans Grand Prix
v S. Davis	0-5	5th round	Rothmans Grand Prix
v Edmonds	9-8	3rd round	Coral UK Open
v F. Davis	9-2	4th round	Coral UK Open
v White	6-9	5th round	Coral UK Open
v Thorburn	5-4	1st round	Kit Kat
v S. Davis	1-6	Semi-final	Kit Kat
1986 v Fisher	5-0	3rd round	Mercantile Credit Classic
v Cripsey	5-2	4th round	Mercantile Credit Classic
v Dennis Taylor	5-4	5th round	Mercantile Credit Classic
v Williams	2-5	Quarter-final	Mercantile Credit Classic
v Dennis Taylor	5-1	1st round	BCE Belgian Classic
v Stevens	4-5	Semi-final	BCE Belgian Classic
v Griffiths	4-5	1st round	Benson & Hedges Masters
v Bradley	5-3	3rd round	Dulux British Open
v Hallett	5-1	4th round	Dulux British Open
v P. Francisco	5-2	5th round	Dulux British Open
v Werbeniuk	5-1	Quarter-final	Dulux British Open
v S. Davis	3-9	Semi-final	Dulux British Open
v Meo	4-5	1st round	Benson & Hedges Irish Masters
v Spencer	10-7	1st round	Embassy World Championship
v Griffiths	12-13	2nd round	Embassy World Championship
v J. McLaughlin	6-2	Quarter-final	Strongbow Irish Championship
v E. Hughes	6-2	Semi-final	Strongbow Irish Championship
v Dennis Taylor	7-10	Final	Strongbow Irish Championship
v White	1-5	1st round	Carlsberg Challenge
v Johnson	5-2	1st round	Langs Scottish Masters
v Stevens	6-2	Semi-final	Langs Scottish Masters
v Thorburn	8-9	Final	Langs Scottish Masters
v Sinclair	5-3	3rd round	BCE International
v P. Francisco	4-5	4th round	BCE International
v F. Davis	5-0	3rd round	Rothmans Grand Prix
v Martin	5-2	4th round	Rothmans Grand Prix
v Williams	1-5	5th round	Rothmans Grand Prix
v Johnson	5-3	1st round	BCE Canadian Masters
v S. Davis	2-8	Semi-final	BCE Canadian Masters
v Hendry	9-8	3rd round	Tennents UK Open
v Martin	9-6	4th round	Tennents UK Open
v Hallett	9-7	5th round	Tennents UK Open
v W. Jones	9-5	Quarter-final	Tennents UK Open
v S. Davis	3-9	Semi-final	Tennents UK Open
1987 v Roscoe	5-2	3rd round	Mercantile Credit Classic
v Parrott	2-5	4th round	Mercantile Credit Classic
v Griffiths	5-4	1st round	Benson & Hedges Masters
v Johnson	5-1	Quarter-final	Benson & Hedges Masters
v Meo	6-2	Semi-final	Benson & Hedges Masters
v Dennis Taylor	8-9	Final	Benson & Hedges Masters
v J. McLaughlin	4-5	3rd round	Dulux British Open
v Griffiths	1-5	1st round	Benson & Hedges Irish Masters
v Wright	10-6	1st round	Embassy World Championship

Alex Higgins

	v Griffiths	10-13	2nd round	Embassy World Championship
	v White	3-5	1st round	Langs Scottish Masters
	v Duggan	9-4	3rd round	Tennents UK Open
	v David Taylor	9-6	4th round	Tennents UK Open
	v S. Davis	2-9	5th round	Tennents UK Open
1988	v T. Jones	5-0	3rd round	Mercantile Credit Classic
	v S. Davis	0-5	4th round	Mercantile Credit Classic
	v Knowles	5-4	1st round	Benson & Hedges Masters
	v Hallett	2-5	2nd round	Benson & Hedges Masters
	v O'Boye	4-6	Quarter-final	Irish Championship
	v T. Jones	3-5	3rd round	MIM Britannia British Open
	v Dennis Taylor	5-3	1st round	Benson & Hedges Irish Masters
	v Thorburn	5-3	Quarter-final	Benson & Hedges Irish Masters
	v Davis	2-6	Semi-final	Benson & Hedges Irish Masters
	v Drago	2-10	1st round	Embassy World Championship

PAT HOULIHAN (England)

Born 7.11.29. **Turned professional** 1969. **World ranking** 59 (65). **Amateur career** 1965 English champion. **Best professional performance** Last 32 1987 Rothmans Grand Prix.

1972	v Dunning	10-11	Qualifying	World Championship
1973	v Jack Rea	9-2	1st round	World Championship
	v Higgins	3-16	2nd round	World Championship
1977	v Meadowcroft	1-5	1st round	Super Crystalate UK
1978	v Ross	9-1	Prelim	Embassy World Championship
	v Meadowcroft	9-6	Qualifying	Embassy World Championship
	v Thorburn	8-13	1st round	Embassy World Championship
	v Andrewartha	3-9	Qualifying	Coral UK Championship
1979	v Barrie	9-5	Prelim	Embassy World Championship
	v Mountjoy	6-9	Qualifying	Embassy World Championship
	v Jack Rea	9-3	2nd round	Coral UK Championship
	v Higgins	3-9	3rd round	Coral UK Championship
1980	v Meo	1-9	Qualifying	Embassy World Championship
	v Meo	1-9	1st round	Coral UK Championship
1981	v Spencer	1-9	1st round	John Courage English
	v French	3-5	Qualifying	Jameson International
	v Kennerley	9-1	Qualifying	Coral UK Championship
	v Black	9-4	Qualifying	Coral UK Championship
	v Meadowcroft	9-4	Qualifying	Coral UK Championship
	v Miles	3-9	2nd round	Coral UK Championship
1982	v Anderson	9-5	Qualifying	Embassy World Championship
	v Martin	3-9	Qualifying	Embassy World Championship
	v E. McLaughlin	2-5	Qualifying	Jameson International
	v Knowles	4-5	1st round	Professional Players Tournament
	v Mountjoy	3-9	1st round	Coral UK Championship
1983	v Murphy	9-10	Qualifying	Embassy World Championship
	v Scott	0-5	Qualifying	Jameson International
	v Sheehan	2-5	Qualifying	Professional Players Tournament
	v V. Harris	6-9	Qualifying	Coral UK Championship
1984	v Williamson	5-10	Qualifying	Embassy World Championship
	v Hargreaves	2-5	Qualifying	Jameson International
	v Everton	3-5	Qualifying	Rothmans Grand Prix
	v Chappel	3-9	Qualifying	Coral UK Open
1985	v Foldvari	1-5	Qualifying	Mercantile Credit Classic
	v T. Jones	1-9	Qualifying	Tolly Cobbold English Championship
	v Jim Bear	2-5	1st round	Goya Matchroom Trophy
	v Robinson	5-0	1st round	Rothmans Grand Prix
	v T. Jones	4-5	2nd round	Rothmans Grand Prix
	v Watson	9-4	1st round	Coral UK Open

	v Newbury	3-9	2nd round	Coral UK Open
1986	v Bennett	5-0	1st round	Mercantile Credit Classic
	v Foldvari	5-4	2nd round	Mercantile Credit Classic
	v Reynolds	1-5	3rd round	Mercantile Credit Classic
	v Hargreaves	9-5	1st round	Tolly Cobbold English Championship
	v Dunning	*wo*	2nd round	Tolly Cobbold English Championship
	v Spencer	5-9	3rd round	Tolly Cobbold English Championship
	v Longworth	3-5	2nd round	Dulux British Open
	v Sheehan	7-10	Qualifying	Embassy World Championship
	v Chalmers	5-1	1st round	BCE International
	v Cripsey	5-1	2nd round	BCE International
	v Meo	5-4	3rd round	BCE International
	v E. Hughes	1-5	4th round	BCE International
	v Grace	1-5	1st round	Rothmans Grand Prix
1987	v Owers	1-5	1st round	Mercantile Credit Classic
	v N. Gilbert	4-5	1st round	Dulux British Open
	v Wright	4-10	Qualifying	Embassy World Championship
	v D. Gilbert	3-5	2nd round	Fidelity International
	v Heaton	5-0	2nd round	Rothmans Grand Prix
	v Reynolds	5-4	3rd round	Rothmans Grand Prix
	v Chaperon	0-5	4th round	Rothmans Grand Prix
	v Miles	3-9	2nd round	Tennents UK Open
1988	v James	2-5	2nd round	Mercantile Credit Classic
	v Marshall	4-6	2nd round	English Championship
	v Bear	0-5	2nd round	MIM Britannia British Open
	v Cripsey	4-10	Qualifying	Embassy World Championship

DENNIS HUGHES (England)

Born 30.1.37. **Turned professional** 1981. **World ranking** 111 (106)

1981	v Jack Rea	5-4	Qualifying	Jameson International
	v Demarco	1-5	Qualifying	Jameson International
	v Hallett	6-9	Qualifying	Coral UK Championship
1982	v Higgins	2-6	Semi-final	Irish Championship
	v Everton	9-4	Qualifying	Embassy World Championship
	v Meo	4-9	Qualifying	Embassy World Championship
	v Edmonds	0-5	Qualifying	Jameson International
	v Charlton	2-5	1st round	Professional Players Tournament
	v Meadowcroft	8-9	Qualifying	Coral UK Championship
1983	v Parkin	5-0	Qualifying	Jameson International
	v Johnson	1-5	Qualifying	Jameson International
	v Medati	1-5	Qualifying	Professional Players Tournament
	v Medati	2-9	Qualifying	Coral UK Championship
1984	v Parrott	3-10	Qualifying	Embassy World Championship
	v Oliver	4-5	Qualifying	Jameson International
	v Dunning	0-5	Qualifying	Rothmans Grand Prix
	v G. Foulds	7-9	Qualifying	Coral UK Open
1985	v Watchorn	0-5	Prelim	Mercantile Credit Classic
	v Watterson	9-5	Qualifying	Tolly Cobbold English Championship
	v N. Foulds	3-9	1st round	Tolly Cobbold English Championship
	v Mikkelsen	0-6	Qualifying	Dulux British Open
	v French	10-5	Qualifying	Embassy World Championship
	v Newbury	9-10	Qualifying	Embassy World Championship
	v Kearney	5-1	1st round	Goya Matchroom Trophy
	v Gauvreau	5-4	2nd round	Goya Matchroom Trophy
	v Higgins	1-5	3rd round	Goya Matchroom Trophy
	v Bennett	5-4	1st round	Rothmans Grand Prix
	v Morra	2-5	2nd round	Rothmans Grand Prix
	v Kearney	9-8	1st round	Coral UK Open
	v King	0-9	2nd round	Coral UK Open
1986	v Burke	3-5	1st round	Mercantile Credit Classic

Eugene Hughes

	v F. Davis	6-9	2nd round	Tolly Cobbold English Championship
	v Hendry	1-5	1st round	Dulux British Open
	v Agrawal	6-10	Qualifying	Embassy World Championship
	v Roe	2-5	1st round	BCE International
	v Jack Rea	2-5	1st round	Rothmans Grand Prix
	v Ellis	9-6	1st round	Tennents UK Open
	v Murphy	0-9	2nd round	Tennents UK Open
1987	v Wright	2-5	1st round	Mercantile Credit Classic
	v P. Gibson	3-6	1st round	Tolly Ales English Championship
	v Whitthread	1-5	1st round	Dulux British Open
	v Parkin	10-5	Qualifying	Embassy World Championship
	v B. Harris	2-10	Qualifying	Embassy World Championship
	v Rowswell	1-5	1st round	Fidelity International
	v Donnelly	1-5	1st round	Rothmans Grand Prix
	v Edmonds	4-9	2nd round	Tennents UK Open
1988	v Williamson	5-3	1st round	Mercantile Credit Classic
	v Chappel	3-5	2nd round	Mercantile Credit Classic
	v Fitzmaurice	6-1	1st round	English Championship
	v Wildman	6-0	2nd round	English Championship
	v Williams	1-6	3rd round	English Championship
	v Fagan	5-4	1st round	MIM Britannia British Open
	v F. Davis	2-5	2nd round	MIM Britannia British Open
	v Miles	3-10	Qualifying	Embassy World Championship

EUGENE HUGHES (Republic of Ireland)

Born 4.11.55. **Turned professional** 1981. **World ranking** 21 (24). **Amateur career** Republic of Ireland champion 1978, 1979. **Best professional performances** Semi-finals 1984 Jameson International, 1986 BCE International.

	v M. Owen	5-1	Qualifying	Jameson International
	v Fitzmaurice	5-3	Qualifying	Jameson International
	v Sinclair	5-2	Qualifying	Jameson International
	v Edmonds	4-5	1st round	Jameson International
1982	v Mountjoy	4-5	1st round	Benson & Hedges Irish Masters
	v Jack Rea	6-1	Quarter-final	Irish Championship
	v Higgins	2-6	Semi-final	Irish Championship
	v Knowles	7-9	Qualifying	Embassy World Championship
	v Parkin	5-2	Qualifying	Jameson International
	v Martin	5-4	Qualifying	Jameson International
	v Reardon	3-5	1st round	Jameson International
	v Stevens	2-5	1st round	Professional Players Tournament
1983	v Burke	6-2	Quarter-final	Irish Championship
	v Higgins	2-6	Semi-final	Irish Championship
	v Fitzmaurice	10-7	Qualifying	Embassy World Championship
	v Sinclair	10-8	Qualifying	Embassy World Championship
	v Reardon	7-10	1st round	Embassy World Championship
	v Fisher	5-4	Qualifying	Jameson International
	v G. Foulds	5-1	Qualifying	Jameson International
	v S. Davis	1-5	1st round	Jameson International
	v Sinclair	5-4	1st round	Professional Players Tournament
	v Werbeniuk	5-0	2nd round	Professional Players Tournament
	v Griffiths	5-2	3rd round	Professional Players Tournament
	v Thorne	1-5	Quarter-final	Professional Players Tournament
1984	v Knowles	1-5	Qualifying	Lada Classic
	v Dennis Taylor	1-5	1st round	Benson & Hedges Irish Masters
	v Mifsud	5-10	Qualifying	Embassy World Championship
	v Roscoe	5-1	Qualifying	Jameson International
	v Mountjoy	5-1	1st round	Jameson International
	v Reardon	5-1	2nd round	Jameson International
	v Thorne	5-2	Quarter-final	Jameson International

Note: The 1981 year label appears at the start of the first group (v M. Owen).

	v S. Davis	3-9	Semi-final	Jameson International
	v John Rea	4-5	1st round	Rothmans Grand Prix
	v Morra	9-8	Qualifying	Coral UK Open
	v Meo	4-9	1st round	Coral UK Open
1985	v Newbury	5-3	Qualifying	Mercantile Credit Classic
	v Meo	5-4	1st round	Mercantile Credit Classic
	v Reardon	1-5	2nd round	Mercantile Credit Classic
	v Watchorn	6-4	1st round	Dulux British Open
	v B. Harris	5-4	2nd round	Dulux British Open
	v Macleod	5-2	3rd round	Dulux British Open
	v Higgins	2-5	Quarter-final	Dulux British Open
	v Reardon	5-0	1st round	Benson & Hedges Irish Masters
	v S. Davis	4-5	Quarter-final	Benson & Hedges Irish Masters
	v Kelly	6-2	Quarter-final	Irish Championship
	v Dennis Taylor	5-6	Semi-final	Irish Championship
	v Newbury	10-6	Qualifying	Embassy World Championship
	v Reardon	9-10	1st round	Embassy World Championship
	v Murphy	3-5	3rd round	Goya Matchroom Trophy
	v Simngam	5-1	3rd round	Rothmans Grand Prix
	v Meo	3-5	4th round	Rothmans Grand Prix
	v West	3-9	3rd round	Coral UK Open
1986	v Wych	5-2	3rd round	Mercantile Credit Classic
	v F. Davis	5-3	4th round	Mercantile Credit Classic
	v Johnson	1-5	5th round	Mercantile Credit Classic
	v Longworth	4-5	3rd round	Dulux British Open
	v Reardon	5-2	1st round	Benson & Hedges Irish Masters
	v Thorburn	1-5	Quarter-final	Benson & Hedges Irish Masters
	v Murphy	10-7	Qualifying	Embassy World Championship
	v David Taylor	10-7	1st round	Embassy World Championship
	v Thorburn	6-13	2nd round	Embassy World Championship
	v Sheehan	5-0	1st round	Strongbow Irish Championship
	v Burke	6-3	Quarter-final	Strongbow Irish Championship
	v Higgins	2-6	Semi-final	Strongbow Irish Championship
	v Chappel	5-4	3rd round	BCE International
	v Houlihan	5-1	4th round	BCE International
	v Chaperon	5-0	5th round	BCE International
	v S. Davis	5-4	Quarter-final	BCE International
	v N. Foulds	8-9	Semi-final	BCE International
	v Hendry	1-5	3rd round	Rothmans Grand Prix
	v Roscoe	9-8	3rd round	Tennents UK Open
	v Reardon	9-5	4th round	Tennents UK Open
	v W. Jones	5-9	5th round	Tennents UK Open
1987	v Wright	4-5	3rd round	Mercantile Credit Classic
	v V. Harris	5-0	3rd round	Dulux British Open
	v Johnson	3-5	4th round	Dulux British Open
	v Dennis Taylor	4-5	1st round	Benson & Hedges Irish Masters
	v Medati	10-2	Qualifying	Embassy World Championship
	v Johnson	9-10	1st round	Embassy World Championship
	v Watchorn	5-2	1st round	Matchroom Irish Championship
	v Kearney	6-1	Quarter-final	Matchroom Irish Championship
	v O'Boye	3-6	Semi-final	Matchroom Irish Championship
	v Owers	5-4	3rd round	Fidelity International
	v Wych	5-4	4th round	Fidelity International
	v S. Francisco	5-4	5th round	Fidelity International
	v Thorburn	1-5	Quarter-final	Fidelity International
	v Fisher	4-5	3rd round	Rothmans Grand Prix
	v N. Gilbert	9-7	3rd round	Tennents UK Open
	v White	4-9	4th round	Tennents UK Open
1988	v Newbury	1-5	3rd round	Mercantile Credit Classic
	v Watchorn	2-5	1st round	Irish Championship
	v Cripsey	3-5	3rd round	MIM Britannia British Open
	v Johnson	4-5	1st round	Benson & Hedges Irish Masters
	v James	6-10	Qualifying	Embassy World Championship

STEVE JAMES (England)

Born 2.5.61. **Turned professional** 1986. **World ranking** 32 (67). **Best professional performance** Quarter-finals 1988 Embassy World Championship.

1986	v N. Gilbert	5-2	1st round	BCE International
	v Edmonds	2-5	2nd round	BCE International
	v Morra	3-5	1st round	Rothmans Grand Prix
	v Rigitano	9-5	1st round	Tennents UK Open
	v King	8-9	2nd round	Tennents UK Open
1987	v Jonik	4-5	1st round	Mercantile Credit Classic
	v Hargreaves	6-5	1st round	Tolly Ales English Championship
	v F. Davis	6-2	2nd round	Tolly Ales English Championship
	v Longworth	6-2	3rd round	Tolly Ales English Championship
	v Johnson	3-6	4th round	Tolly Ales English Championship
	v Darrington	5-3	1st round	Dulux British Open
	v Miles	5-2	2nd round	Dulux British Open
	v Campbell	5-1	3rd round	Dulux British Open
	v Williams	2-5	4th round	Dulux British Open
	v Watterson	10-2	Qualifying	Embassy World Championship
	v Edmonds	1-10	Qualifying	Embassy World Championship
	v B. Harris	5-0	2nd round	Fidelity International
	v Campbell	5-4	3rd round	Fidelity International
	v Row	3-5	4th round	Fidelity International
	v G. Foulds	5-0	2nd round	Rothmans Grand Prix
	v Johnson	4-5	3rd round	Rothmans Grand Prix
	v T. Jones	6-9	2nd round	Tennents UK Open
1988	v Houlihan	5-2	2nd round	Mercantile Credit Classic
	v White	1-5	3rd round	Mercantile Credit Classic
	v Greaves	5-6	1st round	English Championship
	v King	5-2	2nd round	MIM Britannia British Open
	v Charlton	5-2	3rd round	MIM Britannia British Open
	v White	1-5	4th round	MIM Britannia British Open
	v O'Boye	10-7	Qualifying	Embassy World Championship
	v Browne	10-1	Qualifying	Embassy World Championship
	v E. Hughes	10-6	Qualifying	Embassy World Championship
	v Williams	10-6	1st round	Embassy World Championship
	v Johnson	13-9	2nd round	Embassy World Championship
	v Thorburn	11-13	Quarter-final	Embassy World Championship

GREG JENKINS (Australia)

Turned professional 1985. **World ranking** 104 (94).

1985	v Wilkinson	2-6	1st round	Australian Championship
	v Burke	9-5	1st round	Coral UK Open
	v Bradley	3-9	2nd round	Coral UK Open
1986	v Watterson	2-5	2nd round	Mercantile Credit Classic
	v Demarco	5-1	1st round	Dulux British Open
	v Meadowcroft	5-2	2nd round	Dulux British Open
	v Wildman	4-5	3rd round	Dulux British Open
	v Gibson	4-10	Qualifying	Embassy World Championship
	v Foldvari	3-6	2nd round	Australian Championship
	v Everton	5-3	1st round	BCE International
	v Gauvreau	1-5	2nd round	BCE International
	v Kearney	3-5	1st round	Rothmans Grand Prix
	v Mienie	9-6	1st round	Tennents UK Open
	v O'Kane	5-9	2nd round	Tennents UK Open
1987	v Parkin	5-2	1st round	Mercantile Credit Classic
	v Scott	5-4	2nd round	Mercantile Credit Classic
	v S. Davis	0-5	3rd round	Mercantile Credit Classic
	v Rowswell	1-5	1st round	Dulux British Open

	v Grace	10-9	Qualifying	Embassy World Championship
	v Murphy	4-10	Qualifying	Embassy World Championship
	v King	4-6	Quarter-final	Australian Championship
	v Whitthread	5-1	1st round	Fidelity International
	v Wych	4-5	2nd round	Fidelity International
	v Anderson	2-5	1st round	Rothmans Grand Prix
	v Gary Wilkinson	3-9	1st round	Tennents UK Open
1988	v A. Harris	4-5	1st round	Mercantile Credit Classic
	v J. Smith	5-3	1st round	MIM Britannia British Open
	v O'Boye	1-5	2nd round	MIM Britannia British Open

JOE JOHNSON (England)

Born 29.7.52. **Turned professional** 1979. **World ranking** 11 (5). **Amateur career** Runner-up 1978 World Championship. **Best professional performances** Winner 1986 Embassy World Championship; runner-up 1987 Embassy World Championship.

1979	v Werbeniuk	3-9	2nd round	Coral UK Championship
1980	v Dunning	9-6	Qualifying	Coral UK Championship
	v Fagan	4-9	1st round	Coral UK Championship
1981	v Knowles	9-2	Qualifying	John Courage English
	Johnson wo		1st round	John Courage English
	v Edmonds	5-9	2nd round	John Courage English
	v Meo	8-9	Qualifying	Embassy World Championship
	v Donnelly	5-4	Qualifying	Jameson International
	v Macleod	5-1	Qualifying	Jameson International
	v Wych	5-2	1st round	Jameson International
	v Miles	3-5	2nd round	Jameson International
	v Murphy	9-1	Qualifying	Coral UK Championship
	v Watterson	9-3	Qualifying	Coral UK Championship
	v Wilson	9-5	Qualifying	Coral UK Championship
	v Spencer	9-5	2nd round	Coral UK Championship
	v Reardon	7-9	3rd round	Coral UK Championship
1982	v Harris	9-4	Qualifying	Embassy World Championship
	v Hallett	8-9	Qualifying	Embassy World Championship
	v Wilson	4-5	Qualifying	Jameson International
	v Miles	5-1	1st round	Professional Players Tournament
	v Stevens	5-1	2nd round	Professional Players Tournament
	v Wildman	5-4	3rd round	Professional Players Tournament
	v Virgo	1-5	Quarter-final	Professional Players Tournament
	v V. Harris	9-8	Qualifying	Coral UK Championship
	v Griffiths	1-9	1st round	Coral UK Championship
1983	v Watchorn	10-0	Qualifying	Embassy World Championship
	v Wilson	8-10	Qualifying	Embassy World Championship
	v D. Hughes	5-1	Qualifying	Jameson International
	v Charlton	2-5	1st round	Jameson International
	v Burke	5-3	1st round	Professional Players Tournament
	v White	5-3	2nd round	Professional Players Tournament
	v Charlton	5-0	3rd round	Professional Players Tournament
	v Thorburn	5-1	Quarter-final	Professional Players Tournament
	v Meo	9-6	Semi-final	Professional Players Tournament
	v Knowles	8-9	Final	Professional Players Tournament
	v Gibson	9-6	Qualifying	Coral UK Championship
	v Virgo	9-6	1st round	Coral UK Championship
	v David Taylor	9-3	2nd round	Coral UK Championship
	v Griffiths	2-9	Quarter-final	Coral UK Championship
1984	v Spencer	4-5	Qualifying	Lada Classic
	v Gibson	10-3	Qualifying	Embassy World Championship
	v Dennis Taylor	1-10	1st round	Embassy World Championship
	v Morra	5-0	Qualifying	Jameson International
	v Charlton	5-1	1st round	Jameson International

Joe Johnson

v Dennis Taylor	2-5	2nd round	Jameson International
v Medati	5-1	1st round	Rothmans Grand Prix
v Williamson	4-5	2nd round	Rothmans Grand Prix
v John Rea	9-6	Qualifying	Coral UK Open
v Spencer	9-6	1st round	Coral UK Open
v Stevens	2-9	2nd round	Coral UK Open
1985 v Edmonds	5-4	Qualifying	Mercantile Credit Classic
v Knowles	5-1	1st round	Mercantile Credit Classic
v Wilson	5-0	2nd round	Mercantile Credit Classic
v King	5-3	Quarter-final	Mercantile Credit Classic
v Thorburn	2-9	Semi-final	Mercantile Credit Classic
v Scott	9-1	1st round	Tolly Cobbold English Championship
v Virgo	4-9	2nd round	Tolly Cobbold English Championship
v W. Jones	5-6	1st round	Dulux British Open
v G. Foulds	10-6	Qualifying	Embassy World Championship
v Werbeniuk	8-10	1st round	Embassy World Championship
v White	4-5	Quarter-final	Winfield Australian Masters
v Jim Bear	5-1	3rd round	Goya Matchroom Trophy
v Bradley	5-2	4th round	Goya Matchroom Trophy
v Wilson	5-1	5th round	Goya Matchroom Trophy
v N. Foulds	2-5	Quarter-final	Goya Matchroom Trophy
v Gilbert	5-2	3rd round	Rothmans Grand Prix
v Hallett	5-4	4th round	Rothmans Grand Prix
v Thorburn	1-5	5th round	Rothmans Grand Prix
v Simngam	9-4	3rd round	Coral UK Open
v N. Foulds	8-9	4th round	Coral UK Open
1986 v B. Harris	5-4	3rd round	Mercantile Credit Classic
v Mans	5-2	4th round	Mercantile Credit Classic
v E. Hughes	5-1	5th round	Mercantile Credit Classic
v Thorburn	4-5	Quarter-final	Mercantile Credit Classic
v Thorburn	3-5	1st round	Benson & Hedges Masters
v Fowler	9-7	3rd round	Tolly Cobbold English Championship
v Spencer	9-7	4th round	Tolly Cobbold English Championship
v Hallett	6-9	Quarter-final	Tolly Cobbold English Championship
v J. McLaughlin	5-2	3rd round	Dulux British Open
v Werbeniuk	5-2	4th round	Dulux British Open
v Martin	10-3	1st round	Embassy World Championship
v Hallett	13-6	2nd round	Embassy World Championship
v Griffiths	13-12	Quarter-final	Embassy World Championship
v Knowles	16-8	Semi-final	Embassy World Championship
v S. Davis	**18-12**	**Final**	**Embassy World Championship**
v Dennis Taylor	3-5	1st round	Carlsberg Challenge
v Higgins	2-5	1st round	Langs Scottish Masters
v Murphy	5-4	3rd round	BCE International
v David Taylor	3-5	4th round	BCE International
v Browne	2-5	3rd round	Rothmans Grand Prix
v Higgins	3-5	1st round	BCE Canadian Masters
v Parrott	1-9	3rd round	Tennents UK Open
1987 v Sinclair	5-0	3rd round	Mercantile Credit Classic
v P. Francisco	3-5	4th round	Mercantile Credit Classic
v Reardon	5-2	1st round	Benson & Hedges Masters
v Higgins	1-5	Quarter-final	Benson & Hedges Masters
v Miles	6-3	3rd round	Tolly Ales English Championship
v James	6-2	4th round	Tolly Ales English Championship
v Williams	6-5	Quarter-final	Tolly Ales English Championship
v Dodd	5-9	Semi-final	Tolly Ales English Championship
v Drago	5-0	3rd round	Dulux British Open
v E. Hughes	5-3	4th round	Dulux British Open
v Spencer	3-5	5th round	Dulux British Open
v Griffiths	0-5	Quarter-final	Benson & Hedges Irish Masters
v E. Hughes	10-9	1st round	Embassy World Championship
v Macleod	13-7	2nd round	Embassy World Championship
v Hendry	13-12	Quarter-final	Embassy World Championship

v N. Foulds	16-9	Semi-final	Embassy World Championship
v S. Davis	14-18	Final	Embassy World Championship
v N. Foulds	5-4	1st round	Carling Champions
v Dennis Taylor	5-8	Final	Carling Champions
v Hendry	5-2	1st round	Langs Scottish Masters
v Thorburn	6-3	Semi-final	Langs Scottish Masters
v Griffiths	**9-7**	**Final**	**Langs Scottish Masters**
v Wych	4-5	3rd round	Fidelity International
v James	5-4	3rd round	Rothmans Grand Prix
v P. Francisco	2-5	4th round	Rothmans Grand Prix
v Thorburn	3-5	1st round	Labatts Canadian Masters (WS)
v Bear	9-5	3rd round	Tennents UK Open
v West	9-6	4th round	Tennents UK Open
v Chappel	9-4	5th round	Tennents UK Open
v Hallett	9-7	Quarter-final	Tennents UK Open
v White	4-9	Semi-final	Tennents UK Open
1988 v Chappel	5-2	3rd round	Mercantile Credit Classic
v Hendry	3-5	4th round	Mercantile Credit Classic
v Thorne	5-4	1st round	Benson & Hedges Masters
v White	5-3	Quarter-final	Benson & Hedges Masters
v S. Davis	3-6	Semi-final	Benson & Hedges Masters
v J. Smith	6-5	3rd round	English Championship
v Martin	6-4	4th round	English Championship
v Knowles	6-4	Quarter-final	English Championship
v Reynolds	8-9	Semi-final	English Championship
v Lawlor	5-1	3rd round	MIM Britannia British Open
v Rowswell	5-2	4th round	MIM Britannia British Open
v O'Kane	2-5	5th round	MIM Britannia British Open
v E. Hughes	5-4	1st round	Benson & Hedges Irish Masters
v S. Davis	0-5	Quarter-final	Benson & Hedges Irish Masters
v Wilson	10-7	1st round	Embassy World Championship
v James	9-13	2nd round	Embassy World Championship

TONY JONES (England)

Born 15.4.60. **Turned professional** 1983. **World ranking** 49 (46). **Amateur career** 1983 English champion. **Best professional performance** Last 16 1988 MIM Britannia British Open.

1983 v Oliver	5-2	Qualifying	Professional Players Tournament
v Werbeniuk	4-5	1st round	Professional Players Tournament
v Sinclair	9-3	Qualifying	Coral UK Championship
v Knowles	5-9	1st round	Coral UK Championship
1984 v King	9-10	Qualifying	Embassy World Championship
v French	5-1	Qualifying	Jameson International
v Duggan	2-5	Qualifying	Jameson International
v Sinclair	5-4	Qualifying	Rothmans Grand Prix
v Griffiths	5-3	1st round	Rothmans Grand Prix
v N. Foulds	0-5	2nd round	Rothmans Grand Prix
v Chaperon	9-1	Qualifying	Coral UK Open
v Fagan	9-2	Qualifying	Coral UK Open
v Wildman	9-2	Qualifying	Coral UK Open
v Higgins	7-9	1st round	Coral UK Open
1985 v Greaves	5-2	Qualifying	Mercantile Credit Classic
v Gibson	5-0	Qualifying	Mercantile Credit Classic
v Dodd	5-1	Qualifying	Mercantile Credit Classic
v S. Francisco	1-5	Qualifying	Mercantile Credit Classic
v Houlihan	9-1	Qualifying	Tolly Cobbold English Championship
v Williams	6-9	1st round	Tolly Cobbold English Championship
v G. Foulds	6-0	Qualifying	Dulux British Open
v White	5-6	1st round	Dulux British Open
v Darrington	10-2	Qualifying	Embassy World Championship

v Duggan	10-8	Qualifying	Embassy World Championship
v Fitzmaurice	10-4	Qualifying	Embassy World Championship
v Sinclair	10-2	Qualifying	Embassy World Championship
v Knowles	8-10	1st round	Embassy World Championship
v Kelly	5-3	2nd round	Goya Matchroom Trophy
v David Taylor	4-5	3rd round	Goya Matchroom Trophy
v Houlihan	5-4	2nd round	Rothmans Grand Prix
v Meo	2-5	3rd round	Rothmans Grand Prix
v Jonik	9-4	2nd round	Coral UK Open
v Griffiths	5-9	3rd round	Coral UK Open
1986 v Gilbert	5-3	2nd round	Mercantile Credit Classic
v Thorne	5-3	3rd round	Mercantile Credit Classic
v Werbeniuk	3-5	4th round	Mercantile Credit Classic
v B. Harris	9-5	2nd round	Tolly Cobbold English Championship
v Virgo	7-9	3rd round	Tolly Cobbold English Championship
v O'Boye	5-2	2nd round	Dulux British Open
v S. Francisco	2-5	3rd round	Dulux British Open
v V. Harris	10-7	Qualifying	Embassy World Championship
v Gilbert	7-10	Qualifying	Embassy World Championship
v Burke	4-5	2nd round	BCE International
v Smith	5-0	2nd round	Rothmans Grand Prix
v White	0-5	3rd round	Rothmans Grand Prix
v Fitzmaurice	9-0	2nd round	Tennents UK Open
v West	9-4	3rd round	Tennents UK Open
v Knowles	2-9	4th round	Tennents UK Open
1987 v Oliver	5-0	2nd round	Mercantile Credit Classic
v Parrott	2-5	3rd round	Mercantile Credit Classic
v Oliver	6-1	2nd round	Tolly Ales English Championship
v Williams	4-6	3rd round	Tolly Ales English Championship
v Donnelly	5-2	2nd round	Dulux British Open
v Macleod	5-4	3rd round	Dulux British Open
v Griffiths	3-5	4th round	Dulux British Open
v Chalmers	10-1	Qualifying	Embassy World Championship
v Van Rensberg	10-0	Qualifying	Embassy World Championship
v Virgo	9-10	Qualifying	Embassy World Championship
v P. Gibson	4-5	2nd round	Fidelity International
v Roscoe	5-1	2nd round	Rothmans Grand Prix
v Thorburn	2-5	3rd round	Rothmans Grand Prix
v James	9-6	2nd round	Tennents UK Open
v Hallett	2-9	3rd round	Tennents UK Open
1988 v A. Harris	5-2	2nd round	Mercantile Credit Classic
v Higgins	0-5	3rd round	Mercantile Credit Classic
v J. Smith	0-5	2nd round	English Championship
v Fitzmaurice	5-3	2nd round	MIM Britannia British Open
v Higgins	5-3	3rd round	MIM Britannia British Open
v Chaperon	5-4	4th round	MIM Britannia British Open
v Hendry	3-5	5th round	MIM Britannia British Open
v Foldvari	9-10	Qualifying	Embassy World Championship

WAYNE JONES (Wales)

Born 24.12.59. **Turned professional** 1984. **World ranking** 34 (34). **Amateur career** 1983 Welsh champion. **Best professional performance** Quarter-finals 1986 Tennents UK Open.

1984 v Watchorn	5-0	Qualifying	Jameson International
v Gibson	5-2	Qualifying	Jameson International
v Scott	5-0	Qualifying	Jameson International
v Wildman	5-0	Qualifying	Jameson International
v David Taylor	4-5	1st round	Jameson International
v Watterson	5-3	Qualifying	Rothmans Grand Prix
v Campbell	4-5	1st round	Rothmans Grand Prix

	v O'Kane	7-9	Qualifying	Coral UK Open
1985	v O'Kane	5-0	Qualifying	Mercantile Credit Classic
	v Duggan	0-5	Qualifying	Mercantile Credit Classic
	v Donnelly	6-1	Qualifying	Dulux British Open
	v Johnson	6-5	1st round	Dulux British Open
	v Chaperon	2-5	2nd round	Dulux British Open
	v Jack Rea	10-3	Qualifying	Embassy World Championship
	v Dunning	10-6	Qualifying	Embassy World Championship
	v Watterson	10-5	Qualifying	Embassy World Championship
	v Miles	10-8	Qualifying	Embassy World Championship
	v White	4-10	1st round	Embassy World Championship
	v Newbury	2-6	1st round	BCE Welsh Championship
	v Smith	5-3	2nd round	Goya Matchroom Trophy
	v Parrott	3-5	3rd round	Goya Matchroom Trophy
	v John Rea	5-0	2nd round	Rothmans Grand Prix
	v Thorne	5-0	3rd round	Rothmans Grand Prix
	v P. Francisco	3-5	4th round	Rothmans Grand Prix
	v Fitzmaurice	9-3	2nd round	Coral UK Open
	v Virgo	7-9	3rd round	Coral UK Open
1986	v Van Rensberg	4-5	2nd round	Mercantile Credit Classic
	v Everton	6-2	1st round	Zetters Welsh Championship
	v Reardon	6-4	Quarter-final	Zetters Welsh Championship
	v Mountjoy	7-9	Semi-final	Zetters Welsh Championship
	v Rigitano	5-1	2nd round	Dulux British Open
	v Mans	2-5	3rd round	Dulux British Open
	v Grace	10-3	Qualifying	Embassy World Championship
	v Hendry	8-10	Qualifying	Embassy World Championship
	v Jack Rea	5-1	2nd round	BCE International
	v Reardon	4-5	3rd round	BCE International
	v Foldvari	5-3	2nd round	Rothmans Grand Prix
	v David Taylor	5-1	3rd round	Rothmans Grand Prix
	v S. Francisco	4-5	4th round	Rothmans Grand Prix
	v Hargreaves	9-0	2nd round	Tennents UK Open
	v Campbell	9-3	3rd round	Tennents UK Open
	v Dennis Taylor	9-2	4th round	Tennents UK Open
	v E. Hughes	9-5	5th round	Tennents UK Open
	v Higgins	5-9	Quarter-final	Tennents UK Open
1987	v Everton	5-0	2nd round	Mercantile Credit Classic
	v Dennis Taylor	5-2	3rd round	Mercantile Credit Classic
	v Kearney	5-1	4th round	Mercantile Credit Classic
	v Wilson	3-5	5th round	Mercantile Credit Classic
	v M. Bennett	6-3	1st round	Matchroom Welsh Championship
	v Griffiths	2-6	Quarter-final	Matchroom Welsh Championship
	v Gilbert	3-5	2nd round	Dulux British Open
	v Donnelly	10-3	Qualifying	Embassy World Championship
	v M. Bennett	3-10	Qualifying	Embassy World Championship
	v Dunning	5-1	2nd round	Fidelity International
	v Reynolds	5-4	3rd round	Fidelity International
	v N. Gilbert	4-5	4th round	Fidelity International
	v Donnelly	5-3	2nd round	Rothmans Grand Prix
	v Stevens	1-5	3rd round	Rothmans Grand Prix
	v Meakin	9-1	2nd round	Tennents UK Open
	v Wilson	6-9	3rd round	Tennents UK Open
1988	v Roscoe	4-5	2nd round	Mercantile Credit Classic
	v Reardon	6-5	Quarter-final	Welsh Championship
	v Mountjoy	9-5	Semi-final	Welsh Championship
	v Griffiths	3-9	Final	Welsh Championship
	v John Rea	5-3	2nd round	MIM Britannia British Open
	v Campbell	3-5	3rd round	MIM Britannia British Open
	v Glen Wilkinson	10-4	Qualifying	Embassy World Championship
	v Morra	10-8	Qualifying	Embassy World Championship
	v Martin	10-5	Qualifying	Embassy World Championship
	v N. Foulds	7-10	1st round	Embassy World Championship

FRANK JONIK (Canada)

Born 2.12.57. **Turned professional** 1979. **World ranking** 106 (96).

Year	Opponent	Score	Round	Tournament
1980	v Wildman	9-7	Qualifying	Embassy World Championship
	v Wilson	6-9	Qualifying	Embassy World Championship
1981	v Hallett	1-9	Qualifying	Embassy World Championship
1982	v John Bear	4-9	Qualifying	Embassy World Championship
	v Hallett	2-5	Qualifying	Jameson International
	v Mountjoy	5-3	1st round	Professional Players Tournament
	v Meo	0-5	2nd round	Professional Players Tournament
1983	v Edmonds	4-10	Qualifying	Embassy World Championship
	v Chaperon	9-4	2nd round	Canadian Championship
	v Wych	9-5	Quarter-final	Canadian Championship
	v Thorburn	9-6	Semi-final	Canadian Championship
	v Stevens	**8-9**	**Final**	**Canadian Championship**
	v Wildman	4-5	1st round	Professional Players Tournament
1984	v Mikkelsen	9-10	Qualifying	Embassy World Championship
	v J. McLaughlin	5-2	Qualifying	Jameson International
	v Gauvreau	1-5	Qualifying	Jameson International
	v Bradley	1-5	Qualifying	Rothmans Grand Prix
	v Newbury	3-9	Qualifying	Coral UK Open
1985	v G. Foulds	2-5	Qualifying	Mercantile Credit Classic
	v J. McLaughlin	6-2	Qualifying	Dulux British Open
	v Spencer	0-6	1st round	Dulux British Open
	v O'Kane	5-10	Qualifying	Embassy World Championship
	v Mikkelsen	6-4	Quarter-final	Canadian Championship
	v Chaperon	3-6	Semi-final	Canadian Championship
	v Newbury	4-5	2nd round	Goya Matchroom Trophy
	v Fowler	4-5	2nd round	Rothmans Grand Prix
	v T. Jones	4-9	2nd round	Coral UK Open
1986	v P. Francisco	2-5	2nd round	Mercantile Credit Classic
	v Dodd	4-5	2nd round	Dulux British Open
	v Chaperon	8-10	Qualifying	Embassy World Championship
	v Rigitano	6-1	1st round	Canadian Championship
	v Chaperon	6-3	2nd round	Canadian Championship
	v Thorburn	3-6	Semi-final	Canadian Championship
	v Miles	1-5	2nd round	Rothmans Grand Prix
	v Wilkinson	8-9	1st round	Tennents UK Open
1987	v James	5-4	1st round	Mercantile Credit Classic
	v Drago	5-2	2nd round	Mercantile Credit Classic
	v West	4-5	3rd round	Mercantile Credit Classic
	v Owers	4-5	1st round	Dulux British Open
	v Morra	2-6	Quarter-final	Canadian Championship
	v N. Gilbert	5-3	1st round	Rothmans Grand Prix
	v Chappel	4-5	2nd round	Rothmans Grand Prix
	v M. Smith	5-9	1st round	Tennents UK Open
1988	v Dunning	2-5	1st round	Mercantile Credit Classic
	v Wildman	4-5	2nd round	Mercantile Credit Classic
	v Dunning	3-5	1st round	MIM Britannia British Open

TONY KEARNEY (Republic of Ireland)

Born 24.6.54. **Turned professional** 1984. **World ranking** 80 (66). **Amateur career** 1981 Republic of Ireland champion. **Best professional performance** Last 32 1987 Mercantile Credit Classic.

Year	Opponent	Score	Round	Tournament
1984	v Burke	4-5	Qualifying	Jameson International
	v Chaperon	1-5	Qualifying	Rothmans Grand Prix
	v Murphy	2-9	Qualifying	Coral UK Open
1985	v French	5-1	Qualifying	Mercantile Credit Classic
	v Williamson	3-5	Qualifying	Mercantile Credit Classic

	v Watterson	6-4	Qualifying	Dulux British Open
	v S. Francisco	4-6	1st round	Dulux British Open
	v Burke	4-6	Qualifying	Irish Championship
	v Anderson	8-10	Qualifying	Embassy World Championship
	v D. Hughes	1-5	1st round	Goya Matchroom Trophy
	v Jim Bear	5-3	1st round	Rothmans Grand Prix
	v Edmonds	2-5	2nd round	Rothmans Grand Prix
	v D. Hughes	8-9	1st round	Coral UK Open
1986	v Jim Bear	5-0	1st round	Mercantile Credit Classic
	v Medati	2-5	2nd round	Mercantile Credit Classic
	v Smith	5-2	1st round	Dulux British Open
	v Foldvari	5-2	2nd round	Dulux British Open
	v Wilkinson	10-5	Qualifying	Embassy World Championship
	v Scott	8-10	Qualifying	Embassy World Championship
	v Fagan	5-0	1st round	Strongbow Irish Championship
	v Murphy	2-6	Quarter-final	Strongbow Irish Championship
	v Medati	3-5	2nd round	BCE International
	v Jenkins	5-3	1st round	Rothmans Grand Prix
	v Chappel	1-5	2nd round	Rothmans Grand Prix
	v Dunning	6-9	1st round	Tennents UK Open
1987	v Agrawal	5-0	1st round	Mercantile Credit Classic
	v Wildman	5-3	2nd round	Mercantile Credit Classic
	v Macleod	5-0	3rd round	Mercantile Credit Classic
	v W. Jones	1-5	4th round	Mercantile Credit Classic
	v Chappel	3-5	2nd round	Dulux British Open
	v Medati	8-10	Qualifying	Embassy World Championship
	v Murphy	5-1	1st round	Matchroom Irish Championship
	v E. Hughes	1-6	Quarter-final	Matchroom Irish Championship
	v Foldvari	1-5	2nd round	Fidelity International
	v Darrington	5-0	2nd round	Rothmans Grand Prix
	v Griffiths	0-5	3rd round	Rothmans Grand Prix
	v Fowler	7-9	2nd round	Tennents UK Open
1988	v Newbury	1-5	2nd round	Mercantile Credit Classic
	v Fagan	5-3	1st round	Irish Championship
	v Dennis Taylor	3-6	Quarter-final	Irish Championship
	v Fowler	1-5	2nd round	MIM Britannia British Open
	v Kelly	4-10	Qualifying	Embassy World Championship

BILLY KELLY (Republic of Ireland)

Born 1.5.45. **Turned professional** 1981. **World ranking** 110 (103).

	v Macleod	1-5	Qualifying	Jameson International
	v G. Foulds	7-9	Qualifying	Coral UK Championship
1982	v Sinclair	8-9	Qualifying	Embassy World Championship
	v G. Foulds	5-4	Qualifying	Jameson International
	v Williamson	5-1	Qualifying	Jameson International
	v Higgins	3-5	1st round	Jameson International
	v Wych	0-5	1st round	Professional Players Tournament
	v Fitzmaurice	8-0 retd	Qualifying	Coral UK Championship
	v Virgo	2-9	1st round	Coral UK Championship
1983	v Dennis Taylor	0-6	Quarter-final	Irish Championship
	v Demarco	10-4	Qualifying	Embassy World Championship
	v S. Francisco	5-10	Qualifying	Embassy World Championship
	v F. Davis	1-5	Qualifying	Jameson International
	v Hallett	0-5	1st round	Professional Players Tournament
1984	v Burke	7-10	Qualifying	Embassy World Championship
	v Hargreaves	5-2	Qualifying	Jameson International
	v King	5-4	Qualifying	Jameson International
	v S. Francisco	3-5	Qualifying	Jameson International
	v O'Kane	4-5	Qualifying	Rothmans Grand Prix
	v Bradley	6-9	Qualifying	Coral UK Open

	v Bales	3-5	Qualifying	Mercantile Credit Classic
	v P. Francisco	3-6	Qualifying	Dulux British Open
	v Watchorn	6-2	Qualifying	Irish Championship
	v E. Hughes	2-6	Quarter-final	Irish Championship
	v Rigitano	6-10	Qualifying	Embassy World Championship
1985	v P. Francisco	3-6	Qualifying	Dulux British Open
	v Watchorn	6-2	Qualifying	Irish Championship
	v E. Hughes	2-6	Quarter-final	Irish Championship
	v Rigitano	6-10	Qualifying	Embassy World Championship
	v T. Jones	3-5	2nd round	Goya Matchroom Trophy
	v Donnelly	5-4	2nd round	Rothmans Grand Prix
	v S. Francisco	2-5	3rd round	Rothmans Grand Prix
	v Medati	1-9	2nd round	Coral UK Open
1986	v F. Davis	3-5	2nd round	Mercantile Credit Classic
	v F. Davis	4-5	2nd round	Dulux British Open
	v Edmonds	0-10	Qualifying	Embassy World Championship
	v Jack Rea	5-0	1st round	Strongbow Irish Championship
	v Dennis Taylor	1-6	Quarter-final	Strongbow Irish Championship
	v Whitthread	5-1	1st round	BCE International
	v Van Rensberg	1-5	2nd round	BCE International
	v Parkin	5-2	1st round	Rothmans Grand Prix
	v V. Harris	3-5	2nd round	Rothmans Grand Prix
	v Watchorn	8-9	1st round	Tennents UK Open
1987	v Jack Rea	3-5	1st round	Mercantile Credit Classic
	v B. Bennett	5-2	1st round	Dulux British Open
	v B. Harris	2-5	2nd round	Dulux British Open
	v B. Bennett	10-0	Qualifying	Embassy World Championship
	v Gibson	9-10	Qualifying	Embassy World Championship
	v O'Boye	0-5	1st round	Matchroom Irish Championship
	v Darrington	5-4	1st round	Fidelity International
	v Wright	2-5	2nd round	Fidelity International
	v Dodd	2-5	2nd round	Rothmans Grand Prix
	v Williamson	5-9	1st round	Tennents UK Open
1988	v Roe	1-5	1st round	Mercantile Credit Classic
	v Murphy	1-5	1st round	Irish Championship
	v Meadowcroft	1-5	1st round	MIM Britannia British Open
	v Kearney	10-4	Qualifying	Embassy World Championship
	v Browne	8-10	Qualifying	Embassy World Championship

WARREN KING (Australia)

Born 1.4.55. **Turned professional** 1982. **World ranking** 44 (39). **Amateur career** Australian champion 1980, 1981. **Best professional performances** Last 32 1987, 1988 Embassy World Championship, 1985 Goya Matchroom Trophy, 1986 BCE International, 1986 Rothmans Grand Prix, 1987 Dulux British Open; 1986, 1987 Australian champion.

	v Anderson	10-6	Qualifying	Embassy World Championship
1983	v Hallett	6-10	Qualifying	Embassy World Championship
	v Black	5-3	Qualifying	Jameson International
	v Miles	3-5	Qualifying	Jameson International
	v B. Harris	5-3	Qualifying	Professional Players Tournament
	v Meo	2-5	1st round	Professional Players Tournament
1984	v Jones	10-9	Qualifying	Embassy World Championship
	v Watterson	10-8	Qualifying	Embassy World Championship
	v Martin	10-8	Qualifying	Embassy World Championship
	v S. Davis	3-10	1st round	Embassy World Championship
	v Kelly	4-5	Qualifying	Jameson International
	v Greaves	5-0	Qualifying	Rothmans Grand Prix
	v Macleod	4-5	1st round	Rothmans Grand Prix
	v Browne	9-5	Qualifying	Coral UK Open
	v Virgo	9-4	Qualifying	Coral UK Open
	v Dennis Taylor	5-9	1st round	Coral UK Open

1985	v Duggan	5-4	Qualifying	Mercantile Credit Classic
	v Reynolds	5-2	Qualifying	Mercantile Credit Classic
	v Spencer	5-2	1st round	Mercantile Credit Classic
	v White	5-2	2nd round	Mercantile Credit Classic
	v Johnson	3-5	Quarter-final	Mercantile Credit Classic
	v Medati	6-4	Qualifying	Dulux British Open
	v Reardon	5-6	1st round	Dulux British Open
	v Medati	9-10	Qualifying	Embassy World Championship
	v Anderson	8-2	Quarter-final	Australian Championship
	v Campbell	6-9	Semi-final	Australian Championship
	v Caggianello	5-0	2nd round	Goya Matchroom Trophy
	v Williams	5-3	3rd round	Goya Matchroom Trophy
	v White	2-5	4th round	Goya Matchroom Trophy
	v Drago	4-5	2nd round	Rothmans Grand Prix
	v D. Hughes	9-0	2nd round	Coral UK Open
	v Williams	5-9	3rd round	Coral UK Open
1986	v Duggan	5-2	2nd round	Mercantile Credit Classic
	v Mountjoy	4-5	3rd round	Mercantile Credit Classic
	v John Rea	1-5	2nd round	Dulux British Open
	v Sheehan	10-4	Qualifying	Embassy World Championship
	v Roscoe	10-5	Qualifying	Embassy World Championship
	v Reynolds	7-10	Qualifying	Embassy World Championship
	v Charlton	8-6	Semi-final	Australian Championship
	v Campbell	**10-3**	**Final**	**Australian Championship**
	v Rigitano	5-0	2nd round	BCE International
	v Longworth	5-0	3rd round	BCE International
	v S. Davis	4-5	4th round	BCE International
	v Donnelly	5-2	2nd round	Rothmans Grand Prix
	v Werbeniuk	5-2	3rd round	Rothmans Grand Prix
	v Thorne	2-5	4th round	Rothmans Grand Prix
	v James	9-8	2nd round	Tennents UK Open
	v Hallett	5-9	3rd round	Tennents UK Open
1987	v Burke	5-0	2nd round	Mercantile Credit Classic
	v Reynolds	4-5	3rd round	Mercantile Credit Classic
	v Williamson	5-3	2nd round	Dulux British Open
	v Parrott	5-1	3rd round	Dulux British Open
	v N. Foulds	4-5	4th round	Dulux British Open
	v Roe	10-4	Qualifying	Embassy World Championship
	v Owers	10-4	Qualifying	Embassy World Championship
	v Charlton	10-4	Qualifying	Embassy World Championship
	v S. Davis	7-10	1st round	Embassy World Championship
	v Jenkins	6-4	Quarter-final	Australian Championship
	v Foldvari	8-1	Semi-final	Australian Championship
	v Charlton	**10-7**	**Final**	**Australian Championship**
	v M. Smith	5-3	2nd round	Fidelity International
	v S. Francisco	2-5	3rd round	Fidelity International
	v Foldvari	4-5	2nd round	Rothmans Grand Prix
	v Meadowcroft	9-4	2nd round	Tennents UK Open
	v S. Davis	2-9	3rd round	Tennents UK Open
1988	v Oliver	3-5	2nd round	Mercantile Credit Classic
	v James	2-5	2nd round	MIM Britannia British Open
	v Watchorn	10-4	Qualifying	Embassy World Championship
	v Clark	10-9	Qualifying	Embassy World Championship
	v Spencer	10-7	Qualifying	Embassy World Championship
	v Parrott	4-10	1st round	Embassy World Championship

TONY KNOWLES (England)

Born 13.6.55. **Turned professional** 1980. **World ranking** 8 (7). **Best professional performances** Winner 1982 Jameson International, 1983 Professional Players Tournament.

1980	v Andrewartha	8-9	Qualifying	Coral UK Championship
1981	v Johnson	2-9	Qualifying	John Courage English Professional

	v Ross	7-0	Qualifying	Embassy World Championship
	v Wych	9-3	Qualifying	Embassy World Championship
	v Miles	8-10	1st round	Embassy World Championship
	v Hallet	5-2	1st round	Jameson International
	v Virgo	2-5	2nd round	Jameson International
	v G. Foulds	9-1	Qualifying	Coral UK Championship
	v F. Davis	9-6	2nd round	Coral UK Championship
	v Mountjoy	9-6	3rd round	Coral UK Championship
	v Griffiths	5-9	Quarter-final	Coral UK Championship
1982	v Dennis Taylor	2-5	Semi-final	Tolly Cobbold Classic
	v E. Hughes	9-7	Qualifying	Embassy World Championship
	v S. Davis	10-1	1st round	Embassy World Championship
	v Miles	13-7	2nd round	Embassy World Championship
	v Charlton	11-13	Quarter-final	Embassy World Championship
	v S. Davis	4-5	1st round	Langs Scottish Masters
	v Sinclair	5-2	1st round	Jameson International
	v Reardon	5-2	2nd round	Jameson International
	v Wilson	5-4	Quarter-final	Jameson International
	v Stevens	9-8	Semi-final	Jameson International
	v David Taylor	**9-6**	**Final**	**Jameson International**
	v Houlihan	5-4	1st round	Professional Players Tournament
	v Wilson	4-5	2nd round	Professional Players Tournament
	v Donnelly	9-6	1st round	Coral UK Championship
	v Spencer	6-9	2nd round	Coral UK Championship
1983	v Stevens	0-5	1st round	Lada Classic
	v Mountjoy	1-5	1st round	Benson & Hedges Irish Masters
	v Miles	10-3	1st round	Embassy World Championship
	v Reardon	13-12	2nd round	Embassy World Championship
	v Meo	13-9	Quarter-final	Embassy World Championship
	v Thorburn	15-16	Semi-final	Embassy World Championship
	v Werbeniuk	0-5	Semi-final	Winfield Masters
	v Meo	5-4	1st round	Langs Scottish Masters
	v Thorburn	6-2	Semi-final	Langs Scottish Masters
	v S. Davis	6-9	Final	Langs Scottish Masters
	v Edmonds	5-1	1st round	Jameson International
	v Spencer	4-5	2nd round	Jameson International
	v Medati	5-1	1st round	Professional Players Tournament
	v Williams	5-4	2nd round	Professional Players Tournament
	v S. Francisco	5-0	3rd round	Professional Players Tournament
	v Campbell	5-3	Quarter-final	Professional Players Tournament
	v Thorne	9-7	Semi-final	Professional Players Tournament
	v Johnson	**9-8**	**Final**	**Professional Players Tournament**
	v T. Jones	9-5	1st round	Coral UK Championship
	v Mountjoy	9-5	2nd round	Coral UK Championship
	v Higgins	5-9	Quarter-final	Coral UK Championship
1984	v E. Hughes	5-1	Qualifying	Lada Classic
	v Hallett	5-3	1st round	Lada Classic
	v Parrott	1-5	Quarter-final	Lada Classic
	v Dennis Taylor	5-2	1st round	Benson & Hedges Masters
	v Higgins	5-1	Quarter-final	Benson & Hedges Masters
	v Griffiths	4-6	Semi-final	Benson & Hedges Masters
	v Griffiths	0-5	Quarter-final	Benson & Hedges Irish Masters
	v White	5-1	1st round	Tolly Cobbold Classic
	v Thorburn	5-3	Semi-final	Tolly Cobbold Classic
	v S. Davis	2-8	Final	Tolly Cobbold Classic
	v Parrott	7-10	1st round	Embassy World Championship
	v White	5-3	Quarter-final	Winfield Australian Masters
	v Charlton	6-0	Semi-final	Winfield Australian Masters
	v Virgo	**7-3**	**Final**	**Winfield Australian Masters**
	v Griffiths	5-3	1st round	Langs Scottish Masters
	v White	5-6	Semi-final	Langs Scottish Masters
	v Higgins	5-3	1st round	Carlsberg Challenge
	v White	7-9	Final	Carlsberg Challenge

	v Reynolds	5-1	1st round	Jameson International
	v Newbury	5-4	2nd round	Jameson International
	v White	5-4	Quarter-final	Jameson International
	v S. Francisco	9-6	Semi-final	Jameson International
	v S. Davis	2-9	Final	Jameson International
	v V. Harris	5-1	1st round	Rothmans Grand Prix
	v Dunning	5-1	2nd round	Rothmans Grand Prix
	v Williamson	5-2	3rd round	Rothmans Grand Prix
	v N. Foulds	2-5	Quarter-final	Rothmans Grand Prix
	v Gauvreau	9-5	1st round	Coral UK Open
	v Dennis Taylor	9-2	2nd round	Coral UK Open
	v Stevens	7-9	Quarter-final	Coral UK Open
1985	v Johnson	1-5	1st round	Mercantile Credit Classic
	v Mountjoy	3-5	1st round	Benson & Hedges Masters
	v Bradley	9-8	1st round	Tolly Cobbold English Championship
	v Martin	9-3	2nd round	Tolly Cobbold English Championship
	v David Taylor	9-2	Quarter-final	Tolly Cobbold English Championship
	v Longworth	9-6	Semi-final	Tolly Cobbold English Championship
	v S. Davis	2-9	Final	Tolly Cobbold English Championship
	v French	6-2	1st round	Dulux British Open
	v Longworth	5-2	2nd round	Dulux British Open
	v Meo	2-5	3rd round	Dulux British Open
	v Charlton	5-3	Quarter-final	Benson & Hedges Irish Masters
	v White	4-6	Semi-final	Benson & Hedges Irish Masters
	v T. Jones	10-8	1st round	Embassy World Championship
	v Mountjoy	13-6	2nd round	Embassy World Championship
	v White	13-10	Quarter-final	Embassy World Championship
	v Dennis Taylor	5-16	Semi-final	Embassy World Championship
	v S. Francisco	4-5	1st round	Langs Scottish Masters
	v E. McLaughlin	5-1	3rd round	Goya Matchroom Trophy
	v N. Foulds	4-5	4th round	Goya Matchroom Trophy
	v Gibson	5-1	3rd round	Rothmans Grand Prix
	v Edmonds	5-3	4th round	Rothmans Grand Prix
	v Campbell	5-2	5th round	Rothmans Grand Prix
	v Stevens	5-4	Quarter-final	Rothmans Grand Prix
	v Dennis Taylor	6-9	Semi-final	Rothmans Grand Prix
	v Reardon	5-2	1st round	BCE Canadian Masters
	v O'Boye	9-5	3rd round	Coral UK Open
	v Spencer	9-7	4th round	Coral UK Open
	v David Taylor	9-7	5th round	Coral UK Open
	v White	4-9	Quarter-final	Coral UK Open
1986	v Rigitano	5-4	3rd round	Mercantile Credit Classic
	v Macleod	5-4	4th round	Mercantile Credit Classic
	v Williams	2-5	5th round	Mercantile Credit Classic
	v White	5-3	1st round	BCE Belgian Classic
	v Griffiths	2-5	Semi-final	BCE Belgian Classic
	v S. Francisco	5-1	1st round	Benson & Hedges Masters
	v Charlton	5-4	Quarter-final	Benson & Hedges Masters
	v Thorburn	4-6	Semi-final	Benson & Hedges Masters
	v Bales	9-4	3rd round	Tolly Cobbold English Championship
	v Hallett	5-9	4th round	Tolly Cobbold English Championship
	v Williamson	5-1	3rd round	Dulux British Open
	v Wych	4-5	4th round	Dulux British Open
	v Fagan	4-5	Quarter-final	Benson & Hedges Irish Masters
	v N. Foulds	10-9	1st round	Embassy World Championship
	v S. Francisco	13-10	2nd round	Embassy World Championship
	v Stevens	13-9	Quarter-final	Embassy World Championship
	v Johnson	8-16	Semi-final	Embassy World Championship
	v Stevens	3-5	1st round	Langs Scottish Masters
	v Spencer	5-0	3rd round	BCE International
	v Charlton	5-1	4th round	BCE International
	v Wilson	4-5	5th round	BCE International
	v Roe	5-3	3rd round	Rothmans Grand Prix

Tony Knowles

	Opponent	Score	Round	Tournament
	v P. Francisco	5-3	4th round	Rothmans Grand Prix
	v Mountjoy	5-1	5th round	Rothmans Grand Prix
	v S. Francisco	2-5	Quarter-final	Rothmans Grand Prix
	v Thorburn	5-1	1st round	BCE Canadian Masters
	v Thorne	7-8	Semi-final	BCE Canadian Masters
	v John Rea	9-4	3rd round	Tennents UK Open
	v T. Jones	9-2	4th round	Tennents UK Open
	v Griffiths	9-6	5th round	Tennents UK Open
	v Parrott	4-9	Quarter-final	Tennents UK Open
1987	v Fowler	4-5	3rd round	Mercantile Credit Classic
	v S. Francisco	2-5	1st round	Benson & Hedges Masters
	v Dodd	2-6	3rd round	Tolly Ales English Championship
	v Fowler	5-4	3rd round	Dulux British Open
	v Reynolds	5-0	4th round	Dulux British Open
	v Murphy	5-3	5th round	Dulux British Open
	v Dennis Taylor	5-4	Quarter-final	Dulux British Open
	v N. Foulds	2-9	Semi-final	Dulux British Open
	v Meo	2-5	1st round	Benson & Hedges Irish Masters
	v Hallett	6-10	1st round	Embassy World Championship
	v Fowler	5-4	3rd round	Fidelity International
	v David Taylor	5-2	4th round	Fidelity International
	v Virgo	2-5	5th round	Fidelity International
	v J. McLaughlin	5-0	3rd round	Rothmans Grand Prix
	v Roe	5-2	4th round	Rothmans Grand Prix
	v Charlton	5-0	5th round	Rothmans Grand Prix
	v Hendry	2-5	Quarter-final	Rothmans Grand Prix
	v White	1-5	1st round	Labatts Canadian Masters (WS)
	v John Rea	9-6	3rd round	Tennents UK Open
	v Stevens	9-8	4th round	Tennents UK Open
	v Parrott	4-9	5th round	Tennents UK Open
1988	v Wright	5-1	3rd round	Mercantile Credit Classic
	v Roscoe	5-0	4th round	Mercantile Credit Classic
	v Murphy	5-3	5th round	Mercantile Credit Classic
	v Dennis Taylor	5-1	Quarter-final	Mercantile Credit Classic
	v Parrott	4-9	Semi-final	Mercantile Credit Classic
	v Higgins	4-5	1st round	Benson & Hedges Masters
	v Wright	6-2	3rd round	English Championship
	v Owers	6-4	4th round	English Championship
	v Johnson	4-6	Quarter-final	English Championship
	v M. Gibson	5-4	3rd round	MIM Britannia British Open
	v Macleod	4-5	4th round	MIM Britannia British Open
	v Thorne	5-3	1st round	Benson & Hedges Irish Masters
	v N. Foulds	3-5	Quarter-final	Benson & Hedges Irish Masters
	v Fowler	10-8	1st round	Embassy World Championship
	v Charlton	13-7	2nd round	Embassy World Championship
	v White	6-13	Quarter-final	Embassy World Championship

ERIC LAWLOR (England)

Born 1.7.37. **Turned professional** 1987. **World ranking** 93.

	Opponent	Score	Round	Tournament
1987	v Roscoe	4-5	1st round	Fidelity International
	v D. Gilbert	2-5	1st round	Rothmans Grand Prix
	v Fitzmaurice	9-0	1st round	Tennents UK Open
	v Wright	9-7	2nd round	Tennents UK Open
	v P. Francisco	4-9	3rd round	Tennents UK Open
1988	v Sinclair	3-5	1st round	Mercantile Credit Classic
	v Roe	6-5	1st round	English Championship
	v Bradley	6-5	2nd round	English Championship
	v Parrott	3-6	3rd round	English Championship

v Sinclair	5-3	1st round	MIM Britannia British Open
v B. Harris	5-2	2nd round	MIM Britannia British Open
v Johnson	1-5	3rd round	MIM Britannia British Open
v Newbury	3-10	Qualifying	Embassy World Championship

STEVE LONGWORTH (England)

Born 27.7.48. **Turned professional** 1984. **World ranking** 30 (31). **Amateur career** 1984 English champion. **Best professional performances** Last 16 1987 Embassy World Championship, 1985 Rothmans Grand Prix, 1986 Tennents UK Open.

1984	v Newbury	4-5	Qualifying	Jameson International
	v E. McLaughlin	2-5	Qualifying	Rothmans Grand Prix
	v Darrington	9-5	Qualifying	Coral UK Open
	v Burke	9-4	Qualifying	Coral UK Open
	v Morra	1-9	Qualifying	Coral UK Open
1985	v P. Francisco	5-4	Qualifying	Mercantile Credit Classic
	v Oliver	5-1	Qualifying	Mercantile Credit Classic
	v Fisher	5-1	Qualifying	Mercantile Credit Classic
	v N. Foulds	5-3	Qualifying	Mercantile Credit Classic
	v David Taylor	5-4	1st round	Mercantile Credit Classic
	v Thorburn	3-5	2nd round	Mercantile Credit Classic
	v Edmonds	9-4	Qualifying	Tolly Cobbold English Championship
	v Wildman	9-3	1st round	Tolly Cobbold English Championship
	v Medati	9-7	2nd round	Tolly Cobbold English Championship
	v White	9-5	Quarter-final	Tolly Cobbold English Championship
	v Knowles	6-9	Semi-final	Tolly Cobbold English Championship
	v F. Davis	6-1	Qualifying	Dulux British Open
	v Wilson	6-3	1st round	Dulux British Open
	v Knowles	2-5	2nd round	Dulux British Open
	v Giannaros	10-1	Qualifying	Embassy World Championship
	v Cripsey	10-8	Qualifying	Embassy World Championship
	v Van Rensberg	7-10	Qualifying	Embassy World Championship
	v Wilkinson	5-0	2nd round	Goya Matchroom Trophy
	v Thorburn	3-5	3rd round	Goya Matchroom Trophy
	v Hargreaves	5-2	2nd round	Rothmans Grand Prix
	v Parrott	5-2	3rd round	Rothmans Grand Prix
	v David Taylor	5-1	4th round	Rothmans Grand Prix
	v Stevens	3-5	5th round	Rothmans Grand Prix
	v Gibson	9-2	2nd round	Coral UK Open
	v Meo	5-9	3rd round	Coral UK Open
1986	v O'Boye	1-5	2nd round	Mercantile Credit Classic
	v Duggan	9-4	2nd round	Tolly Cobbold English Championship
	v Reynolds	5-9	3rd round	Tolly Cobbold English Championship
	v Houlihan	5-3	2nd round	Dulux British Open
	v E. Hughes	5-4	3rd round	Dulux British Open
	v P. Francisco	2-5	4th round	Dulux British Open
	v Watchorn	10-7	Qualifying	Embassy World Championship
	v John Rea	10-4	Qualifying	Embassy World Championship
	v Virgo	8-10	Qualifying	Embassy World Championship
	v King	0-5	3rd round	BCE International
	v Wildman	2-5	3rd round	Rothmans Grand Prix
	v Rowswell	9-3	3rd round	Tennents UK Open
	v Mountjoy	9-1	4th round	Tennents UK Open
	v Parrott	6-9	5th round	Tennents UK Open
1987	v Murphy	5-3	3rd round	Mercantile Credit Classic
	v Meo	0-5	4th round	Mercantile Credit Classic
	v James	2-6	3rd round	Tolly Ales English Championship
	v Duggan	2-5	3rd round	Dulux British Open
	v Murphy	10-2	Qualifying	Embassy World Championship
	v Stevens	10-4	1st round	Embassy World Championship

	v Hendry	7-13	2nd round	Embassy World Championship
	v Williamson	5-4	3rd round	Fidelity International
	v White	1-5	4th round	Fidelity International
	v Gary Wilkinson	4-5	3rd round	Rothmans Grand Prix
	v Werbeniuk	9-5	3rd round	Tennents UK Open
	v Chappel	6-9	4th round	Tennents UK Open
1988	v Edmonds	5-3	3rd round	Mercantile Credit Classic
	v S. Francisco	2-5	4th round	Mercantile Credit Classic
	v Chambers	6-4	3rd round	English Championship
	v Meo	4-6	4th round	English Championship
	v Rowswell	4-5	3rd round	MIM Britannia British Open
	v Cripsey	10-2	Qualifying	Embassy World Championship
	v Griffiths	1-10	1st round	Embassy World Championship

EDDIE McLAUGHLIN (Scotland)

Born 27.6.52. **Turned professional** 1981. **World ranking** 131 (107).

1981	v Black	5-3	Qualifying	Jameson International
	v Wildman	5-3	Qualifying	Jameson International
	v Greaves	5-1	Qualifying	Jameson International
	v Ross	5-3	Quarter-final	Scottish Championship
	v Black	3-6	Semi-final	Scottish Championship
	v Meo	2-5	1st round	Jameson International
	v Medati	5-9	Qualifying	Coral UK Championship
1982	v Macleod	8-9	Qualifying	Embassy World Championship
	v Gibson	3-6	Quarter-final	Scottish Championship
	v Houlihan	5-2	Qualifying	Jameson International
	v Williams	1-5	Qualifying	Jameson International
	v Mans	2-5	1st round	Professional Players Tournament
	v Wilson	6-9	Qualifying	Coral UK Championship
1983	v Greaves	10-7	Qualifying	Embassy World Championship
	v Fisher	9-10	Qualifying	Embassy World Championship
	v Black	4-6	1st round	Scottish Championship
	v Campbell	5-2	Qualifying	Jameson International
	v Edmonds	1-5	Qualifying	Jameson International
	v Charlton	0-5	1st round	Professional Players Tournament
	v B. Harris	8-9	Qualifying	Coral UK Championship
1984	v Stevens	4-5	Qualifying	Lada Classic
	v Hargreaves	10-5	Qualifying	Embassy World Championship
	v Andrewartha	8-10	Qualifying	Embassy World Championship
	v O'Kane	1-5	Qualifying	Jameson International
	v Longworth	5-2	Qualifying	Rothmans Grand Prix
	v Mountjoy	4-5	1st round	Rothmans Grand Prix
	v Bales	4-9	Qualifying	Coral UK Open
1985	v Sheehan	5-2	Qualifying	Mercantile Credit Classic
	v F. Davis	5-1	Qualifying	Mercantile Credit Classic
	v Macleod	4-5	Qualifying	Mercantile Credit Classic
	v Macleod	4-6	1st round	Scottish Championship
	v French	0-6	Qualifying	Dulux British Open
	v Chalmers	9-10	Qualifying	Embassy World Championship
	v Hendry	5-3	2nd round	Goya Matchroom Trophy
	v Knowles	1-5	3rd round	Goya Matchroom Trophy
	v Van Rensberg	4-5	2nd round	Rothmans Grand Prix
1986	v J. McLaughlin	2-5	2nd round	Mercantile Credit Classic
	v West	3-5	2nd round	Dulux British Open
	v Black	4-6	Quarter-final	Canada Dry Scottish Championship
	v John Rea	6-10	Qualifying	Embassy World Championship
1987	v Demarco	0-6	1st round	Scottish Championship
1988	v Roscoe	1-10	Qualifying	Embassy World Championship

JACK McLAUGHLIN (Northern Ireland)

Born 29.1.59. **Turned professional** 1984. **World ranking** 64 (51). **Amateur career** Northern Ireland champion 1983, 1984. **Best professional performances** 1988 Irish champion, last 32 1987 Dulux British Open, 1986 Rothmans Grand Prix.

1984	v Greaves	5-3	Qualifying	Jameson International
	v Jonik	2-5	Qualifying	Jameson International
	v Meadowcroft	5-1	Qualifying	Rothmans Grand Prix
	v Wildman	3-5	1st round	Rothmans Grand Prix
	v French	9-3	Qualifying	Coral UK Open
	v Roscoe	9-8	Qualifying	Coral UK Open
	v Miles	9-8	Qualifying	Coral UK Open
	v Thorburn	4-9	1st round	Coral UK Open
1985	v Demarco	5-1	Qualifying	Mercantile Credit Classic
	v Black	5-0	Qualifying	Mercantile Credit Classic
	v Scott	4-5	Qualifying	Mercantile Credit Classic
	v Jonik	2-6	Qualifying	Dulux British Open
	v Sheehan	6-3	Qualifying	Irish Championship
	v Williamson	3-5	2nd round	Goya Matchroom Trophy
	v Medati	5-2	2nd round	Rothmans Grand Prix
	v Griffiths	4-5	3rd round	Rothmans Grand Prix
	v Chaperon	9-5	Qualifying	Coral UK Open
	v Reynolds	7-9	1st round	Coral UK Open
1986	v E. McLaughlin	5-2	2nd round	Mercantile Credit Classic
	v Thorburn	1-5	3rd round	Mercantile Credit Classic
	v Fisher	5-3	2nd round	Dulux British Open
	v Johnson	2-5	3rd round	Dulux British Open
	v Murphy	7-10	Qualifying	Embassy World Championship
	v Watchorn	5-0	1st round	Strongbow Irish Championship
	v Higgins	2-6	Quarter-final	Strongbow Irish Championship
	v B. Bennett	5-0	1st round	BCE International
	v Fowler	5-2	2nd round	BCE International
	v Wilson	2-5	3rd round	BCE International
	v Owers	5-2	1st round	Rothmans Grand Prix
	v Gauvreau	5-3	2nd round	Rothmans Grand Prix
	v West	5-1	3rd round	Rothmans Grand Prix
	v White	2-5	4th round	Rothmans Grand Prix
	v Gauvreau	9-8	2nd round	Tennents UK Open
	v Mountjoy	6-9	3rd round	Tennents UK Open
1987	v M. Gibson	5-3	2nd round	Mercantile Credit Classic
	v Werbeniuk	1-5	3rd round	Mercantile Credit Classic
	v Gibson	5-1	2nd round	Dulux British Open
	v Higgins	5-4	3rd round	Dulux British Open
	v David Taylor	2-5	4th round	Dulux British Open
	v Van Rensberg	6-10	Qualifying	Embassy World Championship
	v Sheehan	4-5	1st round	Matchroom Irish Championship
	v N. Gilbert	4-5	2nd round	Fidelity International
	v Oliver	5-2	2nd round	Rothmans Grand Prix
	v Knowles	0-5	3rd round	Rothmans Grand Prix .
	v John Rea	5-9	2nd round	Tennents UK Open
1988	v P. Gibson	5-4	2nd round	Mercantile Credit Classic
	v Martin	2-5	3rd round	Mercantile Credit Classic
	v Burke	5-3	1st round	Irish Championship
	v Watchorn	6-5	Quarter-final	Irish Championship
	v O'Boye	6-4	Semi-final	Irish Championship
	v Dennis Taylor	**9-4**	**Final**	**Irish Championship**
	v Rowswell	2-5	2nd round	MIM Britannia British Open
	v M. Smith	3-10	Qualifying	Embassy World Championship

MURDO MACLEOD (Scotland)

Born 14.1.47. **Turned professional** 1981. **World ranking** 48 (30). **Best professional performances** Last 16 1988 MIM Britannia British Open, 1987 Embassy World Championship, 1986 Coral UK Open, 1985 Goya Matchroom Trophy; Scottish champion, 1983, 1985.

Year	Opponent	Score	Round	Tournament
1981	v Kelly	5-1	Qualifying	Jameson International
	v Johnson	1-5	Qualifying	Jameson International
	v Black	4-5	Quarter-final	Scottish Championship
	v Roscoe	7-9	Qualifying	Coral UK Championship
1982	v E. McLaughlin	9-8	Qualifying	Embassy World Championship
	v Dunning	4-9	Qualifying	Embassy World Championship
	v Donnelly	6-5	1st round	Scottish Championship
	v Black	0-6	Quarter-final	Scottish Championship
	v Dodd	1-5	Qualifying	Jameson International
	v Thorne	5-2	2nd round	Professional Players Tournament
	v Reardon	2-5	3rd round	Professional Players Tournament
	v Martin	6-9	Qualifying	Coral UK Championship
1983	v M. Owen	10-5	Qualifying	Embassy World Championship
	v Martin	7-10	Qualifying	Embassy World Championship
	v Gibson	6-5	1st round	Scottish Championship
	v Black	6-2	Semi-final	Scottish Championship
	v Sinclair	**11-9**	**Final**	**Scottish Championship**
	v S. Davis	1-5	1st round	Langs Supreme Scottish Masters
	v Medati	5-3	Qualifying	Jameson International
	v Reardon	2-5	1st round	Jameson International
	v Murphy	0-5	1st round	Professional Players Tournament
	v Bennett	9-0	Qualifying	Coral UK Championship
	v Higgins	6-9	1st round	Coral UK Championship
1984	v David Taylor	5-4	Qualifying	Lada Classic
	v Stevens	1-5	1st round	Lada Classic
	v Gauvreau	6-10	Qualifying	Embassy World Championship
	v White	0-5	1st round	Langs Supreme Scottish Masters
	v Black	5-3	Qualifying	Jameson International
	v Meo	1-5	1st round	Jameson International
	v King	5-4	1st round	Rothmans Grand Prix
	v Thorne	3-5	2nd round	Rothmans Grand Prix
	v Scott	9-5	Qualifying	Coral UK Open
	v David Taylor	6-9	1st round	Coral UK Open
1985	v E. McLaughlin	5-4	Qualifying	Mercantile Credit Classic
	v Charlton	5-1	1st round	Mercantile Credit Classic
	v Virgo	0-5	2nd round	Mercantile Credit Classic
	v E. McLaughlin	6-4	1st round	Scottish Championship
	v M. Gibson	6-4	Semi-final	Scottish Championship
	v Sinclair	**10-2**	**Final**	**Scottish Championship**
	v Murphy	6-5	1st round	Dulux British Open
	v Thorne	5-0	2nd round	Dulux British Open
	v E. Hughes	2-5	3rd round	Dulux British Open
	v P. Francisco	10-7	Qualifying	Embassy World Championship
	v Mountjoy	5-10	1st round	Embassy World Championship
	v Thorburn	1-5	1st round	Langs Scottish Masters
	v Fitzmaurice	5-1	3rd round	Goya Matchroom Trophy
	v Chaperon	5-4	4th round	Goya Matchroom Trophy
	v S. Davis	1-5	5th round	Goya Matchroom Trophy
	v Drago	3-5	3rd round	Rothmans Grand Prix
	v Murphy	9-7	3rd round	Coral UK Open
	v Reardon	9-5	4th round	Coral UK Open
	v West	4-9	5th round	Coral UK Open
1986	v Sinclair	5-3	3rd round	Mercantile Credit Classic
	v Knowles	4-5	4th round	Mercantile Credit Classic
	v F. Davis	5-4	3rd round	Dulux British Open

	v S. Francisco	5-1	4th round	Dulux British Open
	v Griffiths	2-5	5th round	Dulux British Open
	v Hendry	5-6	Quarter-final	Canada Dry Scottish Championship
	v Fowler	6-10	Qualifying	Embassy World Championship
	v Gauvreau	4-5	3rd round	BCE International
	v M. Bennett	1-5	3rd round	Rothmans Grand Prix
	v Grace	6-9	3rd round	Tennents UK Open
1987	v Kearney	0-5	3rd round	Mercantile Credit Classic
	v Donnelly	2-6	1st round	Scottish Championship
	v T. Jones	4-5	3rd round	Dulux British Open
	v Edmonds	10-7	Qualifying	Embassy World Championship
	v Williams	10-5	1st round	Embassy World Championship
	v Johnson	7-13	2nd round	Embassy World Championship
	v N. Gilbert	1-5	3rd round	Fidelity International
	v Wych	4-5	3rd round	Rothmans Grand Prix
	v Edmonds	4-9	3rd round	Tennents UK Open
1988	v Donnelly	4-5	3rd round	Mercantile Credit Classic
	v Donnelly	6-5	Quarter-final	Scottish Championship
	v John Rea	6-5	Semi-final	Scottish Championship
	v Hendry	4-10	Final	Scottish Championship
	v D. Gilbert	5-4	3rd round	MIM Britannia British Open
	v Knowles	5-4	4th round	MIM Britannia British Open
	v Hallett	2-5	5th round	MIM Britannia British Open
	v Fowler	3-10	Qualifying	Embassy World Championship

ROBERT MARSHALL (England)

Born 25.8.64. **Turned professional** 1987. **World ranking** 119.

1987	v V. Harris	1-5	1st round	Fidelity International
	v Sheehan	5-1	1st round	Rothmans Grand Prix
	v Wych	2-5	2nd round	Rothmans Grand Prix
	v Roe	3-9	1st round	Tennents UK Open
1988	v Morra	0-5	1st round	Mercantile Credit Classic
	v Oliver	6-3	1st round	English Championship
	v Houlihan	6-4	2nd round	English Championship
	v Thorne	3-6	3rd round	English Championship
	v Rigitano	2-5	1st round	MIM Britannia British Open
	v Chaperon	3-10	Qualifying	Embassy World Championship

DAVE MARTIN (England)

Born 9.5.48. **Turned professional** 1981. **World ranking** 36 (27). **Best professional performances** Semi-finals 1981 Jameson International, quarter-finals 1988 Mercantile Credit Classic.

1981	v Anderson	9-3	Qualifying	Embassy World Championship
	v Pulman	9-2	Qualifying	Embassy World Championship
	v Werbeniuk	4-10	1st round	Embassy World Championship
	v Dunning	5-2	1st round	Jameson International
	v Werbeniuk	5-2	2nd round	Jameson International
	v Charlton	5-2	3rd round	Jameson International
	v Miles	5-1	Quarter-final	Jameson International
	v Dennis Taylor	1-9	Semi-final	Jameson International
	v Sinclair	9-7	Qualifying	Coral UK Championship
	v Higgins	7-9	2nd round	Coral UK Championship
1982	v Houlihan	9-3	Qualifying	Embassy World Championship
	v Miles	5-10	Qualifying	Embassy World Championship
	v E. Hughes	4-5	Qualifying	Jameson International
	v Gibson	5-2	1st round	Professional Players Tournament

	v Spencer	3-5	2nd round	Professional Players Tournament
	v Macleod	9-6	Qualifying	Coral UK Championship
	v Higgins	7-9	1st round	Coral UK Championship
1983	v Parkin	10-1	Qualifying	Embassy World Championship
	v Macleod	10-7	Qualifying	Embassy World Championship
	v Werbeniuk	4-10	Qualifying	Embassy World Championship
	v Greaves	5-1	Qualifying	Jameson International
	v Fagan	5-0	Qualifying	Jameson International
	v Higgins	5-2	1st round	Jameson International
	v Mountjoy	0-5	2nd round	Jameson International
	v Fitzmaurice	5-0	1st round	Professional Players Tournament
	v Watterson	5-4	2nd round	Professional Players Tournament
	v Campbell	0-5	3rd round	Professional Players Tournament
	v French	9-3	Qualifying	Coral UK Championship
	v Griffiths	4-9	Qualifying	Coral UK Championship
1984	v King	8-10	Qualifying	Embassy World Championship
	v Fowler	0-5	Qualifying	Jameson International
	v Chaperon	5-4	1st round	Rothmans Grand Prix
	v Meo	4-5	2nd round	Rothmans Grand Prix
	v Murphy	8-9	Qualifying	Coral UK Open
1985	v Foldvari	2-5	Qualifying	Mercantile Credit Classic
	v Miles	9-7	1st round	Tolly Cobbold English Championship
	v Knowles	3-9	2nd round	Tolly Cobbold English Championship
	v Bennett	6-0	1st round	Dulux British Open
	v Reardon	5-4	2nd round	Dulux British Open
	v O'Kane	4-5	3rd round	Dulux British Open
	v O'Kane	8-10	Qualifying	Embassy World Championship
	v Sinclair	5-1	3rd round	Goya Matchroom Trophy
	v Thorburn	3-5	4th round	Goya Matchroom Trophy
	v Morra	5-2	3rd round	Rothmans Grand Prix
	v S. Francisco	3-5	4th round	Rothmans Grand Prix
	v Darrington	9-3	3rd round	Coral UK Open
	v S. Francisco	6-9	4th round	Coral UK Open
1986	v Murphy	5-3	3rd round	Mercantile Credit Classic
	v P. Francisco	2-5	4th round	Mercantile Credit Classic
	v F. Davis	9-8	3rd round	Tolly Cobbold English Championship
	v S. Davis	4-9	4th round	Tolly Cobbold English Championship
	v B. Harris	5-1	3rd round	Dulux British Open
	v S. Davis	1-5	4th round	Dulux British Open
	v Gilbert	10-5	Qualifying	Embassy World Championship
	v Johnson	3-10	1st round	Embassy World Championship
	v Chaperon	4-5	3rd round	BCE International
	v Higgins	2-5	4th round	Rothmans Grand Prix
	v Williamson	9-5	3rd round	Tennents UK Open
	v Higgins	6-9	4th round	Tennents UK Open
1987	v G. Foulds	5-4	3rd round	Mercantile Credit Classic
	v Griffiths	4-5	4th round	Mercantile Credit Classic
	v Spencer	6-5	3rd round	Tolly Ales English Championship
	v Thorne	3-6	4th round	Tolly Ales English Championship
	v Scott	5-3	3rd round	Dulux British Open
	v Spencer	2-5	4th round	Dulux British Open
	v Hendry	7-10	Qualifying	Embassy World Championship
	v D. Gilbert	2-5	3rd round	Fidelity International
	v Roe	4-5	3rd round	Rothmans Grand Prix
	v V. Harris	7-9	3rd round	Tennents UK Open
1988	v J. McLaughlin	5-2	3rd round	Mercantile Credit Classic
	v Mountjoy	5-4	4th round	Mercantile Credit Classic
	v White	5-2	5th round	Mercantile Credit Classic
	v Knowles	1-5	Quarter-final	Mercantile Credit Classic
	v M. Smith	6-5	3rd round	English Championship
	v Johnson	4-6	4th round	English Championship
	v Browne	4-5	3rd round	MIM Britannia British Open
	v W. Jones	5-10	Qualifying	Embassy World Championship

JIM MEADOWCROFT (England)

Born 15.12.46. **Turned professional** 1971. **World ranking** 94 (92). **Best professional performances** Quarter-finals 1976 Embassy World Championship, 1977 Super Crystalate UK Championship.

1973 v Reardon	10-16	2nd round	World Championship
1974 v Kennerley	8-5	1st round	World Championship
v Reardon	3-15	2nd round	World Championship
1975 v Werbeniuk	9-15	Qualifying	World Championship
1976 v Wheelwright	8-1	Qualifying	Embassy World Championship
v Gross	8-4	Qualifying	Embassy World Championship
v Thorne	8-5	Qualifying	Embassy World Championship
v Williams	15-7	1st round	Embassy World Championship
v Mans	8-15	Quarter-final	Embassy World Championship
1977 v Fagan	9-11	Qualifying	Embassy World Championship
v Houlihan	5-1	1st round	Super Crystalate UK Championship
v Reardon	5-4	2nd round	Super Crystalate UK Championship
v Fagan	4-5	Quarter-final	Super Crystalate UK Championship
1978 v Houlihan	6-9	Qualifying	Embassy World Championship
v Jack Rea	9-5	Qualifying	Coral UK Championship
v Higgins	6-9	1st round	Coral UK Championship
1979 v Van Rensberg	9-7	Prelim	Embassy World Championship
v Griffiths	6-9	Qualifying	Embassy World Championship
v Edmonds	3-9	2nd round	Coral UK Championship
1980 v Sinclair	9-1	Qualifying	Embassy World Championship
v Virgo	2-10	1st round	Embassy World Championship
v Greaves	9-1	Qualifying	Coral UK Championship
v Thorne	1-9	1st round	Coral UK Championship
1981 v Barrie	9-3	Qualifying	John Courage English
v S. Davis	2-9	1st round	John Courage English
v White	8-9	Qualifying	Embassy World Championship
v Roscoe	5-4	Qualifying	Jameson International
v Wilson	5-4	1st round	Jameson International
v Stevens	1-5	2nd round	Jameson International
v Houlihan	4-9	Qualifying	Coral UK Championship
1982 v Watterson	9-7	Qualifying	Embassy World Championship
v Higgins	5-10	1st round	Embassy World Championship
v Ross	5-0	Qualifying	Jameson International
v White	1-5	1st round	Jameson International
v Bennett	5-4	1st round	Professional Players Tournament
v Sinclair	3-5	2nd round	Professional Players Tournament
v D. Hughes	9-8	Qualifying	Coral UK Championship
v Dennis Taylor	7-9	1st round	Coral UK Championship
1983 v Bennett	10-3	Qualifying	Embassy World Championship
v Cripsey	10-6	Qualifying	Embassy World Championship
v David Taylor	2-10	1st round	Embassy World Championship
v Roscoe	5-4	1st round	Professional Players Tournament
v Thorburn	1-5	2nd round	Professional Players Tournament
v N. Foulds	2-9	Qualifying	Coral UK Championship
1984 v Meo	1-5	Qualifying	Lada Classic
v N. Foulds	2-10	Qualifying	Embassy World Championship
v Chalmers	5-1	Qualifying	Jameson International
v Williams	4-5	Qualifying	Jameson International
v J. McLaughlin	1-5	Qualifying	Rothmans Grand Prix
v Bradley	7-9	Qualifying	Coral UK Open
1985 v Fowler	2-5	Qualifying	Mercantile Credit Classic
v Chalmers	3-9	Qualifying	Tolly Cobbold English Championship
v B. Harris	1-6	Qualifying	Dulux British Open
v P. Francisco	5-10	Qualifying	Embassy World Championship
v Chappel	2-5	2nd round	Goya Matchroom Trophy
v West	2-5	2nd round	Rothmans Grand Prix

	v	Hargreaves	9-8	2nd round	Coral UK Open
	v	Hallett	1-9	3rd round	Coral UK Open
1986	v	West	0-5	2nd round	Mercantile Credit Classic
	v	Cripsey	1-9	2nd round	Tolly Cobbold English Championship
	v	Jenkins	2-5	2nd round	Dulux British Open
	v	Darrington	6-10	Qualifying	Embassy World Championship
	v	P. Gibson	2-5	1st round	BCE International
	v	Greaves	5-2	1st round	Rothmans Grand Prix
	v	Mans	wo	2nd round	Rothmans Grand Prix
	v	Martin	scr	3rd round	Rothmans Grand Prix
	v	Demarco	9-2	1st round	Tennents UK Open
	v	Bradley	2-9	2nd round	Tennents UK Open
1987	v	Newbury	1-5	2nd round	Mercantile Credit Classic
	v	Grace	4-5	1st round	Dulux British Open
	v	Mienie	10-3	Qualifying	Embassy World Championship
	v	Cripsey	9-10	Qualifying	Embassy World Championship
	v	Greaves	5-1	1st round	Fidelity International
	v	Owers	3-5	2nd round	Fidelity International
	v	A. Harris	5-3	1st round	Rothmans Grand Prix
	v	Browne	3-5	2nd round	Rothmans Grand Prix
	v	King	4-9	2nd round	Tennents UK Open
1988	v	Everton	3-5	1st round	Mercantile Credit Classic
	v	Heaton	0-6	1st round	English Championship
	v	Kelly	5-1	1st round	MIM Britannia British Open
	v	Murphy	4-5	2nd round	MIM Britannia British Open
	v	B. Bennett	10-5	Qualifying	Embassy World Championship
	v	Cripsey	3-10	Qualifying	Embassy World Championship

STEVE MEAKIN (England)

Born 19.7.61. **Turned professional** 1987. **World ranking** 117.

1987	v	Foldvari	3-5	1st round	Fidelity International
	v	Morra	5-2	1st round	Rothmans Grand Prix
	v	Newbury	1-5	2nd round	Rothmans Grand Prix
	v	Glen Wilkinson	9-0	1st round	Tennents UK Open
	v	W. Jones	1-9	2nd round	Tennents UK Open
1988	v	Darrington	5-4	1st round	Mercantile Credit Classic
	v	F. Davis	4-5	2nd round	Mercantile Credit Classic
	v	Darrington	6-3	1st round	English Championship
	v	Owers	2-6	2nd round	English Championship
	v	Williamson	1-5	1st round	MIM Britannia British Open
	v	Morra	5-10	Qualifying	Embassy World Championship

PAUL MEDATI (England)

Born 14.11.44. **Turned professional** 1981. **World ranking** 68 (68). **Best professional performances** Last 32 1988 MIM Britannia British Open, 1986 Dulux British Open.

1981	v	Watterson	3-5	Qualifying	Jameson International
	v	E. McLaughlin	9-5	Qualifying	Coral UK Championship
	v	Donnelly	9-7	Qualifying	Coral UK Championship
	v	Thorne	6-9	Qualifying	Coral UK Championship
1982	v	Phillips	9-3	Qualifying	Embassy World Championship
	v	Wilson	5-9	Qualifying	Embassy World Championship
	v	Williams	3-5	Qualifying	Jameson International
	v	Thorburn	1-5	1st round	Professional Players Tournament
	v	Bennett	9-1	Qualifying	Coral UK Championship
	v	White	7-9	1st round	Coral UK Championship
1983	v	John Bear	10-7	Qualifying	Embassy World Championship

	v Black	4-10	Qualifying	Embassy World Championship
	v V. Harris	5-0	Qualifying	Jameson International
	v Macleod	3-5	Qualifying	Jameson International
	v D. Hughes	5-1	Qualifying	Professional Players Tournament
	v Knowles	1-5	1st round	Professional Players Tournament
	v D. Hughes	9-2	Qualifying	Coral UK Championship
	v Edmonds	9-7	Qualifying	Coral UK Championship
	v Reynolds	9-3	1st round	Coral UK Championship
	v Higgins	1-9	2nd round	Coral UK Championship
1984	v Mikkelsen	8-10	Qualifying	Embassy World Championship
	v Gibson	3-5	Qualifying	Jameson International
	v Dodd	5-4	Qualifying	Rothmans Grand Prix
	v Johnson	1-5	1st round	Rothmans Grand Prix
	v Hargreaves	6-9	Qualifying	Coral UK Open
1985	v Cripsey	5-4	Qualifying	Mercantile Credit Classic
	v Roscoe	5-4	Qualifying	Mercantile Credit Classic
	v Parrott	5-3	Qualifying	Mercantile Credit Classic
	v Stevens	4-5	1st round	Mercantile Credit Classic
	v Hargreaves	9-8	Qualifying	Tolly Cobbold English Championship
	v Spencer	9-4	1st round	Tolly Cobbold English Championship
	v Longworth	7-9	2nd round	Tolly Cobbold English Championship
	v King	4-6	Qualifying	Dulux British Open
	v Bennett	10-4	Qualifying	Embassy World Championship
	v Williamson	10-8	Qualifying	Embassy World Championship
	v King	10-9	Qualifying	Embassy World Championship
	v S. Francisco	7-10	Qualifying	Embassy World Championship
	v Cripsey	2-5	2nd round	Goya Matchroom Trophy
	v J. McLaughlin	2-5	2nd round	Rothmans Grand Prix
	v Kelly	9-1	2nd round	Coral UK Open
	v Campbell	7-9	3rd round	Coral UK Open
1986	v Kearney	5-2	2nd round	Mercantile Credit Classic
	v O'Kane	0-5	3rd round	Mercantile Credit Classic
	v Greaves	9-4	2nd round	Tolly Cobbold English Championship
	v Thorne	2-9	3rd round	Tolly Cobbold English Championship
	v Everton	5-1	2nd round	Dulux British Open
	v David Taylor	5-1	3rd round	Dulux British Open
	v Campbell	4-5	4th round	Dulux British Open
	v Simngam	10-9	Qualifying	Embassy World Championship
	v Gibson	10-6	Qualifying	Embassy World Championship
	v Wilson	6-10	Qualifying	Embassy World Championship
	v Kearney	5-3	2nd round	BCE International
	v Griffiths	3-5	3rd round	BCE International
	v Rigitano	5-1	2nd round	Rothmans Grand Prix
	v P. Francisco	1-5	3rd round	Rothmans Grand Prix
	v Grace	5-9	2nd round	Tennents UK Open
1987	v Dodd	4-5	2nd round	Mercantile Credit Classic
	v N. Gibson	6-2	2nd round	Tolly Ales English Championship
	v Virgo	1-6	3rd round	Tolly Ales English Championship
	v Ellis	5-0	2nd round	Dulux British Open
	v Charlton	4-5	3rd round	Dulux British Open
	v Kearney	10-8	Qualifying	Embassy World Championship
	v Gauvreau	10-3	Qualifying	Embassy World Championship
	v E. Hughes	2-10	Qualifying	Embassy World Championship
	v Murphy	3-5	2nd round	Fidelity International
	v M. Bennett	4-5	2nd round	Rothmans Grand Prix
	v Dodd	6-9	2nd round	Tennents UK Open
1988	v Chaperon	3-5	2nd round	Mercantile Credit Classic
	v B. Bennett	6-0	1st round	English Championship
	v Fowler	1-6	2nd round	English Championship
	v Gauvreau	5-1	2nd round	MIM Britannia British Open
	v David Taylor	5-4	3rd round	MIM Britannia British Open
	v Thorburn	2-5	4th round	MIM Britannia British Open

| v Gary Wilkinson | 10-9 | Qualifying | Embassy World Championship |
| v Dodd | 6-10 | Qualifying | Embassy World Championship |

TONY MEO (England)

Born 4.10.59. **Turned professional** 1979. **World ranking** 31 (20). **Best professional performances** Runner-up 1984 Lada Classic; English champion 1986, 1987.

1979	v David Taylor	9-7	2nd round	Coral UK Championship
	v Virgo	6-9	3rd round	Coral UK Championship
1980	v Van Rensberg	9-1	Qualifying	Embassy World Championship
	v Houlihan	9-1	Qualifying	Embassy World Championship
	v Higgins	9-10	1st round	Embassy World Championship
	v Hood	9-5	Qualifying	Coral UK Championship
	v Houlihan	9-1	1st round	Coral UK Championship
	v Virgo	9-1	2nd round	Coral UK Championship
	v S. Davis	5-9	Quarter-final	Coral UK Championship
1981	v Virgo	9-6	Qualifying	John Courage English
	v Miles	9-7	2nd round	John Courage English
	v Thorne	9-8	Semi-final	John Courage English
	v S. Davis	3-9	Final	John Courage English
	v Johnson	9-8	Qualifying	Embassy World Championship
	v Hallett	9-4	Qualifying	Embassy World Championship
	v Virgo	10-6	1st round	Embassy World Championship
	v Griffiths	6-13	2nd round	Embassy World Championship
	v E. McLaughlin	5-2	1st round	Jameson International
	v Mans	3-5	2nd round	Jameson International
	v Williams	9-8	2nd round	Coral UK Championship
	v Thorburn	9-6	3rd round	Coral UK Championship
	v Higgins	9-4	Quarter-final	Coral UK Championship
	v Griffiths	3-9	Semi-final	Coral UK Championship
1982	v David Taylor	5-2	1st round	Benson & Hedges Masters
	v Thorburn	5-0	Quarter-final	Benson & Hedges Masters
	v S. Davis	4-6	Semi-final	Benson & Hedges Masters
	v Spencer	5-3	1st round	Benson & Hedges Irish Masters
	v Griffiths	3-5	Quarter-final	Benson & Hedges Irish Masters
	v D. Hughes	9-4	Qualifying	Embassy World Championship
	v Mans	8-10	1st round	Embassy World Championship
	v Sinclair	3-5	Qualifying	Jameson International
	v M. Owen	5-4	1st round	Professional Players Tournament
	v Jonik	5-0	2nd round	Professional Players Tournament
	v Charlton	3-5	3rd round	Professional Players Tournament
	v Scott	9-5	Qualifying	Coral UK Championship
	v Miles	9-4	1st round	Coral UK Championship
	v David Taylor	9-6	2nd round	Coral UK Championship
	v Virgo	9-6	Quarter-final	Coral UK Championship
	v Griffiths	7-9	Semi-final	Coral UK Championship
1983	v Charlton	3-5	1st round	Benson & Hedges Masters
	v Burke	5-0	1st round	Benson & Hedges Irish Masters
	v Reardon	4-5	Quarter-final	Benson & Hedges Irish Masters
	v V. Harris	10-0	Qualifying	Embassy World Championship
	v G. Foulds	10-4	Qualifying	Embassy World Championship
	v White	10-8	1st round	Embassy World Championship
	v Mountjoy	13-11	2nd round	Embassy World Championship
	v Knowles	9-13	Quarter-final	Embassy World Championship
	v Knowles	4-5	1st round	Langs Supreme Scottish Masters
	v Watterson	3-5	1st round	Jameson International
	v King	5-2	1st round	Professional Players Tournament
	v Reynolds	5-0	2nd round	Professional Players Tournament
	v Hallett	5-3	3rd round	Professional Players Tournament
	v Stevens	5-3	Quarter-final	Professional Players Tournament
	v Johnson	6-9	Semi-final	Professional Players Tournament

v Parrott	9-7	1st round	Coral UK Championship
v Spencer	9-5	2nd round	Coral UK Championship
v Davis	4-9	Quarter-final	Coral UK Championship
1984 v Meadowcroft	5-1	Qualifying	Lada Classic
v Williams	5-3	1st round	Lada Classic
v Stevens	5-2	Quarter-final	Lada Classic
v Wildman	5-3	Semi-final	Lada Classic
v S. Davis	8-9	Final	Lada Classic
v S. Davis	0-5	1st round	Benson & Hedges Masters
v White	5-4	1st round	Benson & Hedges Irish Masters
v S. Davis	4-5	Quarter-final	Benson & Hedges Irish Masters
v Thorburn	4-5	1st round	Tolly Cobbold Classic
v S. Francisco	5-10	1st round	Embassy World Championship
v Stevens	5-1	Quarter-final	Winfield Australian Masters
v Virgo	2-6	Semi-final	Winfield Australian Masters
v Macleod	5-1	1st round	Jameson International
v White	1-5	2nd round	Jameson International
v Burke	5-1	1st round	Rothmans Grand Prix
v Martin	5-4	2nd round	Rothmans Grand Prix
v Thorburn	4-5	3rd round	Rothmans Grand Prix
v E. Hughes	9-4	1st round	Coral UK Open
v S. Davis	7-9	2nd round	Coral UK Open
1985 v E. Hughes	4-5	1st round	Mercantile Credit Classic
v Fisher	9-3	1st round	Tolly Cobbold English Championship
v Hallett	9-4	2nd round	Tolly Cobbold English Championship
v Reynolds	9-4	Quarter-final	Tolly Cobbold English Championship
v S. Davis	8-9	Semi-final	Tolly Cobbold English Championship
v Foldvari	6-0	1st round	Dulux British Open
v Hallett	5-4	2nd round	Dulux British Open
v Knowles	5-2	3rd round	Dulux British Open
v S. Francisco	4-5	Quarter-final	Dulux British Open
v White	1-5	1st round	Benson & Hedges Irish Masters
v Virgo	10-6	1st round	Embassy World Championship
v White	11-13	2nd round	Embassy World Championship
v Virgo	5-3	Quarter-final	Winfield Australian Masters
v White	6-3	Semi-final	Winfield Australian Masters
v Campbell	**7-2**	**Final**	**Winfield Australian Masters**
v Dunning	5-0	3rd round	Goya Matchroom Trophy
v Parrott	4-5	4th round	Goya Matchroom Trophy
v T. Jones	5-2	3rd round	Rothmans Grand Prix
v E. Hughes	5-3	4th round	Rothmans Grand Prix
v Dennis Taylor	3-5	5th round	Rothmans Grand Prix
v Longworth	9-5	3rd round	Coral UK Open
v Fowler	9-2	4th round	Coral UK Open
v S. Davis	5-9	5th round	Coral UK Open
1986 v O'Boye	5-3	3rd round	Mercantile Credit Classic
v West	5-1	4th round	Mercantile Credit Classic
v Thorburn	1-5	5th round	Mercantile Credit Classic
v White	4-5	1st round	Benson & Hedges Masters
v Scott	9-1	3rd round	Tolly Cobbold English Championship
v Wildman	9-3	4th round	Tolly Cobbold English Championship
v Reynolds	9-4	Quarter-final	Tolly Cobbold English Championship
v S. Davis	9-7	Semi-final	Tolly Cobbold English Championship
v N. Foulds	**9-7**	**Final**	**Tolly Cobbold English Championship**
v Donnelly	5-3	3rd round	Dulux British Open
v Newbury	5-0	4th round	Dulux British Open
v Thorburn	5-3	5th round	Dulux British Open
v Virgo	3-5	Quarter-final	Dulux British Open
v Higgins	5-4	1st round	Benson & Hedges Irish Masters
v White	2-5	Quarter-final	Benson & Hedges Irish Masters
v Parrott	6-10	1st round	Embassy World Championship
v Griffiths	3-6	1st round	Matchroom Trophy
v Houlihan	5-1	3rd round	BCE International

	Opponent	Score	Round	Tournament
	v Chappel	5-1	3rd round	Rothmans Grand Prix
	v Parrott	5-3	4th round	Rothmans Grand Prix
	v Dennis Taylor	5-2	5th round	Rothmans Grand Prix
	v N. Foulds	3-5	Quarter-final	Rothmans Grand Prix
	v O'Boye	9-3	3rd round	Tennents UK Open
	v Hallett	4-9	4th round	Tennents UK Open
1987	v John Rea	5-4	3rd round	Mercantile Credit Classic
	v Longworth	5-0	4th round	Mercantile Credit Classic
	v S. Davis	2-5	5th round	Mercantile Credit Classic
	v White	5-4	1st round	Benson & Hedges Masters
	v Mountjoy	5-4	Quarter-final	Benson & Hedges Masters
	v Higgins	2-6	Semi-final	Benson & Hedges Masters
	v Duggan	6-3	3rd round	Tolly Ales English Championship
	v Fowler	6-0	4th round	Tolly Ales English Championship
	v Parrott	6-3	Quarter-final	Tolly Ales English Championship
	v Thorne	9-3	Semi-final	Tolly Ales English Championship
	v Dodd	**9-5**	**Final**	**Tolly Ales English Championship**
	v Spencer	1-5	3rd round	Dulux British Open
	v Knowles	5-2	1st round	Benson & Hedges Irish Masters
	v S. Davis	2-5	Quarter-final	Benson & Hedges Irish Masters
	v Parrott	8-10	1st round	Embassy World Championship
	v Wright	5-2	3rd round	Fidelity International
	v S. Davis	3-5	4th round	Fidelity International
	v Newbury	0-5	3rd round	Rothmans Grand Prix
	v S. Davis	5-6	1st round	Matchroom Trophy
	v Watchorn	9-1	3rd round	Tennents UK Open
	v Hallett	5-9	4th round	Tennents UK Open
1988	v Morra	5-1	3rd round	Mercantile Credit Classic
	v Higgins	3-5	4th round	Mercantile Credit Classic
	v F. Davis	6-3	3rd round	English Championship
	v Longworth	6-4	4th round	English Championship
	v Reynolds	4-6	Quarter-final	English Championship
	v Gary Wilkinson	2-5	3rd round	MIM Britannia British Open
	v Werbeniuk	4-10	Qualifying	Embassy World Championship

DEREK MIENIE (South Africa)

Turned professional 1978. **World ranking** 121 (115).

	Opponent	Score	Round	Tournament
1979	v Mountjoy	1-9	Prelim	Embassy World Championship
1985	v Edmonds	1-6	Qualifying	Dulux British Open
	v Bradley	4-10	Qualifying	Embassy World Championship
	v Fagan	4-5	2nd round	Goya Matchroom Trophy
	v Simngam	3-5	1st round	Rothmans Grand Prix
	v Hargreaves	7-9	1st round	Coral UK Open
1986	v Smith	1-5	1st round	Mercantile Credit Classic
	v Thornley	3-10	Qualifying	Embassy World Championship
	v Hines	6-5	1st round	South African Championship
	v Van Rensberg	1-7	2nd round	South African Championship
	v Oliver	4-5	1st round	BCE International
	v Fitzmaurice	5-2	1st round	Rothmans Grand Prix
	v M. Gibson	4-5	2nd round	Rothmans Grand Prix
	v Jenkins	6-9	1st round	Tennents UK Open
1987	v Cripsey	0-5	2nd round	Mercantile Credit Classic
	v Roscoe	2-5	1st round	Dulux British Open
	v Meadowcroft	3-10	Qualifying	Embassy World Championship
1988	v Bear	4-10	Qualifying	Embassy World Championship

BERNIE MIKKELSEN (Canada)

Born 11.4.50. **Turned professional** 1979. **World ranking** 97 (74). **Best professional performance** Last 32 1986 Mercantile Credit Classic.

1981	v White	4-9	Qualifying	Embassy World Championship
1982	v Roscoe	6-9	Qualifying	Embassy World Championship
1983	v Rigitano	9-4	2nd round	Canadian Championship
	v Thorburn	2-9	Quarter-final	Canadian Championship
1984	v Medati	10-8	Qualifying	Embassy World Championship
	v Jonik	10-9	Qualifying	Embassy World Championship
	v Thorne	3-10	Qualifying	Embassy World Championship
	v Chappel	5-4	Qualifying	Jameson International
	v Everton	5-0	Qualifying	Jameson International
	v Roscoe	1-5	Qualifying	Jameson International
	v Sheehan	3-5	Qualifying	Rothmans Grand Prix
1985	v Chalmers	5-1	Prelim	Mercantile Credit Classic
	v Watchorn	1-5	Qualifying	Mercantile Credit Classic
	v D. Hughes	6-0	Qualifying	Dulux British Open
	v Bradley	9-10	Qualifying	Embassy World Championship
	v Watson	5-3	1st round	Canadian Championship
	v Jonik	4-6	Quarter-final	Canadian Championship
	v Fisher	5-3	2nd round	Goya Matchroom Trophy
	v Reynolds	0-5	3rd round	Goya Matchroom Trophy
	v Murphy	5-4	2nd round	Rothmans Grand Prix
	v Hallett	3-5	3rd round	Rothmans Grand Prix
	v Williamson	9-3	2nd round	Coral UK Open
	v David Taylor	6-9	3rd round	Coral UK Open
1986	v Scott	5-1	2nd round	Mercantile Credit Classic
	v Reardon	5-3	3rd round	Mercantile Credit Classic
	v Campbell	2-5	4th round	Mercantile Credit Classic
	v Roscoe	4-5	2nd round	Dulux British Open
	v Hargreaves	10-7	Qualifying	Embassy World Championship
	v Watterson	2-10	Qualifying	Embassy World Championship
	v Sanderson	6-1	1st round	Canadian Championship
	v Wych	3-6	2nd round	Canadian Championship
	v O'Boye	4-5	2nd round	BCE International
	v G. Foulds	1-5	2nd round	Rothmans Grand Prix
	v Sinclair	9-8	2nd round	Tennents UK Open
	v Reynolds	6-9	3rd round	Tennents UK Open
1987	v Foldvari	5-1	2nd round	Mercantile Credit Classic
	v Hallett	3-5	3rd round	Mercantile Credit Classic
	v Foldvari	3-5	2nd round	Dulux British Open
	v M. Bennett	4-10	Qualifying	Embassy World Championship
	v Bear	0-6	1st round	Canadian Championship
1988	v Jack Rea	10-3	Qualifying	Embassy World Championship
	v Wildman	5-10	Qualifying	Embassy World Championship

GRAHAM MILES (England)

Born 11.5.41. Turned professional 1969. World ranking 65 (69). Best professional performance Runner-up 1974 World Professional Championship.

1972	v Bennett	15-6	Qualifying	World Championship
	v Dunning	5-11	Qualifying	World Championship
1973	v Thompson	9-5	1st round	World Championship
	v Pulman	16-10	2nd round	World Championship
	v Charlton	6-16	Quarter-final	World Championship
1974	v Morgan	15-7	2nd round	World Championship
	v Dunning	15-13	Quarter-final	World Championship
	v Williams	15-7	Semi-final	World Championship
	v Reardon	12-22	Final	World Championship
1975	v Reardon	3-5	Quarter-final	Benson & Hedges Masters
	v Thorburn	2-15	2nd round	World Championship
1976	v Spencer	5-4	Semi-final	Benson & Hedges Masters

	v Reardon	3-7	Final	Benson & Hedges Masters
	v Mans	10-15	1st round	Embassy World Championship
1977	v Reardon	2-5	Semi-final	Benson & Hedges Masters
	v Thorne	13-4	1st round	Embassy World Championship
	v Pulman	10-13	Quarter-final	Embassy World Championship
	v Ross	5-1	2nd round	Super Crystalate UK Championship
	v Virgo	2-5	Quarter-final	Super Crystalate UK Championship
1978	v David Taylor	13-10	1st round	Embassy World Championship
	v Mans	7-13	Quarter-final	Embassy World Championship
	v Williams	9-8	1st round	Coral UK Championship
	v Thorne	9-1	Quarter-final	Coral UK Championship
	v Mountjoy	1-9	Semi-final	Coral UK Championship
1979	v Higgins	6-3	Semi-final	Holsten Lager International
	v Spencer	7-11	Final	Holsten Lager International
	v Williams	9-5	Qualifying	Embassy World Championship
	v Reardon	8-13	1st round	Embassy World Championship
	v Fagan	5-9	3rd round	Coral UK Championship
1980	v Stevens	3-10	1st round	Embassy World Championship
	v Sinclair	5-9	1st round	Coral UK Championship
1981	v Hood	9-1	1st round	John Courage English
	v Meo	7-9	2nd round	John Courage English
	v Knowles	10-8	1st round	Embassy World Championship
	v Thorburn	2-13	2nd round	Embassy World Championship
	v Johnson	5-3	2nd round	Jameson International
	v Thorburn	5-0	3rd round	Jameson International
	v Martin	1-5	Quarter-final	Jameson International
	v Houlihan	9-5	2nd round	Coral UK Championship
	v Griffiths	4-9	3rd round	Coral UK Championship
1982	v S. Davis	2-5	Semi-final	Tolly Cobbold Classic
	v Martin	10-5	1st round	Embassy World Championship
	v Knowles	7-13	2nd round	Embassy World Championship
	v Edmonds	1-5	Qualifying	Jameson International
	v Johnson	1-5	1st round	Professional Players Tournament
	v Meo	4-9	1st round	Coral UK Championship
1983	v Morgan	10-6	Qualifying	Embassy World Championship
	v Knowles	3-10	1st round	Embassy World Championship
	v King	5-3	Qualifying	Jameson International
	v Griffiths	2-5	1st round	Jameson International
	v Gauvreau	5-3	1st round	Professional Players Tournament
	v Campbell	2-5	2nd round	Professional Players Tournament
	v Hallett	4-9	1st round	Coral UK Championship
1984	v Williamson	10-6	Qualifying	Embassy World Championship
	v Spencer	3-10	1st round	Embassy World Championship
	v Newbury	1-5	Qualifying	Jameson International
	v Murphy	5-3	1st round	Rothmans Grand Prix
	v S. Davis	0-5	2nd round	Rothmans Grand Prix
	v J. McLaughlin	8-9	Qualifying	Coral UK Open
1985	v Browne	3-5	Qualifying	Mercantile Credit Classic
	v Martin	7-9	1st round	Tolly Cobbold English Championship
	v Edmonds	6-1	1st round	Dulux British Open
	v Spencer	2-5	2nd round	Dulux British Open
	v Stevens	2-5	3rd round	Dulux British Open
	v W. Jones	8-10	Qualifying	Embassy World Championship
	v O'Boye	5-2	2nd round	Goya Matchroom Trophy
	v Virgo	2-5	3rd round	Goya Matchroom Trophy
	v Rigitano	5-4	2nd round	Rothmans Grand Prix
	v Reynolds	5-3	3rd round	Rothmans Grand Prix
	v Stevens	2-5	4th round	Rothmans Grand Prix
	v Oliver	9-4	2nd round	Coral UK Open
	v Reardon	4-9	3rd round	Coral UK Open
1986	v Hendry	1-5	2nd round	Mercantile Credit Classic
	v Fitzmaurice	9-5	2nd round	Tolly Cobbold English Championship
	v Williams	6-9	3rd round	Tolly Cobbold English Championship

	v Agrawal	5-4	2nd round	Dulux British Open
	v Stevens	3-5	3rd round	Dulux British Open
	v Everton	10-3	Qualifying	Embassy World Championship
	v Foldvari	7-10	Qualifying	Embassy World Championship
	v Roe	5-1	2nd round	BCE International
	v N. Foulds	2-5	3rd round	BCE International
	v Jonik	5-1	2nd round	Rothmans Grand Prix
	v N. Foulds	1-5	3rd round	Rothmans Grand Prix
	v Sheehan	9-8	2nd round	Tennents UK Open
	v Virgo	7-9	3rd round	Tennents UK Open
1987	v Sinclair	1-5	2nd round	Mercantile Credit Classic
	v Johnson	3-6	3rd round	Tolly Ales English Championship
	v Greaves	10-7	Qualifying	Embassy World Championship
	v Murphy	7-10	Qualifying	Embassy World Championship
	v Wildman	3-5	2nd round	Fidelity International
	v Scott	5-2	2nd round	Rothmans Grand Prix
	v Davis	1-5	3rd round	Rothmans Grand Prix
	v Houlihan	9-3	2nd round	Tennents UK Open
	v Spencer	9-5	3rd round	Tennents UK Open
	v Fowler	4-9	4th round	Tennents UK Open
1988	v M. Bennett	1-5	2nd round	Mercantile Credit Classic
	v M. Smith	1-6	1st round	English Championship
	v Owers	5-3	2nd round	MIM Britannia British Open
	v Dennis Taylor	1-5	3rd round	MIM Britannia British Open
	v D. Hughes	10-3	Qualifying	Embassy World Championship
	v Bales	10-7	Qualifying	Embassy World Championship
	v Chappel	7-10	Qualifying	Embassy World Championship

MARIO MORRA (Canada)

Born 8.9.53. **Turned professional** 1979. **World ranking** 82 (78).

1981	v Thorne	5-9	Qualifying	Embassy World Championship
	v Wildman	3-5	Qualifying	Jameson International
1982	v Murphy	9-5	Qualifying	Embassy World Championship
	v Fitzmaurice	7-9	Qualifying	Embassy World Championship
	v Demarco	5-2	Qualifying	Jameson International
	v Reynolds	1-5	Qualifying	Jameson International
	v Wilson	2-5	1st round	Professional Players Tournament
1983	v Black	9-10	Qualifying	Embassy World Championship
	v Jim Bear	8-9	2nd round	Canadian Championship
	v Watchorn	5-3	Qualifying	Jameson International
	v Hallett	5-3	Qualifying	Jameson International
	v White	5-3	1st round	Jameson International
	v Charlton	3-5	2nd round	Jameson International
	v Hargreaves	5-0	Qualifying	Professional Players Tournament
	v S. Francisco	3-5	1st round	Professional Players Tournament
	v Burke	5-2	Qualifying	Lada Classic
	v Everton	5-0	Qualifying	Lada Classic
	v S. Francisco	1-5	Qualifying	Lada Classic
1984	v G. Foulds	10-2	Qualifying	Embassy World Championship
	v Murphy	10-5	Qualifying	Embassy World Championship
	v Reynolds	10-7	Qualifying	Embassy World Championship
	v Thorburn	3-10	1st round	Embassy World Championship
	v Bradley	5-3	Qualifying	Jameson International
	v Johnson	0-5	Qualifying	Jameson International
	v Cripsey	5-3	Qualifying	Rothmans Grand Prix
	v S. Davis	2-5	1st round	Rothmans Grand Prix
	v Longworth	9-1	Qualifying	Coral UK Open
	v E. Hughes	8-9	Qualifying	Coral UK Open
1985	v Newbury	2-5	Qualifying	Mercantile Credit Classic
	v Bradley	2-6	Qualifying	Dulux British Open

Dene O'Kane

	v	Browne	10-6	Qualifying	Embassy World Championship
	v	Campbell	9-10	Qualifying	Embassy World Championship
	v	John Bear	4-5	1st round	Canadian Championship
	v	Oliver	5-1	2nd round	Goya Matchroom Trophy
	v	Campbell	2-5	3rd round	Goya Matchroom Trophy
	v	D. Hughes	5-2	2nd round	Rothmans Grand Prix
	v	Martin	2-5	3rd round	Rothmans Grand Prix
	v	Agrawal	9-8	2nd round	Coral UK Open
	v	Mountjoy	2-9	3rd round	Coral UK Open
1986	v	B. Harris	3-5	2nd round	Mercantile Credit Classic
	v	Gilbert	4-5	2nd round	Dulux British Open
	v	Gibson	9-10	Qualifying	Embassy World Championship
	v	Thornley	4-6	1st round	Canadian Championship
	v	Ellis	5-3	1st round	BCE International
	v	Drago	3-5	2nd round	BCE International
	v	James	5-3	1st round	Rothmans Grand Prix
	v	Black	5-4	2nd round	Rothmans Grand Prix
	v	Griffiths	9-3	3rd round	Rothmans Grand Prix
	v	B. Bennett	9-3	1st round	Tennents UK Open
	v	Drago	6-9	2nd round	Tennents UK Open
1987	v	Ellis	5-1	1st round	Mercantile Credit Classic
	v	Mans	5-0	2nd round	Mercantile Credit Classic
	v	Williams	2-5	3rd round	Mercantile Credit Classic
	v	M. Bennett	5-4	1st round	Dulux British Open
	v	Van Rensberg	5-1	2nd round	Dulux British Open
	v	Virgo	3-5	3rd round	Dulux British Open
	v	P. Gibson	10-6	Qualifying	Embassy World Championship
	v	Chappel	8-10	Qualifying	Embassy World Championship
	v	Chaperon	6-5	1st round	Canadian Championship
	v	Jonik	6-2	Quarter-final	Canadian Championship
	v	Thorburn	4-7	Semi-final	Canadian Championship
	v	Hargreaves	5-4	1st round	Fidelity International
	v	Dodd	5-3	2nd round	Fidelity International
	v	David Taylor	3-5	3rd round	Fidelity International
	v	Meakin	2-5	1st round	Rothmans Grand Prix
	v	A. Harris	8-9	1st round	Tennents UK Open
1988	v	Marshall	5-0	1st round	Mercantile Credit Classic
	v	Gauvreau	5-4	2nd round	Mercantile Credit Classic
	v	Meo	1-5	3rd round	Mercantile Credit Classic
	v	Watchorn	5-1	1st round	MIM Britannia British Open
	v	M. Bennett	5-2	2nd round	MIM Britannia British Open
	v	Griffiths	1-5	3rd round	MIM Britannia British Open
	v	Meakin	10-5	Qualifying	Embassy World Championship
	v	Edmonds	10-8	Qualifying	Embassy World Championship
	v	W. Jones	8-10	Qualifying	Embassy World Championship

DOUG MOUNTJOY (Wales)

Born 8.6.42. **Turned professional** 1976. **World ranking** 24 (14). **Amateur career** 1976 World champion; Welsh champion 1968, 1976. **Best professional performances** Winner 1978 Coral UK Championship, 1977 Benson & Hedges Masters, 1979 Benson & Hedges Irish Masters; Welsh champion 1982, 1984, 1987.

1977	v	Higgins	5-3	Semi-final	Benson & Hedges Masters
	v	**Reardon**	**7-6**	**Final**	**Benson & Hedges Masters**
	v	Jack Rea	11-9	Qualifying	Embassy World Championship
	v	Higgins	13-12	1st round	Embassy World Championship
	v	Dennis Taylor	11-13	Quarter-final	Embassy World Championship
	v	Andrewartha	5-2	1st round	Super Crystalate UK Championship
	v	Spencer	5-3	2nd round	Super Crystalate UK Championship

v Thorne	5-4	Quarter-final	Super Crystalate UK Championship
v Higgins	9-2	Semi-final	Super Crystalate UK Championship
v Fagan	9-12	Final	Super Crystalate UK Championship
1978 v Spencer	3-5	Final	Benson & Hedges Irish Masters
v Andrewartha	9-3	Qualifying	Embassy World Championship
v Reardon	9-13	1st round	Embassy World Championship
v Barrie	9-5	Qualifying	Coral UK Championship
v Dennis Taylor	9-4	1st round	Coral UK Championship
v Andrewartha	9-4	Quarter-final	Coral UK Championship
v Miles	9-1	Semi-final	Coral UK Championship
v David Taylor	**15-9**	**Final**	**Coral UK Championship**
1979 v F. Davis	5-2	1st round	Benson & Hedges Masters
v Spencer	5-0	Quarter-final	Benson & Hedges Masters
v Higgins	1-5	Semi-final	Benson & Hedges Masters
v Reardon	**6-5**	**Final**	**Benson & Hedges Irish Masters**
v Mienie	9-1	Prelim	Embassy World Championship
v Houlihan	9-6	Qualifying	Embassy World Championship
v Charlton	6-13	1st round	Embassy World Championship
v S. Davis	5-9	3rd round	Coral UK Championship
v Griffiths	9-6	1st round	Woodpecker Welsh Championship
v Reardon	**9-6**	**Final**	**Woodpecker Welsh Championship**
1980 v Griffiths	8-9	Final	Benson & Hedges Irish Masters
v Wilson	10-6	1st round	Embassy World Championship
v Thorburn	10-13	2nd round	Embassy World Championship
v Williams	8-9	1st round	Coral UK Championship
1981 v Charlton	5-0	1st round	Benson & Hedges Masters
v Higgins	1-5	Quarter-final	Benson & Hedges Masters
v Wilson	6-9	Semi-final	Woodpecker Welsh Championship
v Thorne	10-6	1st round	Embassy World Championship
v Charlton	13-7	2nd round	Embassy World Championship
v Dennis Taylor	13-8	Quarter-final	Embassy World Championship
v Reardon	16-10	Semi-final	Embassy World Championship
v S. Davis	12-18	Final	Embassy World Championship
v S. Davis	0-5	Quarter-final	Langs Supreme Scottish Masters
v Higgins	1-5	3rd round	Jameson International
v Dennis Taylor	5-4	1st round	Northern Ireland Classic
v White	8-9	Semi-final	Northern Ireland Classic
v Knowles	6-9	3rd round	Coral UK Championship
1982 v Spencer	5-4	1st round	Benson & Hedges Masters
v S. Davis	2-5	Quarter-final	Benson & Hedges Masters
v Andrewartha	6-3	1st round	Welsh Championship
v Reardon	9-7	Semi-final	Welsh Championship
v Griffiths	**9-8**	**Final**	**Welsh Championship**
v E. Hughes	5-4	1st round	Benson & Hedges Irish Masters
v S. Davis	2-5	Quarter-final	Benson & Hedges Irish Masters
v Williams	10-3	1st round	Embassy World Championship
v Higgins	12-13	2nd round	Embassy World Championship
v Wilson	4-5	1st round	Jameson International
v Jonik	3-5	1st round	Professional Players Tournament
v Houlihan	9-3	1st round	Coral UK Championship
v Virgo	5-9	2nd round	Coral UK Championship
1983 v Griffiths	5-1	1st round	Lada Classic
v Werbeniuk	2-5	Quarter-final	Lada Classic
v Virgo	5-1	1st round	Benson & Hedges Masters
v S. Davis	5-4	Quarter-final	Benson & Hedges Masters
v Reardon	3-6	Semi-final	Benson & Hedges Masters
v M. Owen	6-0	Quarter-final	Woodpecker Welsh Championship
v Wilson	9-3	Semi-final	Woodpecker Welsh Championship
v Reardon	1-9	Final	Woodpecker Welsh Championship
v Knowles	5-1	1st round	Benson & Hedges Irish Masters
v Griffiths	4-5	Quarter-final	Benson & Hedges Irish Masters
v Wilson	10-2	1st round	Embassy World Championship
v Meo	11-13	2nd round	Embassy World Championship

	v Wildman	5-4	1st round	Jameson International
	v Martin	5-0	2nd round	Jameson International
	v Thorburn	2-5	Quarter-final	Jameson International
	v Campbell	3-5	1st round	Professional Players Tournament
	v Watterson	9-2	1st round	Coral UK Championship
	v Knowles	5-9	2nd round	Coral UK Championship
1984	v Parrott	4-5	Qualifying	Lada Classic
	v Higgins	2-5	1st round	Benson & Hedges Masters
	v Everton	6-1	1st round	Strongbow Welsh Championship
	v Griffiths	9-5	Semi-final	Strongbow Welsh Championship
	v Wilson	**9-3**	**Final**	**Strongbow Welsh Championship**
	v Hallett	10-4	1st round	Embassy World Championship
	v N. Foulds	13-6	2nd round	Embassy World Championship
	v Dennis Taylor	8-13	Quarter-final	Embassy World Championship
	v E. Hughes	1-5	1st round	Jameson International
	v E. McLaughlin	5-4	1st round	Rothmans Grand Prix
	v Wildman	5-0	2nd round	Rothmans Grand Prix
	v Charlton	5-4	3rd round	Rothmans Grand Prix
	v Thorburn	3-5	Quarter-final	Rothmans Grand Prix
	v Hallett	9-2	1st round	Coral UK Open
	v White	2-9	2nd round	Coral UK Open
1985	v Wilson	4-5	1st round	Mercantile Credit Classic
	v Knowles	5-3	1st round	Benson & Hedges Masters
	v Meo	5-4	Quarter-final	Benson & Hedges Masters
	v Griffiths	6-2	Semi-final	Benson & Hedges Masters
	v Thorburn	6-9	Final	Benson & Hedges Masters
	v V. Harris	5-6	1st round	Dulux British Open
	v Macleod	10-5	1st round	Embassy World Championship
	v Knowles	6-13	2nd round	Embassy World Championship
	v Newbury	6-5	Quarter-final	BCE Welsh Championship
	v Wilson	9-2	Semi-final	BCE Welsh Championship
	v Griffiths	4-9	Final	BCE Welsh Championship
	v Wych	5-1	3rd round	Goya Matchroom Trophy
	v Campbell	1-5	4th round	Goya Matchroom Trophy
	v Chappel	5-1	3rd round	Rothmans Grand Prix
	v Campbell	2-5	4th round	Rothmans Grand Prix
	v Morra	9-2	3rd round	Coral UK Open
	v West	4-9	4th round	Coral UK Open
1986	v King	5-4	3rd round	Mercantile Credit Classic
	v O'Kane	5-3	4th round	Mercantile Credit Classic
	v Werbeniuk	5-3	5th round	Mercantile Credit Classic
	v N. Foulds	5-3	Quarter-final	Mercantile Credit Classic
	v Thorburn	6-9	Semi-final	Mercantile Credit Classic
	v Dennis Taylor	2-5	1st round	Benson & Hedges Masters
	v Roscoe	6-4	Quarter-final	Zetters Welsh Championship
	v W. Jones	9-7	Semi-final	Zetters Welsh Championship
	v Griffiths	3-9	Final	Zetters Welsh Championship
	v Fagan	1-5	3rd round	Dulux British Open
	v̄ Mans	10-3	1st round	Embassy World Championship
	v S. Davis	5-13	2nd round	Embassy World Championship
	v M. Gibson	5-3	3rd round	BCE International
	v Reynolds	2-5	4th round	BCE International
	v B. Harris	5-2	3rd round	Rothmans Grand Prix
	v Wych	5-1	4th round	Rothmans Grand Prix
	v Knowles	1-5	5th round	Rothmans Grand Prix
	v J. McLaughlin	9-6	3rd round	Tennents UK Open
	v Longworth	1-9	4th round	Tennents UK Open
1987	v Dodd	4-5	3rd round	Mercantile Credit Classic
	v S. Davis	2-5	1st round	Benson & Hedges Masters
	v Meo	4-5	Quarter-final	Benson & Hedges Masters
	v Roscoe	6-2	Quarter-final	Matchroom Welsh Championship
	v Chappel	9-2	Semi-final	Matchroom Welsh Championship
	v Newbury	**9-7**	**Final**	**Matchroom Welsh Championship**

	v Owers	5-3	3rd round	Dulux British Open
	v P. Francisco	5-3	4th round	Dulux British Open
	v Thorburn	4-5	5th round	Dulux British Open
	v David Taylor	10-5	1st round	Embassy World Championship
	v O'Kane	5-13	2nd round	Embassy World Championship
	v Roe	4-5	3rd round	Fidelity International
	v Chambers	2-5	3rd round	Rothmans Grand Prix
	v M. Smith	9-7	3rd round	Tennents UK Open
1988	v F. Davis	5-0	3rd round	Mercantile Credit Classic
	v Martin	4-5	4th round	Mercantile Credit Classic
	v White	0-5	1st round	Benson & Hedges Masters
	v M. Bennett	6-3	Quarter-final	Welsh Championship
	v W. Jones	5-9	Semi-final	Welsh Championship
	v O'Kane	3-5	3rd round	MIM Britannia British Open
	v West	10-6	1st round	Embassy World Championship
	v N. Foulds	1-13	2nd round	Embassy World Championship

TOMMY MURPHY (Northern Ireland)

Born 8.1.62. **Turned professional** 1981. **World ranking** 42 (44.) **Amateur career** 1981 Northern Ireland champion. **Best professional performances** Last 16 1988 Mercantile Credit Classic, 1987 Dulux British Open.

1981	v Johnson	1-9	Qualifying	Coral UK Championship
1982	v Fagan	6-2	Quarter-final	Irish Championship
	v Dennis Taylor	0-6	Semi-final	Irish Championship
	v Morra	5-9	Qualifying	Embassy World Championship
	v Fisher	1-5	Qualifying	Jameson International
	v Reardon	0-5	1st round	Professional Players Tournament
	v Everton	9-4	Qualifying	Coral UK Championship
	v Sinclair	5-9	Qualifying	Coral UK Championship
1983	v Fagan	4-6	Quarter-final	Irish Championship
	v Houlihan	10-9	Qualifying	Embassy World Championship
	v Virgo	8-10	Qualifying	Embassy World Championship
	v Sheehan	5-2	Qualifying	Jameson International
	v Thorne	2-5	Qualifying	Jameson International
	v Macleod	5-0	1st round	Professional Players Tournament
	v Stevens	1-5	2nd round	Professional Players Tournament
	v Demarco	9-4	Qualifying	Coral UK Championship
	v Donnelly	9-4	Qualifying	Coral UK Championship
	v Dennis Taylor	6-9	1st round	Coral UK Championship
1984	v Fitzmaurice	10-8	Qualifying	Embassy World Championship
	v Morra	5-10	Qualifying	Embassy World Championship
	v Bales	4-5	Qualifying	Jameson International
	v G. Foulds	5-1	Qualifying	Rothmans Grand Prix
	v Miles	3-5	1st round	Rothmans Grand Prix
	v Kearney	9-2	Qualifying	Coral UK Open
	v Watterson	9-4	Qualifying	Coral UK Open
	v Martin	9-8	Qualifying	Coral UK Open
	v S. Davis	1-9	1st round	Coral UK Open
1985	v Fowler	0-5	Qualifying	Mercantile Credit Classic
	v Sheehan	6-3	Qualifying	Dulux British Open
	v Macleod	5-6	1st round	Dulux British Open
	v Browne	6-3	Qualifying	Irish Championship
	v Fagan	2-6	Quarter-final	Irish Championship
	v P. Francisco	4-10	Qualifying	Embassy World Championship
	v Jack Rea	5-1	2nd round	Goya Matchroom Trophy
	v E. Hughes	5-3	3rd round	Goya Matchroom Trophy
	v Higgins	2-5	4th round	Goya Matchroom Trophy
	v Mikkelsen	4-5	2nd round	Rothmans Grand Prix

	v Everton	9-4	2nd round	Coral UK Open
	v Macleod	7-9	3rd round	Coral UK Open
1986	v Chappel	5-4	2nd round	Mercantile Credit Classic
	v Martin	3-5	3rd round	Mercantile Credit Classic
	v Duggan	1-5	2nd round	Dulux British Open
	v J. McLaughlin	10-7	Qualifying	Embassy World Championship
	v Thornley	10-3	Qualifying	Embassy World Championship
	v E. Hughes	7-10	Qualifying	Embassy World Championship
	v O'Boye	5-0	1st round	Strongbow Irish Championship
	v Kearney	6-2	Quarter-final	Strongbow Irish Championship
	v Dennis Taylor	3-6	Semi-final	Strongbow Irish Championship
	v Donnelly	5-2	2nd round	BCE International
	v Johnson	4-5	3rd round	BCE International
	v Anderson	4-5	2nd round	Rothmans Grand Prix
	v D. Hughes	9-0	2nd round	Tennents UK Open
	v Thorne	4-9	3rd round	Tennents UK Open
1987	v Bales	5-2	2nd round	Mercantile Credit Classic
	v Longworth	3-5	3rd round	Mercantile Credit Classic
	v D. Gilbert	5-4	2nd round	Dulux British Open
	v Wych	5-1	3rd round	Dulux British Open
	v Reardon	5-4	4th round	Dulux British Open
	v Knowles	3-5	5th round	Dulux British Open
	v Jenkins	10-4	Qualifying	Embassy World Championship
	v Miles	10-7	Qualifying	Embassy World Championship
	v Longworth	2-10	Qualifying	Embassy World Championship
	v Kearney	1-5	1st round	Matchroom Irish Championship
	v Medati	5-3	2nd round	Fidelity International
	v Virgo	1-5	3rd round	Fidelity International
	v Van Rensberg	4-5	2nd round	Rothmans Grand Prix
	v M. Gibson	9-0	2nd round	Tennents UK Open
	v Drago	9-7	3rd round	Tennents UK Open
	v Thorne	4-9	4th round	Tennents UK Open
1988	v V. Harris	5-2	2nd round	Mercantile Credit Classic
	v Campbell	5-3	3rd round	Mercantile Credit Classic
	v Reynolds	5-4	4th round	Mercantile Credit Classic
	v Knowles	3-5	5th round	Mercantile Credit Classic
	v Kelly	5-1	1st round	Irish Championship
	v Browne	5-6	Quarter-final	Irish Championship
	v Meadowcroft	5-4	2nd round	MIM Britannia British Open
	v Virgo	1-5	3rd round	MIM Britannia British Open
	v Roscoe	10-8	Qualifying	Embassy World Championship
	v Chaperon	5-10	Qualifying	Embassy World Championship

STEVE NEWBURY (Wales)

Born 21.4.56. **Turned professional** 1984. **World ranking** 25 (45). **Amateur career** 1980 Welsh champion. **Best professional performance** Semi-finals 1988 Mercantile Credit Classic.

1984	v Longworth	5-4	Qualifying	Jameson International
	v Burke	5-0	Qualifying	Jameson International
	v Fagan	5-0	Qualifying	Jameson International
	v Miles	5-1	Qualifying	Jameson International
	v Werbeniuk	5-2	1st round	Jameson International
	v Knowles	4-5	2nd round	Jameson International
	v Fisher	5-0	Qualifying	Rothmans Grand Prix
	v Thorne	2-5	1st round	Rothmans Grand Prix
	v Rigitano	9-6	Qualifying	Coral UK Open
	v Jonik	9-3	Qualifying	Coral UK Open
	v Dodd	6-9	Qualifying	Coral UK Open
1985	v V. Harris	5-3	Qualifying	Mercantile Credit Classic

v Burke	5-1	Qualifying	Mercantile Credit Classic
v Morra	5-2	Qualifying	Mercantile Credit Classic
v E. Hughes	3-5	Qualifying	Mercantile Credit Classic
v Browne	6-0	Qualifying	Dulux British Open
v Sinclair	6-3	1st round	Dulux British Open
v Griffiths	5-3	2nd round	Dulux British Open
v Dennis Taylor	3-5	3rd round	Dulux British Open
v D. Hughes	10-9	Qualifying	Embassy World Championship
v Burke	10-3	Qualifying	Embassy World Championship
v Scott	10-2	Qualifying	Embassy World Championship
v E. Hughes	6-10	Qualifying	Embassy World Championship
v W. Jones	6-2	1st round	BCE Welsh Championship
v Mountjoy	5-6	Quarter-final	BCE Welsh Championship
v Jonik	5-4	2nd round	Goya Matchroom Trophy
v Griffiths	2-5	3rd round	Goya Matchroom Trophy
v Burke	5-3	2nd round	Rothmans Grand Prix
v David Taylor	2-5	3rd round	Rothmans Grand Prix
v Houlihan	9-3	2nd round	Coral UK Open
v Stevens	7-9	3rd round	Coral UK Open
1986 v Cripsey	4-5	2nd round	Mercantile Credit Classic
v Wilson	4-6	Quarter-final	Zetters Welsh Championship
v Oliver	5-2	2nd round	Dulux British Open
v O'Kane	5-3	3rd round	Dulux British Open
v Meo	0-5	4th round	Dulux British Open
v Agrawal	10-5	Qualifying	Embassy World Championship
v Black	10-2	Qualifying	Embassy World Championship
v Spencer	7-10	Qualifying	Embassy World Championship
v Dunning	5-4	2nd round	BCE International
v S. Francisco	4-5	3rd round	BCE International
v D. Gilbert	5-1	2nd round	Rothmans Grand Prix
v Reynolds	5-0	3rd round	Rothmans Grand Prix
v O'Boye	5-2	4th round	Rothmans Grand Prix
v S. Francisco	2-5	5th round	Rothmans Grand Prix
v Owers	8-9	2nd round	Tennents UK Open
1987 v Meadowcroft	5-1	2nd round	Mercantile Credit Classic
v White	4-5	3rd round	Mercantile Credit Classic
v Wilson	6-2	Quarter-final	Matchroom Welsh Championship
v Griffiths	9-6	Semi-final	Matchroom Welsh Championship
v Mountjoy	7-9	Final	Matchroom Welsh Championship
v Roscoe	3-5	2nd round	Dulux British Open
v Dodd	10-7	Qualifying	Embassy World Championship
v Rigitano	10-4	Qualifying	Embassy World Championship
v Hallett	4-10	Qualifying	Embassy World Championship
v Fisher	5-0	2nd round	Fidelity International
v P. Francisco	5-2	3rd round	Fidelity International
v Thorburn	3-5	4th round	Fidelity International
v Meakin	5-1	2nd round	Rothmans Grand Prix
v Meo	5-0	3rd round	Rothmans Grand Prix
v Thorburn	5-0	4th round	Rothmans Grand Prix
v Gary Wilkinson	5-3	5th round	Rothmans Grand Prix
v Dennis Taylor	2-5	Quarter-final	Rothmans Grand Prix
v Foldvari	9-5	2nd round	Tennents UK Open
v Parrott	5-9	3rd round	Tennents UK Open
1988 v Kearney	5-1	2nd round	Mercantile Credit Classic
v E. Hughes	5-1	3rd round	Mercantile Credit Classic
v Thorburn	5-3	4th round	Mercantile Credit Classic
v Clark	5-2	5th round	Mercantile Credit Classic
v Griffiths	5-4	Quarter-final	Mercantile Credit Classic
v S. Davis	2-9	Semi-final	Mercantile Credit Classic
v Wilson	3-6	Quarter-final	Welsh Championship
v Oliver	5-3	2nd round	MIM Britannia British Open
v Thorburn	2-5	3rd round	MIM Britannia British Open
v Lawlor	10-3	Qualifying	Embassy World Championship

v M. Smith	10-9	Qualifying	Embassy World Championship
v West	8-10	Qualifying	Embassy World Championship

JOE O'BOYE (Republic of Ireland)

Born 6.3.60. **Turned professional** 1985. **World ranking** 35 (56). **Amateur career** 1980 English champion. **Best professional performances** Quarter-finals 1987 Fidelity International, 1988 MIM Britannia British Open.

1985	v Parkin	5-3	1st round	Goya Matchroom Trophy
	v Miles	2-5	2nd round	Goya Matchroom Trophy
	v Hendry	5-4	1st round	Rothmans Grand Prix
	v Chaperon	5-3	2nd round	Rothmans Grand Prix
	v Mans	5-3	3rd round	Rothmans Grand Prix
	v White	4-5	4th round	Rothmans Grand Prix
	v Bennett	9-3	1st round	Coral UK Open
	v Gauvreau	9-5	2nd round	Coral UK Open
	v Knowles	5-9	3rd round	Coral UK Open
1986	v Wilkinson	5-1	1st round	Mercantile Credit Classic
	v Longworth	5-1	2nd round	Mercantile Credit Classic
	v Meo	3-5	3rd round	Mercantile Credit Classic
	v Jim Bear	5-1	1st round	Dulux British Open
	v T. Jones	2-5	2nd round	Dulux British Open
	v Oliver	8-10	Qualifying	Embassy World Championship
	v Murphy	0-5	1st round	Strongbow Irish Championship
	v Mikkelsen	5-4	2nd round	BCE International
	v Williams	0-5	3rd round	BCE International
	v Edmonds	5-2	2nd round	Rothmans Grand Prix
	v Thorburn	5-4	3rd round	Rothmans Grand Prix
	v Newbury	2-5	4th round	Rothmans Grand Prix
	v Duggan	9-4	2nd round	Tennents UK Open
	v Meo	3-9	3rd round	Tennents UK Open
1987	v V. Harris	5-1	2nd round	Mercantile Credit Classic
	v Griffiths	1-5	3rd round	Mercantile Credit Classic
	v Bradley	5-1	2nd round	Dulux British Open
	v Reardon	5-4	3rd round	Dulux British Open
	v N. Gilbert	10-5	Qualifying	Embassy World Championship
	v Bradley	7-10	Qualifying	Embassy World Championship
	v Kelly	5-0	1st round	Matchroom Irish Championship
	v Higgins	wo	Quarter-final	Matchroom Irish Championship
	v E. Hughes	6-3	Semi-final	Matchroom Irish Championship
	v Dennis Taylor	2-9	Final	Matchroom Irish Championship
	v Fagan	5-1	2nd round	Fidelity International
	v Stevens	5-1	3rd round	Fidelity International
	v Foldvari	5-4	4th round	Fidelity International
	v Clark	5-2	5th round	Fidelity International
	v Hendry	2-5	Quarter-final	Fidelity International
	v Chambers	3-5	2nd round	Rothmans Grand Prix
	v Donnelly	9-2	2nd round	Tennents UK Open
	v Stevens	8-9	3rd round	Tennents UK Open
1988	v Sheehan	5-3	2nd round	Mercantile Credit Classic
	v Reynolds	3-5	3rd round	Mercantile Credit Classic
	v Sheehan	5-0	1st round	Irish Championship
	v Higgins	6-4	Quarter-final	Irish Championship
	v J. McLaughlin	4-6	Semi-final	Irish Championship
	v Jenkins	5-1	2nd round	MIM Britannia British Open
	v Reynolds	5-2	3rd round	MIM Britannia British Open
	v Campbell	5-1	4th round	MIM Britannia British Open
	v Roe	5-1	5th round	MIM Britannia British Open
	v Hallett	4-5	Quarter-final	MIM Britannia British Open
	v James	7-10	Qualifying	Embassy World Championship

DENE O'KANE (New Zealand)

Born 24.2.63. **Turned professional** 1984. **World ranking** 23 (35). **Amateur career** 1980 New Zealand champion. **Best professional performances** Quarter-finals 1987 Embassy World Championship, 1988 MIM Britannia British Open.

Year	Opponent	Score	Round	Tournament
1984	v Parkin	5-2	Qualifying	Jameson International
	v E. McLaughlin	5-1	Qualifying	Jameson International
	v Fitzmaurice	5-4	Qualifying	Jameson International
	v Hallett	5-4	Qualifying	Jameson International
	v Thorne	3-5	1st round	Jameson International
	v Kelly	5-4	Qualifying	Rothmans Grand Prix
	v David Taylor	1-5	1st round	Rothmans Grand Prix
	v W. Jones	9-7	Qualifying	Coral UK Open
	v Duggan	9-6	Qualifying	Coral UK Open
	v Scott	7-9	Qualifying	Coral UK Open
1985	v W. Jones	0-5	Qualifying	Mercantile Credit Classic
	v Cripsey	6-4	Qualifying	Dulux British Open
	v Campbell	6-4	1st round	Dulux British Open
	v V. Harris	5-3	2nd round	Dulux British Open
	v Martin	5-4	3rd round	Dulux British Open
	v S. Davis	1-5	Quarter-final	Dulux British Open
	v J. McLaughlin	wo	Qualifying	Embassy World Championship
	v V. Harris	10-5	Qualifying	Embassy World Championship
	v Jonik	10-5	Qualifying	Embassy World Championship
	v Dodd	10-7	Qualifying	Embassy World Championship
	v Martin	10-8	Qualifying	Embassy World Championship
	v David Taylor	4-10	1st round	Embassy World Championship
	v B. Harris	3-5	3rd round	Goya Matchroom Trophy
	v Edmonds	2-5	3rd round	Rothmans Grand Prix
	v Chappel	5-9	3rd round	Coral UK Open
1986	v Medati	5-0	3rd round	Mercantile Credit Classic
	v Mountjoy	3-5	4th round	Mercantile Credit Classic
	v Newbury	3-5	3rd round	Dulux British Open
	v Hendry	9-10	Qualifying	Embassy World Championship
	v Oliver	5-2	2nd round	BCE International
	v Hallett	5-1	3rd round	BCE International
	v Owers	0-5	4th round	BCE International
	v M. Bennett	2-5	2nd round	Rothmans Grand Prix
	v Jenkins	9-5	2nd round	Tennents UK Open
	v Werbeniuk	9-5	3rd round	Tennents UK Open
	v Griffiths	0-9	4th round	Tennents UK Open
1987	v G. Foulds	4-5	2nd round	Mercantile Credit Classic
	v Rowswell	4-5	2nd round	Dulux British Open
	v D. Gilbert	10-2	Qualifying	Embassy World Championship
	v Black	10-2	Qualifying	Embassy World Championship
	v P. Francisco	10-5	Qualifying	Embassy World Championship
	v Thorburn	10-5	1st round	Embassy World Championship
	v Mountjoy	13-5	2nd round	Embassy World Championship
	v White	6-13	Quarter-final	Embassy World Championship
	v Van Rensberg	5-3	2nd round	Fidelity International
	v S. Davis	2-5	3rd round	Fidelity International
	v Gary Wilkinson	2-5	2nd round	Rothmans Grand Prix
	v Rowswell	9-2	2nd round	Tennents UK Open
	v Charlton	9-8	3rd round	Tennents UK Open
	v Dennis Taylor	9-7	4th round	Tennents UK Open
	v Thorne	7-9	5th round	Tennents UK Open
1988	v Rowswell	4-5	2nd round	Mercantile Credit Classic
	v Whitthread	5-2	2nd round	MIM Britannia British Open
	v Mountjoy	5-3	3rd round	MIM Britannia British Open
	v Browne	5-2	4th round	MIM Britannia British Open

v Johnson	5-2	5th round	MIM Britannia British Open
v Parrott	2-5	Quarter-final	MIM Britannia British Open
v Sinclair	9-10	Qualifying	Embassy World Championship

BILL OLIVER (England)
Born 3.12.48. **Turned professional** 1983. **World ranking** 84 (85).

1983 v T. Jones	2-5	Qualifying	Professional Players Tournament
v Andrewartha	1-9	Qualifying	Coral UK Championship
1984 v Dunning	10-3	Qualifying	Embassy World Championship
v Caggianello	10-7	Qualifying	Embassy World Championship
v Williams	8-10	Qualifying	Embassy World Championship
v D. Hughes	5-4	Qualifying	Jameson International
v Chalmers	4-5	Qualifying	Jameson International
v Bennett	5-3	Qualifying	Rothmans Grand Prix
v White	1-5	1st round	Rothmans Grand Prix
v Fowler	3-9	Qualifying	Coral UK Open
1985 v Longworth	1-5	Qualifying	Mercantile Credit Classic
v Fowler	7-9	Qualifying	Tolly Cobbold English Championship
v Thorne	3-6	1st round	Dulux British Open
v Foldvari	3-10	Qualifying	Embassy World Championship
v Morra	1-5	2nd round	Goya Matchroom Trophy
v Fagan	5-4	2nd round	Rothmans Grand Prix
v Thorburn	0-5	3rd round	Rothmans Grand Prix
v Miles	4-9	2nd round	Coral UK Open
1986 v Bradley	3-5	2nd round	Mercantile Credit Classic
v Dodd	9-5	2nd round	Tolly Cobbold English Championship
v Parrott	0-9	3rd round	Tolly Cobbold English Championship
v Newbury	2-5	2nd round	Dulux British Open
v O'Boye	10-8	Qualifying	Embassy World Championship
v Fowler	8-10	Qualifying	Embassy World Championship
v Mienie	5-4	1st round	BCE International
v O'Kane	2-5	2nd round	BCE International
v Anderson	4-5	1st round	Rothmans Grand Prix
v Chalmers	9-6	1st round	Tennents UK Open
v Hendry	1-9	2nd round	Tennents UK Open
1987 v Greaves	5-4	1st round	Mercantile Credit Classic
v T. Jones	0-5	2nd round	Mercantile Credit Classic
v T. Jones	1-6	2nd round	Tolly Ales English Championship
v Jack Rea	5-1	1st round	Dulux British Open
v Drago	1-5	2nd round	Dulux British Open
v Watchorn	3-5	1st round	Fidelity International
v J. McLaughlin	2-5	2nd round	Rothmans Grand Prix
v Burke	9-1	1st round	Tennents UK Open
v Scott	9-4	2nd round	Tennents UK Open
v Thorne	3-9	3rd round	Tennents UK Open
1988 v Burke	5-2	1st round	Mercantile Credit Classic
v King	5-3	2nd round	Mercantile Credit Classic
v West	3-5	3rd round	Mercantile Credit Classic
v Marshall	3-6	1st round	English Championship
v M. Smith	5-0	1st round	MIM Britannia British Open
v Newbury	3-5	2nd round	MIM Britannia British Open
v Chalmers	10-9	Qualifying	Embassy World Championship
v Reardon	10-6	Qualifying	Embassy World Championship
v Robidoux	10-2	Qualifying	Embassy World Championship
v Wilson	6-10	Qualifying	Embassy World Championship

KEN OWERS (England)
Born 30.3.53. **Turned professional** 1986. **World ranking** 53 (53). **Best professional performance** Last 16 1986 BCE International.

1986 v Scott	5-1	2nd round	BCE International

	v White	5-2	3rd round	BCE International
	v O'Kane	5-0	4th round	BCE International
	v N. Foulds	1-5	5th round	BCE International
	v J. McLaughlin	2-5	1st round	Rothmans Grand Prix
	v D. Gilbert	9-8	1st round	Tennents UK Open
	v Newbury	9-8	2nd round	Tennents UK Open
	v S. Francisco	3-9	3rd round	Tennents UK Open
1987	v Houlihan	5-1	1st round	Mercantile Credit Classic
	v John Rea	2-5	2nd round	Mercantile Credit Classic
	v Bales	6-5	2nd round	Tolly Ales English Championship
	v N. Foulds	6-3	3rd round	Tolly Ales English Championship
	v Hallett	2-6	4th round	Tolly Ales English Championship
	v Jonik	5-4	1st round	Dulux British Open
	v F. Davis	5-3	2nd round	Dulux British Open
	v Mountjoy	1-5	3rd round	Dulux British Open
	v Fisher	10-5	Qualifying	Embassy World Championship
	v F. Davis	10-5	Qualifying	Embassy World Championship
	v King	4-10	Qualifying	Embassy World Championship
	v Meadowcroft	5-3	2nd round	Fidelity International
	v E. Hughes	4-5	3rd round	Fidelity International
	v Glen Wilkinson	4-5	2nd round	Rothmans Grand Prix
	v Roe	7-9	2nd round	Tennents UK Open
1988	v Fisher	5-0	2nd round	Mercantile Credit Classic
	v Williams	5-3	3rd round	Mercantile Credit Classic
	v P. Francisco	0-5	4th round	Mercantile Credit Classic
	v Meakin	6-2	2nd round	English Championship
	v David Taylor	6-3	3rd round	English Championship
	v Knowles	4-6	4th round	English Championship
	v Miles	3-5	2nd round	MIM Britannia British Open
	v Roe	10-7	Qualifying	Embassy World Championship
	v Wright	8-10	Qualifying	Embassy World Championship

JOHN PARROTT (England)

Born 11.5.64. **Turned professional** 1983. **World ranking** 7 (13). **Best professional performance** Runner-up 1988 Mercantile Credit Classic, winner 1988 Kent Cup.

1983	v Watchorn	5-0	Qualifying	Professional Players Tournament
	v Fagan	5-2	1st round	Professional Players Tournament
	v Griffiths	1-5	2nd round	Professional Players Tournament
	v Scott	9-7	Qualifying	Coral UK Championship
	v Fisher	9-0	Qualifying	Coral UK Championship
	v Meo	7-9	1st round	Coral UK Championship
1984	v Mountjoy	5-4	Qualifying	Lada Classic
	v Higgins	5-2	1st round	Lada Classic
	v Knowles	5-1	Qualifying	Lada Classic
	v S. Davis	4-5	Semi-final	Lada Classic
	v D. Hughes	10-3	Qualifying	Embassy World Championship
	v Everton	10-2	Qualifying	Embassy World Championship
	v Mans	10-0	Qualifying	Embassy World Championship
	v Knowles	10-7	1st round	Embassy World Championship
	v Dennis Taylor	11-13	2nd round	Embassy World Championship
	v Gauvreau	4-5	Qualifying	Jameson International
	v Gauvreau	5-3	1st round	Rothmans Grand Prix
	v Charlton	1-5	2nd round	Rothmans Grand Prix
	v Fitzmaurice	9-6	Qualifying	Coral UK Open
	v Thorne	7-9	1st round	Coral UK Open
1985	v Medati	3-5	Qualifying	Mercantile Credit Classic
	v G. Foulds	9-4	1st round	Tolly Cobbold English Championship
	v David Taylor	6-9	2nd round	Tolly Cobbold English Championship

John Parrott

v John Rea	6-4	1st round	Dulux British Open
v Dennis Taylor	2-5	2nd round	Dulux British Open
v Fowler	10-2	Qualifying	Embassy World Championship
v Spencer	10-3	1st round	Embassy World Championship
v Stevens	13-6	2nd round	Embassy World Championship
v Reardon	12-13	Quarter-final	Embassy World Championship
v Thorne	5-0	Quarter-final	Winfield Australian Masters
v Campbell	4-6	Semi-final	Winfield Australian Masters
v White	3-5	Semi-final	Carlsberg Trophy
v W. Jones	5-3	3rd round	Goya Matchroom Trophy
v Meo	5-4	4th round	Goya Matchroom Trophy
v Griffiths	5-1	5th round	Goya Matchroom Trophy
v Dennis Taylor	1-5	Quarter-final	Goya Matchroom Trophy
v Longworth	2-5	3rd round	Rothmans Grand Prix
v Dennis Taylor	1-5	1st round	BCE Canadian Masters
v Sinclair	9-2	3rd round	Coral UK Open
v Thorburn	6-9	4th round	Coral UK Open
1986 v Van Rensberg	3-5	3rd round	Mercantile Credit Classic
v Oliver	9-0	3rd round	Tolly Cobbold English Championship
v Virgo	6-9	4th round	Tolly Cobbold English Championship
v Roscoe	5-2	3rd round	Dulux British Open
v Fagan	5-0	4th round	Dulux British Open
v Wych	4-5	5th round	Dulux British Open
v Foldvari	10-6	Qualifying	Embassy World Championship
v Meo	10-4	1st round	Embassy World Championship
v White	8-13	2nd round	Embassy World Championship
v Thorburn	1-5	1st round	Langs Scottish Masters
v Hendry	3-5	3rd round	BCE International
v Cripsey	5-4	3rd round	Rothmans Grand Prix
v Meo	3-5	4th round	Rothmans Grand Prix
v Bradley	9-4	3rd round	Tennents UK Open
v Johnson	9-1	4th round	Tennents UK Open
v Longworth	9-6	5th round	Tennents UK Open
v Knowles	9-4	Quarter-final	Tennents UK Open
v N. Foulds	3-9	Semi-final	Tennents UK Open
1987 v T. Jones	5-2	3rd round	Mercantile Credit Classic
v Higgins	5-2	4th round	Mercantile Credit Classic
v Charlton	5-4	5th round	Mercantile Credit Classic
v S. Davis	4-5	Quarter-final	Mercantile Credit Classic
v Wildman	6-1	3rd round	Tolly Ales English Championship
v Virgo	6-2	4th round	Tolly Ales English Championship
v Meo	3-6	Quarter-final	Tolly Ales English Championship
v King	1-5	3rd round	Dulux British Open
v Fowler	10-3	Qualifying	Embassy World Championship
v Meo	10-8	1st round	Embassy World Championship
v White	11-13	2nd round	Embassy World Championship
v Chappel	5-1	3rd round	Fidelity International
v Chaperon	5-1	4th round	Fidelity International
v S. Davis	2-5	5th round	Fidelity International
v Dodd	5-1	3rd round	Rothmans Grand Prix
v Stevens	5-0	4th round	Rothmans Grand Prix
v Griffiths	5-4	5th round	Rothmans Grand Prix
v Chaperon	5-2	Quarter-final	Rothmans Grand Prix
v Hendry	7-9	Semi-final	Rothmans Grand Prix
v Newbury	9-5	3rd round	Tennents UK Open
v Wych	9-6	4th round	Tennents UK Open
v Knowles	9-4	5th round	Tennents UK Open
v S. Davis	5-9	Quarter-final	Tennents UK Open
1988 v Wildman	5-2	3rd round	Mercantile Credit Classic
v David Taylor	5-0	4th round	Mercantile Credit Classic
v Virgo	5-0	5th round	Mercantile Credit Classic
v Dennis Taylor	5-1	Quarter-final	Mercantile Credit Classic
v Knowles	9-4	Semi-final	Mercantile Credit Classic

v S. Davis	11-13	Final	Mercantile Credit Classic
v Foulds	5-4	1st round	Benson & Hedges Masters
v Thorburn	5-4	Quarter-final	Benson & Hedges Masters
v Hallett	5-6	Semi-final	Benson & Hedges Masters
v Lawlor	6-3	3rd round	English Championship
v Reynolds	2-6	4th round	English Championship
v Foldvari	5-1	3rd round	MIM Britannia British Open
v Virgo	5-1	4th round	MIM Britannia British Open
v N. Foulds	5-0	5th round	MIM Britannia British Open
v O'Kane	5-2	Quarter-final	MIM Britannia British Open
v Hallett	8-9	Semi-final	MIM Britannia British Open
v Clark	5-1	Final	Kent Cup
v King	10-4	1st round	Embassy World Championship
v Thorburn	10-13	2nd round	Embassy World Championship

JACK REA (Northern Ireland)

Born 6.4.21. **Turned professional** 1948. **World ranking** 99 (112). **Amateur career** 1947 Northern Ireland champion. **Best professional performance** Runner-up 1957 World Championship.

1969	v G. Owen	17-25	Quarter-final	World Championship
1970	v Spencer	15-31	Quarter-final	World Championship
1972	v Higgins	11-19	1st round	World Championship
1973	v Houlihan	2-9	1st round	World Championship
1976	v Anderson	8-5	Qualifying	Embassy World Championship
1977	v John Rea	9-11	Qualifying	Embassy World Championship
	v Fagan	1-5	1st round	Super Crystalate UK Championship
1978	v Meadowcroft	5-9	Qualifying	Coral UK Championship
1979	v Dunning	5-9	Prelim	Embassy World Championship
	v Bennett	9-8	1st round	Coral UK Championship
	v Houlihan	3-9	2nd round	Coral UK Championship
1980	v Thorne	1-9	Qualifying	Embassy World Championship
1981	v D. Hughes	4-5	Qualifying	Jameson International
1982	v E. Hughes	1-6	Quarter-final	Irish Championship
	v Bennett	8-5	Qualifying	Embassy World Championship
	v Werbeniuk	2-5	2nd round	Professional Players Tournament
	v Roscoe	6-9	Qualifying	Coral UK Championship
1983	v Higgins	3-6	Quarter-final	Irish Championship
	v David Taylor	7-8	Qualifying	Embassy World Championship
	v Edmonds	1-5	Qualifying	Jameson International
	v French	5-9	Qualifying	Coral UK Championship
1984	v Bradley	2-5	Qualifying	Jameson International
1985	v Foldvari	4-5	Qualifying	Mercantile Credit Classic
	v Dennis Taylor	0-6	Quarter-final	Irish Championship
	v Murphy	1-5	2nd round	Goya Matchroom Trophy
1986	v Fisher	3-5	2nd round	Mercantile Credit Classic
	v Bradley	1-5	2nd round	Dulux British Open
	v Kelly	0-5	1st round	Strongbow Irish Championship
	v Darrington	5-4	1st round	BCE International
	v W. Jones	1-5	2nd round	BCE International
	v D. Hughes	5-2	1st round	Rothmans Grand Prix
	v B. Harris	0-5	2nd round	Rothmans Grand Prix
	v B. Harris	5-9	2nd round	Tennents UK Open
1987	v Kelly	5-3	1st round	Mercantile Credit Classic
	v Hendry	1-5	2nd round	Mercantile Credit Classic
	v Oliver	1-5	1st round	Dulux British Open
	v Bear	5-10	Qualifying	Embassy World Championship
	v Browne	3-5	1st round	Matchroom Irish Championship
	v Burke	5-1	1st round	Fidelity International
	v G. Foulds	5-4	2nd round	Fidelity International
	v Spencer	0-5	3rd round	Fidelity International
	v Rigitano	4-5	1st round	Rothmans Grand Prix

	v Watterson	9-6	1st round	Tennents UK Open
	v Chaperon	6-9	2nd round	Tennents UK Open
1988	v D. Gilbert	2-5	1st round	Mercantile Credit Classic
	v Browne	0-5	1st round	Irish Championship
	v Rowswell	1-5	1st round	MIM Britannia British Open
	v Mikkelsen	3-10	Qualifying	Embassy World Championship

JOHN REA (Scotland)

Born 5.12.51. **Turned professional** 1984. **World ranking** 81 (70). **Best professional performance** Last 32 1986 Dulux British Open.

1984	v Browne	2-5	Qualifying	Jameson International
	v Fitzmaurice	5-2	Qualifying	Rothmans Grand Prix
	v E. Hughes	5-4	1st round	Rothmans Grand Prix
	v David Taylor	1-5	2nd round	Rothmans Grand Prix
	v Bennett	9-5	Qualifying	Coral UK Open
	v Dunning	9-3	Qualifying	Coral UK Open
	v Edmonds	9-6	Qualifying	Coral UK Open
	v Johnson	6-9	Qualifying	Coral UK Open
1985	v Sheehan	2-5	Qualifying	Mercantile Credit Classic
	v Donnelly	6-2	1st round	Scottish Championship
	v Sinclair	2-6	Semi-final	Scottish Championship
	v Fisher	6-0	Qualifying	Dulux British Open
	v Parrott	4-6	1st round	Dulux British Open
	v W. Jones	3-10	Qualifying	Embassy World Championship
	v Bradley	1-5	2nd round	Goya Matchroom Trophy
	v W. Jones	0-5	2nd round	Rothmans Grand Prix
	v F. Davis	8-9	2nd round	Coral UK Open
1986	v Williamson	5-4	2nd round	Mercantile Credit Classic
	v Hallett	2-5	3rd round	Mercantile Credit Classic
	v King	5-1	2nd round	Dulux British Open
	v Reardon	5-3	3rd round	Dulux British Open
	v Virgo	0-5	4th round	Dulux British Open
	v Donnelly	6-1	Quarter-final	Canada Dry Scottish Championship
	v Gibson	0-6	Semi-final	Canada Dry Scottish Championship
	v E. McLaughlin	10-6	Qualifying	Embassy World Championship
	v Longworth	4-10	Qualifying	Embassy World Championship
	v Anderson	5-1	2nd round	BCE International
	v S. Davis	1-5	3rd round	BCE International
	v Sinclair	5-4	2nd round	Rothmans Grand Prix
	v Wych	2-5	3rd round	Rothmans Grand Prix
	v N. Gilbert	9-8	2nd round	Tennents UK Open
	v Knowles	4-9	3rd round	Tennents UK Open
1987	v Owers	5-2	2nd round	Mercantile Credit Classic
	v Meo	4-5	3rd round	Mercantile Credit Classic
	v Black	6-1	1st round	Scottish Championship
	v Hendry	0-6	Semi-final	Scottish Championship
	v Hargreaves	5-3	2nd round	Dulux British Open
	v Griffiths	2-5	3rd round	Dulux British Open
	v Rempe	9-10	Qualifying	Embassy World Championship
	v Bales	5-2	2nd round	Fidelity International
	v Thorne	3-5	3rd round	Fidelity International
	v Bradley	5-1	2nd round	Rothmans Grand Prix
	v P. Francisco	3-5	3rd round	Rothmans Grand Prix
	v J. McLaughlin	9-5	2nd round	Rothmans Grand Prix
	v Knowles	6-9	3rd round	Tennents UK Open
1988	v Bales	5-0	2nd round	Mercantile Credit Classic
	v Spencer	3-5	3rd round	Mercantile Credit Classic
	v Sinclair	6-5	Quarter-final	Scottish Championship
	v W. Jones	3-5	2nd round	MIM Britannia British Open
	v N. Gilbert	5-10	Qualifying	Embassy World Championship

RAY REARDON M.B.E. (Wales)

Born 8.10.32. **Turned professional** 1967. **World ranking** 40 (38). **Amateur career** 1950–55 Welsh champion, 1964 English champion. **Best professional performances** Winner World Championship 1970, 1973–76, 1978, Professional Players Tournament 1982, Benson & Hedges Masters 1976; Welsh champion 1981, 1983.

1969	v F. Davis	24-25	Quarter-final	World Championship
1970	v F. Davis	31-26	Quarter-final	World Championship (Apr)
	v Spencer	37-33	Semi-final	World Championship (Apr)
	v Pulman	**39-34**	**Final**	**World Championship (Apr)**
	v Spencer	15-34	Semi-final	World Championship (Nov)
1972	v Williams	23-25	Quarter-final	World Championship
1973	v Meadowcroft	16-10	2nd round	World Championship
	v G. Owen	16-6	Quarter-final	World Championship
	v Spencer	23-22	Semi-final	World Championship
	v Charlton	**38-32**	**Final**	**World Championship**
1974	v Meadowcroft	15-3	2nd round	World Championship
	v M. Owen	15-11	Quarter-final	World Championship
	v F. Davis	15-3	Semi-final	World Championship
	v Miles	**22-12**	**Final**	**World Championship**
1975	v Miles	5-3	Quarter-final	Benson & Hedges Masters
	v Williams	5-4	Semi-final	Benson & Hedges Masters
	v Spencer	8-9	Final	Benson & Hedges Masters
	v Simpson	15-11	2nd round	World Championship
	v Spencer	19-17	Quarter-final	World Championship
	v Higgins	19-14	Semi-final	World Championship
	v Charlton	**31-30**	**Final**	**World Championship**
1976	v Charlton	5-4	Semi-final	Benson & Hedges Masters
	v Miles	**7-3**	**Final**	**Benson & Hedges Masters**
	v Dunning	15-7	1st round	Embassy World Championship
	v Dennis Taylor	15-2	Quarter-final	Embassy World Championship
	v Mans	20-10	Semi-final	Embassy World Championship
	v Higgins	**27-16**	**Final**	**Embassy World Championship**
1977	v Miles	5-2	Semi-final	Benson & Hedges Masters
	v Mountjoy	6-7	Final	Benson & Hedges Masters
	v Fagan	13-7	1st round	Embassy World Championship
	v Spencer	6-13	Quarter-final	Embassy World Championship
	v Meadowcroft	4-5	2nd round	Super Crystalate UK Championship
1978	v Higgins	1-5	Semi-final	Benson & Hedges Masters
	v Mountjoy	13-9	1st round	Embassy World Championship
	v Werbeniuk	13-6	Quarter-final	Embassy World Championship
	v Charlton	18-14	Semi-final	Embassy World Championship
	v Mans	**25-18**	**Final**	**Embassy World Championship**
	v Thorne	6-9	1st round	Coral UK Championship
1979	v David Taylor	5-2	Quarter-final	Benson & Hedges Masters
	v Mans	3-5	Semi-final	Benson & Hedges Masters
	v Mountjoy	5-6	Final	Benson & Hedges Masters
	v Miles	13-8	1st round	Embassy World Championship
	v Dennis Taylor	8-13	Quarter-final	Embassy World Championship
1980	v Dennis Taylor	5-3	Quarter-final	Benson & Hedges Masters
	v Higgins	2-5	Semi-final	Benson & Hedges Masters
	v Higgins	1-5	Final	British Gold Cup
	v Wilson	9-3	1st round	Woodpecker Welsh Championship
	v Mountjoy	6-9	Final	Woodpecker Welsh Championship
	v Werbeniuk	13-6	2nd round	Embassy World Championship
	v David Taylor	11-13	Quarter-final	Embassy World Championship
	v Andrewartha	9-3	2nd round	Coral UK Championship
	v Williams	9-4	Quarter-final	Coral UK Championship
	v Higgins	7-9	Semi-final	Coral UK Championship
1981	v Spencer	1-5	Quarter-final	Benson & Hedges Masters
	v Griffiths	9-6	Semi-final	Woodpecker Welsh Championship

v **Wilson**	**9-6**	**Final**	**Woodpecker Welsh Championship**
v Higgins	6-5	Semi-final	Benson & Hedges Irish Masters
v Griffiths	7-9	Final	Benson & Hedges Irish Masters
v Spencer	13-11	2nd round	Embassy World Championship
v Werbeniuk	13-10	Quarter-final	Embassy World Championship
v Mountjoy	10-16	Semi-final	Embassy World Championship
v White	4-5	Quarter-final	Langs Supreme Scottish Masters
v Virgo	3-5	3rd round	Jameson International
v Johnson	9-7	3rd round	Coral UK Championship
v White	8-9	Quarter-final	Coral UK Championship
1982 v David Taylor	5-1	1st round	Lada Classic
v S. Davis	4-5	Semi-final	Lada Classic
v Dennis Taylor	5-3	1st round	Benson & Hedges Masters
v Griffiths	3-5	Quarter-final	Benson & Hedges Masters
v Everton	6-1	1st round	Welsh Championship
v Mountjoy	7-9	Semi-final	Welsh Championship
v Dennis Taylor	5-4	Quarter-final	Benson & Hedges Irish Masters
v Griffiths	3-6	Semi-final	Benson & Hedges Irish Masters
v Donnelly	10-5	1st round	Embassy World Championship
v Virgo	13-8	2nd round	Embassy World Championship
v S. Francisco	13-8	Quarter-final	Embassy World Championship
v Charlton	16-11	Semi-final	Embassy World Championship
v Higgins	15-18	Final	Embassy World Championship
v Griffiths	3-5	1st round	Langs Supreme Scottish Masters
v E. Hughes	5-3	1st round	Jameson International
v Knowles	2-5	2nd round	Jameson International
v Murphy	5-0	1st round	Professional Players Tournament
v Higgins	5-2	2nd round	Professional Players Tournament
v Macleod	5-2	3rd round	Professional Players Tournament
v Werbeniuk	5-3	Quarter-final	Professional Players Tournament
v Charlton	10-7	Semi-final	Professional Players Tournament
v **White**	**10-5**	**Final**	**Professional Players Tournament**
v Wildman	9-5	1st round	Coral UK Championship
v Hallett	9-8	2nd round	Coral UK Championship
v White	9-8	Quarter-final	Coral UK Championship
v Higgins	6-9	Semi-final	Coral UK Championship
1983 v Spencer	3-5	1st round	Lada Classic
v Reynolds	5-1	1st round	Benson & Hedges Masters
v White	5-2	Quarter-final	Benson & Hedges Masters
v Mountjoy	6-3	Semi-final	Benson & Hedges Masters
v Thorburn	7-9	Final	Benson & Hedges Masters
v **White**	**9-6**	**Final**	**Yamaha International Masters**
v Andrewartha	6-2	Quarter-final	Woodpecker Welsh Championship
v Griffiths	9-4	Semi-final	Woodpecker Welsh Championship
v **Mountjoy**	**9-1**	**Final**	**Woodpecker Welsh Championship**
v Meo	5-4	Quarter-final	Benson & Hedges Irish Masters
v Higgins	6-3	Semi-final	Benson & Hedges Irish Masters
v S. Davis	2-9	Final	Benson & Hedges Irish Masters
v E. Hughes	10-7	1st round	Embassy World Championship
v Knowles	12-13	2nd round	Embassy World Championship
v Macleod	5-2	1st round	Jameson International
v Thorne	0-5	2nd round	Jameson International
v Ganim	5-4	1st round	Professional Players Tournament
v Duggan	5-2	2nd round	Professional Players Tournament
v Thorne	3-5	3rd round	Professional Players Tournament
v B. Harris	9-7	1st round	Coral UK Championship
v Wilson	9-4	2nd round	Coral UK Championship
v White	4-9	Quarter-final	Coral UK Championship
1984 v Williams	4-5	Qualifying	Lada Classic
v Virgo	5-3	1st round	Benson & Hedges Masters
v White	3-5	Quarter-final	Benson & Hedges Masters
v M. Owen	6-1	1st round	Strongbow Welsh Championship
v Wilson	4-9	Semi-final	Strongbow Welsh Championship

	v Higgins	2-5	Quarter-final	Benson & Hedges Irish Masters
	v Wych	10-7	1st round	Embassy World Championship
	v S. Francisco	13-8	2nd round	Embassy World Championship
	v Stevens	2-13	Quarter-final	Embassy World Championship
	v Dodd	5-4	1st round	Jameson International
	v E. Hughes	1-5	2nd round	Jameson International
	v Roscoe	5-1	1st round	Rothmans Grand Prix
	v Wilson	5-4	2nd round	Rothmans Grand Prix
	v Dennis Taylor	3-5	3rd round	Rothmans Grand Prix
	v Fowler	9-2	1st round	Coral UK Open
	v David Taylor	9-4	2nd round	Coral UK Open
	v Thorburn	8-9	Quarter-final	Coral UK Open
1985	v Hallett	5-3	1st round	Mercantile Credit Classic
	v E. Hughes	5-1	2nd round	Mercantile Credit Classic
	v S. Davis	1-5	Quarter-final	Mercantile Credit Classic
	v David Taylor	5-1	1st round	Benson & Hedges Masters
	v Thorburn	0-5	Quarter-final	Benson & Hedges Masters
	v King	6-5	1st round	Dulux British Open
	v Martin	4-5	2nd round	Dulux British Open
	v E. Hughes	0-5	1st round	Benson & Hedges Irish Masters
	v E. Hughes	10-9	1st round	Embassy World Championship
	v Fagan	13-9	2nd round	Embassy World Championship
	v Parrott	13-12	Quarter-final	Embassy World Championship
	v S. Davis	5-16	Semi-final	Embassy World Championship
	v Everton	6-2	Quarter-final	BCE Welsh Championship
	v Griffiths	3-9	Semi-final	BCE Welsh Championship
	v Duggan	3-5	3rd round	Goya Matchroom Trophy
	v Scott	4-5	3rd round	Rothmans Grand Prix
	v Knowles	5-2	1st round	BCE Canadian Masters
	v Dennis Taylor	3-8	Semi-final	BCE Canadian Masters
	v Miles	9-4	3rd round	Coral UK Open
	v Macleod	5-9	4th round	Coral UK Open
	v Griffiths	2-5	1st round	Kit Kat
1986	v Mikkelsen	3-5	3rd round	Mercantile Credit Classic
	v Stevens	1-5	1st round	BCE Belgian Classic
	v Thorne	4-5	1st round	Benson & Hedges Masters
	v W. Jones	4-6	Quarter-final	Zetters Welsh Championship
	v John Rea	3-5	3rd round	Dulux British Open
	v E. Hughes	2-5	1st round	Benson & Hedges Irish Masters
	v Campbell	8-10	1st round	Embassy World Championship
	v W. Jones	5-4	3rd round	BCE International
	v Gauvreau	2-5	4th round	BCE International
	v Chaperon	3-5	3rd round	Rothmans Grand Prix
	v M. Gibson	9-6	3rd round	Tennents UK Open
	v E. Hughes	5-9	4th round	Tennents UK Open
1987	v Hendry	3-5	3rd round	Mercantile Credit Classic
	v Johnson	2-5	1st round	Benson & Hedges Masters
	v Chappel	4-6	Quarter-final	Matchroom Welsh Championship
	v O'Boye	5-4	3rd round	Dulux British Open
	v Murphy	4-5	4th round	Dulux British Open
	v West	10-5	1st round	Embassy World Championship
	v S. Davis	4-13	2nd round	Embassy World Championship
	v Rowswell	5-4	2nd round	Fidelity International
	v Charlton	4-5	3rd round	Fidelity International
	v Burke	5-2	2nd round	Rothmans Grand Prix
	v Dennis Taylor	1-5	3rd round	Rothmans Grand Prix
	v Van Rensberg	9-7	2nd round	Tennents UK Open
	v S. Francisco	3-9	3rd round	Tennents UK Open
1988	v Gary Wilkinson	5-3	2nd round	Mercantile Credit Classic
	v Thorburn	3-5	3rd round	Mercantile Credit Classic
	v W. Jones	5-6	Quarter-final	Welsh Championship
	v Van Rensberg	5-3	2nd round	MIM Britannia British Open
	v S. Davis	5-0	3rd round	MIM Britannia British Open

| v Roe | 2-5 | 4th round | MIM Britannia British Open |
| v Oliver | 6-10 | Qualifying | Embassy World Championship |

JIM REMPE (USA)

Born 4.11.47. **Turned professional** 1980. **World ranking** 108 (102).

1985	v Burke	5-3	1st round	Goya Matchroom Trophy
	v Wych	1-5	2nd round	Goya Matchroom Trophy
	v Agrawal	2-5	1st round	Rothmans Grand Prix
1987	v Smith	10-9	Qualifying	Embassy World Championship
	v John Rea	10-9	Qualifying	Embassy World Championship
	v Hendry	4-10	Qualifying	Embassy World Championship
1988	v Foldvari	4-10	Qualifying	Embassy World Championship

DEAN REYNOLDS (England)

Born 11.1.63. **Turned professional** 1981. **World ranking** 22 (15). **Best professional performances** Semi-finals 1987 Mercantile Credit Classic, 1988 English champion.

1982	v Sheehan	9-5	Qualifying	Embassy World Championship
	v Edmonds	9-6	Qualifying	Embassy World Championship
	v F. Davis	10-7	1st round	Embassy World Championship
	v S. Francisco	8-13	2nd round	Embassy World Championship
	v Morra	5-1	Qualifying	Jameson International
	v Thorne	5-3	1st round	Jameson International
	v S. Davis	0-5	2nd round	Jameson International
	v Fitzmaurice	5-0	2nd round	Professional Players Tournament
	v Wilson	5-1	3rd round	Professional Players Tournament
	v Charlton	2-5	Quarter-final	Professional Players Tournament
	v Fisher	9-6	1st round	Coral UK Championship
	v Higgins	8-9	2nd round	Coral UK Championship
1983	v Reardon	1-5	1st round	Benson & Hedges Masters
	v Edmonds	10-6	Qualifying	Embassy World Championship
	v Higgins	4-10	1st round	Embassy World Championship
	v Williams	5-3	Qualifying	Jameson International
	v Dennis Taylor	3-5	1st round	Jameson International
	v Greaves	5-1	1st round	Professional Players Tournament
	v Meo	0-5	2nd round	Professional Players Tournament
	v Medati	3-9	1st round	Coral UK Championship
1984	v Griffiths	2-5	Qualifying	Lada Classic
	v Morra	7-10	Qualifying	Embassy World Championship
	v Bales	5-4	Qualifying	Jameson International
	v Knowles	1-5	1st round	Jameson International
	v Fowler	5-2	1st round	Rothmans Grand Prix
	v P. Francisco	5-4	2nd round	Rothmans Grand Prix
	v S. Francisco	5-1	3rd round	Rothmans Grand Prix
	v S. Davis	0-5	Quarter-final	Rothmans Grand Prix
	v Chappel	6-9	Qualifying	Coral UK Open
1985	v King	2-5	Qualifying	Mercantile Credit Classic
	v Fitzmaurice	9-2	1st round	Tolly Cobbold English Championship
	v Thorne	9-6	2nd round	Tolly Cobbold English Championship
	v Meo	4-9	Quarter-final	Tolly Cobbold English Championship
	v Giannaros	6-3	1st round	Dulux British Open
	v Thorburn	3-5	2nd round	Dulux British Open
	v Gauvreau	10-1	Qualifying	Embassy World Championship
	v Higgins	4-10	1st round	Embassy World Championship
	v Mikkelsen	5-0	3rd round	Goya Matchroom Trophy
	v Gibson	5-0	4th round	Goya Matchroom Trophy
	v White	1-5	5th round	Goya Matchroom Trophy
	v Miles	3-5	3rd round	Rothmans Grand Prix

Dean Reynolds

	v J. McLaughlin	9-7	3rd round	Coral UK Open
	v Griffiths	7-9	4th round	Coral UK Open
1986	v Houlihan	5-1	3rd round	Mercantile Credit Classic
	v Dennis Taylor	4-5	4th round	Mercantile Credit Classic
	v Longworth	9-5	3rd round	Tolly Cobbold English Championship
	v Thorne	9-8	4th round	Tolly Cobbold English Championship
	v Meo	4-9	Quarter-final	Tolly Cobbold English Championship
	v Wych	3-5	3rd round	Dulux British Open
	v Stevens	6-10	1st round	Embassy World Championship
	v Dodd	5-2	3rd round	BCE International
	v Mountjoy	5-2	4th round	BCE International
	v David Taylor	5-1	5th round	BCE International
	v N. Foulds	2-5	Quarter-final	BCE International
	v Newbury	0-5	3rd round	Rothmans Grand Prix
	v Mikkelsen	9-6	3rd round	Tennents UK Open
	v S. Francisco	9-8	4th round	Tennents UK Open
	v S. Davis	5-9	5th round	Tennents UK Open
1987	v King	5-4	3rd round	Mercantile Credit Classic
	v Thorburn	5-4	4th round	Mercantile Credit Classic
	v West	5-3	5th round	Mercantile Credit Classic
	v Wilson	5-1	Quarter-final	Mercantile Credit Classic
	v White	8-9	Semi-final	Mercantile Credit Classic
	v Edmonds	6-3	3rd round	Tolly Ales English Championship
	v White	6-5	4th round	Tolly Ales English Championship
	v Thorne	4-6	Quarter-final	Tolly Ales English Championship
	v N. Gilbert	5-3	3rd round	Dulux British Open
	v Knowles	0-5	4th round	Dulux British Open
	v Oliver	10-7	Qualifying	Embassy World Championship
	v White	8-10	1st round	Embassy World Championship
	v W. Jones	4-5	3rd round	Fidelity International
	v Houlihan	4-5	3rd round	Rothmans Grand Prix
	v Chappel	5-9	3rd round	Tennents UK Open
1988	v O'Boye	5-3	3rd round	Mercantile Credit Classic
	v Murphy	4-5	4th round	Mercantile Credit Classic
	v S. Davis	2-5	1st round	Benson & Hedges Masters
	v D. Gilbert	6-3	3rd round	English Championship
	v Parrott	6-2	4th round	English Championship
	v Meo	6-4	Quarter-final	English Championship
	v Johnson	9-8	Semi-final	English Championship
	v N. Foulds	**9-5**	**Final**	**English Championship**
	v O'Boye	2-5	3rd round	MIM Britannia British Open
	v Hendry	6-10	1st round	Embassy World Championship

GINO RIGITANO (Canada)

Born 14.8.57. **Turned professional** 1983. **World ranking** 91 (86).

1983	v Gauvreau	9-6	1st round	Canadian Championship
	v Mikkelsen	4-9	2nd round	Canadian Championship
1984	v Gibson	7-10	Qualifying	Embassy World Championship
	v Foldvari	2-5	Qualifying	Jameson International
	v Edmonds	5-3	Qualifying	Rothmans Grand Prix
	v Thorburn	4-5	1st round	Rothmans Grand Prix
	v Newbury	6-9	Qualifying	Coral UK Open
1985	v Fowler	0-5	Qualifying	Mercantile Credit Classic
	v Thorburn	3-6	1st round	Dulux British Open
	v Sheehan	10-9	Qualifying	Embassy World Championship
	v B. Harris	10-4	Qualifying	Embassy World Championship
	v Kelly	10-6	Qualifying	Embassy World Championship
	v Fisher	10-2	Qualifying	Embassy World Championship
	v N. Foulds	8-10	Qualifying	Embassy World Championship
	v Black	4-5	2nd round	Goya Matchroom Trophy
	v Miles	4-5	2nd round	Rothmans Grand Prix

1986 v Dodd	5-3	2nd round	Mercantile Credit Classic
v Knowles	4-5	3rd round	Mercantile Credit Classic
v W. Jones	1-5	2nd round	Dulux British Open
v Foldvari	6-10	Qualifying	Embassy World Championship
v Jonik	1-6	1st round	Canadian Championship
v Greaves	5-3	1st round	BCE International
v King	0-5	2nd round	BCE International
v Everton	5-1	1st round	Rothmans Grand Prix
v Medati	1-5	2nd round	Rothmans Grand Prix
v James	5-9	1st round	Tennents UK Open
1987 v Grace	5-4	1st round	Mercantile Credit Classic
v Gauvreau	0-5	2nd round	Mercantile Credit Classic
v Demarco	5-1	1st round	Dulux British Open
v Browne	5-4	2nd round	Dulux British Open
v Hallett	0-5	3rd round	Dulux British Open
v Morgan	4-0 retd	Qualifying	Embassy World Championship
v V. Harris	10-6	Qualifying	Embassy World Championship
v Newbury	4-10	Qualifying	Embassy World Championship
v Wych	4-6	1st round	Canadian Championship
v Gary Wilkinson	1-5	1st round	Fidelity International
v Jack Rea	5-4	1st round	Rothmans Grand Prix
v Wright	0-5	2nd round	Rothmans Grand Prix
v P. Gibson	5-9	1st round	Tennents UK Open
1988 v Fowler	5-2	2nd round	Mercantile Credit Classic
v Virgo	2-5	3rd round	Mercantile Credit Classic
v Marshall	5-2	1st round	MIM Britannia British Open
v Chaperon	2-5	2nd round	MIM Britannia British Open
v Dunning	10-7	Qualifying	Embassy World Championship
v M. Bennett	4-10	Qualifying	Embassy World Championship

DAVID ROE (England)

Born 11.9.65. **Turned professional** 1986. **World ranking** 39 (84). **Best professional performances** Last 16 1987 Tennents UK Open, 1988 MIM Britannia British Open.

1986 v D. Hughes	5-2	1st round	BCE International
v Miles	1-5	2nd round	BCE International
v Hargreaves	5-1	1st round	Rothmans Grand Prix
v Van Rensberg	5-3	2nd round	Rothmans Grand Prix
v Knowles	3-5	3rd round	Rothmans Grand Prix
v G. Foulds	7-1	1st round	Tennents UK Open
v Van Rensberg	9-6	2nd round	Tennents UK Open
v Dennis Taylor	6-9	3rd round	Tennents UK Open
1987 v Darrington	5-0	1st round	Mercantile Credit Classic
v Chaperon	4-5	2nd round	Mercantile Credit Classic
v Greaves	6-1	1st round	Tolly Ales English Championship
v Williamson	4-6	2nd round	Tolly Ales English Championship
v Watterson	5-3	1st round	Dulux British Open
v Black	5-0	2nd round	Dulux British Open
v N. Foulds	1-5	3rd round	Dulux British Open
v King	4-10	Qualifying	Embassy World Championship
v Ellis	5-4	1st round	Fidelity International
v F. Davis	5-3	2nd round	Fidelity International
v Mountjoy	5-4	3rd round	Fidelity International
v James	3-5	4th round	Fidelity International
v Whitthread	5-1	1st round	Rothmans Grand Prix
v Wildman	5-3	2nd round	Rothmans Grand Prix
v Martin	5-4	3rd round	Rothmans Grand Prix
v Knowles	2-5	4th round	Rothmans Grand Prix
v Marshall	9-3	1st round	Tennents UK Open

THE PLAYERS 157

v Owers	9-7	2nd round	Tennents UK Open
v Williams	9-7	3rd round	Tennents UK Open
v V. Harris	9-5	4th round	Tennents UK Open
v White	5-9	5th round	Tennents UK Open
1988 v Kelly	5-1	1st round	Mercantile Credit Classic
v Dodd	2-5	2nd round	Mercantile Credit Classic
v Lawlor	5-6	1st round	English Championship
v Chambers	5-3	1st round	MIM Britannia British Open
v Edmonds	5-1	2nd round	MIM Britannia British Open
v Drago	5-3	3rd round	MIM Britannia British Open
v Reardon	5-2	4th round	MIM Britannia British Open
v O'Boye	1-5	5th round	MIM Britannia British Open
v Demarco	10-2	Qualifying	Embassy World Championship
v Owers	7-10	Qualifying	Embassy World Championship

COLIN ROSCOE (Wales)

Born 30.6.45. **Turned professional** 1981. **World ranking** 67 (79). **Amateur career** 1981 Welsh champion. **Best professional performance** Last 32 1988 Mercantile Credit Classic.

1981 v Macleod	9-7	Qualifying	Coral UK Championship
v Williams	4-9	Qualifying	Coral UK Championship
v Andrewartha	5-2	Qualifying	Jameson International
v Sheehan	5-1	Qualifying	Jameson International
v Meadowcroft	4-5	Qualifying	Jameson International
1982 v Griffiths	2-6	1st round	Welsh Championship
v Mikkelsen	9-6	Qualifying	Embassy World Championship
v Thorne	1-9	Qualifying	Embassy World Championship
v Dunning	5-2	Qualifying	Jameson International
v French	5-2	Qualifying	Jameson International
v S. Davis	0-5	1st round	Jameson International
v Griffiths	1-5	1st round	Professional Players Tournament
v Jack Rea	9-6	Qualifying	Coral UK Championship
v Wildman	4-9	Qualifying	Coral UK Championship
1983 v Wilson	4-6	Quarter-final	Woodpecker Welsh Championship
v Sinclair	2-10	Qualifying	Jameson International
v Hallett	2-5	Qualifying	Jameson International
v Meadowcroft	4-5	1st round	Professional Players Tournament
v N. Foulds	2-9	Qualifying	Coral UK Championship
1984 v Ganim	5-3	Qualifying	Lada Classic
v Miles	5-2	Qualifying	Lada Classic
v Werbeniuk	5-4	1st round	Lada Classic
v Griffiths	2-5	2nd round	Lada Classic
v Wilson	2-6	1st round	Strongbow Welsh Championship
v Demarco	10-7	Qualifying	Embassy World Championship
v Browne	4-10	Qualifying	Embassy World Championship
v Mikkelsen	5-1	Qualifying	Jameson International
v French	5-0	Qualifying	Rothmans Grand Prix
v Reardon	1-5	1st round	Rothmans Grand Prix
v J. McLaughlin	8-9	Qualifying	Coral UK Open
1985 v Medati	4-5	Qualifying	Mercantile Credit Classic
v Giannaros	1-6	Qualifying	Dulux British Open
v G. Foulds	7-10	Qualifying	Embassy World Championship
v Wilson	3-6	Quarter-final	BCE Welsh Championship
v G. Foulds	5-3	2nd round	Goya Matchroom Trophy
v Wilson	1-5	3rd round	Goya Matchroom Trophy
v Watson	2-5	2nd round	Rothmans Grand Prix
v West	5-9	2nd round	Coral UK Open
1986 v V. Harris	1-5	2nd round	Mercantile Credit Classic
v Mountjoy	4-6	Quarter-final	Zetters Welsh Championship
v Mikkelsen	5-4	2nd round	Dulux British Open

	v Parrott	2-5	3rd round	Dulux British Open
	v G. Foulds	10-3	Qualifying	Embassy World Championship
	v King	5-10	Qualifying	Embassy World Championship
	v Parkin	5-1	1st round	BCE International
	v Chappel	3-5	2nd round	BCE International
	v Burke	3-5	1st round	Rothmans Grand Prix
	v Parkin	9-1	1st round	Tennents UK Open
	v Wildman	9-6	2nd round	Tennents UK Open
	v E. Hughes	8-9	3rd round	Tennents UK Open
1987	v Whitthread	5-1	1st round	Mercantile Credit Classic
	v Fagan	wo	2nd round	Mercantile Credit Classic
	v Higgins	2-5	3rd round	Mercantile Credit Classic
	v Everton	6-2	1st round	Matchroom Welsh Championship
	v Mountjoy	2-6	Quarter-final	Matchroom Welsh Championship
	v Mienie	5-2	1st round	Dulux British Open
	v Newbury	5-3	2nd round	Dulux British Open
	v Dennis Taylor	1-5	3rd round	Dulux British Open
	v Whitthread	10-2	Qualifying	Embassy World Championship
	v Duggan	7-10	Qualifying	Embassy World Championship
	v Lawlor	5-4	1st round	Fidelity International
	v Browne	5-2	2nd round	Fidelity International
	v Hallett	3-5	3rd round	Fidelity International
	v T. Jones	1-5	1st round	Rothmans Grand Prix
	v Chambers	4-9	1st round	Tennents UK Open
1988	v Watchorn	5-2	1st round	Mercantile Credit Classic
	v W. Jones	5-4	2nd round	Mercantile Credit Classic
	v Charlton	5-3	3rd round	Mercantile Credit Classic
	v Knowles	0-5	4th round	Mercantile Credit Classic
	v Chappel	4-6	1st round	Welsh Championship
	v P. Gibson	5-4	1st round	MIM Britannia British Open
	v Wildman	5-0	2nd round	MIM Britannia British Open
	v Wilson	2-5	3rd round	MIM Britannia British Open
	v E. McLaughlin	10-1	Qualifying	Embassy World Championship
	v Murphy	8-10	Qualifying	Embassy World Championship

BRIAN ROWSWELL (England)

Born 18.3.67. **Turned professional** 1986. **World ranking** 70 (91). **Best professional performance** Last 32 MIM Britannia British Open.

	v Sheehan	5-4	1st round	BCE International
1986	v Sheehan	5-4	1st round	BCE International
	v Wildman	2-5	2nd round	BCE International
	v D. Gilbert	1-5	1st round	Rothmans Grand Prix
	v F. Davis	9-4	2nd round	Tennents UK Open
	v Longworth	3-9	3rd round	Tennents UK Open
1987	v Watterson	5-1	1st round	Mercantile Credit Classic
	v Bradley	4-5	2nd round	Mercantile Credit Classic
	v Smith	5-6	1st round	Tolly Ales English Championship
	v Jenkins	5-1	1st round	Dulux British Open
	v O'Kane	5-4	2nd round	Dulux British Open
	v S. Francisco	0-5	3rd round	Dulux British Open
	v Bradley	6-10	Qualifying	Embassy World Championship
	v D. Hughes	5-1	1st round	Fidelity International
	v Reardon	4-5	2nd round	Fidelity International
	v J. Smith	5-3	1st round	Rothmans Grand Prix
	v Chaperon	4-5	2nd round	Rothmans Grand Prix
	v Everton	4-9	1st round	Tennents UK Open
	v O'Kane	2-9	2nd round	Tennents UK Open
1988	v Chambers	5-2	1st round	Mercantile Credit Classic
	v O'Kane	5-4	2nd round	Mercantile Credit Classic
	v S. Francisco	3-5	3rd round	Mercantile Credit Classic
	v Gary Wilkinson	1-6	1st round	English Championship

v Jack Rea	5-1	1st round	MIM Britannia British Open
v J. McLaughlin	5-2	2nd round	MIM Britannia British Open
v Longworth	5-4	3rd round	MIM Britannia British Open
v Johnson	2-5	4th round	MIM Britannia British Open
v Thornley	10-7	Qualifying	Embassy World Championship
v Werbeniuk	6-10	Qualifying	Embassy World Championship

GEORGE SCOTT (England)

Born 16.9.29. **Turned professional** 1981. **World ranking** 90 (61). **Best professional performances** Last 32 1985 Goya Matchroom Trophy, 1985 Rothmans Grand Prix.

1982 v B. Harris	5-4	Qualifying	Jameson International
v Thorburn	1-5	1st round	Jameson International
v Meo	5-9	Qualifying	Coral UK Championship
1983 v Houlihan	5-0	Qualifying	Jameson International
v Gibson	5-3	Qualifying	Jameson International
v Werbeniuk	5-3	1st round	Jameson International
v Griffiths	0-5	2nd round	Jameson International
v Dennis Taylor	5-4	1st round	Professional Players Tournament
v S. Francisco	1-5	2nd round	Professional Players Tournament
v Parrott	7-9	Qualifying	Coral UK Championship
1984 v Heywood	10-7	Qualifying	Embassy World Championship
v Wych	6-10	Qualifying	Embassy World Championship
v W. Jones	0-5	Qualifying	Jameson International
v Chappel	1-5	Qualifying	Rothmans Grand Prix
v O'Kane	9-7	Qualifying	Coral UK Open
v Macleod	5-9	Qualifying	Coral UK Open
1985 v J. McLaughlin	5-4	Qualifying	Mercantile Credit Classic
v Campbell	5-4	Qualifying	Mercantile Credit Classic
v Thorburn	1-5	1st round	Mercantile Credit Classic
v V. Harris	9-7	Qualifying	Tolly Cobbold English Championship
v Johnson	1-9	1st round	Tolly Cobbold English Championship
v Darrington	6-3	Qualifying	Dulux British Open
v Dennis Taylor	2-6	1st round	Dulux British Open
v Newbury	2-10	Qualifying	Embassy World Championship
v Van Rensberg	5-4	2nd round	Goya Matchroom Trophy
v Wildman	5-1	3rd round	Goya Matchroom Trophy
v Thorne	1-5	4th round	Goya Matchroom Trophy
v Chalmers	5-2	2nd round	Rothmans Grand Prix
v Reardon	5-4	3rd round	Rothmans Grand Prix
v Wilson	3-5	4th round	Rothmans Grand Prix
v Sheehan	6-9	2nd round	Coral UK Open
1986 v Mikkelsen	1-5	2nd round	Mercantile Credit Classic
v Bennett	9-1	2nd round	Tolly Cobbold English Championship
v Meo	1-9	3rd round	Tolly Cobbold English Championship
v Chalmers	5-1	2nd round	Dulux British Open
v Griffiths	3-5	3rd round	Dulux British Open
v Kearney	10-8	Qualifying	Embassy World Championship
v Fowler	7-10	Qualifying	Embassy World Championship
v Owers	1-5	2nd round	BCE International
v Dodd	2-5	2nd round	Rothmans Grand Prix
v Watchorn	9-7	2nd round	Tennents UK Open
v Stevens	2-9	3rd round	Tennents UK Open
1987 v Jenkins	4-5	2nd round	Mercantile Credit Classic
v Fitzmaurice	2-6	2nd round	Tolly Ales English Championship
v Burke	5-2	2nd round	Dulux British Open
v Martin	3-5	3rd round	Dulux British Open
v Dunning	10-7	Qualifying	Embassy World Championship
v Oliver	5-10	Qualifying	Embassy World Championship
v Gary Wilkinson	2-5	2nd round	Fidelity International

	v Miles	2-5	2nd round	Rothmans Grand Prix
	v Oliver	4-9	2nd round	Tennents UK Open
1988	v Bear	5-3	2nd round	Mercantile Credit Classic
	v Drago	3-5	3rd round	Mercantile Credit Classic
	v Chambers	3-6	2nd round	English Championship
	v Dunning	3-5	2nd round	MIM Britannia British Open
	v Clark	4-10	Qualifying	Embassy World Championship

DESSIE SHEEHAN (Republic of Ireland)

Born 3.9.49. **Turned professional** 1981. **World ranking** 115 (95). **Amateur career** Republic of Ireland champion, 1970, 1971, 1980.

	v V. Harris	5-1	Qualifying	Jameson International
1981	v Roscoe	1-5	Qualifying	Jameson International
1982	v E. Hughes	1-6	1st round	Irish Championship
	v V. Harris	3-5	Qualifying	Jameson International
	v Dennis Taylor	3-5	1st round	Benson & Hedges Irish Masters
	v Reynolds	5-9	Qualifying	Embassy World Championship
	v Fitzmaurice	1-5	1st round	Professional Players Tournament
1983	v Donnelly	6-10	Qualifying	Embassy World Championship
	v Murphy	2-5	Qualifying	Jameson International
	v Houlihan	5-2	Qualifying	Professional Players Tournament
	v Williams	1-5	1st round	Professional Players Tournament
1984	v B. Harris	3-10	Qualifying	Embassy World Championship
	v Bales	2-5	Qualifying	Jameson International
	v Mikkelsen	5-3	Qualifying	Rothmans Grand Prix
	v Hallett	1-5	1st round	Rothmans Grand Prix
	v P. Francisco	5-9	Qualifying	Coral UK Open
1985	v John Rea	5-2	Qualifying	Mercantile Credit Classic
	v E. McLaughlin	2-5	Qualifying	Mercantile Credit Classic
	v Murphy	3-6	Qualifying	Dulux British Open
	v J. McLaughlin	3-6	Qualifying	Irish Championship
	v Rigitano	9-10	Qualifying	Embassy World Championship
	v Smith	2-5	1st round	Goya Matchroom Trophy
	v Watson	1-5	1st round	Rothmans Grand Prix
	v Watchorn	9-7	1st round	Coral UK Open
	v Scott	9-6	2nd round	Coral UK Open
	v S. Davis	1-9	3rd round	Coral UK Open
1986	v Hendry	2-5	1st round	Mercantile Credit Classic
	v Simngam	5-2	1st round	Dulux British Open
	v Watterson	wo	2nd round	Dulux British Open
	v Thorburn	0-5	3rd round	Dulux British Open
	v Houlihan	10-7	Qualifying	Embassy World Championship
	v King	4-10	Qualifying	Embassy World Championship
	v E. Hughes	0-5	1st round	Strongbow Irish Championship
	v Rowswell	4-5	1st round	BCE International
	v Demarco	5-1	1st round	Rothmans Grand Prix
	v Browne	4-5	2nd round	Rothmans Grand Prix
	v M. Bennett	9-8	1st round	Tennents UK Open
	v Miles	8-9	2nd round	Tennents UK Open
1987	v M. Bennett	3-5	1st round	Mercantile Credit Classic
	v Wright	5-2	1st round	Dulux British Open
	v V. Harris	4-5	2nd round	Dulux British Open
	v N. Gilbert	6-10	Qualifying	Embassy World Championship
	v J. McLaughlin	5-4	1st round	Matchroom Irish Championship
	v Dennis Taylor	3-6	Quarter-final	Matchroom Irish Championship
	v Dunning	1-5	1st round	Fidelity International
	v Marshall	1-5	1st round	Rothmans Grand Prix
	v Ellis	8-9	1st round	Tennents UK Open
1988	v Heaton	5-2	1st round	Mercantile Credit Classic
	v O'Boye	3-5	2nd round	Mercantile Credit Classic

v O'Boye	0-5	1st round	Irish Championship
v N. Gilbert	3-5	1st round	MIM Britannia British Open
v P. Gibson	9-10	Qualifying	Embassy World Championship

EDDIE SINCLAIR (Scotland)

Born 5.5.37. **Turned professional** 1979. **World ranking** 85 (77). **Amateur career** Scottish champion 1960, 1963, 1967, 1968, 1973, 1975 and 1976.

1980 v Meadowcroft	1-9	Qualifying	Embassy World Championship
v Kennerley	9-1	Qualifying	Coral UK Championship
v Miles	9-5	1st round	Coral UK Championship
v Dennis Taylor	6-9	2nd round	Coral UK Championship
1981 v Donnelly	0-5	Quarter-final	Scottish Championship
v Morgan	9-8	Qualifying	Embassy World Championship
v Wilson	4-9	Qualifying	Embassy World Championship
v E. Hughes	2-5	Qualifying	Jameson International
v Wildman	9-8	Qualifying	Coral UK Championship
v Hood	9-0	Qualifying	Coral UK Championship
v Martin	7-9	Qualifying	Coral UK Championship
1982 v Kelly	9-8	Qualifying	Embassy World Championship
v Donnelly	8-9	Qualifying	Embassy World Championship
v Phillips	6-3	Quarter-final	Scottish Championship
v Gibson	6-2	Semi-final	Scottish Championship
v Black	**11-7**	**Final**	**Scottish Championship**
v Higgins	1-5	1st round	Langs Supreme Scottish Masters
v Anderson	5-2	Qualifying	Jameson International
v Meo	5-3	Qualifying	Jameson International
v Knowles	2-5	1st round	Jameson International
v F. Davis	5-2	1st round	Professional Players Tournament
v Meadowcroft	5-3	2nd round	Professional Players Tournament
v Griffiths	3-5	3rd round	Professional Players Tournament
v Murphy	9-5	Qualifying	Coral UK Championship
v Spencer	8-9	1st round	Coral UK Championship
1983 v Roscoe	10-2	Qualifying	Embassy World Championship
v E. Hughes	8-10	Qualifying	Embassy World Championship
v Donnelly	6-5	Semi-final	Scottish Championship
v Macleod	9-11	Final	Scottish Championship
v Andrewartha	5-4	Qualifying	Jameson International
v Thorburn	0-5	1st round	Jameson International
v E. Hughes	4-5	1st round	Professional Players Tournament
v T. Jones	3-9	Qualifying	Coral UK Championship
1984 v S. Davis	2-5	Qualifying	Lada Classic
v Browne	10-1	Qualifying	Embassy World Championship
v Stevens	1-10	1st round	Embassy World Championship
v Duggan	5-0	Qualifying	Jameson International
v Mans	5-2	Qualifying	Jameson International
v Higgins	1-5	1st round	Jameson International
v T. Jones	4-5	Qualifying	Rothmans Grand Prix
v P. Francisco	9-8	Qualifying	Coral UK Open
v S. Francisco	4-9	Qualifying	Coral UK Open
v Demarco	6-3	1st round	Scottish Championship
v John Rea	6-2	Semi-final	Scottish Championship
v Macleod	2-10	Final	Scottish Championship
1985 v Newbury	3-6	1st round	Dulux British Open
v T. Jones	2-10	Qualifying	Embassy World Championship
v Darrington	5-0	2nd round	Goya Matchroom Trophy
v Martin	1-5	3rd round	Goya Matchroom Trophy
v Fitzmaurice	3-5	2nd round	Rothmans Grand Prix
v G. Foulds	9-4	2nd round	Coral UK Open
v Parrott	2-9	3rd round	Coral UK Open

1986	v Greaves	5-1	2nd round	Mercantile Credit Classic
	v Macleod	2-5	3rd round	Mercantile Credit Classic
	v B. Harris	3-5	2nd round	Dulux British Open
	v Gibson	4-6	Quarter-final	Canada Dry Scottish Championship
	v Morgan	10-8	Qualifying	Embassy World Championship
	v Van Rensberg	2-10	Qualifying	Embassy World Championship
	v Fagan	5-0	2nd round	BCE International
	v Higgins	3-5	3rd round	BCE International
	v John Rea	4-5	2nd round	Rothmans Grand Prix
	v Mikkelsen	8-9	2nd round	Tennents UK Open
1987	v Miles	5-1	2nd round	Mercantile Credit Classic
	v Johnson	0-5	3rd round	Mercantile Credit Classic
	v M. Gibson	6-2	1st round	Scottish Championship
	v Donnelly	4-6	Semi-final	Scottish Championship
	v Hendry	5-2	2nd round	Dulux British Open
	v P. Francisco	3-5	3rd round	Dulux British Open
	v Drago	10-9	Qualifying	Embassy World Championship
	v Edmonds	6-10	Qualifying	Embassy World Championship
	v Heaton	5-3	1st round	Fidelity International
	v Edmonds	5-4	2nd round	Fidelity International
	v Wilson	1-5	3rd round	Fidelity International
	v Ellis	5-4	1st round	Rothmans Grand Prix
	v Edmonds	2-5	2nd round	Rothmans Grand Prix
	v N. Gilbert	8-9	1st round	Tennents UK Open
1988	v Lawlor	5-3	1st round	Mercantile Credit Classic
	v Wright	3-5	2nd round	Mercantile Credit Classic
	v John Rea	5-6	Quarter-final	Scottish Championship
	v Lawlor	3-5	1st round	MIM Britannia British Open
	v Burke	10-2	Qualifying	Embassy World Championship
	v O'Kane	10-9	Qualifying	Embassy World Championship
	v B. Harris	0-10	Qualifying	Embassy World Championship

JASON SMITH (England)
Born 6.1.64. **Turned professional** 1987. **World ranking** 118.

1987	v Bradley	1-5	2nd round	Fidelity International
	v Rowswell	3-5	1st round	Rothmans Grand Prix
	v Black	8-9	1st round	Tennents UK Open
1988	v Bear	3-5	1st round	Mercantile Credit Classic
	v V. Harris	6-3	1st round	English Championship
	v T. Jones	6-5	2nd round	English Championship
	v Johnson	5-6	3rd round	English Championship
	v Jenkins	3-5	1st round	MIM Britannia British Open
	v Donnelly	10-4	Qualifying	Embassy World Championship
	v Wych	3-10	Qualifying	Embassy World Championship

MARTIN SMITH (England)
Born 12.6.61. **Turned professional** 1985. **World ranking** 72 (108). **Best professional performance** Last 32 Tennents UK Open.

1985	v Sheehan	5-2	1st round	Goya Matchroom Trophy
	v W. Jones	3-5	2nd round	Goya Matchroom Trophy
	v Bales	1-5	1st round	Rothmans Grand Prix
	v Wilkinson	4-9	1st round	Coral UK Open
1986	v Mienie	5-1	1st round	Mercantile Credit Classic
	v Edmonds	5-2	2nd round	Mercantile Credit Classic
	v Mans	4-5	3rd round	Mercantile Credit Classic
	v Edmonds	8-9	2nd round	Tolly Cobbold English Championship
	v Kearney	2-5	1st round	Dulux British Open

	v Greaves	10-4	Qualifying	Embassy World Championship
	v Donnelly	6-10	Qualifying	Embassy World Championship
	v M. Bennett	4-5	1st round	BCE International
	v Hines	5-2	1st round	Rothmans Grand Prix
	v T. Jones	0-5	2nd round	Rothmans Grand Prix
	v Wright	7-9	1st round	Tennents UK Open
1987	v N. Gilbert	2-5	1st round	Mercantile Credit Classic
	v Rowswell	6-5	1st round	Tolly Ales English Championship
	v Dodd	3-6	2nd round	Tolly Ales English Championship
	v Ellis	2-5	1st round	Dulux British Open
	v Rempe	9-10	Qualifying	Embassy World Championship
	v Donnelly	5-3	1st round	Fidelity International
	v King	3-5	2nd round	Fidelity International
	v Black	5-0	1st round	Rothmans Grand Prix
	v Gauvreau	3-5	2nd round	Rothmans Grand Prix
	v Jonik	9-5	1st round	Tennents UK Open
	v Browne	9-4	2nd round	Tennents UK Open
	v Mountjoy	9-7	3rd round	Tennents UK Open
	v Campbell	8-9	4th round	Tennents UK Open
1988	v Fitzmaurice	5-2	1st round	Mercantile Credit Classic
	v Browne	5-1	2nd round	Mercantile Credit Classic
	v David Taylor	3-5	3rd round	Mercantile Credit Classic
	v Miles	6-1	1st round	English Championship
	v B. Harris	6-4	2nd round	English Championship
	v Martin	5-6	3rd round	English Championship
	v Oliver	0-5	1st round	MIM Britannia British Open
	v V. Harris	10-6	Qualifying	Embassy World Championship
	v J. McLaughlin	10-3	Qualifying	Embassy World Championship
	v Newbury	9-10	Qualifying	Embassy World Championship

JOHN SPENCER (England)

Born 18.9.35. **Turned professional** 1967. **World ranking** 27 (28). **Amateur career** Runner-up 1966 World Championship, 1966 English amateur champion. **Best professional performances** Winner World Championship 1969, 1970, 1977, Benson & Hedges Masters 1975, Benson & Hedges Irish Masters 1978.

1969	v Pulman	30-19	Quarter-final	World Championship
	v Williams	55-18	Semi-final	World Championship
	v G. Owen	**46-27**	**Final**	**World Championship**
1970	v Jack Rea	31-15	Quarter-final	World Championship (Apr)
	v Reardon	33-37	Semi-final	World Championship (Apr)
	v Reardon	34-15	Semi-final	World Championship (Nov)
	v Simpson	**42-31**	**Final**	**World Championship (Nov)**
1972	v F. Davis	31-21	Quarter-final	World Championship
	v Charlton	37-32	Semi-final	World Championship
	v Higgins	32-37	Final	World Championship
1973	v David Taylor	16-5	2nd round	World Championship
	v Williams	16-7	Quarter-final	World Championship
	v Reardon	22-23	Semi-final	World Championship
1974	v Mans	13-15	2nd round	World Championship
1975	v Pulman	5-3	Quarter-final	Benson & Hedges Masters
	v Charlton	5-2	Semi-final	Benson & Hedges Masters
	v Reardon	**9-8**	**Final**	**Benson & Hedges Masters**
	v Pulman	15-10	2nd round	World Championship
	v Reardon	17-19	Quarter-final	World Championship
1976	v Miles	4-5	Semi-final	Benson & Hedges Masters
	v David Taylor	15-5	1st round	Embassy World Championship
	v Higgins	14-15	Quarter-final	Embassy World Championship
1977	v Virgo	13-9	1st round	Embassy World Championship
	v Reardon	13-6	Quarter-final	Embassy World Championship
	v Pulman	18-16	Semi-final	Embassy World Championship

	v Thorburn	**25-21**	Final	**Embassy World Championship**
	v Mountjoy	3-5	2nd round	Super Crystalate UK Championship
1978	v Thorburn	3-5	Semi-final	Benson & Hedges Masters
	v Mountjoy	**5-3**	**Final**	**Benson & Hedges Irish Masters**
	v Mans	8-13	1st round	Embassy World Championship
	v Andrewartha	8-9	1st round	Coral UK Championship
1979	v Williams	6-2	Semi-final	Holsten Lager International
	v Miles	**11-7**	**Final**	**Holsten Lager International**
	v Mountjoy	0-5	Quarter-final	Benson & Hedges Masters
	v Werbeniuk	11-13	1st round	Embassy World Championship
	v Werbeniuk	8-9	3rd round	Coral UK Championship
1980	v Charlton	5-2	Quarter-final	Benson & Hedges Masters
	v Griffiths	0-5	Semi-final	Benson & Hedges Masters
	v Stevens	8-13	2nd round	Embassy World Championship
	v Wildman	7-9	1st round	Coral UK Championship
1981	v Dennis Taylor	5-2	1st round	Benson & Hedges Masters
	v Reardon	5-1	Quarter-final	Benson & Hedges Masters
	v Griffiths	5-6	Semi-final	Benson & Hedges Masters
	v Houlihan	9-1	1st round	John Courage English
	v S. Davis	7-9	2nd round	John Courage English
	v Edmonds	10-9	1st round	Embassy World Championship
	v Reardon	11-13	2nd round	Embassy World Championship
	v Edmonds	5-3	2nd round	Jameson International
	v Griffiths	2-5	3rd round	Jameson International
	v Johnson	5-9	2nd round	Coral UK Championship
1982	v S. Davis	2-5	1st round	Lada Classic
	v Mountjoy	4-5	1st round	Benson & Hedges Masters
	v Meo	3-5	1st round	Benson & Hedges Irish Masters
	v Dunning	10-4	1st round	Embassy World Championship
	v Thorne	5-13	2nd round	Embassy World Championship
	v Edmonds	5-2	1st round	Jameson International
	v Virgo	4-5	2nd round	Jameson International
	v G. Foulds	5-1	1st round	Professional Players Tournament
	v Martin	5-3	2nd round	Professional Players Tournament
	v Virgo	1-5	3rd round	Professional Players Tournament
	v Sinclair	9-8	1st round	Coral UK Championship
	v Knowles	9-6	2nd round	Coral UK Championship
	v Higgins	5-9	Quarter-final	Coral UK Championship
1983	v Reardon	5-3	1st round	Lada Classic
	v David Taylor	5-2	Quarter-final	Lada Classic
	v S. Davis	4-5	Semi-final	Lada Classic
	v Hallett	10-7	1st round	Embassy World Championship
	v Charlton	11-13	2nd round	Embassy World Championship
	v Higgins	2-3	1st round	Winfield Masters
	v Morgan	5-1	1st round	Jameson International
	v Knowles	5-4	2nd round	Jameson International
	v Griffiths	4-5	Quarter-final	Jameson International
	v Black	5-2	1st round	Professional Players Tournament
	v Thorne	1-5	2nd round	Professional Players Tournament
	v Dunning	9-7	1st round	Coral UK Championship
	v Meo	5-9	2nd round	Coral UK Championship
1984	v Johnson	5-4	Qualifying	Lada Classic
	v S. Davis	1-5	1st round	Lada Classic
	v Thorburn	5-4	1st round	Benson & Hedges Masters
	v Griffiths	4-5	Quarter-final	Benson & Hedges Masters
	v Miles	10-3	1st round	Embassy World Championship
	v S. Davis	5-13	2nd round	Embassy World Championship
	v S. Francisco	2-5	1st round	Jameson International
	v P. Francisco	2-5	1st round	Rothmans Grand Prix
	v Johnson	6-9	1st round	Coral UK Open
1985	v King	2-5	1st round	Mercantile Credit Classic
	v Charlton	5-3	1st round	Benson & Hedges Masters
	v White	2-5	Quarter-final	Benson & Hedges Masters

	v Medati	4-9	1st round	Tolly Cobbold English Championship
	v Jonik	6-0	1st round	Dulux British Open
	v Miles	3-5	2nd round	Dulux British Open
	v Parrott	3-10	1st round	Embassy World Championship
	v Foldvari	5-4	3rd round	Goya Matchroom Trophy
	v Griffiths	1-5	4th round	Goya Matchroom Trophy
	v B. Harris	2-5	3rd round	Rothmans Grand Prix
	v V. Harris	9-5	3rd round	Coral UK Open
	v Knowles	7-9	4th round	Coral UK Open
	v S. Davis	2-5	1st round	Kit Kat
1986	v Cripsey	1-5	3rd round	Mercantile Credit Classic
	v Houlihan	9-5	3rd round	Tolly Cobbold English Championship
	v Johnson	7-9	4th round	Tolly Cobbold English Championship
	v Browne	0-5	3rd round	Dulux British Open
	v Higgins	7-10	1st round	Embassy World Championship
	v Williamson	5-2	2nd round	BCE International
	v Knowles	0-5	3rd round	BCE International
	v Burke	5-3	2nd round	Rothmans Grand Prix
	v S. Francisco	4-5	3rd round	Rothmans Grand Prix
	v Foldvari	9-6	2nd round	Tennents UK Open
	v Wilson	9-5	3rd round	Tennents UK Open
	v Stevens	9-4	4th round	Tennents UK Open
	v Thorburn	2-9	5th round	Tennents UK Open
1987	v D. Gilbert	5-4	2nd round	Mercantile Credit Classic
	v Thorne	5-3	3rd round	Mercantile Credit Classic
	v Campbell	3-5	4th round	Mercantile Credit Classic
	v Wright	6-1	2nd round	Tolly Ales English Championship
	v Martin	5-6	3rd round	Tolly Ales English Championship
	v Whitthread	5-2	2nd round	Dulux British Open
	v Meo	5-1	3rd round	Dulux British Open
	v Martin	5-2	4th round	Dulux British Open
	v Johnson	5-3	5th round	Dulux British Open
	v White	3-5	Quarter-final	Dulux British Open
	v Bales	10-3	Qualifying	Embassy World Championship
	v Chaperon	10-4	Qualifying	Embassy World Championship
	v West	5-10	Qualifying	Embassy World Championship
	v Jack Rea	5-0	3rd round	Fidelity International
	v Hallett	2-5	4th round	Fidelity International
	v Chappel	1-5	3rd round	Rothmans Grand Prix
	v Miles	5-9	3rd round	Tennents UK Open
1988	v John Rea	5-3	3rd round	Mercantile Credit Classic
	v White	1-5	4th round	Mercantile Credit Classic
	v Fowler	3-6	3rd round	English Championship
	v F. Davis	5-0	3rd round	MIM Britannia British Open
	v Dennis Taylor	5-0	4th round	MIM Britannia British Open
	v Williams	4-5	5th round	MIM Britannia British Open
	v King	7-10	Qualifying	Embassy World Championship

KIRK STEVENS (Canada)

Born 17.8.58. **Turned professional** 1978. **World ranking** 37 (21). **Best professional performances** Semi-finals Embassy World Championship 1980, 1984; runner-up 1985 Dulux British Open.

	v Amdor	9-1	Prelim	Embassy World Championship
1979	v Pulman	9-0	Qualifying	Embassy World Championship
	v F. Davis	8-13	1st round	Embassy World Championship
1980	v Hallett	9-3	Qualifying	Embassy World Championship
	v Miles	10-3	1st round	Embassy World Championship
	v Spencer	13-8	2nd round	Embassy World Championship
	v Charlton	13-7	Quarter-final	Embassy World Championship
	v Higgins	13-16	Semi-final	Embassy World Championship

Dennis Taylor

Year	Opponent	Score	Round	Tournament
1981	v F. Davis	4-5	1st round	Benson & Hedges Masters
	v David Taylor	3-5	Semi-final	Yamaha International Masters
	v Dunning	10-4	1st round	Embassy World Championship
	v Dennis Taylor	11-13	2nd round	Embassy World Championship
	v Thorburn	1-5	Quarter-final	Langs Supreme Scottish Masters
	v Meadowcroft	5-1	2nd round	Jameson International
	v David Taylor	0-5	3rd round	Jameson International
	v Griffiths	0-5	1st round	Northern Ireland Classic
	v Hallett	9-4	2nd round	Coral UK Championship
	v Werbeniuk	7-9	3rd round	Coral UK Championship
1982	v Fitzmaurice	10-4	1st round	Embassy World Championship
	v Fagan	13-7	2nd round	Embassy World Championship
	v White	9-13	Quarter-final	Embassy World Championship
	v Watterson	5-3	1st round	Jameson International
	v Mans	5-2	2nd round	Jameson International
	v Griffiths	5-3	Quarter-final	Jameson International
	v Knowles	3-9	Semi-final	Jameson International
	v E. Hughes	5-2	1st round	Professional Players Tournament
	v Johnson	1-5	2nd round	Professional Players Tournament
1983	v Knowles	5-0	1st round	Lada Classic
	v Thorburn	5-3	Quarter-final	Lada Classic
	v Werbeniuk	2-5	Semi-final	Lada Classic
	v Griffiths	3-5	1st round	Benson & Hedges Masters
	v Fisher	10-2	1st round	Embassy World Championship
	v Mans	13-3	2nd round	Embassy World Championship
	v Thorburn	12-13	Quarter-final	Embassy World Championship
	v Thorburn	2-5	Semi-final	Winfield Masters
	v Caggianello	9-0	Quarter-final	Canadian Championship
	v Jim Bear	9-8	Semi-final	Canadian Championship
	v Jonik	**9-8**	**Final**	**Canadian Championship**
	v Edmonds	5-1	1st round	Professional Players Tournament
	v Murphy	5-1	2nd round	Professional Players Tournament
	v Wildman	5-0	3rd round	Professional Players Tournament
	v Meo	3-5	Quarter-final	Professional Players Tournament
1984	v E. McLaughlin	5-4	Qualifying	Lada Classic
	v Macleod	5-1	1st round	Lada Classic
	v Meo	2-5	Quarter-final	Lada Classic
	v David Taylor	5-1	1st round	Benson & Hedges Masters
	v S. Davis	5-3	Quarter-final	Benson & Hedges Masters
	v White	4-6	Semi-final	Benson & Hedges Masters
	v Charlton	5-3	1st round	Tolly Cobbold Classic
	v S. Davis	4-5	Semi-final	Tolly Cobbold Classic
	v Sinclair	10-1	1st round	Embassy World Championship
	v David Taylor	13-10	2nd round	Embassy World Championship
	v Reardon	13-2	Quarter-final	Embassy World Championship
	v White	14-16	Semi-final	Embassy World Championship
	v Meo	1-5	Quarter-final	Winfield Australian Masters
	v Higgins	2-5	1st round	Langs Supreme Scottish Masters
	v White	0-5	1st round	Carlsberg Challenge
	v Gauvreau	1-5	1st round	Jameson International
	v Chappel	5-3	1st round	Rothmans Grand Prix
	v Williams	5-3	2nd round	Rothmans Grand Prix
	v Hallett	5-3	3rd round	Rothmans Grand Prix
	v Dennis Taylor	2-5	Quarter-final	Rothmans Grand Prix
	v Chappel	9-7	1st round	Coral UK Open
	v Johnson	9-2	2nd round	Coral UK Open
	v Knowles	9-7	Quarter-final	Coral UK Open
	v S. Davis	2-9	Semi-final	Coral UK Open
1985	v Medati	5-4	1st round	Mercantile Credit Classic
	v Thorne	1-5	2nd round	Mercantile Credit Classic
	v Meo	2-5	1st round	Benson & Hedges Masters
	v Gauvreau	6-3	1st round	Dulux British Open
	v Wildman	5-2	2nd round	Dulux British Open

	v Miles	5-2	3rd round	Dulux British Open
	v Dennis Taylor	5-2	Quarter-final	Dulux British Open
	v S. Davis	9-7	Semi-final	Dulux British Open
	v S. Francisco	9-12	Final	Dulux British Open
	v Higgins	3-5	Quarter-final	Benson & Hedges Irish Masters
	v Edmonds	10-8	1st round	Embassy World Championship
	v Parrott	6-13	2nd round	Embassy World Championship
	v Chaperon	4-6	Quarter-final	Canadian Championship
	v Chappel	3-5	3rd round	Goya Matchroom Trophy
	v Watson	5-0	3rd round	Rothmans Grand Prix
	v Miles	5-2	4th round	Rothmans Grand Prix
	v Longworth	5-3	5th round	Rothmans Grand Prix
	v Knowles	4-5	Quarter-final	Rothmans Grand Prix
	v Newbury	9-7	3rd round	Coral UK Open
	v Hallett	9-5	4th round	Coral UK Open
	v Williams	9-7	5th round	Coral UK Open
	v Dennis Taylor	1-9	Quarter-final	Coral UK Open
1986	v F. Davis	2-5	3rd round	Mercantile Credit Classic
	v Reardon	5-1	1st round	BCE Belgian Classic
	v Higgins	5-4	Semi-final	BCE Belgian Classic
	v Griffiths	7-9	Final	BCE Belgian Classic
	v Charlton	4-5	1st round	Benson & Hedges Masters
	v Miles	5-3	3rd round	Dulux British Open
	v Wilson	5-0	4th round	Dulux British Open
	v Thorne	4-5	5th round	Dulux British Open
	v Reynolds	10-6	1st round	Embassy World Championship
	v Charlton	13-12	2nd round	Embassy World Championship
	v Knowles	9-13	Quarter-final	Embassy World Championship
	v Thornley	6-2	2nd round	Canadian Championship
	v Wych	2-6	Semi-final	Canadian Championship
	v Knowles	5-3	1st round	Langs Scottish Masters
	v Higgins	2-6	Semi-final	Langs Scottish Masters
	v Bales	3-5	3rd round	BCE International
	v Dodd	4-5	3rd round	Rothmans Grand Prix
	v Scott	9-2	3rd round	Tennents UK Open
	v Spencer	4-9	4th round	Tennents UK Open
1987	v Chaperon	5-3	3rd round	Mercantile Credit Classic
	v West	3-5	4th round	Mercantile Credit Classic
	v Thorne	3-5	1st round	Benson & Hedges Masters
	v Chaperon	5-4	3rd round	Dulux British Open
	v West	5-4	4th round	Dulux British Open
	v David Taylor	2-5	5th round	Dulux British Open
	v Thorne	1-5	1st round	Benson & Hedges Irish Masters
	v Longworth	4-10	1st round	Embassy World Championship
	v Caggianello	6-0	Quarter-final	Canadian Championship
	v Bear	2-7	Semi-final	Canadian Championship
	v O'Boye	1-5	3rd round	Fidelity International
	v W. Jones	5-1	3rd round	Rothmans Grand Prix
	v Parrott	0-5	4th round	Rothmans Grand Prix
	v O'Boye	9-8	3rd round	Tennents UK Open
	v Knowles	8-9	4th round	Tennents UK Open
1988	v M. Bennett	2-5	3rd round	Mercantile Credit Classic
	v M. Bennett	10-7	Qualifying	Embassy World Championship
	v Thorburn	6-10	1st round	Embassy World Championship

DAVID TAYLOR (England)

Born 29.7.43. **Turned professional** 1968. **World ranking** 28 (25). **Amateur career** 1968 World and English champion. **Best professional performances** Semi-finals 1980 Embassy World Championship; runner-up 1978 Coral UK, 1982 Jameson International.

1970	v Bennett	11-8	1st round	World Championship
	v Pulman	22-39	Quarter-final	World Championship
1972	v Charlton	25-31	Quarter-final	World Championship
1973	v Dunning	9-4	1st round	World Championship
	v Spencer	5-16	2nd round	World Championship
1974	v Dunning	6-8	1st round	World Championship
1975	v King	15-8	1st round	World Championship
	v Higgins	2-15	2nd round	World Championship
1976	v Greaves	8-1	Qualifying	Embassy World Championship
	v Jack Rea	8-7	Qualifying	Embassy World Championship
	v Spencer	5-15	1st round	Embassy World Championship
1977	v Greaves	11-0	Qualifying	Embassy World Championship
	v Charlton	5-13	1st round	Embassy World Championship
	v Greaves	5-4	1st round	Super Crystalate UK Championship
	v Higgins	4-5	2nd round	Super Crystalate UK Championship
1978	v Morgan	9-7	Qualifying	Embassy World Championship
	v Miles	10-13	1st round	Embassy World Championship
	v Parkin	9-2	Qualifying	Coral UK Championship
	v Fagan	9-7	1st round	Coral UK Championship
	v Virgo	9-2	Quarter-final	Coral UK Championship
	v Higgins	9-5	Semi-final	Coral UK Championship
	v Mountjoy	9-15	Final	Coral UK Championship
1979	v Fagan	5-4	1st round	Benson & Hedges Masters
	v Reardon	2-5	Quarter-final	Benson & Hedges Masters
	v Dunning	9-8	Qualifying	Embassy World Championship
	v Higgins	5-13	1st round	Embassy World Championship
	v Meo	7-9	2nd round	Coral UK Championship
1980	v Edmonds	10-3	1st round	Embassy World Championship
	v F. Davis	13-5	2nd round	Embassy World Championship
	v Reardon	13-11	Quarter-final	Embassy World Championship
	v Thorburn	7-16	Semi-final	Embassy World Championship
	v Williams	7-9	2nd round	Coral UK Championship
1981	v Stevens	5-3	Semi-final	Yamaha International Masters
	v S. Davis	6-9	Final	Yamaha International Masters
	v Dunning	8-9	1st round	John Courage English
	v Wilson	10-6	1st round	Embassy World Championship
	v F. Davis	13-3	2nd round	Embassy World Championship
	v Thorburn	6-13	Quarter-final	Embassy World Championship
	v Stevens	5-0	3rd round	Jameson International
	v S. Davis	1-5	Quarter-final	Jameson International
	v Higgins	5-9	3rd round	Coral UK Championship
1982	v Reardon	1-5	1st round	Lada Classic
	v Meo	2-5	1st round	Benson & Hedges Masters
	v Fagan	9-10	1st round	Embassy World Championship
	v Fisher	5-1	1st round	Jameson International
	v Werbeniuk	5-2	2nd round	Jameson International
	v S. Davis	5-3	Quarter-final	Jameson International
	v Virgo	9-5	Semi-final	Jameson International
	v Knowles	6-9	Final	Jameson International
	v Anderson	5-1	1st round	Professional Players Tournament
	v Dennis Taylor	1-5	2nd round	Professional Players Tournament
	v Dodd	9-7	1st round	Coral UK Championship
	v Meo	6-9	2nd round	Coral UK Championship
1983	v White	5-3	1st round	Lada Classic
	v Spencer	2-5	Quarter-final	Lada Classic
	v White	2-5	1st round	Benson & Hedges Masters
	v Charlton	4-5	1st round	Benson & Hedges Irish Masters
	v Meadowcroft	10-2	1st round	Embassy World Championship
	v Werbeniuk	10-13	2nd round	Embassy World Championship
	v Donnelly	3-5	1st round	Jameson International
	v Morgan	5-3	1st round	Professional Players Tournament
	v Wildman	3-5	2nd round	Professional Players Tournament
	v N. Foulds	9-4	1st round	Coral UK Championship

	v Johnson	3-9	2nd round	Coral UK Championship
1984	v Macleod	4-5	Qualifying	Lada Classic
	v Stevens	1-5	1st round	Benson & Hedges Masters
	v Gauvreau	10-5	1st round	Embassy World Championship
	v Stevens	10-13	2nd round	Embassy World Championship
	v Charlton	4-5	Quarter-final	Winfield Australian Masters
	v W. Jones	5-4	1st round	Jameson International
	v S. Davis	1-5	2nd round	Jameson International
	v O'Kane	5-1	1st round	Rothmans Grand Prix
	v John Rea	5-1	2nd round	Rothmans Grand Prix
	v S. Davis	1-5	3rd round	Rothmans Grand Prix
	v Macleod	9-6	1st round	Coral UK Open
	v Reardon	4-9	2nd round	Coral UK Open
1985	v Longworth	4-5	1st round	Mercantile Credit Classic
	v Reardon	1-5	1st round	Benson & Hedges Masters
	v Cripsey	9-5	1st round	Tolly Cobbold English Championship
	v Parrott	9-6	2nd round	Tolly Cobbold English Championship
	v Knowles	2-9	Quarter-final	Tolly Cobbold English Championship
	v Bradley	3-6	1st round	Dulux British Open
	v O'Kane	10-4	1st round	Embassy World Championship
	v S. Davis	4-13	2nd round	Embassy World Championship
	v White	0-4	1st round	Winfield Australian Masters
	v T. Jones	5-4	3rd round	Goya Matchroom Trophy
	v Werbeniuk	5-4	4th round	Goya Matchroom Trophy
	v N. Foulds	4-5	5th round	Goya Matchroom Trophy
	v Newbury	5-2	3rd round	Rothmans Grand Prix
	v Longworth	1-5	4th round	Rothmans Grand Prix
	v Mikkelsen	9-6	3rd round	Coral UK Open
	v Campbell	9-4	4th round	Coral UK Open
	v Knowles	7-9	5th round	Coral UK Open
1986	v Gauvreau	3-5	3rd round	Mercantile Credit Classic
	v S. Davis	4-5	1st round	Benson & Hedges Masters
	v Edmonds	6-9	3rd round	Tolly Cobbold English Championship
	v Medati	1-5	3rd round	Dulux British Open
	v E. Hughes	7-10	1st round	Embassy World Championship
	v Edmonds	5-4	3rd round	BCE International
	v Johnson	5-3	4th round	BCE International
	v Reynolds	1-5	5th round	BCE International
	v W. Jones	1-5	3rd round	Rothmans Grand Prix
	v Chaperon	9-8	3rd round	Tennents UK Open
	v Thorburn	4-9	4th round	Tennents UK Open
1987	v Bradley	1-5	3rd round	Mercantile Credit Classic
	v Fitzmaurice	6-1	3rd round	Tolly Ales English Championship
	v Williams	2-6	4th round	Tolly Ales English Championship
	v Wilkinson	5-4	3rd round	Dulux British Open
	v J. McLaughlin	5-2	4th round	Dulux British Open
	v Stevens	5-2	5th round	Dulux British Open
	v Thorburn	3-5	Quarter-final	Dulux British Open
	v Cripsey	10-7	Qualifying	Embassy World Championship
	v Mountjoy	5-10	1st round	Embassy World Championship
	v Morra	5-3	3rd round	Fidelity International
	v Knowles	2-5	4th round	Fidelity International
	v Chaperon	3-5	3rd round	Rothmans Grand Prix
	v Chaperon	9-6	3rd round	Tennents UK Open
	v Higgins	6-9	4th round	Tennents UK Open
1988	v M. Smith	5-3	3rd round	Mercantile Credit Classic
	v Parrott	0-5	4th round	Mercantile Credit Classic
	v Owers	3-6	3rd round	English Championship
	v Medati	4-5	3rd round	MIM Britannia British Open
	v Chaperon	6-10	Qualifying	Embassy World Championship

DENNIS TAYLOR (Northern Ireland)
Born 19.1.49. Turned professional 1971. World ranking 10 (8). Best professional performances Winner 1985 Embassy World Championship, 1984 Rothmans Grand Prix, 1987 Benson & Hedges Masters, 1987 British Caledonian Tokyo Masters, Carling Champion, 1987 Labatts Canadian Masters, 1987 Matchroom Trophy, Irish champion 1982, 1985, 1986, 1987

1973	v Thorburn	8-9	1st round	World Championship
1974	v M. Owen	1-8	Qualifying	World Championship
1975	v Mans	15-12	1st round	World Championship
	v F. Davis	15-14	2nd round	World Championship
	v G. Owen	19-9	Quarter-final	World Championship
	v Charlton	12-19	Semi-final	World Championship
1976	v G. Owen	15-9	1st round	Embassy World Championship
	v Reardon	2-15	Quarter-final	Embassy World Championship
1977	v Karnehm	11-0	Qualifying	Embassy World Championship
	v Mans	13-11	1st round	Embassy World Championship
	v Mountjoy	13-11	Quarter-final	Embassy World Championship
	v Thorburn	16-18	Semi-final	Embassy World Championship
1978	v F. Davis	9-13	1st round	Embassy World Championship
	v Mountjoy	4-9	1st round	Coral UK Championship
1979	v S. Davis	13-11	1st round	Embassy World Championship
	v Reardon	13-8	Quarter-final	Embassy World Championship
	v Virgo	19-12	Semi-final	Embassy World Championship
	v Griffiths	16-24	Final	Embassy World Championship
	v Thorne	9-8	3rd round	Coral UK Championship
	v Fagan	9-6	Quarter-final	Coral UK Championship
	v Virgo	4-9	Semi-final	Coral UK Championship
1980	v Reardon	3-5	Quarter-final	Benson & Hedges Masters
	v Wych	10-13	2nd round	Embassy World Championship
	v Sinclair	9-6	2nd round	Coral UK Championship
	v Griffiths	2-9	Quarter-final	Coral UK Championship
1981	v Spencer	2-5	1st round	Benson & Hedges Masters
	v S. Davis	2-5	Semi-final	Yamaha International Masters
	v Stevens	13-11	2nd round	Embassy World Championship
	v Mountjoy	8-13	Quarter-final	Embassy World Championship
	v Williams	5-1	3rd round	Jameson International
	v Virgo	5-2	Quarter-final	Jameson International
	v Martin	9-1	Semi-final	Jameson International
	v S. Davis	0-9	Final	Jameson International
	v Mountjoy	4-5	1st round	Northern Ireland Classic
	v White	5-9	3rd round	Coral UK Championship
1982	v Higgins	1-5	1st round	Lada Classic
	v Reardon	3-5	1st round	Benson & Hedges Masters
	v Knowles	5-2	Semi-final	Tolly Cobbold Classic
	v S. Davis	3-8	Final	Tolly Cobbold Classic
	v Murphy	6-0	Semi-final	Irish Championship
	v Higgins	**16-13**	**Final**	**Irish Championship**
	v Sheehan	5-3	1st round	Benson & Hedges Irish Masters
	v Reardon	4-5	Quarter-final	Benson & Hedges Irish Masters
	v S. Francisco	7-10	1st round	Embassy World Championship
	v White	5-4	1st round	Langs Supreme Scottish Masters
	v S. Davis	1-6	Semi-final	Langs Supreme Scottish Masters
	v Wildman	5-2	1st round	Jameson International
	v Thorburn	5-2	2nd round	Jameson International
	v Virgo	3-5	Quarter-final	Jameson International
	v Edmonds	5-4	1st round	Professional Players Tournament
	v David Taylor	5-1	2nd round	Professional Players Tournament
	v White	3-5	3rd round	Professional Players Tournament
	v Meadowcroft	9-7	1st round	Coral UK Championship
	v Griffiths	7-9	2nd round	Coral UK Championship

1983	v S. Davis	2-5	1st round	Lada Classic
	v S. Davis	1-5	Semi-final	Tolly Cobbold Classic
	v Kelly	6-0	Quarter-final	Irish Championship
	v Fagan	6-1	Semi-final	Irish Championship
	v Higgins	11-16	Final	Irish Championship
	v White	4-5	1st round	Benson & Hedges Irish Masters
	v S. Francisco	10-9	1st round	Embassy World Championship
	v S. Davis	11-13	2nd round	Embassy World Championship
	v Reynolds	5-3	1st round	Jameson International
	v Thorburn	3-5	2nd round	Jameson International
	v Scott	4-5	1st round	Professional Players Tournament
	v Murphy	9-6	1st round	Coral UK Championship
	v White	4-9	2nd round	Coral UK Championship
1984	v Hallett	4-5	Qualifying	Lada Classic
	v Knowles	2-5	1st round	Benson & Hedges Masters
	v E. Hughes	5-1	1st round	Benson & Hedges Irish Masters
	v Thorburn	5-2	Quarter-final	Benson & Hedges Irish Masters
	v Griffiths	4-5	Semi-final	Benson & Hedges Irish Masters
	v Johnson	10-1	1st round	Embassy World Championship
	v Parrott	13-11	2nd round	Embassy World Championship
	v Mountjoy	13-8	Quarter-final	Embassy World Championship
	v S. Davis	9-16	Semi-final	Embassy World Championship
	v Fowler	5-0	1st round	Jameson International
	v Watchorn	5-1	1st round	Rothmans Grand Prix
	v Virgo	5-3	2nd round	Rothmans Grand Prix
	v Reardon	5-3	3rd round	Rothmans Grand Prix
	v Stevens	5-2	Quarter-final	Rothmans Grand Prix
	v N. Foulds	9-3	Semi-final	Rothmans Grand Prix
	v Thorburn	**10-2**	**Final**	**Rothmans Grand Prix**
	v King	9-5	1st round	Coral UK Open
	v Knowles	2-9	2nd round	Coral UK Open
1985	v Williams	3-5	1st round	Mercantile Credit Classic
	v Thorburn	3-5	1st round	Benson & Hedges Masters
	v Scott	6-2	1st round	Dulux British Open
	v Parrott	5-2	2nd round	Dulux British Open
	v Newbury	5-3	3rd round	Dulux British Open
	v Stevens	2-5	Quarter-final	Dulux British Open
	v Charlton	4-5	1st round	Benson & Hedges Irish Masters
	v Jack Rea	6-0	Quarter-final	Irish Championship
	v E. Hughes	6-5	Semi-final	Irish Championship
	v Higgins	**10-5**	**Final**	**Irish Championship**
	v S. Francisco	10-2	1st round	Embassy World Championship
	v Charlton	13-6	2nd round	Embassy World Championship
	v Thorburn	13-5	Quarter-final	Embassy World Championship
	v Knowles	16-5	Semi-final	Embassy World Championship
	v S. Davis	**18-17**	**Final**	**Embassy World Championship**
	v Thorne	3-5	1st round	Langs Scottish Masters
	v Cripsey	5-1	3rd round	Goya Matchroom Trophy
	v B. Harris	5-3	4th round	Goya Matchroom Trophy
	v Higgins	5-1	5th round	Goya Matchroom Trophy
	v Parrott	5-1	Quarter-final	Goya Matchroom Trophy
	v Thorburn	5-9	Semi-final	Goya Matchroom Trophy
	v West	5-1	3rd round	Rothmans Grand Prix
	v Williams	5-2	4th round	Rothmans Grand Prix
	v Meo	5-3	5th round	Rothmans Grand Prix
	v Wilson	5-2	Quarter-final	Rothmans Grand Prix
	v Knowles	9-6	Semi-final	Rothmans Grand Prix
	v S. Davis	9-10	Final	Rothmans Grand Prix
	v Parrott	5-1	1st round	BCE Canadian Masters
	v Reardon	8-3	Semi-final	BCE Canadian Masters
	v S. Davis	**9-5**	**Final**	**BCE Canadian Masters**
	v Jim Bear	9-3	3rd round	Coral UK Open
	v Cripsey	9-2	4th round	Coral UK Open

	v N. Foulds	9-5	5th round	Coral UK Open
	v Stevens	9-1	Quarter-final	Coral UK Open
	v Thorne	7-9	Semi-final	Coral UK Open
	v F. Davis	5-0	1st round	Kit Kat
	v Griffiths	6-4	Semi-final	Kit Kat
	v S. Davis	**9-5**	**Final**	**Kit Kat**
1986	v Fitzmaurice	5-1	3rd round	Mercantile Credit Classic
	v Reynolds	5-4	4th round	Mercantile Credit Classic
	v Higgins	4-5	5th round	Mercantile Credit Classic
	v Higgins	1-5	1st round	BCE Belgian Classic
	v Mountjoy	5-2	1st round	Benson & Hedges Masters
	v White	3-5	Quarter-final	Benson & Hedges Masters
	v Bales	4-5	3rd round	Dulux British Open
	v Thorne	2-5	Quarter-final	Benson & Hedges Irish Masters
	v Hallett	6-10	1st round	Embassy World Championship
	v Kelly	6-1	Quarter-final	Strongbow Irish Championship
	v Murphy	6-3	Semi-final	Strongbow Irish Championship
	v Higgins	**10-7**	**Final**	**Strongbow Irish Championship**
	v Griffiths	5-4	Semi-final	Camus Hong Kong Masters
	v Thorne	3-8	Final	Camus Hong Kong Masters
	v Johnson	5-3	1st round	Carlsberg Challenge
	v White	**8-3**	**Final**	**Carlsberg Challenge**
	v Thorne	5-6	Semi-final	Matchroom Trophy
	v Foldvari	5-1	3rd round	BCE International
	v Hendry	5-3	4th round	BCE International
	v S. Francisco	0-5	5th round	BCE International
	v Wright	5-3	3rd round	Rothmans Grand Prix
	v Virgo	5-3	4th round	Rothmans Grand Prix
	v Meo	2-5	5th round	Rothmans Grand Prix
	v Thorne	4-5	1st round	BCE Canadian Masters
	v Roe	9-6	3rd round	Tennents UK Open
	v W. Jones	2-9	4th round	Tennents UK Open
1987	v W. Jones	2-5	3rd round	Mercantile Credit Classic
	v N. Foulds	5-2	1st round	Benson & Hedges Masters
	v S. Francisco	5-3	Quarter-final	Benson & Hedges Masters
	v Thorburn	6-5	Semi-final	Benson & Hedges Masters
	v Higgins	**9-8**	**Final**	**Benson & Hedges Masters**
	v Roscoe	5-1	3rd round	Dulux British Open
	v Charlton	5-1	4th round	Dulux British Open
	v Griffiths	5-4	5th round	Dulux British Open
	v Knowles	4-5	Quarter-final	Dulux British Open
	v E. Hughes	5-4	1st round	Benson & Hedges Irish Masters
	v Thorburn	5-1	Quarter-final	Benson & Hedges Irish Masters
	v Thorne	6-2	Semi-final	Benson & Hedges Irish Masters
	v M. Bennett	10-4	1st round	Embassy World Championship
	v N. Foulds	10-13	2nd round	Embassy World Championship
	v Sheehan	6-3	Quarter-final	Matchroom Irish Championship
	v Browne	6-1	Semi-final	Matchroom Irish Championship
	v O'Boye	**9-2**	**Final**	**Matchroom Irish Championship**
	v Griffiths	**6-3**	**Final**	**British Caledonian Tokyo Masters (WS)**
	v S. Davis	4-5	Semi-final	Riley Hong Kong Masters (WS)
	v Hendry	5-3	1st round	Carling Champions
	v Johnson	**8-5**	**Final**	**Carling Champions**
	v Thorburn	2-5	1st round	Langs Scottish Masters
	v Bradley	5-0	3rd round	Fidelity International
	v Clark	0-5	4th round	Fidelity International
	v Reardon	5-1	3rd round	Rothmans Grand Prix
	v Werbeniuk	5-3	4th round	Rothmans Grand Prix
	v Wilson	5-2	5th round	Rothmans Grand Prix
	v Newbury	5-2	Quarter-final	Rothmans Grand Prix
	v P. Francisco	9-4	Semi-final	Rothmans Grand Prix
	v Hendry	7-10	Final	Rothmans Grand Prix
	v S. Davis	5-1	1st round	Labatts Canadian Masters (WS)

	v Thorburn	8-5	Semi-final	Labatts Canadian Masters (WS)
	v White	**9-7**	**Final**	**Labatts Canadian Masters (WS)**
	v White	6-2	1st round	Matchroom Trophy
	v S. Davis	3-6	Semi-final	Matchroom Trophy
	v Thorne	**10-3**	**Final**	**Matchroom Trophy**
	v Dodd	9-8	3rd round	Tennents UK Open
	v O'Kane	7-9	4th round	Tennents UK Open
1988	v Whitthread	5-2	3rd round	Mercantile Credit Classic
	v Drago	5-0	4th round	Mercantile Credit Classic
	v P. Francisco	5-3	5th round	Mercantile Credit Classic
	v Parrott	1-5	Quarter-final	Mercantile Credit Classic
	v Hallett	3-5	1st round	Benson & Hedges Masters
	v Kearney	6-3	Quarter-final	Irish Championship
	v Browne	6-5	Semi-final	Irish Championship
	v J. McLaughlin	4-9	Final	Irish Championship
	v Miles	5-1	3rd round	MIM Britannia British Open
	v Spencer	0-5	4th round	MIM Britannia British Open
	v Higgins	3-5	1st round	Benson & Hedges Irish Masters
	v Werbeniuk	10-8	1st round	Embassy World Championship
	v Drago	5-13	2nd round	Embassy World Championship

CLIFF THORBURN C.M. (Canada)

Born 16.1.48. **Turned professional** 1973. **World ranking** 6 (4). **Best professional performances** Winner 1980 Embassy World Championship, 1985 Goya Matchroom Trophy, 1983, 1985, 1986 Benson & Hedges Masters; Canadian champion 1985, 1986, 1987.

1973	v Dennis Taylor	9-8	1st round	World Championship
	v Williams	15-16	2nd round	World Championship
1974	v Morgan	4-8	1st round	World Championship
1975	v Pulman	3-5	1st round	Benson & Hedges Masters
	v Morgan	15-6	1st round	World Championship
	v Miles	15-2	2nd round	World Championship
	v Charlton	12-19	Quarter-final	World Championship
1976	v Higgins	14-15	1st round	Embassy World Championship
1977	v Ross	11-0	Qualifying	Embassy World Championship
	v Williams	13-6	1st round	Embassy World Championship
	v Charlton	13-12	Quarter-final	Embassy World Championship
	v Dennis Taylor	18-16	Semi-final	Embassy World Championship
	v Spencer	21-25	Final	Embassy World Championship
1978	v Mountjoy	4-2	Quarter-final	Benson & Hedges Masters
	v Spencer	5-3	Semi-final	Benson & Hedges Masters
	v Higgins	5-7	Final	Benson & Hedges Masters
	v Houlihan	13-8	1st round	Embassy World Championship
	v Charlton	12-13	Quarter-final	Embassy World Championship
1979	v Mans	4-5	Quarter-final	Benson & Hedges Masters
	v Virgo	10-13	1st round	Embassy World Championship
1980	v Virgo	5-3	1st round	Benson & Hedges Masters
	v Griffiths	3-5	Quarter-final	Benson & Hedges Masters
	v Mountjoy	13-10	2nd round	Embassy World Championship
	v Wych	13-6	Quarter-final	Embassy World Championship
	v David Taylor	16-7	Semi-final	Embassy World Championship
	v Higgins	**18-16**	**Final**	**Embassy World Championship**
1981	v Mans	5-4	Quarter-final	Benson & Hedges Masters
	v Higgins	5-6	Semi-final	Benson & Hedges Masters
	v Griffiths	5-6	Semi-final	Benson & Hedges Irish Masters
	v Miles	13-2	2nd round	Embassy World Championship
	v David Taylor	13-6	Quarter-final	Embassy World Championship
	v S. Davis	10-16	Semi-final	Embassy World Championship
	v Stevens	5-1	Quarter-final	Langs Scottish Masters
	v Higgins	6-2	Semi-final	Langs Scottish Masters

Cliff Thorburn

v White	4-9	Final	Langs Scottish Masters
v Miles	0-5	3rd round	Jameson International
v White	2-5	1st round	Northern Ireland Classic
v Meo	6-9	3rd round	Coral UK Championship
1982 v Griffiths	1-5	1st round	Lada Classic
v Meo	0-5	Quarter-final	Benson & Hedges Masters
v Higgins	4-5	Quarter-final	Benson & Hedges Irish Masters
v White	4-10	1st round	Embassy World Championship
v Scott	5-1	1st round	Jameson International
v Dennis Taylor	2-5	2nd round	Jameson International
v Medati	5-1	1st round	Professional Players Tournament
v Everton	5-2	2nd round	Professional Players Tournament
v Werbeniuk	2-5	3rd round	Professional Players Tournament
1983 v Wilson	5-3	1st round	Lada Classic
v Stevens	3-5	Quarter-final	Lada Classic
v Johnson	5-2	1st round	Benson & Hedges Masters
v Griffiths	5-3	Quarter-final	Benson & Hedges Masters
v Charlton	6-5	Semi-final	Benson & Hedges Masters
v Reardon	**9-7**	**Final**	**Benson & Hedges Masters**
v Campbell	10-5	1st round	Embassy World Championship
v Griffiths	13-12	2nd round	Embassy World Championship
v Stevens	13-12	Quarter-final	Embassy World Championship
v Knowles	16-15	Semi-final	Embassy World Championship
v S. Davis	6-18	Final	Embassy World Championship
v Stevens	5-2	Semi-final	Winfield Masters
v Werbeniuk	**7-3**	**Final**	**Winfield Masters**
v Mikkelsen	9-2	Quarter-final	Canadian Championship
v Jonik	6-9	Semi-final	Canadian Championship
v Griffiths	5-1	1st round	Langs Scottish Masters
v Knowles	2-6	Semi-final	Langs Scottish Masters
v Sinclair	5-0	1st round	Jameson International
v Dennis Taylor	5-3	2nd round	Jameson International
v Mountjoy	5-2	Quarter-final	Jameson International
v Griffiths	9-8	Semi-final	Jameson International
v S. Davis	4-9	Final	Jameson International
v V. Harris	5-1	1st round	Professional Players Tournament
v Meadowcroft	5-1	2nd round	Professional Players Tournament
v Wilson	5-3	3rd round	Professional Players Tournament
v Johnson	1-5	Quarter-final	Professional Players Tournament
1984 v S. Francisco	1-5	Qualifying	Lada Classic
v Spencer	4-5	1st round	Benson & Hedges Masters
v Dennis Taylor	2-5	Quarter-final	Benson & Hedges Irish Masters
v Meo	5-4	1st round	Tolly Cobbold Classic
v Knowles	3-5	Semi-final	Tolly Cobbold Classic
v Morra	10-3	1st round	Embassy World Championship
v Thorne	13-11	2nd round	Embassy World Championship
v White	8-13	Quarter-final	Embassy World Championship
v S. Davis	2-5	1st round	Langs Scottish Masters
v Virgo	0-5	1st round	Jameson International
v Rigitano	5-4	1st round	Rothmans Grand Prix
v Campbell	5-1	2nd round	Rothmans Grand Prix
v Meo	5-4	3rd round	Rothmans Grand Prix
v Mountjoy	5-3	Quarter-final	Rothmans Grand Prix
v S. Davis	9-7	Semi-final	Rothmans Grand Prix
v Dennis Taylor	2-10	Final	Rothmans Grand Prix
v J. McLaughlin	9-4	1st round	Coral UK Open
v Wilson	9-3	2nd round	Coral UK Open
v Reardon	9-8	Quarter-final	Coral UK Open
v Higgins	7-9	Semi-final	Coral UK Open
1985 v Scott	5-1	1st round	Mercantile Credit Classic
v Longworth	5-3	2nd round	Mercantile Credit Classic
v Griffiths	5-4	Quarter-final	Mercantile Credit Classic
v Johnson	9-2	Semi-final	Mercantile Credit Classic

v Thorne	8-13	Final	Mercantile Credit Classic
v Dennis Taylor	5-3	1st round	Benson & Hedges Masters
v Reardon	5-0	Quarter-final	Benson & Hedges Masters
v White	6-4	Semi-final	Benson & Hedges Masters
v Mountjoy	**9-6**	**Final**	**Benson & Hedges Masters**
v Rigitano	6-3	1st round	Dulux British Open
v Reynolds	5-3	2nd round	Dulux British Open
v Higgins	2-5	3rd round	Dulux British Open
v White	3-5	Quarter-final	Benson & Hedges Irish Masters
v Hallett	10-8	1st round	Embassy World Championship
v Werbeniuk	13-3	2nd round	Embassy World Championship
v Dennis Taylor	5-13	Quarter-final	Embassy World Championship
v Caggianello	6-2	Quarter-final	Canadian Championship
v Wych	6-5	Semi-final	Canadian Championship
v Chaperon	**6-4**	**Final**	**Canadian Championship**
v Higgins	4-5	Semi-final	Carlsberg Trophy
v Macleod	5-1	1st round	Langs Scottish Masters
v S. Francisco	6-0	Semi-final	Langs Scottish Masters
v Thorne	**9-7**	**Final**	**Langs Scottish Masters**
v Longworth	5-3	3rd round	Goya Matchroom Trophy
v Martin	5-3	4th round	Goya Matchroom Trophy
v Campbell	5-0	5th round	Goya Matchroom Trophy
v Duggan	5-2	Quarter-final	Goya Matchroom Trophy
v Dennis Taylor	9-5	Semi-final	Goya Matchroom Trophy
v White	**12-10**	**Final**	**Goya Matchroom Trophy**
v Oliver	5-0	3rd round	Rothmans Grand Prix
v Wildman	5-2	4th round	Rothmans Grand Prix
v Johnson	5-1	5th round	Rothmans Grand Prix
v Griffiths	5-1	Quarter-final	Rothmans Grand Prix
v S. Davis	5-9	Semi-final	Rothmans Grand Prix
v White	5-3	1st round	BCE Canadian Masters
v S. Davis	1-8	Semi-final	BCE Canadian Masters
v Dodd	9-4	3rd round	Coral UK Open
v Parrott	9-6	4th round	Coral UK Open
v Thorne	7-9	5th round	Coral UK Open
v Higgins	4-5	1st round	Kit Kat
1986 v J. McLaughlin	5-1	3rd round	Mercantile Credit Classic
v Hallett	5-3	4th round	Mercantile Credit Classic
v Meo	5-1	5th round	Mercantile Credit Classic
v Johnson	5-4	Quarter-final	Mercantile Credit Classic
v Mountjoy	9-6	Semi-final	Mercantile Credit Classic
v White	12-13	Final	Mercantile Credit Classic
v Johnson	5-3	1st round	Benson & Hedges Masters
v Griffiths	5-2	Quarter-final	Benson & Hedges Masters
v Knowles	6-4	Semi-final	Benson & Hedges Masters
v White	**9-5**	**Final**	**Benson & Hedges Masters**
v Sheehan	5-0	3rd round	Dulux British Open
v Wildman	5-1	4th round	Dulux British Open
v Meo	3-5	5th round	Dulux British Open
v E. Hughes	5-1	Quarter-final	Benson & Hedges Irish Masters
v Thorne	4-6	Semi-final	Benson & Hedges Irish Masters
v Werbeniuk	10-5	1st round	Embassy World Championship
v E. Hughes	13-6	2nd round	Embassy World Championship
v Thorne	13-6	Quarter-final	Embassy World Championship
v S. Davis	12-16	Semi-final	Embassy World Championship
v Watson	6-1	Quarter-final	Canadian Championship
v Jonik	6-3	Semi-final	Canadian Championship
v Wych	**6-2**	**Final**	**Canadian Championship**
v Parrott	5-1	1st round	Langs Scottish Masters
v White	6-2	Semi-final	Langs Scottish Masters
v Higgins	**9-8**	**Final**	**Langs Scottish Masters**
v Burke	5-0	3rd round	BCE International
v Wych	5-3	4th round	BCE International

v Griffiths	5-4	5th round	BCE International
v Wilson	5-1	Quarter-final	BCE International
v P. Francisco	9-7	Semi-final	BCE International
v N. Foulds	9-12	Final	BCE International
v O'Boye	4-5	3rd round	Rothmans Grand Prix
v Knowles	1-5	1st round	BCE Canadian Masters
v Fowler	9-7	3rd round	Tennents UK Open
v David Taylor	9-4	4th round	Tennents UK Open
v Spencer	9-2	5th round	Tennents UK Open
v N. Foulds	2-9	Quarter-final	Tennents UK Open
1987 v Cripsey	5-0	3rd round	Mercantile Credit Classic
v Reynolds	4-5	4th round	Mercantile Credit Classic
v Williams	5-1	1st round	Benson & Hedges Masters
v Thorne	5-3	Quarter-final	Benson & Hedges Masters
v Dennis Taylor	5-6	Semi-final	Benson & Hedges Masters
v Wildman	5-3	3rd round	Dulux British Open
v Cripsey	5-2	4th round	Dulux British Open
v Mountjoy	5-4	5th round	Dulux British Open
v David Taylor	5-3	Quarter-final	Dulux British Open
v White	5-9	Semi-final	Dulux British Open
v Dennis Taylor	1-5	Quarter-final	Benson & Hedges Irish Masters
v O'Kane	5-10	1st round	Embassy World Championship
v Watson	6-3	Quarter-final	Canadian Championship
v Morra	7-4	Semi-final	Canadian Championship
v Bear	**8-4**	**Final**	**Canadian Championship**
v Dennis Taylor	5-2	1st round	Langs Scottish Masters
v Johnson	3-6	Semi-final	Langs Scottish Masters
v Grace	5-1	3rd round	Fidelity International
v Newbury	5-3	4th round	Fidelity International
v James	5-0	5th round	Fidelity International
v E. Hughes	5-1	Quarter-final	Fidelity International
v Hendry	9-1	Semi-final	Fidelity International
v S. Davis	5-12	Final	Fidelity International
v T. Jones	5-2	3rd round	Rothmans Grand Prix
v Newbury	0-5	4th round	Rothmans Grand Prix
v Johnson	5-3	1st round	Labatts Canadian Masters (WS)
v Dennis Taylor	5-8	Semi-final	Labatts Canadian Masters (WS)
v Cripsey	9-6	3rd round	Tennents UK Open
v Virgo	9-6	4th round	Tennents UK Open
v Campbell	9-4	5th round	Tennents UK Open
v Thorne	8-9	Quarter-final	Tennents UK Open
1988 v Reardon	5-3	3rd round	Mercantile Credit Classic
v Newbury	3-5	4th round	Mercantile Credit Classic
v Williams	5-3	1st round	Benson and Hedges Masters
v Parrott	4-5	Quarter-final	Benson and Hedges Masters
v Newbury	5-2	3rd round	MIM Britannia British Open
v Medati	5-2	4th round	MIM Britannia British Open
v Thorne	5-2	5th round	MIM Britannia British Open
v Williams	5-2	Quarter-final	MIM Britannia British Open
v Hendry	5-9	Semi-final	MIM Britannia British Open
v Higgins	3-5	Quarter-final	Benson & Hedges Irish Masters
v Stevens	10-6	1st round	Embassy World Championship
v Parrott	13-10	2nd round	Embassy World Championship
v James	13-11	Quarter-final	Embassy World Championship
v S. Davis	8-16	Semi-final	Embassy World Championship

WILLIE THORNE (England)

Born 4.3.54. **Turned professional** 1975. **World ranking** 13 (11). **Best professional performance** Winner 1985 Mercantile Credit Classic.

1976 v Condo	8-3	Qualifying	Embassy World Championship

	v Meadowcroft	5-8	Qualifying	Embassy World Championship
1977	v Bennett	11-4	Qualifying	Embassy World Championship
	v Miles	4-13	1st round	Embassy World Championship
	v Bennett	5-1	1st round	Super Crystalate UK Championship
	v Williams	5-4	2nd round	Super Crystalate UK Championship
	v Mountjoy	4-5	Quarter-final	Super Crystalate UK Championship
1978	v Williams	9-3	Qualifying	Embassy World Championship
	v Charlton	12-13	1st round	Embassy World Championship
	v Bennett	9-4	Qualifying	Coral UK Championship
	v Reardon	9-6	1st round	Coral UK Championship
	v Miles	1-9	Quarter-final	Coral UK Championship
1979	v Jim Charlton	9-3	Prelim	Embassy World Championship
	v Virgo	8-9	Qualifying	Embassy World Championship
	v Andrewartha	9-4	2nd round	Coral UK Championship
	v Dennis Taylor	8-9	3rd round	Coral UK Championship
1980	v Jack Rea	9-1	Qualifying	Embassy World Championship
	v Werbeniuk	9-10	1st round	Embassy World Championship
	v Meadowcroft	9-1	1st round	Coral UK Championship
	v Higgins	7-9	2nd round	Coral UK Championship
1981	v Wildman	9-2	1st round	John Courage English
	v Dunning	9-0	2nd round	John Courage English
	v Meo	8-9	Semi-final	John Courage English
	v Morra	9-5	Qualifying	Embassy World Championship
	v Greaves	9-3	Qualifying	Embassy World Championship
	v Mountjoy	6-10	1st round	Embassy World Championship
	v Medati	9-6	Qualifying	Coral UK Championship
	v Edmonds	9-4	2nd round	Coral UK Championship
	v S. Davis	2-9	3rd round	Coral UK Championship
1982	v Roscoe	9-1	Qualifying	Embassy World Championship
	v Griffiths	10-6	1st round	Embassy World Championship
	v Spencer	13-5	2nd round	Embassy World Championship
	v Higgins	10-13	Quarter-final	Embassy World Championship
	v Reynolds	3-5	1st round	Jameson International
	v Demarco	5-3	1st round	Professional Players Tournament
	v Macleod	4-5	2nd round	Professional Players Tournament
	v Wilson	7-9	1st round	Coral UK Championship
	v Virgo	10-3	1st round	Embassy World Championship
	v Higgins	8-13	2nd round	Embassy World Championship
1983	v Murphy	5-2	Qualifying	Jameson International
	v Virgo	5-2	1st round	Jameson International
	v Reardon	5-0	2nd round	Jameson International
	v Charlton	0-5	Quarter-final	Jameson International
	v Everton	5-1	1st round	Professional Players Tournament
	v Spencer	5-1	2nd round	Professional Players Tournament
	v Reardon	5-3	3rd round	Professional Players Tournament
	v E. Hughes	5-1	Quarter-final	Professional Players Tournament
	v Knowles	7-9	Semi-final	Professional Players Tournament
	v Wildman	9-5	1st round	Coral UK Championship
	v S. Davis	3-9	2nd round	Coral UK Championship
1984	v S. Davis	2-5	1st round	Tolly Cobbold Classic
	v Mikkelsen	10-3	Qualifying	Embassy World Championship
	v Virgo	10-9	1st round	Embassy World Championship
	v Thorburn	11-13	2nd round	Embassy World Championship
	v Virgo	3-5	Quarter-final	Winfield Australian Masters
	v O'Kane	5-3	1st round	Jameson International
	v Gauvreau	5-3	2nd round	Jameson International
	v E. Hughes	2-5	Quarter-final	Jameson International
	v Newbury	5-2	1st round	Rothmans Grand Prix
	v Macleod	5-3	2nd round	Rothmans Grand Prix
	v N. Foulds	1-5	3rd round	Rothmans Grand Prix
	v Parrot	9-7	1st round	Coral UK Open
	v Charlton	9-7	2nd round	Coral UK Open
	v Higgins	5-9	Quarter-final	Coral UK Open

1985	v Foldvari	5-2	1st round	Mercantile Credit Classic
	v Stevens	5-1	2nd round	Mercantile Credit Classic
	v Virgo	5-1	Quarter-final	Mercantile Credit Classic
	v S. Davis	9-8	Semi-final	Mercantile Credit Classic
	v Thorburn	**13-8**	**Final**	**Mercantile Credit Classic**
	v White	2-5	1st round	Benson & Hedges Masters
	v Dodd	9-1	1st round	Tolly Cobbold English Championship
	v Reynolds	6-9	2nd round	Tolly Cobbold English Championship
	v Oliver	6-3	1st round	Dulux British Open
	v Macleod	0-5	2nd round	Dulux British Open
	v Fagan	6-10	1st round	Embassy World Championship
	v Parrott	0-5	Quarter-final	Winfield Australian Masters
	v Dennis Taylor	5-3	1st round	Langs Scottish Masters
	v White	6-2	Semi-final	Langs Scottish Masters
	v Thorburn	7-9	Final	Langs Scottish Masters
	v Fowler	5-1	3rd round	Goya Matchroom Trophy
	v Scott	5-1	4th round	Goya Matchroom Trophy
	v Duggan	4-5	5th round	Goya Matchroom Trophy
	v W. Jones	0-5	3rd round	Rothmans Grand Prix
	v Browne	9-6	3rd round	Coral UK Open
	v Virgo	9-8	4th round	Coral UK Open
	v Thorburn	9-7	5th round	Coral UK Open
	v Griffiths	9-7	Quarter-final	Coral UK Open
	v Dennis Taylor	9-7	Semi-final	Coral UK Open
	v S. Davis	14-16	Final	Coral UK Open
1986	v T. Jones	3-5	3rd round	Mercantile Credit Classic
	v Reardon	5-4	1st round	Benson & Hedges Masters
	v S. Davis	4-5	Quarter-final	Benson & Hedges Masters
	v Medati	9-2	3rd round	Tolly Cobbold English Championship
	v Reynolds	8-9	4th round	Tolly Cobbold English Championship
	v Dodd	5-2	3rd round	Dulux British Open
	v Mans	5-1	4th round	Dulux British Open
	v Stevens	5-4	5th round	Dulux British Open
	v Griffiths	5-4	Quarter-final	Dulux British Open
	v Virgo	9-4	Semi-final	Dulux British Open
	v S. Davis	7-12	Final	Dulux British Open
	v Griffiths	5-2	1st round	Benson & Hedges Irish Masters
	v Dennis Taylor	5-2	Quarter-final	Benson & Hedges Irish Masters
	v Thorburn	6-4	Semi-final	Benson & Hedges Irish Masters
	v White	5-9	Final	Benson & Hedges Irish Masters
	v Hendry	10-8	1st round	Embassy World Championship
	v Campbell	13-9	2nd round	Embassy World Championship
	v Thorburn	6-13	Quarter-final	Embassy World Championship
	v S. Davis	5-2	Semi-final	Camus Hong Kong Masters
	v Dennis Taylor	**8-3**	**Final**	**Camus Hong Kong Masters**
	v N. Foulds	6-3	1st round	Matchroom Trophy
	v Dennis Taylor	6-5	Semi-final	Matchroom Trophy
	v S. Davies	**10-9**	**Final**	**Matchroom Trophy**
	v Drago	2-5	3rd round	BCE International
	v Duggan	5-0	3rd round	Rothmans Grand Prix
	v King	5-2	4th round	Rothmans Grand Prix
	v N. Foulds	3-5	5th round	Rothmans Grand Prix
	v Dennis Taylor	5-4	1st round	BCE Canadian Masters
	v Knowles	8-7	Semi-final	BCE Canadian Masters
	v S. Davis	3-9	Final	BCE Canadian Masters
	v Murphy	9-4	3rd round	Tennents UK Open
	v Grace	9-1	4th round	Tennents UK Open
	v Drago	5-9	5th round	Tennents UK Open
1987	v Spencer	3-5	3rd round	Mercantile Credit Classic
	v Stevens	5-3	1st round	Benson & Hedges Masters
	v Thorburn	3-5	Quarter-final	Benson & Hedges Masters
	v B. Harris	6-2	3rd round	Tolly Ales English Championship
	v Martin	6-3	4th round	Tolly Ales English Championship

Willie Thorne

	v Reynolds	6-4	Quarter-final	Tolly Ales English Championship
	v Meo	3-9	Semi-final	Tolly Ales English Championship
	v R. Harris	5-1	3rd round	Dulux British Open
	v Duggan	5-2	4th round	Dulux British Open
	v N. Foulds	2-5	5th round	Dulux British Open
	v Stevens	5-1	1st round	Benson & Hedges Irish Masters
	v White	5-4	Quarter-final	Benson & Hedges Irish Masters
	v Dennis Taylor	6-2	Semi-final	Benson & Hedges Irish Masters
	v S. Davis	1-9	Final	Benson & Hedges Irish Masters
	v Hendry	7-10	1st round	Embassy World Championship
	v John Rea	5-3	3rd round	Fidelity International
	v Virgo	4-5	4th round	Fidelity International
	v Bear	5-1	3rd round	Rothmans Grand Prix
	v Bales	5-2	4th round	Rothmans Grand Prix
	v Drago	5-2	5th round	Rothmans Grand Prix
	v P. Francisco	3-5	Quarter-final	Rothmans Grand Prix
	v N. Foulds	6-5	Semi-final	Matchroom Trophy
	v Dennis Taylor	3-10	Final	Matchroom Trophy
	v Oliver	9-3	3rd round	Tennents UK Open
	v Murphy	9-4	4th round	Tennents UK Open
	v O'Kane	9-7	5th round	Tennents UK Open
	v Thorburn	9-8	Quarter-final	Tennents UK Open
	v S. Davis	2-9	Semi-final	Tennents UK Open
1988	v Bradley	5-1	3rd round	Mercantile Credit Classic
	v West	2-5	4th round	Mercantile Credit Classic
	v Johnson	4-5	1st round	Benson & Hedges Masters
	v Marshall	6-3	3rd round	English Championship
	v Virgo	6-0	4th round	English Championship
	v N. Foulds	2-6	Quarter-final	English Championship
	v Wych	5-1	3rd round	MIM Britannia British Open
	v Wilson	5-3	4th round	MIM Britannia British Open
	v Thorburn	2-5	5th round	MIM Britannia British Open
	v Knowles	3-5	1st round	Benson & Hedges Irish Masters
	v P. Francisco	10-6	1st round	Embassy World Championship
	v Griffiths	9-13	2nd round	Embassy World Championship

PAUL THORNLEY (Canada)
Turned professional 1979. **World ranking** 124 (110).

1983	v Caggianello	7-9	2nd round	Canadian Championship
1984	v Fisher	8-10	Qualifying	Embassy World Championship
	v Crispey	3-5	Qualifying	Jameson International
	v Williamson	2-5	Qualifying	Rothmans Grand Prix
1985	v Chaperon	1-5	1st round	Canadian Championship
	v Mienie	10-3	Qualifying	Embassy World Championship
	v Fagan	10-7	Qualifying	Embassy World Championship
	v Murphy	3-10	Qualifying	Embassy World Championship
1986	v Morra	6-4	1st round	Canadian Championship
	v Stevens	2-6	2nd round	Canadian Championship
1987	v Greaves	6-10	Qualifying	Embassy World Championship
	v Watson	4-6	1st round	Canadian Championship
1988	v V. Harris	5-4	1st round	MIM Britannia British Open
	v Wych	1-5	2nd round	MIM Britannia British Open
	v Rowswell	7-10	Qualifying	Embassy World Championship

JIMMY VAN RENSBERG (South Africa)
Born 24.10.31. **Turned professional** 1978. **World ranking** 87 (72). **Amateur career** 11 times South African champion between 1953 and 1973. **Best professional performance** Last 32 1986 Mercantile Credit Classic.

1979	v Meadowcroft	7-9	Prelim	Embassy World Championship
1980	v Meo	1-9	Qualifying	Embassy World Championship
1984	v V. Harris	10-7	Qualifying	Embassy World Championship
	v Edmonds	10-9	Qualifying	Embassy World Championship
	v S. Francisco	3-10	Qualifying	Embassy World Championship
1985	v Longworth	10-7	Qualifying	Embassy World Championship
	v Gauvreau	9-10	Qualifying	Embassy World Championship
	v Scott	4-5	2nd round	Goya Matchroom Trophy
	v E. McLaughlin	5-4	2nd round	Rothmans Grand Prix
	v Campbell	4-5	3rd round	Rothmans Grand Prix
	v Edmonds	5-9	2nd round	Coral UK Open
1986	v W. Jones	5-4	2nd round	Mercantile Credit Classic
	v Parrott	5-3	3rd round	Mercantile Credit Classic
	v S. Davis	1-5	4th round	Mercantile Credit Classic
	v Wych	0-5	2nd round	Dulux British Open
	v Williamson	10-9	Qualifying	Embassy World Championship
	v Sinclair	10-2	Qualifying	Embassy World Championship
	v Campbell	6-10	Qualifying	Embassy World Championship
	v Mienie	7-1	2nd round	South African Championship
	v Ellis	2-8	Semi-final	South African Championship
	v Kearney	5-3	2nd round	BCE International
	v West	3-5	3rd round	BCE International
	v Roe	3-5	2nd round	Rothmans Grand Prix
	v Roe	6-9	2nd round	Tennents UK Open
1987	v N. Gilbert	5-3	2nd round	Mercantile Credit Classic
	v S. Francisco	4-5	3rd round	Mercantile Credit Classic
	v Morra	1-5	2nd round	Dulux British Open
	v J. McLaughlin	10-6	Qualifying	Embassy World Championship
	v T. Jones	0-10	Qualifying	Embassy World Championship
	v O'Kane	3-5	2nd round	Fidelity International
	v Murphy	5-4	2nd round	Rothmans Grand Prix
	v Charlton	1-5	3rd round	Rothmans Grand Prix
	v Whitthread	9-5	1st round	Tennents UK Open
	v Reardon	7-9	2nd round	Tennents UK Open
1988	v Grace	5-3	2nd round	Mercantile Credit Classic
	v Griffiths	2-5	3rd round	Mercantile Credit Classic
	v Reardon	3-5	2nd round	MIM Britannia British Open

JOHN VIRGO (England)

Born 4.3.46. **Turned professional** 1976. **World ranking** 15 (19). **Best professional performance** Winner 1979 Coral UK Championship.

1977	v Andrewartha	11-1	Prelim	Embassy World Championship
	v Dunning	11-6	Qualifying	Embassy World Championship
	v Spencer	9-13	1st round	Embassy World Championship
	v Dennis Taylor	5-2	2nd round	Super Crystalate UK Championship
	v Miles	5-2	Quarter-final	Super Crystalate UK Championship
	v Fagan	8-9	Semi-final	Super Crystalate UK Championship
1978	v F. Davis	8-9	Qualifying	Embassy World Championship
	v Edmonds	9-4	Qualifying	Coral UK Championship
	v Pulman	9-3	1st round	Coral UK Championship
	v David Taylor	2-9	Quarter-final	Coral UK Championship
1979	v Parkin	9-0	Prelim	Embassy World Championship
	v Thorne	9-8	Qualifying	Embassy World Championship
	v Thorburn	13-10	1st round	Embassy World Championship
	v Werbeniuk	13-9	Quarter-final	Embassy World Championship
	v Dennis Taylor	12-19	Semi-final	Embassy World Championship
	v Meo	9-6	3rd round	Coral UK Championship
	v S. Davis	9-7	Quarter-final	Coral UK Championship
	v Dennis Taylor	9-4	Semi-final	Coral UK Championship

	v Griffiths	**14-13**	**Final**	**Coral UK Championship**
1980	v Thorburn	3-5	1st round	Benson & Hedges Masters
	v Meadowcroft	10-2	1st round	Embassy World Championship
	v Charlton	12-13	2nd round	Embassy World Championship
	v Meo	1-9	2nd round	Coral UK Championship
1981	v Meo	6-9	1st round	John Courage English
	v Meo	6-10	1st round	Embassy World Championship
	v Knowles	5-2	2nd round	Jameson International
	v Reardon	5-3	3rd round	Jameson International
	v Dennis Taylor	2-5	Quarter-final	Jameson International
	v White	6-9	2nd round	Coral UK Championship
1982	v Hallett	10-4	1st round	Embassy World Championship
	v Reardon	8-13	2nd round	Embassy World Championship
	v V. Harris	5-2	Qualifying	Jameson International
	v Charlton	5-4	1st round	Jameson International
	v Spencer	5-4	2nd round	Jameson International
	v Dennis Taylor	5-3	Quarter-final	Jameson International
	v David Taylor	5-9	Semi-final	Jameson International
	v Black	5-2	1st round	Professional Players Tournament
	v Hallett	5-2	2nd round	Professional Players Tournament
	v Spencer	5-1	3rd round	Professional Players Tournament
	v Johnson	5-1	Quarter-final	Professional Players Tournament
	v White	4-10	Semi-final	Professional Players Tournament
	v Kelly	9-2	1st round	Coral UK Championship
	v Mountjoy	9-5	2nd round	Coral UK Championship
	v Meo	6-9	Quarter-final	Coral UK Championship
1983	v Charlton	2-5	1st round	Lada Classic
	v Mountjoy	1-5	1st round	Benson & Hedges Masters
	v Murphy	10-8	Qualifying	Embassy World Championship
	v Thorne	3-10	1st round	Embassy World Championship
	v Thorne	2-5	1st round	Jameson International
	v French	5-4	1st round	Professional Players Tournament
	v Wilson	2-5	2nd round	Professional Players Tournament
	v Johnson	6-9	1st round	Coral UK Championship
1984	v Wildman	2-5	Qualifying	Lada Classic
	v Reardon	3-5	1st round	Benson & Hedges Masters
	v Thorburn	9-10	1st round	Embassy World Championship
	v Thorne	5-3	Quarter-final	Winfield Australian Masters
	v Meo	6-2	Semi-final	Winfield Australian Masters
	v Knowles	3-7	Final	Winfield Australian Masters
	v F. Davis	5-3	Qualifying	Jameson International
	v Thorburn	5-0	1st round	Jameson International
	v S. Francisco	2-5	2nd round	Jameson International
	v Bradley	5-0	1st round	Rothmans Grand Prix
	v Dennis Taylor	3-5	2nd round	Rothmans Grand Prix
	v King	4-9	Qualifying	Coral UK Open
1985	v Bales	5-1	Qualifying	Mercantile Credit Classic
	v Werbeniuk	5-2	1st round	Mercantile Credit Classic
	v Macleod	5-0	2nd round	Mercantile Credit Classic
	v Thorne	1-5	Quarter-final	Mercantile Credit Classic
	v Darrington	9-0	1st round	Tolly Cobbold English Championship
	v Johnson	9-4	2nd round	Tolly Cobbold English Championship
	v S. Davis	2-9	Quarter-final	Tolly Cobbold English Championship
	v P. Francisco	6-2	1st round	Dulux British Open
	v S. Davis	2-5	2nd round	Dulux British Open
	v Wych	10-4	Qualifying	Embassy World Championship
	v Meo	6-10	1st round	Embassy World Championship
	v Meo	3-5	Quarter-final	Winfield Australian Masters
	v Miles	5-2	3rd round	Goya Matchroom Trophy
	v S. Davis	1-5	4th round	Goya Matchroom Trophy
	v P. Francisco	4-5	3rd round	Rothmans Grand Prix
	v W. Jones	9-7	3rd round	Coral UK Open
	v Thorne	8-9	4th round	Coral UK Open

1986	v Gibson	5-3	3rd round	Mercantile Credit Classic
	v White	2-5	4th round	Mercantile Credit Classic
	v T. Jones	9-7	3rd round	Tolly Cobbold English Championship
	v Parrott	9-6	4th round	Tolly Cobbold English Championship
	v S. Davis	2-9	Quarter-final	Tolly Cobbold English Championship
	v Fowler	5-1	3rd round	Dulux British Open
	v John Rea	5-0	4th round	Dulux British Open
	v Charlton	5-4	5th round	Dulux British Open
	v Meo	5-3	Quarter-final	Dulux British Open
	v Thorne	4-9	Semi-final	Dulux British Open
	v White	7-10	1st round	Embassy World Championship
	v Newbury	5-4	3rd round	BCE International
	v S. Francisco	0-5	4th round	BCE International
	v Fagan	5-2	3rd round	Rothmans Grand Prix
	v Dennis Taylor	3-5	4th round	Rothmans Grand Prix
	v Miles	9-7	3rd round	Tennents UK Open
	v Drago	6-9	4th round	Tennents UK Open
1987	v M. Bennett	5-3	3rd round	Mercantile Credit Classic
	v S. Davis	2-5	4th round	Mercantile Credit Classic
	v Medati	6-1	3rd round	Tolly Ales English Championship
	v Parrott	2-6	4th round	Tolly Ales English Championship
	v Morra	5-3	3rd round	Dulux British Open
	v S. Davis	5-4	4th round	Dulux British Open
	v Wilson	5-2	5th round	Dulux British Open
	v N. Foulds	3-5	Quarter-final	Dulux British Open
	v T. Jones	10-9	Qualifying	Embassy World Championship
	v N. Foulds	4-10	1st round	Embassy World Championship
	v Murphy	5-1	3rd round	Fidelity International
	v Thorne	5-4	4th round	Fidelity International
	v Knowles	5-2	5th round	Fidelity International
	v S. Davis	2-5	Quarter-final	Fidelity International
	v Gauvreau	5-1	3rd round	Rothmans Grand Prix
	v Wilson	3-5	4th round	Rothmans Grand Prix
	v F. Davis	9-4	3rd round	Tennents UK Open
	v Thorburn	6-9	4th round	Tennents UK Open
1988	v Rigitano	5-2	3rd round	Mercantile Credit Classic
	v N. Foulds	5-3	4th round	Mercantile Credit Classic
	v Parrott	0-5	5th round	Mercantile Credit Classic
	v Dodd	6-3	3rd round	English Championship
	v Thorne	0-6	4th round	English Championship
	v Murphy	5-1	3rd round	MIM Britannia British Open
	v Parrott	1-5	4th round	MIM Britannia British Open
	v Duggan	10-5	Qualifying	Embassy World Championship
	v S. Davis	8-10	1st round	Embassy World Championship

PAUL WATCHORN (Republic of Ireland)
Born 19.7.58. **Turned professional** 1982. **World ranking** 98 (114).

1983	v Johnson	0-10	Qualifying	Embassy World Championship
	v Morra	3-5	Qualifying	Jameson International
	v Parrott	0-5	Qualifying	Professional Players Tournament
1984	v Donnelly	7-10	Qualifying	Embassy World Championship
	v W. Jones	0-5	Qualifying	Jameson International
	v Dennis Taylor	1-5	1st round	Rothmans Grand Prix
	v B. Harris	9-7	Qualifying	Coral UK Open
	v Everton	9-6	Qualifying	Coral UK Open
	v Fisher	5-9	Qualifying	Coral UK Open
1985	v D. Hughes	5-0	Prelim	Mercantile Credit Classic
	v Mikkelsen	5-1	Qualifying	Mercantile Credit Classic
	v Donnelly	1-5	Qualifying	Mercantile Credit Classic
	v Fitzmaurice	6-1	Qualifying	Dulux British Open
	v E. Hughes	4-6	1st round	Dulux British Open

John Virgo

	v Kelly	2-6	Qualifying	Irish Championship
	v Hines	4-10	Qualifying	Embassy World Championship
	v Agrawal	2-5	1st round	Goya Matchroom Trophy
	v Drago	2-5	1st round	Rothmans Grand Prix
	v Sheehan	9-7	1st round	Coral UK Open
1986	v Greaves	4-5	1st round	Mercantile Credit Classic
	v Wilkinson	4-5	1st round	Dulux British Open
	v Longworth	7-10	Qualifying	Embassy World Championship
	v J. McLaughlin	0-5	1st round	Strongbow Irish Championship
	v Bear	1-5	1st round	BCE International
	v Darrington	5-2	1st round	Rothmans Grand Prix
	v Drago	3-5	2nd round	Rothmans Grand Prix
	v Kelly	9-8	1st round	Tennents UK Open
	v Scott	7-9	2nd round	Tennents UK Open
1987	v Donnelly	5-0	1st round	Mercantile Credit Classic
	v Duggan	1-5	2nd round	Mercantile Credit Classic
	v Dunning	5-2	1st round	Dulux British Open
	v Cripsey	4-5	2nd round	Dulux British Open
	v G. Foulds	6-10	Qualifying	Embassy World Championship
	v E. Hughes	2-5	1st round	Matchroom Irish Championship
	v Oliver	5-3	1st round	Fidelity International
	v Fowler	1-5	2nd round	Fidelity International
	v Fisher	4-5	1st round	Rothmans Grand Prix
	v Darrington	9-2	1st round	Tennents UK Open
	v Bradley	9-5	2nd round	Tennents UK Open
	v Meo	1-9	3rd round	Tennents UK Open
1988	v Roscoe	2-5	1st round	Mercantile Credit Classic
	v E. Hughes	5-2	1st round	Irish Championship
	v J. McLaughlin	5-6	Quarter-final	Irish Championship
	v Morra	1-5	1st round	MIM Britannia British Open
	v M. Gibson	10-7	Qualifying	Embassy World Championship
	v King	4-10	Qualifying	Embassy World Championship

GERRY WATSON (Canada)

Born 28.9.49. **Turned professional** 1983. **World ranking** 133 (109).

	v Chaperon	5-9	1st round	Canadian Championship
1983	v Chaperon	5-9	1st round	Canadian Championship
1984	v Anderson	4-10	Qualifying	Embassy World Championship
	v Mikkelsen	3-5	1st round	Canadian Championship
	v Sheehan	5-1	1st round	Rothmans Grand Prix
	v Roscoe	5-2	2nd round	Rothmans Grand Prix
	v Stevens	0-5	3rd round	Rothmans Grand Prix
	v Houlihan	4-9	1st round	Coral UK Open
1986	v Gilbert	4-5	1st round	Mercantile Credit Classic
1987	v Thornley	6-4	1st round	Canadian Championship
	v Thorburn	3-6	Quarter-final	Canadian Championship

MIKE WATTERSON (England)

Born 26.8.42. **Turned professional** 1981. **World ranking** 107 (82).

	v Medati	5-3	Qualifying	Jameson International
1981	v Medati	5-3	Qualifying	Jameson International
	v Everton	5-4	Qualifying	Jameson International
	v Fagan	2-5	Qualifying	Jameson International
	v Bennett	9-4	Qualifying	Coral UK Championship
	v Johnson	3-9	Qualifying	Coral UK Championship
1982	v Demarco	9-6	Qualifying	Embassy World Championship
	v Meadowcroft	7-9	Qualifying	Embassy World Championship
	v Everton	5-1	Qualifying	Jameson International
	v Fagan	5-1	Qualifying	Jameson International
	v Stevens	3-5	1st round	Jameson International

	v Donnelly	5-4	1st round	Professional Players Tournament
	v Griffiths	2-5	2nd round	Professional Players Tournament
	v B. Harris	3-9	Qualifying	Coral UK Championship
1983	v Campbell	6-10	Qualifying	Embassy World Championship
	v Demarco	5-3	Qualifying	Jameson International
	v Mans	5-4	Qualifying	Jameson International
	v Meo	5-3	1st round	Jameson International
	v S. Davis	0-5	2nd round	Jameson International
	v Higgins	5-2	1st round	Professional Players Tournament
	v Martin	4-5	2nd round	Professional Players Tournament
	v Everton	9-6	Qualifying	Coral UK Championship
	v F. Davis	9-6	Qualifying	Coral UK Championship
	v Mountjoy	2-9	1st round	Coral UK Championship
1984	v Bennett	10-5	Qualifying	Embassy World Championship
	v King	8-10	Qualifying	Embassy World Championship
	v Black	3-5	Qualifying	Jameson International
	v W. Jones	3-5	Qualifying	Rothmans Grand Prix
	v Murphy	4-9	Qualifying	Coral UK Open
1985	v Edmonds	2-5	Qualifying	Mercantile Credit Classic
	v Kearney	4-6	Qualifying	Dulux British Open
	v W. Jones	5-10	Qualifying	Embassy World Championship
	v Fitzmaurice	2-5	2nd round	Goya Matchroom Trophy
	v Caggianello	5-1	2nd round	Rothmans Grand Prix
	v Williams	2-5	3rd round	Rothmans Grand Prix
	v Jim Bear	0-9	2nd round	Coral UK Open
1986	v Jenkins	5-2	2nd round	Mercantile Credit Classic
	v Williams	0-5	3rd round	Mercantile Credit Classic
	v G. Foulds	1-9	2nd round	Tolly Cobbold English Championship
	v Mikkelsen	10-2	Qualifying	Embassy World Championship
	v Dodd	1-10	Qualifying	Embassy World Championship
	v Wright	1-5	1st round	BCE International
	v M. Bennett	1-5	1st round	Rothmans Grand Prix
	v Burke	9-0	1st round	Tennents UK Open
	v Black	9-3	2nd round	Tennents UK Open
	v P. Francisco	4-9	3rd round	Tennents UK Open
1987	v Rowswell	1-5	1st round	Mercantile Credit Classic
	v Roe	3-5	1st round	Dulux British Open
	v James	2-10	Qualifying	Embassy World Championship
	v Anderson	3-5	1st round	Fidelity International
	v Jack Rea	6-9	1st round	Tennents UK Open
1988	v Chambers	3-10	Qualifying	Embassy World Championship

BILL WERBENIUK (Canada)

Born 14.1.47. **Turned professional** 1973. **World ranking** 47 (33). **Best professional performances** Semi-finals 1983 Lada Classic, 1979 Coral UK Championship.

1974	v Thompson	8-3	1st round	World Championship
	v F. Davis	5-15	2nd round	World Championship
1975	v Higgins	0-5	1st round	Benson & Hedges Masters
	v Meadowcroft	15-9	1st round	Embassy World Championship
	v Charlton	11-15	2nd round	Embassy World Championship
1976	v F. Davis	12-15	1st round	Embassy World Championship
1978	v Parkin	9-2	Qualifying	Embassy World Championship
	v Pulman	13-4	1st round	Embassy World Championship
	v Reardon	6-13	Quarter-final	Embassy World Championship
1979	v Andrewartha	9-2	Qualifying	Embassy World Championship
	v Spencer	13-11	1st round	Embassy World Championship
	v Virgo	9-13	Quarter-final	Embassy World Championship
	v Johnson	9-3	2nd round	Coral UK Championship
	v Spencer	9-8	3rd round	Coral UK Championship
	v Edmonds	9-8	Quarter-final	Coral UK Championship

	v Griffiths	3-9	Semi-final	Coral UK Championship
1980	v Thorne	10-9	1st round	Embassy World Championship
	v Reardon	6-13	2nd round	Embassy World Championship
	v S. Davis	3-9	2nd round	Coral UK Championship
1981	v Martin	10-4	1st round	Embassy World Championship
	v Mans	13-5	2nd round	Embassy World Championship
	v Reardon	10-13	Quarter-final	Embassy World Championship
	v Martin	2-5	2nd round	Jameson International
	v Stevens	9-7	3rd round	Coral UK Championship
	v S. Davis	5-9	Quarter-final	Coral UK Championship
1982	v John Bear	10-7	1st round	Embassy World Championship
	v Charlton	5-13	2nd round	Embassy World Championship
	v Wych	5-3	1st round	Jameson International
	v David Taylor	2-5	2nd round	Jameson International
	v Morgan	5-3	1st round	Professional Players Tournament
	v Jack Rea	5-2	2nd round	Professional Players Tournament
	v Thorburn	5-2	3rd round	Professional Players Tournament
	v Reardon	3-5	Quarter-final	Professional Players Tournament
1983	v Higgins	5-4	1st round	Lada Classic
	v Mountjoy	5-2	Quarter-final	Lada Classic
	v Stevens	5-2	Semi-final	Lada Classic
	v S. Davis	5-9	Final	Lada Classic
	v Higgins	5-4	1st round	Benson & Hedges Masters
	v Charlton	3-5	Quarter-final	Benson & Hedges Masters
	v Griffiths	3-5	Semi-final	Tolly Cobbold Classic
	v Martin	10-4	1st round	Embassy World Championship
	v David Taylor	13-10	2nd round	Embassy World Championship
	v Higgins	11-13	Quarter-final	Embassy World Championship
	v Knowles	5-0	Semi-final	Winfield Masters
	v Thorburn	3-7	Final	Winfield Masters
	v Scott	3-5	1st round	Jameson International
	v T. Jones	5-4	1st round	Professional Players Tournament
	v E. Hughes	0-5	2nd round	Professional Players Tournament
1984	v Roscoe	4-5	Qualifying	Lada Classic
	v Griffiths	1-5	1st round	Benson & Hedges Masters
	v Griffiths	2-5	1st round	Benson & Hedges Irish Masters
	v F. Davis	10-4	1st round	Embassy World Championship
	v Griffiths	5-10	2nd round	Embassy World Championship
	v Williamson	2-5	1st round	Rothmans Grand Prix
	v Williams	1-9	1st round	Coral UK Open
1985	v Virgo	2-5	1st round	Mercantile Credit Classic
	v Griffiths	2-5	1st round	Benson & Hedges Masters
	v Chaperon	1-6	1st round	Dulux British Open
	v Johnson	10-8	1st round	Embassy World Championship
	v Thorburn	3-13	2nd round	Embassy World Championship
	v Williamson	5-2	3rd round	Goya Matchroom Trophy
	v David Taylor	4-5	4th round	Goya Matchroom Trophy
	v Fowler	1-5	3rd round	Rothmans Grand Prix
	v F. Davis	7-9	3rd round	Coral UK Open
1986	v G. Foulds	5-3	3rd round	Mercantile Credit Classic
	v T. Jones	5-3	4th round	Mercantile Credit Classic
	v Mountjoy	3-5	5th round	Mercantile Credit Classic
	v Foldvari	5-4	3rd round	Dulux British Open
	v Johnson	5-3	4th round	Dulux British Open
	v Williams	5-3	5th round	Dulux British Open
	v Higgins	1-5	Quarter-final	Dulux British Open
	v Thorburn	5-10	1st round	Embassy World Championship
	v G. Foulds	2-5	3rd round	BCE International
	v King	2-5	3rd round	Rothmans Grand Prix
	v O'Kane	5-9	3rd round	Tennents UK Open
1987	v J. McLaughlin	5-1	3rd round	Mercantile Credit Classic
	v Duggan	0-5	4th round	Mercantile Credit Classic
	v Cripsey	2-5	3rd round	Dulux British Open

	v M. Bennett	8-10	Qualifying	Embassy World Championship
	v Cripsey	5-1	3rd round	Fidelity International
	v S. Francisco	3-5	4th round	Fidelity International
	v Foldvari	5-1	3rd round	Rothmans Grand Prix
	v Dennis Taylor	3-5	4th round	Rothmans Grand Prix
	v Black	9-5	2nd round	Tennents UK Open
	v Longworth	5-9	3rd round	Tennents UK Open
1988	v Glen Wilkinson	5-2	2nd round	Mercantile Credit Classic
	v Hendry	2-5	3rd round	Mercantile Credit Classic
	v N. Gilbert	1-5	2nd round	MIM Britannia British Open
	v Rowswell	10-6	Qualifying	Embassy World Championship
	v Bradley	10-8	Qualifying	Embassy World Championship
	v Meo	10-4	Qualifying	Embassy World Championship
	v Dennis Taylor	9-10	1st round	Embassy World Championship

BARRY WEST (England)

Born 24.10.58. **Turned professional** 1985. **World ranking** 26 (29). **Best professional performance** Quarter-finals 1985 Coral UK Open.

1985	v Hendry	4-5	1st round	Goya Matchroom Trophy
	v Meadowcroft	5-2	2nd round	Rothmans Grand Prix
	v Dennis Taylor	1-5	3rd round	Rothmans Grand Prix
	v Roscoe	9-5	2nd round	Coral UK Open
	v E. Hughes	9-3	3rd round	Coral UK Open
	v Mountjoy	9-4	4th round	Coral UK Open
	v Macleod	9-4	5th round	Coral UK Open
	v S. Davis	1-9	Quarter-final	Coral UK Open
1986	v Darrington	5-0	1st round	Mercantile Credit Classic
	v Meadowcroft	5-0	2nd round	Mercantile Credit Classic
	v Wildman	5-2	3rd round	Mercantile Credit Classic
	v Meo	1-5	4th round	Mercantile Credit Classic
	v Gilbert	8-9	1st round	Tolly Cobbold English Championship
	v Bennett	5-1	1st round	Dulux British Open
	v E. McLaughlin	5-3	2nd round	Dulux British Open
	v Campbell	4-5	3rd round	Dulux British Open
	v Dunning	10-3	Qualifying	Embassy World Championship
	v Donnelly	10-5	Qualifying	Embassy World Championship
	v Werbeniuk	8-10	Qualifying	Embassy World Championship
	v Van Rensberg	5-3	3rd round	BCE International
	v Griffiths	1-5	4th round	BCE International
	v J. McLaughlin	1-5	3rd round	Rothmans Grand Prix
	v T. Jones	4-9	3rd round	Tennents UK Open
1987	v Jonik	5-4	3rd round	Mercantile Credit Classic
	v Stevens	5-3	4th round	Mercantile Credit Classic
	v Reynolds	3-5	5th round	Mercantile Credit Classic
	v V. Harris	6-3	3rd round	Tolly Ales English Championship
	v Dodd	3-6	4th round	Tolly Ales English Championship
	v Grace	5-2	3rd round	Dulux British Open
	v Stevens	4-5	4th round	Dulux British Open
	v Spencer	10-5	Qualifying	Embassy World Championship
	v Reardon	5-10	1st round	Embassy World Championship
	v Chaperon	4-5	3rd round	Fidelity International
	v Cripsey	3-5	3rd round	Rothmans Grand Prix
	v Gauvreau	9-6	3rd round	Tennents UK Open
	v Johnson	6-9	4th round	Tennents UK Open
1988	v Oliver	5-3	3rd round	Mercantile Credit Classic
	v Thorne	5-2	4th round	Mercantile Credit Classic
	v Griffiths	2-5	5th round	Mercantile Credit Classic
	v Greaves	6-5	3rd round	English Championship
	v White	6-2	4th round	English Championship
	v Hallett	6-5	Quarter-final	English Championship

v N. Foulds	6-9	Semi-final	English Championship
v Dunning	5-0	3rd round	MIM Britannia British Open
v Williams	0-5	4th round	MIM Britannia British Open
v Newbury	10-8	Qualifying	Embassy World Championship
v Mountjoy	6-10	1st round	Embassy World Championship

JIMMY WHITE (England)

Born 2.5.62. **Turned professional** 1980. **World ranking** 2 (2). **Amateur career** 1980 World champion, 1979 English champion. **Best professional performances** Winner 1986 Mercantile Credit Classic, 1986 Rothmans Grand Prix, 1987 Dulux British Open, 1984 Benson & Hedges Masters, 1985 & 1986 Benson & Hedges Irish Masters.

1981	v Mikkelsen	9-4	Qualifying	Embassy World Championship
	v Meadowcroft	9-8	Qualifying	Embassy World Championship
	v S. Davis	8-10	1st round	Embassy World Championship
	v Reardon	5-4	Quarter-final	Langs Supreme Scottish Masters
	v S. Davis	6-5	Semi-final	Langs Supreme Scottish Masters
	v Thorburn	**9-4**	**Final**	**Langs Supreme Scottish Masters**
	v Williams	1-5	1st round	Jameson International
	v Thorburn	5-2	1st round	Northern Ireland Classic
	v Mountjoy	9-8	Semi-final	Northern Ireland Classic
	v S. Davis	**11-9**	**Final**	**Northern Ireland Classic**
	v Everton	9-4	Qualifying	Coral UK Championship
	v Virgo	9-6	2nd round	Coral UK Championship
	v Dennis Taylor	9-5	3rd round	Coral UK Championship
	v Reardon	9-8	Quarter-final	Coral UK Championship
	v S. Davis	0-9	Semi-final	Coral UK Championship
1982	v Charlton	4-5	1st round	Benson & Hedges Masters
	v Wildman	9-4	Qualifying	Embassy World Championship
	v Thorburn	10-4	1st round	Embassy World Championship
	v Mans	13-6	2nd round	Embassy World Championship
	v Stevens	13-9	Quarter-final	Embassy World Championship
	v Higgins	15-16	Semi-final	Embassy World Championship
	v Dennis Taylor	4-5	1st round	Langs Supreme Scottish Masters
	v Meadowcroft	5-1	1st round	Jameson International
	v Wilson	2-5	2nd round	Jameson International
	v Wych	5-0	2nd round	Professional Players Tournament
	v Dennis Taylor	5-3	3rd round	Professional Players Tournament
	v Griffiths	5-2	Quarter-final	Professional Players Tournament
	v Virgo	10-4	Semi-final	Professional Players Tournament
	v Reardon	5-10	Final	Professional Players Tournament
	v Medati	9-7	1st round	Coral UK Championship
	v Wilson	9-5	2nd round	Coral UK Championship
	v Reardon	8-9	Quarter-final	Coral UK Championship
1983	v David Taylor	3-5	1st round	Lada Classic
	v David Taylor	5-2	1st round	Benson & Hedges Masters
	v Reardon	2-5	Quarter-final	Benson & Hedges Masters
	v Reardon	6-9	Final	Yamaha International Masters
	v Dennis Taylor	5-4	1st round	Benson & Hedges Irish Masters
	v Higgins	2-5	Quarter-final	Benson & Hedges Irish Masters
	v Meo	8-10	1st round	Embassy World Championship
	v Higgins	3-5	1st round	Langs Supreme Scottish Masters
	v Morra	3-5	1st round	Jameson International
	v Williamson	5-2	1st round	Professional Players Tournament
	v Johnson	3-5	2nd round	Professional Players Tournament
	v Black	9-1	1st round	Coral UK Championship
	v Dennis Taylor	9-4	2nd round	Coral UK Championship
	v Reardon	9-4	Quarter-final	Coral UK Championship
	v S. Davis	4-9	Semi-final	Coral UK Championship
1984	v Campbell	5-1	Qualifying	Lada Classic

	v Charlton	3-5	1st round	Lada Classic
	v Charlton	5-2	1st round	Benson & Hedges Masters
	v Reardon	5-3	Quarter-final	Benson & Hedges Masters
	v Stevens	6-4	Semi-final	Benson & Hedges Masters
	v Griffiths	**9-5**	**Final**	**Benson & Hedges Masters**
	v Meo	4-5	1st round	Benson & Hedges Irish Masters
	v Knowles	1-5	1st round	Tolly Cobbold Classic
	v Williams	10-6	1st round	Embassy World Championship
	v Charlton	13-7	2nd round	Embassy World Championship
	v Thorburn	13-8	Quarter-final	Embassy World Championship
	v Stevens	16-14	Semi-final	Embassy World Championship
	v S. Davis	16-18	Final	Embassy World Championship
	v Knowles	3-5	Quarter-final	Winfield Australian Masters
	v Macleod	5-0	1st round	Langs Supreme Scottish Masters
	v Knowles	6-5	Semi-final	Langs Supreme Scottish Masters
	v S. Davis	4-9	Final	Langs Supreme Scottish Masters
	v Stevens	5-0	1st round	Carlsberg Challenge
	v Knowles	**9-7**	**Final**	**Carlsberg Challenge**
	v Williams	5-3	1st round	Jameson International
	v Meo	5-1	2nd round	Jameson International
	v Knowles	4-5	Quarter-final	Jameson International
	v Oliver	5-1	1st round	Rothmans Grand Prix
	v S. Francisco	1-5	2nd round	Rothmans Grand Prix
	v Campbell	9-7	1st round	Coral UK Open
	v Mountjoy	9-2	2nd round	Coral UK Open
	v S. Davis	4-9	Quarter-final	Coral UK Open
1985	v Browne	5-2	1st round	Mercantile Credit Classic
	v King	2-5	2nd round	Mercantile Credit Classic
	v Thorne	5-2	1st round	Benson & Hedges Masters
	v Spencer	5-2	Quarter-final	Benson & Hedges Masters
	v Thorburn	4-6	Semi-final	Benson & Hedges Masters
	v Chalmers	9-5	1st round	Tolly Cobbold English Championship
	v N. Foulds	9-7	2nd round	Tolly Cobbold English Championship
	v Longworth	5-9	Quarter-final	Tolly Cobbold English Championship
	v T. Jones	6-5	1st round	Dulux British Open
	v S. Francisco	4-5	2nd round	Dulux British Open
	v Meo	5-1	1st round	Benson & Hedges Irish Masters
	v Thorburn	5-3	Quarter-final	Benson & Hedges Irish Masters
	v Knowles	6-4	Semi-final	Benson & Hedges Irish Masters
	v Higgins	**9-5**	**Final**	**Benson & Hedges Irish Masters**
	v W. Jones	10-4	1st round	Embassy World Championship
	v Meo	13-11	2nd round	Embassy World Championship
	v Knowles	10-13	Quarter-final	Embassy World Championship
	v Johnson	5-4	Quarter-final	Winfield Australian Masters
	v Meo	3-6	Semi-final	Winfield Australian Masters
	v Higgins	5-0	1st round	Langs Scottish Masters
	v Thorne	2-6	Semi-final	Langs Scottish Masters
	v Parrott	5-3	Semi-final	Carlsberg Challenge
	v Higgins	**8-3**	**Final**	**Carlsberg Challenge**
	v Fagan	5-2	3rd round	Goya Matchroom Trophy
	v King	5-2	4th round	Goya Matchroom Trophy
	v Reynolds	5-1	5th round	Goya Matchroom Trophy
	v S. Davis	5-3	Quarter-final	Goya Matchroom Trophy
	v N. Foulds	9-5	Semi-final	Goya Matchroom Trophy
	v Thorburn	10-12	Final	Goya Matchroom Trophy
	v Fitzmaurice	5-0	3rd round	Rothmans Grand Prix
	v O'Boye	5-4	4th round	Rothmans Grand Prix
	v S. Francisco	4-5	5th round	Rothmans Grand Prix
	v Thorburn	3-5	1st round	BCE Canadian Masters
	v Bradley	9-4	3rd round	Coral UK Open
	v Chappel	9-5	4th round	Coral UK Open
	v Higgins	9-6	5th round	Coral UK Open
	v Knowles	9-4	Quarter-final	Coral UK Open

Jimmy White

	v S. Davis	5-9	Semi-final	Coral UK Open
1986	v Fowler	5-1	3rd round	Mercantile Credit Classic
	v Virgo	5-2	4th round	Mercantile Credit Classic
	v Gauvreau	5-2	5th round	Mercantile Credit Classic
	v S. Davis	5-2	Quarter-final	Mercantile Credit Classic
	v Williams	9-7	Semi-final	Mercantile Credit Classic
	v Thorburn	**13-12**	**Final**	**Mercantile Credit Classic**
	v Knowles	3-5	1st round	BCE Belgian Classic
	v Meo	5-4	1st round	Benson & Hedges Masters
	v Dennis Taylor	5-3	Quarter-final	Benson & Hedges Masters
	v S. Davis	6-3	Semi-final	Benson & Hedges Masters
	v Thorburn	5-9	Final	Benson & Hedges Masters
	v Williamson	9-1	3rd round	Tolly Cobbold English Championship
	v Williams	9-5	4th round	Tolly Cobbold English Championship
	v N. Foulds	4-9	Quarter-final	Tolly Cobbold English Championship
	v P. Francisco	4-5	3rd round	Dulux British Open
	v Meo	5-2	Quarter-final	Benson & Hedges Irish Masters
	v Fagan	6-0	Semi-final	Benson & Hedges Irish Masters
	v Thorne	**9-5**	**Final**	**Benson & Hedges Irish Masters**
	v Virgo	10-7	1st round	Embassy World Championship
	v Parrott	13-8	2nd round	Embassy World Championship
	v S. Davis	5-13	Quarter-final	Embassy World Championship
	v Higgins	5-1	1st round	Carlsberg Challenge
	v Dennis Taylor	3-8	Final	Carlsberg Challenge
	v Hendry	5-1	1st round	Langs Scottish Masters
	v Thorburn	2-6	Semi-final	Langs Scottish Masters
	v Owers	2-5	3rd round	BCE International
	v T. Jones	5-0	3rd round	Rothmans Grand Prix
	v J. McLaughlin	5-2	4th round	Rothmans Grand Prix
	v Hallett	5-3	5th round	Rothmans Grand Prix
	v Hendry	5-4	Quarter-final	Rothmans Grand Prix
	v S. Francisco	9-6	Semi-final	Rothmans Grand Prix
	v Williams	**10-6**	**Final**	**Rothmans Grand Prix**
	v S. Davis	2-5	1st round	BCE Canadian Masters
	v Edmonds	9-4	3rd round	Tennents UK Open
	v P. Francisco	9-5	4th round	Tennents UK Open
	v N. Foulds	7-9	5th round	Tennents UK Open
1987	v Newbury	5-4	3rd round	Mercantile Credit Classic
	v Bradley	5-0	4th round	Mercantile Credit Classic
	v Duggan	5-2	5th round	Mercantile Credit Classic
	v Griffiths	5-3	Quarter-final	Mercantile Credit Classic
	v Reynolds	9-8	Semi-final	Mercantile Credit Classic
	v S. Davis	12-13	Final	Mercantile Credit Classic
	v Meo	4-5	1st round	Benson & Hedges Masters
	v Cripsey	6-4	3rd round	Tolly Ales English Championship
	v Reynolds	5-6	4th round	Tolly Ales English Championship
	v Chappel	5-1	3rd round	Dulux British Open
	v Hallett	5-2	4th round	Dulux British Open
	v Williams	5-0	5th round	Dulux British Open
	v Spencer	5-3	Quarter-final	Dulux British Open
	v Thorburn	9-5	Semi-final	Dulux British Open
	v N. Foulds	**13-9**	**Final**	**Dulux British Open**
	v Thorne	4-5	Quarter-final	Benson & Hedges Irish Masters
	v Reynolds	10-8	1st round	Embassy World Championship
	v Parrott	13-11	2nd round	Embassy World Championship
	v O'Kane	13-6	Quarter-final	Embassy World Championship
	v S. Davis	11-16	Semi-final	Embassy World Championship
	v Hendry	2-5	Semi-final	Riley Hong Kong Masters (WS)
	v Higgins	5-3	1st round	Langs Scottish Masters
	v Griffiths	2-6	Semi-final	Langs Scottish Masters
	v M. Bennett	5-3	3rd round	Fidelity International
	v Longworth	5-1	4th round	Fidelity International
	v Hallett	4-5	5th round	Fidelity International

v Wright	5-4	3rd round	Rothmans Grand Prix
v Drago	3-5	4th round	Rothmans Grand Prix
v Knowles	5-1	1st round	Labatts Canadian Masters (WS)
v N. Foulds	8-7	Semi-final	Labatts Canadian Masters (WS)
v Dennis Taylor	7-9	Final	Labatts Canadian Masters (WS)
v Dennis Taylor	2-6	1st round	Matchroom Trophy
v Dunning	9-0	3rd round	Tennents UK Open
v E. Hughes	9-4	4th round	Tennents UK Open
v Roe	9-5	5th round	Tennents UK Open
v Griffiths	9-7	Quarter-final	Tennents UK Open
v Johnson	9-4	Semi-final	Tennents UK Open
v S. Davis	14-16	Final	Tennents UK Open
1988 v James	5-1	3rd round	Mercantile Credit Classic
v Spencer	5-1	4th round	Mercantile Credit Classic
v Martin	2-5	5th round	Mercantile Credit Classic
v Mountjoy	5-0	1st round	Benson & Hedges Masters
v Johnson	3-5	Quarter-final	Benson & Hedges Masters
v Clark	6-5	3rd round	English Championship
v West	2-6	4th round	English Championship
v Clark	5-2	3rd round	MIM Britannia British Open
v James	5-1	4th round	MIM Britannia British Open
v Gary Wilkinson	5-1	5th round	MIM Britannia British Open
v Hendry	4-5	Quarter-final	MIM Britannia British Open
v Griffiths	2-5	Quarter-final	Benson & Hedges Irish Masters
v Campbell	10-3	1st round	Embassy World Championship
v Hendry	13-12	2nd round	Embassy World Championship
v Knowles	13-6	Quarter-final	Embassy World Championship
v Griffiths	11-16	Semi-final	Embassy World Championship

TERRY WHITTHREAD (England)

Born 7.7.64. **Turned professional** 1986. **World ranking** 101 (116). **Amateur career** 1985 English champion.

1986 v Kelly	1-5	1st round	BCE International
v Duggan	1-5	1st round	Rothmans Grand Prix
v Darrington	8-9	1st round	Tennents UK Open
1987 v Roscoe	1-5	1st round	Mercantile Credit Classic
v Fisher	3-6	1st round	Tolly Ales English Championship
v D. Hughes	5-1	1st round	Dulux British Open
v Spencer	2-5	2nd round	Dulux British Open
v Roscoe	2-10	Qualifying	Embassy World Championship
v Jenkins	1-5	1st round	Fidelity International
v Roe	1-5	1st round	Rothmans Grand Prix
v Van Rensberg	5-9	1st round	Tennents UK Open
1988 v Fagan	5-2	1st round	Mercantile Credit Classic
v G. Foulds	5-3	2nd round	Mercantile Credit Classic
v Dennis Taylor	2-5	3rd round	Mercantile Credit Classic
v D. Gilbert	1-6	1st round	English Championship
v Glen Wilkinson	5-4	1st round	MIM Britannia British Open
v O'Kane	2-5	2nd round	MIM Britannia British Open

MARK WILDMAN (England)

Born 25.1.36. **Turned professional** 1979. **World ranking** 76 (47). **Best professional performance** Semi-final 1984 Lada Classic.

1980 v Jonik	7-9	Qualifying	Embassy World Championship
v Wilson	9-8	Qualifying	Coral UK Championship
v Spencer	9-7	1st round	Coral UK Championship
v F. Davis	6-9	2nd round	Coral UK Championship

1981	v Bennett	9-3	Qualifying	John Courage English
	v Thorne	2-9	1st round	John Courage English
	v Edmonds	3-9	Qualifying	Embassy World Championship
	v Morra	5-3	Qualifying	Jameson International
	v E. McLaughlin	3-5	Qualifying	Jameson International
	v Sinclair	8-9	Qualifying	Coral UK Championship
1982	v G. Foulds	9-8	Qualifying	Embassy World Championship
	v White	4-9	Qualifying	Embassy World Championship
	v Gibson	5-1	Qualifying	Jameson International
	v Hallett	5-2	Qualifying	Jameson International
	v Dennis Taylor	2-5	1st round	Jameson International
	v Dunning	5-4	1st round	Professional Players Tournament
	v Mans	5-4	2nd round	Professional Players Tournament
	v Johnson	4-5	3rd round	Professional Players Tournament
	v Roscoe	9-4	Qualifying	Coral UK Championship
	v Reardon	5-9	1st round	Coral UK Championship
1983	v S. Davis	2-5	1st round	Benson & Hedges Masters
	v B. Harris	10-7	Qualifying	Embassy World Championship
	v Griffiths	8-10	1st round	Embassy World Championship
	v B. Harris	5-2	Qualifying	Jameson International
	v Mountjoy	4-5	1st round	Jameson International
	v Jonik	5-4	1st round	Professional Players Tournament
	v David Taylor	5-3	2nd round	Professional Players Tournament
	v Stevens	0-5	3rd round	Professional Players Tournament
	v Greaves	9-5	Qualifying	Coral UK Championship
	v Thorne	5-9	1st round	Coral UK Championship
1984	v Virgo	5-2	Qualifying	Lada Classic
	v S. Francisco	5-1	1st round	Lada Classic
	v Charlton	5-4	Quarter-final	Lada Classic
	v Meo	3-5	Semi-final	Lada Classic
	v Andrewartha	9-10	Qualifying	Embassy World Championship
	v W. Jones	0-5	Qualifying	Jameson International
	v J. McLaughlin	5-3	1st round	Rothmans Grand Prix
	v Mountjoy	0-5	2nd round	Rothmans Grand Prix
	v T. Jones	2-9	Qualifying	Coral UK Open
1985	v Fagan	3-5	Qualifying	Mercantile Credit Classic
	v Longworth	3-9	1st round	Tolly Cobbold English Championship
	v Gibson	6-1	1st round	Dulux British Open
	v Stevens	2-5	2nd round	Dulux British Open
	v Edmonds	7-10	Qualifying	Embassy World Championship
	v Scott	1-5	3rd round	Goya Matchroom Trophy
	v Duggan	5-4	3rd round	Rothmans Grand Prix
	v Thorburn	2-5	4th round	Rothmans Grand Prix
	v Drago	5-9	3rd round	Coral UK Open
1986	v West	2-5	3rd round	Mercantile Credit Classic
	v Cripsey	9-5	3rd round	Tolly Cobbold English Championship
	v Meo	3-9	4th round	Tolly Cobbold English Championship
	v Jenkins	5-4	3rd round	Dulux British Open
	v Thorburn	1-5	4th round	Dulux British Open
	v Edmonds	9-10	Qualifying	Embassy World Championship
	v Rowswell	5-2	2nd round	BCE International
	v P. Francisco	2-5	3rd round	BCE International
	v Ellis	5-1	2nd round	Rothmans Grand Prix
	v Longworth	5-2	3rd round	Rothmans Grand Prix
	v Williams	1-5	4th round	Rothmans Grand Prix
	v Roscoe	6-9	2nd round	Tennents UK Open
1987	v Kearney	3-5	2nd round	Mercantile Credit Classic
	v Parrott	1-6	3rd round	Tolly Ales English Championship
	v Chalmers	5-0	2nd round	Dulux British Open
	v Thorburn	3-5	3rd round	Dulux British Open
	v Foldvari	10-5	Qualifying	Embassy World Championship
	v Wright	0-10	Qualifying	Embassy World Championship
	v Miles	5-3	2nd round	Fidelity International

	v Griffiths	1-5	3rd round	Fidelity International
	v Roe	3-5	2nd round	Rothmans Grand Prix
	v Chambers	5-9	2nd round	Tennents UK Open
1988	v Jonik	5-4	2nd round	Mercantile Credit Classic
	v Parrott	2-5	3rd round	Mercantile Credit Classic
	v D. Hughes	0-6	2nd round	English Championship
	v Roscoe	0-5	2nd round	MIM Britannia British Open
	v Mikkelsen	10-5	Qualifying	Embassy World Championship
	v Foldvari	1-10	Qualifying	Embassy World Championship

GARY WILKINSON (England)

Born 7.4.66. **Turned professional** 1987. **World ranking** 45 (unranked). **Best professional performances** Last 16 1987 Rothmans Grand Prix, 1988 MIM Britannia British Open.

	v Rigitano	5-1	1st round	Fidelity International
1987	v Rigitano	5-1	1st round	Fidelity International
	v Scott	5-2	2nd round	Fidelity International
	v Hendry	4-5	3rd round	Fidelity International
	v V. Harris	5-0	1st round	Rothmans Grand Prix
	v O'Kane	5-2	2nd round	Rothmans Grand Prix
	v Longworth	5-4	3rd round	Rothmans Grand Prix
	v S. Francisco	5-3	4th round	Rothmans Grand Prix
	v Newbury	3-5	5th round	Rothmans Grand Prix
	v Jenkins	9-3	1st round	Tennents UK Open
	v Grace	9-5	2nd round	Tennents UK Open
	v Griffiths	5-9	3rd round	Tennents UK Open
1988	v Reardon	3-5	2nd round	Mercantile Credit Classic
	v Rowswell	6-1	1st round	English Championship
	v Edmonds	6-3	2nd round	English Championship
	v N. Foulds	3-6	3rd round	English Championship
	v Black	5-2	1st round	MIM Britannia British Open
	v Bales	5-1	2nd round	MIM Britannia British Open
	v Meo	5-2	3rd round	MIM Britannia British Open
	v S. Francisco	5-3	4th round	MIM Britannia British Open
	v White	1-5	5th round	MIM Britannia British Open
	v Medati	9-10	Qualifying	Embassy World Championship

GLEN WILKINSON (Australia)

Born 4.7.59. **Turned professional** 1985. **World ranking** 95 (97). **Amateur career** 1985 Australian champion.

	v Jenkins	6-2	1st round	Australian Championship
1985	v Jenkins	6-2	1st round	Australian Championship
	v Heywood	7-3	2nd round	Australian Championship
	v Charlton	2-8	Quarter-final	Australian Championship
	v Demarco	5-2	1st round	Goya Matchroom Trophy
	v Longworth	0-5	2nd round	Goya Matchroom Trophy
	v Gilbert	4-5	1st round	Rothmans Grand Prix
	v Smith	9-4	1st round	Coral UK Open
	v Fowler	6-9	2nd round	Coral UK Open
1986	v O'Boye	1-5	1st round	Mercantile Credit Classic
	v Watchorn	5-4	1st round	Dulux British Open
	v Donnelly	4-5	2nd round	Dulux British Open
	v Kearney	5-10	Qualifying	Embassy World Championship
	v Heywood	6-0	2nd round	Australian Championship
	v Campbell	1-6	Quarter-final	Australian Championship
	v Bradley	4-5	2nd round	BCE International
	v G. Foulds	3-5	1st round	Rothmans Grand Prix
	v Jonik	9-8	1st round	Tennents UK Open
	v Chappel	2-9	2nd round	Tennents UK Open
1987	v Fitzmaurice	5-2	1st round	Mercantile Credit Classic

	v Fowler	1-5	2nd round	Mercantile Credit Classic
	v Fitzmaurice	5-0	1st round	Dulux British Open
	v Mans	5-2	2nd round	Dulux British Open
	v David Taylor	4-5	3rd round	Dulux British Open
	v Campbell	4-6	Quarter-final	Australian Championship
	v P. Gibson	3-5	1st round	Fidelity International
	v Owers	5-4	2nd round	Rothmans Grand Prix
	v Wilson	4-5	3rd round	Rothmans Grand Prix
	v Meakin	0-9	1st round	Tennents UK Open
1988	v Chalmers	5-3	1st round	Mercantile Credit Classic
	v Werbeniuk	2-5	2nd round	Mercantile Credit Classic
	v Whitthread	4-5	1st round	MIM Britannia British Open
	v Everton	10-2	Qualifying	Embassy World Championship
	v W. Jones	4-10	Qualifying	Embassy World Championship

REX WILLIAMS (England)

Born 20.7.33. **Turned professional** 1951. **World ranking** 18 (12). **Amateur career** 1951 English champion. **Best professional performance** Runner-up 1986 Rothmans Grand Prix.

1969	v Bennett	38-11	Quarter-final	World Championship
	v Spencer	18-55	Semi-final	World Championship
1970	v G. Owen	11-31	Quarter-final	World Championship (Apr)
1972	v Reardon	25-23	Quarter-final	World Championship
	v Higgins	30-31	Semi-final	World Championship
1973	v Thorburn	16-15	2nd round	World Championship
	v Spencer	7-16	Quarter-final	World Championship
1974	v Pulman	15-12	2nd round	World Championship
	v Mans	15-4	Quarter-final	World Championship
	v Miles	7-15	Semi-final	World Championship
1975	v Higgins	5-3	Quarter-final	Benson & Hedges Masters
	v Reardon	4-5	Semi-final	Benson & Hedges Masters
	v Anderson	15-4	2nd round	World Championship
	v Higgins	12-19	Quarter-final	World Championship
1976	v Meadowcroft	7-15	1st round	Embassy World Championship
1977	v Thorburn	6-13	1st round	Embassy World Championship
1978	v Thorne	3-9	Qualifying	Embassy World Championship
	v Griffiths	9-8	Qualifying	Coral UK Championship
	v Miles	8-9	1st round	Coral UK Championship
1979	v Spencer	2-6	Semi-final	Holsten Lager International
	v Greaves	9-2	Prelim	Embassy World Championship
	v Miles	5-9	Qualifying	Embassy World Championship
1980	v Wych	7-9	Qualifying	Embassy World Championship
	v Barrie	9-1	Qualifying	Coral UK Championship
	v Mountjoy	9-8	1st round	Coral UK Championship
	v David Taylor	9-7	2nd round	Coral UK Championship
	v Reardon	4-9	Quarter-final	Coral UK Championship
1981	v Hood	9-4	Qualifying	Embassy World Championship
	v Edmonds	7-9	Qualifying	Embassy World Championship
	v French	5-0	Qualifying	Jameson International
	v White	5-1	1st round	Jameson International
	v F. Davis	5-0	2nd round	Jameson International
	v Dennis Taylor	1-5	3rd round	Jameson International
	v French	9-3	Qualifying	Coral UK Championship
	v Roscoe	9-4	Qualifying	Coral UK Championship
	v Dunning	9-4	Qualifying	Coral UK Championship
	v Meo	8-9	2nd round	Coral UK Championship
1982	v Black	9-2	Qualifying	Embassy World Championship
	v Mountjoy	3-10	1st round	Embassy World Championship
	v Medati	5-3	Qualifying	Jameson International
	v E. McLaughlin	5-1	Qualifying	Jameson International

	v Griffiths	2-5	1st round	Jameson International
	v Ross	5-0	1st round	Professional Players Tournament
	v Charlton	2-5	2nd round	Professional Players Tournament
	v G. Foulds	9-7	Qualifying	Coral UK Championship
	v S. Davis	6-9	1st round	Coral UK Championship
	v Darrington	10-0	Qualifying	Embassy World Championship
	v F. Davis	10-1	Qualifying	Embassy World Championship
	v S. Davis	4-10	1st round	Embassy World Championship
1983	v French	5-1	Qualifying	Jameson International
	v Reynolds	3-5	Qualifying	Jameson International
	v Sheehan	5-1	1st round	Professional Players Tournament
	v Knowles	4-5	2nd round	Professional Players Tournament
	v V. Harris	9-6	Qualifying	Coral UK Championship
	v Wilson	4-9	1st round	Coral UK Championship
1984	v Reardon	5-4	Qualifying	Lada Classic
	v Meo	3-5	1st round	Lada Classic
	v Oliver	10-8	Qualifying	Embassy World Championship
	v White	6-10	1st round	Embassy World Championship
	v Meadowcroft	5-4	Qualifying	Jameson International
	v White	3-5	Qualifying	Jameson International
	v Chalmers	5-0	1st round	Rothmans Grand Prix
	v Stevens	3-5	2nd round	Rothmans Grand Prix
	v Fisher	9-8	Qualifying	Coral UK Open
	v Werbeniuk	9-1	1st round	Coral UK Open
	v Higgins	7-9	2nd round	Coral UK Open
1985	v Donnelly	5-3	Qualifying	Mercantile Credit Classic
	v Dennis Taylor	5-3	1st round	Mercantile Credit Classic
	v Griffiths	3-5	2nd round	Mercantile Credit Classic
	v T. Jones	9-6	1st round	Tolly Cobbold English Championship
	v S. Davis	2-9	2nd round	Tolly Cobbold English Championship
	v Fowler	4-6	1st round	Dulux British Open
	v F. Davis	10-6	Qualifying	Embassy World Championship
	v Griffiths	3-10	1st round	Embassy World Championship
	v King	3-5	3rd round	Goya Matchroom Trophy
	v Watterson	5-2	3rd round	Rothmans Grand Prix
	v Dennis Taylor	2-5	4th round	Rothmans Grand Prix
	v King	9-5	3rd round	Coral UK Open
	v P. Francisco	9-7	4th round	Coral UK Open
	v Stevens	7-9	5th round	Coral UK Open
1986	v Watterson	5-0	3rd round	Mercantile Credit Classic
	v V. Harris	5-1	4th round	Mercantile Credit Classic
	v Knowles	5-2	5th round	Mercantile Credit Classic
	v Higgins	5-2	Quarter-final	Mercantile Credit Classic
	v White	7-9	Semi-final	Mercantile Credit Classic
	v Miles	9-6	3rd round	Tolly Cobbold English Championship
	v White	5-9	4th round	Tolly Cobbold English Championship
	v Drago	5-1	3rd round	Dulux British Open
	v Bales	5-4	4th round	Dulux British Open
	v Werbeniuk	3-5	5th round	Dulux British Open
	v S. Francisco	4-10	1st round	Embassy World Championship
	v O'Boye	5-0	3rd round	BCE International
	v Duggan	5-4	4th round	BCE International
	v S. Davis	4-5	5th round	BCE International
	v Bear	5-2	3rd round	Rothmans Grand Prix
	v Wildman	5-1	4th round	Rothmans Grand Prix
	v Higgins	5-1	5th round	Rothmans Grand Prix
	v S. Davis	5-1	Quarter-final	Rothmans Grand Prix
	v N. Foulds	9-8	Semi-final	Rothmans Grand Prix
	v White	6-10	Final	Rothmans Grand Prix
	v Drago	7-9	3rd round	Tennents UK Open
1987	v Morra	5-2	3rd round	Mercantile Credit Classic
	v Charlton	4-5	4th round	Mercantile Credit Classic
	v Thorburn	1-5	1st round	Benson & Hedges Masters

	v T. Jones	6-4	3rd round	Tolly Ales English Championship
	v David Taylor	6-2	4th round	Tolly Ales English Championship
	v Johnson	5-4	Quarter-final	Tolly Ales English Championship
	v Foldvari	5-4	3rd round	Dulux British Open
	v James	5-2	4th round	Dulux British Open
	v White	0-5	5th round	Dulux British Open
	v Macleod	5-10	1st round	Embassy World Championship
	v Foldvari	0-5	3rd round	Fidelity International
	v Edmonds	3-5	3rd round	Rothmans Grand Prix
	v Roe	7-9	3rd round	Tennents UK Open
1988	v Owers	3-5	3rd round	Mercantile Credit Classic
	v Thorburn	3-5	1st round	Benson & Hedges Masters
	v D. Hughes	6-1	3rd round	English Championship
	v Hallett	3-6	4th round	English Championship
	v N. Gilbert	5-2	3rd round	MIM Britannia British Open
	v West	5-0	4th round	MIM Britannia British Open
	v Spencer	5-4	5th round	MIM Britannia British Open
	v Thorburn	2-5	Quarter-final	MIM Britannia British Open
	v Griffiths	1-5	1st round	Benson & Hedges Irish Masters
	v James	6-10	1st round	Embassy World Championship

IAN WILLIAMSON (England)

Born 1.12.58. **Turned professional** 1982. **World ranking** 89 (81).

1982	v Donnelly	5-3	Qualifying	Jameson International
	v Kelly	1-5	Qualifying	Jameson International
	v Dodd	1-9	Qualifying	Coral UK Championship
1983	v French	10-8	Qualifying	Embassy World Championship
	v Dodd	9-10	Qualifying	Embassy World Championship
	v Darrington	3-5	Qualifying	Jameson International
	v White	2-5	1st round	Professional Players Tournament
	v Hargreaves	9-4	Qualifying	Coral UK Championship
	v Black	6-9	Qualifying	Coral UK Championship
1984	v Houlihan	10-5	Qualifying	Embassy World Championship
	v Hines	10-6	Qualifying	Embassy World Championship
	v Miles	6-10	Qualifying	Embassy World Championship
	v V. Harris	5-0	Qualifying	Jameson International
	v G. Foulds	4-5	Qualifying	Jameson International
	v Thornley	5-2	Qualifying	Rothmans Grand Prix
	v Werbeniuk	5-2	1st round	Rothmans Grand Prix
	v Johnson	5-4	2nd round	Rothmans Grand Prix
	v Knowles	2-5	3rd round	Rothmans Grand Prix
	v P. Francisco	2-9	Qualifying	Coral UK Open
1985	v Kearney	5-3	Qualifying	Mercantile Credit Classic
	v Fagan	1-5	Qualifying	Mercantile Credit Classic
	v Bradley	8-9	Qualifying	Tolly Cobbold English Championship
	v Chappel	5-6	Qualifying	Dulux British Open
	v Medati	8-10	Qualifying	Embassy World Championship
	v J. McLaughlin	5-3	2nd round	Goya Matchroom Trophy
	v Werbeniuk	2-5	3rd round	Goya Matchroom Trophy
	v Gilbert	4-5	2nd round	Rothmans Grand Prix
	v Mikkelsen	3-9	2nd round	Coral UK Championship
1986	v John Rea	4-5	2nd round	Mercantile Credit Classic
	v Parkin	9-4	2nd round	Tolly Cobbold English Championship
	v White	1-9	3rd round	Tolly Cobbold English Championship
	v Cripsey	5-4	2nd round	Dulux British Open
	v Knowles	1-5	3rd round	Dulux British Open
	v Van Rensberg	9-10	Qualifying	Embassy World Championship
	v Spencer	4-5	2nd round	BCE International
	v Hendry	1-5	2nd round	Rothmans Grand Prix
	v Browne	9-4	2nd round	Tennents UK Open
	v Martin	5-9	3rd round	Tennents UK Open

Cliff Wilson

1987	v Edmonds	5-2	2nd round	Mercantile Credit Classic
	v Wilson	4-5	3rd round	Mercantile Credit Classic
	v Roe	6-4	2nd round	Tolly Ales English Championship
	v Hallett	2-6	3rd round	Tolly Ales English Championship
	v King	3-5	2nd round	Dulux British Open
	v Black	8-10	Qualifying	Embassy World Championship
	v Everton	5-0	1st round	Fidelity International
	v Gauvreau	5-1	2nd round	Fidelity International
	v Longworth	4-5	3rd round	Fidelity International
	v Clark	1-5	1st round	Rothmans Grand Prix
	v Kelly	9-5	1st round	Tennents UK Open
	v Duggan	7-9	2nd round	Tennents UK Open
1988	v D. Hughes	3-5	1st round	Mercantile Credit Classic
	v Dunning	6-5	1st round	English Championship
	v Duggan	2-6	2nd round	English Championship
	v Meakin	5-1	1st round	MIM Britannia British Open
	v Bradley	5-3	2nd round	MIM Britannia British Open
	v Hallett	0-5	3rd round	MIM Britannia British Open
	v Bradley	9-10	Qualifying	Embassy World Championship

CLIFF WILSON (Wales)

Born 10.5.34. **Turned professional** 1979. **World ranking** 16 (17). **Amateur career** World champion 1978, Welsh champion 1956, 1977, 1979. **Best professional performances** Quarter-finals 1982 Jameson International, 1986 BCE International, 1985 Rothmans Grand Prix, 1987 Mercantile Credit Classic.

1979	v Pulman	9-7	2nd round	Coral UK Championship
	v Griffiths	4-9	3rd round	Coral UK Championship
	v Reardon	3-9	1st round	Woodpecker Welsh Championship
1980	v Jonik	9-6	Qualifying	Embassy World Championship
	v Mountjoy	6-10	1st round	Embassy World Championship
	v Wildman	8-9	Qualifying	Coral UK Championship
1981	v Andrewartha	6-5	Prelim	Woodpecker Welsh Championship
	v Mountjoy	9-6	Semi-final	Woodpecker Welsh Championship
	v Reardon	6-9	Final	Woodpecker Welsh Championship
	v Andrewartha	9-4	Qualifying	Embassy World Championship
	v Sinclair	9-4	Qualifying	Embassy World Championship
	v David Taylor	6-10	1st round	Embassy World Championship
	v Meadowcroft	4-5	1st round	Jameson International
	v Johnson	5-9	Qualifying	Coral UK Championship
1982	v M. Owen	6-0	1st round	Welsh Championship
	v Griffiths	6-9	Semi-final	Welsh Championship
	v Medati	9-5	Qualifying	Embassy World Championship
	v Charlton	5-10	1st round	Embassy World Championship
	v Johnson	5-4	Qualifying	Jameson International
	v Mountjoy	5-4	1st round	Jameson International
	v White	5-2	2nd round	Jameson International
	v Knowles	4-5	Quarter-final	Jameson International
	v Morra	5-2	1st round	Professional Players Tournament
	v Knowles	5-4	2nd round	Professional Players Tournament
	v Reynolds	1-5	3rd round	Professional Players Tournament
	v E. McLaughlin	9-6	Qualifying	Coral UK Championship
	v Thorne	9-7	1st round	Coral UK Championship
	v White	5-9	2nd round	Coral UK Championship
1983	v Thorburn	3-5	1st round	Lada Classic
	v Roscoe	6-4	Quarter-final	Woodpecker Welsh Championship
	v Mountjoy	3-9	Semi-final	Woodpecker Welsh Championship
	v Everton	10-1	Qualifying	Embassy World Championship
	v Johnson	10-8	Qualifying	Embassy World Championship
	v Mountjoy	2-10	1st round	Embassy World Championship
	v Donnelly	1-5	Qualifying	Jameson International

	v Bennett	5-1	1st round	Professional Players Tournament
	v Virgo	5-2	2nd round	Professional Players Tournament
	v Thorburn	3-5	3rd round	Professional Players Tournament
	v Williams	9-4	1st round	Coral UK Championship
	v Reardon	4-9	2nd round	Coral UK Championship
1984	v Charlton	0-5	Qualifying	Lada Classic
	v Roscoe	6-2	1st round	Strongbow Welsh Championship
	v Reardon	9-4	Semi-final	Strongbow Welsh Championship
	v Mountjoy	3-9	Final	Strongbow Welsh Championship
	v Mifsud	8-10	Qualifying	Embassy World Championship
	v Dodd	1-5	Qualifying	Jameson International
	v Donnelly	5-2	1st round	Rothmans Grand Prix
	v Reardon	4-5	2nd round	Rothmans Grand Prix
	v Dodd	9-8	Qualifying	Coral UK Open
	v Griffiths	9-6	1st round	Coral UK Open
	v Thorburn	3-9	2nd round	Coral UK Open
1985	v Fowler	5-4	Qualifying	Mercantile Credit Classic
	v Mountjoy	5-4	1st round	Mercantile Credit Classic
	v Johnson	0-5	2nd round	Mercantile Credit Classic
	v Longworth	3-6	1st round	Dulux British Open
	v Fagan	9-10	Qualifying	Embassy World Championship
	v Roscoe	6-3	Quarter-final	BCE Welsh Championship
	v Mountjoy	2-9	Semi-final	BCE Welsh Championship
	v Roscoe	5-1	3rd round	Goya Matchroom Trophy
	v Chappel	5-0	4th round	Goya Matchroom Trophy
	v Johnson	1-5	5th round	Goya Matchroom Trophy
	v Bales	5-1	3rd round	Rothmans Grand Prix
	v Scott	5-3	4th round	Rothmans Grand Prix
	v Drago	5-2	5th round	Rothmans Grand Prix
	v Dennis Taylor	2-5	Quarter-final	Rothmans Grand Prix
	v Cripsey	7-9	3rd round	Coral UK Open
1986	v Browne	3-5	3rd round	Mercantile Credit Classic
	v Newbury	6-4	Quarter-final	Zetters Welsh Championship
	v Griffiths	1-9	Semi-final	Zetters Welsh Championship
	v Chaperon	5-3	3rd round	Dulux British Open
	v Stevens	0-5	4th round	Dulux British Open
	v Charlton	6-10	1st round	Embassy World Championship
	v J. McLaughlin	5-2	3rd round	BCE International
	v Bales	5-1	4th round	BCE International
	v Knowles	5-4	5th round	BCE International
	v Thorburn	1-5	Quarter-final	BCE International
	v Anderson	5-4	3rd round	Rothmans Grand Prix
	v N. Foulds	0-5	4th round	Rothmans Grand Prix
	v Spencer	5-9	3rd round	Tennents UK Open
1987	v Williamson	5-4	3rd round	Mercantile Credit Classic
	v Dodd	5-4	4th round	Mercantile Credit Classic
	v W. Jones	5-3	5th round	Mercantile Credit Classic
	v Reynolds	1-5	Quarter-final	Mercantile Credit Classic
	v Newbury	2-6	Quarter-final	Matchroom Welsh Championship
	v G. Foulds	5-3	3rd round	Dulux British Open
	v S. Francisco	5-4	4th round	Dulux British Open
	v Virgo	2-5	5th round	Dulux British Open
	v Wright	4-10	Qualifying	Embassy World Championship
	v Sinclair	5-1	3rd round	Fidelity International
	v D. Gilbert	1-5	4th round	Fidelity International
	v Glen Wilkinson	5-4	3rd round	Rothmans Grand Prix
	v Virgo	5-3	4th round	Rothmans Grand Prix
	v Dennis Taylor	2-5	5th round	Rothmans Grand Prix
	v W. Jones	9-6	3rd round	Tennents UK Open
	v S. Francisco	1-9	4th round	Tennents UK Open
1988	v D. Gilbert	5-3	3rd round	Mercantile Credit Classic
	v Griffiths	2-5	4th round	Mercantile Credit Classic
	v Newbury	6-3	Quarter-final	Welsh Championship

v Griffiths	7-9	Semi-final	Welsh Championship
v Roscoe	5-2	3rd round	MIM Britannia British Open
v Thorne	3-5	4th round	MIM Britannia British Open
v Oliver	10-6	Qualifying	Embassy World Championship
v Johnson	7-10	1st round	Embassy World Championship

JON WRIGHT (England)

Born 10.8.62. **Turned professional** 1986. **World ranking** 61 (54). **Best professional performances** Last 32 1987 Embassy World Championship, 1987 Mercantile Credit Classic.

1986	v Watterson	5-1	1st round	BCE International
	v Black	1-5	2nd round	BCE International
	v Fisher	5-1	1st round	Rothmans Grand Prix
	v Bradley	5-0	2nd round	Rothmans Grand Prix
	v Dennis Taylor	3-5	3rd round	Rothmans Grand Prix
	v Smith	9-7	1st round	Tennents UK Open
	v Fagan	9-0	2nd round	Tennents UK Open
	v Johnson	1-9	3rd round	Tennents UK Open
1987	v D. Hughes	5-2	1st round	Mercantile Credit Classic
	v Chappel	5-4	2nd round	Mercantile Credit Classic
	v E. Hughes	5-4	3rd round	Mercantile Credit Classic
	v Hendry	1-5	4th round	Mercantile Credit Classic
	v Chalmers	6-5	1st round	Tolly Ales English Championship
	v Spencer	1-6	2nd round	Tolly Ales English Championship
	v Sheehan	2-5	1st round	Dulux British Open
	v Houlihan	10-4	Qualifying	Embassy World Championship
	v Browne	10-6	Qualifying	Embassy World Championship
	v Wildman	10-0	Qualifying	Embassy World Championship
	v Wilson	10-4	Qualifying	Embassy World Championship
	v Higgins	6-10	1st round	Embassy World Championship
	v Kelly	5-2	2nd round	Fidelity International
	v Meo	2-5	3rd round	Fidelity International
	v Rigitano	5-0	2nd round	Rothmans Grand Prix
	v White	4-5	3rd round	Rothmans Grand Prix
	v Lawlor	7-9	2nd round	Tennents UK Open
1988	v Sinclair	5-3	2nd round	Mercantile Credit Classic
	v Knowles	1-5	3rd round	Mercantile Credit Classic
	v Fisher	6-2	2nd round	English Championship
	v Knowles	2-6	3rd round	English Championship
	v D. Gilbert	2-5	2nd round	MIM Britannia British Open
	v Chambers	10-2	Qualifying	Embassy World Championship
	v Owers	10-8	Qualifying	Embassy World Championship
	v Hendry	4-10	Qualifying	Embassy World Championship

JIM WYCH (Canada)

Born 11.1.55. **Turned professional** 1979. **World ranking** 38 (36). **Amateur career** 1979 Canadian champion. **Best professional performances** Quarter finals 1980 Embassy World Championship, 1986 Dulux British Open.

1980	v John Bear	9-5	Qualifying	Embassy World Championship
	v Williams	9-7	Qualifying	Embassy World Championship
	v Pulman	10-5	1st round	Embassy World Championship
	v Dennis Taylor	13-10	2nd round	Embassy World Championship
	v Thorburn	6-13	Quarter-final	Embassy World Championship
1981	v Knowles	3-9	Qualifying	Embassy World Championship
	v Johnson	2-5	1st round	Jameson International
1982	v Higgins	3-5	1st round	Benson & Hedges Irish Masters
	v John Bear	4-9	Qualifying	Embassy World Championship

	v Bennett	5-0	Qualifying	Jameson International
	v Werbeniuk	3-5	1st round	Jameson International
	v Kelly	5-0	1st round	Professional Players Tournament
	v White	0-5	2nd round	Professional Players Tournament
1983	v Jonik	5-9	Quarter-final	Canadian Championship
1984	v Ganim	10-1	Qualifying	Embassy World Championship
	v Scott	10-6	Qualifying	Embassy World Championship
	v Fagan	10-3	Qualifying	Embassy World Championship
	v Reardon	7-10	1st round	Embassy World Championship
1985	v Bradley	10-7	Qualifying	Embassy World Championship
	v Virgo	4-10	Qualifying	Embassy World Championship
	v Sanderson	5-2	1st round	Canadian Championship
	v John Bear	6-3	Quarter-final	Canadian Championship
	v Thorburn	5-6	Semi-final	Canadian Championship
	v Rempe	5-1	2nd round	Goya Matchroom Trophy
	v Mountjoy	1-5	3rd round	Goya Matchroom Trophy
	v V. Harris	3-5	2nd round	Rothmans Grand Prix
	v Duggan	9-5	2nd round	Coral UK Open
	v S. Francisco	8-9	3rd round	Coral UK Open
1986	v Demarco	5-0	2nd round	Mercantile Credit Classic
	v E. Hughes	2-5	3rd round	Mercantile Credit Classic
	v Van Rensberg	5-0	2nd round	Dulux British Open
	v Reynolds	5-3	3rd round	Dulux British Open
	v Knowles	5-4	4th round	Dulux British Open
	v Parrott	5-4	5th round	Dulux British Open
	v S. Davis	2-5	Quarter-final	Dulux British Open
	v Chappel	10-6	Qualifying	Embassy World Championship
	v Duggan	10-5	Qualifying	Embassy World Championship
	v Hallett	7-10	Qualifying	Embassy World Championship
	v Mikkelsen	6-3	2nd round	Canadian Championship
	v Stevens	6-2	Semi-final	Canadian Championship
	v Thorburn	2-6	Final	Canadian Championship
	v Bradley	5-2	3rd round	BCE International
	v Thorburn	3-5	4th round	BCE International
	v John Rea	5-2	3rd round	Rothmans Grand Prix
	v Mountjoy	1-5	4th round	Rothmans Grand Prix
	v B. Harris	9-6	3rd round	Tennents UK Open
	v N. Foulds	3-9	4th round	Tennents UK Open
1987	v B. Harris	3-5	3rd round	Mercantile Credit Classic
	v Murphy	1-5	3rd round	Dulux British Open
	v Bradley	10-7	Qualifying	Embassy World Championship
	v Griffiths	4-10	1st round	Embassy World Championship
	v Bear	4-6	Quarter-final	Canadian Championship
	v Jenkins	5-4	2nd round	Fidelity International
	v Johnson	5-4	3rd round	Fidelity International
	v E. Hughes	4-5	4th round	Fidelity International
	v Marshall	5-2	2nd round	Rothmans Grand Prix
	v Macleod	5-4	3rd round	Rothmans Grand Prix
	v S. Davis	1-5	4th round	Rothmans Grand Prix
	v Fisher	9-6	2nd round	Tennents UK Open
	v Hendry	9-7	3rd round	Tennents UK Open
	v Parrott	6-9	4th round	Tennents UK Open
1988	v Clark	2-5	2nd round	Mercantile Credit Classic
	v Thornley	5-1	2nd round	MIM Britannia British Open
	v Thorne	1-5	3rd round	MIM Britannia British Open
	v J. Smith	10-3	Qualifying	Embassy World Championship
	v M. Bennett	5-10	Qualifying	Embassy World Championship

At the end of the 1987–88 season, the following players became non-tournament playing members of the WPBSA: Clive Everton (Wales), Derek Mienie (South Africa), John Hargreaves (England), Derek

Heaton (England), Paul Thornley (Canada), David Greaves (England), Joe Caggianello (Canada), Eddie McLaughlin (Scotland) and Gerry Watson (Canada).

Other non-tournament playing members are: Mike Hines (South Africa), Maurice Parkin (England), Bert Demarco (Scotland), Bernard Bennett (England), Steve Mizerak (USA), Paddy Morgan (Australia), James Giannaros (Australia), Lou Condo (Australia), Mannie Francisco (South Africa) and Wayne Saunderson (Canada).

George Ganim resigned during the 1987-88 season, and Perrie Mans resigned at the end of the 1986-87 season.

The nine players who qualified for professional status for the 1988-89 season were: Darren Morgan (Wales), Mark Rowing (England), Mark Johnston-Allen (England), Ian Graham (England), Mick Price (England), Craig Edwards (England), Steve Campbell (England), Tony Wilson (England) and Nick Terry (England). Alain Robidoux (Canada), by virtue of acquiring one merit point through receiving two walkovers at the World Championship, qualified for full tournament status.

SNOOKER GREATS

JOE DAVIES O.B.E. (1901–1978)

Although only one of the 'Big Four' at billiards, Joe Davis was undoubtedly the number one at snooker. With his friend Bill Camkin, a Birmingham billiard trader, he promoted and won the first World Professional Snooker Championship in 1927. He went on to win the title every year until 1940. The Championship was suspended until 1946, at which point Davis beat Horace Lindrum 78–67 to take the title for the 15th time,

Davis then retired from Championship play. He continued to play in other tournaments and in the public's mind he was still the champion, whoever had won the World Championship in his absence.

His expertise at the three-ball game carried him to four World Professional Billiards titles but his name will always be synonymous with snooker. It was he who developed the modern break-making methods, using the black as the key colour, and it was he who brought the sport to the public's attention.

WALTER DONALDSON (1907–1973)

Consistent and steady, Walter Donaldson reached eight consecutive World Championship finals between 1948 and 1954. In 1947 and 1950 he beat Fred Davis to take the title.

As professional snooker's appeal dwindled in the mid-1950s, a disillusioned Donaldson turned his billiard room into a cowshed and broke up the slates of his table for crazy paving.

JOHN PULMAN (born 1926)

After winning the English Amateur Championship in 1946, John Pulman turned professional but was at his peak when the professional game was going through a period in the doldrums. He was never able to capitalise fully on his natural talent.

He won the world title in 1957 and then successfully withstood a series of challengers. When the influx of new professionals led to the Championship being restored to a tournament format, he once reached the final, losing to Ray Reardon.

An accident led to his retirement from playing in 1982 but he is still involved on the circuit as a member of ITV's commentary team.

THE CIRCUIT

WINFIELD AUSTRALIAN MASTERS

Having existed for four years as the Australian version of Pot Black, the Winfield Australian Masters was expanded in 1983 to an authentic tournament format although the final stages were still played in a television studio. In 1986, however, the event reverted to its original format and consequently those results are not listed.

1983
First round: C. Thorburn beat W. King 3-1; J. White beat I. Anderson 3-2; K. Stevens beat D. Mountjoy 3-1; E. Charlton beat P. Morgan 3-2; A. Higgins beat J. Spencer 3-2; B. Werbeniuk beat Dennis Taylor 3-2; T. Meo beat David Taylor 3-0; A. Knowles beat J. Campbell 3-1
Quarter-finals: Thorburn beat White 4-2; Stevens beat Charlton 4-1; Werbeniuk beat Higgins 4-0; Knowles beat Meo 4-3
Semi-finals: Thorburn beat Stevens 5-2; Werbeniuk beat Knowles 5-0
Final: Thorburn beat Werbeniuk 7-3

1984
First round: W. Thorne beat C. Thorburn 4-1; J. Virgo beat D. Mountjoy 4-1; T. Meo beat B. Werbeniuk 4-0; K. Stevens beat P. Morgan 4-2; E. Charlton beat W. King 4-1; David Taylor beat I. Anderson 4-2; J. White beat J. Campbell 4-0; A. Knowles beat Dennis Taylor 4-2
Quarter-finals: Virgo beat Thorne 5-3; Charlton beat David Taylor 5-4; Meo beat Stevens 5-1; Knowles beat White 5-3
Semi-finals: Virgo beat Meo 6-2; Knowles beat Charlton 6-0
Final: Knowles beat Virgo 7-3

1985
First round: E. Charlton beat I. Anderson 4-2; J. Campbell beat A. Higgins 4-1; W. Thorne beat P. Morgan 4-2; J. Parrott beat S. Francisco 4-3; J. Johnson beat B. Werbeniuk 4-1; J. White beat David Taylor 4-0; T. Meo beat W. King 4-1; J. Virgo beat A. Knowles 4-1
Quarter-finals: Campbell beat Charlton 5-4; Parrott beat Thorne 5-0; White beat Johnson 5-4; Meo beat Virgo 5-3
Semi-finals: Campbell beat Parrott 6-4; Meo beat White 6-3
Final: Meo beat Campbell 7-2

CAMUS HONG KONG MASTERS

First staged 1984*. **Sponsors** Camus. **Venue** Queen Elizabeth Stadium. **Prize-money last season** £86,800. **TV** Hong Kong.
The first two events, in 1984 and 1985, were small, pathfinding events which do not meet the conditions required for full inclusion in this book.

1986
Semi-finals: Dennis Taylor beat T. Griffiths 5-4; W. Thorne beat S. Davis 5-2
Final: Thorne beat Dennis Taylor 8-3

1987
See World Series

CARLING CHAMPIONS

First staged 1984. **Sponsors** Carlsberg (1984–86), Carling (1987–). **Venue** RTE Studios. **Initial prize-money** £20,000. **Prize-money last season** £34,000. **TV** RTE.

1984
First round: A. Knowles beat A. Higgins 5-3; J. White beat K. Stevens 5-0
Final: White beat Knowles 9-7

1985
First round: J. White beat J. Parrott 5-3; A. Higgins beat C. Thorburn 5-4
Final: White beat Higgins 8-3

1986
First round: J. White beat A. Higgins 5-1; Dennis Taylor beat J. Johnson 5-3
Final: Dennis Taylor beat White 8-3

1987
First round: J. Johnson beat N. Foulds 5-4; Dennis Taylor beat S. Hendry 5-3
Final: Taylor beat Johnson 8-5

LANGS SCOTTISH MASTERS

First staged 1981. **Sponsors** Langs. **Venue** Kelvin Hall, Glasgow (1981), Holiday Inn, Glasgow (1982), Skean Dhu Hotel (re-named Hospitality Inn), Glasgow (1983–). **Initial prize-money** £20,500. **Prize-money this season** £50,000. **TV** BBC Scotland.

1981
Preliminary round: V. Harris beat I. Black 4-0
First round: J. White beat R. Reardon 5-4; S. Davis beat D. Mountjoy 5-0; C. Thorburn beat K. Stevens 5-1; A. Higgins beat V. Harris 5-3
Semi-finals: White beat Davis 6-5; Thorburn beat Higgins 6-2
Final: White beat Thorburn 9-4

1982
First round: Dennis Taylor beat J. White 5-4; S. Davis beat A. Knowles 5-4; T. Griffiths beat R. Reardon 5-3; A. Higgins beat E. Sinclair 5-1
Semi-finals: S. Davis beat Dennis Taylor 6-1; Higgins beat Griffiths 6-5
Final: S. Davis beat Higgins 9-4

1983
First round: C. Thorburn beat T. Griffiths 5-1; S. Davis beat M. Macleod 5-1; A. Knowles beat T. Meo 5-4; A. Higgins beat J. White 5-3
Semi-finals: Knowles beat Thorburn 6-2; S. Davis beat Higgins 6-2
Final: S. Davis beat Knowles 9-6

1984
First round: A. Knowles beat T. Griffiths 5-3; J. White beat M. Macleod 5-0; S. Davis beat C. Thorburn 5-2; A. Higgins beat K. Stevens 5-2
Semi-finals: White beat Knowles 6-5; S. Davis beat Higgins 6-4
Final: S. Davis beat White 9-4

1985
First round: J. White beat A. Higgins 5-0; C. Thorburn beat M. Macleod 5-1;
S. Francisco beat A. Knowles 5-4; W. Thorne beat Dennis Taylor 5-2
Semi-finals: Thorne beat White 6-2; Thorburn beat Francisco 6-0
Final: Thorburn beat Thorne 9-7

1986
First round: C. Thorburn beat J. Parrott 5-1; J. White beat S. Hendry 5-1; K. Stevens
beat A. Knowles 5-3; A. Higgins beat J. Johnson 5-2
Semi-finals: Thorburn beat White 6-2; Higgins beat Stevens 6-2
Final: Thorburn beat Higgins 9-8

1987
First round: C. Thorburn beat Dennis Taylor 5-2; J. Johnson beat S. Hendry 5-2;
T. Griffiths beat N. Foulds 5-4; J. White beat A. Higgins 5-3
Semi-finals: Johnson beat Thorburn 6-3; Griffiths beat White 6-2
Final: Johnson beat Griffiths 9-7

FIDELITY INTERNATIONAL

First staged 1981. **Sponsors** Jameson (1981–84), Goya (1985), BCE (1986),
Fidelity (1987–). **Venue** Assembly Rooms, Derby (1981–82), Eldon Square
Recreation Centre, Newcastle upon Tyne (1983–84), Trentham Gardens, Stoke
(1985–). **Initial prize-money** £66,000. **Prize-money last season** £200,000. **TV**
ITV.

1981 (*Jameson*)
Qualifying groups
1   M. Gibson beat S. Hood 5-3; Gibson beat M. Parkin 5-3; J. Dunning beat Gibson
    5-3
2   C. Roscoe beat R. Andrewartha 5-2; D. Sheehan beat V. Harris 5-1; Roscoe beat
    Sheehan 5-1; J. Meadowcroft beat Roscoe 5-4
3   C. Everton beat K. Kennerley 5-4; M. Watterson beat P. Medati 5-3; Watterson beat
    Everton 5-4; P. Fagan beat Watterson 5-2
4   P. Houlihan wo J. Barrie scr; D. French beat G. Foulds 5-2; French beat Houlihan
    5-3; R. Williams beat French 5-0
5   B. Demarco wo B. Mikkelsen scr; D. Hughes beat Jack Rea 5-4; Demarco beat
    Hughes 5-1; M. Hallett beat Demarco 5-4
6   E. Hughes beat M. Owen 5-1; J. Fitzmaurice beat B. Bennett 5-1; E. Hughes beat
    Fitzmaurice 5-3; E. Hughes beat E. Sinclair 5-2
7   E. McLaughlin beat I. Black 5-3; M. Wildman beat M. Morra 5-3; E. McLaughlin
    beat Wildman 5-3; E. McLaughlin beat D. Greaves 5-1
8   M. Macleod beat B. Kelly 5-1; J. Johnson beat J. Donnelly 5-4; Johnson beat
    Macleod 5-1; Johnson wo J. Pulman scr
First round: J. Johnson beat J. Wych 5-2; D. Martin beat J. Dunning 5-2; R. Williams
beat J. White 5-1; A. Knowles beat M. Hallett 5-2; R. Edmonds beat E. Hughes 5-4;
J. Meadowcroft beat C. Wilson 5-4; T. Meo beat E. McLaughlin 5-2
Second round: G. Miles beat Johnson 5-3; Martin beat B. Werbeniuk 5-2; Williams beat
F. Davis 5-0; A. Higgins beat P. Fagan 5-3; J. Spencer beat Edmonds 5-3; J. Virgo beat
Knowles 5-2; K. Stevens beat Meadowcroft 5-1; P. Mans beat Meo 5-3
Third round: Miles beat C. Thorburn 5-0; Martin beat E. Charlton 5-2; Virgo beat
R. Reardon 5-3; David Taylor beat Stevens 5-0; Dennis Taylor beat Williams 5-1;
Higgins beat D. Mountjoy 5-1; T. Griffiths beat Spencer 5-2; S. Davis beat Mans 5-3
Quarter-finals: Martin beat Miles 5-1; Higgins beat Griffiths 5-2; Dennis Taylor beat
Virgo 5-2; S. Davis beat David Taylor 5-1
Semi-finals: Dennis Taylor beat Martin 9-1; S. Davis beat Higgins 9-8
Final: S. Davis beat Dennis Taylor 9-0

1982 (*Jameson*)
Qualifying groups
1   R. Edmonds beat D. Hughes 5-0; Edmonds beat G. Miles 5-1
2   V. Harris beat D. Sheehan 5-3; J. Virgo beat Harris 5-2
3   M. Fisher beat T. Murphy 5-1; Fisher beat F. Davis 5-3
4   B. Bennett beat M. Owen 5-2; J. Wych beat Bennett 5-0
5   M. Morra beat B. Demarco 5-2; D. Reynolds beat Morra 5-1
6   M. Watterson beat C. Everton 5-1; Watterson beat P. Fagan 5-1
7   E. Sinclair beat I. Anderson 5-2; Sinclair beat T. Meo 5-3
8   G. Scott beat B. Harris 5-4; Scott *wo* John Bear *scr*
9   J. Johnson *wo* J. Phillips *scr*; C. Wilson beat Johnson 5-4
10 E. Hughes beat M. Parkin 5-2; Hughes beat D. Martin 5-4
11 C. Ross *wo* D. Greaves *scr*; J. Meadowcroft beat Ross 5-0
12 I. Williamson beat J. Donnelly 5-3; B. Kelly beat G. Foulds 5-4; Kelly beat Williamson 5-1
13 C. Roscoe beat J. Dunning 5-2; D. French beat G. Cripsey 5-1; Roscoe beat French 5-2
14 M. Hallett beat F. Jonik 5-2; M. Wildman beat M. Gibson 5-1; Wildman beat Hallett 5-2
15 J. Fitzmaurice beat I. Black 5-3; L. Dodd beat M. Macleod 5-1; Dodd beat Fitzmaurice 5-3
16 R. Williams beat P. Medati 5-3; E. McLaughlin beat P. Houlihan 5-2; Williams beat McLaughlin 5-1
First round: A. Knowles beat Sinclair 5-2; Reynolds beat W. Thorne 5-3; S. Davis beat Roscoe 5-0; B. Werbeniuk beat Wych 5-3; David Taylor beat Fisher 5-1; K. Stevens beat Watterson 5-3; T. Griffiths beat Williams 5-2; J. Spencer beat Edmonds 5-2; Dennis Taylor beat Wildman 5-2; Virgo beat E. Charlton 5-4; P. Mans beat Dodd 5-3; J. White beat Meadowcroft 5-1; R. Reardon beat E. Hughes 5-3; C. Thorburn beat Scott 5-1; A. Higgins beat Kelly 5-3; Wilson beat D. Mountjoy 5-4
Second round: S. Davis beat Reynolds 5-0; David Taylor beat Werbeniuk 5-2; Stevens beat Mans 5-2; Griffiths beat Higgins 5-2; Dennis Taylor beat Thorburn 5-2; Wilson beat White 5-2; Virgo beat Spencer 5-4; Knowles beat Reardon 5-2
Quarter-finals: Virgo beat Dennis Taylor 5-3; David Taylor beat S. Davis 5-3; Knowles beat Wilson 5-4; Stevens beat Griffiths 5-3
Semi-finals: Knowles beat Stevens 9-3; David Taylor beat Virgo 9-5
Final: Knowles beat David Taylor 9-6

1983 (*Jameson*)
Qualifying groups
1   M. Watterson beat B. Demarco 5-3; Watterson beat P. Mans 5-4
2   T. Murphy beat D. Sheehan 5-2; W. Thorne beat Murphy 5-2
3   R. Williams beat D. French 5-1; D. Reynolds beat Williams 5-3
4   J. Donnelly beat B. Bennett 5-1; Donnelly beat C. Wilson 5-1
5   M. Darrington beat I. Williamson 5-3; S. Francisco beat Darrington 5-2
6   W. King beat I. Black 5-3; G. Miles beat King 5-3
7   D. Hughes beat M. Parkin 5-0; J. Johnson beat Hughes 5-1
8   B. Harris beat J. Dunning 5-3; M. Wildman beat Harris 5-2
9   D. Martin beat D. Greaves 5-1; Martin beat P. Fagan 5-0
10 R. Andrewartha beat C. Everton 5-1; E. Sinclair beat Andrewartha 5-4
11 P. Medati beat V. Harris 5-0; M. Macleod beat Medati 5-3
12 F. Davis beat B. Kelly 5-1; P. Morgan beat J. Fitzmaurice 5-4; Morgan beat Davis 5-3
13 M. Hallett beat C. Roscoe 5-2; M. Morra beat P. Watchorn 5-3; Morra beat Hallett 5-3

14 G. Foulds beat P. Burke 5-2; E. Hughes beat M. Fisher 5-4; Hughes beat Foulds 5-1
15 M. Gibson beat L. Dodd 5-1; G. Scott beat P. Houlihan 5-0; Scott beat Gibson 5-3
16 E. McLaughlin beat J. Campbell 5-2; R. Edmonds beat Jack Rea 5-1; Edmonds beat
    McLaughlin 5-1
First round: Dennis Taylor beat Reynolds 5-3; R. Reardon beat Macleod 5-2; Thorne
beat J. Virgo 5-2; Morra beat J. White 5-3; D. Mountjoy beat Wildman 5-4; Martin beat
A. Higgins 5-2; Watterson beat T. Meo 5-3; Scott beat B. Werbeniuk 5-3; T. Griffiths
beat Miles 5-2; S. Davis beat Hughes 5-1; Donnelly beat David Taylor 5-3; Francisco *wo*
K. Stevens *scr*; E. Charlton beat Johnson 5-2; Thorburn beat Sinclair 5-0; J. Spencer beat
Morgan 5-1; A. Knowles beat Edmonds 5-1
Second round: Griffiths beat Scott 5-0; Spencer beat Knowles 5-4; Thorburn beat Dennis
Taylor 5-3; Mountjoy beat Martin 5-0; Charlton beat Morra 5-3; Thorne beat Reardon
5-0; S. Francisco beat Donnelly 5-1; S. Davis beat Watterson 5-0
Quarter-finals: Griffiths beat Spencer 5-4; Thorburn beat Mountjoy 5-2; Charlton beat
Thorne 5-0; S. Davis beat S. Francisco 5-1
Semi-finals: Thorburn beat Griffiths 9-8; S. Davis beat Charlton 9-2
Final: S. Davis beat Thorburn 9-4

1984 (*Jameson*)
Qualifying groups
1   G. Foulds beat P. Francisco 5-4; I. Williamson beat V. Harris 5-0; Foulds beat
    Williamson 5-4; Foulds beat J. Donnelly 5-3; J. Campbell beat Foulds 5-3
2   W. Jones beat P. Watchorn 5-0; M. Gibson beat P. Medati 5-3; Jones beat Gibson
    5-2; Jones beat G. Scott 5-0; Jones beat M. Wildman 5-0
3   T. Jones beat D. French 5-1; S. Duggan beat Jones 5-2; E. Sinclair beat Duggan 5-0;
    Sinclair beat P. Mans 5-2
4   B. Bennett beat B. Demarco 5-1; Bennett *wo* P. Morgan *scr*; Bennett *wo* J. Wych *scr*;
    N. Foulds beat Bennett 5-0
5   R. Foldvari beat G. Rigitano 5-2; Foldvari beat R. Edmonds 5-1; L. Dodd beat
    Foldvari 5-3; Dodd beat C. Wilson 5-1
6   B. Mikkelsen beat T. Chappel 5-4; Mikkelsen beat C. Everton 5-0; C. Roscoe beat
    Mikkelsen 5-1; E. Hughes beat Roscoe 5-1
7   D. O'Kane beat M. Parkin 5-2; O'Kane beat E. McLaughlin 5-1; O'Kane beat
    J. Fitzmaurice 5-4; O'Kane beat M. Hallett 5-4
8   J. McLaughlin beat D. Greaves 5-3; F. Jonik beat McLaughlin 5-2; M. Gauvreau
    beat Jonik 5-1; Gauvreau beat J. Parrott 5-4
9   G. Cripsey beat P. Thornley 5-3; J. Dunning beat Cripsey 5-3; F. Davis beat
    Dunning 5-4; J. Virgo beat Davis 5-3
10 J. Hargreaves beat P. Houlihan 5-2; B. Kelly beat Hargreaves 5-2; Kelly beat
    W. King 5-4; S. Francisco beat Kelly 5-3
11 D. Fowler beat R. Chaperon 5-0; Fowler *wo* P. Mifsud *scr*; Fowler beat
    R. Andrewartha 5-0; Fowler beat D. Martin 5-0
12 M. Bradley beat M. Darrington 5-3; Bradley beat Jack Rea 5-2; M. Morra beat
    Bradley 5-3; J. Johnson beat Morra 5-0
13 D. Chalmers *wo* Condo *scr*; W. Oliver beat D. Hughes 5-4; Chalmers beat Oliver
    5-4; J. Meadowcroft beat Chalmers 5-1; R. Williams beat Meadowcroft 5-4
14 P. Browne beat John Rea 5-2; I. Black beat Browne 5-4; Black beat M. Watterson
    5-3; M. Macleod beat Black 5-3
15 S. Newbury beat S. Longworth 5-4; P. Burke beat A. Kearney 5-4; Newbury beat
    Burke 5-0; Newbury beat P. Fagan 5-0; Newbury beat G. Miles 5-1
16 R. Bales beat D. Sheehan 5-2; Bales beat T. Murphy 5-4; Bales beat M. Fisher 5-3;
    D. Reynolds beat Bales 5-4
First round: S. Davis beat Campbell 5-1; A. Higgins beat Sinclair 5-1; T. Griffiths beat
N. Foulds 5-3; R. Reardon beat Dodd 5-4; E. Hughes beat D. Mountjoy 5-1; W. Thorne
beat O'Kane 5-3; Gauvreau beat K. Stevens 5-1; Virgo beat C. Thorburn 5-0;

S. Francisco beat J. Spencer 5-2; Dennis Taylor beat Fowler 5-0; Johnson beat
E. Charlton 5-1; J. White beat Williams 5-3; T. Meo beat Macleod 5-1; Newbury beat
B. Werbeniuk 5-2; A. Knowles beat Reynolds 5-1; David Taylor beat W. Jones 5-4
Second round: S. Davis beat David Taylor 5-1; Higgins beat Griffiths 5-4; E. Hughes
beat Reardon 5-1; Thorne beat Gauvreau 5-3; S. Francisco beat Virgo 5-2; Dennis
Taylor beat Johnson 5-2; White beat Meo 5-1; Knowles beat Newbury 5-4
Quarter-finals: S. Davis beat Higgins 5-1; E. Hughes beat Thorne 5-2; S. Francisco *wo*
Dennis Taylor *scr*; Knowles beat White 5-4
Semi-finals: S. Davis beat E. Hughes 9-3; Knowles beat S. Francisco 9-6
Final: S. Davis beat Knowles 9-2

1985 (*Goya Matchroom*)
First round: M. Darrington beat D. Gilbert 5-2; O. Agrawal beat P. Watchorn 5-2;
M. Smith beat D. Sheehan 5-2; S. Simngam beat D. Greaves 5-2; G. Wilkinson beat
B. Demarco 5-2; J. Rempe beat P. Burke 5-3; S. Hendry beat B. West 5-4; Jim Bear beat
P. Houlihan 5-2; J. Caggianello beat J. Hargreaves 5-2; D. Mienie *wo* G. Watson *scr*;
J. O'Boye beat M. Parkin 5-3; R. Bales beat T. Drago 5-2; D. Hughes beat A. Kearney
5-1; G. Cripsey beat B. Bennett 5-3
Second round: B. Mikkelsen beat M. Fisher 5-3; M. Gibson beat P. Francisco 5-4;
P. Fagan beat Mienie 5-4; W. King beat Caggianello 5-0; R. Chaperon beat D. Chalmers
5-2; Bales beat R. Edmonds 5-0; G. Miles beat O'Boye 5-2; J. Fitzmaurice beat
M. Watterson 5-2; T. Chappel beat J. Meadowcraft 5-2; C. Roscoe beat G. Foulds 5-3;
E. McLaughlin beat Hendry 5-3; Jim Bear beat J. Donnelly 5-2; T. Jones beat W. Kelly
5-3; M. Bradley beat John Rea 5-1; L. Dodd beat Simngam 5-4; Williamson beat
J. McLaughlin 5-3; J. Dunning beat C. Everton 5-2; M. Morra beat B. Oliver 5-1;
D. Fowler beat Agrawal 5-2; J. Wych beat Rempe 5-1; E. Sinclair beat Darrington 5-0;
S. Longworth beat Wilkinson 5-0; Cripsey beat P. Medati 5-2; S. Newbury beat F. Jonik
5-4; S. Duggan beat F. Davis 5-1; I. Black beat G. Rigitano 5-4; R. Foldvari beat
V. Harris 5-4; G. Scott beat J. Van Rensberg 5-4; T. Murphy beat Jack Rea 5-1;
B. Harris beat P. Browne 5-3; W. Jones beat Smith 5-3; D. Hughes beat M. Gauvreau 5-4
Third round: S. Davis beat Bales 5-2; J. Virgo beat Miles 5-2; Chaperon beat S. Francisco
5-3; M. Macleod beat Fitzmaurice 5-1; Gibson beat E. Charlton 5-4; D. Reynolds beat
Mikkelsen 5-0; J. White beat Fagan 5-2; King beat R. Williams 5-3; Chappel beat
K. Stevens 5-3; C. Wilson beat Roscoe 5-1; J. Johnson beat Jim Bear 5-1; Bradley beat
M. Hallett 5-4; David Taylor beat T. Jones 5-4; B. Werbeniuk beat Williamson 5-2;
A. Knowles beat E. McLaughlin 5-1; N. Foulds beat Dodd 5-3; C. Thorburn beat
Longworth 5-3; D. Martin beat Sinclair 5-1; D. Mountjoy beat Wych 5-1; J. Campbell
beat Morra 5-2; W. Thorne beat Fowler 5-1; Scott beat M. Wildman 5-1; Duggan beat
R. Reardon 5-4; Black beat P. Mans 5-4; T. Griffiths beat Newbury 5-2; J. Spencer beat
Foldvari 5-4; T. Meo beat Dunning 5-0; J. Parrott beat W. Jones 5-3; A. Higgins beat
D. Hughes 5-1; Murphy beat E. Hughes 5-3; Dennis Taylor beat Cripsey 5-1; B. Harris
beat D. O'Kane 5-3
Fourth round: S. Davis beat Virgo 5-1; Macleod beat Chaperon 5-4; Reynolds beat
Gibson 5-0; White beat King 5-2; Wilson beat Chappel 5-0; Johnson beat Bradley 5-2;
David Taylor beat Werbeniuk 5-4; N. Foulds beat Knowles 5-3; Thorburn beat Martin
5-3; Campbell beat Mountjoy 5-1; Thorne beat Scott 5-1; Duggan beat Black 5-1;
Griffiths beat Spencer 5-1; Parrott beat Meo 5-4; Higgins beat Murphy 5-2; Dennis
Taylor beat B. Harris 5-3
Fifth round: S. Davis beat Macleod 5-1; White beat Reynolds 5-1; Johnson beat Wilson
5-1; N. Foulds beat David Taylor 5-4; Thorburn beat Campbell 5-0; Duggan beat Thorne
5-4; Parrott beat Griffiths 5-1; Dennis Taylor beat Higgins 5-1
Quarter-finals: White beat S. Davis 5-3; N. Foulds beat Johnson 5-2; Thorburn beat
Duggan 5-2; Dennis Taylor beat Parrott 5-1
Semi-finals: White beat N. Foulds 9-5; Thorburn beat Dennis Taylor 9-5
Final: Thorburn beat White 12-10

1986 (*BCE*)
First round: P. Burke beat J. Fitzmaurice 5-4; G. Wilkinson *wo* F. Jonik *scr*; A. Kearney
wo S. Simngam *scr*; B. Kelly beat T. Whitthread 5-1; J. McLaughlin beat B. Bennett 5-0;
J. Wright beat M. Watterson 5-1; B. Rowswell beat D. Sheehan 5-4; Jack Rea beat
M. Darrington 5-4; G. Jenkins beat C. Everton 5-3; J. Dunning beat B. Demarco 5-4;
M. Bennett beat M. Smith 5-4; P. Gibson beat J. Meadowcroft 5-2; I. Anderson *wo*
E. McLaughlin *scr*; G. Rigitano beat D. Greaves 5-3; J. Bear beat P. Watchorn 5-1;
P. Houlihan beat D. Chalmers 5-1; C. Roscoe beat M. Parkin 5-1; M. Morra beat F. Ellis
5-3; N. Gilbert beat O. Agrawal 5-0; K. Owers beat J. Hargreaves 5-3; B. Oliver beat
D. Mienie 5-4; D. Roe beat D. Hughes 5-2; G. Foulds *wo* L. Heywood *scr*; M. Hines beat
M. Fisher 5-2; J. Donnelly *wo* R. Grace *scr*; S. James beat D. Gilbert 5-2
Second round: Burke beat T. Jones 5-4; M. Bradley beat Wilkinson 5-4; P. Medati beat
Kearney 5-3; J. Van Rensberg beat Kelly 5-1; R. Bales beat F. Davis 5-4; J. McLaughlin
beat D. Fowler 5-2; J. Spencer beat I. Williamson 5-4; I. Black beat Wright 5-1;
E. Sinclair beat P. Fagan 5-0; M. Wildman beat Rowswell 5-2; W. Jones beat Jack Rea
5-1; M. Gauvreau beat Jenkins 5-1; S. Newbury beat Dunning 5-4; M. Bennett beat
P. Browne 5-1; R. Foldvari beat B. Harris 5-0; S. Hendry beat P. Gibson 5-2; John Rea
beat Anderson 5-1; W. King beat Rigitano 5-0; J. O'Boye beat B. Mikkelsen 5-4;
S. Duggan beat Bear 5-4; Houlihan beat G. Cripsey 5-1; T. Chappel beat Roscoe 5-3;
J. Drago beat Morra 5-3; R. Chaperon beat N. Gilbert 5-3; Owers beat G. Scott 5-1;
D. O'Kane beat Oliver 5-2; G. Miles beat Roe 5-1; G. Foulds beat V. Harris 5-4;
M. Gibson beat Hines 5-1; L. Dodd *wo* P. Mans *scr*; T. Murphy beat Donnelly 5-2;
R. Edmonds beat James 5-2
Third round: C. Thorburn beat Burke 5-0; J. Wych beat Bradley 5-2; T. Griffiths beat
Medati 5-3; B. West beat Van Rensberg 5-3; Bales beat K. Stevens 5-3; C. Wilson beat
J. McLaughlin 5-2; T. Knowles beat Spencer 5-0; E. Charlton beat Black 5-0; A. Higgins
beat Sinclair 5-3; P. Francisco beat Wildman 5-2; R. Reardon beat W. Jones 5-4;
Gauvreau beat M. Macleod 5-4; S. Francisco beat Newbury 5-4; J. Virgo beat
M. Bennett 5-1; Dennis Taylor beat Foldvari 5-1; Hendry beat J. Parrott 5-3; S. Davis
beat John Rea 5-1; King beat S. Longworth 5-0; R. Williams beat O'Boye 5-0; Duggan
beat J. Campbell 5-3; Houlihan beat T. Meo 5-4; E. Hughes beat Chappel 5-4; Drago
beat W. Thorne 5-2; Chaperon beat D. Martin 5-4; Owers beat J. White 5-2; O'Kane
beat M. Hallet 5-1; N. Foulds beat Miles 5-2; G. Foulds beat B. Werbeniuk 5-2;
D. Mountjoy beat M. Gibson 5-3; D. Reynolds beat Dodd 5-2; J. Johnson beat Murphy
5-4; David Taylor beat Edmonds 5-4
Fourth round: Thorburn beat Wych 5-3; Griffiths beat West 5-1; Wilson beat Bales 5-1;
Knowles beat Charlton 5-1; P. Francisco beat Higgins 5-4; Gauvreau beat Reardon 5-2;
S. Francisco beat Virgo 5-0; Dennis Taylor beat Hendry 5-3; S. Davis beat King 5-4;
Williams beat Duggan 5-4; E. Hughes beat Houlihan 5-1; Chaperon beat Drago 5-1;
Owers beat O'Kane 5-0; N. Foulds beat G. Foulds 5-0; Reynolds beat Mountjoy 5-2;
David Taylor beat Johnson 5-3
Fifth round: Thorburn beat Griffiths 5-4; Wilson beat Knowles 5-4; P. Francisco beat
Gauvreau 5-2; S. Francisco beat Dennis Taylor 5-0; S. Davis beat Williams 5-4; E.
Hughes beat Chaperon 5-0; N. Foulds beat Owers 5-1; Reynolds beat David Taylor 5-1
Quarter-finals: Thorburn beat Wilson 5-1; P. Francisco beat S. Francisco 5-3; E. Hughes
beat S. Davis 5-4; N. Foulds beat Reynolds 5-2
Semi-finals: Thorburn beat P. Francisco 9-7; N. Foulds beat E. Hughes 9-8
Final: N. Foulds beat Thorburn 12-9

1987
First round: P. Gibson beat Glen Wilkinson 5-3; Gary Wilkinson beat G. Rigitano 5-1;
E. Sinclair beat D. Heaton 5-3; D. Gilbert beat A. Harris 5-4; R. Foldvari beat
S. Meakin 5-3; P. Fagan *wo* E. McLaughlin *scr*; J. Smith *wo* F. Jonik *scr*; M. Clark beat
J. Bear 5-2; G. Jenkins beat T. Whitthread 5-1; J. Meadowcroft beat D. Greaves 5-1;
M. Smith beat J. Donnelly 5-3; I. Anderson beat M. Watterson 5-3; D. Roe beat F. Ellis
5-4; J. Chambers *wo* B. Mikkelsen *scr*; M. Fisher *wo* J. Rempe *scr*; D. Chalmers beat

J. Fitzmaurice 5-4; I. Williamson beat C. Everton 5-0; C. Roscoe beat E. Lawler 5-4; Jack Rea beat P. Burke 5-1; J. Dunning beat D. Sheehan 5-1; N. Gilbert beat I. Black 5-3; R. Rowswell beat D. Hughes 5-1; P. Watchorn beat B. Oliver 5-3; M. Morra beat J. Hargreaves 5-4; V. Harris beat R. Marshall 5-1; B. Kelly beat M. Darrington 5-4
Second round: P. Gibson beat T. Jones 5-4; Gary Wilkinson beat G. Scott 5-2; Sinclair beat R. Edmonds 5-4; D. Gilbert beat P. Houlihan 5-3; Foldvari beat A. Kearney 5-1; J. O'Boye beat Fagan 5-1; M. Bradley beat J. Smith 5-1; Clark beat S. Duggan 5-2; J. Wych beat Jenkins 5-4; K. Owers beat Meadowcroft 5-3; W. King beat M. Smith 5-3; G. Cripsey beat Anderson 5-4; Roe beat F. Davis 5-3; S. James beat B. Harris 5-0; R. Grace beat Chambers 5-4; S. Newbury beat Fisher 5-0; M. Bennett beat Chambers 5-4; Williamson beat M. Gauvreau 5-1; Roscoe beat P. Browne 5-2; Jack Rea beat G. Foulds 5-4; W. Jones beat Dunning 5-1; N. Gilbert beat J. McLaughlin 5-4; M. Wildman beat Miles 5-3; R. Reardon beat Rowswell 5-4; D. Fowler beat Watchorn 5-1; Morra beat L. Dodd 5-3; John Rea beat R. Bales 5-2; T. Murphy beat P. Medati 5-3; T. Chappel beat M. Gibson 5-2; R. Chaperon beat V. Harris 5-4; D. O'Kane beat J. Van Rensberg 5-3; J. Wright beat Kelly 5-2
Third round: N. Foulds beat P. Gibson 5-2; S. Hendry beat Gary Wilkinson 5-4; C. Wilson beat Sinclair 5-1; D. Gilbert beat D. Martin 5-2; Foldvari beat R. Williams 5-0; O'Boye beat K. Stevens 5-1; Dennis Taylor beat Bradley 5-0; Clark beat T. Drago 5-2; Wych beat J. Johnson 5-4; E. Hughes beat Owers 5-4; S. Francisco beat King 5-2; B. Werbeniuk beat Cripsey 5-1; Roe beat D. Mountjoy 5-4; James beat J. Campbell 5-4; C. Thorburn beat Grace 5-1; Newbury beat P. Francisco 5-2; J. White beat M. Bennett 5-3; S. Longworth beat Williamson 5-4; M. Hallett beat Roscoe 5-3; J. Spencer beat Jack Rea 5-0; W. Jones beat D. Reynolds 5-4; N. Gilbert beat M. Macleod 5-1; T. Griffiths beat Wildman 5-1; E. Charlton beat Reardon 5-4; A. Knowles beat Fowler 5-4; David Taylor beat Morra 5-3; W. Thorne beat John Rea 5-3; J. Virgo beat Murphy 5-1; J. Parrott beat Chappel 5-1; Chaperon beat B. West 5-4; S. Davis beat O'Kane 5-2; T. Meo beat Wright 5-2
Fourth round: Hendry beat N. Foulds 5-2; D. Gilbert beat Wilson 5-1; O'Boye beat Foldvari 5-4; Clark beat Dennis Taylor 5-0; E. Hughes beat Wych 5-4; S. Francisco beat Werbeniuk 5-3; James beat Roe 5-3; Thorburn beat Newbury 5-3; White beat Longworth 5-1; Hallett beat Spencer 5-2; N. Gilbert beat W. Jones 5-4; Charlton beat Griffiths 5-2; Knowles beat David Taylor 5-2; Virgo beat Thorne 5-4; Parrott beat Chaperon 5-1; S. Davis beat Meo 5-3
Fifth round: Hendry beat D. Gilbert 5-0; O'Boye beat Clark 5-2; E. Hughes beat S. Francisco 5-4; Thorburn beat James 5-0; Hallett beat White 5-4; Charlton beat N. Gilbert 5-0; Virgo beat Knowles 5-2; S. Davis beat Parrott 5-2
Quarter-finals: Hendry beat O'Boye 5-2; Thorburn beat E. Hughes 5-1; Hallett beat Charlton 5-4; S. Davis beat Virgo 5-2
Semi-finals: Thorburn beat Hendry 9-1; S. Davis beat Hallett 9-3
Final: S. Davis beat Thorburn 12-5

ROTHMANS GRAND PRIX

First staged 1982. **Sponsors** WPBSA (1982–83 when entitled Professional Players Tournament), Rothmans (1984–). **Venue** La Reserve, Sutton Coldfield & International Snooker Club, Aston, Birmingham (1982), Redwood Lodge Country Club (1983), Hexagon, Reading (1984–). **Initial prize-money** £32,000. **Prize-money last season** £300,000. **TV** BBC.

1982 (*Professional Players Tournament*)
First round: E. Sinclair beat F. Davis 5-2; J. Meadowcroft beat B. Bennett 5-4; M. Watterson beat J. Donnelly 5-4; T. Griffiths beat C. Roscoe 5-1; A. Higgins beat D. French 5-3; R. Reardon beat T. Murphy 5-0; B. Werbeniuk beat P. Morgan 5-3; C. Everton beat P. Fagan 5-2; C. Thorburn beat P. Medati 5-1; David Taylor beat

I. Anderson 5-1; Dennis Taylor beat R. Edmonds 5-4; J. Wych beat B. Kelly 5-0;
R. Williams beat C. Ross 5-0; P. Mans beat E. McLaughlin 5-2; W. Thorne beat
B. Demarco 5-3; M. Wildman beat J. Dunning 5-4; J. Johnson beat G. Miles 5-1;
E. Charlton beat D. Hughes 5-2; F. Jonik beat D. Mountjoy 5-3; K. Stevens beat
E. Hughes 5-2; T. Meo beat M. Owen 5-4; C. Wilson beat M. Morra 5-2; A. Knowles
beat P Houlihan 5-4; J. Virgo beat I. Black 5-2; M. Hallett beat V. Harris 5-3; D. Martin
beat M. Gibson 5-2; J. Fitzmaurice beat D. Sheehan 5-1; J. Spencer beat G. Foulds 5-1
Second round: Werbeniuk beat Jack Rea 5-2; Sinclair beat Meadowcroft 5-3; Thorburn
beat Everton 5-2; Griffiths beat Watterson 5-2; Reardon beat Higgins 5-2; Dennis
Taylor beat David Taylor 5-1; Wildman beat Mans 5-4; Charlton beat Williams 5-2;
M. Macleod beat Thorne 5-4; White beat Wych 5-0; Johnson beat Stevens 5-1; Meo beat
Jonik 5-0; Wilson beat Knowles 5-4; Virgo beat Hallett 5-2; Spencer beat Martin 5-3;
Reynolds beat Fitzmaurice 5-0
Third round: Werbeniuk beat Thorburn 5-2; Johnson beat Wildman 5-4; Reynolds beat
Wilson 5-1; Virgo beat Spencer 5-1; Charlton beat Meo 5-3; White beat Dennis Taylor
5-3; Griffiths beat Sinclair 5-3; Reardon beat Macleod 5-2
Quarter-finals: White beat Griffiths 5-2; Virgo beat Johnson 5-1; Reardon beat
Werbeniuk 5-3; Charlton beat Reynolds 5-1
Semi-finals: White beat Virgo 10-4; Reardon beat Charlton 10-7
Final: Reardon beat White 10-5

1983 (*Professional Players Tournament*)
Qualifying: G. Ganim Jr beat G. Cripsey 5-4; S. Duggan beat M. Darrington 5-4;
T. Jones beat W. Oliver 5-2; D. French beat N. Foulds 5-2; B. Bennett beat B. Demarco
5-4; P. Burke beat G. Foulds 5-4; V. Harris *wo* P. Mifsud *scr*; P. Medati beat D. Hughes
5-1; T. Murphy beat P. Browne 5-2; J. Parrott beat P. Watchorn 5-0; D. Sheehan beat
P. Houlihan 5-2; M. Morra beat J. Hargreaves 5-0; D. Greaves beat R. Andrewartha 5-2;
W. King beat B. Harris 5-3; P. Morgan beat M. Gibson 5-4
First round: R. Reardon beat Ganim 5-4; C. Thorburn beat V. Harris 5-1;
J. Meadowcroft beat C. Roscoe 5-4; Duggan beat J. Dunning 5-2; J. Virgo beat French
5-4; J. Spencer beat I. Black 5-2; W. Thorne beat C. Everton 5-1; C. Wilson beat Bennett
5-1; T. Griffiths beat L. Dodd 5-3; J. White beat I. Williamson 5-2; Parrott beat
P. Fagan 5-2; J. Johnson beat Burke 5-3; E. Hughes beat E. Sinclair 5-4; M. Fisher beat
F. Davis 5-4; B. Werbeniuk beat T. Jones 5-4; E. Charlton beat E. McLaughlin 5-0;
M. Watterson beat A. Higgins 5-2; K. Stevens beat R. Edmonds 5-1; D. Martin beat
J. Fitzmaurice 5-0; T. Murphy beat Macleod 5-0; J. Campbell beat D. Mountjoy 5-3;
David Taylor beat P. Morgan 5-3; G. Miles beat M. Gauvreau 5-3; M. Wildman beat
F. Jonik 5-4; G. Scott beat Dennis Taylor 5-4; T. Meo beat W. King 5-2; S. Francisco
beat M. Morra 5-3; D. Reynolds beat D. Greaves 5-1; R. Williams beat D. Sheehan 5-1;
M. Hallett beat B. Kelly 5-0; A. Knowles beat P. Medati 5-1; S. Davis beat J. Donnelly
5-1
Second round: Reardon beat Duggan 5-2; Thorburn beat Meadowcroft 5-1; Thorne beat
Spencer 5-1; Wilson beat Virgo 5-2; Griffiths beat Parrott 5-1; Johnson beat White 5-3;
E. Hughes beat Werbeniuk 5-0; Charlton beat Fisher 5-4; Stevens beat Murphy 5-1;
Martin beat Watterson 5-4; Wildman beat David Taylor 5-3; Campbell beat Miles 5-2;
Meo beat Reynolds 5-0; S. Francisco beat Scott 5-1; Knowles beat Williams 5-4; Hallett
beat S. Davis 5-2
Third round: Thorne beat Reardon 5-3; Thorburn beat Wilson 5-3; E. Hughes beat
Griffiths 5-2; Johnson beat Charlton 5-0; Stevens beat Wildman 5-0; Campbell beat
Martin 5-0; Knowles beat S. Francisco 5-0; Meo beat Hallett 5-3
Quarter-finals: Johnson beat Thorburn 5-1; Thorne beat E. Hughes 5-1; Meo beat
Stevens 5-3; Knowles beat Campbell 5-3
Semi-finals: Knowles beat Thorne 9-7; Johnson beat Meo 9-6
Final: Knowles beat Johnson 9-8

1984
Qualifying: I. Williamson beat P. Thornley 5-2; Donnelly beat J. Hargreaves 5-4;
B. Demarco *wo* P. Fagan *scr*; V. Harris beat F. Davis 5-1; J. Dunning beat D. Hughes
5-0; D. O'Kane beat B. Kelly 5-4; M. Gauvreau beat R. Foldvari 5-2; E. McLaughlin
beat S. Longworth 5-2; M. Morra beat G. Cripsey 5-3; S. Duggan beat P. Browne 5-2;
D. Sheehan *wo* L. Condo *scr*; Sheehan beat B. Mikkelsen 5-3; P. Burke beat
M. Darrington 5-3; D. Chalmers beat R. Andrewartha 5-2; W. King beat D. Greaves
5-0; P. Medati beat L. Dodd 5-4; R. Chaperon beat A. Kearney 5-1; Chaperon beat
M. Gibson 5-4; P. Francisco beat I. Black 5-4; G. Rigitano beat R. Edmonds 5-3;
M. Bradley beat F. Jonik 5-1; W. Jones beat M. Watterson 5-3; John Rea beat
J. Fitzmaurice 5-2; R. Bales *wo* J. Wych *scr*; S. Newbury beat M. Fisher 5-0; W. Oliver
beat B. Bennett 5-3; C. Everton beat P. Houlihan 5-3; J. McLaughlin beat
J. Meadowcroft 5-1; T. Chappel beat G. Scott 5-1; T. Murphy beat G. Foulds 5-1;
T. Jones beat E. Sinclair 5-4; C. Roscoe beat D. French 5-0; P. Watchorn *wo* P. Morgan
scr; D. Fowler *wo* P. Mifsud *scr*
First round: A. Knowles beat V. Harris 5-1; Dunning beat P. Mans 5-4; Williamson beat
B. Werbeniuk 5-2; J. Johnson beat Medati 5-1; W. Thorne beat Newbury 5-2;
M. Macleod beat King 5-4; N. Foulds beat Demarco 5-2; T. Jones beat T. Griffiths 5-3;
R. Reardon beat Roscoe 5-1; C. Wilson beat Donnelly 5-2; Dennis Taylor beat Watchorn
5-1; J. Virgo beat Bradley 5-0; A. Higgins beat Bales 5-1; M. Hallett beat Sheehan 5-1;
R. Williams beat Chalmers 5-0; K. Stevens beat Chappel 5-3; C. Thorburn beat Rigitano
5-4; J. Campbell beat W. Jones 5-4; T. Meo beat Burke 5-1; D. Martin beat Chaperon
5-4; D. Mountjoy beat E. McLaughlin 5-4; M. Wildman beat J. McLaughlin 5-3;
J. Parrott beat Gauvreau 5-3; E. Charlton beat Everton 5-1; J. White beat Oliver 5-1;
S. Francisco beat Duggan 5-3; P. Francisco beat J. Spencer 5-2; D. Reynolds beat Fowler
5-2; David Taylor beat O'Kane 5-1; John Rea beat E. Hughes 5-4; G. Miles beat
Murphy 5-3; S. Davis beat Morra 5-2
Second round: Knowles beat Dunning 5-1; Williamson beat Johnson 5-4; Thorne beat
Macleod 5-3; N. Foulds beat T. Jones 5-0; Reardon beat Wilson 5-4; Dennis Taylor beat
Virgo 5-3; Hallett beat Higgins 5-3; Stevens beat Williams 5-3; Thorburn beat Campbell
5-1; Meo beat Martin 5-4; Mountjoy beat Wildman 5-0; Charlton beat Parrott 5-1;
S. Francisco beat White 5-1; David Taylor beat John Rea 5-1; S. Davis beat Miles 5-0;
Reynolds beat P. Francisco 5-4
Third round: Knowles beat Williamson 5-2; N. Foulds beat Thorne 5-1; Dennis Taylor
beat Reardon 5-3; Stevens beat Hallett 5-3; Thorburn beat Meo 5-4; Mountjoy beat
Charlton 5-4; Reynolds beat S. Francisco 5-1; S. Davis beat David Taylor 5-1
Quarter-finals: N. Foulds beat Knowles 5-2; Dennis Taylor beat Stevens 5-2; Thorburn
beat Mountjoy 5-3; S. Davis beat Reynolds 5-0
Semi-finals: Dennis Taylor beat N. Foulds 9-3; Thorburn beat S. Davis 9-7
Final: Dennis Taylor beat Thorburn 10-2

1985
First round: B. West beat B. Demarco 5-2; P. Houlihan *wo* G. Robinson *scr*; S. Simngam
beat D. Mienie 5-3; T. Drago beat P. Watchorn 5-2; R. Bales beat M. Smith 5-1;
G. Watson beat D. Sheehan 5-1; J. Hargreaves beat G. Cripsey 5-1; A. Kearney beat Jim
Bear 5-3; D. Gilbert beat G. Wilkinson 5-4; J. O'Boye beat S. Hendry 5-4; D. Hughes
beat B. Bennett 5-4; M. Darrington beat D. Greaves 5-2; O. Agrawal beat J. Rempe 5-2
Second round: West beat J. Meadowcroft 5-2; M. Watterson beat J. Caggianello 5-1;
T. Jones beat Houlihan 5-4; Simngam beat F. Davis 5-3; G. Foulds beat Black 5-3;
Drago beat W. King 5-4; G. Scott beat D. Chalmers 5-2; Bales beat M. Fisher 5-3;
Watson beat C. Roscoe 5-2; G. Miles beat Rigitano 5-4; S. Newbury beat P. Burke 5-3;
S. Longworth beat Hargreaves 5-2; T. Chappel beat L. Dodd 5-2; J. Van Rensberg beat
E. McLaughlin 5-4; M. Gibson beat M. Bradley 5-4; R. Edmonds beat Kearney 5-2;
B. Oliver beat P. Fagan 5-4; S. Duggan beat M. Gauvreau 5-4; Gilbert beat I. Williams
5-4; B. Mikkelsen beat T. Murphy 5-4; W. Jones beat John Rea 5-0; P. Francisco beat
C. Everton 5-0; J. McLaughlin beat P. Medati 5-2; B. Harris beat P. Browne 5-3;

J. Fitzmaurice beat E. Sinclair 5-3; O'Boye beat R. Chaperon 5-3; B. Kelly beat
J. Donnelly 5-4; M. Morra beat D. Hughes 5-2; V. Harris beat J. Wych 5-3; Darrington
beat R. Foldvari 5-3; Agrawal *wo* J. Dunning *scr*; D. Fowler beat F. Jonik 5-4
Third round: Dennis Taylor beat West 5-1; R. Williams beat Watterson 5-2; T. Meo beat
T. Jones 5-2; E. Hughes beat Simngam 5-1; E. Charlton beat G. Foulds 5-1; Drago beat
M. Macleod 5-3; Scott beat R. Reardon 5-4; C. Wilson beat Bales 5-1; K. Stevens beat
Watson 5-0; Miles beat D. Reynolds 5-3; David Taylor beat Newbury 5-2; Longworth
beat J. Parrott 5-2; D. Mountjoy beat Chappel 5-1; J. Campbell beat Van Rensberg 5-4;
A. Knowles beat Gibson 5-1; Edmonds beat D. O'Kane 5-2; C. Thorburn beat Oliver
5-0; M. Wildman beat Duggan 5-4; J. Johnson beat Gilbert 5-2; M. Hallett beat
Mikkelsen 5-3; W. Jones beat W. Thorne 5-0; P. Francisco beat J. Virgo 5-4; T. Griffiths
beat J. McLaughlin 5-4; B. Harris beat J. Spencer 5-2; J. White beat Fitzmaurice 5-0;
O'Boye beat P. Mans 5-3; S. Francisco beat Kelly 5-2; D. Martin beat Morra 5-2;
A. Higgins beat V. Harris 5-1; N. Foulds beat Darrington 5-0; S. Davis beat Agrawal
5-0; Fowler beat B. Werbeniuk 5-1
Fourth round: Dennis Taylor beat Williams 5-2; Meo beat E. Hughes 5-3; Drago beat
Charlton 5-3; Wilson beat Scott 5-3; Stevens beat Miles 5-2; Longworth beat David
Taylor 5-1; Campbell beat Mountjoy 5-2; Knowles beat Edmonds 5-3; Thorburn beat
Wildman 5-2; Johnson beat Hallett 5-4; P. Francisco beat W. Jones 5-3; Griffiths beat
B. Harris 5-3; White beat O'Boye 5-4; S. Francisco beat Martin 5-3; Higgins beat
N. Foulds 5-3; S. Davis beat Fowler 5-1
Fifth round: Dennis Taylor beat Meo 5-3; Wilson beat Drago 5-2; Stevens beat
Longworth 5-3; Knowles beat Campbell 5-4; Thorburn beat Johnson 5-1; Griffiths beat
P. Francisco 5-2; S. Francisco beat White 5-4; S. Davis beat Higgins 5-0
Quarter-finals: Dennis Taylor beat Wilson 5-2; Knowles beat Stevens 5-4; Thorburn beat
Griffiths 5-1; S. Davis beat S. Francisco 5-2
Semi-finals: Dennis Taylor beat Knowles 9-6; S. Davis beat Thorburn 9-5
Final: S. Davis beat Dennis Taylor 10-9

1986
First round: D. Mienie beat J. Fitzmaurice 5-2; Watchorn beat M. Darrington 5-2;
M. Morra beat S. James 5-3; G. Foulds beat G. Wilkinson 5-3; J. Bear beat B. Bennett
5-2; F. Ellis *wo* E. McLaughlin *scr*; J. Meadowcroft beat D. Greaves 5-2; T. Whitthread
wo S. Simngam *scr*; J. Donnelly beat N. Gilbert 5-1; F. Jonik *wo* L. Heywood *scr*;
I. Anderson beat B. Oliver 5-4; A. Kearney beat G. Jenkins 5-3; P. Gibson beat
J. Dunning 5-1; J. Wright beat M. Fisher 5-1; R. Grace beat P. Houlihan 5-1; D. Gilbert
beat B. Rowswell 5-1; P. Burke beat C. Roscoe 5-3; Jack Rea beat D. Hughes 5-2;
D. Roe beat J. Hargreaves 5-1; G. Rigitano beat C. Everton 5-1; M. Smith beat M. Hines
5-2; J. McLaughlin beat K. Owers 5-2; B. Kelly beat M. Parkin 5-2; D. Chalmers beat
O. Agrawal 5-1; D. Sheehan beat B. Demarco 5-1; M. Bennett beat M. Watterson 5-1
Second round: M. Gibson beat Mienie 5-4; T. Drago beat Watchorn 5-3; Morra beat
I. Black 5-4; G. Foulds beat B. Mikkelsen 5-1; Bear beat D. Fowler 5-2; M. Wildman
beat Ellis 5-1; F. Davis beat R. Bales 5-4; Meadowcroft *wo* P. Mans *scr*; S. Duggan beat
Whitthread 5-1; W. King beat Donnelly 5-2; G. Miles beat Jonik 5-1; Anderson beat
T. Murphy 5-4; T. Chappel beat Kearney 5-1; G. Cripsey beat P. Gibson 5-3; Wright
beat M. Bradley 5-0; P. Fagan beat Grace 5-3; J. O'Boye beat R. Edmonds 5-2;
S. Newbury beat D. Gilbert 5-1; J. Spencer beat Burke 5-3; W. Jones beat R. Foldvari
5-3; B. Harris beat Jack Rea 5-0; John Rea beat E. Sinclair 5-4; Roe beat J. Van
Rensberg 5-3; P. Medati beat Rigitano 5-1; T. Jones beat Smith 5-0; J. McLaughlin beat
M. Gauvreau 5-3; L. Dodd beat G. Scott 5-2; V. Harris beat Kelly 5-3; R. Chaperon beat
Chalmers 5-2; S. Hendry beat I. Williamson 5-1; P. Browne beat Sheehan 5-4;
M. Bennett beat D. O'Kane 5-2
Third round: S. Davis beat M. Gibson 5-1; Drago beat E. Charlton 5-4; T. Griffiths beat
Morra 5-3; J. Campbell beat G. Foulds 5-0; R. Williams beat Bear 5-2; Wildman beat
S. Longworth 5-2; A. Higgins beat F. Davis 5-0; D. Martin *wo* Meadowcroft *scr*;
W. Thorne beat Duggan 5-0; King beat B. Werbeniuk 5-2; N. Foulds beat Miles 5-1;

C. Wilson beat Anderson 5-4; T. Meo beat Chappel 5-1; J. Parrott beat Cripsey 5-4; Dennis Taylor beat Wright 5-3; J. Virgo beat Fagan 5-2; O'Boye beat C. Thorburn 5-4; Newbury beat D. Reynolds 5-0; S. Francisco beat Spencer 5-4; W. Jones beat David Taylor 5-1; D. Mountjoy beat B. Harris 5-2; J. Wych beat John Rea 5-2; A. Knowles beat Roe 5-3; P. Francisco beat Medati 5-1; J. White beat T. Jones 5-0; J. McLaughlin beat B. West 5-1; Dodd beat K. Stevens 5-4; M. Hallett beat V. Harris 5-2; Chaperon beat R. Reardon 5-3; Hendry beat E. Hughes 5-1; Browne beat J. Johnson 5-2; M. Bennett beat M. Macleod 5-1

Fourth round: S. Davis beat Drago 5-1; Griffiths beat Campbell 5-1; Williams beat Wildman 5-1; Higgins beat Martin 5-2; Thorne beat King 5-2; N. Foulds beat Wilson 5-0; Meo beat Parrott 5-3; Dennis Taylor beat Virgo 5-3; Newbury beat O'Boye 5-2; S. Francisco beat W. Jones 5-4; Mountjoy beat Wych 5-1; Knowles beat P. Francisco 5-3; White beat J. McLaughlin 5-2; Hallett beat Dodd 5-2; Hendry beat Chaperon 5-2; Browne beat M. Bennett 5-0

Fifth round: S. Davis beat Griffiths 5-2; Williams beat Higgins 5-1; N. Foulds beat Thorne 5-3; Meo beat Dennis Taylor 5-2; S. Francisco beat Newbury 5-2; Knowles beat Mountjoy 5-1; White beat Hallett 5-3; Hendry beat Browne 5-3

Quarter-finals: Williams beat S. Davis 5-1; N. Foulds beat Meo 5-3; S. Francisco beat Knowles 5-2; White beat Hendry 5-4

Semi-finals: Williams beat N. Foulds 9-8; White beat S. Francisco 9-6

Final: White beat Williams 10-6

1987

First round: G. Rigitano beat Jack Rea 5-4; J. Meadowcroft beat A. Harris 5-3; J. Bear beat D. Greaves 5-0; I. Anderson beat G. Jenkins 5-2; P. Gibson beat P. Fagan 5-0; P. Burke beat C. Everton 5-1; R. Foldvari beat J. Dunning 5-0; Glen Wilkinson *wo* J. Rempe *scr*; M. Smith beat I. Black 5-0; D. Gilbert beat E. Lawlor 5-2; Gary Wilkinson beat B. Harris 5-0; C. Roscoe *wo* J. Hargreaves *scr*; S. Meakin beat M. Morra 5-2; M. Clark beat I. Williamson 5-1; M. Fisher beat P. Watchorn 5-4; D. Heaton *wo* M. Watterson *scr*; B. Rowswell beat J. Smith 5-3; B. Kelly *wo* B. Mikkelsen *scr*; J. Donnelly beat D. Hughes 5-1; M. Darrington beat D. Chalmers 5-2; F. Jonik beat N. Gilbert 5-3; B. Oliver *wo* E. McLaughlin *scr*; D. Roe beat T. Whitthread 5-1; E. Sinclair beat F. Ellis 5-4; J. Chambers beat J. Fitzmaurice 5-2; R. Marshall beat D. Sheehan 5-1

Second round: J. Wright beat Rigitano 5-0; Meadowcroft beat P. Browne 5-3; Bear beat B. Harris 5-3; R. Bales beat Anderson 5-1; P. Gibson beat S. Duggan 5-4; G. Cripsey beat M. Gibson 5-2; S. James beat G. Foulds 5-0; John Rea beat M. Bradley 5-1; R. Reardon beat Burke 5-2; Foldvari beat W. King 5-4; Glen Wilkinson beat K. Owers 5-4; M. Gauvreau beat M. Smith 5-3; D. Fowler beat D. Gilbert 5-1; Gary Wilkinson beat D. O'Kane 5-2; T. Jones beat Roscoe 5-1; S. Newbury beat Meakin 5-1; Clark beat R. Grace 5-1; Fisher beat F. Davis 5-0; P. Houlihan beat Heaton 5-0; R. Chaperon beat Rowswell 5-4; L. Dodd beat Kelly 5-2; W. Jones beat Donnelly 5-3; A. Kearney beat Darrington 5-0; T. Chappel beat Jonik 5-4; J. McLaughlin beat Oliver 5-2; Roe beat M. Wildman 5-3; R. Edmonds beat Sinclair 5-2; J. Van Rensberg beat T. Murphy 5-4; Chambers beat J. O'Boye 5-3; M. Bennett beat R. Medati 5-4; G. Miles beat G. Scott 5-2; J. Wych beat Marshall 5-2

Third round: J. White beat Wright 5-4; T. Drago beat Meadowcroft 5-1; W. Thorne beat Bear 5-4; Bales beat J. Campbell 5-3; P. Gibson beat M. Hallett 5-4; Cripsey beat B. West 5-3; J. Johnson beat James 5-4; P. Francisco beat John Rea 5-3; Dennis Taylor beat Reardon 5-1; B. Werbeniuk beat Foldvari 5-1; C. Wilson beat Glen Wilkinson 5-4; J. Virgo beat Gauvreau 5-1; S. Francisco beat Fowler 5-1; Gary Wilkinson beat S. Longworth 5-4; C. Thorburn beat T. Jones 5-2; Newbury beat T. Meo 5-0; Clark beat N. Foulds 5-4; Fisher beat E. Hughes 5-4; Houlihan beat D. Reynolds 5-4; Chaperon beat David Taylor 5-3; J. Parrott beat Dodd 5-1; K. Stevens beat W. Jones 5-1; T. Griffiths beat Kearney 5-0; Chappel beat J. Spencer 5-1; T. Knowles beat J. McLaughlin 5-0; Roe beat D. Martin 5-4; Edmonds beat R. Williams 5-3; E. Charlton

beat Van Rensberg 5-3; Chambers beat D. Mountjoy 5-2; S. Hendry beat M. Bennett 5-1; S. Davis beat Miles 5-1; Wych beat M. Macleod 5-4
Fourth round: Drago beat White 5-3; Thorne beat Bales 5-2; Cripsey beat P. Gibson 5-4; P. Francisco beat Johnson 5-2; Dennis Taylor beat Werbeniuk 5-3; Wilson beat Virgo 5-3; Gary Wilkinson beat S. Francisco 5-3; Newbury beat Thorburn 5-0; Fisher beat Clark 5-4; Chaperon beat Houlihan 5-0; Parrott beat Stevens 5-0; Griffiths beat Chappel 5-3; Knowles beat Roe 5-2; Charlton beat Edmonds 5-3; Hendry beat Chambers 5-1; S. Davis beat Wych 5-1
Fifth round: Thorne beat Drago 5-2; P. Francisco beat Cripsey 5-1; Dennis Taylor beat Wilson 5-2; Newbury beat Gary Wilkinson 5-3; Chaperon beat Fisher 5-2; Parrott beat Griffiths 5-4; Knowles beat Charlton 5-0; Hendry beat S. Davis 5-2
Quarter-finals: P. Francisco beat Thorne 5-3; Dennis Taylor beat Newbury 5-2; Parrott beat Chaperon 5-2; Hendry beat Knowles 5-2
Semi-finals: Dennis Taylor beat P. Francisco 9-4; Hendry beat Parrott 9-7
Final: Hendry beat Dennis Taylor 10-7

BCE CANADIAN MASTERS

First staged 1985. **Sponsors** BCE. **Venue** CBC Studios, Toronto. **Initial prize-money** £50,000. **Prize-money last season** £62,500. **TV** CBC.

1985
First round: Dennis Taylor beat J. Parrott 5-1; R. Reardon beat A. Knowles 5-2; C. Thorburn beat J. White 5-3; S. Davis beat T. Griffiths 5-4
Semi-finals: Taylor beat Reardon 8-3; S. Davis beat Thorburn 8-1
Final: Taylor beat S. Davis 9-5

1986
First round: W. Thorne beat Dennis Taylor 5-4; A. Knowles beat C. Thorburn 5-1; S. Davis beat J. White 5-2; A. Higgins beat J. Johnson 5-3
Semi-finals: Thorne beat Knowles 8-7; S. Davis beat Higgins 8-2
Final: S. Davis beat Thorne 9-3

1987
See World Series

TENNENTS UK OPEN

First staged 1977. **Sponsors** Super Crystalate (1977), Coral (1979-85), Tennents (1986-). **Venue** Blackpool Tower Circus (1977), Guild Hall, Preston (1978-). **Initial prize-money** £7,000. **Prize-money last season** £300,000. **TV** BBC.

1977 (*Super Crystalate UK Championship*)
First round: J. Virgo *wo* J. Barrie *scr*; C. Ross beat J. Karnehm 5-4; P. Fagan beat Jack Rea 5-1; J. Meadowcroft beat P. Houlihan 5-1; D. Mountjoy beat R. Andrewartha 5-2; W. Thorne beat B. Bennett 5-1; J. Dunning beat M. Parkin 5-4; David Taylor beat D. Greaves 5-4
Second round: Virgo beat Dennis Taylor 5-2; G. Miles beat Ross 5-1; Fagan beat F. Davis 5-0; Meadowcroft beat R. Reardon 5-4; Mountjoy beat J. Spencer 5-3; Thorne beat R. Williams 5-4; Dunning *wo* J. Pulman *scr*; A. Higgins beat David Taylor 5-4
Quarter-finals: Virgo beat Miles 5-2; Fagan beat Meadowcroft 5-4; Mountjoy beat Thorne 5-4; Higgins beat Dunning 5-0
Semi-finals: Fagan beat Virgo 9-8; Mountjoy beat Higgins 9-2
Final: Fagan beat Mountjoy 12-9

1978 (*Coral UK Championship*)
Qualifying: W. Thorne beat B. Bennett 9-4; R. Andrewartha beat P. Houlihan 9-3;
D. Mountjoy beat J. Barrie 9-5; R. Williams beat T. Griffiths 9-8; J. Dunning beat
D. Greaves 9-3; J. Virgo beat R. Edmonds 9-4; David Taylor beat M. Parkin 9-2;
J. Meadowcroft beat Jack Rea 9-5
First round: David Taylor beat Fagan 9-7; Virgo beat J. Pulman 9-3; F. Davis beat
Dunning 9-2; A. Higgins beat Meadowcroft 9-6; Thorne beat R. Reardon 9-6; G. Miles
beat Williams 9-8; Mountjoy beat Dennis Taylor 9-4; Andrewartha beat J. Spencer 9-8
Quarter-finals: David Taylor beat Virgo 9-2; Higgins beat F. Davis 9-4; Miles beat
Thorne 9-1; Mountjoy beat Andrewartha 9-4
Semi-finals: David Taylor beat Higgins 9-5; Mountjoy beat Miles 9-1
Final: Mountjoy beat David Taylor 15-9

1979 (*Coral UK Championship*)
Qualifying: Jack Rea beat B. Bennett 9-8; M. Hallett beat M. Parkin 9-1; J. Dunning
beat D. Greaves 9-8
First round: W. Thorne beat R. Andrewartha 9-4; P. Houlihan beat Jack Rea 9-3;
S. Davis beat Dunning 9-3; P. Fagan beat Hallett 9-4; B. Werbeniuk beat J. Johnson 9-3;
R. Edmonds beat J. Meadowcroft 9-3; T. Meo beat David Taylor 9-7; C. Wilson beat
J. Pulman 9-7
Second round: S. Davis beat D. Mountjoy 9-5; T. Griffiths beat Wilson 9-4; A. Higgins
beat Houlihan 9-3; Fagan beat G. Miles 9-5; Werbeniuk beat J. Spencer 9-8; Dennis
Taylor beat Thorne 9-8; J. Virgo beat Meo 9-6; Edmonds beat F. Davis 9-6
Quarter-finals: Werbeniuk beat Edmonds 9-8; Dennis Taylor beat Fagan 9-6; Virgo beat
S. Davis 9-7; Griffiths beat Higgins 9-7
Semi-finals: Virgo beat Dennis Taylor 9-4; Griffiths beat Werbeniuk 9-3
Final: Virgo beat Griffiths 14-13

1980 (*Coral UK Championship*)
Preliminary round: M. Hallett beat B. Bennett 9-4; S. Hood beat C. Ross 9-3
Qualifying: Hallett beat R. Edmonds 9-8; E. Sinclair beat K. Kennerley 9-1; M. Wildman
beat C. Wilson 9-8; J. Meadowcroft beat D. Greaves 9-1; R. Andrewartha beat
A. Knowles 9-8; R. Williams beat J. Barrie 9-1; J. Johnson beat J. Dunning 9-6; T. Meo
beat Hood 9-5
First round: Meo beat P. Houlihan 9-1; S. Davis beat Hallett 9-1; P. Fagan beat Johnson
9-4; Sinclair beat G. Miles 9-5; Thorne beat Meadowcroft 9-1; Wildman beat J. Spencer
9-7; Williams beat D. Mountjoy 9-8; Andrewartha beat J. Pulman 9-6
Second round: Meo beat J. Virgo 9-1; S. Davis beat B. Werbeniuk 9-3; Dennis Taylor
beat Sinclair 9-6; T. Griffiths beat Fagan 9-8; A. Higgins beat Thorne 9-7; F. Davis beat
Wildman 9-6; R. Reardon beat Andrewartha 9-3; Williams beat David Taylor 9-7
Quarter-finals: S. Davis beat Meo 9-5; Griffiths beat Dennis Taylor 9-2; Higgins beat
F. Davis 9-6; Reardon beat Williams 9-4
Semi-finals: S. Davis beat Griffiths 9-0; Higgins beat Reardon 9-7
Final: S. Davis beat Higgins 16-6

1981 (*Coral UK Championship*)
Qualifying groups
1 P. Medati beat E. McLaughlin 9-5; Medati beat J. Donnelly 9-7; W. Thorne beat
   Medati 9-6
2 M. Hallett beat V. Harris 9-4; Hallett beat D. Hughes 9-6; Hallett beat P. Fagan 9-5
3 M. Gibson beat J. Fitzmaurice 9-6; C. Everton beat Gibson 9-7; J. White beat
   Everton 9-4
4 J. Johnson beat T. Murphy 9-1; M. Watterson beat B. Bennett 9-4; Johnson beat
   Watterson 9-3; Johnson beat C. Wilson 9-5
5 P. Houlihan beat K. Kennerley 9-1; Houlihan beat I. Black 9-4; Houlihan beat
   J. Meadowcroft 9-4
6 G. Foulds beat B. Kelly 9-7; A. Knowles beat Foulds 9-1

7　E. Sinclair beat M. Wildman 9-8; Sinclair beat S. Hood 9-0; D. Martin beat Sinclair 9-7
8　R. Williams beat D. French 9-3; C. Roscoe beat M. Macleod 9-7; Williams beat Roscoe 9-4; Williams beat J. Dunning 9-4
First round: Thorne beat R. Edmonds 9-4; K. Stevens beat Hallet 9-4; White beat J. Virgo 9-6; Johnson beat J. Spencer 9-5; G. Miles beat Houlihan 9-5; Knowles beat F. Davis 9-6; A. Higgins beat Martin 9-7; T. Meo beat Williams 9-8
Second round: S. Davis beat Thorne 9-2; B. Werbeniuk beat Stevens 9-7; White beat Dennis Taylor 9-5; R. Reardon beat Johnson 9-7; T. Griffiths beat Miles 9-4; Knowles beat D. Mountjoy 9-6; Higgins beat David Taylor 9-5; Meo beat C. Thorburn 9-6
Quarter-finals: S. Davis beat Werbeniuk 9-5; White beat Reardon 9-8; Griffiths beat Knowles 9-5; Meo beat Higgins 9-4
Semi-finals: S. Davis beat White 9-0; Griffiths beat Meo 9-3
Final: S. Davis beat Griffiths 16-3

1982 (*Coral UK Championship*)
Qualifying groups
1　T. Meo beat G. Scott 9-5
2　C. Wilson beat E. McLaughlin 9-6
3　D. Martin beat M. Macleod 9-6
4　J. Meadowcroft beat D. Hughes 9-8
5　J. Donnelly beat C. Ross 9-5
6　P. Houlihan *wo* J. Dunning *scr*
7　M. Hallett beat B. Demarco 9-1
8　B. Kelly beat J. Fitzmaurice 9-0
9　G. Foulds beat M. Gibson 9-2; R. Williams beat Foulds 9-7
10　V. Harris beat M. Owen 9-4; J. Johnson beat Harris 9-8
11　T. Murphy beat C. Everton 9-4; E. Sinclair beat Murphy 9-5
12　B. Harris beat G. Cripsey 9-6; Harris beat M. Watterson 9-3
13　M. Fisher beat I. Black 9-3; Fisher beat R. Edmonds 9-8
14　L. Dodd beat I. Williamson 9-1; Dodd beat D. French 9-7
15　B. Bennett *wo* J. Phillips *scr*; P. Medati beat Bennett 9-1
16　C. Roscoe beat Jack Rea 9-6; M. Wildman beat Roscoe 9-4
First round: S. Davis beat Williams 9-6; P. Fagan beat B. Harris 9-6; T. Griffiths beat Johnson 9-1; Dennis Taylor beat Meadowcroft 9-7; David Taylor beat Dodd 9-7; Meo beat G. Miles 9-4; J. Virgo beat Kelly 9-2; D. Mountjoy beat Houlihan 9-3; R. Reardon beat Wildman 9-5; Hallett beat F. Davis 9-7; Wilson beat W. Thorne 9-7; J. White beat Medati 9-7; J. Spencer beat Sinclair 9-8; A. Knowles beat Donnelly 9-6; D. Reynolds beat Fisher 9-6; A. Higgins beat Martin 9-7
Second round: S. Davis beat Fagan 9-3; Griffiths beat Dennis Taylor 9-7; Meo beat David Taylor 9-6; Virgo beat Mountjoy 9-5; Reardon beat Hallett 9-8; White beat Wilson 9-5; Spencer beat Knowles 9-6; Higgins beat Reynolds 9-8
Quarter-finals: Griffiths beat S. Davis 9-6; Meo beat Virgo 9-6; Reardon beat White 9-8; Higgins beat Spencer 9-5
Semi-finals: Griffiths beat Meo 9-7; Higgins beat Reardon 9-6
Final: Griffiths beat Higgins 16-15

1983 (*Coral UK Championship*)
Qualifying groups
1　J. Johnson beat M. Gibson 9-6
2　T. Jones beat E. Sinclair 9-3
3　M. Wildman beat D. Greaves 9-5
4　M. Macleod beat B. Bennett 9-0
5　M. Watterson beat C. Everton 9-6; Watterson beat F. Davis 9-6
6　M. Darrington beat G. Cripsey 9-3; M. Hallett beat Darrington 9-1
7　N. Foulds beat C. Roscoe 9-2; Foulds beat J. Meadowcroft 9-2

 8 V. Harris beat P. Houlihan 9-6; R. Williams beat Harris 9-6
 9 D. French beat Jack Rea 9-5; D. Martin beat French 9-3
10 G. Foulds beat S. Duggan 9-8; Foulds beat L. Dodd 9-7
11 J. Parrott beat G. Scott 9-7; Parrott beat M. Fisher 9-0
12 R. Andrewartha beat W. Oliver 9-1; J. Dunning beat Andrewartha 9-2
13 T. Murphy beat B. Demarco 9-4; Murphy beat Donnelly 9-4
14 P. Medati beat D. Hughes 9-3; Medati beat R. Edmonds 9-7
15 B. Harris beat E. McLaughlin 9-8; Harris beat J. Fitzmaurice 9-3
16 I. Williamson beat J. Hargreaves 9-4; I. Black beat Williamson 9-6
First round: T. Griffiths beat Martin 9-4; Hallett beat G. Miles 9-4; Johnson beat
J. Virgo 9-6; David Taylor beat N. Foulds 9-4; A. Knowles beat J. Jones 9-5;
D. Mountjoy beat Watterson 9-2; A. Higgins beat Macleod 9-6; Medati beat D. Reynolds
9-3; C. Wilson beat Williams 9-4; R. Reardon beat B. Harris 9-7; Dennis Taylor beat
Murphy 9-6; J. White beat Black 9-1; J. Spencer beat Dunning 9-7; T. Meo beat Parrott
9-7; W. Thorne beat Wildman 9-5; S. Davis beat G. Foulds 9-1
Second round: Griffiths beat Hallett 9-5; Johnson beat David Taylor 9-3; Knowles beat
Mountjoy 9-5; Higgins beat Medati 9-1; Reardon beat Wilson 9-4; White beat Dennis
Taylor 9-4; Meo beat Spencer 9-5; S. Davis beat Thorne 9-3
Quarter-finals: White beat Reardon 9-4; Griffiths beat Johnson 9-2; Higgins beat
Knowles 9-5; S. Davis beat Meo 9-4
Semi-finals: Higgins beat Griffiths 9-4; S. Davis beat White 9-4
Final: Higgins beat S. Davis 16-15

1984 (*Coral UK Open*)
Qualifying rounds
 1 T. Jones beat R. Chaperon 9-1; Jones beat P. Fagan 9-2; Jones beat M. Wildman 9-2
 2 P. Watchorn beat B. Harris 9-7; Watchorn beat C. Everton 9-6; M. Fisher beat
    Watchorn 9-5; R. Williams beat Fisher 9-8
 3 R. Foldvari beat D. Greaves 9-5; G. Cripsey beat Foldvari 9-7; J. Fitzmaurice beat
    Cripsey 9-8; J. Parrott beat Fitzmaurice 9-6
 4 P. Francisco beat D. Sheehan 9-5; P. Francisco beat I. Williamson 9-2; E. Sinclair
    beat P. Francisco 9-8; S. Francisco beat Sinclair 9-4
 5 D. Fowler beat B. Demarco 9-3; Fowler beat W. Oliver 9-3; Fowler beat F. Davis
    9-4; Fowler beat N. Foulds 9-6
 6 D. O'Kane beat W. Jones 9-7; O'Kane beat S. Duggan 9-6; G. Scott beat O'Kane
    9-7; M. Macleod beat Scott 9-5
 7 S. Newbury beat G. Rigitano 9-6; Newbury beat F. Jonik 9-3; L. Dodd beat
    Newbury 9-6; C. Wilson beat Dodd 9-8
 8 J. McLaughlin beat D. French 9-3; McLaughlin *wo* P. Morgan *scr*; McLaughlin beat
    C. Roscoe 9-8; McLaughlin beat G. Miles 9-8
 9 R. Bales beat D. Chalmers 9-2; Bales beat E. McLaughlin 9-4; M. Gauvreau beat
    Bales 9-8; Gauvreau beat P. Mans 9-6
10 G. Foulds beat D. Hughes 9-7; P. Browne beat Foulds 9-5; W. King beat Browne
    9-5; King beat J. Virgo 9-4
11 John Rea beat B. Bennett 9-5; Rea beat F. Dunning 9-3; Rea beat R. Edmonds 9-6;
    J. Johnson beat Rea 9-6
12 T. Chappel beat P. Houlihan 9-3; Chappel beat I. Black 9-3; Chappel *wo*
    R. Andrewartha *scr*; Chappel beat D. Reynolds 9-6
13 J. Hargreaves beat P. Medati 9-6; M. Gibson beat Hargreaves 9-8; J. Donnelly beat
    Gibson 9-6; J. Campbell beat Donnelly 9-6
14 M. Bradley beat V. Harris 9-8; Bradley beat B. Kelly 9-6; Bradley beat
    J. Meadowcroft 9-7; M. Hallett beat Bradley 9-8
15 S. Longworth beat M. Darrington 9-5; Longworth beat P. Burke 9-4; M. Morra beat
    Longworth 9-1; E. Hughes beat Morra 9-8
16 T. Murphy beat A. Kearney 9-2; Murphy beat M. Watterson 9-4; Murphy beat
    D. Martin 9-8

First round: A. Higgins beat T. Jones 9-7; S. Davis beat Murphy 9-1; J. White beat
Campbell 9-7; Williams beat B. Werbeniuk 9-1; W. Thorne beat Parrott 9-7; E. Charlton
beat S. Francisco 9-4; D. Mountjoy beat Hallett 9-2; T. Meo beat E. Hughes 9-4;
R. Reardon beat Fowler 9-2; K. Stevens beat Chappel 9-7; Dennis Taylor beat King 9-5;
Wilson beat T. Griffiths 9-6; Johnson beat J. Spencer 9-6; David Taylor beat Macleod
9-6; A. Knowles beat Gauvreau 9-5; C. Thorburn beat J. McLaughlin 9-4
Second round: Thorne beat Charlton 9-7; White beat Mountjoy 9-2; Higgins beat
Williams 9-7; Stevens beat Johnson 9-2; Reardon beat David Taylor 9-4; Thorburn beat
Wilson 9-3; Knowles beat Dennis Taylor 9-2; S. Davis beat Meo 9-7
Quarter-finals: Higgins beat Thorne 9-5; S. Davis beat White 9-4; Thorburn beat
Reardon 9-8; Stevens beat Knowles 9-7
Semi-finals: Higgins beat Thorburn 9-7; S. Davis beat Stevens 9-2
Final: S. Davis beat Higgins 16-8

1985 (*Coral UK Open*)

First round: D. Sheehan beat P. Watchorn 9-7; T. Drago beat D. Gilbert 9-5;
G. Wilkinson beat M. Smith 9-4; O. Agrawal beat S. Hendry 9-2; B. West *wo*
G. Robinson *scr*; G. Jenkins beat P. Burke 9-5; J. O'Boye beat B. Bennett 9-3;
M. Darrington *wo* M. Parkin *scr*; P. Houlihan beat G. Watson 9-4; J. Hargreaves beat
D. Mienie 9-7; D. Hughes beat A. Kearney 9-8; S. Simngam beat R. Bales 9-2; Jim Bear
beat B. Demarco 9-1; G. Cripsey beat D. Greaves 9-4
Second round: Sheehan beat G. Scott 9-6; Drago beat J. Donnelly 9-8; S. Longworth beat
M. Gibson 9-2; D. Fowler beat Wilkinson 9-6; M. Morra beat Agrawal 9-8; West beat
C. Roscoe 9-5; G. Miles beat B. Oliver 9-4; T. Murphy beat C. Everton 9-4; M. Bradley
beat Jenkins 9-3; T. Chappell *wo* J. McLaughlin *scr*; R. Edmonds beat J. Van Rensberg
9-5; F. Davis beat John Rea 9-8; B. Mikkelsen beat I. Williamson 9-3; P. Medati beat
W. Kelly 9-1; O'Boye beat M. Gauvreau 9-5; V. Harris beat I. Black 9-3; L. Dodd *wo*
Jack Rea *scr*; E. Sinclair beat G. Foulds 9-4; P. Browne beat D. Chalmers 9-4; W. Jones
beat J. Fitzmaurice 9-3; J. Wych beat S. Duggan 9-5; Darrington beat R. Foldvari 9-6;
T. Jones beat F. Jonik 9-4; J. McLaughlin beat R. Chaperon 9-5; S. Newbury beat
Houlihan 9-3; J. Meadowcroft beat Hargreaves 9-8; P. Francisco *wo* G. Rigitano *scr*;
W. King beat D. Hughes 9-0; Simngam beat M. Fisher 9-4; P. Fagan beat B. Harris 9-2;
Jim Bear beat M. Watterson 9-0; Cripsey *wo* J. Dunning *scr*
Third round: S. Davis beat Sheehan 9-1; Drago beat M. Wildman 9-5; T. Meo beat
Longworth 9-5; Fowler beat P. Mans 9-2; D. Mountjoy beat Morra 9-2; West beat
E. Hughes 9-3; R. Reardon beat Miles 9-4; M. Macleod beat Murphy 9-7; J. White beat
Bradley 9-4; Chappel beat D. O'Kane 9-5; A. Higgins beat Edmonds 9-8; F. Davis beat
B. Werbeniuk 9-7; David Taylor beat Mikkelsen 9-6; J. Campbell beat Medati 9-7;
A. Knowles beat O'Boye 9-5; J. Spencer beat V. Harris 9-5; C. Thorburn beat Dodd 9-4;
J. Parrott beat Sinclair 9-2; W. Thorne beat Browne 9-6; J. Virgo beat W. Jones 9-7;
S. Francisco beat Wych 9-8; D. Martin beat Darrington 9-3; T. Griffiths beat T. Jones
9-5; D. Reynolds beat J. McLaughlin 9-7; K. Stevens beat Newbury 9-7; M. Hallett beat
Meadowcroft 9-1; P. Francisco beat E. Charlton 9-5; R. Williams beat King 9-5;
J. Johnson beat Simngam 9-4; N. Foulds beat Fagan 9-5; Dennis Taylor beat Jim Bear
9-3; Cripsey beat C. Wilson 9-7
Fourth round: S. Davis beat Drago 9-2; Meo beat Fowler 9-2; West beat Mountjoy 9-4;
Macleod beat Reardon 9-5; White beat Chappel 9-5; Higgins beat F. Davis 9-2; David
Taylor beat Campbell 9-4; Knowles beat Spencer 9-7; Thorburn beat Parrott 9-6; Thorne
beat Virgo 9-8; S. Francisco beat Martin 9-6; Griffiths beat Reynolds 9-7; Stevens beat
Hallett 9-5; Williams beat P. Francisco 9-7; N. Foulds beat Johnson 9-8; Dennis Taylor
beat Cripsey 9-2
Fifth round: S. Davis beat Meo 9-5; West beat Macleod 9-4; White beat Higgins 9-6;
Knowles beat David Taylor 9-7; Thorne beat Thorburn 9-7; Griffiths beat S. Francisco
9-5; Stevens beat Williams 9-7; Dennis Taylor beat N. Foulds 9-5
Quarter-finals: S. Davis beat West 9-1; White beat Knowles 9-4; Thorne beat Griffiths
9-7; Dennis Taylor beat Stevens 9-1

Semi-finals: S. Davis beat White 9-5; Thorne beat Dennis Taylor 9-7
Final: S. Davis beat Thorne 16-14

1986

First round: G. Wilkinson beat F. Jonik 9-8; M. Fisher beat D. Greaves 9-4; K. Owers beat D. Gilbert 9-8; M. Morra beat B. Bennett 9-3; D. Sheehan beat M. Bennett 9-8; D. Hughes beat F. Ellis 9-6; R. Grace beat P. Houlihan 9-6; B. Oliver beat D. Chalmers 9-6; S. James beat G. Rigitano 9-5; J. Dunning beat A. Kearney 9-6; C. Roscoe beat M. Parkin 9-1; D. Roe beat G. Foulds 7-1 (*retd*); J. Hargreaves *wo* L. Heywood *scr*; M. Darrington beat T. Whitthread 9-8; P. Watchorn beat B. Kelly 9-8; Jack Rea *wo* S. Simngam *scr*; J. Bear beat C. Everton 9-1; M. Watterson beat P. Burke 9-0; N. Gilbert beat J. Donnelly 9-8; J. Fitzmaurice beat M. Hines 9-4; P. Gibson beat O. Agrawal 9-6; G. Jenkins beat D. Mienie 9-6; B. Rowswell *wo* E. McLaughlin *scr*; J. Wright beat M. Smith 9-7; J. Meadowcroft beat B. Demarco 9-2
Second round: T. Chappel beat Wilkinson 9-2; V. Harris beat Fisher 9-4; Owers beat S. Newbury 9-8; B. Mikkelsen beat E. Sinclair 9-8; T. Drago beat Morra 9-6; G. Miles beat Sheehan 9-8; T. Murphy beat D. Hughes 9-0; Grace beat P. Medati 9-5; S. Hendry beat Oliver 9-1; I. Williamson beat P. Browne 9-4; J. O'Boye beat S. Duggan 9-4; W. King beat James 9-8; M. Gibson beat Dunning 9-2; Roscoe beat M. Wildman 9-6; Roe beat J. Van Rensberg 9-6; W. Jones beat Hargreaves 9-0; D. Fowler beat Darrington 9-6; R. Chaperon beat Dodd 9-4; G. Scott beat Watchorn 9-7; J. Spencer beat R. Foldvari 9-6; G. Cripsey beat R. Bales 9-6; B. Harris beat Jack Rea 9-5; R. Edmonds beat Bear 9-6; Watterson beat I. Black 9-3; John Rea beat N. Gilbert 9-8; T. Jones beat Fitzmaurice 9-0; P. Gibson *wo* P. Mans *scr*; D. O'Kane beat Jenkins 9-5; J. McLaughlin beat Gauvreau 9-8; Rowswell beat F. Davis 9-4; Wright beat P. Fagan 9-0; M. Bradley beat Meadowcroft 9-2
Third round: S. Davis beat Chappel 9-7; E. Charlton beat V. Harris 9-2; S. Francisco beat Owers 9-3; D. Reynolds beat Mikkelsen 9-6; Drago beat R. Williams 9-7; J. Virgo beat Miles 9-7; W. Thorne beat Murphy 9-4; Grace beat M. Macleod 9-6; A. Higgins beat Hendry 9-8; D. Martin beat Williamson 9-5; T. Meo beat O'Boye 9-3; M. Hallett beat King 9-5; R. Reardon beat M. Gibson 9-6; E. Hughes beat Roscoe 9-8; Dennis Taylor beat Roe 9-6; W. Jones beat J. Campbell 9-3; C. Thorburn beat Fowler 9-7; David Taylor beat Chaperon 9-8; K. Stevens beat Scott 9-2; Spencer beat C. Wilson 9-5; N. Foulds beat Cripsey 9-7; J. Wych beat B. Harris 9-6; J. White beat Edmonds 9-4; P. Francisco beat Watterson 9-4; A. Knowles beat John Rea 9-4; T. Jones beat B. West 9-4; T. Griffiths beat P. Gibson 9-3; O'Kane beat B. Werbeniuk 9-5; D. Mountjoy beat J. McLaughlin 9-6; S. Longworth beat Rowswell 9-3; J. Johnson beat Wright 9-1; J. Parrott beat Bradley 9-4
Fourth round: S. Davis beat Charlton 9-6; Reynolds beat S. Francisco 9-8; Drago beat Virgo 9-6; Thorne beat Grace 9-1; Higgins beat Martin 9-6; Hallett beat Meo 9-4; E. Hughes beat Reardon 9-5; W. Jones beat Dennis Taylor 9-2; Thorburn beat David Taylor 9-4; Spencer beat Stevens 9-4; N. Foulds beat Wych 9-3; White beat P. Francisco 9-5; Knowles beat T. Jones 9-2; Griffiths beat O'Kane 9-0; Longworth beat Mountjoy 9-1; Parrott beat Johnson 9-1
Fifth round: S. Davis beat Reynolds 9-5; Drago beat Thorne 9-5; Higgins beat Hallet 9-7; W. Jones beat E. Hughes 9-5; Thorburn beat Spencer 9-2; N. Foulds beat White 9-7; Knowles beat Griffiths 9-6; Parrott beat Longworth 9-6
Quarter-finals: S. Davis beat Drago 9-8; Higgins beat W. Jones 9-5; N. Foulds beat Thorburn 9-2; Parrott beat Knowles 9-4
Semi-finals: S. Davis beat Higgins 9-3; N. Foulds beat Parrott 9-3
Final: S. Davis beat N. Foulds 16-7

1987

First round: J. Meadowcroft *wo* E. McLaughlin *scr*; E. Lawlor beat J. Fitzmaurice 9-0; I. Williamson beat B. Kelly 9-5; Jack Rea beat M. Watterson 9-6; R. Foldvari beat M. Clark 9-8; M. Fisher *wo* J. Hargreaves *scr*; J. Donnelly beat I. Anderson 9-4;

B. Rowswell beat C. Everton 9-4; B. Oliver beat P. Burke 9-1; M. Smith beat F. Jonik
9-5; J. Chambers beat C. Roscoe 9-4; P. Gibson beat G. Rigitano 9-5; F. Ellis beat
D. Sheehan 9-8; P. Watchorn beat M. Darrington 9-2; D. Gilbert beat D. Heaton 9-5;
I. Black beat J. Smith 9-8; J. Bear beat D. Chalmers 9-5; A. Harris beat M. Morra 9-8;
Gary Wilkinson beat G. Jenkins 9-3; D. Hughes *wo* B. Mikkelsen *scr*; J. Van Rensberg
beat T. Whitthread 9-5; S. Meakin beat Glen Wilkinson 9-0; D. Roe beat R. Marshall
9-3; V. Harris beat D. Greaves 9-1; J. Dunning beat P. Fagan 9-4; N. Gilbert beat
E. Sinclair 9-8

Second round: W. King beat Meadowcroft 9-4; Lawlor beat J. Wright 9-7; S. Duggan
beat Williamson 9-7; R. Chaperon beat Jack Rea 9-6; S. Newbury beat Foldvari 9-5;
J. Wych beat Fisher 9-6; John Rea beat J. McLaughlin 9-5; J. O'Boye beat Donnelly 9-2;
L. Dodd beat Medati 9-6; D. O'Kane beat Rowswell 9-2; Oliver beat G. Scott 9-4;
T. Murphy beat M. Gibson 9-0; M. Smith beat P. Browne 9-4; Chambers beat
M. Wildman 9-5; G. Cripsey beat P. Gibson 9-6; F. Davis beat Ellis 9-6; D. Fowler beat
Kearney 9-7; Miles beat P. Houlihan 9-3; T. Jones beat S. James 9-6; Watchorn beat
M. Bradley 9-5; T. Chappel beat D. Gilbert 9-2; B. Werbeniuk beat Black 9-5; Bear beat
B. Harris 9-4; M. Gauvreau beat A. Harris 9-3; Gary Wilkinson beat R. Grace 9-5;
R. Edmonds beat D. Hughes 9-4; R. Reardon beat Van Rensberg 9-7; W. Jones beat
Meakin 9-1; Roe beat K. Owers 9-7; V. Harris beat M. Bennett 9-7; Dunning beat
R. Bales 9-8; N. Gilbert beat G. Foulds 9-4

Third round: S. Davis beat King 9-2; P. Francisco beat Lawlor 9-4; A. Higgins beat
Duggan 9-4; David Taylor beat Chaperon 9-6; J. Parrott beat Newbury 9-5; Wych beat
S. Hendry 9-7; T. Knowles beat John Rea 9-6; K. Stevens beat O'Boye 9-8; Dennis
Taylor beat Dodd 9-8; O'Kane beat E. Charlton 9-8; Thorne beat Oliver 9-3; Murphy
beat T. Drago 9-7; M. Smith beat Mountjoy 9-7; J. Campbell beat Chambers 9-7;
C. Thorburn beat Cripsey 9-6; J. Virgo beat F. Davis 9-4; Fowler beat N. Foulds 9-5;
Miles beat J. Spencer 9-5; M. Hallett beat T. Jones 9-2; T. Meo beat Watchorn 9-1;
Chappel beat D. Reynolds 9-5; S. Longworth beat Werbeniuk 9-5; J. Johnson beat Bear
9-5; B. West beat Gauvreau 9-6; T. Griffiths beat Gary Wilkinson 9-5; Edmonds beat
M. Macleod 9-4; S. Francisco beat Reardon 9-3; C. Wilson beat W. Jones 9-6; Roe beat
R. Williams 9-7; V. Harris beat D. Martin 9-7; J. White beat Dunning 9-0; E. Hughes
beat N. Gilbert 9-7

Fourth round: S. Davis beat P. Francisco 9-6; Higgins beat David Taylor 9-6; Parrott
beat Wych 9-6; Knowles beat Stevens 9-8; O'Kane beat Dennis Taylor 9-7; Thorne beat
Murphy 9-4; Campbell beat M. Smith 9-8; Thorburn beat Virgo 9-6; Fowler beat Miles
9-4; Hallett beat Meo 9-5; Chappel beat Longworth 9-6; Johnson beat West 9-6;
Griffiths beat Edmonds 9-5; S. Francisco beat Wilson 9-1; Roe beat V. Harris 9-5; White
beat E. Hughes 9-4

Fifth round: S. Davis beat Higgins 9-2; Parrott beat Knowles 9-4; Thorne beat O'Kane
9-7; Thorburn beat Campbell 9-4; Hallett beat Fowler 9-4; Johnson beat Chappel 9-4;
Griffiths beat S. Francisco 9-3; White beat Roe 9-5

Quarter-finals: S. Davis beat Parrott 9-5; Thorne beat Thorburn 9-8; Johnson beat
Hallett 9-7; White beat Griffiths 9-7

Semi-finals: S. Davis beat Thorne 9-2; White beat Johnson 9-4

Final: S. Davis beat White 16-14

MATCHROOM TROPHY

First staged 1986. **Sponsors** Matchroom. **Venue** Cliffs Pavilion, Southend. **Initial
prize-money** £100,000. **Prize-money last season** £125,000. **TV** Super Channel.

1986
First round: T. Griffiths beat T. Meo 6-3; W. Thorne beat N. Foulds 6-3
Semi-finals: S. Davis beat Griffiths 6-2; Thorne beat Dennis Taylor 6-5
Final: Thorne beat S. Davis 10-9

1987
First round: S. Davis beat T. Meo 6-5; N. Foulds beat T. Griffiths 6-2; Dennis Taylor
beat J. White 6-2
Semi-finals: W. Thorne beat Foulds 6-5; Dennis Taylor beat S. Davis 6-3
Final: Dennis Taylor beat Thorne 10-3

FOSTERS WORLD DOUBLES CHAMPIONSHIP

First staged 1982. **Sponsors** Hofmeister (1982–86), Fosters (1987–). **Venue**
Crystal Palace (1982), Derngate, Northampton (1983–). **Initial prize-money**
£60,000. **Prize-money last season** £250,000. **TV** ITV.

1982 (*Hofmeister*)
Qualifying groups
1   J. Johnson & C. Wilson *wo* M. Morra & F. Joṇik *scr*; Johnson & Wilson beat
    R. Edmonds & J. Meadowcroft 6-4; R. Reardon & J. Spencer beat Johnson &
    Wilson 6-2
2   D. Martin & Dennis Taylor beat L. Dodd & D. French 6-2; T. Griffiths &
    D. Mountjoy beat Martin & Taylor 6-0
3   F. Davis & P. Medati beat J. Dunning & B. Demarco 6-0; A. Higgins & E. Charlton
    beat Davis & Medati 6-3
4   P. Houlihan & B. Bennett beat E. Sinclair & I. Black 6-2; D. Reynolds &
    M. Watterson beat Houlihan & Bennett 6-3; S. Davis & T. Meo beat Reynolds &
    Watterson 6-3
5   M. Hallett & G. Cripsey beat M. Macleod & E. McLaughlin 6-3; Hallett & Cripsey
    beat P. Fagan & G. Foulds 6-2; K. Stevens & J. Wych beat Hallett & Cripsey 6-4
6   V. Harris & I. Williamson beat T. Murphy & E. Hughes 6-1; R. Williams &
    J. Fitzmaurice beat Harris & Williamson 6-1; G. Miles & B. Werbeniuk beat
    Williams & Fitzmaurice 6-5
7   J. White & A. Knowles beat G. Scott & D. Hughes 6-2; White & Knowles beat
    David Taylor & W. Thorne 6-1
8   M. Fisher & M. Wildman beat C. Everton & C. Roscoe 6-3; Fisher & Wildman beat
    J. Donnelly & M. Gibson 6-5; C. Thorburn & J. Virgo beat Fisher & Wildman 6-2
First round: Griffiths & Mountjoy beat Stevens & Wych 6-1; S. Davis & Meo beat
Thorburn & Virgo 6-2; White & Knowles beat Reardon & Spencer 6-2; Higgins &
Charlton beat Miles & Werbeniuk 6-3
Semi-finals: Griffiths & Mountjoy beat Charlton & Higgins 10-7; S. Davis & Meo beat
White & Knowles 10-5
Final: S. Davis & Meo beat Griffiths & Mountjoy 13-2

1983 (*Hofmeister*)
Preliminary round: B. Bennett & P. Houlihan beat M. Gibson & M. Macleod 5-2;
S. Duggan & J. Hargreaves beat W. Oliver & P. Browne 5-1; G. Scott & J. Parrott beat
G. Foulds & N. Foulds 5-4; B. Harris & M. Morra beat D. Sheehan & E. McLaughlin 5-2
Qualifying: T. Murphy & P. Morgan beat P. Burke & D. Martin 5-4; J. Fitzmaurice &
V. Harris beat Bennett & Houlihan 5-4; J. Donnelly & C. Roscoe beat W. King &
J. Campbell 5-3; Duggan & Hargreaves beat D. Hughes & B. Kelly 5-0; J. Dunning &
B. Demarco beat M. Hallett & G. Cripsey 5-4; R. Edmonds & J. Meadowcroft beat
D. French & C. Everton 5-2; E. Hughes & L. Dodd beat Scott & Parrott 5-2; B. Harris &
Morra beat M. Darrington & I. Williamson 5-1
First round: Murphy & Morgan beat I. Black & E. Sinclair 5-1; Dennis Taylor &
R. Williams beat Fitzmaurice & V. Harris 5-1; T. Jones & S. Francisco beat Donnelly &
Roscoe 5-2; G. Miles & G. Ganim beat Duggan & Hargreaves 5-3; F. Davis &
M. Watterson beat Dunning & Demarco 5-3; D. Reynolds & P. Fagan beat Edmonds &
Meadowcroft 5-0; E. Hughes & Dodd beat C. Wilson & J. Johnson 5-1; B. Harris &

Morra beat M. Fisher & M. Wildman 5-2
Second round: S. Davis & T. Meo beat Murphy & Morgan 5-2; David Taylor &
W. Thorne beat Dennis Taylor & Williams 5-4; E. Charlton & B. Werbeniuk beat
T. Jones & S. Francisco 5-3; A. Higgins & K. Stevens *wo* Miles & Ganim *scr*; R. Reardon
& J. Spencer beat F. Davis & Watterson 5-2; J. Virgo & C. Thorburn beat Reynolds &
Fagan 5-2; T. Griffiths & D. Mountjoy beat E. Hughes & Dodd 5-3; A. Knowles &
J. White beat B. Harris & Morra 5-4
Quarter-finals: S. Davis & Meo beat David Taylor & Thorne 5-3; Charlton & Werbeniuk
beat Higgins & Stevens 5-1; Thorburn & Virgo beat Reardon & Spencer 5-0; Knowles &
White beat Griffiths & Mountjoy 5-0
Semi-finals: S. Davis & Meo beat Charlton & Werbeniuk 9-1; Knowles & White beat
Thorburn & Virgo 9-7
Final: S. Davis & Meo beat Knowles & White 10-2

1984 (*Hofmeister*)
Qualifying: J. Donnelly & C. Roscoe beat S. Longworth & D. French 5-3; D. Chalmers &
J. McLaughlin beat P. Fagan & B. Harris 5-0; M. Morra & M. Bradley beat
I. Williamson & M. Darrington 5-1; G. Miles & P. Francisco beat J. Hargreaves &
S. Duggan 5-1; T. Chappel & S. Newbury beat G. Rigitano & G. Scott 5-0; M. Gauvreau
& D. Fowler beat B. Bennett & P. Houlihan 5-1; R. Bales & W. Oliver beat John Rea &
E. McLaughlin 5-2; J. Meadowcroft & R. Edmonds beat F. Jonik & R. Chaperon 5-4;
V. Harris & J. Fitzmaurice beat P. Burke & B. Kelly 5-2; D. Sheehan & P. Watchorn
beat M. Macleod & M. Gibson 5-0; F. Davis & M. Watterson beat C. Everton &
R. Foldvari 5-3; P. Medati & P. Browne beat I. Black & E. Sinclair 5-1; D. Hughes &
A. Kearney *wo* J. Dunning & B. Demarco *scr*
First round: D. Mountjoy & W. Jones beat Chappel & Newbury 5-1; S. Francisco &
T. Jones beat J. Campbell & W. King 5-4; A. Higgins & J. White beat D. Martin &
G. Cripsey 5-2; David Taylor & M. Hallett beat E. Hughes & L. Dodd 5-3; P. Francisco
& Miles beat C. Wilson & J. Johnson 5-4; D. Reynolds & D. O'Kane beat Gauvreau &
Fowler 5-4; Dennis Taylor & R. Williams beat Medati & Browne 5-0; Bales & Oliver
beat G. Foulds & N. Foulds 5-2; S. Davis & T. Meo beat D. Hughes & Kearney 5-2;
R. Reardon & T. Murphy beat F. Davis & Watterson 5-2; M. Fisher & M. Wildman beat
Edmonds & Meadowcroft 5-3; E. Charlton & B. Werbeniuk beat Sheehan & Watchorn
5-2; T. Griffiths & J. Parrott beat Chalmers & J. McLaughlin 5-0; J. Virgo & K. Stevens
beat Morra & Bradley 5-1; A. Knowles & J. Spencer beat V. Harris & Fitzmaurice 5-2
Second round: S. Davis & Meo beat Miles & P. Francisco 5-2; Virgo & Stevens beat
Dennis Taylor & Williams 5-3; Higgins & White beat Reynolds & O'Kane 5-4; Thorburn
& Thorne beat Mountjoy & W. Jones 5-3; Reardon & Murphy beat S. Francisco &
T. Jones 5-3; Griffiths & Parrott beat Bales & Oliver 5-4; David Taylor & Hallett beat
Charlton & Werbeniuk 5-4; Knowles & Spencer beat Fisher & Wildman 5-4
Quarter-finals: Knowles & Spencer beat Reardon & Murphy 5-4; Higgins & White beat
Griffiths & Parrott 5-2; Thorburn & Thorne beat Virgo & Stevens 5-3; S. Davis & Meo
beat Hallett & David Taylor 5-1
Semi-finals: Thorburn & Thorne beat Knowles & Spencer 9-1; Higgins & White beat
S. Davis & Meo 9-6
Final: Higgins & White beat Thorburn & Thorne 10-2

1985 (*Hofmeister*)
First round: P. Watchorn & D. Sheehan beat D. Greaves & G. Jenkins 5-4; G. Cripsey &
G. Wilkinson beat P. Houlihan & B. Bennett 5-2; R. Bales & J. McLaughlin beat
S. Simngam & O. Agrawal 5-3; J. Hargreaves & P. Burke beat T. Drago & J. O'Boye 5-3
Second round: D. Fowler & B. West beat R. Chaperon & M. Gauvreau 5-4; P. Mans &
J. Campbell beat Watchorn & Sheehan 5-1; P. Medati & B. Browne beat R. Foldvari &
M. Fisher 5-3; Cripsey & Wilkinson beat M. Gibson & D. O'Kane 5-4; T. Murphy &
P. Fagan beat A. Kearney & D. Hughes 5-2; M. Bradley & D. Chalmers beat W. Oliver
& M. Darrington 5-4; Bales & J. McLaughlin beat B. Mikkelsen & J. Meadowcroft 5-4;

M. Wildman & R. Edmonds beat S. Hendry & G. Rigitano 5-3; T. Chappel & F. Jonik
beat E. Sinclair & I. Black 5-1; I. Williamson & S. Duggan beat D. Gilbert & B. Harris
5-1; M. Watterson & F. Davis *wo* J. Fitzmaurice & V. Harris *scr*; D. Reynolds &
S. Longworth beat J. Van Rensberg & D. Mienie 5-4; Jim Bear & L. Dodd beat
M. Morra & J. Wych 5-1; J. Donnelly & C. Roscoe beat Hargreaves & Burke 5-4; John
Rea & E. McLaughlin beat G. Scott & G. Foulds 5-0; R. Williams & G. Miles *wo*
J. Dunning & B. Demarco *scr*
Third round: Fowler & West beat A. Higgins & J. White 5-4; Mans & Campbell beat
D. Martin & M. Macleod; M. Hallett & David Taylor beat Medati & Browne 5-4;
T. Jones & R. Reardon beat Cripsey & Wilkinson 5-3; A. Knowles & J. Johnson beat
Murphy & Fagan 5-2; W. Jones & D. Mountjoy beat Bradley & Chalmers 5-2; J. Spencer
& S. Newbury beat Bales & J. McLaughlin 5-4; T. Griffiths & Dennis Taylor beat
Wildman & Edmonds 5-4; C. Thorburn & W. Thorne beat Chappel & Jonik 5-1;
W. King & C. Wilson beat Williamson & Duggan 5-3; P. Francisco & S. Francisco beat
Watterson & F. Davis 5-0; J. Virgo & K. Stevens beat Reynolds & Longworth 5-0;
E. Charlton & B. Werbeniuk beat Jim Bear & Dodd 5-4; N. Foulds & J. Parrott beat
Donnelly & Roscoe 5-1; E. Hughes & M. Smith beat John Rea & E. McLaughlin 5-4;
S. Davis & T. Meo beat Williams & Miles 5-2
Fourth round: Mans & Campbell beat Fowler & West 5-4; T. Jones & Reardon beat
Hallett & David Taylor 5-0; W. Jones & Mountjoy beat Knowles & Johnson 5-4;
Griffiths & Dennis Taylor beat Spencer & Newbury 5-0; Thorburn & Thorne beat King
& Wilson 5-2; P. Francisco & S. Francisco beat Virgo & Stevens 5-3; N. Foulds &
Parrott beat Charlton & Werbeniuk 5-4; S. Davis & Meo beat E. Hughes & Smith 5-1
Quarter-finals: T. Jones & Reardon beat Mans & Campbell 5-4; Griffiths & Dennis
Taylor beat W. Jones & Mountjoy 5-2; Thorburn & Thorne beat P. Francisco &
S. Francisco 5-3; S. Davis & Meo beat N. Foulds & Parrott 5-3
Semi-finals: T. Jones & Reardon beat Griffiths & Dennis Taylor 9-6; S. Davis & Meo
beat Thorburn & Thorne 9-6
Final: S. Davis & Meo beat T. Jones & Reardon 12-5

1986 (*Hofmeister*)
First round: J. Hargreaves & P. Burke beat J. Meadowcroft & M. Morra 5-0; J. Wright &
T. Whitthread beat B. Mikkelsen & F. Jonik 5-4; M. Darrington & B. Oliver beat
D. Greaves & O. Agrawal 5-3; S. James & D. Roe beat J. Fitzmaurice & B. Rowswell
5-1; I. Williamson & R. Grace beat G. Jenkins & P. Gibson 5-2; B. Kelly & Jack Rea *wo*
E. McLaughlin & John Rea *scr*; B. Bennett & P. Houlihan beat J. Bear & D. Mienie 5-2;
J. Donnelly & C. Roscoe beat N. Gilbert & M. Fisher 5-1; J. Dunning & B. Demarco *wo*
R. Foldvari & L. Heywood *scr*; P. Watchorn & D. Sheehan beat D. Hughes &
A. Kearney 5-2
Second round: J. Spencer & G. Rigitano beat Hargreaves & Burke 5-1; S. Duggan &
B. West beat Wright & Whitthread 5-3; M. Gauvreau & R. Chaperon beat J. O'Boye &
J. McLaughlin 5-4; V. Harris & D. Gilbert beat D. Reynolds & S. Longworth 5-4;
Darrington & Oliver beat B. Harris & M. Smith 5-1; James & Roe beat F. Davis &
M. Watterson 5-0; Williamson & Grace beat T. Chappel & M. Bennett 5-2; G. Scott &
G. Foulds beat I. Black & E. Sinclair 5-4; M. Wildman & R. Edmonds beat Kelly & Jack
Rea 5-0; T. Drago & K. Owers beat B. Bennett & Houlihan 5-2; M. Gibson &
D. Chalmers *wo* E. Hughes & S. Simngam *scr*; P. Fagan & T. Murphy beat G. Cripsey &
G. Wilkinson 5-1; S. Newbury & R. Bales beat L. Dodd & M. Bradley 5-2; Donnelly &
Roscoe beat P. Browne & P. Medati 5-1; M. Hallett & S. Hendry beat Dunning &
Demarco 5-1; Wych & D. O'Kane beat Watchorn & Sheehan 5-1
Third round: S. Davis & T. Meo beat Spencer & Rigitano 5-1; Duggan & West beat
C. Wilson & W. King 5-4; David Taylor & E. Charlton beat Gauvreau & Chaperon 5-1;
S. Francisco & P. Francisco beat V. Harris & D. Gilbert 5-4; Dennis Taylor &
T. Griffiths beat Darrington & Oliver 5-1; James & Roe beat J. Campbell & P. Mans
5-2; R. Williams & G. Miles beat Williamson & Grace 5-3; J. White & A. Higgins beat
G. Scott & G. Foulds 5-2; J. Johnson & A. Knowles beat Wildman & Edmonds 5-2;

R. Reardon & T. Jones beat Drago & Owers 5-3; D. Mountjoy & W. Jones beat
M. Gibson & Chalmers 5-1; J. Virgo & K. Stevens beat Fagan & Murphy 5-1; J. Parrott
& N. Foulds beat Newbury & Bales 5-3; D. Martin & M. Macleod beat Donnelly &
Roscoe 5-0; Hallett & Hendry beat B. Werbeniuk & D. Fowler 5-3; W. Thorne &
C. Thorburn beat Wych & O'Kane 5-2
Fourth round: S. Davis & Meo beat Duggan & West 5-3; S. Francisco & P. Francisco
beat David Taylor & Charlton 5-1; Dennis Taylor & Griffiths beat James & Roe 5-2;
White & Higgins beat Williams & Miles 5-2; Reardon & T. Jones beat Johnson &
Knowles 5-4; Virgo & Stevens beat Mountjoy & W. Jones 5-4; Parrott & N. Foulds beat
Martin & Macleod 5-2; Hallett & Hendry beat Thorne & Thorburn 5-4
Quarter-finals: S. Davis & Meo beat S. Francisco & P. Francisco 5-0; Dennis Taylor &
Griffiths beat White & Higgins 5-4; Virgo & Stevens beat Reardon & T. Jones 5-2;
Hallett & Hendry beat N. Foulds & Parrott 5-1
Semi-finals: S. Davis & Meo beat Dennis Taylor & Griffiths 9-6; Hallett & Hendry beat
Virgo & Stevens 9-2
Final: S. Davis & Meo beat Hallett & Hendry 12-3

1987
First round: J. Chambers & M. Clark beat P. Fagan & Jack Rea 5-0; E. Lawlor &
A. Harris beat N. Gilbert & M. Fisher 5-3; B. Oliver & M. Darrington beat D. Chalmers
& Gary Wilkinson 5-4; I. Williamson & R. Foldvari beat F. Ellis & J. Smith 5-1;
G. Jenkins & D. Heaton *wo* J. Van Rensberg & J. Hargreaves *scr*; M. Smith & D. Gilbert
beat B. Kelly & S. Meakin 5-0; J. Fitzmaurice & M. Morra *wo* E. McLaughlin &
D. Hughes *scr*; Glen Wilkinson & P. Gibson beat J. Donnelly & C. Roscoe 5-2; J. Bear &
D. Greaves beat T. Kearney & P. Burke 5-2; E. Sinclair & I. Black *wo* P. Watchorn &
D. Sheehan *scr*
Second round: Chambers & Clark beat P. Browne & J. McLaughlin 5-1; S. James &
D. Roe beat M. Bennett & R. Marshall 5-0; R. Bales & S. Newbury beat Lawlor & Harris
5-1; B. West & S. Duggan beat Oliver & Darrington 5-0; M. Bradley & L. Dodd beat G.
Scott & J. Meadowcroft 5-2; Williamson & Foldvari beat V. Harris & G. Foulds 5-2; M.
Wildman & R. Edmonds beat Jenkins & Heaton 5-3; R. Chaperon & M. Gauvreau beat
M. Gibson & John Rea 5-1; D. O'Kane & J. Wych *wo* F. Davis & M. Watterson *scr*;
M. Smith & D. Gilbert beat J. Wright & T. Whitthread 5-1; G. Cripsey & S. Longworth
beat Fitzmaurice & Morra 5-4; R. Reardon & T. Jones beat Glen Wilkinson & Gibson 5-
2; T. Murphy & T. Chappel *wo* B. Mikkelsen & P. Medati *scr*; B. Werbeniuk &
D. Fowler beat R. Grace & G. Rigitano 5-0; J. O'Boye & B. Harris beat Bear & Greaves
5-0; T. Drago & K. Owers beat Sinclair & Black 5-0
Third round: Chambers & Clark beat S. Davis & T. Meo 5-1; James & Roe beat
D. Martin & J. Spencer 5-2; J. Virgo & K. Stevens beat Bales & Newbury 5-3;
D. Reynolds & J. Parrott beat West & Duggan 5-2; J. Johnson & A. Knowles beat
Bradley & Dodd 5-0; M. Macleod & Campbell beat Williamson & Foldvari 5-4; David
Taylor & E. Charlton beat Wildman & Edmonds 5-3; C. Thorburn & Dennis Taylor beat
Chaperon & Gauvreau 5-1; O'Kane & Wych beat J. White & W. Thorne 5-3; C. Wilson
& W. King beat M. Smith & D. Gilbert 5-3; D. Mountjoy & W. Jones beat Cripsey &
Longworth 5-3; S. Francisco & P. Francisco beat Reardon & T. Jones 5-3; A. Higgins &
E. Hughes beat Murphy & Chappel 5-2; M. Hallett & S. Hendry beat Werbeniuk &
Fowler 5-2; R. Williams & G. Miles beat O'Boye & B. Harris 5-1; T. Griffiths &
N. Foulds beat Owers & Drago 5-1
Fourth round: James & Roe beat Chambers & Clark 5-3; Parrott & Reynolds beat Virgo
& Stevens 5-0; Johnson & Knowles beat Macleod & Campbell 5-1; Thorburn & Dennis
Taylor beat David Taylor & Charlton 5-2; O'Kane & Wych beat Wilson & King 5-2; S.
Francisco & P. Francisco beat Mountjoy & W. Jones 5-3; Hallett & Hendry beat Higgins
& E. Hughes 5-2; N. Foulds & Griffiths beat Williams & Miles 5-3
Quarter finals: James & Roe beat Reynolds & Parrott 5-2; Thorburn & Dennis Taylor
beat Johnson & Knowles 5-0; S. Francisco & P. Francisco beat O'Kane & Wych 5-4;
Hallett & Hendry beat N. Foulds & Griffiths 5-1

Semi-finals: Thorburn & Dennis Taylor beat James & Roe 9-1; Hallett & Hendry beat S. Francisco & P. Francisco 9-4
Final: Hallett & Hendry beat Thorburn & Dennis Taylor 12-8

MERCANTILE CREDIT CLASSIC

First staged 1980*. **Sponsors** Wilsons (1980–82), Lada (1983–84), Mercantile Credit (1985–). **Venue** Civic Centre, Oldham (1982), Spectrum Arena, Warrington (1983–86), Norbreck Castle Hotel, Blackpool (1987–). **Initial prize-money** £15,000 (1982). **Prize-money last season** £250,000.
The first two events, both in 1980, were small invitation events which do not meet the conditions required for full inclusion in this book.

1982 (*Wilsons*)
First round: T. Griffiths beat C. Thorburn 5-1; A. Higgins beat Dennis Taylor 5-1; R. Reardon beat David Taylor 5-1; S. Davis beat J. Spencer 5-2
Semi-finals: Griffiths beat Higgins 5-1; S. Davis beat Reardon 5-4
Final: Griffiths beat S. Davis 9-8

1983 (*Lada Classic*)
First round: E. Charlton beat J. Virgo 5-2; J. Spencer beat R. Reardon 5-3; C. Thorburn beat C. Wilson 5-3; D. Mountjoy beat T. Griffiths 5-1; David Taylor beat J. White 5-3; B. Werbeniuk beat A. Higgins 5-4; K. Stevens beat A. Knowles 5-0; S. Davis beat Dennis Taylor 5-2
Quarter-finals: Spencer beat David Taylor 5-2; Werbeniuk beat Mountjoy 5-2; Stevens beat Thorburn 5-3; S. Davis beat Charlton 5-4
Semi-finals: S. Davis beat Spencer 5-4; Werbeniuk beat Stevens 5-2
Final: S. Davis beat Werbeniuk 9-5

1984 (*Lada Classic*)
First qualifying round: G. Foulds beat M. Gauvreau 5-2; B. Demarco beat M. Gibson 5-2; N. Foulds beat P. Houlihan 5-3; M. Morra beat P. Burke 5-2; G. Ganim beat D. Hughes 5-2; I. Williamson beat D. French 5-1; J. Hargreaves beat W. King 5-3; W. Oliver beat D. Sheehan 5-3; T. Jones beat P. Mifsud 5-3; P. Morgan beat M. Darrington 5-3; G. Cripsey beat V. Harris 5-4; J. Parrott beat B. Bennett 5-0; P. Browne beat D. Greaves 5-2; P. Watchorn beat R. Andrewartha 5-2; S. Duggan beat B. Harris 5-2; P. Medati beat T. Murphy 5-4
Second qualifying round: E. McLaughlin beat G. Foulds 5-1; G. Scott beat Demarco 5-2; N. Foulds beat Jack Rea 5-1; Morra beat C. Everton 5-0; C. Roscoe beat Ganim 5-3; F. Jonik beat Williamson 5-1; Hargreaves beat B. Kelly 5-4; Oliver beat J. Donnelly 5-4; Morgan beat M. Watterson 5-3; T. Jones beat I. Black 5-0; J. Campbell beat Cripsey 5-3; Parrott beat J. Fitzmaurice 5-2; R. Edmonds beat Browne 5-1; M. Fisher beat Watchorn 5-4; L. Dodd beat Duggan 5-2; E. Hughes beat Medati 5-1
Third qualifying round: E. McLaughlin beat W. Thorne 5-3; D. Reynolds beat Scott 5-3; C. Wilson beat N. Foulds 5-1; S. Francisco beat Morra 5-1; Roscoe beat G. Miles 5-2; J. Johnson beat Jonik 5-2; M. Wildman beat Hargreaves 5-1; P. Fagan beat Oliver 5-1; E. Sinclair beat Morgan 5-2; M. Macleod beat T. Jones 5-2; Campbell beat F. Davis 5-0; Parrott beat D. Martin 5-1; R. Williams beat Edmonds 5-1; J. Meadowcroft beat Fisher 5-0; M. Hallett beat Dodd 5-1; E. Hughes beat J. Dunning 5-4
First round: K. Stevens beat E. McLaughlin 5-4; T. Griffiths beat Reynolds 5-2; E. Charlton beat Wilson 5-0; S. Francisco beat C. Thorburn 5-1; Roscoe beat B. Werbeniuk 5-4; J. Spencer beat Johnson 5-4; Wildman beat J. Virgo 5-2; A. Higgins beat Fagan 5-3; S. Davis beat Sinclair 5-2; Macleod beat David Taylor 5-4; J. White beat Campbell 5-1; Parrott beat D. Mountjoy 5-4; Williams beat R. Reardon 5-4; T. Meo beat Meadowcroft 5-1; Hallett beat Dennis Taylor 5-4; A. Knowles beat E. Hughes 5-1

Second round: S. Davis beat Spencer 5-1; Charlton beat White 5-2; Wildman beat
S. Francisco 5-1; Knowles beat Hallett 5-3; Stevens beat Macleod 5-1; Griffiths beat
Roscoe 5-2; Meo beat Williams 5-3; Parrott beat Higgins 5-2
Quarter-finals: Wildman beat Charlton 5-4; S. Davis beat Griffiths 5-4; Meo beat
Stevens 5-2; Parrott beat Knowles 5-1
Semi-finals: Meo beat Wildman 5-3; S. Davis beat Parrott 5-4
Final: S. Davis beat Meo 9-8

1985
Preliminary round: P. Watchorn beat D. Hughes 5-0; B. Mikkelsen beat D. Chalmers 5-1
First qualifying round: T. Jones beat D. Greaves 5-2; J. Giannaros beat T. Chappel 5-2;
S. Newbury beat V. Harris 5-3; G. Foulds beat R. Chaperon 5-3; D. Sheehan beat John
Rea 5-2; R. Bales beat B. Bennett 5-1; R. Foldvari beat P. Houlihan 5-1; P. Medati beat
G. Cripsey 5-4; J. McLaughlin beat B. Demarco 5-1; S. Longworth beat P. Francisco 5-4;
A. Kearney beat D. French 5-1; P. Browne beat M. Bradley 5-3; W. Jones beat
D. O'Kane 5-0; D. Fowler beat Rigitano 5-0; J. Hargreaves beat Darrington 5-2
Second qualifying round: T. Jones beat M. Gibson 5-0; Newbury beat P. Burke 5-1;
G. Foulds beat F. Jonik 5-2; E. McLaughlin beat Sheehan 5-2; Bales beat B. Kelly 5-3;
Foldvari beat Jack Rea 5-4; J. McLaughlin beat I. Black 5-0; Longworth beat B. Oliver
5-1; Watchorn beat Mikkelsen 5-1; I. Williamson beat Kearney 5-3; Browne beat
C. Everton 5-0; S. Duggan beat W. Jones 5-0; Fowler beat T. Murphy 5-0; R. Edmonds
beat Hargreaves 5-2
Third qualifying round: T. Jones beat L. Dodd 5-1; M. Gauvreau beat Giannaros 5-3;
Newbury beat M. Morra 5-2; G. Foulds beat J. Fitzmaurice 5-1; E. McLaughlin beat
F. Davis 5-1; Medati beat C. Roscoe 5-4; G. Scott beat J. McLaughlin 5-4; Longworth
beat M. Fisher 5-1; J. Donnelly beat Watchorn 5-1; P. Fagan beat Williamson 5-1;
W. King beat Duggan 5-4; Fowler beat J. Meadowcroft 5-2; Edmonds beat M. Watterson
5-2
Fourth qualifying round: S. Francisco beat T. Jones 5-1; Fagan beat M. Wildman 5-3;
M. Hallett beat G. Foulds 5-4; M. Macleod beat E. McLaughlin 5-4; Medati beat
J. Parrott 5-3; C. Wilson beat Fowler 5-4; Gauvreau beat E. Sinclair 5-1; J. Johnson beat
Edmonds 5-4; Scott beat J. Campbell 5-4; E. Hughes beat Newbury 5-3; King beat
D. Reynolds 5-2; R. Williams beat Donnelly 5-3; J. Virgo beat Bales 5-1; Longworth beat
N. Foulds 5-3; Browne beat G. Miles 5-3
First round: Longworth beat David Taylor 5-4; Johnson beat A. Knowles 5-1;
C. Thorburn beat Scott 5-1; King beat J. Spencer 5-2; T. Griffiths beat Fagan 5-0;
J. White beat Browne 5-2; E. Hughes beat T. Meo 5-4; Macleod beat Charlton 5-1;
A. Higgins beat Gauvreau 5-3; Virgo beat B. Werbeniuk 5-2; Wilson beat D. Mountjoy
5-4; Williams beat Dennis Taylor 5-3; R. Reardon beat Hallett 5-3; S. Davis beat
S. Francisco 5-0; W. Thorne beat Foldvari 5-2; K. Stevens beat Medati 5-4
Second round: Reardon beat E. Hughes 5-1; S. Davis beat Higgins 5-2; Virgo beat
Macleod 5-0; Thorne beat Stevens 5-1; Thorburn beat Longworth 5-3; Griffiths beat
Williams 5-3; Johnson beat Wilson 5-0; King beat White 5-2
Quarter-finals: S. Davis beat Reardon 5-1; Thorburn beat Griffiths 5-4; Johnson beat
King 5-3; Thorne beat Virgo 5-1
Semi-finals: Thorne beat S. Davis 9-8; Thorburn beat Johnson 9-2
Final: Thorne beat Thorburn 13-8

1986
First round: D. Gilbert beat G. Watson 5-4; A. Kearney beat Jim Bear 5-0; S. Hendry
beat D. Sheehan 5-2; B. Demarco beat O. Agrawal 5-4; M. Smith beat D. Mienie 5-1;
J. O'Boye beat G. Wilkinson 5-1; B. West beat M. Darrington 5-0; P. Burke beat
D. Hughes 5-3; S. Simngam beat J. Hargreaves 5-1; R. Bales beat M. Parkin 5-0;
D. Greaves beat P. Watchorn 5-4; G. Jenkins *wo* G. Robinson *scr*; G. Cripsey beat
T. Drago 5-4; P. Houlihan beat B. Bennett 5-0
Second round: T. Jones beat Gilbert 5-3; G. Foulds beat I. Black 5-2; W. King beat

S. Duggan 5-2; P. Medati beat Kearney 5-2; Hendry beat G. Miles 5-1; M. Bradley beat
B. Oliver 5-3; B. Mikkelsen beat G. Scott 5-1; J. Donnelly beat D. Chalmers 5-0;
F. Davis beat B. Kelly 5-3; J. Wych beat Demarco 5-0; B. Harris beat M. Morra 5-3;
Smith beat R. Edmonds 5-2; O'Boye beat S. Longworth 5-1; West beat J. Meadowcroft
5-0; J. McLaughlin beat E. McLaughlin 5-2; John Rea beat I. Williamson 5-4;
R. Chaperon beat Burke 5-2; J. Van Rensberg beat W. Jones 5-4; P. Francisco beat
F. Jonik 5-2; T. Murphy beat T. Chappel 5-4; M. Gauvreau beat Simngam 5-1;
M. Gibson wo J. Dunning scr; P. Browne beat C. Everton 5-0; D. Fowler beat Bales 5-4;
G. Rigitano beat L. Dodd 5-3; E. Sinclair beat Greaves 5-1; V. Harris beat C. Roscoe
5-1; M. Watterson beat Jenkins 5-2; M. Fisher beat Jack Rea 5-3; Cripsey beat
S. Newbury 5-4; J. Fitzmaurice beat P. Fagan 5-3; Houlihan beat R. Foldvari 5-4
Third round: T. Jones beat W. Thorne 5-3; B. Werbeniuk beat G. Foulds 5-3;
D. Mountjoy beat King 5-4; D. O'Kane beat Medati 5-0; Hendry beat S. Francisco 5-4;
N. Foulds beat Bradley 5-3; Mikkelsen beat R. Reardon 5-3; J. Campbell beat Donnelly
5-2; F. Davis beat K. Stevens 5-2; E. Hughes beat Wych 5-2; J. Johnson beat B. Harris
5-4; P. Mans beat Smith 5-4; T. Meo beat O'Boye 5-3; West beat M. Wildman 5-2;
C. Thorburn beat J. McLaughlin 5-1; M. Hallett beat John Rea 5-2; S. Davis beat
Chaperon 5-1; Van Rensberg beat J. Parrott 5-3; P. Francisco beat E. Charlton 5-1;
D. Martin beat Murphy 5-3; Gauvreau beat David Taylor 5-3; Browne beat C. Wilson
5-3; J. White beat Fowler 5-1; J. Virgo beat Gibson 5-3; A. Knowles beat Rigitano 5-4;
M. Macleod beat Sinclair 5-2; V. Harris beat T. Griffiths 5-3; R. Williams beat
Watterson 5-0; A. Higgins beat Fisher 5-0; Cripsey beat J. Spencer 5-1; Dennis Taylor
beat Fitzmaurice 5-1; D. Reynolds beat Houlihan 5-1
Fourth round: Werbeniuk beat T. Jones 5-3; Mountjoy beat O'Kane 5-3; N. Foulds beat
Hendry 5-4; Campbell beat Mikkelsen 5-2; E. Hughes beat F. Davis 5-3; Johnson beat
Mans 5-2; Meo beat West 5-1; Thorburn beat Hallett 5-3; S. Davis beat Van Rensberg
5-1; P. Francisco beat Martin 5-2; Gauvreau beat Browne 5-3; White beat Virgo 5-2;
Knowles beat Macleod 5-4; Williams beat V. Harris 5-1; Higgins beat Cripsey 5-2;
Dennis Taylor beat Reynolds 5-4
Fifth round: Mountjoy beat Werbeniuk 5-3; N. Foulds beat Campbell 5-1; Johnson beat
E. Hughes 5-1; Thorburn beat Meo 5-1; S. Davis beat P. Francisco 5-0; White beat
Gauvreau 5-2; Williams beat Knowles 5-2; Higgins beat Dennis Taylor 5-4
Quarter-finals: Mountjoy beat N. Foulds 5-3; Thorburn beat Johnson 5-4; White beat
S. Davis 5-2; Williams beat Higgins 5-2
Semi-finals: Thorburn beat Mountjoy 9-6; White beat Williams 9-7
Final: White beat Thorburn 13-12

1987

First round: J. Meadowcroft wo L. Heywood scr; B. Rowswell beat M. Watterson 5-1;
P. Watchorn beat J. Donnelly 5-0; G. Foulds beat B. Bennett 5-2; C. Everton wo
E. McLaughlin scr; A. Kearney beat O. Agrawal 5-0; D. Roe beat M. Darrington 5-0;
F. Jonik beat S. James 5-4; D. Mienie wo J. Hargreaves scr; P. Burke wo J. Bear scr;
G. Jenkins beat M. Parkin 5-2; M. Bennett beat D. Sheehan 5-3; K. Owers beat
P. Houlihan 5-1; M. Morra beat F. Ellis 5-1; M. Fisher beat B. Demarco 5-0; C. Roscoe
beat T. Whitthread 5-1; B. Oliver beat D. Greaves 5-4; G. Wilkinson beat J. Fitzmaurice
5-2; Jack Rea beat B. Kelly 5-3; J. Wright beat D. Hughes 5-2; N. Gilbert beat M. Smith
5-0; P. Gibson wo S. Simngam scr; G. Rigitano beat R. Grace 5-4
Second round: S. Newbury beat Meadowcroft 5-1; M. Bradley beat Rowswell 5-4;
S. Duggan beat Watchorn 5-1; J. McLaughlin beat M. Gibson 5-3; J. O'Boye beat
V. Harris 5-1; G. Foulds beat D. O'Kane 5-4; J. Spencer beat D. Gilbert 5-4; P. Browne
beat Dunning 5-1; W. Jones beat Everton 5-0; Kearney beat M. Wildman 5-3; L. Dodd
beat Medati 5-4; I. Williamson beat R. Edmonds 5-2; R. Chaperon beat Roe 5-4; Jonik
beat T. Drago 5-2; G. Cripsey beat Mienie 5-0; W. King beat Burke 5-0; Jenkins beat
G. Scott 5-4; M. Bennett beat I. Black 5-3; John Rea beat Owers 5-2; T. Murphy beat
R. Bales 5-2; Morra wo P. Mans scr; Fisher beat F. Davis 5-2; Roscoe wo P. Fagan scr;
T. Jones beat Oliver 5-0; D. Fowler beat Wilkinson 5-1; B. Mikkelsen beat R. Foldvari

5-1; S. Hendry beat Jack Rea 5-1; Wright beat T. Chappel 5-4; J. Van Rensberg beat
N. Gilbert 5-3; R. Harris beat P. Gibson 5-3; E. Sinclair beat G. Miles 5-1; M. Gauvreau
beat Rigitano 5-0
Third round: J. White beat Newbury 5-4; Bradley beat David Taylor 5-1; Duggan beat
N. Foulds 5-3; B. Werbeniuk beat J. McLaughlin 5-1; T. Griffiths beat O'Boye 5-1;
D. Martin beat G. Foulds 5-4; Spencer beat W. Thorne 5-3; J. Campbell beat Browne
5-2; W. Jones beat Dennis Taylor 5-2; Kearney beat M. Macleod 5-0; Dodd beat
D. Mountjoy 5-4; C. Wilson beat Williamson 5-4; K. Stevens beat Chaperon 5-3; B. West
beat Jonik 5-4; C. Thorburn beat Cripsey 5-0; D. Reynolds beat King 5-4; S. Davis beat
Jenkins 5-0; J. Virgo beat M. Bennett 5-3; T. Meo beat John Rea 5-4; S. Longworth beat
Murphy 5-3; R. Williams beat Morra 5-2; E. Charlton beat Fisher 5-0; A. Higgins beat
Roscoe 5-2; J. Parrott beat T. Jones 5-2; Fowler beat A. Knowles 5-4; M. Hallett beat
Mikkelsen 5-3; Hendry beat R. Reardon 5-3; Wright beat E. Hughes 5-4; S. Francisco
beat Van Rensberg 5-4; B. Harris beat J. Wych 5-3; J. Johnson beat Sinclair 5-0;
P. Francisco beat Gauvreau 5-3
Fourth round: White beat Bradley 5-0; Duggan beat Werbeniuk 5-0; Griffiths beat
Martin 5-4; Campbell beat Spencer 5-3; W. Jones beat Kearney 5-1; Wilson beat Dodd
5-4; West beat Stevens 5-3; Reynolds beat Thorburn 5-4; S. Davis beat Virgo 5-2; Meo
beat Longworth 5-0; Charlton beat Williams 5-4; Parrott beat Higgins 5-2; Fowler beat
Hallett 5-4; Hendry beat Wright 5-1; S. Francisco beat N. Harris 5-3; P. Francisco beat
Johnson 5-3
Fifth round: White beat Duggan 5-2; Griffiths beat Campbell 5-3; Wilson beat W. Jones
5-3; Reynolds beat West 5-3; S. Davis beat Meo 5-2; Parrott beat Charlton 5-4; Hendry
beat Fowler 5-4; S. Francisco beat P. Francisco 5-1
Quarter-finals: White beat Griffiths 5-3; Reynolds beat Wilson 5-1; S. Davis beat Parrott
5-4; Hendry beat S. Francisco 5-0
Semi-finals: White beat Reynolds 9-8; S. Davis beat Hendry 9-3
Final: S. Davis beat White 13-12

1988

First round: D. Roe beat W. Kelly 5-1; J. Donnelly beat N. Gilbert 5-2; A. Harris beat
G. Jenkins 5-4; M. Morra beat R. Marshall 5-0; B. Rowswell beat J. Chambers 5-2;
R. Foldvari beat D. Greaves 5-3; D. Hughes beat I. Williamson 5-3; Glen Wilkinson beat
D. Chalmers 5-3; D. Gilbert beat Jack Rea 5-2; C. Everton beat J. Meadowcroft 5-3;
B. Oliver beat P. Burke 5-2; M. Clark *wo* B. Mikkelsen *scr*; Gary Wilkinson *wo*
M. Watterson *scr*; G. Rigitano *wo* J. Hargreaves *scr*; F. Jonik beat J. Dunning 5-2;
M. Smith beat J. Fitzmaurice 5-2; M. Fisher *wo* E. McLaughlin *scr*; T. Whitthread beat
P. Fagan 5-2; J. Bear beat J. Smith 5-3; E. Sinclair beat E. Lawlor 5-3; C. Roscoe beat
P. Watchorn 5-2; D. Sheehan beat D. Heaton 5-2; V. Harris beat F. Ellis 5-1; S. Meakin
beat M. Darrington 5-4; P. Gibson beat I. Black 5-2
Second round: L. Dodd beat Roe 5-2; Donnelly beat S. Duggan 5-4; T. Jones beat
A. Harris 5-2; Morra beat M. Gauvreau 5-4; Rowswell beat D. O'Kane 5-4; R. Edmonds
beat Foldvari 5-4; T. Chappel beat D. Hughes 5-3; B. Werbeniuk beat Glen Wilkinson
5-2; J. Van Rensberg beat R. Grace 5-3; D. Gilbert beat B. Harris 5-4; M. Bradley beat
Everton 5-2; Oliver beat W. King 5-3; Clark beat J. Wych 5-2; M. Bennett beat Miles
5-1; R. Reardon beat Gary Wilkinson 5-3; S. Newbury beat A. Kearney 5-1;
R. Chaperon beat P. Medati 5-3; Rigitano beat D. Fowler 5-2; M. Wildman beat Jonik
5-4; M. Smith beat P. Browne 5-1; K. Owers beat Fisher 5-0; G. Cripsey beat M. Gibson
5-4; Whitthread beat G. Foulds 5-3; G. Scott beat Bear 5-3; J. Wright beat Sinclair 5-3;
Roscoe beat W. Jones 5-4; J. O'Boye beat Sheehan 5-3; T. Murphy beat V. Harris 5-2;
F. Davis beat Meakin 5-4; J. McLaughlin beat P. Gibson 5-4; S. James beat P. Houlihan
5-2; John Rea beat R. Bales 5-0
Third round: S. Davis beat Dodd 5-0; Donnelly beat M. Macleod 5-4; A. Higgins beat
T. Jones 5-0; T. Meo beat Morra 5-1; S. Francisco beat Rowswell 5-3; S. Longworth beat
Edmonds 5-3; J. Johnson beat Chappel 5-2; S. Hendry beat Werbeniuk 5-2; T. Griffiths
beat Van Rensberg 5-2; C. Wilson beat D. Gilbert 5-3; W. Thorne beat Bradley 5-1;

B. West beat Oliver 5-3; Clark beat M. Hallett 5-4; M. Bennett beat K. Stevens 5-2; C. Thorburn beat Reardon 5-3; Newbury beat E. Hughes 5-1; N. Foulds beat Chaperon 5-1; J. Virgo beat Rigitano 5-2; J. Parrott beat Wildman 5-2; David Taylor beat M. Smith 5-3; Owers beat R. Williams 5-3; P. Francisco beat Cripsey 5-2; Dennis Taylor beat Whitthread 5-2; T. Drago beat Scott 5-3; A. Knowles beat Wright 5-1; Roscoe beat E. Charlton 5-3; D. Reynolds beat O'Boye 5-3; Murphy beat J. Campbell 5-3; D. Mountjoy beat F. Davis 5-0; D. Martin beat J. McLaughlin 5-2; J. White beat James 5-1; J. Spencer beat John Rea 5-3
Fourth round: S. Davis beat Donnelly 5-0; Higgins beat Meo 5-3; S. Francisco beat Longworth 5-2; Hendry beat Johnson 5-2; Griffiths beat Wilson 5-2; West beat Thorne 5-2; Clark beat M. Bennett 5-2; Newbury beat Thorburn 5-3; Virgo beat N. Foulds 5-3; Parrott beat David Taylor 5-0; P. Francisco beat Owers 5-0; Dennis Taylor beat Drago 5-0; Knowles beat Roscoe 5-0; Murphy beat Reynolds 5-4; Martin beat Mountjoy 5-4; White beat Spencer 5-1
Fifth round: S. Davis beat Higgins 5-0; Hendry beat S. Francisco 5-3; Griffiths beat West 5-2; Newbury beat Clark 5-2; Parrott beat Virgo 5-0; Dennis Taylor beat P. Francisco 5-3; Knowles beat Murphy 5-3; Martin beat White 5-2
Quarter-finals: S. Davis beat Hendry 5-3; Newbury beat Griffiths 5-4; Parrott beat Dennis Taylor 5-1; Knowles beat Martin 5-1
Semi-finals: S. Davis beat Newbury 9-2; Parrott beat Knowles 9-4
Final: S. Davis beat Parrott 13-11

BENSON AND HEDGES MASTERS

First staged 1975. **Sponsors** Benson and Hedges. **Venue** West Centre Hotel (1975), New London Theatre (1976–78), Wembley Conference Centre (1979–). **Initial prize-money** £5,000. **Prize-money last season** £225,000. **TV** BBC.

1975
First round: J. Pulman beat C. Thorburn 5-3; A. Higgins beat B. Werbeniuk 5-0
Quarter-finals: E. Charlton beat F. Davis 5-3; J. Spencer beat Pulman 5-3; R. Reardon beat G. Miles 5-3; R. Williams beat Higgins 5-3
Semi-finals: Spencer beat Charlton 5-2; Reardon beat Williams 5-4
Final: Spencer beat Reardon 9-8

1976
First round: F. Davis beat C. Thorburn 4-2; J. Pulman beat Dennis Taylor 4-2
Quarter-finals: G. Miles beat A. Higgins 4-1; R. Reardon beat Pulman 4-1; J. Spencer beat F. Davis 4-0; E. Charlton beat R. Williams 4-1
Semi-finals: Miles beat Spencer 5-4; Reardon beat Charlton 5-4
Final: Reardon beat Miles 7-3

1977
First round: D. Mountjoy beat J. Pulman 4-2; J. Spencer beat Dennis Taylor 4-2
Quarter-finals: R. Reardon beat R. Williams 4-1; G. Miles beat Spencer 4-1; A. Higgins beat P. Mans 4-2; Mountjoy beat F. Davis 4-2
Semi-finals: Mountjoy beat Higgins 5-3; Reardon beat Miles 5-2
Final: Mountjoy beat Reardon 7-6

1978
First round: J. Pulman beat P. Fagan 4-2; G. Miles beat F. Davis 4-3
Quarter-finals: J. Spencer beat Pulman 4-2; A. Higgins beat Dennis Taylor 4-3; C. Thorburn beat D. Mountjoy 4-2; R. Reardon beat Miles 4-1
Semi-finals: Higgins beat Reardon 5-1; Thorburn beat Spencer 5-3
Final: Higgins beat Thorburn 7-5

1979
First round: D. Mountjoy beat F. Davis 5-2; David Taylor beat P. Fagan 5-4
Quarter-finals: A. Higgins beat E. Charlton 5-2; P. Mans beat C. Thorburn 5-4;
Mountjoy beat Spencer 5-0; R. Reardon beat Taylor 5-2
Semi-finals: Higgins beat Mountjoy 5-1; Mans beat Reardon 5-3
Final: Mans beat Higgins 8-4

1980
First round: C. Thorburn beat J. Virgo 5-3; A. Higgins beat F. Davis 5-1
Quarter-finals: R. Reardon beat Dennis Taylor 5-3; T. Griffiths beat Thorburn 5-3;
J. Spencer beat E. Charlton 5-2; Higgins beat P. Mans 5-1
Semi-finals: Griffiths beat Spencer 5-0; Higgins beat Reardon 5-2
Final: Griffiths beat Higgins 9-5

1981
First round: P. Mans beat S. Davis 5-3; D. Mountjoy beat E. Charlton 5-0; F. Davis beat
K. Stevens 5-4; J. Spencer beat Dennis Taylor 5-2
Quarter-finals: A. Higgins beat Mountjoy 5-1; C. Thorburn beat Mans 5-4; Spencer beat
R. Reardon 5-1; T. Griffiths beat F. Davis 5-2
Semi-finals: Higgins beat Thorburn 6-5; Griffiths beat Spencer 6-5
Final: Higgins beat Griffiths 9-6

1982
First round: R. Reardon beat Dennis Taylor 5-3; D. Mountjoy beat J. Spencer 5-4;
T. Meo beat David Taylor 5-2; E. Charlton beat J. White 5-4
Quarter-finals: Meo beat C. Thorburn 5-0; S. Davis beat Mountjoy 5-2; A. Higgins beat
Charlton 5-1; T. Griffiths beat Reardon 5-3
Semi-finals: S. Davis beat Meo 6-4; Griffiths beat Higgins 6-5
Final: S. Davis beat Griffiths 9-5

1983
First round: B. Werbeniuk beat A. Higgins 5-4; E. Charlton beat T. Meo 5-3; T. Griffiths
beat K. Stevens 5-3; C. Thorburn beat J. Johnson 5-2; R. Reardon beat D. Reynolds 5-1;
D. Mountjoy beat J. Virgo 5-1; S. Davis beat M. Wildman 5-2; J. White beat David
Taylor 5-2
Quarter-finals: Charlton beat Werbeniuk 5-3; Thorburn beat Griffiths 5-3; Reardon beat
White 5-2; Mountjoy beat S. Davis 5-4
Semi-finals: Thorburn beat Charlton 6-5; Reardon beat Mountjoy 6-3
Final: Thorburn beat Reardon 9-7

1984
First round: A. Knowles beat Dennis Taylor 5-2; R. Reardon beat J. Virgo 5-3;
J. Spencer beat C. Thorburn 5-4; T. Griffiths beat B. Werbeniuk 5-1; J. White beat
E. Charlton 5-2; A. Higgins beat D. Mountjoy 5-2; K. Stevens beat David Taylor 5-1;
S. Davis beat T. Meo 5-0
Quarter-finals: Griffiths beat Spencer 5-4; Knowles beat Higgins 5-1; White beat
Reardon 5-3; Stevens beat S. Davis 5-3
Semi-finals: Griffiths beat Knowles 6-4; White beat Stevens 6-4
Final: White beat Griffiths 9-5

1985
First round: J. White beat W. Thorne 5-2; J. Spencer beat E. Charlton 5-3; R. Reardon
beat David Taylor 5-1; C. Thorburn beat Dennis Taylor 5-3; D. Mountjoy beat
A. Knowles 5-3; T. Meo beat K. Stevens 5-2; T. Griffiths beat B. Werbeniuk 5-2;
A. Higgins beat S. Davis 5-4
Quarter-finals: White beat Spencer 5-2; Thorburn beat Reardon 5-0; Mountjoy beat Meo
5-4; Griffiths beat Higgins 5-1
Semi-finals: Thorburn beat White 6-4; Mountjoy beat Griffiths 6-2
Final: Thorburn beat Mountjoy 9-6

1986
First round: C. Thorburn beat J. Johnson 5-3; T. Griffiths beat A. Higgins 5-4;
E. Charlton beat K. Stevens 5-4; A. Knowles beat S. Francisco 5-1; S. Davis beat David
Taylor 5-4; W. Thorne beat R. Reardon 5-4; J. White beat T. Meo 5-4; Dennis Taylor
beat D. Mountjoy 5-2
Quarter-finals: Thorburn beat Griffiths 5-2; Knowles beat Charlton 5-4; S. Davis beat
Thorne 5-4; White beat Dennis Taylor 5-3
Semi-finals: Thorburn beat Knowles 6-4; White beat S. Davis 6-3
Final: Thorburn beat White 9-5

1987
First round: C. Thorburn beat R. Williams 5-1; W. Thorne beat K. Stevens 5-3;
S. Francisco beat A. Knowles 5-2; Dennis Taylor beat N. Foulds 5-2; D. Mountjoy beat
S. Davis 5-2; T. Meo beat J. White 5-4; A. Higgins beat T. Griffiths 5-4; J. Johnson beat
R. Reardon 5-2
Quarter-finals: Thorburn beat Thorne 5-3; Taylor beat S. Francisco 5-3; Meo beat
Mountjoy 5-4; Higgins beat Johnson 5-1
Semi-finals: Taylor beat Thorburn 6-5; Higgins beat Meo 6-2
Final: Taylor beat Higgins 9-8

1988
First round: M. Hallett beat Dennis Taylor 5-3; A. Higgins beat A. Knowles 5-4;
C. Thorburn beat R. Williams 5-3; J. Parrott beat N. Foulds 5-4; J. White beat
D. Mountjoy 5-0; J. Johnson beat W. Thorne 5-4; T. Griffiths beat S. Francisco 5-3;
S. Davis beat D. Reynolds 5-2
Quarter-finals: Hallett beat Higgins 5-2; Parrott beat Thorburn 5-4; Johnson beat White
5-3; S. Davis beat Griffiths 5-0
Semi-finals: Hallett beat Parrott 6-5; S. Davis beat Johnson 6-3
Final: S. Davis beat M. Hallett 9-0

MIM BRITANNIA BRITISH OPEN

First staged 1985. **Sponsors** Dulux (1985–87), MIM Britannia (1988). **Venue**
Assembly Rooms, Derby. **Initial prize-money** £250,000. **Prize-money last season**
£300,000. **TV** ITV.

1985 (*Dulux*)
Qualifying: T. Chappel beat I. Williamson 6-5; D. Chalmers beat P. Burke 6-5; John Rea
beat M. Fisher 6-0; W. King beat P. Medati 6-4; D. Fowler beat C. Everton 6-1;
T. Murphy beat D. Sheehan 6-3; R. Foldvari beat S. Duggan 6-4; V. Harris beat L. Dodd
6-1; T. Jones beat G. Foulds 6-0; P. Francisco beat B. Kelly 6-3; D. O'Kane beat
G. Cripsey 6-4; S. Newbury beat P. Browne 6-0; M. Bradley beat M. Morra 6-2;
A. Kearney beat M. Watterson 6-4; D. French beat E. McLaughlin 6-0; R. Chaperon
beat P. Fagan 6-5; B. Harris beat J. Meadowcroft 6-1; S. Longworth beat F. Davis 6-1;
B. Mikkelsen beat D. Hughes 6-0; G. Scott beat M. Darrington 6-3; J. Giannaros beat
C. Roscoe 6-1; F. Jonik beat J. McLaughlin 6-2; W. Jones beat J. Donnelly 6-1;
P. Watchorn beat J. Fitzmaurice 6-1; R. Bales beat I. Black 6-4; M. Gauvreau beat
D. Greaves 6-3; M. Gibson beat B. Demarco 6-1; R. Edmonds beat D. Mienie 6-1
First round: D. Reynolds beat Giannaros 6-3; M. Macleod beat Murphy 6-5; E. Hughes
beat Watchorn 6-4; Longworth beat C. Wilson 6-3; W. Jones beat J. Johnson 6-5;
M. Hallett *wo* Mikkelsen *scr*; C. Thorburn beat G. Rigitano 6-3; A. Higgins beat Bales
6-3; Chaperon beat B. Werbeniuk 6-1; S. Francisco beat Kearney 6-4; T. Meo beat
Foldvari 6-0; W. Thorne beat W. Oliver 6-3; B. Harris beat E. Charlton 6-3; J. White
beat T. Jones 6-5; A. Knowles beat French 6-2; N. Foulds beat J. Hargreaves 6-1;
Newbury beat E. Sinclair 6-3; M. Wildman beat Gibson 6-1; J. Spencer beat Jonik 6-0;

V. Harris beat D. Mountjoy 6-5; O'Kane beat J. Campbell 6-4; G. Miles beat Edmonds 6-1; T. Griffiths beat Chalmers 6-0; R. Reardon beat King 6-5; J. Parrott beat John Rea 6-4; Bradley beat David Taylor 6-3; K. Stevens beat Gauvreau 6-3; J. Virgo beat P. Francisco 6-2; Fowler beat R. Williams 6-4; D. Martin beat B. Bennett 6-0; S. Davis beat Chappel 6-5; Dennis Taylor beat Scott 6-2
Second round: Newbury beat Griffiths 5-3; Bradley beat Fowler 5-4; S. Davis beat Virgo 5-2; Knowles beat Longworth 5-2; O'Kane beat V. Harris 5-3; Thorburn beat Reynolds 5-3; Higgins beat N. Foulds 5-1; Dennis Taylor beat Parrott 5-2; Macleod beat Thorne 5-0; Martin beat Reardon 5-4; Miles beat Spencer 5-3; S. Francisco beat White 5-4; Meo beat Hallett 5-4; E. Hughes beat B. Harris 5-4; Stevens beat Wildman 5-2; Chaperon beat W. Jones 5-2
Third round: Meo beat Knowles 5-2; S. Davis beat Bradley 5-2; O'Kane beat Martin 5-4; S. Francisco beat Chaperon 5-2; Dennis Taylor beat Newbury 5-3; E. Hughes beat Macleod 5-2; Stevens beat Miles 5-2; Higgins beat Thorburn 5-2
Quarter-finals: Stevens beat Dennis Taylor 5-2; S. Davis beat O'Kane 5-1; S. Francisco beat Meo 5-4; Higgins beat E. Hughes 5-2
Semi-finals: Stevens beat S. Davis 9-7; S. Francisco beat Higgins 9-6
Final: S. Francisco beat Stevens 12-9

1986 (*Dulux*)
First round: J. O'Boye beat Jim Bear 5-1; J. Hargreaves *wo* G. Watson *scr*; O. Agrawal beat D. Greaves 5-3; D. Gilbert beat P. Burke 5-1; S. Hendry beat D. Hughes 5-1; G. Wilkinson beat P. Watchorn 5-4; D. Sheehan beat S. Simngam 5-2; G. Jenkins beat B. Demarco 5-1; B. West beat B. Bennett 5-1; G. Cripsey beat M. Darrington 5-4; P. Houlihan *wo* G. Robinson *scr*; A. Kearney beat M. Smith 5-2; R. Bales beat M. Parkin 5-1; T. Drago *wo* D. Mienie *scr*
Second round: T. Jones beat O'Boye 5-2; F. Davis beat W. Kelly 5-4; G. Scott beat D. Chalmers 5-1; Hargreaves beat R. Edmonds 5-3; L. Dodd beat F. Jonik 5-4; W. Jones beat G. Rigitano 5-1; G. Miles beat Agrawal 5-4; R. Chaperon beat V. Harris 5-0; John Rea beat W. King 5-1; D. Fowler beat T. Chappel 5-4; Gilbert beat M. Morra 5-4; P. Browne beat Hendry 5-0; J. Donnelly beat Wilkinson 5-4; S. Newbury beat W. Oliver 5-2; Sheehan *wo* M. Watterson *scr*; Jenkins beat J. Meadowcroft 5-2; I. Black beat M. Gibson 5-0; B. Harris beat E. Sinclair 5-3; P. Medati beat C. Everton 5-1; West beat E. McLaughlin 5-3; P. Fagan beat J. Fitzmaurice 5-4; C. Roscoe beat B. Mikkelsen 5-4; I. Williamson beat Cripsey 5-4; J. Wych beat J. Van Rensberg 5-0; P. Francisco beat G. Foulds 5-2; S. Longworth beat Houlihan 5-3; M. Bradley beat Jack Rea 5-1; S. Duggan beat T. Murphy 5-1; J. McLaughlin beat M. Fisher 5-3; R. Foldvari beat Kearney 5-2; Bales *wo* J. Dunning *scr*; Drago beat M. Gauvreau 5-3
Third round: S. Francisco beat T. Jones 5-2; M. Macleod beat F. Davis 5-4; T. Griffiths beat Scott 5-3; N. Foulds beat Hargreaves 5-4; W. Thorne beat Dodd 5-2; P. Mans beat W. Jones 5-2; K. Stevens beat Miles 5-3; C. Wilson beat Chaperon 5-3; John Rea beat R. Reardon 5-3; J. Virgo beat Fowler 5-1; E. Charlton beat Gilbert 5-2; Browne beat J. Spencer 5-0; T. Meo beat Donnelly 5-3; Newbury beat D. O'Kane 5-3; C. Thorburn beat Sheehan 5-0; M. Wildman beat Jenkins 5-4; S. Davis beat Black 5-2; D. Martin beat B. Harris 5-1; Medati beat David Taylor 5-1; J. Campbell beat West 5-4; Fagan beat D. Mountjoy 5-1; J. Parrott beat Roscoe 5-2; A. Knowles beat Williamson 5-1; Wych beat D. Reynolds 5-3; P. Francisco beat J. White 5-4; Longworth beat E. Hughes 5-4; A. Higgins beat Bradley 5-3; M. Hallett beat Duggan 5-3; J. Johnson beat J. McLaughlin 5-2; B. Werbeniuk beat Foldvari 5-4; Bales beat Dennis Taylor 5-4; R. Williams beat Drago 5-1
Fourth round: Macleod beat S. Francisco 5-1; Griffiths beat N. Foulds 5-3; Thorne beat Mans 5-1; Stevens beat Wilson 5-0; Virgo beat John Rea 5-0; Charlton beat Browne 5-1; Meo beat Newbury 5-0; Thorne beat Wildman 5-1; S. Davis beat Martin 5-1; Campbell beat Medati 5-4; Parrott beat Fagan 5-0; Wych beat Knowles 5-4; P. Francisco beat Longworth 5-2; Higgins beat Hallett 5-1; Werbeniuk beat Johnson 5-3; Williams beat Bales 5-4

Fifth round: Griffiths beat Macleod 5-2; Thorne beat Stevens 5-4; Virgo beat Charlton 5-4; Meo beat Thorburn 5-3; S. Davis beat Campbell 5-0; Wych beat Parrott 5-4; Higgins beat P. Francisco 5-2; Werbeniuk beat Williams 5-3
Quarter-finals: Thorne beat Griffiths 5-4; Virgo beat Meo 5-3; S. Davis beat Wych 5-2; Higgins beat Werbeniuk 5-1
Semi-finals: Thorne beat Virgo 9-4; S. Davis beat Higgins 9-3
Final: S. Davis beat Thorne 12-7

1987 (*Dulux*)
First round: M. Morra beat M. Bennett 5-4; B. Rowswell beat G. Jenkins 5-1; G. Foulds beat D. Greaves 5-3; D. Roe beat M. Watterson 5-3; B. Kelly beat B. Bennett 5-2; P. Gibson beat O. Agrawal 5-0; N. Gilbert beat P. Houlihan 5-4; J. Hargreaves beat M. Parkin 5-4; J. Donnelly *wo* L. Heywood *scr*; C. Roscoe beat D. Mienie 5-2; F. Ellis beat M. Smith 5-2; D. Chalmers *wo* S. Simngam *scr*; P. Watchorn beat J. Dunning 5-2; K. Owers beat F. Jonik 5-4; M. Fisher *wo* C. Everton *scr*; R. Grace beat J. Meadowcroft 5-4; G. Wilkinson beat J. Fitzmaurice 5-0; T. Kearney *wo* Jim Bear *scr*; G. Rigitano beat B. Demarco 5-1; S. James beat M. Darrington 5-3; T. Whitthread beat D. Hughes 5-1; P. Burke *wo* E. McLaughlin *scr*; B. Oliver beat Jack Rea 5-1; D. Sheehan beat J. Wright 5-2
Second round: M. Gauvreau beat R. Bales 5-0; Morra beat J. Van Rensberg 5-1; Rowswell beat D. O'Kane 5-4; G. Foulds beat R. Edmonds 5-3; Roe beat I. Black 5-0; W. King beat Williamson 5-3; B. Harris beat Kelly 5-2; S. Duggan beat Gibson 5-3; D. Fowler beat Dodd 5-1; N. Gilbert beat W. Jones 5-3; J. O'Boye beat M. Bradley 5-1; T. Murphy beat D. Gilbert 5-4; Hargreaves beat John Rea 5-3; T. Jones beat Donnelly 5-2; Roscoe beat S. Newbury 5-3; P. Medati beat Ellis 5-0; M. Wildman beat Chalmers 5-0; G. Cripsey beat Watchorn 5-4; Owers beat F. Davis 5-3; E. Sinclair beat S. Hendry 5-2; R. Chaperon beat Fisher 5-2; Grace beat P. Fagan 5-3; J. McLaughlin beat M. Gibson 5-1; Wilkinson beat Mans 5-2; T. Chappel beat Kearney 5-3; Rigitano beat P. Browne 5-4; R. Foldvari beat B. Mikkelsen 5-3; James beat G. Miles 5-2; J. Spencer beat Whitthread 5-2; G. Scott beat Burke 5-2; T. Drago beat Oliver 5-1; V. Harris beat Sheehan 5-4
Third round: S. Davis beat Gauvreau 5-0; J. Virgo beat Morra 5-3; S. Francisco beat Rowswell 5-0; C. Wilson beat G. Foulds 5-3; N. Foulds beat Roe 5-1; King beat J. Parrott 5-1; W. Thorne beat B. Harris 5-1; Duggan beat S. Longworth 5-2; A. Knowles beat Fowler 5-4; D. Reynolds beat N. Gilbert 5-2; R. Reardon beat O'Boye 5-4; Murphy beat J. Wych 5-1; T. Griffiths beat John Rea 5-2; T. Jones beat M. Macleod 5-4; Dennis Taylor beat Roscoe 5-1; E. Charlton beat Medati 5-4; C. Thorburn beat Wildman 5-3; Cripsey beat B. Werbeniuk 5-2; D. Mountjoy beat Owers 5-1; P. Francisco beat Sinclair 5-3; K. Stevens beat Chaperon 5-4; B. West beat Grace 5-2; J. McLaughlin beat A. Higgins 5-4; David Taylor beat Wilkinson 5-4; J. White beat Chappel 5-1; M. Hallett beat Rigitano 5-1; R. Williams beat Foldvari 5-4; James beat J. Campbell 5-1; Spencer beat T. Meo 5-1; D. Martin beat Scott 5-3; J. Johnson beat Drago 5-0; E. Hughes beat V. Harris 5-1
Fourth round: Virgo beat S. Davis 5-4; Wilson beat S. Francisco 5-4; N. Foulds beat King 5-4; Thorne beat Duggan 5-2; Knowles beat Reynolds 5-0; Murphy beat Reardon 5-4; Griffiths beat T. Jones 5-3; Dennis Taylor beat Charlton 5-1; Thorburn beat Cripsey 5-2; Mountjoy beat P. Francisco 5-3; Stevens beat West 5-4; David Taylor beat J. McLaughlin 5-2; White beat Hallett 5-2; Williams beat James 5-2; Spencer beat Martin 5-2; Johnson beat E. Hughes 5-3
Fifth round: Virgo beat Wilson 5-2; N. Foulds beat Thorne 5-2; Knowles beat Murphy 5-3; Dennis Taylor beat Griffiths 5-4; Thorburn beat Mountjoy 5-4; David Taylor beat Stevens 5-2; White beat Williams 5-0; Spencer beat Johnson 5-3
Quarter-finals: N. Foulds beat Virgo 5-3; Knowles beat Dennis Taylor 5-4; Thorburn beat David Taylor 5-3; White beat Spencer 5-3
Semi-finals: N. Foulds beat Knowles 9-2; White beat Thorburn 9-5
Final: White beat N. Foulds 13-9

1988
First round: M. Clark beat M. Fisher 5-1; J. Bear beat A. Harris 5-2; Gary Wilkinson beat I. Black 5-2; J. Fitzmaurice *wo* C. Everton *scr*; G. Rigitano beat R. Marshall 5-2; M. Morra beat P. Watchorn 5-1; F. Ellis *wo* M. Watterson *scr*; D. Hughes beat P. Fagan 5-4; N. Gilbert beat D. Sheehan 5-3; J. Dunning beat F. Jonik 5-3; P. Thornley beat V. Harris 5-4; C. Roscoe beat P. Gibson 5-4; B. Oliver beat M. Smith 5-0; M. Darrington beat P. Burke 5-4; R. Foldvari beat D. Heaton 5-1; J. Meadowcroft beat B. Kelly 5-1; T. Whitthread beat Glen Wilkinson 5-4; D. Chalmers *wo* B. Mikkelsen *scr*; E. Lawlor beat E. Sinclair 5-3; B. Rowswell beat Jack Rea 5-1; D. Gilbert *wo* E. McLaughlin *scr*; I. Williamson beat S. Meakin 5-1; J. Donnelly beat D. Greaves 5-4; G. Jenkins beat J. Smith 5-3; J. Van Rensberg *wo* J. Hargreaves *scr*; D. Roe beat J. Chambers 5-3
Second round: Clark beat R. Grace 5-0; S. James beat W. King 5-2; Bear beat P. Houlihan 5-0; Gary Wilkinson beat R. Bales 5-1; T. Jones beat Fitzmaurice 5-3; R. Chaperon beat Rigitano 5-2; Morra beat M. Bennett 5-2; T. Chappel beat Ellis 5-0; G. Miles beat K. Owers 5-2; F. Davis beat D. Hughes 5-2; N. Gilbert beat Werbeniuk 5-1; Dunning beat G. Scott 5-3; J. Wych beat Thornley 5-1; Roscoe beat M. Wildman 5-0; S. Newbury beat Oliver 5-3; P. Medati beat M. Gauvreau 5-1; D. Fowler beat A. Kearney 5-1; Darrington beat L. Dodd 5-4; Foldvari beat G. Foulds 5-3; T. Murphy beat Meadowcroft 5-4; D. O'Kane beat Whitthread 5-2; P. Browne beat Chalmers 5-2; Lawlor beat B. Harris 5-2; Rowswell beat J. McLaughlin 5-2; M. Gibson beat S. Duggan 5-2; D. Gilbert beat J. Wright 5-2; Williamson beat M. Bradley 5-3; G. Cripsey beat Donnelly 5-4; J. O'Boye beat Jenkins 5-1; W. Jones beat John Rea 5-3; R. Reardon beat Van Rensberg 5-3; Roe beat R. Edmonds 5-1
Third round: J. White beat Clark 5-2; James beat E. Charlton 5-2; S. Francisco beat Bear 5-0; Gary Wilkinson beat T. Meo 5-2; T. Jones beat A. Higgins 5-3; Chaperon *wo* K. Stevens *scr*; J. Griffiths beat Morra 5-1; S. Hendry beat Chappel 5-1; Dennis Taylor beat Miles 5-1; J. Spencer beat F. Davis 5-0; R. Williams beat N. Gilbert 5-2; B. West beat Dunning 5-0; W. Thorne beat Wych 5-1; C. Wilson beat Roscoe 5-2; C. Thorburn beat Newbury 5-2; Medati beat David Taylor 5-4; N. Foulds beat Fowler 5-3; P. Francisco beat Darrington 5-1; J. Parrott beat Foldvari 5-1; J. Virgo beat Murphy 5-1; O'Kane beat Mountjoy 5-3; Browne beat D. Martin 5-4; J. Johnson beat Lawlor 5-1; Rowswell beat S. Longworth 5-4; A. Knowles beat M. Gibson 5-4; M. Macleod beat D. Gilbert 5-4; M. Hallett beat Williamson 5-0; Cripsey beat E. Hughes 5-3; O'Boye beat Reynolds 5-2; J. Campbell beat W. Jones 5-3; Reardon beat S. Davis 5-0; Roe beat T. Drago 5-3
Fourth round: White beat James 5-1; Gary Wilkinson beat S. Francisco 5-3; T. Jones beat Chaperon 5-4; Hendry beat Griffiths 5-1; Spencer beat Dennis Taylor 5-0; Williams beat West 5-0; Thorne beat Wilson 5-3; Thorburn beat Medati 5-2; N. Foulds beat P. Francisco 5-3; Parrott beat Virgo 5-1; O'Kane beat Browne 5-2; Johnson beat Rowswell 5-2; Macleod beat Knowles 5-4; Hallett beat Cripsey 5-2; O'Boye beat Campbell 5-1; Roe beat Reardon 5-2
Fifth round: White beat Gary Wilkinson 5-1; Hendry beat T. Jones 5-3; Williams beat Spencer 5-4; Thorburn beat Thorne 5-2; Parrott beat N. Foulds 5-0; O'Kane beat Johnson 5-2; Hallett beat Macleod 5-2; O'Boye beat Roe 5-1
Quarter-finals: Hendry beat White 5-4; Thorburn beat Williams 5-2; Parrott beat O'Kane 5-2; Hallett beat O'Boye 5-4
Semi-finals: Hendry beat Thorburn 9-5; Hallett beat Parrott 9-8
Final: Hendry beat Hallett 13-2

FERSINA WORLD CUP

First staged 1979. **Sponsors** State Express (1979–83), Guinness (1985), Car Care Plan (1986), Tuborg (1987), Fersina Windows (1988–). **Venue** The Hexagon, Reading (1979–83), Bournemouth International Centre (1985–). **Initial prize-money** £27,500. **Prize-money last season** £125,000. **TV** BBC.

1979 (*State Express World Team Classic*)
Group A
England (F. Davis, G. Miles, J. Spencer) beat Rest of World (P. Mans, J. Van Rensberg, P. Fagan) 8-7; England beat Northern Ireland (Jack Rea, A. Higgins, Dennis Taylor) 8-7; Northern Ireland beat Rest of World 8-7
Group B
Wales (R. Reardon, T. Griffiths, D. Mountjoy) beat Canada (C. Thorburn, K. Stevens, B. Werbeniuk) 9-6; Australia (E. Charlton, G. Owen, P. Morgan) beat Canada 8-7; Wales beat Australia 9-6
Final: Wales beat England 14-3

1980 (*State Express World Team Classic*)
Group A
Wales (R. Reardon, T. Griffiths, D. Mountjoy) beat Canada (C. Thorburn, K. Stevens, B. Werbeniuk) 10-5; Canada beat Rest of World (J. Rempe, E. Sinclair, P. Mans) 9-6; Wales beat Rest of World 13-2
Group B
England (F. Davis, J. Virgo, David Taylor) beat Ireland (A. Higgins, Dennis Taylor, P. Fagan) 11-4; Australia (E. Charlton, I. Anderson, P. Morgan) beat England 8-7; Ireland beat Australia 10-5
Semi-finals: Wales beat Ireland 8-7; Canada beat England 8-5
Final: Wales beat Canada 8-5

1981 (*State Express World Team Classic*)
Preliminary match: Republic of Ireland (E. Hughes, P. Fagan, D. Sheehan) beat Scotland (I. Black, M. Macleod, E. Sinclair) 4-2
Group A
England (S. Davis, J. Spencer, David Taylor) beat Australia (I. Anderson, E. Charlton, P. Morgan) 4-3; Northern Ireland (T. Murphy, Dennis Taylor, A. Higgins) beat Australia 4-1; England beat Northern Ireland 4-3
Group B
Wales (R. Reardon, D. Mountjoy, T. Griffiths) beat Canada (K. Stevens, C. Thorburn, B. Werbeniuk) 4-2; Wales beat Republic of Ireland 4-0; Canada beat Republic of Ireland 4-2
Semi-finals: England beat Canada 4-2; Wales beat Northern Ireland 4-3
Final: England beat Wales 4-3

1982 (*State Express World Team Classic*)
Preliminary match: Scotland (E. Sinclair, J. Donnelly, I. Black) beat Republic of Ireland (E. Hughes, P. Fagan, D. Sheehan) 4-2
Group A
England (A. Knowles, S. Davis, J. White) beat Northern Ireland (A. Higgins, T. Murphy, Dennis Taylor) 4-3; Scotland beat Northern Ireland 4-1; England beat Scotland 4-1
Group B
Canada (C. Thorburn, B. Werbeniuk, K. Stevens) beat Wales (T. Griffiths, D. Mountjoy, R. Reardon) 4-3; Canada beat Australia (E. Charlton, P. Morgan, I. Anderson) 4-0; Wales beat Australia 4-1

Semi-finals: England beat Wales 4-2; Canada beat Scotland 4-0
Final: Canada beat England 4-2

1983 (*State Express World Team Classic*)

Preliminary match: Scotland (E. Sinclair, M. Macleod, I. Black) beat Republic of Ireland (B. Kelly, E. Hughes, P. Fagan) 4-2

Group A
Wales (D. Mountjoy, R. Reardon, T. Griffiths) beat Canada (C. Thorburn, B. Werbeniuk, K. Stevens) 4-3; Canada beat Australia (E. Charlton, W. King, J. Campbell) 4-2; Wales beat Australia 4-0

Group B
England (S. Davis, A. Knowles, T. Meo) beat Northern Ireland (A. Higgins, T. Murphy, Dennis Taylor) 4-1; Northern Ireland beat Scotland 4-3; England beat Scotland 4-0
Semi-finals: Wales beat Northern Ireland 4-1; England beat Canada 4-2
Final: England beat Wales 4-2

1985 (*Guinness World Cup*)

First round: Wales beat Australia 5-4 (T. Griffiths drew with E. Charlton 1-1; D. Mountjoy beat J. Campbell 2-0; R. Reardon lost to W. King 0-2; Mountjoy drew with Charlton 1-1; Griffiths beat King 1-0); England A beat Scotland 5-4 (S. Davis lost to E. Sinclair 0-2; A. Knowles drew with M. Macleod 1-1; T. Meo beat J. Donnelly 2-0; S. Davis drew with Sinclair 1-1; Knowles beat Macleod 1-0); England B beat Rest of World 5-2 (J. White beat S. Francisco 2-0; W. Thorne drew with J. Rempe 1-1; J. Spencer drew with D. O'Kane 1-1; White beat Francisco 1-0); Ireland beat Canada 5-2 (Dennis Taylor beat K. Stevens 2-0; E. Hughes drew with C. Thorburn 1-1; A. Higgins drew with B. Werbeniuk 1-1; Higgins beat Thorburn 1-0)
Semi-finals: Ireland beat Wales 5-3 (Dennis Taylor drew with Mountjoy 1-1; E. Hughes lost to Griffiths 0-2; Higgins beat Reardon 2-0; Higgins beat Mountjoy 2-0); England A beat England B 5-2 (S. Davis beat Spencer 2-0; Knowles drew with Thorne 1-1; Meo drew with White 1-1; S. Davis beat White 1-0)
Final: Ireland beat England A 9-7 (Dennis Taylor drew with Knowles 1-1; E. Hughes lost to S. Davis 0-2; Higgins drew with Meo 1-1; Dennis Taylor drew with Knowles 1-1; Dennis Taylor drew with S. Davis 1-1; E. Hughes drew with Knowles 1-1; Higgins beat Meo 2-0; Higgins beat S. Davis 2-0)

1986 (*Car Care Plan World Cup*)

First round: Ireland A beat Ireland B 5-0 (A. Higgins beat P. Fagan 2-0; E. Hughes beat T. Murphy 2-0; Dennis Taylor beat P. Browne 1-0); Wales beat Scotland 5-1 (D. Mountjoy beat M. Macleod 2-0; R. Reardon drew with E. Sinclair 1-1; T. Griffiths beat J. Donnelly 2-0); Canada beat Rest of World 5-0 (C. Thorburn beat T. Drago 2-0; K. Stevens beat O. Agrawal 2-0; B. Werbeniuk beat S. Simngam 1-0); England beat Australia 5-2 (A. Knowles drew with J. Campbell 1-1; J. White drew with E. Charlton 1-1; S. Davis beat W. King 2-0; S. Davis beat Campbell 1-0)
Semi-finals: Ireland A beat Wales 5-2 (Higgins beat Mountjoy 2-0; Hughes lost to Reardon 0-2; Dennis Taylor beat Griffiths 2-0; Taylor beat Griffiths 1-0); Canada beat England 5-3 (Thorburn drew with Knowles 1-1; Stevens beat White 2-0; Werbeniuk drew with S. Davis 1-1; Thorburn drew with S. Davis 1-1)
Final: Ireland A beat Canada 9-7 (Dennis Taylor drew with Thorburn 1-1; Hughes lost to Stevens 0-2; Higgins beat Werbeniuk 2-0; Higgins drew with Stevens 1-1; Higgins drew with Thorburn 1-1; Hughes drew with Stevens 1-1; Taylor beat Werbeniuk 2-0; Taylor drew with Thorburn 1-1)

1987 (*Tuborg World Cup*)

First round: Wales beat Australia 5-1 (R. Reardon drew with E. Charlton 1-1; D. Mountjoy beat W. King 2-0; T. Griffiths beat J. Campbell 2-0); Ireland A beat Ireland B 5-1 (E. Hughes beat P. Browne 2-0; A. Higgins beat P. Fagan 2-0; Dennis Taylor drew with T. Murphy 1-1); Canada beat Rest of World 5-4 (K. Stevens beat

S. Francisco 2-0; C. Thorburn drew with T. Drago 1-1; B. Werbeniuk lost to D. O'Kane 0-2; Stevens drew with Drago 1-1; Thorburn beat Francisco 1-0); England beat Scotland 5-1 (J. Johnson drew with S. Hendry 1-1; S. Davis beat M. Gibson 2-0; T. Meo beat M. Macleod 2-0)
Semi-finals: Ireland A beat Wales 5-2 (Taylor lost to Griffiths 0-2; Hughes beat Reardon 2-0; Higgins beat Mountjoy 2-0; Higgins beat Griffiths 1-0); Canada beat England 5-4 (Stevens drew with Johnson 1-1; Thorburn beat Davis 2-0; Werbeniuk drew with Meo 1-1; Stevens lost to Davis 0-2; Thorburn beat Johnson 1-0)
Final: Ireland A beat Canada 9-2 (Hughes drew with Stevens 1-1; Higgins beat Thorburn 2-0; Taylor beat Werbeniuk 2-0; Taylor beat Stevens 2-0; Hughes drew with Stevens 1-1; Taylor beat Thorburn 1-0)

1988
First round: England beat Republic of Ireland 5-1 (S. Davis beat J. O'Boye 2-0; J. White beat E. Hughes 2-0; N. Foulds drew with P. Browne 1-1); Rest of World beat Northern Ireland 5-3 (D. O'Kane lost to D. Taylor 0-2; T. Drago beat A. Higgins 2-0; Drago drew with Taylor 1-1); Australia beat Canada 5-0 (J. Campbell beat J. Wych 2-0; W. King beat B. Werbeniuk 2-0; E. Charlton beat C. Thorburn 1-0); Scotland beat Wales 5-4 (M. Macleod beat D. Mountjoy 2-0; J. Rea drew with T. Griffiths 1-1; S. Hendry drew with C. Wilson 1-1; Hendry lost to Griffiths 0-2; Macleod beat Wilson 1-0)
Semi-finals: England beat Rest of World 5-3 (Davis drew with Drago 1-1; Foulds drew with O'Kane 1-1; White drew with Francisco 1-1; White beat Francisco 2-0); Australia beat Scotland 5-1 (Campbell beat Macleod 2-0; King beat Rea 2-0; Charlton drew with Hendry 1-1)
Final: England beat Australia 9-7 (Davis drew with Campbell 1-1; Foulds drew with King 1-1; White lost to Charlton 0-2; White drew with Charlton 1-1; White drew with King 1-1; Foulds drew with Campbell 1-1; Davis beat Charlton 2-0; Davis beat King 2-0)

BENSON AND HEDGES IRISH MASTERS

First staged 1978. **Sponsors** Benson and Hedges. **Venue** Goffs, Kill, Co Kildare. **Initial prize-money** £3,000. **Prize-money last season** £90,000. **TV** RTE.

1978
Final: J. Spencer beat D. Mountjoy 5-3

1979
Final: D. Mountjoy beat R. Reardon 6-5

1980
Final: T. Griffiths beat D. Mountjoy 9-8

1981
First round: Dennis Taylor beat J. Spencer 4-2; S. Davis beat J. Virgo 4-3
Quarter-finals: T. Griffiths beat K. Stevens 4-0; Thorburn beat D. Mountjoy 4-0; R. Reardon beat S. Davis 4-2; A. Higgins beat Dennis Taylor 4-2
Semi-finals: Griffiths beat Thorburn 6-5; Reardon beat Higgins 6-5
Final: Griffiths beat Reardon 9-7

1982
First round: Dennis Taylor beat D. Sheehan 5-3; T. Meo beat J. Spencer 5-3; A. Higgins beat J. Wych 5-3; D. Mountjoy beat E. Hughes 5-4
Quarter-finals: T. Griffiths beat T. Meo 5-3; R. Reardon beat Dennis Taylor 5-4; S. Davis beat Mountjoy 5-2; Higgins beat C. Thorburn 5-4
Semi-finals: Griffiths beat Reardon 6-3; S. Davis beat Higgins 6-2
Final: Griffiths beat S. Davis 9-5

1983
First round: J. White beat Dennis Taylor 5-4; T. Meo beat P. Burke 5-0; D. Mountjoy beat A. Knowles 5-1; E. Charlton beat David Taylor 5-4
Quarter-finals: R. Reardon beat Meo 5-4; A. Higgins beat White 5-2; S. Davis beat Charlton 5-1; T. Griffiths beat Mountjoy 5-4
Semi-finals: Reardon beat Higgins 6-3; S. Davis beat Griffiths 6-2
Final: S. Davis beat Reardon 9-2

1984
First round: T. Griffiths beat B. Werbeniuk 5-2; Dennis Taylor beat E. Hughes 5-1; T. Meo beat J. White 5-4; A. Higgins beat E. Charlton 5-2
Quarter-finals: Dennis Taylor beat C. Thorburn 5-2; Griffiths beat A. Knowles 5-0; Higgins beat R. Reardon 5-2; S. Davis beat Meo 5-4
Semi-finals: Griffiths beat Dennis Taylor 6-5; S. Davis beat Higgins 6-4
Final: S. Davis beat Griffiths 9-1

1985
First round: E. Charlton beat Dennis Taylor 5-4; J. White beat T. Meo 5-1; E. Hughes beat R. Reardon 5-0; A. Higgins beat T. Griffiths 5-2
Quarter-finals: A. Knowles beat Charlton 5-3; White beat C. Thorburn 5-3; S. Davis beat Hughes 5-4; Higgins beat K. Stevens 5-3
Semi-finals: White beat Knowles 6-4; Higgins beat S. Davis 6-2
Final: White beat Higgins 9-5

1986
First round: E. Hughes beat R. Reardon 5-2; W. Thorne beat T. Griffiths 5-2; T. Meo beat A. Higgins 5-4; P. Fagan wo K. Stevens scr
Quarter-finals: C. Thorburn beat Hughes 5-1; Thorne beat Dennis Taylor 5-2; J. White beat Meo 5-2; Fagan beat A. Knowles 5-4
Semi-finals: Thorne beat Thorburn 6-4; White beat Fagan 6-0
Final: White beat Thorne 9-5

1987
First round: W. Thorne beat K. Stevens 5-1; Dennis Taylor beat E. Hughes 5-4; T. Meo beat A. Knowles 5-2; T. Griffiths beat A. Higgins 5-1
Quarter-finals: Thorne beat J. White 5-4; Taylor beat C. Thorburn 5-1; S. Davis beat Meo 5-2; Griffiths beat J. Johnson 5-0
Semi-finals: Thorne beat Taylor 6-2; Davis beat Griffiths 6-2
Final: Davis beat Thorne 9-1

1988
First round: T. Griffiths beat R. Williams 5-1; T. Knowles beat W. Thorne 5-3; A. Higgins beat Dennis Taylor 5-3; J. Johnson beat E. Hughes 5-4
Quarter-finals: Griffiths beat J. White 5-2; N. Foulds beat Knowles 5-3; Higgins beat C. Thorburn 5-3; S. Davis beat Johnson 5-0
Semi-finals: Foulds beat Griffiths 6-4; Davis beat Higgins 6-2
Final: Davis beat Foulds 9-4

KENT CUP

First staged 1987 (as exhibition tour). Sponsors British American Tobacco. Venue Peking Sports Stadium. Prize-money last season £120,000. TV China TV.

1988
Quarter-finals: D. Reynolds beat A. Higgins 3-2; J. Parrott beat T. Drago 3-1; M. Clark beat E. Hughes 3-1; A. Knowles beat J. Johnson 3-0
Semi-finals: Clark beat Knowles 4-3; Parrott beat Reynolds 4-2
Final: Parrott beat Clark 5-1

EMBASSY WORLD PROFESSIONAL CHAMPIONSHIP

First staged 1927. **Sponsors** Embassy (1976–). **Venue** Crucible Theatre, Sheffield (1977–). **Initial prize-money** £15,300. **Prize-money last season** £475,000. **TV** BBC.

1927
First round: M. Inman beat T. Newman 8-5; T. Carpenter beat N. Butler 8-3
Second round: T. A. Dennis beat F. Lawrence 8-7; A. Cope beat A. Mann 8-6; J. Davis beat J. Brady 10-5; Carpenter beat Inman 8-3
Semi-finals: J. Davis beat Cope 16-7; Dennis beat Carpenter 12-10
Final: J. Davis beat Dennis 20-11

1928
First round: T. Newman beat F. Smith 12-6; A. Mann beat A. Cope 14-9
Second round: Newman beat T. A. Dennis 12-5; F. Lawrence beat Mann 12-11
Third round: Lawrence beat Newman 12-7
Final: J. Davis beat Lawrence 16-13

1929
First round: F. Lawrence beat A. Mann 13-12
Semi-finals: J. Davis beat Lawrence 13-10; T. A. Dennis beat K. Prince 14-6
Final: J. Davis beat Dennis 19-14

1930
First round: F. Lawrence beat A. Mann 13-11; N. Butler beat T. Newman 13-11
Semi-finals: J. Davis beat Lawrence 13-2; T. A. Dennis beat Butler 13-11
Final: J. Davis beat Dennis 25-12

1931
Final: J. Davis beat T. A. Dennis 25-21

1932
First round: C. McConachy beat T. A. Dennis 13-11
Final: J. Davis beat McConachy 30-19

1933
First round: W. Donaldson beat W. Leigh 13-11
Semi-finals: J. Davis beat Donaldson 13-1; W. Smith beat T. A. Dennis 16-9
Final: J. Davis beat Smith 25-18

1934
Final: J. Davis beat T. Newman 25-23

1935
First round: W. Smith beat C. Stanbury 13-12
Semi-finals: Smith beat A. Mann 13-4; J. Davis beat T. Newman 15-10
Final: J. Davis beat Smith 25-20

1936
First round: C. O'Donnell beat S. Lee 16-15; H. Lindrum beat H. Terry 20-11; J. Davis beat T. Newman 29-2; W. Smith beat S. Smith 16-15; C. Stanbury beat A. Mann 22-9
Second round: Alec Brown beat Stanbury 16-15; Lindrum beat O'Donnell 19-6 (*retd*); J. Davis beat W. Smith 22-9; S. Newman *wo*
Semi-finals: J. Davis beat Alec Brown 21-10; Lindrum beat S. Newman 29-2
Final: J. Davis beat Lindrum 34-27

1937
First round: W. A. Withers beat F. Davis 17-14
Second round: J. Davis beat Withers 30-1; H. Lindrum beat S. Lee 20-11; W. Smith beat
T. Newman 16-15; S. Smith beat Alec Brown 18-13
Semi-finals: Lindrum beat W. Smith 20-11; J. Davis beat S. Smith 18-13
Final: J. Davis beat Lindrum 32-29

1938
First qualifying round: H. Holt beat C. W. Read 21-10
Second qualifying round: F. Davis beat Holt 23-8
First round: F. Davis beat Alec Brown 14-6 (*retd ill*); S. Smith beat C. Stanbury 27-4;
J. Davis beat S. Lee 24-7; W. Smith beat T. Newman 16-15
Semi-finals: J. Davis beat W. Smith (*nrs*); S. Smith beat F. Davis (*nrs*)
Final: J. Davis beat S. Smith 37-24

1939
First qualifying round: W. Donaldson beat H. Holt 18-13; H. W. Laws beat S. Newman
19-12
Second qualifying round: Donaldson beat Laws 18-13
First round: S. Smith beat S. Lee 21-10; W. Donaldson beat C. Falkiner 21-10;
T. Newman beat A. Mann 19-12; F. Davis beat C. Stanbury 19-12
Second round: J. Davis beat W. Smith 19-12; F. Davis beat T. Newman 20-11; Alec
Brown beat H. Lindrum 17-14; S. Smith beat Donaldson 16-15
Semi-finals: J. Davis beat F. Davis 17-14; S. Smith beat Alec Brown 20-11
Final: J. Davis beat S. Smith 43-30

1940
Qualifying round: H. Holt beat C. Stanbury 18-13
First round: W. Donaldson beat Holt 24-7; J. Davis beat Alec Brown 20-11; F. Davis
beat S. Lee 20-11; S. Smith beat T. Newman 22-9
Semi-finals: J. Davis beat Donaldson 22-9; F. Davis beat S. Smith 17-14
Final: J. Davis beat F. Davis 37-36

1946
First qualifying round: K. Kennerley beat F. Lawrence 22-9; C. Stanbury beat J. Barrie
18-13; S. Newman beat W. Leigh 16-15
Second qualifying round: Kennerley beat T. Reece 8-2 (*retd*); S. Newman beat Stanbury
17-14
Third qualifying round: S. Newman beat Kennerley 21-10
First round: J. Davis beat W. Donaldson 21-10; S. Newman beat S. Lee 19-12; F. Davis
beat Alec Brown 24-7; H. Lindrum beat H. Holt 17-14
Semi-finals: J. Davis beat S. Newman 21-10; Lindrum beat F. Davis 16-12
Final: J. Davis beat Lindrum 78-67

1947
First qualifying round: Albert Brown beat J. Pulman 21-14; W. Leigh beat H. F. Francis
19-16; S. Lee beat J. Lees 19-16; K. Kennerley beat C. Stanbury 23-12; E. Newman *wo*
H. Holt *scr*
Second qualifying round: J. Barrie beat F. Lawrence 25-10; Albert Brown beat Newman
28-7; Kennerley beat A. Mann 23-12; Leigh beat Lee 25-10
Third qualifying round: Albert Brown beat Barrie 24-11; Kennerley beat Leigh 21-14
Fourth qualifying round: Albert Brown beat Kennerley 21-14
First round: H. Lindrum beat Albert Brown 39-34; S. Smith beat Alec Brown 43-28;
W. Donaldson beat S. Newman 46-25; F. Davis beat C. McConachy 53-20
Semi-finals: Donaldson beat Lindrum 39-32; F. Davis beat Smith 39-32
Final: Donaldson beat F. Davis 82-63

1948
First qualifying round: C. Stanbury beat E. Newman 26-9; W. Leigh beat H. Holt 18-17; J. Barrie beat H. F. Francis 19-16; J. Pulman *wo* S. Lee *scr*
Second qualifying round: Leigh beat Barrie 21-14; Pulman beat Stanbury 19-16
Third qualifying round: Pulman beat Leigh 18-17
First round: F. Davis beat Alec Brown 43-28; C. McConachy beat J. Pulman 42-29; Albert Brown beat S. Smith 36-35; W. Donaldson beat K. Kennerley 46-25
Semi-finals: F. Davis beat McConachy 43-28; Donaldson beat Alec Brown 40-31
Final: F. Davis beat Donaldson 84-61

1949
First qualifying round: C. Stanbury beat H. F. Francis 18-17
Second qualifying round: Stanbury beat Jack Rea 18-17
Third qualifying round: Stanbury beat H. Holt 18-17
First round: W. Donaldson beat Stanbury 58-13; J. Pulman beat Albert Brown 42-29; S. Smith beat Alec Brown 41-30; F. Davis beat K. Kennerley 50-21
Semi-finals: Donaldson beat Pulman 49-22; F. Davis beat Smith 42-29
Final: F. Davis beat Donaldson 80-65

1950
First qualifying round: W. Smith beat W. A. Withers 28-7; H. Holt beat H. W. Laws 26-9; S. Lee beat C. Stanbury 20-15; K. Kennerley beat J. Barrie 21-14
Second qualifying round: Kennerley beat Smith 22-13; Lee beat Holt 16-8 (*retd ill*)
Third qualifying round: Kennerley beat Lee 21-14
First round: Albert Brown beat J. Pulman 37-34; W. Donaldson beat K. Kennerley 42-29; G. Chenier beat P. Mans 37-34; F. Davis beat Alec Brown 44-27
Semi-finals: Donaldson beat Albert Brown 37-34; F. Davis beat Chenier 43-28
Final: Donaldson beat F. Davis 51-46

1951
First qualifying round: J. Barrie beat S. Lee 23-12
Second qualifying round: Barrie beat H. W. Laws 28-7
First round: F. Davis beat Barrie 42-29; H. Lindrum beat Albert Brown 43-28; W. Donaldson beat K. Kennerley 41-30; J. Pulman beat S. Smith 38-33
Semi-finals: Donaldson beat Lindrum 41-30; F. Davis beat Pulman 22-14 (*retd ill*)
Final: F. Davis beat Donaldson 58-39

1952
First round: Alec Brown beat R. Williams 39-22; Jack Rea beat J. Lees 38-32; Albert Brown beat J. Pulman 32-27 (*records incomplete*)
Semi-finals: W. Donaldson beat Albert Brown 31-30
Final: F. Davis beat Donaldson 38-35

1953
First qualifying round: W. Smith beat J. Lees 21-14; K. Kennerley beat R. Williams 25-12
Second qualifying round: Kennerley beat Smith 42-29
First round: Albert Brown beat Alec Brown 35-26; J. Pulman beat Jack Rea 36-25; W. Donaldson beat Kennerley 42-19; F. Davis beat J. Barrie 32-29
Semi-finals: Donaldson beat Brown (*nrs*); F. Davis beat Pulman 36-25
Final: F. Davis beat Donaldson 37-34

1954
First round: J. Pulman beat Jack Rea 31-30
Semi-finals: W. Donaldson beat Alec Brown 36-25; F. Davis beat Pulman 32-29
Final: F. Davis beat Donaldson 39-21

1955
First round: J. Pulman beat R. Williams 22-15; Jack Rea beat H. Stokes (*nrs*)
Semi-finals: F. Davis beat Rea 36-25; Pulman beat Alec Brown (*nrs*)
Final: F. Davis beat Pulman 37-34

1956
Semi-finals: J. Pulman beat Jack Rea 36-25; F. Davis beat R. Williams 35-26
Final: F. Davis beat Pulman 38-35

1957
Semi-finals: J. Pulman beat R. Williams 21-16; Jack Rea beat K. Kennerley 25-12
Final: Pulman beat Rea 39-34

Through lack of public support no Championship was organised between 1957 and 1964. After a truce with the BA and CC a new system was adopted whereby the champion defended his title against a series of single challengers. These matches resulted as follows:

1964
J. Pulman beat F. Davis 19-16; J. Pulman beat R. Williams 40-33

1965
J. Pulman beat F. Davis 37-36; J. Pulman beat R. Williams 25-22 (*matches*); J. Pulman beat F. Van Rensberg 39-12

1966
J. Pulman beat F. Davis 5-2 (*matches*)

1968
J. Pulman beat E. Charlton 39-34

1969 (*Players No. 6*)
First round: J. Spencer beat J. Pulman 25-18; R. Williams beat B. Bennett 25-4; G. Owen beat Jack Rea 25-17; F. Davis beat R. Reardon 25-24
Semi-finals: Spencer beat Williams 37-12; G. Owen beat Davis 37-24
Final: Spencer beat Owen 37-24

1970 (April) (*Players No. 6*)
First round: David Taylor beat B. Bennett 11-8
Quarter-finals: J. Pulman beat David Taylor 31-20; G. Owen beat R. Williams 31-11; R. Reardon beat F. Davis 31-26; J. Spencer beat Jack Rea 31-15
Semi-finals: Pulman beat G. Owen 37-12; Reardon beat Spencer 37-33
Final: Reardon beat Pulman 37-33

1970 (November)
Round robin: J. Spencer beat P. Mans 20-17; beat N. Squire 27-10; beat J. Pulman 23-14
R. Reardon beat Mans 22-15; beat E. Charlton 21-16; beat Spencer 21-16
W. Simpson beat G. Owen 19-18; beat Pulman 21-16; beat Mans 19-18
Charlton beat Squire 27-10; beat Mans 26-11; beat Owen 23-14
Owen beat P. Morgan 26-11; beat Squire 26-11; Morgan beat Simpson 21-16
Semi-finals: Spencer beat Reardon 34-15; Simpson beat Charlton 27-22
Final: Spencer beat Simpson 37-29

1972
First qualifying round: A. Higgins beat R. Gross 15-6; M. Parkin beat G. Thompson 11-10; G. Miles beat B. Bennett 15-6; J. Dunning beat P. Houlihan 11-10
Second qualifying round: Higgins beat Parkin 11-3; Dunning beat Miles 11-5
First round: J. Pulman beat Dunning 19-7; Higgins beat Jack Rea 19-11
Quarter-finals: J. Spencer beat F. Davis 31-21; E. Charlton beat David Taylor 31-25; Higgins beat Pulman 31-23; R. Williams beat R. Reardon 25-23
Semi-finals: Higgins beat Williams 31-30; Spencer beat Charlton 37-32
Final: Higgins beat Spencer 37-32

1973 (*Park Drive*)
First round: P. Houlihan beat Jack Rea 9-2; D. Greaves beat B. Bennett 9-8; G. Miles beat G. Thompson 9-5; P. Mans beat R. Gross 9-2; W. Simpson beat M. Parkin 9-3;

C. Thorburn beat Dennis Taylor 9-8; David Taylor beat J. Dunning 9-4; J. Meadowcroft
wo K. Kennerley scr
Second round: F. Davis beat Greaves 16-1; Miles beat J. Pulman 16-10; E. Charlton beat
Mans 16-8; G. Owen beat Simpson 16-14; R. Reardon beat Meadowcroft 16-10;
R. Williams beat Thorburn 16-15; J. Spencer beat David Taylor 16-5; A. Higgins beat
Houlihan 16-3
Quarter-finals: Higgins beat F. Davis 16-14; Spencer beat Williams 16-7; Charlton beat
Miles 16-6; Reardon beat G. Owen 16-6
Semi-finals: Charlton beat Higgins 23-9; Reardon beat Spencer 23-22
Final: Reardon beat Charlton 38-32

1974 (*Park Drive*)
Qualifying: J. Dunning beat D. Greaves 8-2; W. Simpson beat Jack Rea 8-3;
J. Meadowcroft beat P. Houlihan 8-5; C. Thorburn beat A. McDonald 8-3; J. Pulman
beat J. Karnehm 8-0; David Taylor beat R. Gross 8-7; M. Owen beat Dennis Taylor 8-1
First round: B. Bennett beat Simpson 8-2; B. Werbeniuk beat G. Thompson 8-3;
Meadowcroft beat K. Kennerley 8-5; M. Owen beat M. Parkin 8-5; P. Mans beat
I. Anderson 8-1; Pulman beat S. Lee 8-0; Dunning beat David Taylor 8-6; P. Morgan
beat Thorburn 8-4
Second round: Mans beat J. Spencer 15-13; Dunning beat E. Charlton 15-13; M. Owen
beat G. Owen 15-8; A. Higgins beat Bennett 15-4; G. Miles beat Morgan 15-7;
R. Williams beat Pulman 15-12; F. Davis beat Werbeniuk 15-5; R. Reardon beat
Meadowcroft 15-3
Quarter-finals: Williams beat Mans 15-4; Reardon beat M. Owen 15-11; Miles beat
Dunning 15-13; F. Davis beat Higgins 15-14
Semi-finals: Miles beat Williams 15-7; Reardon beat F. Davis 15-3
Final: Reardon beat Miles 22-12

1975
Qualifying: P. Tarrant beat B. Bennett 15-8; L. Condo beat M. Parkin 15-8; D. Greaves
beat J. Charlton 15-14
First round: W. Simpson beat R. Mares 15-5; J. Pulman beat Tarrant 15-5; David Taylor
beat R. King 15-8; I. Anderson beat Condo 15-8; Dennis Taylor beat P. Mans 15-12;
G. Owen beat Greaves 15-3; B. Werbeniuk beat J. Meadowcroft 15-9; C. Thorburn beat
P. Morgan 15-6
Second round: R. Reardon beat Simpson 15-11; J. Spencer beat Pulman 15-10; A. Higgins
beat David Taylor 15-2; R. Williams beat Anderson 15-4; Dennis Taylor beat F. Davis
15-14; G. Owen beat J. Dunning 15-8; E. Charlton beat Werbeniuk 15-11; Thorburn beat
G. Miles 15-2
Quarter-finals: Reardon beat Spencer 19-17; Higgins beat Williams 19-12; Dennis Taylor
beat G. Owen 19-9; Charlton beat Thorburn 19-12
Semi-finals: Charlton beat Dennis Taylor 19-12; Reardon beat Higgins 19-14
Final: Reardon beat Charlton 31-30

1976
First qualifying round: Jack Rea beat I. Anderson 8-5; D. Greaves beat J. Charlton 8-5;
J. Meadowcroft beat D. Wheelwright 8-1; R. Gross beat M. Parkin 8-5; L. Condo beat
M. Owen 8-6
Second qualifying round: Jack Rea beat B. Bennett 8-5; David Taylor beat Greaves 8-1;
Meadowcroft beat Gross 8-4; W. Thorne beat Condo 8-3
First round: R. Reardon beat J. Dunning 15-7; Dennis Taylor beat G. Owen 15-9;
P. Mans beat G. Miles 15-10; Meadowcroft beat R. Williams 15-7; E. Charlton beat
J. Pulman 15-9; F. Davis beat B. Werbeniuk 15-12; A. Higgins beat C. Thorburn 15-14;
J. Spencer beat David Taylor 15-5
Quarter-finals: Reardon beat Dennis Taylor 15-2; Mans beat Meadowcroft 15-8;
Charlton beat F. Davis 15-13; Higgins beat Spencer 15-14
Semi-finals: Reardon beat Mans 20-10; Higgins beat Charlton 20-18
Final: Reardon beat Higgins 27-16

1977

First qualifying round: J. Virgo beat R. Andrewartha 11-1
Second qualifying round: P. Fagan beat J. Meadowcroft 11-9; Virgo beat J. Dunning 11-6;
W. Thorne beat B. Bennett 11-4; J. Pulman *wo*; David Taylor beat D. Greaves 11-0;
C. Thorburn beat C. Ross 11-0; Dennis Taylor beat J. Karnehm 11-0; D. Mountjoy beat
Jack Rea 11-9
First round: R. Reardon beat Fagan 13-7; J. Spencer beat Virgo 13-9; G. Miles beat
Thorne 13-4; Pulman beat F. Davis 13-12; E. Charlton beat David Taylor 13-5;
Thorburn beat R. Williams 13-6; Dennis Taylor beat P. Mans 13-11; Mountjoy beat
A. Higgins 13-12
Quarter-finals: Spencer beat Reardon 13-6; Pulman beat Miles 13-10; Thorburn beat
Charlton 13-12; Dennis Taylor beat Mountjoy 13-11
Semi-finals: Spencer beat Pulman 18-16; Thorburn beat Dennis Taylor 18-16
Final: Spencer beat Thorburn 25-21

1978

First qualifying round: M. Parkin beat B. Bennett 9-4; R. Andrewartha beat J. Karnehm
9-0; J. Barrie beat D. Greaves 9-3; P. Houlihan beat C. Ross 9-1
Second qualifying round: D. Mountjoy beat Andrewartha 9-3; P. Fagan beat J. Dunning
9-5; W. Thorne beat R. Williams 9-3; B. Werbeniuk beat M. Parkin 9-2; P. Mans beat
Barrie 9-6; David Taylor beat P. Morgan 9-7; Houlihan beat J. Meadowcroft 9-6;
F. Davis beat J. Virgo 9-8
First round: Mans beat J. Spencer 13-8; G. Miles beat David Taylor 13-10; Fagan beat
A. Higgins 13-12; F. Davis beat Dennis Taylor 13-9; E. Charlton beat Thorne 13-12;
C. Thorburn beat Houlihan 13-8; Werbeniuk beat J. Pulman 13-4; R. Reardon beat
Mountjoy 13-9
Quarter-finals: Mans beat Miles 13-7; F. Davis beat Fagan 13-10; Charlton beat
Thorburn 13-12; Reardon beat Werbeniuk 13-6
Semi-finals: Mans beat F. Davis 18-16; Reardon beat Charlton 18-14
Final: Reardon beat Mans 25-18

1979

First qualifying round: D. Mountjoy beat D. Mienie 9-1; T. Griffiths beat B. Bennett 9-2;
P. Houlihan beat J. Barrie 9-5; W. Thorne beat J. Charlton 9-3; J. Virgo beat M. Parkin
9-0; J. Dunning beat Jack Rea 9-5; R. Williams beat D. Greaves 9-2; J. Meadowcroft
beat J. Van Rensberg 9-7; R. Andrewartha beat R. Edmonds 9-8; S. Davis beat
I. Anderson 9-1; K. Stevens beat R. Amdor 9-1
Second qualifying round: Virgo beat Thorne 9-8; B. Werbeniuk beat Andrewartha 9-2;
David Taylor beat Dunning 9-8; Mountjoy beat Houlihan 9-6; S. Davis beat P. Fagan
9-2; Griffiths beat Meadowcroft 9-6; Stevens beat J. Pulman 9-0; G. Miles beat Williams
9-5
First round: E. Charlton beat Mountjoy 13-6; Werbeniuk beat J. Spencer 13-11; Virgo
beat C. Thorburn 13-10; F. Davis beat Stevens 13-8; Dennis Taylor beat S. Davis 13-11;
A. Higgins beat David Taylor 13-5; Griffiths beat P. Mans 13-8; R. Reardon beat Miles
13-8
Quarter-finals: Charlton beat F. Davis 13-4; Dennis Taylor beat Reardon 13-8; Virgo
beat Werbeniuk 13-9; Griffiths beat Higgins 13-12
Semi-finals: Griffiths beat Charlton 19-17; Dennis Taylor beat Virgo 19-12
Final: Griffiths beat Dennis Taylor 24-16

1980

Qualifying groups
1 Jack Rea beat B. Bennett 9-1; W. Thorne beat K. Robitaille 9-4; Thorne beat Rea
   9-1
2 S. Davis beat C. Ross 9-3; P. Morgan beat P. Thornley 9-4; Davis beat Morgan 9-0
3 M. Hallett beat K. Kennerley 9-2; K. Stevens beat D. Greaves 9-3; Stevens beat
   Hallett 9-3

4   J. Johnson beat R. Andrewartha 9-5; P. Houlihan beat Johnson 9-6; T. Meo beat
J. Van Rensberg 9-1; Meo beat Houlihan 9-1
5   R. Amdor beat B. Mikkelsen 9-7; R. Williams beat Amdor 9-4; J. Wych beat John
Bear 9-5; Wych beat Williams 9-7
6   F. Jonik beat M. Wildman 9-7; C. Wilson beat Jonik 9-6
7   R. Edmonds beat M. Parkin 9-2; S. Hood beat J. Dunning 16-7; Edmonds beat
Hood 9-6
8   E. Sinclair beat M. Morra 9-5; Sinclair beat D. Mienie 9-7; J. Meadowcroft beat
Sinclair 9-1
First round: S. Davis beat P. Fagan 10-6; A. Higgins beat Meo 10-9; D. Mountjoy beat
Wilson 10-6; Wych beat J. Pulman 10-5; J. Virgo beat Meadowcroft 10-2; Stevens beat
G. Miles 10-3; David Taylor beat Edmonds 10-3; B. Werbeniuk beat Thorne 10-9
Second round: S. Davis beat T. Griffiths 13-10; Higgins beat P. Mans 13-6; Stevens beat
J. Spencer 13-8; E. Charlton beat Virgo 13-12; C. Thorburn beat Mountjoy 13-10; Wych
beat Dennis Taylor 13-10; R. Reardon beat Werbeniuk 13-6; David Taylor beat F. Davis
13-5
Quarter-finals: David Taylor beat Reardon 13-11; Thorburn beat Wych 13-6; Stevens
beat Charlton 13-7; Higgins beat S. Davis 13-9
Semi-finals: Thorburn beat David Taylor 16-7; Higgins beat Stevens 16-13
Final: Thorburn beat Higgins 18-16

1981
Qualifying groups
1   W. Thorne beat M. Morra 9-5; D. Greaves beat M. Parkin 9-5; Thorne beat Greaves
9-3
2   J. White beat B. Mikkelsen 9-4; White beat J. Meadowcroft 9-8
3   R. Edmonds beat M. Wildman 9-3; R. Williams beat S. Hood 9-4; Edmonds beat
Williams 9-7
4   T. Meo beat J. Johnson 9-8; M. Hallett beat F. Jonik 9-1; Meo beat Hallett 9-4
5   J. Dunning beat B. Bennett 9-6; Dunning beat P. Fagan 9-7
6   D. Martin beat I. Anderson 9-3; Martin beat J. Pulman 9-2
7   C. Wilson beat R. Andrewartha 9-4; E. Sinclair beat P. Morgan 9-8; Wilson beat
Sinclair 9-4
8   A. Knowles beat C. Ross 7-0 (*retd*); Knowles beat J. Wych 9-3
First round: G. Miles beat Knowles 10-8; David Taylor beat Wilson 10-6; D. Mountjoy
beat Thorne 10-6; K. Stevens beat Dunning 10-4; Meo beat J. Virgo 10-6; S. Davis beat
White 10-8; B. Werbeniuk beat Martin 10-4; J. Spencer beat Edmonds 10-9
Second round: C. Thorburn beat Miles 13-2; David Taylor beat F. Davis 13-3; T. Griffiths
beat Meo 13-6; S. Davis beat Alex Higgins 13-8; Mountjoy beat E. Charlton 13-7; Dennis
Taylor beat Stevens 13-11; Werbeniuk beat P. Mans 13-5; R. Reardon beat Spencer 13-11
Quarter-finals: Thorburn beat David Taylor 13-6; S. Davis beat Griffiths 13-9; Mountjoy
beat Dennis Taylor 13-8; Reardon beat Werbeniuk 13-10
Semi-finals: S. Davis beat Thorburn 16-10; Mountjoy beat Reardon 16-10
Final: S. Davis beat Mountjoy 18-12

1982
Qualifying groups
1   John Bear beat F. Jonik 9-4; Bear beat J. Wych 9-4
2   D. Hughes beat C. Everton 9-4; T. Meo beat Hughes 9-4
3   D. Reynolds beat D. Sheehan 9-5; Reynolds beat R. Edmonds 9-6
4   E. Hughes *wo* D. Mienie *scr*; A. Knowles beat Hughes 9-7
5   M. Wildman beat G. Foulds 9-8; J. White beat Wildman 9-4
6   C. Roscoe beat B. Mikkelsen 9-6; W. Thorne beat Roscoe 9-1
7   P. Medati beat J. Phillips 9-3; C. Wilson beat Medati 9-5
8   P. Houlihan beat I. Anderson 9-5; D. Martin beat Houlihan 9-3
9   M. Macleod beat E. McLaughlin 9-8; J. Dunning beat Macleod 9-4
10 M. Watterson beat B. Demarco 9-6; J. Meadowcroft beat Watterson 9-7

11   D. French beat B. Bennett 9-3; P. Fagan beat French 9-6
12   I. Black beat M. Parkin 9-6; R. Williams beat Black 9-2
13   J. Johnson beat V. Harris 9-4; M. Hallett beat Johnson 9-8
14   J. Donnelly beat M. Gibson 9-8; E. Sinclair beat B. Kelly 9-8; Donnelly beat Sinclair 9-8
15   P. Morgan beat D. Greaves 9-2; S. Francisco beat C. Ross 9-0; Francisco beat Morgan 9-1
16   M. Morra beat T. Murphy 9-5; J. Fitzmaurice wo J. Pulman scr; Fitzmaurice beat Morra 9-7

First round: Knowles beat S. Davis 10-1; G. Miles beat Martin 10-5; B. Werbeniuk beat Bear 10-7; E. Charlton beat Wilson 10-5; S. Francisco beat Dennis Taylor 10-7; Reynolds beat F. Davis 10-7; J. Virgo beat Hallett 10-4; R. Reardon beat Donnelly 10-5; A. Higgins beat Meadowcroft 10-5; D. Mountjoy beat Williams 10-3; Fagan beat David Taylor 10-9; K. Stevens beat Fitzmaurice 10-4; P. Mans beat Meo 10-8; White beat C. Thorburn 10-4

Second round: Knowles beat Miles 13-7; Charlton beat Werbeniuk 13-5; S. Francisco beat Reynolds 13-8; Reardon beat Virgo 13-8; Thorne beat Spencer 13-5; Higgins beat Mountjoy 13-12; Stevens beat Fagan 13-7; White beat Mans 13-6

Quarter-finals: Charlton beat Knowles 13-11; Reardon beat S. Francisco 13-8; Higgins beat Thorne 13-10; White beat Stevens 13-9

Semi-finals: Reardon beat Charlton 16-11; Higgins beat White 16-15

Final: Higgins beat Reardon 18-15

1983
Qualifying groups
1   B. Kelly beat B. Demarco 10-4; S. Francisco beat Kelly 10-5
2   P. Morgan beat P. Burke 10-9; G. Miles beat Morgan 10-6
3   T. Murphy beat P. Houlihan 10-9; J. Virgo beat Murphy 10-8
4   R. Williams beat M. Darrington 10-0; Williams beat F. Davis 10-1
5   M. Wildman beat B. Harris 10-7; Wildman wo J. Wych scr
6   R. Edmonds beat F. Jonik 10-4; D. Reynolds beat Edmonds 10-6
7   M. Fisher beat P. Fagan 10-8; E. McLaughlin beat D. Greaves 10-7; Fisher beat McLaughlin 10-9
8   T. Meo beat V. Harris 10-0; G. Foulds beat M. Gibson 10-6; Meo beat Foulds 10-4
9   I. Black beat M. Morra 10-9; P. Medati beat John Bear 10-7; Black beat Medati 10-4
10   C. Wilson beat C. Everton 10-1; J. Johnson beat P. Watchorn 10-0; Wilson beat Johnson 10-8
11   M. Macleod beat M. Owen 10-5; D. Martin beat M. Parkin 10-1; Martin beat Macleod 10-7
12   J. Meadowcroft beat B. Bennett 10-3; G. Cripsey beat D. Hughes 10-2; Meadowcroft beat Cripsey 10-6
13   J. Donnelly beat D. Sheehan 10-6; J. Campbell beat M. Watterson 10-6; Campbell beat Donnelly 10-2
14   L. Dodd wo J. Dunning scr; I. Williamson beat D. French 10-8; Dodd beat Williamson 10-9
15   M. Hallett beat R. Andrewartha 10-7; W. King beat I. Anderson 10-6; Hallett beat King 10-6
16   E. Hughes beat J. Fitzmaurice 10-7; E. Sinclair beat C. Roscoe 10-2; Hughes beat Sinclair 10-8

First round: A. Higgins beat Reynolds 10-4; W. Thorne beat Virgo 10-3; B. Werbeniuk beat Martin 10-4; David Taylor beat Meadowcroft 10-2; E. Charlton beat Dodd 10-7; J. Spencer beat Hallett 10-7; Dennis Taylor beat S. Francisco 10-9; S. Davis beat Williams 10-4; C. Thorburn beat Campbell 10-5; T. Griffiths beat Wildman 10-8; P. Mans beat Black 10-3; K. Stevens beat Fisher 10-2; D. Mountjoy beat Wilson 10-2; Meo beat J. White 10-8; A. Knowles beat Miles 10-3; R. Reardon beat E. Hughes 10-7

Second round: Higgins beat Thorne 13-8; Werbeniuk beat David Taylor 13-10; Charlton beat Spencer 13-11; S. Davis beat Dennis Taylor 13-11; Thorburn beat Griffiths 13-12;

Meo beat Mountjoy 13-11; Knowles beat Reardon 13-12; Stevens beat Mans 13-3
Quarter-finals: Higgins beat Werbeniuk 13-11; S. Davis beat Charlton 13-5; Thorburn
beat Stevens 13-12; Knowles beat Meo 13-9
Semi-finals: Thorburn beat Knowles 16-15; S. Davis beat Higgins 16-5
Final: S. Davis beat Thorburn 18-6

1984
Qualifying groups
1   J. Parrott beat D. Hughes 10-3; Parrott beat C. Everton 10-2; Parrott beat P. Mans
    10-0
2   B. Mikkelsen beat P. Medati 10-8; Mikkelsen beat F. Jonik 10-9; W. Thorne beat
    Mikkelsen 10-3
3   M. Morra beat G. Foulds 10-2; T. Murphy beat J. Fitzmaurice 10-8; Morra beat
    Murphy 10-5; Morra beat D. Reynolds 10-7
4   W. Sanderson beat P. Morgan 10-8; P. Mifsud beat E. Hughes 10-5; Mifsud beat
    Sanderson 10-5; Mifsud beat C. Wilson 10-8
5   J. Van Rensberg beat V. Harris 10-7; R. Edmonds beat D. Greaves 10-0; Van
    Rensberg beat Edmonds 10-9; S. Francisco beat Van Rensberg 10-3
6   I. Williamson beat P. Houlihan 10-5; M. Hines beat I. Black 10-5; Williamson beat
    Hines 10-6; G. Miles beat Williamson 10-6
7   M. Gibson beat G. Rigitano 10-7; M. Fisher beat P. Thornley 10-8; Gibson beat
    Fisher 10-7; J. Johnson beat Gibson 10-3
8   E. McLaughlin beat J. Hargreaves 10-5; R. Andrewartha *wo* John Bear *scr*;
    Andrewartha beat McLaughlin 10-8; Andrewartha beat M. Wildman 10-9
9   J. Wych beat G. Ganim Jr 10-1; G. Scott beat L. Heywood 10-7; Wych beat Scott
    10-6; Wych beat P. Fagan 10-3
10 P. Browne beat S. Duggan 10-9; C. Roscoe beat B. Demarco 10-7; Browne beat
    Roscoe 10-4; E. Sinclair beat Browne 10-1
11 M. Gauvreau beat J. Campbell 10-7; G. Cripsey beat M. Parkin 10-4; Gauvreau
    beat Cripsey 10-1; Gauvreau beat M. Macleod 10-6
12 I. Anderson beat G. Watson 10-4; J. Donnelly beat P. Watchorn 10-7; Donnelly beat
    Anderson 10-6; F. Davis beat Donnelly 10-5
13 W. King beat T. Jones 10-9; M. Watterson beat B. Bennett 10-5; King beat
    Watterson 10-8; King beat Dave Martin 10-8
14 J. Caggianello beat M. Darrington 10-7; W. Oliver beat J. Dunning 10-3; Oliver beat
    Caggianello 10-7; R. Williams beat Oliver 10-8
15 N. Foulds beat D. French 10-5; L. Dodd beat J. Giannaros 10-1; Foulds beat Dodd
    10-4; Foulds beat J. Meadowcroft 10-2
16 B. Harris beat D. Sheehan 10-3; P. Burke beat B. Kelly 10-7; Burke beat Harris
    10-4; M. Hallett beat Burke 10-5
First round: S. Davis beat King 10-3; J. Spencer beat Miles 10-3; T. Griffiths beat
Mifsud 10-2; B. Werbeniuk beat F. Davis 10-4; N. Foulds beat A. Higgins 10-9;
D. Mountjoy beat Hallett 10-4; Dennis Taylor beat Johnson 10-1; Parrott beat
A. Knowles 10-7; C. Thorburn beat Morra 10-3; Thorne beat J. Virgo 10-9; J. White beat
Williams 10-6; E. Charlton beat Andrewartha 10-4; K. Stevens beat Sinclair 10-1; David
Taylor beat Gauvreau 10-5; S. Francisco beat T. Meo 10-5; R. Reardon beat Wych 10-7
Second round: S. Davis beat Spencer 13-5; Griffiths beat Werbeniuk 13-5; Mountjoy beat
N. Foulds 13-6; Dennis Taylor beat Parrott 13-11; Thorburn beat Thorne 13-11; White
beat Charlton 13-7; Stevens beat David Taylor 13-10; Reardon beat S. Francisco 13-8
Quarter-finals: S. Davis beat Griffiths 13-10; Dennis Taylor beat Mountjoy 13-8; White
beat Thorburn 13-8; Stevens beat Reardon 13-2
Semi-finals: S. Davis beat Dennis Taylor 16-9; White beat Stevens 16-14
Final: S. Davis beat White 18-16

1985

Qualifying groups

1 G. Rigitano beat D. Sheehan 10-9; Rigitano beat B. Harris 10-4; Rigitano beat B. Kelly 10-6; Rigitano beat M. Fisher 10-2; N. Foulds beat Rigitano 10-8

2 D. O'Kane *wo* J. McLaughlin *scr*; O'Kane beat V. Harris 10-5; O'Kane beat F. Jonik 10-5; O'Kane beat L. Dodd 10-7; O'Kane beat D. Martin 10-8

3 S. Longworth beat J. Giannaros 10-1; Longworth beat G. Cripsey 10-8; J. Van Rensberg beat Longworth 10-7; M. Gauvreau beat Van Rensberg 10-9; D. Reynolds beat Gauvreau 10-1

4 R. Chaperon beat R. Bales 10-7; Chaperon beat L. Heywood 10-1; Chaperon beat P. Morgan 10-3; F. Davis beat Chaperon 10-9; R. Williams beat F. Davis 10-6

5 D. Hughes beat D. French 10-5; S. Newbury beat Hughes 10-9; Newbury beat P. Burke 10-3; Newbury beat G. Scott 10-2; E. Hughes beat Newbury 10-6

6 M. Hines beat T. Chappel 10-8; Hines beat P. Watchorn 10-4; M. Gibson beat Hines 10-7; P. Fagan beat Gibson 10-8; Fagan beat C. Wilson 10-9

7 D. Fowler beat J. Hargreaves 10-0; Fowler *wo* G. Watson *scr*; Fowler *wo* J. Caggianello *scr*; Fowler beat J. Donnelly 10-0; J. Parrott beat Fowler 10-2

8 R. Foldvari *wo* P. Thornley *scr*; Foldvari beat B. Oliver 10-3; R. Edmonds beat Foldvari 10-3; Edmonds beat M. Wildman 10-7

9 D. Chalmers beat D. Greaves 10-3; Chalmers beat E. McLaughlin 10-9; Chalmers beat I. Black 10-4; M. Hallett beat Chalmers 10-1

10 G. Foulds beat M. Parkin 10-6; Foulds beat C. Everton 10-2; Foulds beat C. Roscoe 10-7; J. Johnson beat Foulds 10-6

11 P. Medati beat B. Bennett 10-4; Medati beat I. Williamson 10-8; Medati beat W. King 10-9; S. Francisco beat Medati 10-7

12 I. Anderson beat A. Kearney 10-8; P. Browne beat Anderson 10-5; M. Morra beat Browne 10-6; J. Campbell beat Morra 10-9

13 W. Jones beat John Rea 10-3; Jones beat J. Dunning 10-6; Jones beat M. Watterson 10-5; Jones beat G. Miles 10-8

14 M. Bradley beat D. Mienie 10-4; Bradley beat B. Mikkelsen 10-9; J. Wych beat Bradley 10-7; J. Virgo beat Wych 10-4

15 P. Francisco beat B. Demarco 10-4; Francisco beat T. Murphy 10-4; Francisco beat J. Meadowcroft 10-5; M. Macleod beat Francisco 10-7

16 T. Jones beat M. Darrington 10-2; Jones beat S. Duggan 10-8; Jones beat J. Fitzmaurice 10-4; Jones beat E. Sinclair 10-2

First round: S. Davis beat N. Foulds 10-8; David Taylor beat O'Kane 10-4; A. Higgins beat Reynolds 10-4; T. Griffiths beat Williams 10-3; R. Reardon beat E. Hughes 10-9; Fagan beat W. Thorne 10-6; Parrott beat J. Spencer 10-3; K. Stevens beat Edmonds 10-8; C. Thorburn beat Hallett 10-8; B. Werbeniuk beat Johnson 10-8; Dennis Taylor beat S. Francisco 10-2; E. Charlton beat Campbell 10-3; J. White beat W. Jones 10-4; T. Meo beat Virgo 10-6; D. Mountjoy beat Macleod 10-5; A. Knowles beat T. Jones 10-8

Second round: S. Davis beat David Taylor 13-4; Griffiths beat Higgins 13-7; Reardon beat Fagan 13-9; Parrott beat Stevens 13-6; Thorburn beat Werbeniuk 13-3; Dennis Taylor beat Charlton 13-6; White beat Meo 13-11; Knowles beat Mountjoy 13-6

Quarter-finals: S. Davis beat Griffiths 13-6; Reardon beat Parrott 13-12; Dennis Taylor beat Thorburn 13-5; Knowles beat White 13-10

Semi-finals: S. Davis beat Reardon 16-5; Dennis Taylor beat Knowles 16-5

Final: Dennis Taylor beat S. Davis 18-17

1986

First qualifying round: D. Gilbert beat R. Bales 10-7; O. Agrawal beat D. Hughes 10-6; A. Kearney beat G. Wilkinson 10-5; B. Oliver beat J. O'Boye 10-8; D. Sheehan beat P. Houlihan 10-7; M. Gibson beat G. Jenkins 10-4; S. Simngam beat B. Bennett 10-0; Jim Bear beat P. Burke 10-8; T. Drago beat G. Cripsey 10-4; M. Smith beat D. Greaves 10-4; B. West *wo* J. Giannaros *scr*; P. Thornley beat D. Mienie 10-3; R. Grace beat M. Parkin 10-8; S. Hendry beat B. Demarco 10-7; P. Watchorn *wo* J. Rempe *scr*;

B. Mikkelsen beat J. Hargreaves 10-7; M. Darrington wo W. Sanderson scr
Second qualifying round: J. Wych beat T. Chappel 10-6; S. Duggan beat M. Fisher 10-3;
T. Jones beat V. Harris 10-7; Gilbert beat M. Bradley 10-7; S. Newbury beat Agrawal
10-5; I. Black beat B. Harris 10-8; G. Scott beat Kearney 10-8; D. Fowler beat Oliver
10-8; C. Roscoe beat G. Foulds 10-3; W. King beat Sheehan 10-4; Gibson beat M. Morra
10-9; P. Medati beat Simngam 10-9; R. Chaperon beat F. Jonik 10-8; M. Gauvreau beat
Jim Bear 10-5; F. Davis beat D. Chalmers 10-6; P. Francisco beat Drago 10-4;
J. Donnelly beat Smith 10-6; West beat J. Dunning 10-3; T. Murphy beat J. McLaughlin
10-7; Thornley beat P. Fagan 10-7; W. Jones beat Grace 10-3; Hendry beat P. Browne
10-9; E. Sinclair beat P. Morgan 10-8; J. Van Rensberg beat I. Williamson 10-9; John
Rea beat E. McLaughlin 10-6; S. Longworth beat Watchorn 10-7; G. Miles beat
C. Everton 10-3; R. Foldvari beat G. Rigitano 10-6; M. Watterson beat Mikkelsen 10-2;
L. Dodd beat J. Fitzmaurice 10-6; Darrington beat J. Meadowcroft 10-6; R. Edmonds
beat B. Kelly 10-0
Third qualifying round: Wych beat Duggan 10-5; Gilbert beat T. Jones 10-7; Newbury
beat Black 10-2; Fowler beat Scott 10-7; King beat Roscoe 10-5; Medati beat Gibson
10-6; Gauvreau beat Chaperon 10-8; P. Francisco beat F. Davis 10-1; West beat
Donnelly 10-5; Murphy beat Thornley 10-3; Hendry beat W. Jones 10-8; Van Rensberg
beat Sinclair 10-2; Longworth beat John Rea 10-4; Foldvari beat Miles 10-7; Dodd beat
Watterson 10-1; Edmonds beat Darrington 10-5
Fourth qualifying round: M. Hallett beat Wych 10-7; D. Martin beat Gilbert 10-5;
J. Spencer beat Newbury 10-7; Fowler beat M. Macleod 10-6; D. Reynolds beat King
10-7; C. Wilson beat Medati 10-6; R. Williams beat Gauvreau 10-3; N. Foulds beat
P. Francisco 10-9; B. Werbeniuk beat West 10-8; E. Hughes beat Murphy 10-7; Hendry
beat O'Kane 10-9; J. Campbell beat Van Rensberg 10-6; J. Virgo beat Longworth 10-8;
J. Parrott beat Foldvari 10-6; P. Mans beat Dodd 10-7; Edmonds beat M. Wildman 10-9
First round: Hallett beat Dennis Taylor 10-6; J. Johnson beat Martin 10-3; A. Higgins
beat J. Spencer 10-2; T. Griffiths beat Fowler 10-2; K. Stevens beat Reynolds 10-6;
E. Charlton beat Wilson 10-6; S. Francisco beat Williams 10-4; A. Knowles beat
N. Foulds 10-9; C. Thorburn beat Werbeniuk 10-5; E. Hughes beat David Taylor 10-7;
W. Thorne beat Hendry 10-8; Campbell beat R. Reardon 10-8; J. White beat Virgo 10-7;
Parrott beat T. Meo 10-4; D. Mountjoy beat Mans 10-3; S. Davis beat Edmonds 10-4
Second round: Johnson beat Hallett 13-6; Griffiths beat Higgins 13-12; Stevens beat
Charlton 13-12; Knowles beat S. Francisco 13-10; Thorburn beat E. Hughes 13-6; Thorne
beat Campbell 13-9; White beat Parrott 13-8; S. Davis beat Mountjoy 13-5
Quarter-finals: Johnson beat Griffiths 13-12; Knowles beat Stevens 13-9; Thorburn beat
Thorne 13-6; S. Davis beat White 13-5
Final: Johnson beat S. Davis 18-12

1987
First qualifying round: J. Bear beat Jack Rea 10-5; A. Kearney wo F. Jonik scr; S. James
beat M. Watterson 10-2; G. Jenkins beat R. Grace 10-9; D. Greaves beat P. Thornley
10-6; M. Darrington beat B. Demarco 10-6; J. Rempe beat M. Smith 10-9; G. Rigitano
beat P. Morgan 4-0; C. Roscoe beat T. Whitthread 10-2; M. Morra beat P. Gibson 10-6;
D. Chalmers wo E. McLaughlin scr; M. Bennett beat J. Hargreaves 10-6; B. Kelly beat
B. Bennett 10-0; J. Meadowcroft beat D. Mienie 10-3; G. Foulds beat P. Watchorn 10-6;
D. Hughes beat M. Parkin 10-5; B. Oliver beat P. Burke 10-5; J. Dunning beat
J. Caggianello 10-7; J. Wright beat P. Houlihan 10-4; B. Rowswell wo S. Simngam scr;
J. Fitzmaurice beat C. Everton 10-2; D. Roe wo O. Agrawal scr; K. Owers beat M. Fisher
10-5
Second qualifying round: M. Gauvreau beat Bear 10-3; P. Medati beat Kearney 10-8;
E. Sinclair beat T. Drago 10-9; R. Edmonds beat James 10-1; T. Murphy beat Jenkins
10-4; G. Miles beat Greaves 10-7; S. Hendry beat Darrington 10-7; Rempe beat John
Rea 10-9; Rigitano beat V. Harris 10-6; S. Newbury beat L. Dodd 10-7; S. Duggan beat
Roscoe 10-7; T. Chappel beat Morra 10-8; T. Jones beat Chalmers 10-1; J. Van Rensberg
beat J. McLaughlin 10-6; M. Bennett beat B. Mikkelsen 10-4; W. Jones beat J. Donnelly

10-3; I. Black beat I. Williamson 10-8; D. O'Kane beat D. Gilbert 10-2; M. Gibson beat
Kelly 10-9; G. Cripsey beat Meadowcroft 10-9; D. Fowler beat G. Foulds 10-6; B. Harris
beat D. Hughes 10-2; Oliver beat P. Fagan 10-2; G. Scott beat Dunning 10-7;
M. Wildman beat Foldvari 10-5; Wright beat Browne 10-6; M. Bradley beat Rowswell
10-6; J. O'Boye beat N. Gilbert 10-5; J. Spencer beat R. Bales 10-2; R. Chaperon beat
Fitzmaurice 10-2; W. King beat Roe 10-4; Owers beat F. Davis 10-5
Third qualifying round: Medati beat Gauvreau 10-3; Edmonds beat Sinclair 10-6; Murphy
beat Miles 10-7; Hendry beat Rempe 10-4; Newbury beat Rigitano 10-4; Chappel beat
Duggan 10-3; T. Jones beat Van Rensberg 10-0; M. Bennett beat W. Jones 10-3; O'Kane
beat Black 10-2; Cripsey beat M. Gibson 10-4; Fowler beat B. Harris 10-5; Oliver beat
Scott 10-5; Wright beat Wildman 10-0; Bradley beat O'Boye 10-7; Spencer beat
Chaperon 10-4; King beat Owers 10-4
Fourth qualifying round: E. Hughes beat Medati 10-2; M. Macleod beat Edmonds 10-7;
S. Longworth beat Murphy 10-2; Hendry beat D. Martin 10-7; M. Hallett beat Newbury
10-4; J. Campbell beat Chappel 10-6; J. Virgo beat T. Jones 10-9; M. Bennett beat
W. Jones 10-3; O'Kane beat P. Francisco 10-5; David Taylor beat Cripsey 10-7;
J. Parrott beat Fowler 10-3; D. Reynolds beat Oliver 10-7; Wright beat C. Wilson 10-4;
J. Wych beat Bradley 10-7; B. West beat Spencer 10-5; King beat E. Charlton 10-4
First round: J. Johnson beat E. Hughes 10-9; Macleod beat R. Williams 10-5; Longworth
beat K. Stevens 10-4; Hendry beat W. Thorne 10-7; Hallett beat A. Knowles 10-6;
S. Francisco beat Campbell 10-3; N. Foulds beat Virgo 10-4; Dennis Taylor beat
M. Bennett 10-4; O'Kane beat Thorburn 10-5; D. Mountjoy beat David Taylor 10-5;
Parrott beat T. Meo 10-8; J. White beat Reynolds 10-8; A. Higgins beat Wright 10-6;
T. Griffiths beat Wych 10-4; R. Reardon beat West 10-5; S. Davis beat King 10-7
Second round: Johnson beat Macleod 13-7; Hendry beat Longworth 1**8**-7; Hallett beat
S. Francisco 13-9; N. Foulds beat Dennis Taylor 13-10; O'Kane beat Mountjoy 13-5;
White beat Parrott 13-11; Griffiths beat Higgins 13-10; S. Davis beat Reardon 13-4
Quarter-finals: Johnson beat Hendry 13-12; N. Foulds beat Hallett 13-9; White beat
O'Kane 13-6; S. Davis beat Griffiths 13-5
Semi-finals: Johnson beat N. Foulds 16-9; S. Davis beat White 16-11
Final: S. Davis beat Johnson 18-14

1988

Preliminary round: A. Harris beat S. Mizerak 10-2
First qualifying round: P. Gibson beat D. Sheehan 10-9; A. Harris beat M. Fisher 10-4;
C. Roscoe beat E. McLaughlin 10-1; G. Miles beat D. Hughes 10-3; N. Gilbert beat
John Rea 10-5; I. Williamson *wo* J. Caggianello *scr*; B. Rowswell beat P. Thornley 10-7;
B. Oliver beat D. Chalmers 10-9; A. Robidoux *wo* F. Jonik *scr*; B. Kelly beat A. Kearney
10-4; S. James *wo* T. Whitthread *scr*; P. Watchorn beat M. Gibson 10-7; M. Clark beat
M. Darrington 10-5; G. Rigitano beat J. Dunning 10-7; J. Smith beat J. Donnelly 10-4;
Glen Wilkinson beat C. Everton 10-2; M. Morra beat S. Meakin 10-5; M. Smith beat V.
Harris 10-6; E. Lawlor *wo* J. Van Rensberg *scr*; B. Mikkelsen beat Jack Rea 10-3; R.
Foldvari beat J. Rempe 10-4; J. Meadowcroft beat B. Bennett 10-5; D. Gilbert beat D.
Heaton 10-2; P. Medati beat Gary Wilkinson 10-9; I. Black *wo* J. Hargreaves *scr*; P.
Fagan beat D. Greaves 10-3; E. Sinclair beat P. Burke 10-2; D. Roe beat B. Demarco
10-2; J. Chambers beat M. Watterson 10-3; J. Bear beat D. Mienie 10-4; J. Fitzmaurice
beat M. Parkin 10-6
Second qualifying round: P. Gibson beat M. Gauvreau 10-9; S. Duggan beat A. Harris
10-4; T. Murphy beat Roscoe 10-8; R. Chaperon beat Marshall 10-3; Miles beat R. Bales
10-7; T. Chappel beat N. Gilbert 10-8; M. Bradley beat Williamson 10-9; B. Werbeniuk
beat Rowswell 10-6; Oliver beat R. Reardon 10-6; Robidoux *wo* R. Grace *scr*; P. Browne
beat Kelly 10-8; James beat J. O'Boye 10-7; W. King beat Watchorn 10-4; Clark beat G.
Scott 10-4; M. Bennett beat Rigitano 10-4; J. Wych beat J. Smith 10-3; W. Jones beat
Glen Wilkinson 10-4; Morra beat R. Edmonds 10-8; M. Smith beat J. McLaughlin 10-3;
S. Newbury beat E. Lawlor 10-3; M. Wildman beat Mikkelsen 10-5; Foldvari beat T.
Jones 10-9; G. Cripsey beat Meadowcroft 10-3; P. Houlihan *wo* D. Gilbert *scr*; L. Dodd

Steve Davis with the 1988 Embassy World Championship Trophy

beat Medati 10-6; D. Fowler beat Black 10-1; B. Harris beat Fagan 10-1; Sinclair beat D. O'Kane 10-9; K. Owers beat Roe 10-7; J. Wright beat Chambers 10-2; Bear beat G. Foulds 10-2; F. Davis beat Fitzmaurice 10-8
Third qualifying round: Duggan beat P. Gibson 10-9; Chaperon beat Murphy 10-5; Chappel beat Miles 10-7; Werbeniuk beat Bradley 10-8; Oliver beat Robidoux 10-2; James beat Browne 10-1; King beat Clark 10-9; M. Bennett beat Wych 10-5; W. Jones beat Morra 10-8; Newbury beat M. Smith 10-9; Foldvari beat Wildman 10-1; Cripsey beat Houlihan 10-4; Fowler beat Dodd 10-8; B. Harris beat Sinclair 10-0; Wright beat Owers 10-8; F. Davis beat Bear 10-4
Fourth qualifying round: J. Virgo beat Duggan 10-5; Chaperon beat David Taylor 10-6; T. Drago beat Chappel 10-7; Werbeniuk beat T. Meo 10-4; C. Wilson beat Oliver 10-6; James beat E. Hughes 10-6; King beat J. Spencer 10-7; K. Stevens beat M. Bennett 10-7; W. Jones beat D. Martin 10-5; B. West beat Newbury 10-8; P. Francisco beat Foldvari 10-5; S. Longworth beat Cripsey 10-2; Fowler beat M. Macleod 10-3; E. Charlton beat B. Harris 10-4; S. Hendry beat Wright 10-4; J. Campbell beat F. Davis 10-3
First round: S. Davis beat Virgo 10-8; M. Hallett beat Chaperon 10-2; Drago beat A. Higgins 10-2; Dennis Taylor beat Werbeniuk 10-8; J. Johnson beat Wilson 10-7; James beat R. Williams 10-6; J. Parrott beat King 10-4; C. Thorburn beat Stevens 10-6; N. Foulds beat W. Jones 10-7; D. Mountjoy beat West 10-6; W. Thorne beat P. Francisco 10-6; T. Griffiths beat Longworth 10-1; T. Knowles beat Fowler 10-8; Charlton beat S. Francisco 10-7; Hendry beat D. Reynolds 10-6; J. White beat Campbell 10-3
Second round: S. Davis beat Hallett 13-1; Drago beat Dennis Taylor 13-5; James beat Johnson 13-9; Thorburn beat Parrott 13-10; N. Foulds beat Mountjoy 13-1; Griffiths beat Thorne 13-9; Knowles beat Charlton 13-7; White beat Hendry 13-12
Quarter-finals: S. Davis beat Drago 13-4; Thorburn beat James 13-11; Griffiths beat Foulds 13-9; White beat Knowles 13-6
Semi-finals: S. Davis beat Thorburn 16-8; Griffiths beat White 16-11
Final: S. Davis beat Griffiths 18-11

ROTHMANS MATCHROOM LEAGUE

Steve Davis, with six wins and three draws, won the Rothmans Matchroom League with a match to spare when he beat Jimmy White 8-0 at the Royal Concert Hall, Nottingham. His second successive League title, secured in front of the largest crowd of the tournament, 2,100 earned him £70,000 and the first leg of a double which could add a £40,000 bonus if he could also win the £65,000 first prize in the 1988 Rothmans Grand Prix.

The bottom two finishers, Dennis Taylor and Joe Johnson were relegated and consequently will not receive invitations to compete in the 1989 event.

The League broke into new ground in Europe in 1988 with matches in Ostend, Amsterdam, Monte Carlo, Marbella and Antwerp.

LEAGUE SCORECARD

Match				
1	Dennis Taylor	2	Cliff Thorburn	6
2	Steve Davis	4	Stephen Hendry	4
3	Tony Meo	5	Neal Foulds	3
4	Jimmy White	6	Terry Griffiths	2
5	Terry Griffiths	4	Cliff Thorburn	4
6	Steve Davis	5	Neal Foulds	3
7	Willie Thorne	5	Joe Johnson	3
8	Cliff Thorburn	3	Neal Foulds	5
9	Dennis Taylor	3	Terry Griffiths	5
10	Jimmy White	5	Tony Meo	3
11	Jimmy White	5	Dennis Taylor	3
12	Neal Foulds	4	Terry Griffiths	4
13	Steve Davis	5	Cliff Thorburn	3
14	Stephen Hendry	6	Tony Meo	2
15	Dennis Taylor	4	Willie Thorne	4
16	Stephen Hendry	2	Willie Thorne	6
17	Jimmy White	6	Joe Johnson	2
18	Steve Davis	5	Tony Meo	3
19	Neal Foulds	5	Willie Thorne	3
20	Dennis Taylor	8	Joe Johnson	0
21	Willie Thorne	4	Tony Meo	4
22	Steve Davis	5	Dennis Taylor	3
23	Neal Foulds	6	Joe Johnson	2
24	Dennis Taylor	1	Stephen Hendry	7
25	Willie Thorne	6	Cliff Thorburn	2
26	Terry Griffiths	5	Joe Johnson	3
27	Dennis Taylor	4	Tony Meo	4
28	Steve Davis	4	Terry Griffiths	4
29	Neal Foulds	4	Stephen Hendry	4
30	Jimmy White	2	Cliff Thorburn	6
31	Tony Meo	4	Cliff Thorburn	4
32	Stephen Hendry	7	Joe Johnson	1
33	Willie Thorne	4	Terry Griffiths	4
34	Jimmy White	4	Neal Foulds	4
35	Joe Johnson	2	Tony Meo	6
36	Jimmy White	4	Stephen Hendry	4
37	Steve Davis	5	Willie Thorne	3

LEAGUE SCORECARD (continued)

Match

38	Steve Davis	8	Jimmy White	0
39	Joe Johnson	1	Cliff Thorburn	7
40	Stephen Hendry	6	Terry Griffiths	2
41	Steve Davis	4	Joe Johnson	4
42	Tony Meo	3	Terry Griffiths	5
43	Stephen Hendry	6	Cliff Thorburn	2
44	Dennis Taylor	2	Neal Foulds	6
45	Jimmy White	2	Willie Thorne	6

LEAGUE TABLE

Player	Prize-money	P	W	D	L	F	A	Pts
Steve Davis	(£70,000)	9	6	3	0	45	27	21
Stephen Hendry	(£30,000)	9	5	3	1	46	26	18
Willie Thorne	(£25,000)	9	4	3	2	41	31	15
Neal Foulds	(£20,000)	9	4	3	2	40	32	15
Jimmy White	(£17,000)	9	4	2	3	34	38	14
Terry Griffiths	(£15,000)	9	3	4	2	35	37	13
Cliff Thorburn	(£13,000)	9	3	2	4	33	39	11
Tony Meo	(£11,000)	9	2	3	4	34	38	9
Dennis Taylor	(£9,000)	9	1	2	6	30	44	5
Joe Johnson	(£5,000)	9	0	1	8	15	54	1

Highest break 147 points Tony Meo (£5,000 prize-money)

WORLD SERIES

Tokyo (*British Caledonian*)

First round: S. Davis beat W. Thorne 2-0; J. White beat S. Hendry 2-0; Dennis Taylor beat T. Meo 2-1; T. Griffiths beat N. Foulds 2-1
Semi-finals: Taylor beat Davis 3-2; Griffiths beat White 3-0
Final: Taylor beat Griffiths 6-3

Hong Kong (*Rileys*)

Quarter-finals: S. Davis beat T. Griffiths 3-0; J. White beat W. Thorne 3-0; Dennis Taylor beat C. Thorburn 3-0; S. Hendry beat N. Foulds 3-2
Semi-finals: Davis beat Taylor 5-4; Hendry beat White 5-2
Final: Davis beat Hendry 9-3

Canada (*Labatt*)

First round: N. Foulds beat T. Griffiths 5-4; J. White beat A. Knowles 5-1; C. Thorburn beat J. Johnson 5-3; Dennis Taylor beat S. Davis 5-1
Semi-finals: White beat N. Foulds 8-7; Dennis Taylor beat Thorburn 8-5
Final: Dennis Taylor beat White 9-7

Where preliminary rounds have been played against local amateur opposition, these results have not been included.

After the conclusion of three of the proposed eight legs, World Series was postponed.

NATIONAL PROFESSIONAL CHAMPIONSHIPS

The WPBSA's prize fund subsidy to national domestic championships of £1,000 per player from 1985 onwards enabled these events to be staged annually and scheduled properly.

There had previously been Australian and Canadian Championships but these had been played in a haphazard way. Eddie Charlton won the Australian title for the first time in 1964 and was beaten only in 1968 until he lost to John Campbell in 1985.

ENGLISH CHAMPIONSHIP

1981 (*John Courage*)
Qualifying: R. Edmonds beat M. Hallett 9-3; J. Johnson beat A. Knowles 9-2; M. Wildman beat B. Bennett 9-3; J. Dunning beat D. Greaves 9-4; J. Meadowcroft beat J. Barrie 9-3
First round: Edmonds beat F. Davis 9-6; T. Meo beat J. Virgo 9-6; G. Miles beat S. Hood 9-1; S. Davis beat Meadowcroft 9-2; J. Spencer beat P. Houlihan 9-1; W. Thorne beat Wildman 9-2; Johnson *wo*; Dunning beat David Taylor 9-8
Quarter-finals: S. Davis beat Spencer 9-7; Meo beat Miles 9-7; Thorne beat Dunning 9-0; Edmonds beat Johnson 9-5
Semi-finals: S. Davis beat Edmonds 9-0; Meo beat Thorne 9-8
Final: S. Davis beat Meo 9-3

1985 (*Tolly Cobbold*)
Qualifying: D. Fowler beat W. Oliver 9-7; M. Bradley beat I. Williamson 9-8; T. Jones beat P. Houlihan 9-1; L. Dodd beat R. Bales 9-5; J. Fitzmaurice beat D. Greaves 9-3; M. Fisher beat D. French 9-8; S. Duggan beat B. Harris 9-8; D. Hughes beat M. Watterson 9-5; D. Chalmers beat J. Meadowcroft 9-3; S. Longworth beat R. Edmonds 9-4; P. Medati beat J. Hargreaves 9-8; G. Foulds beat F. Davis 9-2; G. Cripsey beat B. Bennett 9-0; G. Scott beat V. Harris 9-7
First round: S. Davis beat Fowler 9-3; M. Hallett beat Duggan 9-4; J. Johnson beat Scott 9-1; T. Meo beat Fisher 9-3; J. Virgo beat M. Darrington 9-0; D. Reynolds beat Fitzmaurice 9-2; R. Williams beat T. Jones 9-6; W. Thorne beat Dodd 9-1; Longworth beat M. Wildman 9-3; J. White beat Chalmers 9-5; Medati beat J. Spencer 9-4; N. Foulds beat D. Hughes 9-3; David Taylor beat Cripsey 9-5; J. Parrott beat G. Foulds 9-4; D. Martin beat G. Miles 9-7; A. Knowles beat Bradley 9-8
Second round: Virgo beat Johnson 9-4; Reynolds beat Thorne 9-6; S. Davis beat Williams 9-2; Meo beat Hallett 9-4; Knowles beat Martin 9-3; David Taylor beat Parrott 9-7; White beat N. Foulds 9-7; Longworth beat Medati 9-7
Quarter-finals: Meo beat Reynolds 9-4; Longworth beat White 9-5; Knowles beat David Taylor 9-2; S. Davis beat Virgo 9-2
Semi-finals: Knowles beat Longworth 9-6; S. Davis beat Meo 9-8
Final: S. Davis beat Knowles 9-2

1986 (*Tolly Cobbold*)
First round: D. Gilbert beat B. West 9-8; P. Houlihan beat J. Hargreaves 9-5

Second round: M. Bradley beat Gilbert 9-5; F. Davis beat D. Hughes 9-6; T. Jones beat B. Harris 9-5; W. Oliver beat L. Dodd 9-5; P. Medati beat D. Greaves 9-4; S. Longworth beat S. Duggan 9-4; G. Cripsey beat J. Meadowcroft 9-1; G. Scott beat B. Bennett 9-1; I. Williamson beat M. Watterson 9-1; R. Edmonds beat M. Smith 9-8; D. Fowler beat M. Darrington 9-3; Houlihan *wo* J. Dunning *scr*; D. Chalmers beat Fisher 9-2; R. Bales beat V. Harris 9-7
Third round: S. Davis beat Bradley 9-3; D. Martin beat F. Davis 9-8; J. Virgo beat T. Jones 9-7; J. Parrott beat Oliver 9-0; W. Thorne beat Medati 9-2; D. Reynolds beat Longworth 9-5; M. Wildman beat Cripsey 9-5; T. Meo beat Scott 9-1; J. White beat Williamson 9-1; R. Williams beat Miles 9-6; N. Foulds beat G. Foulds 9-4; Edmonds beat David Taylor 9-6; J. Johnson beat Fowler 9-7; J. Spencer beat Houlihan 9-5; M. Hallett beat Chalmers 9-1; A. Knowles beat Bales 9-4
Fourth round: S. Davis beat Martin 9-4; Virgo beat Parrott 9-6; Reynolds beat Thorne 9-8; Meo beat Wildman 9-3; White beat Williams 9-5; N. Foulds beat Edmonds 9-4; Johnson beat Spencer 9-7; Hallett beat Knowles 9-5
Quarter-finals: S. Davis beat Virgo 9-2; Meo beat Reynolds 9-4; N. Foulds beat White 9-4; Hallett beat Johnson 9-6
Semi-finals: Meo beat S. Davis 9-7; N. Foulds beat Hallett 9-8
Final: Meo beat Foulds 9-7

1987 (*Tolly Ales*)

First round: M. Fisher beat T. Whitthread 6-3; P. Gibson beat D. Hughes 6-3; J. Wright beat D. Chalmers 6-5; B. Bennett beat N. Gilbert 6-5; D. Roe beat D. Greaves 6-1; K. Owers *wo* P. Houlihan *scr*; S. James beat J. Hargeaves 6-5
Second round: S. Duggan beat Fisher 6-0; M. Bradley beat D. Gilbert 6-3; P. Medati beat Gibson 6-2; M. Wildman *wo* M. Watterson *scr*; B. Harris beat G. Foulds 6-1; J. Spencer beat Wright 6-1; R. Edmonds beat Bennett 6-1; G. Cripsey beat J. Dunning 6-1; L. Dodd beat Smith 6-3; V. Harris beat M. Darrington 6-3; I. Williamson beat Roe 6-4; Owers beat R. Bales 6-5; T. Jones beat B. Oliver 6-1; J. Fitzmaurice beat G. Scott 6-2; James beat F. Davis 6-2; G. Miles *wo* J. Meadowcroft *scr*
Third round: T. Meo beat Duggan 6-3; D. Fowler beat Bradley 6-3; J. Virgo beat Medati 6-1; J. Parrott beat Wildman 6-1; W. Thorne beat B. Harris 6-2; D. Martin beat Spencer 6-5; D. Reynolds beat Edmonds 6-3; J. White beat Cripsey 6-4; Dodd beat A. Knowles 6-2; B. West beat V. Harris 6-3; M. Hallett beat Williamson 6-2; Owers beat N. Foulds 6-3; R. Williams beat Jones 6-4; David Taylor beat Fitzmaurice 6-1; James beat S. Longworth 6-2; J. Johnson beat Miles 6-3
Fourth round: Meo beat Fowler 6-0; Parrott beat Virgo 6-2; Thorne beat Martin 6-3; Reynolds beat White 6-5; Dodd beat West 6-3; Hallett beat Owers 6-2; Williams beat David Taylor 6-2; Johnson beat James 6-3
Quarter-finals: Meo beat Parrott 6-3; Thorne beat Reynolds 6-4; Dodd beat Hallett 6-5; Johnson beat Williams 6-5
Semi-finals: Meo beat Thorne 9-3; Dodd beat Johnson 9-5
Final: Meo beat Dodd 9-5

1988

First round: N. Gilbert beat A. Harris 6-3; J. Chambers beat P. Gibson 6-0; D. Gilbert beat T. Whitthread 6-1; E. Lawlor beat D. Roe 6-5; D. Chalmers *wo* M. Fisher *scr*; S. Meakin beat M. Darrington 6-3; M. Smith beat G. Miles 6-1; J. Smith beat V. Harris 6-3; Gary Wilkinson beat B. Rowswell 6-1; P. Medati beat N. Bennett 6-0; D. Heaton beat J. Meadowcroft 6-0; R. Marshall beat B. Oliver 6-3; D. Hughes beat J. Fitzmaurice 6-3; I. Williamson beat J. Dunning 6-5; D. Greaves beat S. James 6-5; M. Clark *wo* M. Watterson *scr*
Second round: F. Davis beat N. Gilbert 6-5; Chambers beat G. Scott 6-3; D. Gilbert beat R. Bales 6-2; Lawlor beat M. Bradley 6-5; J. Wright beat Fisher 6-2; K. Owers beat Meakin 6-2; M. Smith beat B. Harris 6-4; J. Smith beat T. Jones 6-5; Gary Wilkinson beat R. Edmonds 6-3; L. Dodd beat Heaton 6-0; Marshall beat P. Houlihan 6-4;

D. Hughes beat M. Wildman 6-0; S. Duggan beat Williamson 6-2; Greaves beat
G. Cripsey 6-4; Clark beat G. Foulds 6-0
Third round: T. Meo beat F. Davis 6-3; S. Longworth beat Chambers 6-4; D. Reynolds
beat D. Gilbert 6-3; J. Parrott beat Lawlor 6-3; A. Knowles beat Wright 6-2; Owers beat
David Taylor 6-3; D. Martin beat M. Smith 6-5; J. Johnson beat J. Smith 6-5; N. Foulds
beat Gary Wilkinson 6-3; Fowler beat J. Spencer 6-3; J. Virgo beat Dodd 6-3; W. Thorne
beat Marshall 6-3; R. Williams beat D. Hughes 6-1; M. Hallett beat Duggan 6-3; B. West
beat Greaves 6-5; J. White beat Clark 6-5
Fourth round: Meo beat Longworth 6-4; Reynolds beat Parrott 6-2; Knowles beat Owers
6-4; Johnson beat Martin 6-4; N. Foulds beat Fowler 6-1; Thorne beat Virgo 6-0; Hallett
beat Williams 6-3; West beat White 6-2
Quarter-finals: Reynolds beat Meo 6-4; Johnson beat Knowles 6-3; N. Foulds beat
Thorne 6-2; West beat Hallett 6-5
Semi-finals: Reynolds beat Johnson 9-8; N. Foulds beat West 9-6
Final: Reynolds beat N. Foulds 9-5

IRISH CHAMPIONSHIP

1972
Challenge: A. Higgins beat Jack Rea 28-12

1978
Challenge: A. Higgins beat Dennis Taylor 21-7

1979
Challenge: A. Higgins beat P. Fagan 21-13

1980
Challenge: Dennis Taylor beat A. Higgins 21-15

1981
Challenge: Dennis Taylor beat P. Fagan 22-21

1982
First round: E. Hughes beat D. Sheehan 6-1
Quarter-finals: E. Hughes beat Jack Rea 6-0; T. Murphy beat P. Fagan 6-2
Semi-finals: Dennis Taylor beat Murphy 6-0; A. Higgins beat E. Hughes 6-2
Final: Taylor beat Higgins 16-13

1983
First round: Dennis Taylor beat B. Kelly 6-0; P. Fagan beat T. Murphy 6-4; A. Higgins
beat Jack Rea 6-3; E. Hughes beat P. Burke 6-2
Semi-finals: Higgins beat E. Hughes 6-2; Taylor beat Fagan 6-1
Final: Higgins beat Taylor 16-11

1985 (*Strongbow*)
Preliminary: J. McLaughlin beat D. Sheehan 6-3
Qualifying: P. Burke beat A. Kearney 6-4; T. Murphy beat P. Browne 6-3; B. Kelly beat
P. Watchorn 6-2; Jack Rea beat McLaughlin 6-5
Quarter-finals: P. Fagan beat Murphy 6-2; Dennis Taylor beat Jack Rea 6-0; A. Higgins
beat Burke 6-0; E. Hughes beat Kelly 6-2
Semi-finals: Taylor beat Hughes 6-5; Higgins beat Fagan 6-3
Final: Taylor beat Higgins 10-5

1986 (*Strongbow*)
First round: B. Kelly beat Jack Rea 5-0; T. Murphy beat J. O'Boye 5-0; E. Hughes beat

D. Sheehan 5-0; A. Kearney beat P. Fagan 5-0; J. McLaughlin beat P. Watchorn 5-0;
P. Burke beat P. Browne 5-4
Quarter-finals: Dennis Taylor beat Kelly 6-1; Murphy beat Kearney 6-2; A. Higgins beat
McLaughlin 6-2; Hughes beat Burke 6-3
Semi-finals: Taylor beat Murphy 6-3; Higgins beat Hughes 6-2
Final: Taylor beat Higgins 10-7

1987 (Matchroom)
First round: D. Sheehan beat J. McLaughlin 5-4; P. Browne beat Jack Rea 5-3;
T. Kearney beat T. Murphy 5-1; J. O'Boye beat B. Kelly 5-0; P. Burke beat P. Fagan 5-3;
E. Hughes beat P. Watchorn 5-2
Quarter-finals: Dennis Taylor beat Sheehan 6-3; Hughes beat Kearney 6-1; Browne beat
Burke 6-2; O'Boye wo Higgins scr
Semi-finals: Taylor beat Browne 6-1; O'Boye beat Hughes 6-3
Final: Taylor beat O'Boye 9-2

1988
First round: A. Kearney beat P. Fagan 5-3; T. Murphy beat B. Kelly 5-1; P. Browne beat
Jack Rea 5-0; P. Watchorn beat E. Hughes 5-2; J. McLaughlin beat P. Burke 5-3;
J. O'Boye beat D. Sheehan 5-0
Quarter-finals: Dennis Taylor beat Kearney 6-3; Browne beat Murphy 6-5; McLaughlin
beat Watchorn 6-5; O'Boye beat A. Higgins 6-4
Semi-finals: Taylor beat Browne 6-5; McLaughlin beat O'Boye 6-4
Final: McLaughlin beat Taylor 9-4

SCOTTISH CHAMPIONSHIP

1980
Challenge: E. Sinclair beat C. Ross 11-6

1981
First round: M. Gibson beat B. Demarco 5-3; J. Donnelly beat E. Sinclair 5-0;
E. McLaughlin beat C. Ross 5-3; I. Black beat M. Macleod 5-4
Semi-finals: Gibson beat Donnelly 6-4; Black beat E. McLaughlin 6-3
Final: Black beat Gibson 11-7

1982
First round: M. Macleod beat J. Donnelly 6-5
Quarter-finals: C. Ross beat B. Demarco 6-5; M. Gibson beat E. McLaughlin 6-3;
I. Black beat Macleod 6-0; E. Sinclair beat J. Phillips 6-3
Semi-finals: Black beat Ross 6-4; Sinclair beat Gibson 6-2
Final: Sinclair beat Black 11-7

1983
First round: J. Donnelly beat B. Demarco 6-4; I. Black beat E. McLaughlin 6-4;
M. Macleod beat M. Gibson 6-5
Semi-finals: E. Sinclair beat Donnelly 6-5; Macleod beat Black 6-2
Final: Macleod beat Sinclair 11-9

1985
First round: M. Macleod beat E. McLaughlin 6-4; M. Gibson beat I. Black 6-2; John Rea
beat J. Donnelly 6-2; E. Sinclair beat B. Demarco 6-3
Semi-final: Macleod beat Gibson 6-4; Sinclair beat John Rea 6-2
Final: Macleod beat Sinclair 10-2

1986 (Canada Dry)
First round: S. Hendry beat B. Demarco 6-1

Quarter-finals: Hendry beat M. Macleod 6-5; I. Black beat E. McLaughlin 6-4; John Rea beat J. Donnelly 6-1; M.Gibson beat E. Sinclair 6-4
Semi-finals: Hendry beat Black 6-2; Gibson beat John Rea 6-0
Final: Hendry beat Gibson 10-5

1987
First round: S. Hendry beat B. Demarco 6-2; John Rea beat I. Black 6-1; E. Sinclair beat M. Gibson 6-2; J. Donnelly beat M. Macleod 6-2
Semi-finals: Hendry beat Rea 6-0; Donnelly beat Sinclair 6-4
Final: Hendry beat Donnelly 10-7

1988 (*Swish*)
First round: B. Demarco beat E. McLaughlin 6-0
Quarter-finals: S. Hendry beat Demarco 6-0; M. Gibson beat I. Black 6-2; John Rea beat E. Sinclair 6-5; M. Macleod beat J. Donnelly 6-5
Semi-finals: Hendry beat Gibson 6-1; Macleod beat Rea 6-5
Final: Hendry beat Macleod 10-4

WELSH CHAMPIONSHIP

1977 (*William Hill*)
Challenge: R. Reardon beat D. Mountjoy 12-8

1980 (*Woodpecker*)
First round: D. Mountjoy beat T. Griffiths 9-6; R. Reardon beat C. Wilson 9-3
Final: Mountjoy beat Reardon 9-6

1981 (*Woodpecker*)
Qualifying: C. Wilson beat R. Andrewartha 6-5
First round: Wilson beat D. Mountjoy 9-6; R. Reardon beat T. Griffiths 9-6
Final: Reardon beat Wilson 9-6

1982 (*Woodpecker*)
First round: C. Wilson beat M. Owen 6-0; T. Griffiths beat C. Roscoe 6-2; R. Reardon beat C. Everton 6-1; D. Mountjoy beat R. Andrewartha 6-3
Semi-finals: Griffiths beat Wilson 9-6; Mountjoy beat Reardon 9-7
Final: Mountjoy beat Griffiths 9-8

1983 (*Woodpecker*)
First round: T. Griffiths beat C. Everton 6-1; R. Reardon beat R. Andrewartha 6-2; C. Wilson beat C. Roscoe 6-4; D. Mountjoy beat M. Owen 6-0
Semi-finals: Reardon beat Griffiths 9-4; Mountjoy beat Wilson 9-3
Final: Reardon beat Mountjoy 9-1

1984 (*Strongbow*)
First round: D. Mountjoy beat C. Everton 6-1; T. Griffiths beat R. Andrewartha 6-1; R. Reardon beat M. Owen 6-1; C. Wilson beat C. Roscoe 6-2
Semi-finals: Mountjoy beat Griffiths 9-5; Wilson beat Reardon 9-4
Final: Mountjoy beat Wilson 9-3

1985 (*BCE*)
First round: S. Newbury beat W. Jones 6-2; T. Chappel beat M. Owen 6-0
Quarter finals: R. Reardon beat C. Everton 6-2; D. Mountjoy beat Newbury 6-5; C. Wilson beat C. Roscoe 6-3; T. Griffiths beat Chappel 6-0
Semi-finals: Griffiths beat Reardon 9-3; Mountjoy beat Wilson 9-2
Final: Griffiths beat Mountjoy 9-4

1986 (*Zetters*)
First round: T. Chappel *wo* M. Owen *scr*; W. Jones beat C. Everton 6-2
Quarter-finals: T. Griffiths beat Chappel 6-4; C. Wilson beat S. Newbury 6-4;
D. Mountjoy beat C. Roscoe 6-4; W. Jones beat Reardon 6-4
Semi-finals: Griffiths beat Wilson 9-1; Mountjoy beat W. Jones 9-7
Final: Griffiths beat Mountjoy 9-3

1987 (*Matchroom*)
First round: W. Jones beat M. Bennett 6-3; C. Roscoe beat C. Everton 6-2
Quarter-finals: T. Griffiths beat Jones 6-2; S. Newbury beat C. Wilson 6-2; T. Chappel
beat R. Reardon 6-4; D. Mountjoy beat Roscoe 6-2
Semi-finals: Newbury beat Griffiths 9-6; Mountjoy beat Chappel 9-2
Final: Mountjoy beat Newbury 9-7

1988 (*Senator*)
First round: M. Bennett beat C. Everton 6-0; T. Chappel beat C. Roscoe 6-4
Quarter-finals: D. Mountjoy beat Bennett 6-3; W. Jones beat R. Reardon 6-5; C. Wilson
beat S. Newbury 6-3; T. Griffiths beat Chappel 6-4
Semi-finals: Jones beat Mountjoy 9-5; Griffiths beat Wilson 9-7
Final: Griffiths beat Jones 9-3

AUSTRALIAN CHAMPIONSHIP

1985
First round: G. Wilkinson beat G. Jenkins 6-2; G. Robinson beat J. Charlton* 6-0;
L. Condo beat E. Charlton* 6-2
Second round: Wilkinson beat L. Heywood 7-3; R. Foldvari beat Robinson 7-2;
J. Giannaros beat Condo 7-2; I. Anderson *wo* G. Ganim *scr*
Quarter-finals: E. Charlton beat Wilkinson 8-2; P. Morgan beat Giannaros 8-4; W. King
beat Anderson 8-2; J. Campbell beat Foldvari 8-5
Semi-finals: Charlton beat Morgan 9-3; Campbell beat King 9-6
Final: Campbell beat Charlton 10-7

1986
First-round: G. Jenkins beat G. Ganim** 6-2; L. Condo** beat E. Charlton Jr* 6-0;
J. Charlton* beat G. Robinson* 6-4
Second round: Condo beat J. Giannaros 6-4; I. Anderson beat J. Charlton 6-2;
G. Wilkinson beat L. Heywood 6-0; R. Foldvari beat Jenkins 6-3
Quarter-finals: J. Campbell beat Wilkinson 6-1; Foldvari beat P. Morgan 6-2; W. King
beat Condo 6-3; E. Charlton beat Anderson 6-2
Semi-finals: Campbell beat Foldvari 8-3; King beat Charlton 8-6
Final: King beat Campbell 10-3

1987
Qualifying round: S. Frangie* beat W. Potasnyk* 6-4
First round: G. Jenkins beat L. Condo** 6-1; I. Anderson beat L. Heywood* 6-4;
G. Wilkinson beat J. Charlton* 6-0; Frangie beat P. Morgan** 6-5
Quarter-finals: W. King beat Jenkins 6-4; R. Foldvari beat Frangie 6-2; E. Charlton beat
Anderson 6-2; J. Campbell beat Wilkinson 6-4
Semi-finals: King beat Foldvari 8-1; Charlton beat Campbell 8-6
Final: King beat Charlton 10-7

* Member of the Australian Professional Billiards and Snooker Association but not the WPBSA
** Non-tournament member of the WPBSA

CANADIAN CHAMPIONSHIP

1983
First round: G. Rigitano beat M. Gauvreau 9-6; R. Chaperon beat G. Watson 9-5; J. Caggianello beat W. Sanderson 9-5
Second round: B. Mikkelsen beat Rigitano 9-4; F. Jonik beat Chaperon 9-4; Jim Bear beat M. Morra 9-8; Caggianello beat P. Thornley 9-7
Quarter-finals: C. Thorburn beat Mikkelsen 9-2; Jonik beat J. Wych 9-5; Jim Bear beat John Bear 9-5; K. Stevens beat Caggianello 9-0
Semi-finals: Jonik beat Thorburn 9-6; Stevens beat Jim Bear 9-8
Final: Stevens beat Jonik 9-8

1985
First round: J. Caggianello beat Jim Bear 5-4; R. Chaperon beat P. Thornley 5-1; B. Mikkelsen beat G. Watson 5-3; John Bear beat M. Morra 5-4; J. Wych beat W. Sanderson 5-2
Quarter-finals: Chaperon beat K. Stevens 6-4; F. Jonik beat Mikkelsen 6-4; C. Thorburn beat Caggianello 6-2; Wych beat John Bear 6-3
Semi-finals: Chaperon beat Jonik 6-3; Thorburn beat Wych 6-5
Final: Thorburn beat Chaperon 6-4

1986
First round: G. Watson beat J. Caggianello 6-1; F. Jonik beat G. Rigitano 6-1; R. Chaperon beat J. Bear 6-3; B. Mikkelsen beat W. Sanderson 6-1; P. Thornley beat M. Morra 6-4
Second round: C. Thorburn beat Watson 6-1; Jonik beat Chaperon 6-3; J. Wych beat Mikkelsen 6-3; K. Stevens beat Thornley 6-2
Semi-finals: Thorburn beat Jonik 6-3; Wych beat Stevens 6-2
Final: Thorburn beat Wych 6-2

1987 (*BCE*)
First round: G. Watson beat P. Thornley 6-4; F. Jonik beat W. Sanderson 6-0; M. Morra beat R. Chaperon 6-5; J. Wych beat G. Rigitano 6-4; Jim Bear beat B. Mikkelsen 6-0; J. Caggianello beat M. Gauvreau 6-3
Quarter-finals: Morra beat Jonik 6-2; C. Thorburn beat Watson 6-3; Bear beat Wych 6-4; K. Stevens beat Caggianello 6-0
Semi-finals: Bear beat Stevens 7-2; Thorburn beat Morra 7-4
Final: Thorburn beat Bear 8-4

SOUTH AFRICAN CHAMPIONSHIP

1986
First round: P. Francisco beat V. Blignaut* 6-3; D. Mienie beat M. Hines 6-5; F. Ellis beat R. Amdor* 6-2
Second round: S. Francisco beat G. Johnston* 7-0; P. Francisco beat R. Grace 7-1; J. Van Rensberg beat Mienie 7-1; Ellis beat P. Mans 7-6
Semi-finals: S. Francisco beat P. Francisco 8-3; Ellis beat Van Rensberg 8-2
Final: S. Francisco beat Ellis 9-1

1987
Semi-finals: F. Ellis beat R. Grace 9-8; J. Van Rensberg beat P. Mans* 9-4
Final: Ellis beat Van Rensberg 9-4
* Member of the South African Professional Association but not the WPBSA

PROFESSIONAL BILLIARDS

THE WORLD PROFESSIONAL BILLIARDS CHAMPIONSHIP

Founded in 1870, the World Professional Billiards Championship is the oldest of all the game's events but since snooker has become by far the most popular of the billiard table games it has declined steadily in public appeal.

The problems started in the 1930s when the four best players in the world, Walter Lindrum, Joe Davis, Tom Newman and Clark McConachy, mastered all aspects of the game so completely that they effectively killed it as a public entertainment. They did such a thorough job that there was only one Championship between 1934 and 1968 that they did not claim – when Rex Williams travelled to New Zealand and beat McConachy, then 73 and suffering from Parkinson's disease.

Williams successfully defended the title three times against various challengers but lost it in June 1980 to Joe's younger brother Fred, who thus became only the second player to have held world titles at both billiards and snooker – the first, of course, was Joe.

In November 1980, the event reverted to a tournament format and a variety of playing systems was tried: time-limit games, points-up games and, for the first time last season, the best of five games of 400-up. This formula gave frequent climaxes, as in frames of snooker, and also eliminated the possibility of very large breaks.

1985 also saw Channel 4 attempt a 'Pot Black'-style billiards event, the Blue Arrow Masters. Viewing figures for this were encouraging and the BBC agreed to televise the final of the 1986 World Professional Championship which was again played over the best of five games of 400-up.

In 1987, from the Albert Hall, Bolton, both the semi-finals and final were televised. Norman Dagley, who had earlier in the season won the UK Championship, added the professional title to his two world amateur victories by beating Robby Foldvari 3-1 in the final.

For the 1987–88 season, the format of the World, UK, European and a new event, the Yorkshire Bank tournament, was altered to games of 150 up, although none of these events attracted television coverage.

World Professional Billiards Championship (1870–1920)

1870 (Feb)	W. Cook	J. Roberts Sr	1,200-1,083
(Apr)	J. Roberts Jr	W. Cook	1,000- 522
(June)	J. Roberts Jr	A. Bowles	1,000- 759
(Nov)	J. Bennett	J. Roberts Jr	1,000- 905
1871 (Jan)	J. Roberts Jr	J. Bennett	1,000- 637
(May)	W. Cook	J. Roberts Jr	1,000- 985
(Nov)	W. Cook	J. Bennett	1,000- 942
1872 (Mar)	W. Cook	J. Roberts Jr	1,000- 799
1874 (Feb)	W. Cook	J. Roberts Jr	1,000- 784
1875 (May)	J. Roberts Jr	W. Cook	1,000- 837
(Dec)	J. Roberts Jr	W. Cook	1,000- 865
1877 (May)	J. Roberts Jr	W. Cook	1,000- 779
1880 (Nov)	J. Bennett	W. Cook	1,000- 949
1881 (Jan)	J. Bennett	T. Taylor	1,000- 910
1885 (Apr)	J. Roberts Jr	W. Cook	3,000-2,908
(June)	J. Roberts Jr	J. Bennett	3,000-1,360
1899	C. Dawson	J. North	9,000-4,715
1900	C. Dawson	H. W. Stevenson	9,000-6,775
1901	H. W. Stevenson	C. Dawson	9,000-6,406
	C. Dawson	H. W. Stevenson	9,000-5,796
	H. W. Stevenson (*declared champion – no contest*)		
1903	C. Dawson	H. W. Stevenson	9,000-8,700
1908	M. Inman (*declared champion – no contest*)		
1909	M. Inman	A. Williams	9,000-7,662
Under Billiards Control Club Rules			
1909	H. W. Stevenson (*declared champion – no contest*)		
1910	H. W. Stevenson	M. Inman	13,370-13,212
		(*match abandoned*)	
	H. W. Stevenson	M. Inman	18,000-16,907
1911	H. W. Stevenson	M. Inman	18,000-16,914
1912	M. Inman	T. Reece	18,000- 9,675
1913	M. Inman	T. Reece	18,000-16,627
1914	M. Inman	T. Reece	18,000-12,826
1919	M. Inman	H. W. Stevenson	16,000- 9,468
1920	W. Smith	C. Falkiner	16,000-14,500

World Professional Billiards Championship (1921–88)

Winner (*breaks*)	Score (*average*)	Loser (*breaks*)	Score (*average*)
1921			
First round			
C. Falkiner	7,334 (35.3)	H. W. Stevenson	5,084 (24.3)
560			
T. Newman	8,000 (54.0)	T. Tothill	3,267 (22.0)
467			

Winner (breaks)	Score (average)	Loser (breaks)	Score (average)
Semi-finals			
Newman	8,000 (56.7)	Falkiner	6,627 (47.3)
627,531		587	
T. Reece	nr	F. Lawrence	nr
Final			
Newman	16,000 (nr)	Reece	10,744 (nr)
1922			
First round			
T. Reece	8,000 (35.2)	C. McConachy	6,767 (29.9)
Semi-finals			
T. Newman	8,000 (52.6)	J. Davis	5,181 (34.1)
561,512			
C. Falkiner	8,000 (41.9)	Reece	7,289 (38.2)
391		455	
Final			
Newman	16,000 (56.4)	Falkiner	15,167 (52.7)
1923			
First round			
M. Inman	16,000 (nr)	A. Peall	11,758 (nr)
C. Falkiner	16,000 (nr)	T. Reece	14,952 (nr)
Semi-finals			
T. Newman	16,000 (56.3)	Inman	14,506 (51.1)
850, 705, 500 × 4		701	
W. Smith	16,000 (71.7)	Falkiner	8,695 (29.2)
688		782,620	
Final			
Smith	16,000 (46.4)	Newman	15,180 (44.0)
451,446		638, 629, 575	
1924			
First round			
T. Newman	16,000 (71.4)	C. McConachy	8,703 (38.9)
875		349	
Final			
Newman	16,000 (43.5)	T. Reece	14,845 (40.3)
1,021			
1925			
T. Newman	16,000 (68.4)	T. Reece	10,092 (43.1)
957, 672		512	
1926			
T. Newman	16,000 (82.0)	J. Davis	9,505 (49.0)
637, 574, 588		414	
1927			
First round			
M. Inman	8,000 (nr)	T. Reece	5,527 (nr)
459		1,151	
Second round			
J. Davis	8,000 (nr)	Inman	6,895
504, 588			

Winner (breaks)	Score (average)	Loser (breaks)	Score (average)
Challenge round			
T. Newman	16,000 (73.0)	Davis	14,763 (68.0)
787, 1,073, 1,012, 891		2,501 727	
1928			
First round			
T. Carpenter	8,000 (22.4)	T. Reece	7,283 (20.5)
Second round			
J. Davis	8,000 (66.4)	Carpenter	5,602 (41.8)
Challenge round			
Davis	16,000 (74.4)	T. Newman	14,874 (69.5)
529, 525, 501, 425, 408,		564, 489, 467, 455,	
404, 403, 400		451, 427	
1929			
First round			
T. Newman	8,000 (74.1)	T. Carpenter	5,984 (55.4)
553		453	
Final			
J. Davis	18,000 (100.0)	Newman	17,219 (96.2)
838, 609, 599		723, 691, 672, 647, 576	
1930			
First round			
T. Newman	24.001 (85.1)	M. Inman	10,104 (35.8)
1,567, 1,047			
J. Davis	21,975 (82.0)	C. Falkiner	19,815 (74.0)
Final			
Davis	20,918 (113.1)	Newman	20,117 (109.9)
2,052, 500 × 9		500 × 12	
1932			
J. Davis	25,161 (112.0)	C. McConachy	19,259 (98.0)
1,058, 844, 774		1,432, 916, 889	
1933			
First round			
W. Lindrum	21,470 (*nr*)	T. Newman	20,252 (*nr*)
1,578, 984		877, 805	
J. Davis	20,136 (*nr*)	C. McConachy	16,110 (*nr*)
995		675	
Final			
Lindrum	21,815 (92.0)	Davis	21,121 (89.0)
1,492, 1,272, 1,013		792	
1934			
First round			
W. Lindrum	21,903 (*nr*)	C. McConachy	20,795 (*nr*)
1,065, 807		892, 829	
Final			
Lindrum	23,533 (*nr*)	J. Davis	22,678 (*nr*)
1,474, 1,353		824, 728	

Winner (breaks)	Score (average)	Loser (breaks)	Score (average)
1951			
C. McConachy	6,681 (60.0)	J. Barrie	5,057 (44.8)
481, 438, 425, 397, 376		367, 336	
1968			
R. Williams	5,499 (nr)	C. McConachy	5,234 (nr)
293		236, 200	
1971			
R. Williams	9,250 (nr)	B. Bennett	4,058 (nr)
480, 372, 353, 325, 302		132	
1973			
R. Williams	8,360 (50.7)	J. Karnehm	4,336 (26.1)
528, 363, 309		215	
1974			
R. Williams	7,017 (43.6)	E. Charlton	4,916 (30.4)
506, 365, 308, 307		488, 401	
1976			
R. Williams	9,105 (42.1)	E. Charlton	5,149 (23.9)
532, 349, 382, 306		333	
1980 (May)			
Challenge round			
F. Davis	5,978 (39.9)	R. Williams	4,452 (29.9)
403, 225, 234, 239, 275, 583		226, 202, 439, 229	
1980 (Nov)			
Qualifying			
P. Morgan	1,655 (21.5)	J. Dunning	1,107 (12.9)
M. Wildman	1,968 (26.2)	B. Bennett	678 (9.0)
S. Davis	1,809 (16.9)	K. Kennerley	965 (9.1)
Quarter-finals			
J. Barrie	2,186 (53.3)	S. Davis	870 (21.8)
335			
F. Davis	1,907 (43.3)	Morgan	978 (22.2)
309			
R. Edmonds	1,513 (19.4)	J. Karnehm	1,306 (17.0)
Wildman	1,476 (25.9)	R. Williams	1,415 (24.8)
Semi-finals			
F. Davis	1,253 (34.8)	Barrie	1,153 (32.0)
501			
Wildman	1,629 (21.4)	Edmonds	955 (12.6)
204			
Final			
F. Davis	3,037 (30.4)	Wildman	2,064 (20.6)
200, 361			
1982			
First round			
C. Everton	1,500 (23.4)	B. Bennett	556 (8.6)
Quarter-finals			
F. Davis	1,500 (30.6)	Everton	652 (13.6)
R. Williams	1,500 (31.9)	J. Karnehm	569 (11.9)

Winner (breaks)	Score (average)	Loser (breaks)	Score (average)
R. Edmonds	1,500 (16.5)	K. Kennerley	753 (8.2)
M. Wildman	1,500 (21.7)	J. Fitzmaurice	721 (10.5)
Semi-finals			
Williams	1,500 (20.3)	Davis	1,494 (19.9)
Wildman	1,500 (24.2)	Edmonds	765 (12.1)
203			
Final			
Williams	3,000 (26.1)	Wildman	1,785 (15.5)
207, 259, 217			

1983
Qualifying

I. Williamson	1,000 (12.5)	D. Martin	710 (8.8)
B. Bennett	1,000 (11.2)	G. Cripsey	683 (6.3)
First round			
J. Karnehm		M. Darrington	
I	752 (15.0)		679 (13.3)
II	748 (12.1)		520 (8.4)
	1,500 (13.4)		1,199 (10.6)
B. Bennett		J. Fitzmaurice	
I	751 (10.0)		666 (8.8)
II	749 (10.3)		730 (10.1)
	1,500 (10.1)		1,396 (9.4)
C. Everton		I. Williamson	
I	752 (15.0)		591 (11.6)
II	748 (17.8)		494 (12.0)
	1,500 (16.3)		1,085 (11.8)
E. Charlton		T. Murphy	
I	751 (11.7)		694 (10.8)
II	749 (18.3)		411 (10.0)
	1,500 (14.3)		1,105 (10.5)
Quarter-finals			
R. Williams		Bennett	
	751 (30.0)		225 (8.7)
II 233, 228,			
50 (*unf*)	749 (30.6)		218 (9.5)
	1,500 (31.3)		443 (9.0)
F. Davis		Everton	
I (*unf*)	751 (37.6)		236 (11.2)
II (*full*)	749 (39.4)		241 (12.7)
	1,500 (38.5)		477 (11.9)
R. Edmonds		Karnehm	
I	559 (13.0)		750 (17.4)
II 358			
	941 (29.4)		325 (9.8)
	1,500 (20.0)		1,075 (14.1)

Winner (breaks)	Score (average)	Loser (breaks)	Score (average)
Charlton		M. Wildman	
I	750 (15.6)		408 (8.5)
II (unf)	750 (15.0)		370 (7.6)
	1,500 (15.3)		778 (8.0)
Semi-finals			
F. Davis		Charlton	
I	750 (25.9)		410 (14.1)
II 228	750 (30.0)		546 (21.8)
	1,500 (27.8)		956 (17.7)
Williams		Edmonds	
I (unf)	750 (57.7)		288 (22.2)
II (full)	750 (62.5)		383 (31.9)
	1,500 (60.0)		671 (26.8)
Final			
Williams		F. Davis	
I (unf)	751 (32.7)		227 (9.5)
II 212			
	749 (46.8)		378 (23.6)
	1,500 (38.4)		605 (15.1)
1984			
Preliminary round			
T. Murphy		M. Darrington	
I	400 (12.5)		505 (15.8)
II	621 (17.7)		356 (10.2)
	1,021 (15.0)		861 (12.9)
First round			
P. Morgan		B. Bennett	
I	508 (13.0)		306 (8.1)
II	513 (17.7)		333 (11.5)
	1,021 (15.0)		639 (9.5)
I. Williamson		C. Everton	
I	373 (12.4)		189 (6.5)
II	373 (14.3)		307 (11.4)
	746 (13.3)		496 (8.9)
J. Karnehm		G. Ganim Jr	
I	600 (23.1)		383 (14.2)
II	670 (23.1)		350 (12.5)
	1,270 (23.1)		733 (13.3)
Murphy		J. Fitzmaurice	
I (unf)	425 (12.1)		497 (14.2)
II (full)	625 (15.6)		371 (9.3)
	1,050 (14.2)		868 (11.6)
Quarter-finals			
F. Davis		Murphy	
I	550 (21.1)		453 (17.4)
II	692 (26.6)		399 (16.0)
	1,242 (23.9)		852 (16.7)

Winner (breaks)	Score (average)	Loser (breaks)	Score (average)
E. Charlton		Karnehm	
I	343 (16.3)		623 (28.5)
II 319	601 (35.4)		308 (19.3)
	944 (24.8)		931 (24.5)
Williamson		R. Edmonds	
I	407 (22.6)		432 (22.7)
II	511 (31.9)		373 (23.3)
	918 (27.0)		805 (23.0)
M. Wildman		Morgan	
I	749 (37.4)		299 (14.2)
II	598 (15.8)		460 (17.6)
	1,347 (28.7)		759 (15.8)
Semi-finals			
Charlton		F. Davis	
I	795 (29.4)		268 (9.2)
II	641 (27.9)		561 (25.5)
	1,436 (28.7)		829 (16.6)
Wildman		Williamson	
I 226	610 (23.5)		468 (17.3)
II 205	891 (35.6)		381 (15.2)
	1,501 (29.4)		849 (16.4)
Final			
Wildman		Charlton	
I	599 (27.2)		508 (23.1)
II	446 (14.4)		504 (16.3)
	1,045 (19.7)		1,012 (19.1)
1985			
First round			
P. Francisco 3		M. Darrington 0	
I	400 (22.2)		166 (9.2)
II	400 (12.6)		249 (7.5)
III	400 (16.1)		161 (6.7)
I. Williamson 3		B. Bennett 0	
I	400 (17.0)		200 (8.6)
II	400 (30.9)		89 (6.4)
III	400 (15.4)		331 (12.7)
J. Karnehm 3		E. Charlton 0	
I	400 (22.2)		308 (16.2)
II	400 (21.1)		217 (11.4)
III	400 (14.8)		354 (12.6)
R. Edmonds 3		A. Higgins 0	
I	400 (25.0)		188 (11.0)
II	400 (26.7)		221 (14.7)
III	400 (25.0)		110 (6.9)
M. Wildman 3		T. Jones 0	
I	400 (20.0)		237 (11.3)
II	400 (30.9)		144 (11.0)
III	400 (44.4)		125 (12.5)

Winner (breaks)	Score (average)	Loser (breaks)	Score (average)
N. Dagley 3		J. Fitzmaurice 0	
I	400 (16.7)		325 (13.5)
II	400 (44.4)		284 (28.4)
III 253	400 (33.5)		80 (6.7)
R. Foldvari wo		B. Oliver scr	
F. Davis 3		C. Everton 1	
I	400 (16.2)		275 (11.4)
II	400 (28.6)		206 (13.7)
III	293 (20.9)		400 (30.8)
IV	400 (30.8)		156 (11.1)
Quarter-finals			
Dagley 3		Karnehm 0	
I 270 (unf)	400 (80.0)		24 (4.8)
II	400 (21.1)		294 (14.7)
III	400 (44.4)		59 (6.6)
Foldvari 3		F. Davis 0	
I	400 (15.4)		130 (4.8)
II	400 (33.3)		316 (26.3)
III	400 (20.0)		342 (16.3)
Wildman 3		Francisco 0	
I	400 (28.6)		186 (12.4)
II	400 (28.6)		106 (7.6)
III	400 (66.7)		70 (10.0)
Edmonds 3		Williamson 1	
I	378 (15.0)		400 (16.0)
II	400 (25.0)		246 (15.4)
III 252	400 (28.6)		212 (14.1)
IV	400 (23.5)		248 (14.6)
Semi-finals			
Edmonds 3		Wildman 0	
I (unf)	400 (28.6)		313 (22.3)
II	400 (22.3)		196 (10.3)
III (unf)	400 (22.3)		298 (16.6)
Dagley 3		Foldvari 0	
I	400 (22.2)		352 (19.6)
II	400 (25.0)		248 (14.6)
III	400 (15.4)		282 (11.0)
Final			
Edmonds 3		Dagley 1	
I	400 (33.3)	201	395 (30.4)
II	307 (28.0)		400 (40.0)
III	400 (26.6)		315 (19.6)
IV	400 (20.0)		386 (19.3)

Winner (breaks)	Score (average)	Loser (breaks)	Score (average)
1986			
Qualifying			
R. Close 3		E. Hughes 1	
I	319 (12.8)		400 (16.0)
II	400 (50.0)		105 (11.7)
III	400 (15.4)		310 (11.5)
IV	400 (19.1)		338 (16.1)
G. Scott 3		B. Oliver 0	
I	400 (7.8)		344 (6.9)
II	400 (12.9)		164 (5.3)
III	400 (9.3)		398 (9.5)
First round			
E. Charlton 3		T. Jones 0	
I	400 (10.3)		314 (8.1)
II	400 (14.8)		180 (6.7)
III	400 (25.0)		73 (4.6)
I. Williamson 3		Scott 0	
I	400 (14.3)		372 (12.8)
II	400 (13.8)		288 (10.3)
III	400 (12.9)		251 (8.1)
R. Foldvari 3		J. Karnehm 1	
I	400 (12.5)		282 (8.6)
II	273 (9.1)		400 (13.3)
III	400 (18.2)		268 (12.2)
IV 292	400 (36.4)		116 (10.6)
R. Edmonds 3		J. Fitzmaurice 0	
I	400 (19.5)		131 (6.0)
II	400 (25.0)		104 (6.9)
III	400 (12.1)		295 (8.9)
N. Dagley 3		B. Bennett 0	
I	400 (16.0)		148 (5.9)
II	400 (17.4)		190 (8.3)
III	400 (40.0)		107 (10.7)
Close 3		F. Davis 0	
I (*unf*)	400 (50.0)		57 (6.3)
II	400 (21.1)		262 (13.8)
III	400 (40.0)		323 (29.3)
P. Francisco 3		C. Everton 0	
I	400 (11.4)		395 (11.3)
II	400 (11.5)		397 (11.3)
III	400 (10.8)		349 (9.4)
M. Wildman 3		G. Thompson 0	
I	400 (21.0)		240 (12.0)
II	400 (13.8)		203 (9.0)
III	400 (14.8)		317 (11.3)

Winner (breaks)	Score (average)	Loser (breaks)	Score (average)
Quarter-finals			
Edmonds 3		Francisco 0	
I	400 (12.9)		291 (9.1)
II	400 (15.4)		218 (8.4)
III	400 (12.9)		347 (10.8)
Dagley 3		Charlton 0	
I	400 (16.7)		238 (10.0)
II	400 (12.9)		130 (4.0)
III	400 (13.7)		330 (11.3)
Foldvari 3		Close 0	
I	400 (19.0)		231 (11.0)
II	400 (23.6)		358 (20.0)
III	400 (21.5)		241 (12.5)
Wildman 3		Williamson 2	
I	400 (9.5)		272 (6.3)
II	400 (15.4)		355 (13.6)
III	259 (16.2)		400 (25.1)
IV	282 (9.1)		400 (13.3)
V	400 (12.5)		341 (10.3)
Semi-finals			
Dagley 3		Edmonds 1	
I	278 (9.3)		400 (13.8)
II	400 (11.4)		353 (9.9)
III	400 (16.7)		289 (12.0)
IV	400 (18.7)		214 (9.7)
Foldvari 3		Wildman 1	
I	400 (9.8)		394 (9.4)
II	191 (8.0)		400 (17.5)
III	400 (10.8)		301 (7.9)
IV	400 (17.5)		138 (6.0)
Final			
Foldvari 3		Dagley 1	
I	322 (11.1)		400 (13.8)
II	400 (30.8)		200 (15.4)
III	400 (28.6)		178 (11.9)
IV	400 (30.7)		261 (20.0)

1987
First round

G. Thompson 2		J. Fitzmaurice 0	
I	400 (9.8)		305 (7.3)
II	400 (8.5)		373 (7.9)
G. Miles *wo*		L. Dielis *scr*	
T. Jones *wo*		R. Ceulemans *scr*	
C. Everton 2		H. Griffiths 1	
I	317 (7.4)		400 (9.5)
II	400 (10.0)		380 (9.3)
III	400 (18.2)		311 (14.1)

Winner (breaks)	Score (average)	Loser (breaks)	Score (average)
Second round			
R. Foldvari 3		E. Hughes 0	
I	400 (12.9)		288 (9.0)
II	400 (17.4)		208 (9.0)
III	400 (18.2)		308 (14.0)
F. Davis 3		Thompson 0	
I	400 (33.3)		99 (8.3)
II 258	400 (22.3)		399 (22.0)
III	400 (28.6)		364 (26.0)
P. Francisco 3		Miles 0	
I	400 (22.2)		194 (10.8)
II	400 (50.0)		152 (19.0)
III	400 (10.3)		343 (9.0)
R. Edmonds 3		B. Bennett 0	
I	400 (15.4)		166 (6.1)
II	400 (28.6)		177 (12.6)
III	400 (14.3)		210 (7.3)
N. Dagley 3		R. Close 0	
I	400 (18.2)		381 (17.3)
II	400 (20.0)		228 (11.1)
III	400 (36.4)		73 (6.6)
I. Williamson *wo*		Jones *scr*	
E. Charlton 3		J. Karnehm 1	
I	82 (6.3)		400 (33.4)
II	400 (16.8)		281 (11.7)
III	400 (17.4)		300 (12.5)
IV	400 (15.4)		328 (12.6)
M. Wildman 3		Everton 0	
I	400 (16.6)		320 (12.3)
II	400 (23.5)		226 (13.3)
III	400 (18.2)		286 (12.4)
Quarter-finals			
R. Foldvari 3		F. Davis 1	
I	400 (9.3)		369 (8.2)
II	400 (23.5)		235 (13.8)
III	323 (10.0)		400 (12.5)
IV	400 (16.7)		348 (15.1)
R. Edmonds 3		P. Francisco 0	
I	400 (19.0)		300 (14.3)
II	400 (20.0)		221 (11.1)
III	400 (30.8)		194 (12.4)
N. Dagley 3		I. Williamson 1	
I	400 (28.5)		179 (12.8)
II	259 (18.5)		400 (28.6)
III	400 (16.0)		303 (12.1)
IV	400 (33.3)		334 (25.7)

Winner (breaks)	Score (average)	Loser (breaks)	Score (average)
M. Wildman 3		E. Charlton 1	
I	400 (21.1)		179 (9.0)
II	378 (12.2)		400 (13.3)
III	400 (36.4)		160 (13.3)
IV	400 (19.0)		145 (6.9)
Semi-finals			
Foldvari 3		Edmonds 1	
I 206	400 (66.7)		86 (12.3)
II	266 (12.7)		400 (20.0)
III	400 (14.3)		315 (10.5)
IV	400 (23.5)		364 (21.4)
Dagley 3		Wildman 0	
I	400 (23.5)		188 (11.1)
II	400 (18.2)		369 (16.0)
III	400 (44.5)		197 (21.9)
Final			
Dagley 3		Foldvari 1	
I	313 (28.5)	315	400 (40.0)
II	400 (28.6)	207	352 (23.5)
III	400 (23.5)		114 (6.7)
IV	400 (36.4)		365 (30.4)

1988
Preliminary round: H. Griffiths beat G. Cripsey 4-2; M. Ferreira beat J. Fitzmaurice 4-1; T. Murphy beat C. Everton 4-2; H. Nimmo beat G. Thompson 4-3; D. Heaton beat B. Bennett 4-2; E. Hughes *wo* G. Scott *scr*

First round: N. Dagley beat M. Russell 4-0; Griffiths beat J. Karnehm 4-2; I. Williamson beat R. Close 4-2; Ferreira beat M. Wildman 4-2; R. Edmonds beat Hughes 4-0; E. Charlton beat Murphy 4-1; Nimmo beat F. Davis 4-2; R. Foldvari beat Heaton 4-0

Quarter-finals: Dagley beat Griffiths 4-1; Williamson beat Ferreira 4-2; Charlton beat Edmonds 4-3; Foldvari beat Nimmo 4-2

Semi-finals: Dagley beat Williamson 4-1; Charlton beat Foldvari 4-1

Final: Dagley beat Charlton 7-4

United Kingdom Professional Billiards Championship (1934–51)

Winner (breaks)	Score (average)	Loser (breaks)	Score (average)
1934			
J. Davis	18,745	T. Newman	18,301
537, 504		809, 693, 603, 547	
1935			
J. Davis	21,733	T. Newman	19,919
609, 1,264, 548, 564,		848, 677, 749, 732,	
638, 1,002, 545		598	
1936			
First round			
W. Smith	10,373 (60.0)	S. Lee	7,212 (42.0)

Norman Dagley

Winner (breaks)	Score (average)	Loser (breaks)	Score (average)
Semi-finals			
T. Newman	9,561 (75.0)	S. Smith	7,792 (60.0)
J. Davis	10,965 (93.0)	W. Smith	9,566 (80.0)
Final			
J. Davis	21,710 (125.0)	T. Newman	19,790 (114.0)
1937			
First round			
S. Smith	8,135	S. Lee	4,209
(*match abandoned after nine sessions*)			
Semi-finals			
T. Newman	*wo*	W. Smith	*scr*
J. Davis	12,046	S. Smith	8,516
Final			
J. Davis	22,601 (146.0)	T. Newman	18,321 (118.0)
1, 191, 1,179, 1,000,		782, 774, 720, 671,	
997, 793, 592, 587, 580,		670, 603, 593, 588,	
556, 550, 500		547	
1938			
Semi-finals			
T. Newman	8,959	S. Smith	7,227
556, 771, 602, 599		740	
J. Davis	15,238	S. Lee	6,048
1,013, 840, 988, 666			
Final			
J. Davis	20,933	T. Newman	19,542
1939–45 *No contests*			
1946			
J. Barrie	8,972	W. Leigh	6,782
1947			
S. Smith	7,002	J. Barrie	6,428
1948–49 *No contests*			
1950			
First round			
J. Barrie	7,645 (34.8)	S. Lee	5,593 (25.4)
Semi-finals			
J. Barrie	7,009 (46.7)	W. Smith	5,941 (39.6)
K. Kennerley	*wo*		
Final			
J. Barrie	9,046 (48.9)	K. Kennerley	5,069 (27.4)
1951			
F. Davis	8,120	K. Kennerley	6,011

United Kingdom Professional Billiards Championships (1979–83, 1987–88)

1979 (*Super Crystalate*)
Quarter-finals

J. Karnehm	2,041 (35.8)	J. Dunning	760 (13.1)
281, 286			

Winner (breaks)	Score (average)	Loser (breaks)	Score (average)
R. Williams 259, 309	1,557 (31.8)	R. Edmonds	1,350 (27.0)
J. Barrie 238, 404, 206 (unf)	2,292 (46.8)	S. Davis	629 (12.6)
F. Davis	1,953 (34.9)	B. Bennett	679 (12.1)
Semi-finals			
Williams 224, 372	1,539 (32.7)	Karnehm	1,182 (24.6)
Barrie 227, 444	1,548 (43.0)	F. Davis 245	1,031 (28.6)
Final			
Williams 228, 388, 253	2,952 (44.4)	Barrie 379	2,116 (32.0)
1980			
First round			
S. Davis	1,670 (21.7)	S. Hood	1,029 (13.4)
B. Bennett	1,093 (12.0)	C. Ross	933 (10.1)
Quarter-finals			
J. Barrie	2,001 (32.8)	M. Wildman	815 (13.1)
J. Karnehm 322	1,990 (28.0)	K. Kennerley	842 (11.9)
R. Edmonds	1,380 (17.7)	Bennett	914 (11.6)
R. Williams 205	1,871 (33.4)	S. Davis	862 (15.4)
Semi-finals			
Karnehm 225, 230	1,755 (35.1)	Barrie 229	1,085 (21.3)
Williams 230, 234 (unf)	2,159 (41.5)	Edmonds	789 (15.2)
Final			
Karnehm 205, 208	2,518 (28.0)	Williams 256, 423	2,423 (26,6)
1981			
Qualifying			
S. Davis	980	B. Bennett	770
R. Edmonds 206	1,881	G. Miles	473
J. Pulman	1,078	K. Kennerley	879
Quarter-finals			
J. Karnehm 207	1,307 (22.2)	Edmonds	935 (15.8)
J. Barrie 381	1,743 (41.5)	Pulman	509 (12.1)
R. Williams 265, 385, 290	1,575 (50.8)	S. Davis	579 (18.1)
F. Davis 217	1,304 (29.0)	M. Wildman	805 (17.9)

Winner (breaks)	Score (average)	Loser (breaks)	Score (average)
Semi-finals			
Karnehm	1,338 (23.1)	Barrie	1,074 (18.5)
390			
Williams	2,003 (74.2)	F. Davis	999 (37.0)
217, 505, 231			
Final			
Williams	1,592 (45.5)	Karnehm	1,112 (31.8)
393, 385			
1983			
First round			
B. Bennett	750 (10.4)	D. Greaves	280 (3.7)
C. Everton	750 (28.9)	M. Darrington	177 (6.5)
I. Williamson	750 (14.4)	T. Murphy	625 (11.8)
R. Edmonds	750 (19.7)	J. Fitzmaurice	505 (13.3)
Quarter-finals			
Edmonds	1,500 (30.0)	J. Karnehm	1,194 (23.4)
M. Wildman	1,500 (41.7)	Everton	1,170 (33.4)
285, 217		393	
F. Davis	1,500 (42.9)	Williamson	604 (17.3)
292			
R. Williams	1,500 (46.9)	Bennett	230 (7.0)
246, 461 (*unf*)			
Semi-finals			
Wildman	1,500 (45.5)	Williams	1,272 (38.5)
495		225, 307	
F. Davis	1,500 (36.6)	Edmonds	936 (22.8)
208, 201			
Final			
Wildman	1,500 (21.4)	Davis	1,032 (14.5)
1987			
First round			
C. Everton 2		J. Fitzmaurice 1	
I	400 (50.0)		52 (5.8)
II	365 (6.9)		400 (7.7)
III	400 (22.0)		207 (10.9)
H. Griffiths 2		G. Thompson 1	
I	261 (10.9)		400 (17.4)
II	400 (18.2)		354 (15.4)
III	400 (14.3)		335 (11.6)
B. Bennett 2		D. Greaves 0	
I	400 (12.1)		148 (4.4)
II	400 (11.1)		218 (6.0)
Second round			
M. Wildman *wo*		G. Miles *scr*	
R. Close *wo*		T. Jones *scr*	
E. Hughes *wo*		P. Francisco *scr*	

Winner (breaks)	Score (average)	Loser (breaks)	Score (average)
R. Edmonds 3		M. Darrington 0	
I	400 (16.0)		226 (8.7)
II	400 (23.5)		138 (8.1)
III	400 (15.4)		151 (5.6)
N. Dagley *wo*		J. Karnehm *scr*	
I. Williamson 3		Everton 1	
I	400 (30.8)		142 (10.1)
II	400 (21.1)		245 (12.9)
III	184 (11.5)		400 (25.0)
IV	400 (21.1)		253 (13.3)
F. Davis 3		Griffiths 0	
I	400 (12.9)		287 (9.3)
II	400 (20.0)		267 (12.7)
III	400 (14.8)		271 (10.0)
R. Foldvari 3		Bennett 0	
I	400 (12.4)		360 (11.3)
II	400 (16.7)		268 (10.7)
III	400 (19.0)		170 (8.1)
Quarter-finals			
Wildman 3		Close 1	
I	400 (20.0)		262 (13.1)
II	242 (13.4)		400 (22.2)
III	400 (21.0)		271 (14.3)
IV	400 (18.2)		366 (15.9)
Edmonds 3		Hughes 2	
I	400 (16.0)		200 (8.0)
II	267 (9.2)		400 (14.3)
III	400 (20.8)		110 (7.9)
IV	277 (12.0)		400 (18.2)
V	400 (26.6)		204 (12.8)
Dagley 3		Williamson 1	
I 205	205 (18.3)		400 (23.5)
II	400 (26.7)		202 (13.5)
III	400 (21.2)		296 (14.8)
IV	400 (30.8)		156 (12.0)
Foldvari 3		Davis 2	
I	400 (13.3)		327 (10.5)
II	294 (10.0)		400 (14.4)
III	400 (28.6)		302 (20.0)
IV	160 (14.6)		400 (40.1)
V	400 (18.2)		341 (14.8)
Semi-finals			
Edmonds 3		Wildman 0	
I	400 (16.7)		12 (5.1)
II 241	400 (36.4)		132 (11.0)
III 227	400 (33.5)		243 (20.0)

Winner (breaks)	Score (average)	Loser (breaks)	Score (average)
Dagley 3		Foldvari 2	
I	322 (16.0)		400 (21.5)
II	400 (23.5)		240 (14.1)
III	112 (5.1)		400 (19.0)
IV	400 (22.2)		86 (4.5)
V 249	400 (25.1)		290 (18.1)
Final			
Dagley 3		Edmonds 1	
I	400 (16.0)		344 (13.8)
II	286 (17.9)		400 (25.0)
III	400 (33.3)		339 (28.3)
IV	400 (18.2)		352 (15.3)

1988 (*Strachan*)
Preliminary round: C. Everton beat T. Murphy 4-2; M. Russell beat G. Scott 4-0; G. Cripsey beat H. Griffiths 4-2; H. Nimmo beat B. Bennett 4-0

First round: N. Dagley beat Everton 4-1; I. Williamson beat E. Hughes 4-0; E. Charlton beat G. Thompson 4-2; Russell beat M. Wildman 4-3; R. Close beat R. Edmonds 4-3; F. Davis beat Cripsey 4-0; Nimmo beat J. Karnehm 4-2; R. Foldvari beat M. Ferreira 4-1

Quarter-finals: Williamson beat Dagley 4-2; Russell beat Charlton 4-2; Close beat Davis 4-0; Foldvari beat Nimmo 4-0

Semi-finals: Williamson beat Russell 4-2; Foldvari beat Close 4-1

Final: Williamson beat Foldvari 7-3

EUROPEAN BILLIARDS CHAMPIONSHIP

1987
First round: Robbie Foldvari (Australia) beat Clive Everton (Wales) 4-0; Mike Russell (England) beat Bob Close (England) 4-2; Jack Karnehm (England) beat Howard Griffiths (Wales) 4-1; Michael Ferreira (India) beat Ray Edmonds (England) 4-3; Norman Dagley (England) beat Graham Cripsey (England) 4-0; Ian Williamson (England) beat Eugene Hughes (Republic of Ireland) 4-3; Eddie Charlton (Australia) beat Bernard Bennett (England) 4-0; Mark Wildman (England) beat Geoff Thompson (England) 4-1
Quarter-finals: Foldvari beat Russell 4-1; Karnehm beat Ferreira 4-3; Dagley beat Williamson 4-2; Wildman beat Charlton 4-1
Semi-finals: Foldvari beat Karnehm 4-2; Dagley beat Wildman 4-2
Final: Dagley beat Foldvari 7-5

1988
Group A: M. Ferreira beat H. Nimmo 4-0; N. Dagley beat B. Close 4-1; Close beat
Nimmo 4-1; Dagley beat Ferreira 4-1; Close beat Ferreira 4-1; Dagley beat Nimmo 4-1
Group B: I. Williamson beat C. Everton 4-0
Group C: G. Cripsey beat H. Griffiths 4-1; R. Edmonds beat Griffiths 4-0; Edmonds
beat Cripsey 4-0
Group D: M. Russell beat G. Thompson 4-0; R. Foldvari beat J. Karnehm 4-2;
Thompson beat Karnehm 4-2; Foldvari beat Russell 4-0; Russell beat Karnehm 4-0;
Foldvari beat Thompson 4-1
Semi-final Group A: Close beat Williamson 4-3; Dagley beat Everton 4-3; Close beat
Everton 4-1; Dagley beat Williamson 4-0; Dagley beat Close 4-2; Williamson beat
Everton 4-0
Semi-final Group B: Foldvari beat Cripsey 4-0; Russell beat Edmonds 4-0; Edmonds beat
Foldvari 4-3; Russell beat Cripsey 4-0; Edmonds beat Cripsey 4-0; Russell beat Foldvari
4-3
Semi-finals: Dagley beat Edmonds 4-1; Russell beat Close 4-3
Final: Russell beat Dagley 7-4

YORKSHIRE BANK OPEN

1988
Preliminary round: H. Nimmo beat B. Bennett 4-0; H. Griffiths beat D. Heaton 4-0; C.
Everton beat G. Cripsey 4-2; M. Russell *wo* G. Scott *scr*
First round: N. Dagley beat E. Hughes 4-1; R. Close beat F. Davis 4-3; Nimmo beat I.
Williamson 4-3; M. Ferreira beat M. Wildman 4-3; R. Edmonds beat Griffiths 4-0; G.
Thompson beat J. Karnehm 4-0; E. Charlton beat Everton 4-0; Russell beat R. Foldvari
4-2
Quarter finals: Dagley beat Close 4-1; Ferreira beat Nimmo 4-0; Edmonds beat
Thompson 4-2; Russell beat Charlton 4-3
Semi-finals: Ferreira beat Dagley 4-2; Edmonds beat Russell 4-0
Final: Edmonds beat Ferreira 7-3

BILLIARDS PROFESSIONALS

It was not until 1984 that Norman Dagley could envisage a financial return from professional billiards appropriate for him to relinquish an amateur career which brought him two world and fifteen English amateur titles. After twice losing in the final of the World Professional Billiards Championship, he won the event in 1987 to complete a unique set of titles: English Amateur, World Amateur, UK Professional (1987) and World Professional. In the 1986-87 season, in fact, he won all three professional billiards titles on offer – the World, UK and European Championships. In 1987-88 he retained the world title and did well enough in the UK, European and a new ranking event, the Yorkshire Bank Open, to retain top place in the world rankings. The season saw, though, initial professional titles for Ian Williamson (UK) and Mike Russell (European), the latter making the 18-year-old Tees-sider the youngest-ever winner of a professional billiards title. Ray Edmonds, the 1985 world champion, won the Yorkshire Bank Open.

The billiards-only members of the WPBSA are: Howard Griffiths (Wales), Bob Close (England), Jack Karnehm (England), Geoff Thompson (England), Michael Ferreira (India), Hugh Nimmo (Scotland) and Peter Gilchrist (England).

Ranking List at end of 1987-88 season:
1. Norman Dagley (25 pts); 2. Robby Foldvari (18); 3. Ray Edmonds (14); 4. Ian Williamson (11); 5. Mike Russell (9); 6. Eddie Charlton (8); 7. Mark Wildman (8); 8. Bob Close (7); 9. Michael Ferreira (5); 10. Hugh Nimmo (3); 11. Fred Davis (3); 12. Jack Karnehm (2); 13. Peter Francisco (2); 14. Howard Griffiths (1); 15. Geoff Thompson (1); 16 Clive Everton (1); 17. Graham Cripsey (1); 18. Eugene Hughes (1).

THE WOMEN'S GAME

Ann-Marie Farren's surprise capture of the 1987 Women's World Championship illustrated the improving overall standard in the women's game, but Allison Fisher nevertheless remained the outstanding woman player, even though she concentrated chiefly on Open events which attracted a predominantly male entry.

Now aged 20, Fisher finished 16th at the end of the four 'professional ticket' tournaments which are held to decide which amateurs may play off against the bottom ranked professionals to earn professional status. The World Professional Billiards and Snooker Association could therefore soon be in a position of accepting its first woman member.

There has been a Women's Championship since 1933, but in reality it was only for British players. It was discontinued in 1980 when there was a change in governing body.

The Women's World Open Championship, attracting several overseas players, was first staged in 1976 and then three more times until 1983 when, in what proved a retrograde step, the game split into professional and amateur ranks. Although no world professional event was staged, two World Amateur Championships were, with Stacey Hillyard winning the first and Fisher the second.

However, there was a reconciliation between the professional and amateur factions and the game was declared 'Open', with the World Ladies' Billiards and Snooker Association promoting a Women's World Championship for the past two seasons. Fisher beat a Canadian, Sue LeMaich, to win the title in 1986 for the loss of only one frame, but was beaten in the 1987 semi-finals by Hillyard.

Hillyard became the first woman to make a century in competition when, in January 1985, she made a break of 114 in the Bournemouth League. Fisher, who holds the world championship break record with 84, made a break of 103 in the final of the Billiards and Snooker Control Council's tournament in May 1987, the first woman to make a century in a women's event. Last season, Kim Shaw joined the exclusive club of women who have made centuries in competition when she recorded a break of 104 in a tournament at Breaks, Coventry.

WOMEN'S WORLD CHAMPIONSHIP

1986
Last 16: A. Fisher (England) beat L. Horsbrough (England) 3-0; G. Aplin (England) beat C. Walch (England) 3-1; M. Fisher (England) beat S. Newbury (Wales) 3-0; A. Jones (England) beat S. Martin (Australia) 3-0; S. Hillyard (England) beat J. Dowen (England) 3-1; S. LeMaich (Canada) beat A. Davies (Wales) 3-1; K. Shaw (England) beat S. Sinanan (England) 3-1; M. Tart (England) beat H. Isitt (Wales) 3-0

Quarter-finals: A. Fisher beat Aplin 4-0; Jones beat M. Fisher 4-1; LeMaich beat Hillyard 4-3; Shaw beat Tart 4-0

Semi-finals: A. Fisher beat Jones 4-1; LeMaich beat Shaw 4-3

Final: A. Fisher beat LeMaich 5-0

1987
Last 16: A-M. Farren (England) beat A. Davies (Wales) 3-1; A. Jones (England) beat L. Horsburgh (England) 3-1; J. Banks (England) beat M. O'Driscoll (Republic of Ireland) 3-2; M. Fisher (England) beat R. Clements (England) 3-1; S. Hillyard (England) beat J. Heyhurst (England) 3-1; G. Aplin (England) beat J. Dowen (England) 3-0; K. Leech (England) beat M. Tart (England) 3-0; A. Fisher (England) beat L. Gordon (England) 3-0

Quarter-finals: Farren beat Jones 4-1; M. Fisher beat Banks 4-1; Hillyard beat Aplin 4-1; A. Fisher beat Leech 4-0

Semi-finals: Farren beat M. Fisher 4-0; Hillyard beat A. Fisher 4-3

Final: Farren beat Hillyard 5-1

TUBORG WOMEN'S UK CHAMPIONSHIP

1987
Quarter-finals: A. Fisher (England) beat M. Tart (England) 4-0; A-M. Farren (England) beat S. Hillyard (England) 4-3; G. Aplin (England) beat K. Shaw (England) 4-1; M. Fisher (England) beat R. Clements (England) 4-1

Semi-finals: A. Fisher beat Farren 4-0; M. Fisher beat Aplin 4-0

Finals: A. Fisher beat M. Fisher 5-1

1988
Quarter-finals: A-M. Farren (England) beat C. Walch (England) 4-3; S. Hillyard (England) beat L. Gordon (England) 4-0; J. Dowen (England) beat M. Fisher (England) 4-3; A. Fisher (England) beat K. Corr (England) 4-0

Semi-finals: Hillyard beat Farren 4-1; A. Fisher beat Dowen 4-0

Final: A. Fisher beat Hillyard 5-2

THE AMATEUR GAME

THE WORLD AMATEUR SNOOKER CHAMPIONSHIP

The English Amateur Billiards Championship is the oldest domestic amateur title. It was started in 1888 and was followed in 1916 by the English Amateur Snooker Championship. It was not until 1926 that the first World Amateur Billiards Championship, then called the British Empire Championship, was staged, and in 1963, the inaugural World Amateur Snooker Championship was held in Calcutta.

The two events then took place in alternate years until it was decided that from 1985 the snooker would become an annual event. For that first Championship in 1963 there were only five entries from four countries – England, Australia, India and Ceylon (now Sri Lanka). The 1987 Championship in Bangalore, India, attracted 47 players representing 26 countries – an indication of just how fast the game is developing all over the world.

Before India's Omprakesh Agrawal captured the title in Dublin, the event had been dominated by British players. Gary Owen (England) won it in 1963 and 1966 and another Englishman, David Taylor, in 1968. Jonathan Barron gave England their fourth title in 1970 and Ray Edmonds made it six in a row when he won both in 1972 and 1974.

Welshman Doug Mountjoy broke the stranglehold by taking the 1976 title and his fellow countryman Cliff Wilson won it in 1978 before England gave the Championship its youngest ever titleholder when Jimmy White won in 1980 at the age of 18. The title went back to Wales with Terry Parsons in 1982 and Parsons again reached the final in 1984 only to lose to Agrawal.

Each country affiliated to the International Billiards and Snooker Federation is entitled to send two competitors who are initially split into round robin groups with the quarter-finals onwards being knockout.

The biggest innovation in amateur snooker came in 1972 when the then world governing body, the Billiards and Snooker Control Council (now effectively the English body), lifted all restrictions on amateurs accepting prize-money or fees for exhibitions. This brought about a new breed of full-time amateur players who capitalise fully on a variety of privately organised tournaments which carry thousands of pounds in prize-money.

However, the money available in the 'amateur' game pales into insignificance when compared to the prosperity at the top of the professional game. Consequently, there is a high turnover of top amateurs who, as soon as they become eligible, join the professional ranks.

World Amateur Snooker Championships

	Wins	For	Agst
1963 (*Calcutta*)			
G. Owen (England)	4	23	7
F. Harris (Australia)	3	21	17
M. J. M. Lafir (Ceylon)	2	19	18
T. Monteiro (India)	1	14	19
W. Jones (India)	0	7	24
1966 (*Karachi*)			
G. Owen (England)	5	30	7
J. Spencer (England)	4	26	14
W. Barrie (Australia)	3	23	22
M. J. M. Lafir (Ceylon)	2	22	20
L. U. Demarco (Scotland)	1	14	28
H. Karim (Pakistan)	0	6	30
1968 (*Sydney*)			
Group A			
David Taylor (England)	4	24	13
J. Van Rensberg (S. Africa)	3	22	14
H. Andrews (Australia)	2	17	16
T. Monteiro (India)	1	17	22
L. Napper (N. Zealand)	0	9	24
Group B			
M. Williams (Australia)	3	22	14
P. Morgan (Ireland)	3	19	14
M. J. M. Lafir (Ceylon)	2	19	16
S. Shroff (India)	2	20	19
R. Flutey (N. Zealand)	0	7	24

Play-offs
Semi-finals: Williams beat Van Rensberg 8-7; David Taylor beat Morgan 8-3
Final: David Taylor beat Williams 8-7

	Wins	For	Agst
1970 (*Edinburgh*)			
Group A			
S. Hood (England)	5	20	9
P. Mifsud (Malta)	4	22	11
M. J. M. Lafir (Sri Lanka)	4	20	16
J. Phillips (Scotland)	4	19	18
D. Sneddon (Scotland)	2	17	17
L. Glozier (N. Zealand)	2	10	21
J. Clint (N. Ireland)	0	8	24
Group B			
J. Barron (England)	5	21	13
D. May (Wales)	4	22	18
S. Shroff (India)	3	18	14
E. Sinclair (Scotland)	3	16	16
J. Rogers (Ireland)	3	16	19

	Wins	*For*	*Agst*
L. U. Demarco (Scotland)	2	15	19
H. Andrews (Australia)	1	13	22

Final: Barron beat Hood 11-7

1972 (*Cardiff*)

Group A

J. Van Rensberg (S. Africa)	3	12	6
K. Tristram (N. Zealand)	1	8	8
G. Thomas (Wales)	1	6	8
L. U. Demarco (Scotland)	1	6	10

Group B

M. Francisco (S. Africa)	3	15	5
J. Barron (England)	3	15	10
A. Borg (Malta)	2	12	11
A. Lloyd (Wales)	2	11	14
T. Monteiro (India)	0	3	16

Group C

P. Mifsud (Malta)	4	16	5
R. Edmonds (England)	3	14	7
J. Rogers (Ireland)	2	8	8
M. Berni (Wales)	1	7	12
B. Bennett (N. Zealand)	0	3	16

Group D

A. Savur (India)	2	10	6
M. Williams (Australia)	2	9	7
D. Sneddon (Scotland)	2	9	9
D. May (Wales)	0	6	12

Semi-final groups

Group A

Barron	3	12	4
Savur	2	10	8
Tristram	1	6	8
Mifsud	0	6	12

Group B

M. Francisco	2	11	9
Edmonds	2	11	9
Van Rensberg	1	8	10
Williams	1	9	11

Semi-finals: Edmonds beat Barron 8-6; M. Francisco beat Savur 8-7(51, 72)

Final: Edmonds beat M. Francisco 11-10

1974 (*Dublin*)

Group A

R. Edmonds (England)	7	31	11
M. J. M. Lafir (Sri Lanka)	6	30	19
E. Sinclair (Scotland)	6	28	21
G. Thomas (Wales)	4	24	22
D. Sheehan (Ireland)	4	25	24
P. Donnelly (N. Ireland)	3	21	28
S. Shroff (India)	3	16	26

	Wins	For	Agst
N. Stockman (N. Zealand)	2	18	29
J. Sklazeski (Canada)	1	18	31
Group B			
A. Lloyd (Wales)	8	32	14
W. Hill (N. Zealand)	5	26	21
P. Burke (Ireland)	4	26	20
L. Condo (Australia)	4	26	21
A. Borg (Malta)	4	27	23
D. Sneddon (Scotland)	4	23	21
A. Savur (India)	4	24	23
R. Cowley (Isle of Man)	3	16	27
N. J. Rahim (Sri Lanka)	0	2	32

Quarter-finals: Edmonds beat Condo 4(60)-3; Sinclair beat Hill 4-2; Burke beat Lafir 4-3; Thomas beat Lloyd 4-2

Semi-finals: Edmonds beat Sinclair 8(54)-4(79); Thomas beat Burke 8-2

Final: Edmonds beat Thomas 11-9

1976 (*Johannesburg*)

Group A

D. Mountjoy (Wales)	7	28	9
J. Van Rensberg (S. Africa)	5	24	16
R. Edmonds (England)	4	20	18
N. Stockman (N. Zealand)	4	21	19
E. Sinclair (Scotland)	4	21	21
P. Burke (Ireland)	2	17	25
J. Van Niekerk (S. Africa)	1	17	27
P. Reynolds (Isle of Man)	1	14	27

Group B

P. Mifsud (Malta)	6	25	9
S. Francisco (S. Africa)	6	27	12
T. Griffiths (Wales)	5	23	14
C. Ross (England)	4	19	17
R. Paquette (Canada)	4	22	22
E. Swaffield (N. Ireland)	1	16	26
L. Heywood (Australia)	1	13	27
L. Watson (Ireland)	1	9	27

Group C

M. Francisco (S. Africa)	6	27	12
R. Atkins (Australia)	6	25	12
R. Andrewartha (England)	5	25	14
J. Clint (N. Ireland)	4	17	18
L. U. Demarco (Scotland)	3	21	21
B. Mikkelsen (Canada)	3	19	22
K. Tristram (N. Zealand)	1	9	27
R. Cowley (Isle of Man)	0	11	28

Elimination match: Griffiths beat Andrewartha 4(51)-0

Quarter-finals: Mountjoy beat Atkins 5(80)-1; Van Rensberg beat Griffiths 5-3(52); S. Francisco beat M. Francisco 5-1; Mifsud beat Edmonds 5-1

	Wins	For	Agst

Semi-finals: Mountjoy beat S. Francisco 8(51)-2; Mifsud beat Van Rensberg 8(50)-4
Final: Mountjoy beat Mifsud 11(62, 79)-1

1978 (*Malta*)
Group A

	Wins	For	Agst
K. Burles (Australia)	6	26	10
P. Mifsud (Malta)	6	26	10
J. Johnson (England)	5	23	9
J. Donnelly (Scotland)	5	20	13
D. McVeigh (N. Ireland)	2	15	20
P. Reynolds (Isle of Man)	2	10	22
V. Cremona (Malta)	2	9	25
M. Mohideen (Sri Lanka)	0	8	28

Group B

	Wins	For	Agst
A. Lloyd (Wales)	6	26	12
K. Stevens (Canada)	5	23	16
J. Grech (Malta)	4	23	16
E. Hughes (Ireland)	4	23	21
M. J. M. Lafir (Sri Lanka)	3	19	20
D. Meredith (N. Zealand)	3	18	20
S. Shroff (India)	2	14	23
L. McCann (N. Ireland)	1	10	27

Group C

	Wins	For	Agst
C. Wilson (Wales)	8	32	10
R. Paquette (Canada)	5	24	14
D. Kwok (N. Zealand)	5	23	20
A. Savur (India)	5	26	22
I. Williamson (England)	3	22	24
R. Atkins (Australia)	3	21	24
R. Miller (Scotland)	3	18	24
A. Borg (Malta)	2	15	27
C. Cooper (Isle of Man)	2	13	29

Elimination match: Grech beat Kwok 4-0
Quarter-finals: Burles beat Paquette 5-4; Stevens beat Mifsud 5-0; Johnson beat Lloyd 5(72)-0; Wilson beat Grech 5-4
Semi-finals: Johnson beat Burles 8(85)-4; Wilson beat Stevens 8(64)-2(81)
Final: Wilson beat Johnson 11(87)-5(66)

1980 (*Launceston*)
Group A

	Wins	For	Agst
J. White (England)	6	24	9
A. Savur (India)	4	20	11
E. Hughes (Ireland)	4	21	13
J. Grech (Malta)	3	19	18
L. Adams (N. Zealand)	3	15	18
Loo Yap Long (Singapore)	1	6	23
R. Burke (N. Ireland)	0	11	24

Group B

	Wins	For	Agst
J. Giannaros (Australia)	6	24	11
S. Newbury (Wales)	4	20	14

	Wins	For	Agst
R. Paquette (Canada)	4	20	15
D. Meredith (N. Zealand)	4	20	16
G. Parikh (India)	2	17	18
S. Clarke (N. Ireland)	1	10	22
Lau Weng Yew (Singapore)	0	8	24
Group C			
P. Mifsud (Malta)	6	24	3
R. Atkins (Australia)	4	19	15
J. Bonner (Australia)	4	17	17
W. King (Australia)	3	19	15
E. McLaughlin (Scotland)	3	16	16
J. O'Boye (England)	1	14	21
S. Padayachi (Fiji)	0	2	24
Group D			
A. Lloyd (Wales)	6	24	4
J. Campbell (Australia)	5	22	8
D. Sheehan (Ireland)	4	17	14
M. Gibson (Scotland)	3	16	20
H. Boteju (Sri Lanka)	2	16	20
P. Reynolds (Isle of Man)	1	11	23
W. Barrie (Australia)	0	7	24

Quarter-finals: Savur beat Lloyd 5(54)-3; Atkins beat Giannaros 5(53)-3(82); Mifsud beat Campbell 5(63)-3; White beat Newbury 5(70)-4
Semi-finals: Atkins beat Savur 8-6; White beat Mifsud 8(100)-6(83)
Final: White beat Atkins 11(80, 101)-2(60)

1982 (*Calgary*)
Group A

	Wins	For	Agst
J. Grech (Malta)	6	28	13
A. Kearney (Ireland)	6	26	15
D. O'Kane (N. Zealand)	6	28	18
B. McConnell (Canada)	5	26	19
P. Kippie (Scotland)	5	23	16
S. Habib (India)	4	22	21
V. Saengthong (Thailand)	3	20	28
Lui Yew Keong (Singapore)	1	13	30
J. A. Wahid (Sri Lanka)	0	6	32
Group B			
T. Parsons (Wales)	7	31	7
P. Browne (Ireland)	7	31	12
G. Kwok Kwan Shing (Hong Kong)	7	28	12
G. Parikh (India)	5	27	21
A. Thomson (Zimbabwe)	4	17	23
G. Kwok (N. Zealand)	3	17	26
H. Boteju (Sri Lanka)	2	15	28
W. Craig (Isle of Man)	1	14	29
T. Dada (Pakistan)	0	10	32

	Wins	For	Agst
Group C			
J. Bear (Canada)	7	30	12
M. Bradley (England)	7	30	12
J. Jorgensen (Canada)	6	25	17
W. Mills (N. Ireland)	5	26	17
J. Giannaros (Australia)	5	25	21
P. Reynolds (Isle of Man)	3	23	23
Cheung Che-Ming (Hong Kong)	2	17	25
E. Amro (Egypt)	1	11	31
V. Yassa (Sudan)	0	3	32
Group D			
W. Jones (Wales)	6	27	13
P. Mifsud (Malta)	6	29	15
W. King (Australia)	6	29	17
R. Chaperon (Canada)	5	24	18
D. Chalmers (England)	5	25	24
R. Lane (Scotland)	3	23	23
S. Pavis (N. Ireland)	3	19	27
Lau Weng Yew (Singapore)	2	15	29
S. Sherif (Egypt)	0	7	32

Quarter-finals: W. Jones beat Kearney 5-1; Parsons beat Bradley 5(69, 54)-0; Grech beat Browne 5(55)-3; Bear beat Mifsud 5-2
Semi-finals: Parsons beat Jones 8(103, 87)-5(54); Bear beat Grech 8-7
Final: Parsons beat Bear 11(61, 58, 58)-8(57, 69)

1984 (*Dublin*)

	Wins	For	Agst
Group A			
A. Micallef (Malta)	9	38	16
T. Parsons (Wales)	8	37	11
P. Ennis (Ireland)	8	34	28
V. Saengthong (Thailand)	7	34	19
J. Sigurossonn (Iceland)	6	29	29
T. Finstad (Canada)	4	28	28
B. Bjorkman (Sweden)	4	26	27
A. Thomson (Zimbabwe)	3	24	34
D. Feeney (U.S.A.)	3	21	35
K. Sirisoma (Sri Lanka)	3	16	33
L. Talman (Belgium)	0	11	40
Group B			
D. John (Wales)	9	37	10
T. Drago (Malta)	8	35	15
A. Robidou (Canada)	8	36	20
S. Simngam (Thailand)	7	33	20
J. Long (Ireland)	6	30	24
M. G. Jayaram (India)	5	30	23
A. Campbell (Australia)	4	25	29
J. McIntyre (N. Ireland)	4	21	30
R. Cowley (Isle of Man)	3	20	30

	Wins	For	Agst
M. Sedupathi (Sri Lanka)	1	6	36
C. D'Avoine (Mauritius)	0	3	40
Group C			
G. Wilkinson (Australia)	8	30	13
J. Wright (England)	7	27	14
H. Haenga (N. Zealand)	7	26	14
H. Bakahati (Egypt)	6	26	21
M. Colquitt (Isle of Man)	5	24	20
S. Hendry (Scotland)	5	23	22
T. Kollins (U.S.A.)	3	16	27
K. Friopjofssonn (Iceland)	3	15	28
H. Thwaites (Belgium)	1	3	32
Lui Yew Keong (Singapore)	scr		
Group D			
C. Archer (England)	9	32	15
O. Agrawal (India)	7	33	16
D. Kwok (N. Zealand)	5	27	21
G. Kwok Kwan Shing (Hong Kong)	5	26	23
H. Morgan (N. Ireland)	5	27	27
J. Selby (Wales)	4	24	23
L. Yew (Singapore)	3	25	28
G. Carnegie (Scotland)	3	22	32
M. Hallgren (Sweden)	2	17	32
M. Sadek (Egypt)	2	15	31

Quarter-finals: Agrawal beat John 5-4; Wright beat A. Micallef 5(69, 70)-1; Archer beat Drago 5-4; Parsons beat Wilkinson 5(66)-2

Semi-finals: Agrawal beat Wright 8(75)-5; Parsons beat Archer 8(58, 78, 52)-3

Final: Agrawal beat Parsons 11(69, 74, 62, 54)-7

1985 (*Blackpool*)

Group A

	Wins	For	Agst
P. Mifsud (Malta)	8	37	16
R. Marshall (England)	7	33	21
G. Lackenby (Australia)	7	35	23
S. Robertson (N. Zealand)	7	33	24
J. Long (Ireland)	6	31	28
A. Essam (Egypt)	5	28	25
K. Erwin (Ireland)	5	28	27
J. Allan (Scotland)	5	27	29
M. Lemoy (Belgium)	3	22	35
M. Hallgren (Sweden)	2	23	32
I. Adam (Mauritius)	0	3	40

Group B

	Wins	For	Agst
J. McNellan (Scotland)	10	40	11
T. Whitthread (England)	8	34	11
T. Saelim (Thailand)	8	37	18
D. Kwok (N. Zealand)	6	28	22
S. Sawant (India)	6	28	22
L. K. Guan (Singapore)	5	25	27

	Wins	For	Agst
T. Dada (Pakistan)	4	27	27
A. Thomson (Zimbabwe)	3	20	31
H. Boteju (Sri Lanka)	3	17	32
P. Reynolds (Isle of Man)	2	18	35
P. Rivet (Mauritius)	0	2	40
Group C			
J. Grech (Malta)	9	39	12
D. John (Wales)	8	37	14
J. Bonner (Australia)	8	35	20
G. Kwok Kwan Shing (Hong Kong)	7	35	22
W. Pu-Ob-Orm (Thailand)	6	29	23
M. Sobala (Canada)	5	29	27
L. A. Bux (Pakistan)	5	24	28
H. Bakhaty (Egypt)	3	23	31
K. Sirisoma (Sri Lanka)	2	14	33
H. Ramj (Kenya)	1	13	37
A. Agustsson (Iceland)	1	10	38
Group D			
M. Bennett (Wales)	11	40	16
G. Sethi (India)	9	34	15
A. Robidoux (Canada)	8	34	22
G. Burns (Ireland)	8	30	23
J. Wright (England)	6	25	19
S. Pavis (N. Ireland)	5	28	27
B. Bjorkman (Sweden)	5	26	30
M. Colquitt (Isle of Man)	5	25	30
K. Fridthjofsson (Iceland)	3	14	32
L. Nazarali (Kenya)	3	15	34
D. Barron (Zimbabwe)	3	22	35

Quarter-finals: Marshall beat McNellan 5(50)-1; John beat Bennett 5(44, 37)-2(30); Mifsud beat Whitthread 5(32, 39, 39)-2; Grech beat Sethi 5(42, 59, 50)-2(41, 30)
Semi-finals: John beat Marshall 8(37, 30, 40, 30, 46, 40, 32, 31)-4; Mifsud beat Grech 8(41, 58, 35)-4(56, 82, 40)
Final: Mifsud beat John 11(68, 32, 34, 59, 31, 39)-6(31, 47, 31, 48)

1986 (*New Zealand*)
Group A

G. Burns (Ireland)	9	36	15
J. Griffiths (Wales)	7	29	20
B. Lui (Singapore)	6	26	21
A. Harris (England)	6	31	22
N. Nopkachorn (Thailand)	6	30	22
P. Hawkes (Australia)	4	27	23
M. Lannoye (Belgium)	3	23	26
B. Bjorkman (Sweden)	2	15	30
P. De Groot (N. Zealand)	1	19	33
A. Thomson (Zimbabwe)	1	11	35

	Wins	For	Agst
Group B			
K. Jones (Wales)	7	29	9
M. Colquitt (Isle of Man)	6	24	12
M. Haenga (N. Zealand)	4	25	20
L. Amir Bux (Pakistan)	4	20	20
G. Sethi (India)	3	23	19
C. Sewell (N. Ireland)	3	20	19
M. Raibin (Sri Lanka)	1	10	24
A. Verny (Mauritius)	0	1	28
Group C			
G. Grennan (England)	9	36	17
S. Sawant (India)	6	31	15
J. Allan (Scotland)	5	28	22
W. Pu-Ob-Orm (Thailand)	5	26	22
K. Doherty (Rep. of Ireland)	5	26	27
R. Johansson (Sweden)	4	23	27
G. Natale (Canada)	4	22	31
G. Campbell (N. Ireland)	3	23	31
F. Chan (Hong Kong)	2	23	33
H. Bakhaty (Egypt)	2	20	33
Group D			
P. Mifsud (Malta)	9	36	10
B. Gollan (Canada)	8	34	8
G. Miller (Australia)	6	29	17
S. Leung (Hong Kong)	5	25	19
L. Weng Yew (Singapore)	5	26	24
T. Dada (Pakistan)	3	20	28
R. Young (N. Zealand)	3	16	29
L. Cameron (Scotland)	2	15	29
H. Boteju (Sri Lanka)	2	14	34
Y. Van Velthoven (Belgium)	1	15	32

Quarter-finals: Grennan beat Griffiths 5(38, 91)-2(39, 88, 39, 48); Jones beat Gollan 5(64)-1; Burns beat Colquitt 5(60)-0; Mifsud beat Sawant 5(66, 81)-2

Semi-finals: Mifsud beat Burns 8(52, 56)-5(57, 60); Jones beat Grennan 8(37, 41, 51, 83, 40)-7(45, 38, 48, 36)

Final: Mifsud beat Jones 11(41, 55, 60, 34, 43, 42)-9(99, 57, 63, 45, 43, 44, 52, 45, 66)

1988 (*Bangalore*)

	Wins	For	Agst
Group A			
J. Allan (Scotland)	5	20	7
P. Mifsud (Malta)	4	19	6
B. Bjorkman (Sweden)	3	15	14
B. Lui (Singapore)	2	14	16
R. Karaitiana (N.Z.)	1	8	16
S. Mahboob (Bangladesh)	0	3	20
Group B			
J. Wattana (Thailand)	5	20	9
J. White (Canada)	3	17	14
S. Tong (Hong Kong)	3	14	13

	Wins	For	Agst
Y. Mirza (India)	3	13	12
M. Rowing (England)	1	14	17
M. Loon Hong (Malaysia)	0	7	20
Group C			
D. Morgan (Wales)	5	20	3
S. McClarey (N. Ireland)	3	15	10
S. Lannigan (England)	3	15	10
P. Su Liang (Malaysia)	3	13	11
M. Yousef (Pakistan)	1	3	16
Group D			
A. Robidoux (Canada)	5	20	2
J. Long (Rep. of Ireland)	3	14	9
F. Chan (Hong Kong)	3	14	11
H. Boteju (Sri Lanka)	3	13	12
P. Houke (Netherlands)	1	10	16
Group E			
G. Sethi (India)	4	19	11
M. Henson (W. Germany)	4	17	12
K. Doherty (Rep. of Ireland)	3	18	8
R. Farebrother (Australia)	3	13	12
T. Dada (Pakistan)	1	10	18
A. Borg (Malta)	0	4	20
Group F			
J. Swail (N. Ireland)	5	20	4
P. Hawkes (Australia)	4	17	8
D. Barron (Zimbabwe)	2	13	15
S. Agrawal (India)	2	13	16
S. Lemmens (Belgium)	1	8	14
R. Ameen (Bangladesh)	0	6	20
Group G			
J. Grech (Malta)	6	24	9
B. L'Orange (Norway)	4	22	13
S. Nivison (Scotland)	4	19	14
J. Herbert (Wales)	3	19	15
Lim Koon Guan (Singapore)	2	16	19
A. A. Aziz (Egypt)	2	10	17
K. Hossen (Mauritius)	0	1	24
Group H			
U. Kaimuk (Thailand)	5	20	5
M. Lanoye (Belgium)	3	14	14
D. Meredith (N.Z.)	2	15	14
R. Dikstra (Netherlands)	2	12	13
P. Reynolds (Isle of Man)	2	12	17
K. Sirisoma (Sri Lanka)	1	9	18

Pre-quarter finals: Darren Morgan beat B. L'Orange 5-0: 69(40)-45(34), 64(44)-30, 67(50)-28, 70(61)-2, 108(89)-0; J. Wattana beat M. Lanoye 5-3: 96(44, 39)-8, 13-71, 18-56, 72(52)-50, 72-15, 16-64(40), 86(45)-5, 68(50)-41; A. Robidoux beat M. Henson 5-1: 27-76(38), 49-34, 67(54)-61(36), 84(55)-10, 66(39)-41, 86(32)-36; J. Allan beat P. Hawkes 5-3: 45-72(32), 67-55, 31-

88(38, 35), 40-62, 80(41)-38, 88(42)-29, 61-28, 88-31; P. Mifsud beat J. Swail 5-3: 0-102(102), 23-79(59), 73(36)-16, 55-18, 62-8, 63-64(42), 57-50, 60-19; G. Sethi beat J. White: 65(36)-17, 97(55)-5, 33-74(30, 31), 75(31, 36)-58(43), 77(36)-5, 24-67(32), 54-52; J. Grech beat S. McClarey 5-0: 66-28, 60(38)-22, 69(30, 33)-21, 56-24, 76(35, 32); U. Kaimuk beat J. Long 5-3: 13-73, 72(36)-30, 92(34)-17, 92(32)-28, 41-64, 8-82(65), 64-20, 65(37)-10

Quarter-finals: D. Morgan beat J. Wattana 5-3: 95(36, 35)-2, 67(37)-23, 20-114(71), 78(77)-0, 5-66(60), 29-76(60), 73-35, 84(80)-47(45); A. Robidoux beat J. Allan 5-4: 84(67)-34, 78(36)-14, 64(32)-42, 45-78(37), 1-74(67), 38-61, 13-93(68), 51-31, 63-34; G. Sethi beat P. Mifsud 5-4: 104(40)-48, 22-70(38), 89(48)-31, 61(33)-39, 8-71, 6-71(69), 75(58)-1, 7-61, 80(49)-42; J. Grech beat U. Kaimuk 5-4: 26-81(30), 71(31)-63, 63(40)-67(67), 84(32)-35, 69(40)-56, 9-90(71), 55-62, 84(31)-28, 59-56(44)

Semi-finals: D. Morgan beat A. Robidoux 8-5: 72(38)-14, 83(82)-43, 94(64)-8, 87(53)-24, 72(40)-9, 64(37)-49, 21-79(44, 35); 39-71(48), 47-86(56), 39(34)-75, 19-73(59), 102(69, 33)-23, 63-52(30); J. Grech beat G. Sethi 8-3: 72-29, 72-45(40), 46-71, 69-44(35), 71(63)-17, 26-86(60), 101(45, 56)-45(3); 116(86)-13, 6-58(36), 55-35, 70(31)-13

Match for 3rd and 4th place: A. Robidoux beat G. Sethi 4-1: 55-67, 136(81, 42)-0, 81(52)-46(38), 84(84)-5, 64(31, 33)-62

Final: D. Morgan beat J. Grech 11-4: 86(30)-11, 92(60)-28, 62(37)-51, 18-94(52), 89(68)-31, 73(42)-30, 98(90)-0; 22-71(50), 31-73(49), 69-29, 84(66)-15, 78(50)-20, 33-73(38), 84(39)-7, 73(40)-59

World Amateur Billiards Championships

	Won	Score (average)	Highest break	No of centuries
1926 (*London*)				
J. Earlham (England)	4	8,000 (25.6)	282	18
G. Shailer (Australia)	3	7,394 (16.8)	203	13
M. Smith (Scotland)	2	6,569 (12.7)	130	4
P. Rutledge (S. Africa)	1	5,902 (12.5)	142	2
T. McCluney (N. Ireland)	0	5,617 (11.9)	144	4
1927 (*London*)				
A. Prior (S. Africa)	3	6,000 (16.6)	184	9
H. F. Coles (Wales)	2	5,533 (12.2)	164	2
L. Steeples (England)	1	5,506 (14.8)	236	9
M. Smith (Scotland)	0	4,499 (12.6)	158	1
1929 (*Johannesburg*)				
L. Hayes (Australia)	3	6,000 (15.5)	136	6
A. Prior (S. Africa)	2	5,512 (16.0)	226	7
H. F. Coles (England)	1	5,592 (14.7)	170	7
P. Rutledge (S. Africa)	0	2,882 (10.9)	164	1
1931 (*Sydney*)				
L. Steeples (England)	4	8,000 (37.3)	461	24
S. Lee (England)	3	7,126 (22.1)	433	18
L. Hayes (Australia)	2	6,113 (15.3)	167	6
H. Goldsmith (Australia)	1	4,995 (13.0)	179	4
W. Hackett (N. Zealand)	0	3,549 (7.7)	97	0

	Won	Score (average)	Highest break	No of centuries
1933 (*London*)				
S. Lee (England)	4	12,402 (28.0)	394	31
T. Jones (Wales)	3	9,883 (18.7)	144	8
A. Prior (S. Africa)	2	9,113 (18.3)	235	13
M. Smith (Scotland)	1	8,292 (17.5)	166	5
J. Blackburn (N. Ireland)	0	6,362 (12.5)	94	0
1935 (*London*)				
H. F. Coles (England)	4	13,665 (28.4)	267	33
J. McGhie (Scotland)	3	9,359 (19.4)	207	11
I. Edwards (Wales)	2	9,814 (18.1)	196	11
S. Fenning (Ireland)	1	9,068 (17.4)	161	6
P. Deb (India)	0	7,461 (13.1)	123	5
1936 (*Johannesburg*)				
R. Marshall (Australia)	3	8,526 (22.0)	248	24
A. Prior (S. Africa)	2	7,014 (17.7)	197	11
J. Thompson (England)	1	7,705 (21.2)	245	15
A. Bowlly (S. Africa)	0	4,548 (9.0)	93	0
Three 2 hour sessions				
1938 (*Melbourne*)				
R. Marshall (Australia)	6	17,626 (39.0)	427	59
K. Kennerley (England)	5	14,528 (30.1)	472	45
T. Cleary (Australia)	4	8,535 (19.7)	322	17
S. Moses (N. Zealand)	2	6,727 (13.1)	129	4
M. M. Begg (India)	2	6,685 (13.4)	111	2
A. Burke (S. Africa)	1	5,993 (12.0)	119	1
A. Albertson (N. Zealand)	1	5,805 (12.4)	107	1
1951 (*London*)				
R. Marshall (Australia)	6	14,735 (38.1)	423	42
F. Edwards (England)	5	13,459 (26.7)	345	36
T. Cleary (Australia)	4	12,373 (25.5)	330	31
W. Ramage (Scotland)	3	7,638 (19.1)	151	8
W. Pierce (Wales)	2	6,029 (13.6)	225	3
W. Jones (India)	1	7,202 (16.6)	138	10
E. Haslem (N. Ireland)	0	5,896 (14.1)	125	3
1952 (*Calcutta*)				
L. Driffield (England)	5	8,529 (34.5)	278	31
R. Marshall (Australia)	3	9,237 (37.3)	351	27
C. Hirjee (India)	3	7,701 (22.7)	230	14
W. Ramage (Scotland)	3	6,525 (20.8)	211	10
W. Jones (India)	1	6,731 (23.3)	253	6
A. Yunoos (Burma)	0	3,768 (11.0)	79	0
1954 (*Sydney*)				
T. Cleary (Australia)	4	11,496 (33.5)	682	35
R. Marshall (Australia)	3	11,488 (36.0)	407	35
F. Edwards (England)	2	9,053 (24.7)	328	26
W. Jones (India)	1	8,523 (20.5)	209	17
T. G. Rees (S. Africa)	0	6,271 (16.9)	207	6

	Won	Score (average)	Highest break	No of centuries
1958 (*Calcutta*)				
W. Jones (India)	5	16,493	501	56
L. Driffield (England)	4	14,370	499	48
T. Cleary (Australia)	3	13,626	431	52
C. Hirjee (India)	2	12,853	226	38
W. Asciak (Malta)	1	6,329	154	7
M. Hman (Burma)	0	5,633	215	8
1960 (*Edinburgh*)				
J. H. Beetham (England)	7	9,351	277	29
J. Long (Australia)	6	10,634	353	26
W. Jones (India)	5	12,397	589	30
M. Francisco (S. Africa)	4	7,773	148	11
W. Ramage (Scotland)	3	7,938	283	12
W. Asciak (Malta)	2	8,408	194	11
W. Dennison (N. Ireland)	1	6,231	155	4
A. Ramage (Scotland)	0	5,706	101	2
1962 (*Perth*)				
R. Marshall (Australia)	5	12,367 (35.6)	348	57
W. Jones (India)	5	10,805 (26.9)	489	34
T. Cleary (Australia)	4	9,808 (27.0)	315	27
J. H. Beetham (England)	3	7,626 (22.9)	283	18
S. Benajee (India)	3	8,332 (17.2)	219	9
R. A. Karim (Pakistan)	1	5,657 (11.9)	130	3
W. Harcourt (N. Zealand)	0	5,623 (14.3)	123	5

Play off: Marshall beat Jones 3,623-2,891

	Won	Score (average)	Highest break	No of centuries
1964 (*Pukekohe*)				
W. Jones (India)	9	16,628 (24.5)	294	49
J. Karnehm (England)	8	12,953 (21.8)	390	28
M. Ferreira (India)	7	13,345 (19.0)	182	29
M. Francisco (S. Africa)	6	12,957 (22.0)	518	38
A. Nolan (England)	5	12,126 (19.9)	259	26
T. Cleary (Australia)	4	10,781 (13.9)	241	19
H. Robinson (N. Zealand)	3	7,643 (10.5)	85	0
T. Yesberg (N. Zealand)	2	7,528 (10.4)	80	0
M. Mavalwala (Pakistan)	1	8,404 (11.3)	174	1
A. E. Redmond (S. Africa)	0	6,914 (9.0)	107	1
1967 (*Colombo*)				
L. Driffield (England)	8	13,556 (30.5)	421	53
M. J. M. Lafir (Ceylon)	7	12,562 (18.4)	218	31
M. Francisco (S. Africa)	6	12,477 (20.4)	301	32
M. Ferreira (India)	5	11,140 (19.5)	507	22
J. Long (Australia)	4	11,068 (17.5)	261	27
T. Cleary (Australia)	3	9,252 (11.6)	322	15
N. J. Rahim (Ceylon)	2	6,895 (8.8)	116	3
M. S. M. Marzuq (Ceylon)	1	7,153 (7.9)	88	0
F. Holz (N. Zealand)	0	5,350 (7.1)	68	0

	Won	Score (average)	Highest break	No of centuries
1969 (*London*)				
J. Karnehm (England)	9	12,902	232	27
M. Ferreira (India)	7	14,115	629	34
M. Francisco (S. Africa)	7	13,760	335	35
M. J. M. Lafir (Ceylon)	7	12,934	296	28
R. Marshall (Australia)	6	13,033	216	33
M. Wildman (England)	6	11,739	274	22
R. Oriel (Wales)	5	13,306	297	30
S. Mohan (India)	5	13,407	219	24
P. Mifsud (Malta)	2	10,410	173	8
A. Twohill (N. Zealand)	1	10,016	146	12
F. Holz (N. Zealand)	0	6,061	65	0
1971 (*Malta*)				
Group A				
M. Francisco (S. Africa)	4	6,450	321	15
M. J. M. Lafir (Ceylon)	3	4,757	233	4
P. Mifsud (Malta)	2	4,142	134	2
D. Sneddon (Scotland)	1	3,160	121	2
L. Napper (N. Zealand)	0	3,798	87	0
Group B				
S. Mohan (India)	4	5,839	188	11
N. Dagley (England)	3	5,454	330	11
M. Ferreira (India)	2	4,423	227	4
C. Everton (Wales)	1	3,893	205	5
W. Asciak (Malta)	0	4,511	188	7
Play-offs:				
Dagley	3	6,041	348	17
M. Francisco	2	3,981	353	11
Mohan	1	3,822	327	11
Lafir	0	2,514	211	5
1973 (*Bombay*)				
M. J. M. Lafir (Sri Lanka)	9	16,956 (34.1)	859	43
S. Mohan (India)	7	17,016 (30.8)	468	53
M. Ferreira (India)	7	15,639 (25.4)	421	41
P. Tarrant (Australia)	6	13,200 (24.4)	373	36
C. Everton (Wales)	5	9,921 (18.2)	240	17
A. Nolan (England)	4	12,709 (20.8)	265	31
P. Mifsud (Malta)	4	12,253 (18.8)	203	23
E. Simons (N. Zealand)	2	8,521 (12.4)	94	0
B. Kirkness (N. Zealand)	1	8,464 (13.5)	195	7
L. U. Demarco (Scotland)	0	7,488 (10.4)	87	0
1975 (*Auckland*)				
Group A				
N. Dagley (England)	5	9,257	477	24
D. Sneddon (Scotland)	4	6,272	124	4
G. Parikh (India)	3	6,471	197	16
J. Reece (Australia)	2	4,058	125	4

	Won	Score (average)	Highest break	No of centuries
H. Robinson (N. Zealand)	1	4,529	123	2
M. Shaharwardi (Sri Lanka)	0	4,032	121	1
Group B				
M. Ferreira (India)	5	9,022	411	26
C. Everton (Wales)	4	6,043	272	13
R. Close (England)	3	5,449	164	10
T. Yesberg (N. Zealand)	2	4,373	131	3
J. Long (Australia)	1	4,598	157	5
B. Bennett (N. Zealand)	0	3,684	95	0

Play-offs
Semi-finals: Dagley beat Everton 1,293(222)-775; Ferreira beat Sneddon 2,470(211)-681
Final: Dagley beat Ferreira 3,385(200, 228, 202, 314)-2,268(281)

1977 (*Melbourne*)
Group A

	Won	Score (average)	Highest break	No of centuries
N. Dagley (England)	5	7,546	272	16
C. Everton (Wales)	4	4,962	170	7
S. Aleem (India)	3	7,028	263	11
G. Ganim Sr (Australia)	2	6,322	231	6
H. Robinson (N. Zealand)	1	4,133	93	0
J. Nugent (Scotland)	0	4,131	68	0
Group B				
M. Ferreira (India)	5	12,554	519	33
R. Close (England)	4	7,252	207	15
G. Ganim Jr (Australia)	3	6,424	192	9
T. Yesberg (N. Zealand)	2	4,349	109	1
W. Weerasinghe (Sri Lanka)	1	4,364	97	0
D. Pratt (Scotland)	0	4,316	108	1

Play-offs
Semi-finals: Ferreira beat Everton 2,155-1,310; Close beat Dagley 1,912(234)-1,781(236)
Final: Ferreira beat Close 2,683-2,564(231)

1979 (*Colombo*)
Group A

	Won	Score (average)	Highest break	No of centuries
M. Ferreira (India)	7	14,695	467	40
M. J. M. Lafir (Sri Lanka)	5	12,456	370	30
K. Shirley (England)	5	10,656	195	13
W. Barrie (Australia)	4	8,255	128	2
B. Kirkness (N. Zealand)	4	7,283	214	8
H. Nimmo (Scotland)	2	7,022	105	2
M. S. U. Mohideen (Sri Lanka)	1	6,408	76	0
R. Lim Sin Foo (Singapore)	0	6,433	97	0
Group B				
N. Dagley (England)	6	12,539	466	39
P. Mifsud (Malta)	6	12,193	325	31
S. Agrawal (India)	6	11,924	355	30
G. Ganim Jr (Australia)	3	8,486	267	15
C. Everton (Wales)	3	6,905	211	11
W. A. J. Weerasinghe (Sri Lanka)	3	7,883	202	7

	Won	Score (average)	Highest break	No of centuries
B. Bennett (N. Zealand)	1	6,083	101	1
E. Fisher (Canada)	0	4,198	88	0

Play-offs
Semi-finals: Mifsud beat Ferreira 2,489(338, 285)-1,856; Dagley beat Lafir 2,694(266, 444, 289)-1,692(240)
Final: Mifsud beat Dagley 2,943(361)-2,152

1981 (*New Delhi*)
Group A

	Won	Score (average)	Highest break	No of centuries
N. Dagley (England)	6	11,982	416	42
S. Agrawal (India)	5	12,967	384	39
G. Ganim Jr (Australia)	4	7,934	178	13
A. K. B. Giles (N. Zealand)	3	6,895	162	5
D. Sneddon (Scotland)	2	7,071	123	6
J. W. H. Boteju (Sri Lanka)	1	6,312	107	1
A. A. Essam (Egypt)	0	3,948	59	–

Group B

	Won	Score (average)	Highest break	No of centuries
M. Ferreira (India)	6	13,862	630	58
L. A. Bux (Pakistan)	5	8,712	257	21
R. Close (England)	3	7,161	217	15
J. Grech (Malta)	3	7,388	402	9
D. Meredith (N. Zealand)	3	6,507	154	7
H. Roberts-Thomson (Australia)	2	6,535	151	5
S. M. Shahawardi (Sri Lanka)	0	5,111	77	–

Semi-finals: Dagley beat Bux 2,890(229, 277, 218)-1,505(257); Ferreira beat Agrawal 3,272(213, 532, 327, 527, 630)-1,964(233, 253)
Final: Ferreira beat Dagley 2,725(208, 349, 245, 244)-2,631(223, 296, 281)

1983 (*Malta*)
Group A

	Won	Score (average)	Highest break	No of centuries
M. Ferreira (India)	6		463	31
R. Foldvari (Australia)	5		302	30
L. A. Bux (Pakistan)	4		177	9
H. Nimmo (Scotland)	3		224	6
D. Meredith (N. Zealand)	2		157	7
H. Griffiths (Wales)	1		112	1
A. Micallef (Malta)	0		122	6

Group B

	Won	Score (average)	Highest break	No of centuries
S. Agrawal (India)	5		635	42
N. Dagley (England)	5		368	30
J. Grech (Malta)	5		286	31
V. Ellul (Malta)	2		145	2
R. Lim (Singapore)	2		96	–
W. Loughan (N. Ireland)	2		198	5
H. Boteju (Sri Lanka)	0		120	2

Semi-finals: Agrawal beat Foldvari 2,047(240, 503)-1,900(302, 225, 231); Ferreira beat Dagley 1,983(463)-1,919(258)
Final: Ferreira beat Agrawal 3,933(353, 398, 201, 254)-2,744(242, 212)

	Won	Score (average)	Highest break	No of centuries
1985 (*Malta*)				
Group A				
R. Marshall (Australia)	7		396*	
M. Ferreira (India)	6		341	
L. A. Bux (Pakistan)	5		229	
R. Robinson (N. Zealand)	4		100	
D. Sneddon (Scotland)	3		190	
T. Ward (England)	2		106	
Lau Weng Yew (Singapore)	1		92	
S. Clarke (N. Ireland)	0		101	
Group B				
G. Sethi (India)	7		604	
S. Agrawal (India)	6		599	
R. Close (England)	5		182	
H. Nimmo (Scotland)	3		146	
D. Meredith (N. Zealand)	3		263	
K. Sirisoma (Sri Lanka)	2		118	
F. Humphries	1		131	
A. Micallef (Malta)	1		138	

*unfinished

Semi-finals: Sethi beat Ferreira 2,513(201, 303)-2,379; Marshall beat Agrawal 2,782(300, 204)-1,872

Final: Sethi beat Marshall 3,809(546, 235, 348, 232, 257)-2,453(201)

	Won	Score (average)	Highest break	No of centuries
1987 (*Belfast*)				
Group A				
G. Sethi (India)	8		364	51
D. Edwards (Wales)	7		215	19
D. Elliott (Northern Ireland)	6		192	9
T. Ward (England)	5		130	5
B. Kirkness (New Zealand)	4		196	8
D. Collins (Australia)	3		183	18
J. McIntyre (Northern Ireland)	2		132	1
M. Spoormans (Belgium)	1		77	–
R. Brennan (Republic of Ireland)	0		88	–
Group B				
J. Grech (Malta)	7		447	43
S. Agrawal (India)	7		491	50
P. Gilchrist (England)	7		242	23
D. Meredith (New Zealand)	5		243	21
B. Kelly (Scotland)	4		218	1
S. McClarey (Northern Ireland)	3		136	4
J. Millen (Australia)	2		112	2
T. Martin (Republic of Ireland)	1		95	–
M. De Sutter (Belgium)	0		174	1

Semi-finals: Grech beat Edwards 2971(271, 236, 480)-1748(212); Sethi beat Agrawal 2959(242, 288, 366, 221)-2456

Final: Sethi beat Grech 4846(760, 206, 202, 224, 248, 460)-3256(200, 244, 360, 253, 358, 238)

World Amateur Championship Records

Snooker

T. Drago (Malta)   132   1984

Billiards

T. Cleary (Australia)	682 (2 pots)	1954
M. J. M. Lafir (Sri Lanka)	859 (5 pots)	1973
M. Ferreira (India)	467 (3 pots)	1979

Stephen Hendry making his winner's speech at the 1987 Rothmans Grand Prix

NATIONAL AMATEUR CHAMPIONSHIPS

ENGLAND
Snooker

Year	Champion	Year	Champion	Year	Champion
1916	C. N. Jacques	1939	P. Bendon	1966	J. Spencer
1917	C. N. Jacques	1940	K. Kennerley	1967	M. Owen
1918	T. N. Palmer	*1941–45*	*No contests*	1968	David Taylor
1919	S. H. Fry	1946	H. J. Pulman	1969	R. Edmonds
1920	A. R. Wisdom	1947	H. Morris	1970	J. Barron
1921	M. J. Vaughan	1948	S. Battye	1971	J. Barron
1922	J. McGlynn	1949	T. C. Gordon	1972	J. Barron
1923	W. Coupe	1950	A. Nolan	1973	M. Owen
1924	W. Coupe	1951	R. Williams	1974	R. Edmonds
1925	J. McGlynn	1952	C. Downey	1975	S. Hood
1926	W. Nash	1953	T. C. Gordon	1976	C. Ross
1927	O. T. Jackson	1954	G. Thompson	1977	T. Griffiths
1928	P. H. Matthews	1955	M. Parkin	1978	T. Griffiths
1929	L. Steeples	1956	T. C. Gordon	1979	J. White
1930	L. Steeples	1957	R. Gross	1980	J. O'Boye
1931	P. H. Matthews	1958	M. Owen	1981	V. Harris
1932	W. E. Bach	1959	M. Owen	1982	D. Chalmers
1933	E. Bedford	1960	R. Gross	1983	T. Jones
1934	C. H. Beavis	1961	A. Barnett	1984	S. Longworth
1935	C. H. Beavis	1962	R. Gross	1985	T. Whitthread
1936	P. H. Matthews	1963	G. Owen	1986	A. Harris
1937	K. Kennerley	1964	R. Reardon	1987	M. Rowing
1938	P. H. Matthews	1965	P. Houlihan	1988	B. Pincher

Billiards

Year	Champion	Year	Champion	Year	Champion
1888	{ H. A. O. Lonsdale / A. P. Gaskell	1914	H. C. Virr	1954	A. L. Driffield
1889	{ A. P. Gaskell / A. P. Gaskell	1915	A. W. T. Good	1955	F. Edwards
1890	{ A. P. Gaskell / W. D. Courtney	1916	S. H. Fry	1956	F. Edwards
1891	{ W. D. Courtney / A. P. Gaskell	1917	J. Graham-Symes	1957	A. L. Driffield
1892	{ A. R. Wisdom / S. S. Christey	1918	J. Graham-Symes	1958	A. L. Driffield
1893	{ A. R. Wisdom / S. H. Fry / A. H. Vahid	1919	S. H. Fry	1959	A. L. Driffield
1894	{ H. Mitchell / W. T. Maughan	1920	S. H. Fry	1960	J. H. Beetham
1895	*No contest*	1921	S. H. Fry	1961	J. H. Beetham
1896	S. H. Fry	1922	J. Graham-Symes	1962	A. L. Driffield
1897–98	*No contests*	1923	W. P. McLeod	1963	J. H. Beetham
1899	A. R. Wisdom	1924	W. P. McLeod	1964	A. Nolan
1900	S. H. Fry	1925	S. H. Fry	1965	N. Dagley
1901	S. S. Christey	1926	J. Earlam	1966	N. Dagley
1902	{ A. W. Good / A. W. T. Good	1927	L. Steeples	1967	A. L. Driffield
1903	{ A. R. Wisdom / S. S. Christey	1928	A. Wardle	1968	M. Wildman
1904	W. A. Lovejoy	1929	H. F. E Coles	1969	J. Karnehm
1905	A. W. T. Good	1930	L. Steeples	1970	N. Dagley
1906	E. C. Breed	1931	S. Lee	1971	N. Dagley
1907	H. C. Virr	1932	S. Lee	1972	N. Dagley
1908	H. C. Virr	1933	S. Lee	1973	N. Dagley
1909	Major Fleming	1934	S. Lee	1974	N. Dagley
1910	H. A. O Lonsdale	1935	H. F. E. Coles	1975	N. Dagley
1911	H. C. Virr	1936	J. Thompson	1976	R. Close
1912	H. C. Virr	1937	K. Kennerley	1977	R. Close
1913	H. C. Virr	1938	K. Kennerley	1978	N. Dagley
		1939	K. Kennerley	1979	N. Dagley
		1940	K. Kennerley	1980	N. Dagley
		1941–45	*No contests*	1981	N. Dagley
		1946	M. Showman	1982	N. Dagley
		1947	J. Thompson	1983	N. Dagley
		1948	J. Thompson	1984	N. Dagley
		1949	F. Edwards	1985	R. Close
		1950	F. Edwards	1986	K. Shirley
		1951	F. Edwards	1987	D. Edwards
		1952	A. L. Driffield	1988	P. Gilchrist
		1953	A. L. Driffield		

NORTHERN IRELAND
Snooker

1927	G. Barron	1949	J. Bates	1969	D. Anderson
1928	J. Perry	1950	J. Bates	1970	J. Clint
1929	W. Lyttle	1951	J. Stevenson	1971	S. Crothers
1930	J. Luney	1952	J. Stevenson	1972	P. Donnelly
1931	J. McNally	1953	J. Stevenson	1973	J. Clint
1932	Capt. J. Ross	1954	W. Seeds	1974	P. Donnelly
1933	J. French	1955	J. Stevenson	1975	J. Clint
1934	Capt. J. Ross	1956	S. Brooks	1976	E. Swaffield
1935	W. Agnew	1957	M. Gill	1977	D. McVeigh
1936	W. Lowe	1958	W. Agnew	1978	D. McVeigh
1937	J. Chambers	1959	W. Hanna	1979	R. Burke
1938	J. McNally	1960	M. Gill	1980	S. Clarke
1939	J. McNally	1961	D. Anderson	1981	T. Murphy
1940	No contest	1962	S. McMahon	1982	S. Pavis
1941	J. McNally	1963	D. Anderson	1983	J. McLaughlin Jr
1942–44	No contests	1964	P. Morgan	1984	J. McLaughlin Jr
1945	J. McNally	1965	M. Gill	1985	S. Pavis
1946	J. McNally	1966	S. Crothers	1986	C. Sewell
1947	J. Rea	1967	D. Anderson	1987	S. McClarey
1948	J. Bates	1968	A. Higgins	1988	P. Doran

Billiards

1925	T. McCluney	1948	J. Bates	1968	D. Anderson
1926	T. McCluney	1949	J. Bates	1969	W. Loughan
1927	J. Sloan	1950	J. Bates	1970	S. Crothers
1928	A. Davison	1951	E. Haslem	1971	J. Bates
1929	J. Blackburn	1952	R. Taylor	1972–73	No contests
1930	J. Blackburn	1953	W. Scanlon	1974	P. Donnelly
1931	J. Blackburn	1954	W. Scanlon	1975	P. Donnelly
1932	W. Lowe	1955	D. Turley	1976	P. Donnelly
1933	W. Mills	1956	J. Stevenson	1977	T. Taylor
1934	W. Lowe	1957	W. Scanlon	1978	W. Loughan
1935	W. Morrison	1958	W. Hanna	1979	J. Bates
1936	J. Blackburn	1959	W. Hanna	1980	S. Clarke
1937	J. Blackburn	1960	W. Dennison	1981	W. Loughan
1938	W. Lowe	1961	R. Hanna	1982	P. Donnelly
1939	W. Lowe	1962	N. McQuay	1983	F. Clarke
1940	No contest	1963	W. Hanna	1984	D. Elliott
1941	E. Haslem	1964	{ D. Anderson	1985	S. Clarke
1942–44	No contests		{ D. Turley	1986	D. Elliott
1945	E. Haslem	1965	W. Ashe	1987	D. Elliott
1946	J. Holness	1966	D. Anderson		
1947	J. Bates	1967	W. Loughan		

REPUBLIC OF IRELAND
Snooker

1931	J. Ayres	1952	W. Brown	1971	D. Sheehan
1932	No contest	1953	S. Brooks	1972	J. Rogers
1933	S. Fenning	1954	S. Fenning	1973	F. Murphy
1934	No contest	1955	S. Fenning	1974	P. Burke
1935	S. Fenning	1956	W. Brown	1975	F. Nathan
1936	No contest	1957	J. Connolly	1976	P. Burke
1937	P. J. O'Connor	1958	G. Gibson	1977	J. Clusker
1938–39	No contests	1959–60	No contests	1978	E. Hughes
1940	P. Merrigan	1961	W. Brown	1979	E. Hughes
1941	No contest	1962	J. Weber	1980	D. Sheehan
1942	P. J. O'Connor	1963	J. Rogers	1981	A. Kearney
1943	No contest	1964	J. Rogers	1982	P. Browne
1944	S. Fenning	1965	W. Fields	1983	J. Long
1945–46	No contests	1966	G. Hanway	1984	P. Ennis
1947	C. Downey	1967	P. Morgan	1985	G. Burns
1948	P. Merrigan	1968	G. Hanway	1986	G. Burns
1949	S. Fenning	1969	D. Dally	1987	K. Doherty
1950–51	No contests	1970	D. Sheehan	1988	J. Buckley

Billiards

1931	J. Ayres	1953	D. Turley	1970	L. Drennan
1932	No contest	1954	M. Nolan	1971	L. Codd
1933	J. Ayres	1955	M. Nolan	1972	L. Codd
1934	S. Fenning	1956	M. Nolan	1973	T. Martin
1935	S. Fenning	1957	M. Nolan	1974	T. Doyle
1936	S. Fenning	1958	W. Dennison	1975	P. Fenelon
1937	T. O'Brien	1959–60	No contests	1976	J. Rogers
1938–41	No contests	1961	K. Smyth	1977	E. Hughes
1942	S. Fenning	1962	K. Smyth	1978	E. Hughes
1943	No contest	1963	J. Bates	1979	L. Drennan
1944	S. Fenning	1964	J. Bates	1980	P. Burke
1945–47	No contests	1965	L. Codd	1981	P. Burke
1948	W. Brown	1966	L. Codd	1982	D. Elliott
1949	S. Fenning	1967	P. Morgan	1984	A. Murphy
1950–51	No contests	1968	P. Morgan	1985	A. Roche
1952	M. Nolan	1969	J. Rogers	1987	L. Drennan

SCOTLAND
Snooker

1931	G. Brown	1959	J. Phillips	1974	D. Sneddon
1932–45	No contests	1960	E. Sinclair	1975	E. Sinclair
1946	J. Levey	1961	J. Phillips	1976	E. Sinclair
1947	J. Levey	1962	A. Kennedy	1977	R. Miller
1948	I. Wexelstein	1963	E. Sinclair	1978	J. Donnelly
1949	W. Ramage	1964	J. Phillips	1979	S. Nivison
1950	W. Ramage	1965	L. U. Demarco	1980	M. Gibson
1951	A. Wilson	1966	L. U. Demarco	1981	R. Lane
1952	D. Emerson	1967	E. Sinclair	1982	P. Kippie
1953	P. Spence	1968	E. Sinclair	1983	G. Carnegie
1954	D. Edmond	1969	A. Kennedy	1984	S. Hendry
1955	L. U. Demarco	1970	D. Sneddon	1985	S. Hendry
1956	W. Barrie	1971	J. Phillips	1986	S. Muir
1957	T. Paul	1972	D. Sneddon	1987	S. Nivison
1958	J. Phillips	1973	E. Sinclair	1988	D. Henry

Billiards

1913	Capt. Croneen	1946	J. Levey	1966	W. Ramage
1914–21	No contests	1947	A. Ramage	1967	W. Ramage
1922	H. L. Fleming	1948	W. Ramage	1968	A. Kennedy
1923	M. Smith	1949	W. Ramage	1969	A. Kennedy
1924	No contest	1950	A. Ramage	1970	D. Sneddon
1925	W. D. Greenlees	1951	W. Ramage	1971	D. Sneddon
1926	M. Smith	1952	J. Murray	1972	L. U. Demarco
1927	M. Smith	1953	J. Bates	1973	D. Sneddon
1928	M. Smith	1954	J. Bates	1974	D. Sneddon
1929	J. McGhee	1955	W. Ramage	1975	D. Sneddon
1930	M. Smith	1956	W. Ramage	1976	D. Sneddon
1933	A. Ramage	1957	W. Ramage	1977	J. Nugent
1934	N. Canney	1958	W. Ramage	1978	D. Sneddon
1935	H. King	1959	W. Ramage	1979	H. Nimmo
1936	N. Canney	1960	A. Ramage	1980	D. Sneddon
1937	J. McGhee	1961	P. Spence	1981	D. Sneddon
1938	J. McGhee	1962	W. Ramage	1982	W. Kelly
1939	No contest	1963	W. Ramage	1983	H. Nimmo
1940	W. McCann	1964	W. Ramage	1984	D. Sneddon
1941–45	No contests	1965	W. Ramage	1987	W. Kelly

WALES
Snooker

1930	T. Jones	1954	R. Reardon	1972	G. Thomas
1931	T. Jones	1955	R. Reardon	1973	A. Lloyd
1932	T. Jones	1956	C. Wilson	1974	A. Lloyd
1933	T. Jones	1957	R. D. Meredith	1975	T. Griffiths
1934	T. Jones	1958	A. Kemp	1976	D. Mountjoy
1935	T. Jones	1959	J. R. Price	1977	C. Wilson
1936	T. Jones	1960	L. Luker	1978	A. Lloyd
1937	G. Howells	1961	T. Parsons	1979	C. Wilson
1938	B. Gravenor	1962	A. J. Ford	1980	S. Newbury
1939	W. E. James	1963	R. D. Meredith	1981	C. Roscoe
1940–46	No contests	1964	M. L. Berni	1982	T. Parsons
1947	T. Jones	1965	T. Parsons	1983	W. Jones
1948	R. Smith	1966	L. L. O'Neill	1984	T. Parsons
1949	A. J. Ford	1967	L. L. O'Neill	1985	M. Bennett
1950	R. Reardon	1968	D. Mountjoy	1986	K. Jones
1951	R. Reardon	1969	T. Parsons	1987	D. Morgan
1952	R. Reardon	1970	D. T. May	1988	P. Dawkins
1953	R. Reardon	1971	D. T. May		

Billiards

1920	H. F. E. Coles	1939	B. Gravenor	1963	R. W. Oriel
1921	H. F. E. Coles	1940–45	No contests	1964	R. W. Oriel
1922	H. F. E. Coles	1946	T. G. Rees	1965	R. W. Oriel
1923	H. F. E. Coles	1947	T. C. Morse	1966	R. W. Oriel
1924	H. F. E. Coles	1948	J. Tregoning	1967	R. W. Oriel
1925	Unknown	1949	I. Edwards	1968	D. E. Edwards
1926	Unknown	1950	W. Pierce	1969	R. W. Oriel
1927	Unknown	1951	W. Pierce	1970	R. W. Oriel
1928	G. Moore	1952	J. Tregoning	1971	R. W. Oriel
1929	J. Tregoning	1953	B. Sainsbury	1972	C. Everton
1930	Unknown	1954	R. Smith	1973	C. Everton
1931	L. Prosser	1955	J. Tregoning	1974	R. W. Oriel
1932	T. Jones	1956	A. J. Ford	1975	R. W. Oriel
1933	T. Jones	1957	R. Smith	1976	C. Everton
1934	Unknown	1958	R. W. Oriel	1977	C. Everton
1935	I. Edwards	1959	A. J. Ford	1978	R. W. Oriel
1936	J. Tregoning	1960	C. Everton	1979	R. W. Oriel
1937	B. Gravenor	1961	R. W. Oriel		No further contests
1938	J. Tregoning	1962	R. W. Oriel		

AUSTRALIA
Snooker

1953	W. Simpson	1965	W. Barrie	1977	R. Atkins
1954	W. Simpson	1966	M. Williams	1978	K. Burles
1955	E. Pickett	1967	M. Williams	1979	J. Campbell
1956	R. Marshall	1968	M. Williams	1980	W. King
1957	W. Simpson	1969	W. Barrie	1981	W. King
1958	F. Harris	1970	M. Williams	1982	J. Giannaros
1959	K. Burles	1971	M. Williams	1983	G. Lackenby
1960	K. Burles	1972	M. Williams	1984	G. Wilkinson
1961	M. Williams	1973	M. Williams	1985	J. Bonner
1962	W. Barrie	1974	L. Condo	1986	G. Miller
1963	F. Harris	1975	R. Atkins	1987	P. Hawkes
1964	W. Barrie	1976	R. Atkins		

Billiards

1913	G. B. Shailer	1940–45	No contests	1967	J. Long
1914–19	No contests	1946	R. Marshall	1968	J. Long
1920	J. R. Hooper	1947	T. Cleary	1969	R. Marshall
1921	G. B. Shailer	1948	R. Marshall	1970	R. Marshall
1922	G. B. Shailer	1949	R. Marshall	1971	M. Williams
1923	G. B. Shailer	1950	T. Cleary	1972	P. Tarrant
1924	E. Eccles	1951	R. Marshall	1973	P. Tarrant
1925	G. B. Shailer	1952	R. Marshall	1974	J. Reece
1926	L. W. Hayes	1953	R. Marshall	1975	J. Long
1927	L. W. Hayes	1954	R. Marshall	1976	G. Ganim Jr
1928	L. W. Hayes	1955	R. Marshall	1977	G. Ganim Jr
1929	A. H. Hearndon	1956	J. Long	1978	G. Ganim Jr
1930	S. Ryan	1957	R. Marshall	1979	G. Ganim Jr
1931	H. L. Goldsmith	1958	T. Cleary	1980	G. Ganim Jr
1932	A. Sakzewski	1959	R. Marshall	1981	G. Ganim Jr
1933	L. W. Hayes	1960	J. Long	1982	R. Foldvari
1934	L. W. Hayes	1961	R. Marshall	1983	R. Foldvari
1935	L. W. Hayes	1962	R. Marshall	1984	F. Humphreys
1936	R. Marshall	1963	R. Marshall	1985	R. Marshall
1937	R. Marshall	1964	J. Long	1986	R. Marshall
1938	R. Marshall	1965	T. Cleary	1987	P. Tarrant
1939	R. Marshall	1966	T. Cleary		

CANADA

Snooker

1979	J. Wych	1981	R. Chaperon	1984	T. Finstad
1980	Jim Bear	1983	A. Robidoux	1985	A. Robidoux

Billiards

1979	E. Fisher	1981	R. Chaperon	1982	R. Chaperon
1980	S. Holden				

INDIA

Snooker

1939	P. K. Deb	1956	M. J. M. Lafir	1971	T. Monteiro
1940	P. K. Deb	1957	M. J. M. Lafir	1972	S. Shroff
1941	V. R. Freer	1958	W. Jones	1973	S. Shroff
1942	P. K. Deb	1959	M. J. M. Lafir	1974	M. J. M. Lafir
1943–45	No contests	1960	W. Jones	1975	M. J. M. Lafir
1946	T. A. Selvaraj	1961	M. J. M. Lafir	1976	A. Savur
1947	T. Sadler	1962	R. Marshall	1977	M. J. M. Lafir
1948	W. Jones		(Aust)	1978	A. Savur
1949	T. A. Selvaraj	1963	M. J. M. Lafir	1979	A. Savur
1950	F. Edwards (Eng)	1964	S. Shroff	1980	J. White (Eng)
1951	T. A. Selvaraj	1965	S. Shroff	1981	G. Parikh
1952	W. Jones	1966	T. Monteiro	1984	G. Sethi
1953	A. L. Driffield	1967	S. Shroff	1985	G. Sethi
	(Eng)	1968	S. Mohan	1986	G. Sethi
1954	W. Jones	1969	S. Shroff	1987	G. Sethi
1955	T. A. Selvaraj	1970	S. Shroff	1988	G. Sethi

Billiards

1935	P. K. Deb	1955	W. Jones	1972	S. Mohan
1936	P. K. Deb	1956	C. Hirjee	1973	S. Mohan
1937	M. M. Begg	1957	W. Jones	1974	M. Ferreira
1938	P. K. Deb	1958	C. Hirjee	1975	G. C. Parikh
1939	P. K. Deb	1959	T. Cleary (Aust)	1976	M. Ferreira
1940	S. H. Lyth	1960	W. Jones	1977	M. J. M. Lafir
1941	V. R. Freer	1961	W. Jones	1978	M. Ferreira
1942	V. R. Freer	1962	R. Marshall	1979	M. Ferreira
1943–45	*No contests*		(Aust)	1980	M. Ferreira
1946	C. Hirjee	1963	W. Jones	1981	G. Sethi
1947	C. Hirjee	1964	W. Jones	1982	M. Ferreira
1948	V. R. Freer	1965	W. Jones	1983	S. Agrawal
1949	T. A. Selvaraj	1966	W. Jones	1984	G. Sethi
1950	W. Jones	1967	A. Savur	1985	M. Ferreira
1951	W. Jones	1968	S. Mohan	1986	G. Sethi
1952	W. Jones	1969	M. Ferreira	1987	G. Sethi
1953	L. Driffield (Eng)	1970	S. Mohan	1988	G. Sethi
1954	W. Jones	1971	S. Mohan		

MALTA

Snooker

1947	L. Galea	1961	A. Borg	1975	P. Mifsud
1948	T. B. Oliver	1962	A. Borg	1976	P. Mifsud
1949	L. Galea	1963	M. Tonna	1977	A. Borg
1950	W. Asciak	1964	A. Borg	1978	P. Mifsud
1951	W. Asciak	1965	A. Borg	1979	P. Mifsud
1952	A. Borg	1966	A. Borg	1980	J. Grech
1953	A. Borg	1967	A. Borg	1981	J. Grech
1954	W. Asciak	1968	P. Mifsud	1982	P. Mifsud
1955	A. Borg	1969	P. Mifsud	1983	P. Mifsud
1956	W. Asciak	1970	P. Mifsud	1984	T. Drago
1957	W. Asciak	1971	P. Mifsud	1985	P. Mifsud
1958	W. Asciak	1972	P. Mifsud	1988	P. Mifsud
1959	A. Borg	1973	A. Borg		
1960	A. Borg	1974	A. Borg		

Billiards

1947	V. Micallef	1959	A. Asciak	1972	W. Asciak
1948	*No contests*	1960	A. Asciak	1973	P. Mifsud
1949	E. Bartolo	1961	A. Borg	1974	P. Mifsud
1950	W. Asciak	1962	J. Bartolo	1975	P. Mifsud
1951	W. Asciak	1963	J. Bartolo	1976	P. Mifsud
1952	W. Asciak	1964	W. Asciak	1977	P. Mifsud
1953	W. Asciak	1965	A. Asciak	1978	J. Grech
1954	W. Asciak	1966	A. Asciak	1979	P. Mifsud
1955	W. Asciak	1967	A. Asciak	1980	J. Grech
1956	W. Asciak	1969	P. Mifsud	*1981*	*No contest*
1957	W. Asciak	1970	W. Asciak	1982	V. Ellul
1958	A. Asciak	1971	P. Mifsud	1983	J. Grech

NEW ZEALAND

Snooker

1945	S. Moses	1959	W. Thomas	1973	W. Hill
1946	J. Munro	1960	T. Yesberg	1974	K. Tristram
1947	W. Thompson	1961	F. Franks	1975	K. Tristram
1948	L. Stout	1962	K. Murphy	1976	D. Kwok
1949	L. Stout	1963	W. Harcourt	1977	D. Meredith
1950	L. Stout	1964	T. Yesberg	1978	D. Meredith
1951	N. Lewis	1965	L. Napper	1979	D. Meredith
1952	L. Stout	1966	L. Napper	1980	D. O'Kane
1953	L. Stout	1967	R. Flutey	1981	D. Kwok
1954	R. Franks	1968	L. Napper	1982	D. Kwok
1955	L. Stout	1969	L. Glozier	1983	D. Kwok
1956	L. Stout	1970	K. Tristram	1984	D. Kwok
1957	W. Harcourt	1971	B. J. Bennett	1985	P. de Groot
1958	W. Harcourt	1972	N. Stockman		

Billiards

1908	J. Ryan	1935	L. Holdsworth	1962	W. Harcourt	
1909	No contests	1936	S. Moses	1963	H. C. Robinson	
1910	F. Lovelock	1937	S. Moses	1964	T. Yesberg	
1911	F. Lovelock	1938	L. Holdsworth	1965	L. Napper	
1912	H. Valentine	1939	R. Carrick	1966	A. Twohill	
1913	H. Valentine	1940	S. Moses	1967	A. Twohill	
1914	N. Lynch	1941	R. Carrick	1968	A. Twohill	
1915	W. E. Warren	1942	R. Carrick	1969	E. Simmons	
1916	H. Siedeberg	1943	A. Albertson	1970	L. Napper	
1917	H. Siedeberg	1944	S. Moses	1971	W. Harcourt	
1918	W. E. Warren	1945	J. Shepherd	1972	B. Kirkness	
1919	H. Siedeberg	1946	R. Carrick	1973	H. C. Robinson	
1920	W. E. Warren	1947	C. Peek	1974	H. C. Robinson	
1921	H. Siedeberg	1948	R. Carrick	1975	T. Yesberg	
1922	E. V. Roberts	1949	R. Carrick	1976	H. C. Robinson	
1923	E. V. Roberts	1950	R. Carrick	1977	B. Kirkness	
1924	R. Fredotovich	1951	R. Carrick	1978	B. Kirkness	
1925	C. Mason	1952	L. Stout	1979	R. Adams	
1926	E. V. Roberts	1953	A. Twohill	1980	D. Meredith	
1927	E. V. Roberts	1954	A. Twohill	1981	D. Meredith	
1928	A. Bowie	1955	A. Twohill	1982	D. Meredith	
1929	L. Stout	1956	A. Twohill	1983	D. Meredith	
1930	W. E. Hackett	1957	A. Twohill	1984	D. Meredith	
1931	A. Duncan	1958	A. Albertson	1985	D. Meredith	
1932	C. Mason	1959	A. Twohill	1986	B. Kirkness	
1933	A. Albertson	1960	W. Harcourt			
1934	H. McLean	1961	A. Albertson			

SOUTH AFRICA
Snooker

1937	A. Prior	1957	J. Van Rensberg	1972	J. Van Rensberg	
1938	A. H. Ashby	1958	R. Walker	1973	J. Van Rensberg	
1939	A. Prior	1959	M. Fancisco	1974	S. Francisco	
1940–45	No contests	1960	P. Mans Jr	1975	M. Francisco	
1946	F. Walker	1961	J. Van Rensberg	1976	No contest	
1947	No contest	1962	J. Van Rensberg	1977	S. Francisco	
1948	F. Walker	1963	J. Van Rensberg	1978	J. van Niekerk	
1949	E. Kerr	1964	M. Francisco	1979	F. Ellis	
1950	T. G. Rees	1965	M. Francisco	1980	F. Ellis	
1951	T. G. Rees	1966	M. Francisco	1981	P. Francisco	
1952	T. G. Rees	1967	J. Van Rensberg	1982	P. Francisco	
1953	J. Van Rensberg	1968	S. Francisco	1983	P. Francisco	
1954	J. Van Rensberg	1969	S. Francisco	1984	N. van Niekerk	
1955	J. Van Rensberg	1970	J. Van Rensberg	1985	P. Smallshaw	
1956	F. Walker	1971	M. Francisco	1986	S. Mouton	

Billiards

1920	Sgt Bruyns	1949	T. G. Rees	1968	M. Francisco	
1921	A. Prior	1950	T. G. Rees	1969	M. Francisco	
1922	A. Prior	1951	I. Drapin	1970	M. Francisco	
1923	No contest	1952	T. G. Rees	1971	M. Francisco	
1924	A. Prior	1953	T. G. Rees	1972	S. Francisco	
1925	P. Rutledge	1954	F. Walker	1973	S. Francisco	
1926	A. Prior	1955	F. Walker	1974	M. Francisco	
1927	A. Percival	1956	G. Povall	1975	S. Francisco	
1928	P. Rutledge	1957	F. Walker	1976	No contests	
1929–30	No contests	1958	F. Walker	1977	M. Francisco	
1931	A. Prior	1959	M. Francisco	1978	C. van Dijk	
1932–36	No contests	1960	R. Walker	1979	C. van Dijk	
1937	A. M. Burke	1961	M. Francisco	1980	C. van Dijk	
1938	A. Prior	1962	M. Francisco	1981	P. Spence	
1939	A. Prior	1963	M. Francisco	1982	P. Francisco	
1940–45	No contests	1964	M. Francisco	1983	C. van Dijk	
1946	P. G. Kempen	1965	M. Francisco	1984	C. van Dijk	
1947	No contest	1966	M. Francisco	1985	C. van Dijk	
1948	P. G. Kempen	1967	J. Van Rensberg	1986	C. van Dijk	

SRI LANKA
Snooker

1951	M. S. A. Hassan	1962	M. J. M. Lafir	1973	M. J. M. Lafir
1952	M. J. M Lafir	1963	M. J. M. Izzath	1974	*Abandoned*
1953	M. J. M Lafir	1964	M. J. M. Lafir	1975	N. A. Rahim
1954	M. J. M Lafir	1965	M. J. M. Lafir	1976	M. S. U. Mohideen
1955	M. J. M. Lafir	1966	M. J. M. Lafir	1977	M. S. U. Mohideen
1956	M. J. M. Lafir	1967	N. J. Rahim	1978	N. A. Rahim
1957	M. J. M. Lafir	*1968*	*No contest*	1981	J. W. H. Boteju
1958	M. J. M. Lafir	1969	M. J. M. Lafir	1982	J. A. Wahid
1959	M. J. M. Lafir	1970	N. J. Rahim	1983	J. W. H. Boteju
1960	M. J. M. Lafir	*1971*	*No contest*	1984	K. Scrisoma
1961	M. J. M. Lafir	1972	N. J. Rahim	1985	J. W. H. Boteju

Billiards

1951	M. J. M. Lafir	1962	M. J. M. Lafir	1976	W. Weerasinghe
1952	M. J. M. Lafir	1963	M. H. M. Mujahid	1977	W. Weerasinghe
1953	M. J. M. Lafir	1964	M. J. M. Lafir	1978	J. W. H Boteju
1954	A. C. Cambal	1966	M. J. M. Lafir	1979	W. Weerasinghe
1955	T. A. Selvaraj	1967	J. K. Bakshani	1981	J. W. H Boteju
1956	T. A. Selvaraj	1969	M. J. M. Lafir	1982	J. W. H Boteju
1957	M. J. M. Lafir	1970	M. J. M. Lafir	1983	W. Weerasinghe
1958	M. J. M. Lafir	1972	M. J. M. Lafir	1984	J. W. H Boteju
1959	M. J. M. Lafir	1973	M. J. M. Lafir	1985	K. Scrisoma
1960	M. J. M. Lafir	1974	S. Shaharwardi		
1961	M. J. M. Lafir	1975	M. S. U. Mohideen		

FIXTURES 1988–89

August 28– **September 11**	FIDELITY INTERNATIONAL at Trentham Gardens, Stoke (no play Sept 1) Box office: (0782) 657341
October 10–23	ROTHMANS GRAND PRIX at Hexagon, Reading (no play Oct 14) Box office: (0734) 591591
October 26– **November 5**	CANADIAN MASTERS at venue to be announced
November 11–27	TENNENTS UK OPEN at Guild Hall, Preston (no play Nov 17–18) Box office: (0772) 21721
December 3–11	WORLD MATCHPLAY CHAMPIONSHIP details to be announced Further information: (0708) 24023
January 1–15	MERCANTILE CREDIT CLASSIC at Norbreck Castle Hotel, Blackpool (no play Jan 5) Box office (0253) 52341
January 22–29	BENSON AND HEDGES MASTERS at Wembley Conference Centre Box office: (01) 901 1234
January 30– **February 11**	EUROPEAN OPEN at venue to be announced
February 19– **March 5**	BRITISH OPEN at Assembly Rooms, Derby (no play Feb 23) Box office: (0332) 369311
March 21–24	FERSINA WORLD CUP at International Centre, Bournemouth Box office: (0202) 297297
March 28–April 2	BENSON AND HEDGES IRISH MASTERS at Goffs, Kill, Co Kildare
April 15–May 1	EMBASSY WORLD CHAMPIONSHIP at Crucible Theatre, Sheffield Box office (by post) Crucible Theatre, Norfolk Street, Sheffield SA 1DA